ISBN 978-1-5281-1434-9
PIBN 10907906

1 MONTH OF
FREE
READING

at

www.ForgottenBooks.com

By purchasing this book you are eligible for one month membership to ForgottenBooks.com, giving you unlimited access to our entire collection of over 1,000,000 titles via our web site and mobile apps.

To claim your free month visit:
www.forgottenbooks.com/free907906

English
Français
Deutsche
Italiano
Español
Português

www.forgottenbooks.com

Mythology Photography **Fiction**
Fishing Christianity **Art** Cooking
Essays Buddhism Freemasonry
Medicine **Biology** Music **Ancient**
Egypt Evolution Carpentry Physics
Dance Geology **Mathematics** Fitness
Shakespeare **Folklore** Yoga Marketing
Confidence Immortality Biographies
Poetry **Psychology** Witchcraft
Electronics Chemistry History **Law**
Accounting **Philosophy** Anthropology
Alchemy Drama Quantum Mechanics
Atheism Sexual Health **Ancient History**
Entrepreneurship Languages Sport
Paleontology Needlework Islam
Metaphysics Investment Archaeology
Parenting Statistics Criminology
Motivational

SYNOPSIS

OF THE

PEERAGE OF ENGLAND;

EXHIBITING, UNDER ALPHABETICAL ARRANGEMENT,

The Date of Creation,

DESCENT, AND PRESENT STATE

OF

EVERY TITLE OF PEERAGE WHICH HAS EXISTED IN THIS COUNTRY SINCE THE CONQUEST.

IN TWO VOLUMES.

BY

⋅ NICHOLAS HARRIS NICOLAS, Esq.

OF THE INNER TEMPLE, BARRISTER AT LAW; FELLOW OF THE SOCIETY OF ANTIQUARIES.

VOL. II.

London:

PRINTED BY J. NICHOLS AND SON, 25, PARLIAMENT STREET;

For C. and J. Rivington, St. Paul's Churchyard and Waterloo Place; T. Egerton, Whitehall; J. Cuthell, Middle Row, Holborn; J and W. T. Clarke, Portugal Street, Lincoln's Inn; Longman and Co. Paternoster Row; T. Cadell, Strand; J. Richardson, Royal Exchange; J. Booth, Duke Street, Portland Chapel; J. Booker, New Bond Street; Kingsbury and Co. Leadenhall Street; Baldwin and Co., S. Bagster, and Hamilton and Co., Paternoster Row; J. Hatchard and Son, Piccadilly; J. Harding, St. James's Street; Rodwell and Martin, New Bond Street; G. B. Whittaker, Ave-Maria Lane; B. Lloyd and Son, Harley Street; and R. Saunders, Fleet Street.

1825.

CONTENTS OF VOL II.

SYNOPSIS

OF

THE PEERAGE.

◆

MACARTNEY.

BARON.

I. 1796. George Macartney, 1st Earl Macartney in Ireland; Created Baron Macartney of Parkhurst, co. Surrey, and of Auchinleck in the Stewartry of Kirkcudbright, 8 June, 1796, K. B.; ob. 1806, s. p. when all his titles became

Extinct.

MACCLESFIELD.

EARLS.

I. 1679. 1. Charles Gerard, 1st Baron Gerard of Brandon; Created Viscount Brandon, co. Suffolk, and Earl of Macclesfield, co. Cheshire, 23 July, 1679; ob. 1694.

II. 1694. 2. Charles Gerard, s. and b. ob. 1701, s. p.

III. 1701. 3. Fitton Gerard, brother and heir; ob. 1702, s. p. when his honors became

Extinct.

IV. 1721. 1. Thomas Parker, 1st Baron Parker of Macclesfield; Created Viscount Parker of Ewelme, co. Oxford, and Earl of Macclesfield, co. Cheshire, with remainder, failing his issue male, of the dignities of Baroness and Viscountess Parker and Countess of Macclesfield to his daughter Elizabeth, wife of William Heathcote, Esq. and of the Barony and Viscountcy of Parker and Earldom of Macclesfield to her issue male, 5 Nov. 1721; Lord Chancellor 1718; ob. 1732.

V. 1732. 2. George Parker, s. and b. ob. 1764.

VI. 1764. 3. Thomas Parker, s. and b. ob. 1795.

EARLS.
VII. 1795. 4. George Parker, s. and h. Present Earl of Macclesfield and Viscount and Baron Parker. ⊤

MAHON.
Vide STANHOPE.

MAIDSTONE.

VISCOUNTESS.
I. 1623. 1. Elizabeth, sole dau. and heir of Sir Thomas Heneage, Knt. and widow of Sir Moyle Finch, Bart. Created Viscountess of Maidstone, co. Kent, 8 July, 1623; Created Countess of Winchelsea 12 July, 1628; ob. 1633.

VISCOUNTS.
I. 1632. 2. Sir Thomas Finch, 2d Bart. s. and h. Earl of Winchelsea. Vide WINCHELSEA.

MAINE.

BARONS BY TENURE.
I. H. II. Walter de Maine; held 29 Knight's fees in 1187; ob. ante 1191, and of whose posterity nothing is known.

MALDEN.
VISCOUNTCY, 20 April, 1661.
Vide ESSEX.

MALET.

BARONS BY TENURE.
I. Will. I. 1. William Malet; came into England with William the Conqueror; ob. ....
II. Hen. I. 2. Robert Malet, s. and h. Great Chamberlain of England; disinherited and banished.

———

I. H. II. William Malet, Lord of Danegell, co. Somerset, 1168; his successor was
II. John. William Malet, Lord of Corey Malet, co. Somerset; he was one of the celebrated 25 Barons appointed to enforce the observance of MAG CHARTA; ob ante 1224, s. p. m. leaving t daughters and coheirs, viz. Mabell, wife Hugh de Vivonia, and Helewise, wife, first Sir Hugh Pointz, and secondly, of Robert Muscegros.

MALMESBURY.

MARQUISATE, 1 January, 1715—Forfeited 1728.
Vide WHARTON.

BARONS.   EARLS.
1788.—I. 1800. 1. James Harris ; Created Baron
Malmesbury of Malmesbury, co.
Wilts, 19 Sept. 1788; Created
Viscount Fitz-Harris of Hurn
Court, co. Southampton, and Earl
of Malmesbury, 29 Dec. 1800,
K. B.; ob. 1820.

.... — II. 1820. 2. James Edward Harris, s. and h.
Present Earl and Baron Malmes-
bury, and Viscount Fitz-Harris

MALPAS.

VISCOUNTCY, 27 December, 1706.
Vide CHOLMONDELEY.

MALTON.

BARONS.   EARLS.
1728.—I. 1734. 1. Thomas Wentworth (son and heir
of Thomas Watson, who assumed
the name of Wentworth, 2d son of
Edward 2d Baron Rockingham) ;
Created Baron of Malton, co.York,
28 May, 1728; Created Viscount
Higham of Higham Ferrers, Baron
of Waith, co. York, and of Harrowden, co. Northampton, and Earl
of Malton, co. York, 19 Nov.
1734; succeeded to the Barony of
Rockingam 26 Feb. 1746; and
was created Marquess of Rockingham 19 April, 1746, K. B.; ob.
1750.

.. .. — II. 1750. 2. Charles Watson-Wentworth, Marquess of Rockingham ; Created
Baron and Earl of Malton in Ireland vita patris, 17 Sept. 1750,

A 2

K. G.; ob. 1782, s. p. when all his
honors became

𝕰𝔵𝔱𝔦𝔫𝔠𝔱.

MALTRAVERS.

BARON BY WRIT.

I. 1330. 1. John Maltravers; Summ. to Parl. 5 June,
4 Edward III. 1330, and 18 Nov. 25 Edw. III.
1351. Dugdale states, that John Maltravers,
the father of this Baron, and this John were both Summoned to Parliament 1 Edw. III. but on examining the
Summonses in that year it appears, that they were
merely summoned to be at Newcastle-upon-Tyne, "cum
equis et armis." The Index to his List of Summonses
asserts that this Baron was likewise summoned 35 Edw.
III. but that Writ was evidently not a Summons to Parliament; ob. 1364, leaving his grand-daughter (daughter of
John Maltravers, his eldest son, ob. v. p.) Eleanor, wife of
John Fitz-Alan, 2d son of Richard XII.-9th Earl of Arundel, his next heir, and which John Fitz-Alan is often styled
Baron Maltravers jure uxoris, but he was never Summoned
to Parliament by that title*. John Fitz-Alan his grandson, succeeded as XV.-12th Earl of Arundel; in whose descendants this Barony remained vested, and Thomas, son
and heir apparent of William XVIII.-15th Earl of Arundel, and Henry, eldest son of William XX.-17th Earl of
Arundel, were Summoned to Parliament vita patris as
Barons Maltravers. Mary Fitz-Alan, the dau. and eventually sole heir of the last-mentioned Henry Baron Maltravers (who succeeded as XXI.-18th Earl of Arundel),
carried this Barony to her husband Thomas Howard IX.-
4th Duke of Norfolk, and with the Earldom of Arundel
it descended to their son Philip Howard, who was attainted
32 Eliz. when it became 𝔉𝔬𝔯𝔣𝔢𝔦𝔱𝔢𝔡; it was, however,
restored to his son Thomas XXIII.-20th Earl of Arundel,
and by Act of Parliament 3 Car. I. this Barony, together
with the Baronies of Fitz-Alan, Clun, and Oswaldestre,
was annexed to the title, dignity, and honor of Earl of
Arundel, and settled upon the said Thomas Howard, then
Earl of Arundel and Surrey, and his heirs male, with
remainder to the heirs of his body; remainder to his

---

* It appears however that this John was Summoned to Par-
nent (probably in consequence of his marriage) in the 1st, 2d,
3d of Richard II. as "Johanni de *Arundel.*" Vide p. 29.

uncle Lord William Howard and the heirs male of his body, with remainder to the heirs of his body; remainder to the aforesaid Thomas Earl of Arundel and Surrey, and his heirs for ever; in consequence of which, the Barony of Maltravers, with those above-mentioned, is now vested in his Grace, Bernard Edward present Duke of Norfolk, the heir male of the said Thomas Earl of Arundel and Surrey.   Vide ARUNDEL and NORFOLK.

MAMINOT.

BARON BY TENURE.

I.   Steph. 1. Walcheline Maminot; living 1145.
II. H. II. 2. Walcheline Maminot, s. and h. ob. ante 1192, s. P.

MANCHESTER.

EARLS.

I.   1626. 1. Henry Montagu, 1st Baron Montagu of Kimbolton, and 1st Viscount Mandeville; Created Earl of Manchester 5 Feb. 1626; Lord Treasurer; ob. 1642.

II.   1642. 2. Edward Montagu, s. and h. K.B. and K.G. ob. 1671.

III. 1671. 3. Robert Montagu, s. and h. ob. 1682.

DUKES.

IV.   1682.—I. 1719. 4. Charles Montagu s. and h. Created Duke of Manchester 13 April, 1719; ob. 1722.

V.   ..... —II. 1722. 5. William Montagu, s. and h. ob. 1739, s. P.

VI. ..... —III. 1739. 6. Robert Montagu, brother and heir; ob. 1762.

VII. ..... —IV. 1762. 7. George Montagu, s. and h. ob. 1788.

VIII. ..... —V. 1788. 8. William Montagu, s. and h. Present Duke and Earl of Manchester, Viscount Mandeville and Baron Montagu of Kimbolton.

MANDEVILLE.

BARONS BY TENURE.

I.   Will. I. 1. Geoffrey de Mandevill; obtained divers Lordships from William the Conqueror.
II. H. I. 2. William de Mandeville, s. and h.
III. Steph. 3. Geoffrey de Mandeville, s. and h. Created Earl of Essex by King Stephen. Vide ESSEX.

A 3

MANDEVILLE

OF MERSHWOOD.

BARONS BY TENURE.

I.   John. 1. William de Mandeville, of the same family as
              the above.
II. Hen.III. 2. Robert de Mandeville, s. and h.; living 1265,
              but of whom Dugdale gives no farther account.

I. H.III. 1. Geoffrey de Mandeville; presumed to have
              been brother of Robert, the last Baron; ob.
              1265.
II. Edw.I. 2. John de Mandeville, s. and h. ob. ..... s.p.m.
              Agnes, his daughter, being his heir.

MANDEVILLE.

VISCOUNTS.

I. 1620.   1. Henry Montagu, brother of Edward 1st Baron
              Montagu of Boughton ; Created Baron Mon-
              tagu of Kimbolton, co. Huntingdon, and Visc.
              Mandeville, Dec. 19, 1620 ; Created Earl of
              Manchester Feb. 5, 1626. Vide MANCHESTER.

MANERS.

BARON BY WRIT.

I. 1309.   Baldwin de Maners; Summ. to Parl. 26 Oct.
              3 Edw. II. 1309, but never afterwards ; and
              on his death the dignity became
                        Extinct.

Dugdale gives no account of this Baron in his Baronage.

MANNERS

BARON.   OF FOSTON.

I. 1807.   1. Thomas Manners Sutton, 6th son of George
              Manners (assumed the name of) Sutton, 3d
              son of John 3d Duke of Rutland; Created
              Baron Manners of Foston, co. Lincoln, April
              20. 1807 ; Lord Chancellor of Ireland. Pre-
              sent Baron Manners of Foston. ⚭ .

MANNERS

BARON BY WRIT.   OF HADDON.

I. 1679.   John Manners, s. and h. apparent of John IX.—
              8th Earl of Rutland ; Summ. to Parl. vita pa-
              tris, as "Johanni Manners de Haddon," 29
              April and 7 Oct. 31 Car. II. 1679, and 1

March, 32 Car. II. 1680, though he succeeded
his father as X.-9th Earl of Rutland on the
29th September, 1679; Created Marquess of
Granby and Duke of Rutland, 29 March,
1703; in which dignity this Barony is merged;
ob. 1711. Vide RUTLAND.

MANNY.

BARON BY WRIT.

I.   1347.   Walter de Manny; Summ. to Parl. from 13
Nov. 21 Edw. III. 1347, to 8 Jan. 44 Edw.
Edw. III. 1371. K. G.; ob. 1372, s. P. M.
Anne, his only child, married John Hastings,
XII.-2d Earl of Pembroke; and on the death
of their only issue, John XIII.-3d Earl of
Pembroke, in 1399, s.P. this Barony became
𝕰𝔵𝔱𝔦𝔫𝔠𝔱.

MANSFIELD.

VISCOUNTS.

I.   1620.   William Cavendish, s. and h. of Charles Cavendish (younger brother of William I.-1st
Earl of Devonshire), by Catherine, dau. and
eventually sole heir of Cuthbert, 2d Baron
Ogle; Created Baron Ogle, of Bothal, co.
...... and Viscount Mansfield, co. Nottingham, 3d Nov. 1620; Created Earl of Newcastle 7 March, 1651.   Vide NEWCASTLE.
𝕰𝔵𝔱𝔦𝔫𝔠𝔱 1691.

BARON.   EARLS.

I. 1756.—I. 1776. 1. William Murray, 4th son of David, 5th
   I. 1792.   Viscount Stormont in Scotland; Created Lord Mansfield, Baron Mansfield,
co. Notts, 8 Nov. 1756, to him and his
heirs male; Created Earl of Mansfield,
co. Notts. 31 Oct. 1776, with remainder
of the dignity of Countess Mansfield
to Louisa Viscountess Stormont, wife
of his nephew David Viscount Stormont, and after her decease the Earldom to the heirs male of her body by
her husband, David Viscount Stormont;
Created Earl of Mansfield, co. Middlesex, with remainder, failing his issue
male, to his nephew the said David

Viscount Stormont, Aug. 1, 1792 *;
Lord Chief Justice; ob. 1793, s. p. when
the Barony became Extinct; but the
dignity of Countess of Mansfield, with
the precedence of 31 Oct. 1776, de-

COUNTESS.   volved on

I.   1793. 2. Louisa, dau. of Charles 9th Lord Cathcart
in Scotland, and wife of David, 7th Viscount
Stormont, nephew of the last Earl (her Ladyship afterwards married the Hon. Fulke Greville); Present Countess of Mansfield, co.
Nottingham, and the dignity of Earl of Mansfield in Middlesex, with the precedence of

EARLS.   Aug. 1, 1792, devolved on her first husband,

II.   1793. 3. David Murray, 7th Viscount Stormont in
Scotland, K. T.; ob. 1796.

III.   1796. 4. William Murray, s. and h. Present Earl of
Mansfield in Middlesex, and heir-apparent
to the Earldom of Mansfield, co. Notts; also
Viscount Stormont in Scotland.

MANSELL.

BARONS.

I.   1711. 1. Sir Thomas Mansell, 4th Bart. Created Baron Mansell of Margam, co. Glamorgan, 31
Dec. 1711; ob. 1723.

II.   1723. 2. Thomas Mansell, grandson and heir, being
s. and h. of Robert Mansell (ob. v. p.) eldest
son of the last Baron; ob. 1743, s. p.

III.   1743. 3. Christopher Mansell, uncle and heir, being 2d
son of Thomas, 1st Baron; ob. 1744, s. p.

IV.   1744. 4. Bussy Mansell, brother and heir; ob. 1750,
s. p. m. when the title became
Extinct.

MANVERS.

EARLS.

I.   1806. 1. Charles Meadows (assumed the name of)
Pierrepont, VII.-1st Baron Pierrepont and

---

* The probable cause of these limitations was the doctrine which
was held at the time of his first creation of Earl of Mansfield, that
a Scot's Peer was disqualified from taking an English Peerage
even in remainder. After the contrary was established to be the
law, his Lordship had, by the new creation, the Earldom en-
tailed on his nephew.

EARLS.

Viscount Newark, son of Philip Meadows, by
Frances, sister and heir of Evelyn Pierre-
pont, last Duke of Kingston; Created Earl
Manvers April 9, 1806 ; ob. 1816.

II.   1816. 2. Charles Herbert Pierrepont, s. and h. Present
Earl Manvers, Viscount Newark, and Baron
Pierrepont of Holme Pierrepont. ⚥

MARCH.

EARLS.

I.   1328. 1. Roger Mortimer; Created Earl of March in
1328 ; executed and attainted in 1330, when
the dignity became
Forfeited.

II.   1352. 2. Roger Mortimer, grandson of the last Earl,
viz. s. and h. of Edmund Mortimer, his eldest
son, who survived him, but was not restored
to the Earldom; obtained the reversal of his
grandfather's Attainder in 1352; K. G.; ob.
1360.

III.   1360. 3. Edmund Mortimer, s. and h. He married
Philippa, dau. and heir of Lionel Plantagenet, Duke of Clarence, 3d son of Edward III.
through which alliance this family afterwards
became heirs to the throne; ob. 1381.

IV.   1381. 4. Roger Mortimer, s. and h. ob. 1398.

V.   1398. 5. Edmund Mortimer, s. and h. ob. 1424, s. p.
when the Earldom became *Extinct.* Ann,
his sister and ultimately sole heir, married Richard Plantagenet, Earl of Cambridge,
brother of the Duke of York, and conveyed
the right to the Crown to the House of
York.   Richard Plantagenet, Duke of York,
s. and h. of the said Earl of Cambridge and
Ann Mortimer, is by some writers styled
Earl of March; and which title was also
borne, vita patris, by his son and heir, Edward, afterwards King Edward IV. though
no patent of creation to the dignity ever
appears to have passed the Great Seal.

VI.   1479. 1. Edward Plantagenet, Prince of Wales, s. and
h. apparent of Edward IV. Created Earl of
Salisbury 15 Feb. 1477, and Earl of March

and Pembroke 8 July, 1479; ascended the Throne April 9, 1483, as Edward V. when all his titles became merged in the Crown.

VII. 1619. 1. Esme Stuart, Lord of Aubigny in France, 2d son of Esme Duke of Lenox in Scotland; Created Baron Stuart of Leighton, of Leighton Bromswold, co. Hunts, and Earl of March, 7 June, 1619; ob. 1624.

VIII. 1624. 2. James Stuart, s. and h. Created Duke of Richmond Aug. 1641, with a special remainder; K. G.; ob. 1655.

IX. 1655. 3. Esme Stuart, s. and h. ob. 1660, s. P.

X. 1660. 4. Charles Stuart, Earl of Litchfield, cousin and heir, being s. and h. of George Stuart, 2d son of James VIII.-2d Earl, and 1st Duke of Richmond; Duke of Richmond, K. G.; ob. 1672, s. P. when all his honors became
Extinct.

XI. 1675. 1 Charles Lenox, natural son of Charles II. Created Baron of Setrington, co. York, Earl of March and Duke of Richmond, Aug. 9, 1675.
Vide Richmond.

MARLBOROUGH.

I. 1626. 1. James Ley, 1st Baron Ley; Created Earl of Marlborough, co. Wilts, 1 Feb. 1626; Lord High Treasurer; ob. 1628.

II. 1628. 2. Henry Ley, s. and h. ob. ante 1640.

III. 16... 3. James Ley, s. and h. ob. 1665, s. P.

IV. 1665. 4. William Ley, uncle and heir, being next brother of Henry 2d Earl; ob. 1679, s. P. when all his honors became
Extinct.

IV. 1689.—I. 1702. 1. John Churchill, 1st Baron Churchill, and 1st Baron Churchill in Scotland; Created Earl of Marlborough, co. Wilts, April 9, 1689; Created Marquess of Blandford and Duke of Marlborough 14 Dec. 1702; all his honors were by Act of Parliament Dec. 21, 1706, settled on his daughters and their heirs male; K. G.; ob. 1722, s. P. M.

COUNTESS. DUCHESS.

I.—1. 1722. 2. Henrietta, eldest dau. and coheir of the
last Duke, and wife of Francis Earl of
Godolphin; succeeded by virtue of the
above-mentioned Act of Parliament as
Baroness Churchill, Countess and Duchess of Marlborough, and Marchioness
of Blandford, and as Baroness Church-

EARLS. DUKES.   hill in Scotland; ob. 1733, s. p. m.

V. —II. 1733. 3. Charles Spencer, 5th Earl of Sunderland,
nephew and heir of the Duchess, and
grandson of John, 1st Duke, being 3d
son of Charles third Earl of Sunderland,
by Ann, 2d dau. and coheir of John, 1st
Duke; succeeded, agreeable to the said
Act of Parliament, as Duke and Earl of
Marlborough, Marquess of Blandford,
Baron Churchill, and also as Baron
Churchill in Scotland; succeeded his
brother Robert 2d Earl of Sunderland,
Nov. 27, 1729; K.G.; ob. 1758.

VI. —III. 1758. 4. George Spencer, s. and h. K.G. ob. 1817.

VII.—IV. 1817. 5. George Spencer (assumed the name of)
Churchill, s. and h. Present Duke and
Earl of Marlborough, Marquess of Blandford, Earl of Sunderland, Baron Spencer
of Wormleighton, and Baron Churchill;
also Baron Churchill in Scotland. ☰
♈

MARMION

OF TAMWORTH.

BARONS BY TENURE.

I. Will. I. 1. Robert Marmion obtained the Lordship of
Tamworth from William the Conqueror.

II. H. I. 2. Robert Marmion, s. and h. living 1143.

III. H. II. 3. Robert Marmion, s. and h. ob. circa 1217.

IV. H. III. 4. Robert Marmion, s. and h. ob. 1241.

V. H. III. 5. Philip Marmion, s. and h. ob. 1292, s. p. m.
leaving his daughters his heirs, viz. Joan, the
wife of William le Mostyn; Mazera, who married Ralf de Crumwell; Maud, wife of Ralph de Borde-
laye; and by his second wife a daughter, Joane, who married, first, Sir Thomas Ludlow, whose son, Thomas de
Ludlow, left issue a daughter and heir, Margaret, who
marrying Sir John Dymoke, Knt. brought the manor of

Scrivelsby, co. Lincoln, to that family; which manor being
held by Grand Serjeanty to perform the office of Champion at the King's Coronation, the descendants of the
said Sir John Dymoke have frequently exercised that honorable office as Lords of the said manor. In July 1814
Lewis Dymoke, Esq. the descendant of Sir John Dymoke
above mentioned, presented a petition to his late Majesty, praying him to be pleased to declare the petitioner
entitled to the Barony of Marmion of Scrivelsby, in virtue of the seisure of the manor of Scrivelsby; which Petition was referred to the Attorney General, who having
reported thereon, the same was referred to the House of
Lords, where evidence was received at the bar, and the
Claimant's Counsel summed up, when the Attorney-General was heard in reply, and tendered some documents
on the part of the Crown; but the claimant died before
the judgment of the House was given.

   With respect to this claim, it is to be observed, that
though the manor of Scrivelsby was held by the service of
performing the office of King's Champion by Robert de
Marmyon, in the reign of William the Conqueror, he was
not by seizure thereof a Baron, but by seizure of the
Castle and Barony of TAMWORTH, which he held of the
King in capite by Knight's service; so that, if at this
period Baronies by Tenure were admitted, the possessor
of the Manor and Lordship of Tamworth, (which in the
division of his property fell to the share of Joane, his
eldest daughter, wife of William Mosteyn, and on her
death, s. p. to Alexander Freville, husband of Joan, dau.
and heir of Ralf Cromwell, by Margaret or Mazera, the
next sister of the said Joan de Mosteyn), would possess
the claim to the Barony possessed by Robert de Marmyon above mentioned, he having derived his dignity
from that Barony, instead of from the seizure of the manor of Scrivelsby. Moreover, if Philip Marmion, the last
Baron, had died seized of a Barony in fee, Lewis Dymoke
the claimant was not even a coheir of the said Philip,
though he was the descendant of one of his daughters
and coheirs.

MARMION
OF WITRINGTON.

BARONS BY TENURE.

I,   John.   1. Robert Marmion, younger half-brother of Ro-

BARONS BY WRIT.

bert Marmion, 4th Lord of Tamworth; Lord
of Witrington, co. Lincoln; ob. ....

II.   H. III. 2. William Marmion, s. and h. ob. ....

BY WRIT.

I.   1313. 3. John Marmion, s. and h. Summ. to Parl. from
26 July, 7 Edw. II. 1313, to 14 March, 15
Edw. II. 1322. He was also summoned the
8th June, 22 Edw. I. 1294, and 26 Jan. 25
Edw. I. 1297; but it is doubtful if either of
these Writs can be considered as a regular
Summons to Parl.; vide "CLYVEDON" and
"FITZ JOHN;" ob. 1322.

II.   1322. 4. John Marmion, s. and h. Summ. to Parl. from
3 Dec. 20 Edw. II. 1326, to 1 April, 9 Edw.
III. 1335; ob. 1335.

III.   1335. 5. Robert Marmion, s. and h.; he was never summoned; ob. ...., s. P. leaving his two sis-
ters, viz. Joane, the wife of Sir John Ber-
nack, and Avice, the 2d wife of John II.–5th
Lord Grey of Rotherfield, his heirs, between
whom this Barony fell into ABEYANCE. John,
the eldest son of the said John Lord Grey
by Avice Marmion, assumed the name of
Marmion, and died s P. in 1385, leaving his
niece, Elizabeth, the sole dau. and heir of
Robert, his brother, the 2d son of Avice
Marmion and Lord Grey, his heir; she married Henry III.–11th Baron Fitz-Hugh, K. G.
and the representatives of the Barony of Fitz-
Hugh are consequently coheirs of this Barony.

MARMION
OF ——

BARON BY WRIT.

I.   1264. William Marmion, younger brother of Robert
Marmion, 4th Lord of Tamworth, and also
brother of Robert 1st Lord of Witrington;
Summ. to Parl. 24 Dec. 49 Henry III. 1264,
but never afterwards, and as it does not appear that he left issue, the Barony on his
death probably became
Extinct.

MARNEY.

BARONS.

I. 1523. 1. Henry Marney; Created Baron Marney of Leyr Marney, co. Essex, 9 April, 1523; K.G.; ob. 1524.

II. 1524. 2. John Marney, s. and h. ob. 1525, s. p. m. when the title became
𝕰𝔵𝔱𝔦𝔫𝔠𝔱.

MARSHAL.

BARONS BY TENURE.

I. Hen. I. 1. Gilbert Mareschall, Marshall to the King; ob. ....

II. Steph. 2. John Mareschall, Marshal to the King; ob. ...

III. Ric. I. 3. John Mareschall, s. and h. Marshall to the King; ob. 1199, s. p. leaving his brother William Earl of Pembroke his heir.

MARSHAL

OF ——

BARONS BY TENURRE.

I. John. 1. John Marshal, nephew to William Earl of Pembroke; Created Marshal of Ireland 1207; ob. 1284.

II. 1234. 2. John Marshal, s. and h. ob. 1242.

III. 1242. 3. William Marshal, s. and h. ob. 1264.

IV. 1264. 4. John Marshal, s. and h. ob. 1283.

BY WRIT.

I. 1309. 1. William Marshal, s. and h. Summ. to Parl. from 9 Jan. 2 Edw. II. 1309, to 26 Nov. 7 Edw. II. 1313; ob. circa 1314.

II. 1314. 2. John Marshal, s. and h. he was never Summ. to Parl.; ob. circa 1316, leaving Hawyse, wife of Robert Lord Morley, his sister and heir, in whose descendants, the Barons Morley, this Barony became vested, and it is now in ABEYANCE among the representatives of the Barony of Morley.

Vide MORLEY.

MARSHAM.

VISCOUNTCY, 22 June, 1801.

Vide ROMNEY.

MARTIN.

BARONS BY TENURE.

I. Will.I. 1. Martin de Tours, a Norman ; acquired the
Lordship of Kemys, co. Pembroke.

II. Hen.I. 2. Robert Martin, s. and h. ob. .....

III. H. II. 3. William Martin, s. and h. ob. 1209.

IV. John. 4. William Martin, s. and h. ob. 1215.

V. H. III. 5. Nicholas Martin, s. and h. became Lord of
Barnstaple jure uxoris; ob. 1282.

BARONS BY WRIT.

I. 1295. 6. William Martin, grandson and heir, being
s. and h. of Nicholas Martin (ob. v. p.) eldest
son of the last Baron ; Summ. to Parl. from
23 June, 23 Edw. I. 1295, to 10 Oct. 19 Edw.
II. 1325; ob. 1325.

II. 1325. 7. William Martin, s. and h.; he was never Summ.
to Parl.; ob. 1326, s. p. leaving Eleanor, his
sister, wife of William de Columbers, and
James son of Nicholas de Audley by Joane
Martin, his other sister, his next heirs, among
whose descendants and representatives this
Barony is in ABEYANCE.

MARYBOROUGH.

BARON.

I. 1821. 1. William Wellesley (assumed the name of)
Pole, 2d son of Garret 1st Earl of Morning-
ton in Ireland, and brother of the Marquess
Wellesley, K. G. and of the Duke of Wellington, K. G. ; Created Baron Maryborough
of Maryborough, in Queen's County, 15 Aug.
1821. Present Baron Maryborough.

MASHAM.

BARONS.

I. 1711. 1. Sir Samuel Masham, 4th Bart.; Created Baron Masham of Otes, co. Essex, 31 Dec. 1711;
ob. 1758.

II. 1758. 2. Samuel Masham, s. and h. ob. 1776, s. p.
when the title became
Extinct

B 2

MAUDUIT.

BARONS BY TENURE.

I. Will. I. 1. William Mauduit, Chamberlain to Henry I.
II. Hen. I. 2. Robert Mauduit, s. and h. Chamberlain to the
            King; ob. circa 1135, s. p. m.
III. H. II. 3. William Mauduit, brother of Robert the last
            Baron; Chamberlain to the King; living
            1197. His successor was
IV. John. 4. Robert Mauduit; ob. 1221.
V. H. III. 5. William Mauduit, s. and h. ob. 1256.
VI. H. III. 6. William Mauduit, s. and h. became Earl of
            Warwick jure matris.   Vide WARWICK.

I. John.   Thomas Mauduit, presumed of the same fa-
              mily, living 1241; of whom nothing more is
              recorded.

I. John.   Robert Mauduit, also of this family, Governor
              of Dadington Castle 1216.

MAUDUIT

BARON BY WRIT.   OF ——

I. 1342.   John Mauduit, a branch of the same family;
              Summ. to Parl. 12 Sept. 16 Edw. III. 1342,
              but never afterwards; ob. 1347, leaving John
              his s. and h. but neither this John nor any of
              his posterity were ever Summ. to Parl. or
              ranked among the Barons of the Realm, and
              the Barony on the death of the said Baron
              became   Extinct.

MAULEY.

BARONS BY TENURE.

I. Ric. I. 1. Peter de Mauley; obtained the Barony of
            Mulgrave in right of his wife, Isabel, dau. of
            Robert de Turnham; ob. 1221.
II. H. III. 2. Peter de Mauley, s. and h. ob. 1242.
III. H. III. 3. Peter de Mauley, s. and h. living 1258; ob. ...
BY WRIT.
I. 1295. 4. Peter de Mauley, s. and h. Summ. to Parl. as
            " Petro de Malo-lacu," from 23 June, 23
            Edw. I. 1295, to 12 Dec. 3 Edw. II. 1309; ob.
            1310.

BARONS BY WRIT.

II. 1310. 5. Peter de Mauley, s. and h. Summ. to Parl. as "Petro Malo-lacu," from 19 Dec. 5 Edw. II. 1311, to 22 Jan. 9 Edw. III. 1336, and from 24 Aug. 9 Edw. III. 1336, to 15 March, 28 Edw. II. 1354, as " Petro de Malo-lacu le quint ;" ob. 1355.

III. 1355. 6. Peter de Mauley, s. and h. Summ. to Parl. from 20 Sept. 29 Edw. III. 1355, to 7 Jan. 6 Ric. II. 1383, as "Petro de Malo-lacu le sisme," though in the last few Writs without the addition of " le sisme"; ob. 1383.

IV. 1383. 7. Peter de Mauley, grandson and heir, being s. and h. of Peter de Mauley (ob. v. p.) eldest son of the last Baron ; Summ. to Parl. from 18 Aug. 23 Ric. II. 1399, to 12 Aug. 3 Hen. V. 1415, as " Petro de Malo-lacu ;" ob. 1415, s. p. leaving his sisters, viz. Constance, æt. 30, who married, first, William Fairfax, and 2dly, Sir John Bigot ; and Elizabeth, æt. 25, the wife of George Salvaine, his heirs, amongst whose descendants and representatives this Barony is in ABEYANCE.

MAYNARD.

BARONS.

I. 1628. 1. Sir William Maynard, 1st Bart. and 1st Baron Maynard in Ireland; Created Baron Maynard of Estaines ad Turrim, co. Essex, 14 March, 1628 ; ob. 1639.

II. 1639. 2. William Maynard, s. and h. ob. 1698.

III. 1698. 3. Banastre Maynard, s. and h. ob. 1718.

IV. 1718. 4. Henry Maynard, s. and h. ob. 1742, s. p.

V. 1742. 5. Grey Maynard, brother and heir ; ob. 1745, s.p.

VISCOUNTS.

VI. 1745. ⎫ 6. Charles Maynard, brother and heir;
I. 1766.—I.1766. ⎬ Created Baron Maynard of Much Easton, co. Essex, and Viscount Maynard of Easton Lodge, co. Essex, with remainder, failing his issue male, to his kinsman Sir William Maynard, Bart. 18th Oct. 1766 ; ob. 1775, when the Irish Barony, and the Barony of Maynard of Estaines ad

BARON.   VISC.

Turrim, became **Extinct**; but the
Viscountcy and Barony of Maynard
of Much Easton devolved, agreeable
to the above limitation, on

II. . . . . .—II. 1775.   2. Sir Charles Maynard, 5th Bart. s.
and h. of Sir William Maynard (to
whom the Viscountcy and Barony
was in remainder, as is mentioned
above), descended from Charles
Maynard, a younger brother of William 1st Baron ; ob. 1824, s. P.

III.. . . . .—III.1824.   3. Henry Maynard, nephew and heir,
being s. and h. of William Maynard,
next brother of the last Viscount.
Present Viscount and Baron Maynard
of Much Easton, and a Baronet. ⚌

MEINILL.

BARONS BY WRIT.

I.   1295.   1. Nicholas de Meinill; Summ. to Parl. from 23
June, 23 Edw. I. 1295, to 6 Feb. 27 Edw. I.
1299. He was also summoned 8 June, 22 Edw.
I. 1294 ; but, for the reasons assigned under
"CLYVEDON," it is very doubtful if that Writ
can be considered as a regular Summons to
Parliament ; ob. 1299, s. P. L. when the Bá-
rony became
Extinct.

I.   1313.   1. Nicholas de Meinill, natural son of the last
Baron ; Summ. to Parl. from 22 May, 6 Edw.
II. 1313, to 14 March, 15 Edw. II. 1322 ; ob.
1322, s. P. when this Barony also became
Extinct.

I.   1336.   1. Nicholas de Meinill, called by Dugdale, "Chief
of the family, but how related to the last-
mentioned Nicholas I find not." Summ. to
Parl. from 22 Jan. 9 Edw. III. 1336, to 25
Feb. 16 Edw. III. 1342; ob. 1342, s. P. M.
leaving Elizabeth, his dau. his sole heir ; she
married, 1st, John II.-2d Baron Darcy, and
2dly, Peter III.-6th Baron Mauley. This Barony continued vested in the Barons Darcy
until the death of Philip VI.-11th Baron
Darcy, in 1418, when, with the Barony of

Darcy, it fell into ABEYANCE between his daughters and coheirs. Vide DARCY.

Although the Abeyance of the Baronies of Meinill and Darcy has never been terminated, yet Conyers Darcy, 2d Baron Darcy under the patent of 10 Aug. 1641, and Baron Conyers in right of his grandmother, probably under the presumption that the said patent not only restored the ancient Barony of Darcy, but also that of Meinill, was styled, in the Writs of Summons to Parliament of 7 Oct. 31 Car. II. 1679, and 1 March, 31 Car. II. 1680, " Conyers Darcie de Darcie & *Meinill*, Chl'r." He was created Earl of Holderness in 1682, which title, as well as the Barony of Darcy created by the Patent of 1641, became Extinct in 1778; but it is manifest that the assumption of the title of the Barony of Meinill was without any legal foundation.

MELBOURNE.

BARON.

I.   1615.   1. Peniston Lamb, 1st Viscount Melbourne in Ireland; Created Baron Melbourne of Melbourne, co. Derby, 11 Aug. 1815. Present Baron Melbourne; also Viscount Melbourne in Ireland. ⚓

MELCOMBE.

BARON.

I.   1761.   1. George Dodington; Created Baron Melcombe of Melcombe-Regis, co. Dorset, April 1761; ob. 1762, s. P. when the title became Extinct.

MELDRUM.

BARON.

I.   1815.   1. George Gordon, 5th Earl of Aboyne in Scotland; Created Baron Meldrum of Morven, co. Aberdeen, 11 Aug. 1815. Present Baron Meldrum and Earl of Aboyne in Scotland. ⚓

MELGUND.

VISCOUNTCY, 24 February, 1813.

Vide MINTO.

MELVILLE.

VISCOUNTS.

I. 1802. 1. Henry Dundas; Created Baron Dunira, co, Perth, and Viscount Melville of Melville, co. Edinburgh, Dec. 24, 1802; ob. 1811.

II. 1811. 2. Robert Saunders Dundas, s. and h. Present Viscount Melville and Baron Dunira, K.T.

MENDIP.

BARONS.

I. 1792. 1. Welbore Ellis; Created Baron Mendip of Mendip, co. Somerset, 13 Aug. 1794, with remainder, failing his heirs male, to Henry Welbore Agar, 2d Baron and Viscount Clifden in Ireland, son and heir of James 1st Baron and Viscount Clifden in Ireland, eldest son of Henry Agar, Esq. by Ann Ellis, sister of the said Baron Mendip, and to his heirs male; failing which, to John Ellis Agar and Charles Bagnal Agar, brothers of the said Henry Viscount Clifden, and to their issue male respectively; in default of which, to Welbore Ellis Agar, Esq. and Dr. Charles Agar, Archbishop of Cashel (afterwards created Baron and Viscount Somerton and Earl of Normanton in Ireland) the 2d and 3d sons of the above-mentioned Henry Agar and Ann Ellis, the sister of Lord Mendip, and to the heirs male of their bodies * ; ob. 1802, s.p. when the Barony devolved, agreeable to the above limitation, on

---

* It is worthy of remark, that the only male descendants of Henry Agar and Ann Ellis, *not* included in the limitation of the Barony of Mendip, was the Rev. Henry Agar, their youngest son, whose descendants are still living.

BARONS.

II. 1802. 2. Henry Welbore Agar (assumed the name of)
Ellis, 2d Baron and Viscount Clifden in Ireland. Present Baron Mendip; also Viscount
and Baron Clifden in Ireland. ⚓

MERLEY.

BARONS BY TENURE.

I. Steph. 1. Ranulph Merley, s. and h. of William de Merley; Lord of Wytton.

II. H.II. 2. Roger de Merley, s. and h. ob. 1188.

III. Ric.I. 3. Roger de Merley, s. and h. ob. 1239.

IV. H.III. 4. Roger de Merley, s. and h. ob. 1266, s.p. m. his
three daughters being his coheirs, of whom
Mary married William de Greystock.

MERTON.

VISCOUNTCY, 20 November, 1805.

Vide NELSON.

MESCHINES.

BARON BY TENURE.

I. Hen. I. William de Meschines, brother of Ralph Earl
of Chester; Lord of several Manors in Cumberland; ob. s. p. m. Cecily, his dau. and
heir, married Robert de Romely, Lord of
Skipton.

MIDDLESEX.

EARLS.

I. 1622. 1. Lionel Cranfield, 1st Baron Cranfield; Created Earl of Middlesex 16 Sept. 1622; Lord
Treasurer; ob. 1645.

II. 1645. 2. James Cranfield, s. and h. ob. 1651, s.p.m.

III. 1651. 3. Lionel Cranfield, brother and heir; ob. 1674,
s. p. when the title became
Extinct.

IV. 1675. 1. Charles Sackville, son and heir apparent of
Richard IX.-5th Earl of Dorset, by Frances,

sister and at length sole heir of Lionel the last Earl; Created Baron of Cranfield and Earl of Middlesex Apr. 4, 1675; succeeded as X.-6th Earl of Dorset, Aug. 27, 1677, in which title this Earldom has since been merged. Lionel Cranfield Sackville, his s. and h. Earl of Dorset, was Created Duke of Dorset. Vide Dorset.

MIDDLETON.

BARONS.

I.   1711.   1. Sir Thomas Willoughby, 2d Bart. descended from Thomas Willoughby, a younger brother of William VIII.-7th Baron Willoughby of Eresby; Created Baron Middleton of Middleton, co. Warwick, 31 December, 1711; ob. 1729.

II.   1729.   2. Francis Willoughby, s. and h. ob. 1758.

III.   1758.   3. Francis Willoughby, s. and h. ob. 1774, s. P.

IV.   1774.   4. Thomas Willoughby, brother and heir; ob. 1781, s. P.

V.   1781.   5. Henry Willoughby, cousin and heir; being s. and h. of Thomas Willoughby, next brother of Francis 2d Baron; ob. 1800.

VI.   1800.   6. Henry Willoughby, s. and h. Present Baron Middleton. ═

MILBROKE.

BARON.

I.   1442.   1. John Cornwall, Baron Fanhope, husband of Elizabeth Plantagenet, sister of King Henry IV.; Created Baron of Milbroke, co. Bedford, 30 Jan. 1442, K. G.; ob. 1443, s. P. L. when all his honors became
Extinct.

MILFORD HAVEN.

Earldom, Nov. 9, 1706—Merged in the Crown June 11, 1727.
Vide Cambridge.

MILTON.

VISCOUNTCY, 6 September, 1746.

Vide FITZ-WILLIAM.

MILTON.

OF MILTON ABBEY.

BARONS. VISCOUNTS.

I. 1762.—I. 1792. 1. Joseph Damer, 1st Baron Milton in Ireland; Created Baron Milton of Milton Abbey, co. Dorset, 10 May, 1762; Created Viscount Milton of Milton Abbey aforesaid, and Earl of Dorchester, in the said county, 18 May, 1792; ob. 1798.

II. ......—II. 1798. 2. George Damer, s. and h. Earl of Dorchester; ob. 1808, s. p. when all his honors became

Extinct.

MINSHULL.

John Minshull is said by many writers to have been created Baron Minshull of Minshull, co. Cheshire, in 1642, and it is stated that the title became extinct on his death. Dugdale, however, takes no notice of such a Peter. The probability is, that the patent was never regularly executed; for Banks, in his Dormant and Extinct Peerage, asserts that the said John Minshull left issue male, whose descendants in the male line are still existing, and who, it may be presumed, would assert their claim to the dignity if a valid one could be preferred.

MINSTER.

BARON.

I. 1821. 1. Henry Conyngham, 1st Marquess Conyngham in Ireland; Created Baron Minster of Minster Abbey, co. Kent, July 14, 1821; Lord Steward. Present Baron Minster; also Marquess Conyngham, &c. in Ireland; K. P. ᛏ

MINTO.

BARONS.   EARLS.

I. 1797.—I. 1813. 1. Sir Gilbert Eliot, 4th Bart,.; Created
Baron Minto, co. Roxburgh, Oct. 26,
1797; Created Viscount Melgund of
Melgund, co. Forfar, and Earl of
Minto, co. Roxburgh, 24 Feb. 1813;
ob. 1814.

II. .... —II. 1814. 2. Gilbert Eliot, (assumed the names of)
Murray Knynynmound, son and heir.
Present Earl and Baron Minto and
Viscount Melgund.

MOELS.

BARONS BY TENURE.

I. H. III. 1. Nicholas de Moels, Lord of Caddebury; co.
Somerset; living 1263.

II. Edw. I. 2. Roger de Moels, s. and h. ob. 1294.

BY WRIT.

I. 1299. 3. John de Moels, s. and h. Summ. to Parl. from
6 Feb. 27 Edw. I. 1299, to 16 June, 4 Edw.
II. 1311.   He was also summoned 26 Jan. 25
Edw. I. 1297; but, for the reasons assigned
under "FITZ-JOHN," it is doubtful if that
Writ was a regular Summons to Parliament;
ob. 1311.

II. 1311. 4. Nicholas de Moels, s. and h. Summ. to Parl.
from 19 Oct. 5 Edw. II. 1311, to 6 Oct. 9
Edw. II. 1315; ob. 1316, s. p.

III. 1316. 5. John de Moels, brother and heir; he was
never Summ. to Parl.; ob. 1337, s. p. m.
leaving Isabel, wife of William Lord Botreaux, and Muriel, wife of Sir Thomas
Courtenay, his daughters and coheirs, among
whose descendants and representatives this
Barony is in ABEYANCE.

The heiress of the above William Lord Botreaux car-
ried the Barony of Botreaux with the moiety of that of
Moels to Robert 2d Lord Hungerford, whose mother Ka-
therine Lady Hungerford, dau. and eventually sole heir of
Sir Thomas Peverel by Margaret, dau. and coheir of Sir
Thomas Courtenay and Muriel de Moels his wife above
mentioned, was also the coheir of the other moiety of the
Barony of Moels; which representation, viz. of one

moiety, and of half the other moiety, is now vested in the
present Marquess of Hastings, Baron Hungerford, Molines,
and Botreaux, the heir-general of the body of the said
Robert Baron Hungerford and of Margaret, daughter and
heiress of Lord Botreaux, his wife. Vide HUNGERFORD
and HASTINGS. Muriel, the other daughter and coheir
of Sir Thomas Courtenay and of Muriel his wife, daughter and coheir of John last Baron Moels, married John
Dinham (ancestor of Lord Dinham), among whose descendants the representation of the other part of the
moiety of the Barony of Moels is now vested.

MOHUN.

BARONS BY TENURE.

I. Will.I. 1. William de Mohun; obtained 56 Lordships
from William the Conqueror; Lord of
Dunster.

II. Hen.I. 2. William de Mohun, s. and h. ob. . . . .

III. Steph. 3. William de Mohun, s. and h. said to have been
created Earl of Dorset by the Empress
Maud in 1140; ob. ante 1165.

IV. H. II. 4. William de Mohun, s. and h. living 1196; ob.
ante 1202.

V. John. 5. Reginald de Mohun, s. and h. ob. 1213.

VI. H.III. 6. Reginald de Mohun, s. and h. ob. 1256.

VII. H.III. 7. John de Mohun, s. and h. ob. 1278.

BARONS BY WRIT.

I. 1199. 8. John de Mohun, s. and h. Summ. to Parl. from
6 Feb. 27 Edw. I. 1299, to 23 Oct. 4 Edw.III.
1330; ob. 1330.

II. 1330. 9. John de Mohun, grandson and heir, being son
and heir of John de Mohun (ob. v. p.) eldest
son of the last Baron; Summ. to Parl. from
25 Feb. 16 Edward III. 1342, to 4 Oct. 47
Edward III. 1373; after the 22 Edw. III.
with the addition of " de Dunsterre;" ob.
. . . . s. P. M. leaving his three daughters, viz.
Elizabeth, wife of Edward Plantagenet, Duke
of York; Elizabeth, married to William de
Montacute; and Maude, married to John
Lord Strange of Knocking, his next heirs;
among whose descendants and representatives this Barony is in ABEYANCE.

MOHUN
OF OKEHAMPTON.

BARONS.

I.   1628. 1. Sir John Mohun, 2d Bart. (lineally descended
from Reginald de Mohun, younger son of
John I.-8th Baron, and uncle to John II.-9th
Baron) ; Created Baron Mohun of Okehamp-
ton, co. Devon, 15 April, 1628 ; ob. 1644.

II. 1644. 2. John Mohun, s. and h. ob. 16.., s. P.

III. 16... 3. Warwick Mohun, brother and heir ; ob. 1665.

IV. 1665. 4. Charles Mohun, s. and h. ob. ante 1682.

V.   16... 5. Charles Mohun, s. and h. ob. 1712, s. P. when
the title became
𝕰𝖝𝖙𝖎𝖓𝖈𝖙.

MOLINES.

BARONS BY WRIT.

I.   1347. 1. John de Molines ; Summ. to Parl. 18 February,
21 Edw. III. 1347 ; but never afterwards ; he
died between 1355 and 1367, leaving William
his son and heir, who dying in 1380, was
succeeded by his son Richard ; which Richard
died in 1384, leaving William de Molines his
son and heir, who dying s. P. M. 1428, Alianore his only daughter was his heir. None
of the male descendants of John the 1st
Baron were ever summoned to Parliament,
and the Barony on his death became
𝕰𝖝𝖙𝖎𝖓𝖈𝖙.

II. 1445. Robert Hungerford *, son and heir apparent
of Robert 2d Baron Hungerford, having married the
above-mentioned Alianore, dau. and sole heir of William
de Molines, was Summ. to Parl. as " Roberto Hungerford,
Militi, Domino de Moleyns," from 13 January, 23 Hen.

---

* Although the title of Lord Molines was attributed to each of
the descendants of John the 1st Baron, Robert de Hungerford is
here called the *second* Baron, because it has been decided that a
single Summons to Parliament, without a proof of sitting, does
not constitute a Barony in fee ; and moreover in this instance it
is somewhat doubtful if the Writ to John Molines in 21 Edw. III.
was a *regular* Summons to Parliament.

VI. 1445, to 20 Jan. 31 Hen. VI. 1453; succeeded as third Baron Hungerford in 1459; ATTAINTED 1461, when all his honors became forfeited. Thomas Hungerford his son and heir was attainted in 1468, and dying s. p. m. Mary his daughter was his heir; she married Edward Hastings, afterwards second Lord Hastings of Ashby de la Zouche; and in 1485 the attainder of the said Thomas Hungerford and of Robert Hungerford his father was reversed. George Hastings, son and heir of the said Edward Lord Hastings, succeeded his father in this Barony, and in those of Hastings, Hungerford, and Botreaux in 1507, and was Created Earl of Huntingdon in 1529, when the Baronies of MOLINES, Hungerford, Hastings, and Botreaux, became vested in the Earls of Huntingdon, and so continued until the death of Francis XXII.-10th Earl in 1789, when they devolved on his sister and heir Elizabeth, and are now vested in her son Francis, the present Marquess of Hastings, Baron Hastings, Molines, Botreaux, and Hungerford, &c.

Vide HUNGERFORD and HASTINGS.

MONK.

BARONY, 7 July, 1660—Extinct 1688.

Vide ALBEMARLE.

MONMOUTH.

BARONS BY TENURE.

I. Will.I. 1. William Fitz-Baderon; held 22 lordships temp. Will. I.
II. Hen. I. 2. Witbenock, surnamed de Monmouth, son and heir.
III. H. II. 3. Baderon de Monmouth, s. and h. living 1168; ob. ante 1176.
IV. Ric. I. 4. Gilbert de Monmouth, s. and h. ob. ....
V. John. 5. John de Monmouth, s. and h. ob. 1248.
VI. H.III. 6. John de Monmouth, s. and h. ob. 1257, s.p.m. Albreda de Botereus and Joan de Nevill, being his daughters and coheirs according to Dugdale; but other authorities state, that he died s. p. and that the said Albreda and Joan were sisters to Cecily de Waleran, the mother of this Baron.

c 2

MONMOUTH.

EARLS.

I.   1626. 1. Robert Carey, 1st Baron Carey of Leppington;
          Created Earl of Monmouth 5 Feb. 1626;
          ob. 1639.

II.   1639. 2. Henry Carey, s. and h. ob. 1661, s. p. m. when
          the title became
                    Extinct.

DUKE.

I. 1663. James Fitz-Roy, natural son of Charles II.
          Created Baron of Tyndale, co. Nortbumber-
          land, Viscount Doncaster and Duke of Mon-
          mouth 14 Feb. 1663, K. G.; attainted and
          beheaded 1685, when all his honors became
                    Forfeited.

III.   1689. 1. Charles Mordaunt, 2d Viscount Mordaunt of
          Avalon, being son and heir of John 1st Vis-
          count Mordaunt, by Elizabeth, sole dau. and
          heir of Robert Carey, next brother of Henry
          Carey 2d Earl of Monmouth; was Created
          Earl of Monmouth 9 April, 1689; succeeded
          as 3d Earl of Peterborough in 1697, to which
          title this Earldom was united until 1814,
          when by the death of Charles Henry 5th Earl
          of Peterborough and 3d Earl of Monmouth,
          s. p. both these dignities became
                    Extinct.   Vide PETERBOROUGH.

MONSON.

BARONS.

I.   1728. 1. Sir John Monson, 5th Bart. Created Baron
          Monson of Burton, co. Lincoln, 28 May,
          1728, K. B.; ob. 1748.

II.   1748. 2. John Monson, s. and h. ob. 1774.

III.   1774. 3. John Monson, s. and h. ob. 1806.

IV.   1806. 4. John George Monson, s. and h. ob. 1809.

V.   1809. 5. Frederick John Monson, s. and h. Present
          Baron Monson (a minor).

MONTACUTE or MONTAGU.

BARONS BY TENURE.

I. H. II. Richard de Montacute; living 1160; ob. ante 1165; his successor was

II. .... Drue de Montacute; living 1167; ob. .... to whom succeeded

III. Ric. I. William de Montacute; ob. 1217, s.p. leaving

IV. H.III. William de Montacute, son of Dru de Montacute, his next heir; ob. 1246, leaving his two daughters his heirs.

I. H.III. 1. William de Montacute, son of William de Montacute; ob. ....

BARONS BY WRIT.

I. 1300. 2. Simon de Montacute, s. and h. Summ. to Parl. from 26 September, 28 Edw. I. 1300, to 6 October, 9 Edw. II. 1315; he was also Summoned 8 June, 22 Edw. I. 1294; but it is very doubtful if that Writ was a regular Summons to Parliament, vide " CLYVEDON;" ob. circa 1816.

II. 1317. 3. William de Montacute, s. and h. Summ. to Parl. from 20 Nov. 11 Edw. II. 1317, to 25 Aug. 12 Edward II. 1318; ob. 1319.

III. 1319. 4. William de Montacute, s. and h. Summ. to Parl. from 5 June, 5 Edward III. 1331, to 29 Nov. 10 Edward III. 1336; Created Earl of Salisbury 16 March, 1337. This Barony continued merged in that Earldom until the attainder of John VI.-3d Earl in 1400, when, with his other honors, viz. the Earldom of Salisbury, the Barony of Montagu, created by the Writ of 31 Edward III. (vide p. 436), and the Barony of Monthermer, it became forfeited; Thomas de Montacute his son and heir was Summ. to Parl. in 1409 as Earl of Salisbury, and was fully restored in blood and honors 9 Henry V. 1421; he died S. P. M. in 1428, when this Barony, with those just mentioned, devolved on Alice his sole daughter and heir, who married Richard Nevill; her husband was created Earl of Salisbury in 1442, and was attainted in 1459; but it appears that he was restored in the following year, before the end of which he died, when all his honors devolved on his son Richard Earl of Warwick, and who, jure matris, possessed

c 3

both the Baronies of Montagu and that of Monthermer;
but on his attainder in 1471, these Baronies, with his
other dignities became

Forfeited.

He left two daughters his coheirs, viz. Ann, who married, first, Edward Prince of Wales, and secondly, King
Richard III, but died s. p. s.; and Isabel, who married
George Plantagenet, Duke of Clarence, who was drowned
and attainted in 1477, by whom she left issue Edward,
who was beheaded and attainted in 1499 (ob. s. p.)
and Margaret, wife of Sir Richard Pole, K. G. which Margaret was Created Countess of Salisbury, but was attainted in 1539, and beheaded in 1541; her eldest son

BARON BY WRIT.

I.　1533.　Henry Pole, was Summ. to Parl. 5 January,
24 Henry VIII. 1533, and 18 June, 28 Hen.
VIII. 1536, as "Henrico Pole de Montagu;"
attainted and beheaded in 1539, when this
Barony also became

Forfeited.

He died s. p. m leaving Katherine, wife of Francis
XIX.-3d Earl of Huntingdon (now represented by her
heir-general the Marquess of Hastings), and Winifred,
who married, first, Sir Thomas Hastings, and secondly,
Sir Thomas Barrington, his daughters and coheirs, who
were fully restored in blood and honors 1 Ph. and Mary,
and amongst whose descendants and representatives the
Barony of Montagu, created by the Writ of 24 Henry
VIII. to their father, is in ABEYANCE.

MONTAGU.

BARON.　MARQUESS.

1.　1461.—I. 1470. John Nevill, 3d son of Richard Nevill,
Earl of Salisbury, and Alice Monta-
cute above mentioned, and brother of
Richard Earl of Warwick; Summ. to Parl.
as "Johanni Nevyll, Domino de Montagu,
Cbl'r," 23 May, 1 Edw. IV. 1461, and as
"Johanni Nevyll de Montagu," 22 Dec.
1 Edw. IV. 1462, and 28 Feb. 2 Edward IV.
1463, having on the 30th July, 38 Hen. VI.
1460, been Summoned as " "Johanni Nevill,
Domino Nevill, Cbl'r;" Created Earl of

Northumberland 27 May, 1467; which title
he resigned in 1471, and was created Marquess Montagu 25 March, 1470; ob. 1471,
and being attainted, all his honors became
𝔉𝔬𝔯𝔣𝔢𝔦𝔱𝔢𝔡.

VISCOUNTS.

I.   1554. 1. Anthony Brown, grandson and heir of Anthony Brown and Lucy his wife, widow of
Sir William. Fitz-William, and dau. and
eventually coheir of John Nevill, last Marquess; Created Viscount Montague 2 Sept.
1554, K. G.; ob. 1592.

II.   1592. 2. Anthony Brown, grandson and heir, being
son and heir of Anthony Brown (ob. v. p.)
eldest son of the last Viscount; ob. 1629.

III. 1629. 3. Francis Brown, s. and h. ob. 1682.

IV. 1682. 4. Francis Brown, s. and h. ob. 1708, s. p.

V.   1708. 5. Henry Brown, brother and heir; ob. 1717.

VI. 1717. 6. Anthony Brown, s. and h. ob. 1767,

VII. 1767. 7. Anthony Joseph Brown, s. and h. ob. 1787.

VIII.1787. 8. George Samuel Brown, son and heir; ob.
1793, s. p.

IX. 1793. 9. Mark Anthony Browne, cousin and heir male,
being son and heir of Mark, eldest surviving
son of Stanislaus, son and heir of Stanislaus,
eldest son of John Browne, second son of
Anthony 1st Viscount; ob. 1797, s. p. when
this dignity became
𝔈𝔵𝔱𝔦𝔫𝔠𝔱 *.

---

* A claim to this dignity has been several times asserted by a
Mr. John Browne, of Storington, as the descendant of George
the 2d son of John Browne, 2d son of Anthony the 1st Viscount
Montagu, and he has brought actions of ejectment for the re-
covery of the lands as heir male of the said Viscount, against the
Crown (who came into possession under the reversion of the original grant to Anthony 1st Viscount, his heirs male being considered to have failed); but Mr. Browne has never proceeded to
trial. His claim to this Viscountcy has been lately urged by a
petition to the Crown, and by it referred to the Attorney-General,
from whom his *pretensions* will no doubt receive the consideration
they *deserve*.

MONTAGU

OF ——

BARON BY WRIT.

I.   1342.   Edward de Montagu, younger brother of William IV.-1st Earl of Salisbury, and III.-4th Baron Montagu (vide p. 430); Summ. to Parliament from 25 February 26 Edward III. 1342, to 20 Nov. 34 Edward III. 1360; ob. 1361, S. P. M. leaving Joan, the wife of William de Ufford, afterwards Earl of Suffolk, his dau. and heir; on whose death, s. P. this Barony became

𝔈𝔵𝔱𝔦𝔫𝔠𝔱.

MONTAGU

OF ——

BARONS BY WRIT.

I.   1357.   1. John de Montagu, 2d son of William IV.-1st Earl of Salisbury, and III.-4th Baron Montagu (vide p. 433); he married Margaret, grand-dau. and heir of Ralph Baron Monthermer; Summ. to Parl from 15 Feb. 31 Edward III. 1357, to 6 Dec. 13 Rich. II. 1389, as " John de Montacute; ob. 1390.

II.   1390.   2. John de Montagu, s. and h. Summ. to Parl. from 23 Nov. 16 Rich. II. 1392, to 30 Nov. 20 Rich. II. 1396 as "John de Montacute;" succeeded his uncle in the Barony of Montagu created by the Writ of 26 Sept. 28 Edw. I. 1300, (vide p. 433), and as VI.-3d Earl of Salisbury in 1397.   Vide SALISBURY.

This Barony, together with that of Montagu or Montacute, created by the Writ of 28 Edward I. just mentioned, and the Barony of Monthermer, continued merged in the Earldom of Salisbury until the attainder of John VI.-3d Earl in 1400, when, with his other honors, it became 𝔣𝔬𝔯𝔣𝔢𝔦𝔱𝔢𝔡. Thomas de Montacute his son and heir was fully restored in blood and honors in 1421, and dying s.p.m. in 1428, this Barony, with those above mentioned, devolved on Alice his daughter and sole heir, wife of Richard Nevill, Earl of Salisbury, who was attainted in 1459, but restored in the following year, before the end of which he died, when all his dignities devolved on his son Richard Nevill, Earl of Salisbury and Warwick; but on his attainder in 1471 this Barony, with all his other honors, became

Forfeited.

Vide MONTAGU, p. 433.

MONTAGU

OF BOUGHTON.

BARONS.

I.   1621.   1. Edward Montagu, presumed to have been descended from Simon de Montagu, a younger son of John I.-1st Baron Montagu de Montagu, under the Writ of 31 Edward III. 1357, vide last page ; Created Baron Montagu of Boughton, co. Northampton, 29 June, 1621; ob. 1644.

II.   1644.   2. Edward Montagu, s. and h. ob. 1683.

EARLS.   DUKES.

III. 1683.—I. 1689.—I. 1705. 3. Ralph Montagu, s. and h. Created Viscount Monthermer of Monthermer, co. Essex, and Earl of Montagu, 9 April, 1689; Created Marquess of Monthermer and Duke of Montagu 12 April, 1705; ob. 1709.

IV. .... —III. .... —II. 1709. John Montagu, s. and h. ob. 1749, s. p. m. when all his titles became

Extinct.

V.   1762.   1. John Montagu, son and heir apparent of George 4th Earl of Cardigan, (afterwards Duke of Montagu, vide infra,) by Mary, dau. and coheir of John last Duke of Montagu, and Baron Montagu of Boughton; Created Baron Montagu of Boughton, co. Northampton, 8th May, 1762; ob. vita patris, 1772, s. p. when this Barony again became

Extinct.

DUKE.

VI. 1786.—III. 1766.   1. George Brudenell (assumed the name of) Montagu 4th Earl of

DUKES.

Cardigan, having married Mary, dau. and co-heir of John last Duke of Montagu, was created Marquess of Monthermer and Duke of Montagu 5 Nov. 1766; Created Baron Montagu of Boughton, co. Northampton, 8 August, 1786, with remainder, failing his issue male, to his grandson Henry James Montagu Scott, 2d son of Henry, 3d Duke of Buccleugh, by Elizabeth Montagu his sole dau. and heiress. K. G. ob. 1790, s. p. m. when the Marquisate of Monthermer and Dukedom of Montagu became Extinct; the Earldom of Cardigan devolved on his next heir male, and this Barony descended, agreeable to the above limitation, on his grandson

VII. 1790. 2. Henry James Montagu Scott, above mentioned, uncle of Walter Francis, present Duke of Buccleugh. Present Baron Montagu of Boughton. ⳴

MONTAGU
OF KIMBOLTON.

BARON.

I. 1620. 1. Henry Montagu, brother of Edward 1st Baron Montagu of Boughton; Created Baron Montagu of Kimbolton, co. Huntingdon, and Viscount Mandeville 19 Dec. 1620; Created Earl of Manchester 5 Feb. 1624.

Vide MANCHESTER.

MONTAGU
OF ST. NEOTS.

BARONY, 12 July, 1660.

Vide SANDWICH.

MONTALT.

BARONS BY TENURE.

I. H. II. 1. Robert de Montalt, Lord of Montalt, co. Flint; living 1160.

II. H. II. 2. Robert de Montalt, son and heir.

III. H.III. 3. Roger de Montalt, s. and h. ob. 1260.

BARONS BY TENURE.

IV. H.III. 4. John de Montalt, s. and h. ob. .... s. p.
V. H III. 5. Robert de Montalt, brother and heir; ob.....

BARONS BY WRIT.

L. 1295. 6. Roger de Montalt, s. and h. Summ. to Parl. 23 June, 23 Edward I. 1295; ob. 1297, s. p. when the Barony became

Extinct.

II. 1299. Robert de Montalt, brother and heir; Summ. to Parl. from 6 Feb. 27 Edw. I. 1299, to 13 June, 13 Edward III. 1329; ob. 1329, s. p. when this Barony also became

Extinct.

MONTBEGON.

BARONS BY TENURE.

L. Steph. 1. Roger de Montbegon; held several Lordships in Lincoln temp. Steph.
II. H. II. 2. Adam de Montbegon, s. and h. ob. .....
III. Ric. I. 3. Robert de Montbegon, s. and h. ob. ....
IV. John. 4. Roger de Montbegon, s. and h. ob. 1226 *, s. p.
V. H.III. 5. Henry de Montbegon, cousin and heir; of whom nothing farther is known.

MONTEAGLE.

BARONS BY WRIT.

I. 1514. 1. Edward Stanley, 2d son of Thomas 1st Earl of Derby; proclaimed Lord of Monteagle 1514, and Summ. to Parl. 23 Nov. 6 Henry VIII. 1514, and 12 Nov. 7 Henry VIII. 1515, as "Edwardo Stanley de Mount-Egell, Chl'r," K. G.; ob. 1523.
II. 1523. 2. Thomas Stanley, s. and h. Summ. to Parl. from 3 Nov. 21 Henry VIII. 1529, to 23 Jan. 1 Eliz. 1559; ob. 1560.
III. 1560. 3. William Stanley, s. and h. Summ. to Parl from 11 Jan. 5 Eliz. 1563, to 6 Jan. 23 Eliz. 1581; ob. 1581, s. p. m. Elizabeth his sole

---

* There is much discrepancy in Dugdale's account of these Barons. Vide tome I. p. 618.

BARONS BY WRIT.

dau. and heir, married Edward XI.-11th Baron Morley.

IV. 1605. 4. William Parker, son and heir apparent of the said Edward Baron Morley by Elizabeth his wife, dau. and sole heir of the last Baron; Summ. to Parl. as "Willielmo Parker de Montegle, Chl'r," vita patris, from 5 Nov. 3 Jac. 1605, to 5 April, 12 Jac. 1614; succeeded to the Barony of Morley in 1618, and was Summ. to Parl. 18 Jac. 1620, as "Willielmo Parker de Morley and Montegle, Chl'r;" ob. 1622.

V. 1622. 5. Henry Parker, s. and h. Summ. to Parl. as Baron Morley and Monteagle; ob. 1655.

VI. 1655. 6. Thomas Parker, s. and h. Summ. to Parl. as Baron Morley and Monteagle; ob. circa 1686, s. p. when the Baronies of Parker and Monteagle, with that of Marshal, fell into ABEY-ANCE between the issue of his aunts, viz. Catherine, wife of John V.-2d Earl Rivers, and Elizabeth, who married Edward Cranfield, Esq. among whose descendants and representatives they are now in ABEYANCE.

MONTEAGLE

OF WESTPORT.

BARONS.

I. 1806. 1. John Denis Browne, 1st Marquess of Sligo in Ireland; Created Baron Monteagle of Westport, co. Mayo, 20 Feb. 1806, K. G.; ob. 1809.

II. 1809. 2. Howe Peter Browne, s. and h. Present Baron Monteagle of Westport; also Marquess of Sligo, &c. in Ireland, K. P. ⚓

MONTFICHET.

BARONS BY TENURE.

I. Will. I. 1. William de Montfichet; living 1135.

II. H. II. 2. Gilbert de Motfichet, s. and h. living 1168.

III. Ric. I. 3. Richard de Montfichet, s. and h. ob. 1193.

IV. John. 4. Richard de Montfichet, s. and h.; he was one of the celebrated 25 Barons appointed to enforce the observance of MAGNA CHARTA; living 1258; ob. ...., s. p. leaving his three sisters his heirs, viz, Margery, wife of Hugh de Bolebec; Aveline, married to William Earl of Albemarle; and Philippa, married to Hugh de Plaitz.

MONTFORT.

BARONS BY TENURE.

I. Will. I. 1. Hugh de Montfort; obtained 114 Lordships from William the Conqueror.

II. Will. II. 2. Hugh de Montfort, s. and h. ob. ...., s. p. m. Hugh and Robert, his sons, died s. p.

III. Hen. I. 3. Hugh de Montfort, grandson and heir, being son and heir of Gilbert de Gant, by .... daughter and heir of Hugh the last Baron; assumed the name of Montfort; liv. 1124.

IV. Steph. 4. Robert de Montfort, s. and h. living 1163; ob. ...., s. p.

V. H. II. 5. Thurstan de Montfort, brother and heir; ob. ante 1190.

VI. Ric. I. 6. Henry de Montfort, s. and h. ob. ....; to whom succeeded

VII. John. 7. Thurstan de Montfort; ob. 1216.

VIII. H. III. 8. Peter de Montfort, s. and h. ob. 1264.

IX. H. III. 9. Peter de Montfort, s. and h. ob. 1287.

BY WRIT.

I. 1295. 10. John de Montfort, s. and h. Summ. to Parl. 23 June, 1 October, and 2 Nov. 23 Edward I. 1295; ob. 1296.

II. 1296. 11. John de Montfort, s. and h. Summ. to Parl. 26 July, 7 Edw. II. 1313; ob. circa 1314, s.p.

III. 1314. 12. Peter de Montfort, brother and heir; Summ. to Parl. from 22 Jan. 9 Edward III. 1336, to 10 March, 23 Edward III. 1349; ob. 1367, s. p. his sisters being his heirs; viz. Elizabeth, wife of Sir Baldwin de Freville, Knt. and Maud, wife of .... Sudley; between whose descendants and representatives the Barony created by the Writ of 23 Edward I. to their father is in ABEYANCE.

MONTFORT

OF HORSEHEATH.

BARONS.

I.   1741.   1. Henry Bromley ; Created Lord Montfort, Ba-
                 ron of Horseheath, co. Cambridge, 9 May,
                 1741; ob. 1755.
II. 1755.   2. Thomas Bromley, s. and h. ob. 1799.
III. 1799.   3. Henry Bromley, s. and h.   Present Baron
                 Montfort of Horseheath. ==

MONTGOMERY.

BARON BY WRIT.

I.   1342.   John de Montgomery ; Summ. to Parl. 25
                 Feb. 16 Edw. III. 1342, but never afterwards,
                 nor any of his descendants; Admiral of the
                 King's Fleet; ob. .... when the Barony be-
                 came   Extinct.

MONTGOMERY

OF WALES.

EARL.

I.   1605.   1. Philip Herbert, 2d son of Henry XXI.-2d
                 Earl of Pembroke ; Created Baron Herbert
                 of Shurland in the Isle of Shepey, co. Kent.
                 and Earl of Montgomery in Wales, 4 May,
                 1605 ; succeeded his brother William XXIII.-
                 4th Earl of Pembroke in 1630, K. G. Vide
                 PEMBROKE, in which dignity this Earldom is
                 merged.

MONTGOMERY.

VISCOUNTCY, 24 March, 1687—Extinct 1748.

                                    Vide Powis.

MONTHERMER.

BARONS BY WRIT.

I.   1309.   1. Ralph de Monthermer; he married Joane Plan-
                 tagenet, dau. of King Edward I. and widow
                 of Gilbert Earl of Clare, Gloucester, and Hert-

ford, and whilst she continued his wife he had the titles of Earl of Gloucester and Hertford attributed to him, and was Summ. to Parl. as " Comiti Gloucestr' et Hertf." from 6 Feb. 27 Edw. I. 1299, to 3 Nov. 34 Edw. I. 1306, jure uxoris, but she dying in 1307, he never afterwards used these titles, but was Summ. to Parl. as " Radulpho de Monthermer" only, from 4th March, 2 Edw. II. 1309, to 30 Oct. 18 Edw. II. 1324. Thomas de Monthermer, his son and heir, died vita patris, leaving Margaret, his sole dau. and heir, who married Sir John de Monta-cute, 2d son of William IV.-1st Earl of Salisbury; which Sir John was Summ. to Parl. as "John de Montacute," 31 Edw. III. though probably in consequence of his mar-riage (vide p. 436). John de Montagu, his son and heir, was also Summ. to Parl. and succeeded as VI.-3d Earl of Salisbury, and to the Barony of Montacute, cre-ated by the Writ of 28 Edw. I. 1300, in 1397. He was at-tainted and beheaded in 1400, when this Barony, with his other honors, became Forfeited. Thomas de Montacute, his son and heir, VII.-4th Earl of Salisbury, was restored to his father's dignities in 1421, on whose death, s. p. m. in 1428, the two Baronies of Montagu, and that of Monther-mer, devolved on Alice, his dau. and heir; she married Richard Nevill, who was created Earl of Salisbury, and though Attainted in 1459, appears to have been restored in the following year, when he died, and when his honors fell to his son and heir, Richard Nevill, the celebrated Earl of Warwick and Salisbury, and who, jure matris, succeeded to both the Baronies of Montagu, as well as to that of Monthermer, but on his death and Attainder, in 1471, all his honors became

Forfeited.

Vide MONTAGU, pp. 433, 434, and p. 436.

MONTHERMER

OF ——

BARON BY WRIT.

I. 1337. Edward de Monthermer; supposed by Banks to have been the son of the said Ralph by Joane Plantagenet; Summ. to Parl. 23d April, 11 Edw. III. 1337, but never after,

D 2

and of whom nothing farther is known ; on
his death, this Barony became
𝔈𝔯𝔱𝔦𝔫𝔠𝔱.

MONTHERMER

OF ESSEX.

VISCOUNTCY, 9th April, 1689.
MARQUISATE, 12th April, 1705.
Both 𝔈𝔯𝔱𝔦𝔫𝔠𝔱 1749.
Vide MONTAGU OF BOUGHTON.
MARQUISATE, 5th November, 1766—𝔈𝔯𝔱𝔦𝔫𝔠𝔱 1790.
Vide MONTAGU OF BOUGHTON.

MONTJOY.

BARONS.
I.   1465. 1. Walter Blount; Created Baron Montjoy of
Thurveston, co. Derby, 20 June, 1465; Lord
Treasurer ; K. G.; ob. 1474.
II.   1474. 2. Edward Blount, grandson and heir, being
s. and h. of William Blount (ob. v. p) eldest
son of the last Baron ; ob. 1475, s. p.
III. 1475. 3. John Blount, uncle and heir, being 2d son of
Walter 1st Baron ; ob. 1485.
IV.   1485. 4. William Blount, s. and h. ob. 1535.
V.   1535. 5. Charles Blount, s. and h. ob. 1545.
VI.   1545. 6. James Blount, s. and h. ob. 1593.
VII. 1593. 7. William Blount, s. and h. ob. 1594, s. p.
VIII. 1594. 8. Charles Blount, brother and heir; Created
Earl of Devonshire 21 July, 1603, K. G.; ob.
1606, s. p. L. when all his honors became
𝔈𝔯𝔱𝔦𝔫𝔠𝔱.

IX.   1627. 1. Montjoy-Blount (natural son of the last Ba-
ron), 1st Baron Montjoy of Montjoy Fort, in
Ireland; Created Baron Montjoy of Thurves-
ton co. Derby, ... 1627; Created Earl of
Newport 3 Aug. 1628.   Vide NEWPORT.
𝔈𝔯𝔱𝔦𝔫𝔠𝔱 1681.

MONTJOY
OF THE ISLE OF WIGHT.

BARONS.

I. 1711. 1. Thomas Windsor, 1st Viscount Windsor in Ireland, younger son of Thomas 1st Earl of Plymouth; descended from Andrews Windsor, 1st Baron Windsor, by Elizabeth, sister and coheir of Edward II.-2d Baron Montjoy; Created Baron Montjoy of the Isle of Wight 1 Jan. 1711; ob. 1738.

II. 1738. 2. Herbert Windsor, s. and h. Viscount Windsor in Ireland; ob. 1758, s. p. m. when all his honors became

Extinct.

VISCOUNTCY, 20 February, 1796.

Vide BUTE.

MOORE.

BARONS.

I. 1801. 1. Charles Moore, 1st Marquess of Drogheda in Ireland; Created Baron Moore of Moore Place, co. Kent, 17 Jan. 1801, K. P.; ob. 1822.

II. 1822. 2. Charles Moore, s. and h. Present Baron Moore; also Marquess of Drogheda, &c. in Ireland.

MORDAUNT
OR TURVEY.

BARONS BY WRIT.

I. 1532. 1. John Mordaunt; Summ. to Parl. from 4 May, 21 Henry VIII. to 5 Nov. 5 and 6 Philip and Mary, 1558; ob. 1562.

II. 1562. 2. John Mordaunt, s. and h. Summ. to Parl. from 11 Jan. 5 Eliz. 1563, to 8 May, 14 Eliz. 1572; ob. 1572.

III. 1572. 3. Lewis Mordaunt, s. and h. Summ. to Parl. from 8 Feb. 18 Eliz. 1576, to 24 Oct. 39 Eliz. 1597; ob. 1601.

IV. 1601. 4. Henry Mordaunt, s. and h. Summ. to Parl.

D 3

from 27 Oct. 43 Eliz. 1601, to 5 Nov. 3 Jaq. I. 1605; ob. 1608.

V.   1608. 5. John Mordaunt, s and h. Summ. to Parl. from 30 Jan. 18 Jaq. I. 1620, to 17 May, 23 Jaq. I. 1625; Created Earl of Peterborough in 1628. He married Elizabeth, dau. and sole heir of William Howard, son and heir apparent of Charles Howard, Earl of Nottingham, who in right of her mother Ann, dau. and heir of John 2d Baron St. John of Bletsho, was sole heir of the Barony of Beauchamp of Bletsho; ob. 1642.

VI.   1642. 6. Henry Mordaunt, s. and h. Earl of Peterborough, K. G.; ob. 1697, s. p. m.

BARONESS.

I.   1697. 7. Mary Mordaunt, dau. and sole heir; she married, 1st, Henry Duke of Norfolk, from whom she was divorced; and 2dly, Sir John Germain, Bart.; ob. 1705, s. p.

BARON BY WRIT.

VII. 1705. 8. Charles Mordaunt, III.-3d Earl of Peterborough, and III.-1st Earl of Monmouth, cousin and heir, being s. and h. of John Viscount Mordaunt of Avalon, next brother of Henry 2d Earl of Peterborough, and 6th Baron Mordaunt.

This Barony became merged in the Earldoms of Peterborough and Monmouth, until the death of Charles Henry V.-5th Earl of Peterborough, and V.-3d Earl of Monmouth, s. p. in 1814, when it devolved on

BARONESS.

II. 1814. 9. Mary Anastatia Grace Mordaunt, dau. of Charles IV. Earl of Peterborough, and 7th Baron Mordaunt of Turvey, and half-sister and sole heir of Charles last Earl and last Baron; ob. 1819, s. p. when the Barony devolved on

BARON BY WRIT.

X.   1819. 10. Alexander Gordon, 4th Duke of Gordon in Scotland, and 1st Earl of Norwich in England, cousin and heir, he being heir general of Charles 3d Earl of Peterborough, and VII.-8th Baron Mordaunt, viz. s. and h. of Cosmo 3d Duke of Gordon, eldest son of

Alexander 2d Duke of Gordon, by Henrietta, dau. of the said Charles 3d Earl of Peter-Peterborough and Baron Mordaunt. Present Baron Mordaunt of Turvey, Baron Beauchamp of Bletsho, Baron Gordon, and Earl of Norwich; also Duke of Gordon, &c. in Scotland; K.T. ⚮

MORDAUNT

OF AVALON AND RYEGATE.

BARONS. VISCOUNTS.

I. —I. 1659. 1. John Mordaunt, 2d son of John 1st Earl of Peterborough, and V.-5th Baron Mordaunt of Turvey; Created Baron Mordaunt of Ryegate, co. Surrey, and Viscount Mordaunt of Avalon, co. Somerset, 10 July, 1659; ob. 1675.

II.—II.1675. 2. Charles Mordaunt, s. and h. Created Earl of Monmouth April 9, 1689; succeeded as III.-3d Earl of Peterborough in 1697, and as VII.-8th Baron Mordaunt of Turvey in 1705. The Barony of Mordaunt of Ryegate, and this Viscountcy continued merged in the superior titles of Peterborough and Monmouth, until the death of Charles Henry 5th Earl of Peterborough, V.-3d Earl of Monmouth, IX.-10th Baron Mordaunt of Turvey, and IV.-4th Viscount Mordaunt of Avalon, and Baron Mordaunt of Ryegate, when all his honors became

Extinct.

MORLEY.

BARONS BY WRIT.

I. 1299. 1. William de Morley; Summ. to Parl. from 29 Dec. 28 Edw. I. 1299, to 3 Nov. 34 Edw. I. 1306; ob. . . . .

II. 1317. 2. Robert de Morley, s. and h. Summ. to Parl. from 20 Nov. 11 Edw. II. 1317, to 15 Feb. 31 Edw. III. 1357. He married Hawyse, dau. and heir of John Baron Marshal; ob. 1360.

III· 1360. 3. William de Morley, s. and h. Summ. to Parl. from 4 Dec. 38 Edw. III. 1364, to 3 Dec. 2 Ric. II. 1378; ob. 1380.

IV. 1380. 4. Thomas de Morley, s. and h. Summ. to Parl.
from 16 July, 5 Ric. II. 1381, to 3 Sept. 4
Henry V. 1417; ob. 1417.

V. 1417. 5. Thomas de Morley, grandson and heir, being
s. and h. of Robert de Morley (ob. v. p.) eldest
son of the last Baron; Summ. to Parl. from
15 July, 5 Henry VI. 1427, to 5 July, 13
Henry VI. 1435 *; ob. 1435.

VI. 1435. 6. Robert de Morley, s. and h. Summ. to Parl.
3d Dec. 20 Henry VI. 1441; ob. 1442, s.p. m.

VII. 1469.   William Lovel, 2d son of William Baron Lovel of Tichmersh, having married Alianore,
dau. and sole heir of the last Baron, was
Summ. to Parl. jure uxoris, from 10 Aug.
9 Edw. IV. 1469, to 15 Oct. 10 Edw. IV.
1417, as " Willielmo Lovel de Morley, Chl'r;"
ob. 1476.

VIII. 1476. 7. Henry Lovel, s. and h.; he was never Summ.
to Parl.; ob. 1489, s. P.

IX. 1523. 8. Henry Parker, s. and h. of Sir William Par-
   .   ker, by Alice Lovel, sister and sole heir of
Henry the last Baron; Summ. to Parl. as
"Henrico Parker de Morley, Chl'r." from 15
April, 14 Henry VIII. 1523, to 28 Oct. 2 and
3 Philip and Mary, 1555; ob. 1555.

X. 1555.10. Henry Parker, grandson and heir, being s. and
h of Sir Henry Parker, K. B. (ob. v. p.) eldest
son of the last Baron; Summ. to Parl. from

---

* A *John* de Morley is stated in the List of Summonses to
have been Summ. to Parl. 24 May, 11 Hen. VI. 1433, but as the
name of *Thomas* de Morley regularly occurs in the 5th and 7th
Henry VI. and again the 18th Henry VI. it is presumed to have
been an error; in the year preceding, viz. 10 Henry VI. the
Christian name does not appear in the List of Summonses, as it
stands " ..... de Morley, Chl'r." *Thomas* was Baron Morley
from the death of his grandfather in 1417, to his own death, Dec.
18, 1435, as is stated above. Moreover, in the List of Barons
present in Parliament in the 11th of Henry VI. the very year in
which he is styled in the Writ *John* de Morley, he is properly
called "Thomæ de Morley, Chivaler." Vide Rot. Parl. vol. iv.
p. 422.

20 Jan. 4 and 5 Philip and Mary, 1558, to 8 May, 14 Eliz. 1572; ob. ....

XI. 1581. 11. Edward Parker, s. and h. Summ. to Parl. from 26 Jan. 23 Eliz. 1581, to 5 April 12 Jaq. I. 1614. He married Elizabeth, sole dau. and heir of William Baron Monteagle; ob. 1618.

XII. 1618. 12. William Parker, s. and h. Summ. to Parl. vita patris in right of his mother, as Baron Monteagle; and summoned as "Willielmo Parker de Morley and Monteagle," from 30 Jan. 18 Jaq. I. 1621, to 4 Nov. 19 Jaq. I. 1621; ob. 1622.

XIII. 1622. 13. Henry Parker, s. and h. Summ. to Parl. as " Henrico Parker de Morley and Monteagle," from 12 Feb. 21 Jaq. I. 1624, to 3 Nov. 15 Car. I. 1639; ob. 1655.

XIV. 1655. 14. Thomas Parker, s. and h. Summ. to Parl. as "Thomæ Parker de Morley and Monteagle," from 8 May, 13 Car. II. 1661, to 19 May, 1 Jaq. II. 1685; ob. circa 1686, s. p. when the Baronies of Morley and Monteagle, together with that of Marshal, fell into Abeyance between the issue of his aunts, viz. of Catherine, wife of John Savage, V.-2d Earl Rivers, and of Elizabeth, who married Edward Cranfield, Esq. and among whose descendants and representatives they are still in ABEYANCE.

MORLEY

CO. DEVON.

EARL.

I. 1815. 1. John Parker (descended from a distinct family from that of the above Barons), 2d Baron Boringdon; Created Viscount Boringdon of North Molton, co. Devon, and Earl of Morley, in the said County, 29 Nov. 1815. Present Earl of Morley and Viscount and Baron Boringdon.

MORTIMER

OF WIGMORE,

BARONS BY TENURE.

I. Will.I. 1. Ralph de Mortimer; came into England with William the Conqueror, and obtained the Castle of Wigmore; ob. . . . . .

II. H. I. 2. Hugh de Mortimer, s. and h. ob. 1185.

III. H.II. 3. Roger de Mortimer, s. and h. ob. 1215.

IV. John. 4. Hugh de Mortimer, s. and h. ob. 1227, s. p.

V. H.III. 5. Ralph de Mortimer, half-brother and heir; ob. 1246.

VI. H. III. 6. Roger de Mortimer, s. and h. ob. 1282.

BY WRIT.

I. 1295. 7. Edmund Mortimer, s. and h. Summ. to Parl. from 23 June, 23 Edw. I. 1295, to 2 June, 30 Edw. I. 1302. He was also summoned 8 June, 22 Edw. I. 1294; but, for the reasons assigned under "CLYVEDON," it is doubtful if that Writ can be deemed a regular Summons to Parliament; ob. 1303.

II. 1299. 8. Roger Mortimer, s. and h. Summ. to Parl. from 6 Feb. 27 Edw. I. 1299, to 3 Dec. 20 Edw. II. 1326; after the 1st Edw. II. with the addition of "de Wigmore;" Created Earl of March in 1328; executed and attainted 1330, when all his honors became

Forfeited.

I. 1331. 1. Edmund Mortimer, s. and h. In consequence of his father's Attainder, he did not succeed to his honors, but was Summ. to Parl. 20 Nov. 5 Edw. III. 1331, as "Edmund de Mortuomari;" ob. Dec. 1331.

IV. 1331. 2. ⎱ Roger Mortimer, s. and h. Summ. to Parl.
III. 1353. 9. ⎰ from 20 Nov. 22 Edw. III 1348, to 15 March, 28 Edw. III. 1354, as "Rogero de Mortuomari," excepting in the 24th, 25th, and 27th Edw. III. and then with the addition of "de Wigmore," the Attainder of his grandfather being reversed, in the Parliament of 27 Edw. III. he was summoned to the next Parliament, viz. 20 Sept. 29 Edw. III. 1355, as Earl of March, K. G.   Vide MARCH.

Ann Mortimer, the sister and eventually sole heir of Edmund 6th Earl of March, and VI.-12th Baron Mortimer, married Richard Plantagenet, Earl of Cambridge, and conveyed the right to the Throne to the House of York: their son, Richard Plantagenet, Duke of York, inherited the Baronies of Mortimer created by the Writs of 23 Edw. I. and 5 Edw. III. jure matris, and on the accession of the son and heir of the said Duke to the Throne, by the title of King Edward IV. these Baronies, with all his other dignities, became merged in the Crown.

MORTIMER

OF RICHARD'S CASTLE.

BARONS BY TENURE.

I.   H. II.   1. Robert de Mortimer, of the same family as the preceding, by marrying Margery, dau. and heir of Hugh de Say, acquired Richard's Castle temp. Henry II.; ob. circa 1219.

II.   H. III.   2. Hugh de Mortimer, s. and h. ob. 1275.

III. Edw. I.   3. Robert de Mortimer, s. and h. He married Joyce, dau. and heir of William le Zouche, 2d son of Roger II.-2d Baron Zouche of Ashby; ob. 1287.

BY WRIT.

IV.   1299.   4. Hugh de Mortimer, s. and h. Summ. to Parl. 6 Feb. and 10 April, 27 Edw. I. 1299. He was also summoned 26 Jan. and 9 Sept. 25 Edw. I. 1297; but it is doubtful if the two latter Writs were regular Summonses to Parl. vide "FITZ-JOHN;" ob. 1304, s. P. M. Joan and Margaret being his daughters and heirs; of whom the former married to her second husband Richard Talbot, whose posterity enjoyed the Lordship. (Vide TALBOT of RICHARD'S CASTLE.) This Barony is probably in ABEYANCE among the descendants and representatives of the daughters and coheirs of the last Baron.

MORTIMER
OF ATTILBERG.

BARONS BY TENURE.

I.   John.   Robert de Mortimer, Lord of Attilbergh, co. Norfolk, temp. John; from whom descended

I. Edw.I. 1. William de Mortimer, who was living at Attilberg 1283; Summoned 8 June, 22 Edw. I. 1294, and 26 Jan. 25 Edw. I. 1297; but it is doubtful if either of these Writs can be considered as a regular Summons to Parliament; vide "CLYVEDON" and "FITZ-JOHN;" ob. 1297.

II. 1342. 2. Constantine de Mortimer, s. and h. Summ. to Parl. 25 Feb. 16 Edw. III. 1342; but never after, nor any of his descendants. Unless the Writs of 22 and 25 Edw. I. be considered as regular Writs of Summons to Parliament, this Barony, on the death of Constantine, the last Baron, became
      Extinct.

MORTIMER
OF CHIRKE.

BARON BY WRIT.

I.   1307.   Roger Mortimer, 2d son of Roger V.-5th Baron; Summ. to Parl. from 26 Aug. 1 Edw. II. 1307, to 15 May, 14 Edw. II. 1321, as "Roger de Mortuo-mari de Chirche;" ob. 1336, leaving John his son and heir, whose posterity continued in the male line for several generations, but neither he nor any of his descendants were ever Summoned to Parliament; the Barony is, however, probably in ABEYANCE among the descendants and representatives of the said John de Mortimer.

MORTIMER
OF ———

BARON BY WRIT.

I.   1296.   Simon Mortimer, probably of the same family, though Dugdale gives no account of him;

Summ. to Parl. 26 Aug. 24 Edw. I. 1296, but
never after, and of whom nothing farther is
known; ob. .... when the Barony became
Extinct.

MORTIMER.

EARL.

I. 1711. Robert Harley; Created Baron Harley of Wigmore, co. Hereford, Earl of Oxford, and Earl
Mortimer, with a special remainder, 24 May,
1711.   Vide OXFORD.

MORVILLE.

BARONS BY TENURE.

I. Hen. II. 1. Simon de Morvill, Lord of Burgh, co. Cumberland, jure uxoris; ob. ....
II. Ric. I. 2. Roger de Morvill, s. and h. ob. .....
III. John. 3. Hugh de Morvill, s. and h. ob. 1204, s. p. m.
his two daughters being his heirs.

I. H. II. Richard de Morvill, younger son of Simon 1st
Baron; ob. ...., s. p. m. Helen, his dau.
being his heir.

BY WRIT.

I. 1319. Nicholas de Morville, probably descended from
the same family; Summ. to Parl. 6 Nov. 13
Edw. II. 1319, and 5 Aug. 14 Edward II. 1320, but never
after, and of whom nothing more is known. Dugdale
gives no account of this Baron.

MOREWIC.

BARONS BY TENURE.

I. H. II. 1. Ernulf de Morewic, held one knight's fee co.
Northumberland 1165.
II. H. III. 2. Hugh de Morewic, s. and h. ob. 1190.
III. Ric. I. 3. Hugh de Morewic, s. and h. ob. ....
IV. H. III. 4. Hugh de Morewic, s. and h. ob. 1261, s. p. m.
leaving his three daughters his heirs; viz.
Sybil, wife, 1st, of Roger de Lumley, and 2d,

of Roger de St. Martin; Theophania, of
John de Bulmer; and Beatrix, of John de
Roseles.

MOUNT EDGCUMBE.

VISCOUNTS. EARLS.

I. 1781.—I. 1789. 1. George Edgcumbe, 3d Baron Edgcumbe; Created Viscount Mount
Edgcumb and Valletort, co. Devon,
5 March, 1781; Created Earl of
Mount Edgcumbe aforesaid 31 Aug.
1789; ob. 1795.

II. ......—II. 1795. 2. Richard Edgcumbe, s. and h. Present
Earl of Mount Edgcumbe, Viscount
Mount Edgcumbe and Valletort, and
Baron Edgcumbe. ⚓

MOUNT STUART.

BARONESS.

I. 1761. 1. Mary, only dau. of Edward Wortley Montagu
(grandson of Edward 1st Earl of Sandwich),
and wife of John 3d Earl of Bute in Scotland,
K. G.; Created Baroness Mount Stuart of
Wortley, co. York, 3d April, 1761, with limitation of the Barony to her issue male by

BARONS.   her said husband; ob. 1794.

I. 1794. 2. John Stuart, 4th Earl of Bute in Scotland, s.
and h.; succeeded his mother in this Ba-
rony 13 Nov. 1794; Created Marquess of
Bute, &c. in England.   Vide BUTE.

MOWBRAY.

BARONS BY TENURE.

I. WilL I. 1. Nigel de Albini, obtained divers Lordships
from William the Conqueror; living 1118;
ob. .....

II. Steph. 2. Roger de Mowbray, which name he assumed,
s. and h. living 1145; ob. .....

III. H. III. 3. Nigel de Mowbray, s. and h. ob. 1191.

BARONS BY TENURE.

IV. John. 4. William de Moubray, s. and b.; he was one of the celebrated 25 Barons appointed to enforce the observance of MAGNA CHARTA*; ob. 1222.

V. H. III. 5. Nigel de Mowbray, s. and b. ob. 1228, s. P.

VI. H.III. 6. Roger de Mowbray, brother and heir; ob. 1266.

BY WRIT.

I. 1295. 7. Roger de Mowbray, s. and h. Summ. to Parl. from 23 June, 23 Edw. I. 1295, to 26 Aug. 24 Edw. I. 1296. He was also summoned 8 June, 22 Edw. I. 1294, and 26 Aug. 25 Edw. I. 1297; but it is doubtful if either of those Writs was a regular Summons to Parl. vide "CLYVEDON" and "FITZ JOHN;" ob. 1298.

II. 1298. 8. John de Mowbray, s. and b. Summ. to Parl. from 26 Aug. 1 Edw. II. 1307, to 5 Aug. 14 Edw. II. 1320; ob. 1321.

III. 1321. 9. John de Mowbray, s. and b. Summ. to Parl. from 10 Dec. 1 Edw. III. 1327, to 20 Nov. 34 Edw. III. 1360; ob. 1361.

IV. 1361. 10. John de Mowbray, s. and b. Summ. to Parl. from 14 Aug. 36 Edw. III. 1362, to 20 Jan. 39 Edw. III. 1366, as "Johanni de Mowbray de Axilholm;" he married Elizabeth, dau. and heir of John Baron Segrave, by Margaret, dau. and heir of Thomas Plantagenet, Earl of Norfolk, son of King Edward I.; ob. 1368.

V. 1368. 11. John de Mowbray, s. and b.; Created Earl of Nottingham 1377; ob. 1379, s. P.

VI. 1379. 12. Thomas de Mowbray, brother and heir; Created Earl of Nottingham 1383, and Duke of Norfolk 1400; Earl Marshal; K.G.

Vide NORFOLK.

On the death of Ann Mowbray, dau. and sole heir of

---

* ROGER DE MOWBRAY, a younger brother of this Baron, ought, perhaps, to be ranked among the Barons of that period, as he is generally considered to have been another of the celebrated 25 Barons appointed to enforce the observance of MAGNA CHARTA, though some writers call him Roger de Montbezon. This Roger de Mowbray died s. P.

John IV.-4th Duke of Norfolk, and X.-16th Baron Mowbray, without issue, this Barony fell into ABEYANCE between the descendants of Margaret and Isabel, the daughters of Thomas VI.-12th Baron Mowbray, and I.-1st Duke of Norfolk; which Margaret married Sir Robert Howard, ancestor of the Dukes of Norfolk, and Isabel was the wife of James Baron Berkeley, ancestor of the Earls of Berkeley. The Abeyance was not determined until the 13th April, 1639, when Henry Howard, son and heir apparent of Thomas Earl of Arundel, Norfolk, and Surrey, was Summ. to Parl. as Baron Mowbray; his eldest son was restored to the Dukedom of Norfolk, in which dignity this Barony continued merged until the death of Edward XIV.-11th Duke, in 1777, when, together with several other Baronies, it again fell into ABEYANCE between the two daughters and coheirs of Philip Howard, younger brother of the said Duke; and between the Lords Petre and Stourton, as the descendants and representatives of the said coheirs, this Barony, with those of Howard, Furnival, &c. is now in ABEYANCE.   Vide FURNIVAL AND NORFOLK,

MULGRAVE.

EARLS.

I.   1626. 1. Edmund Sheffield, 3d Baron Sheffield; Created Earl of Mulgrave 7 Feb. 1626, K. G.; ob. 1646.

II.   1646. 2. Edmund Sheffield, grandson and heir, being son and heir of Sir John Sheffield (ob. v. p.) eldest son of the last Earl; ob. 1658.

III.   1658. 3. John Sheffield, s. and h. Created Marquess of Normanby, co. Lincoln, 10 May, 1694; Created Duke of Normanby 9 March, 1703; Created Duke of Buckingham 23d of the same month, K. G.; ob. 1721.

IV.   1721. 4. Edmund Sheffield, s. and h. Duke of Normanby and Buckingham; ob. 1735, s. p. when all his titles became
                Extinct.

BARONS.

I.   1790.   Constantine John Phipps, 2d Baron Mulgrave in Ireland; Created Baron Mulgrave of Mul-

grave, co. York, 16 June, 1790; ob. 1792,
s. p. m. when the English Barony became
Extinct.

BARON. EARL.
JI. 1798.—V. 1812. 1. Henry Phipps, 3d Baron Mulgrave in
Ireland, brother and heir of the last
Baron; Created Baron Mulgrave of
Mulgrave, co. York, 13 Aug. 1798;
Created Viscount Normanby of Nor-
manby, co. York, and Earl of Mul-
grave in the said county, 7 Sept.
1812. Present Earl and Baron Mul-
grave and Viscount Normanby; also
Baron Mulgrave in Ireland, G. C. B.

MULTON
OF GILLESLAND.

BARONS BY TENURE.

I. H. I. Thomas de Multon, Lord of Multon, co. Lincoln; to whom succeeded

II. H. II. Lambert de Multon; living 1165; his successor was

III. John. 1. Thomas de Multon, who married, secondly,
Ada, dau. and coheir of Hugh de Morville;
ob. 1240.

IV. H. III. 2. Thomas de Multon, eldest son by the 2d wife;
he married Maud, dau. and heir of Hubert
de Vaux of Gillesland; ob. 1270.

V. H. III. 3. Thomas de Multon, s. and h. ob. 1293.

VI. Edw. I. 4. Thomas de Multon, s. and h. ob. 1295.

BARON BY WRIT.

I. 1307. 5. Thomas de Multon, s. and h. Summ. to Parl.
from 26 August, 1 Edw. II. 1307, to 26 Nov.
7 Edw. II. 1313, as "Thomæ de Multon de
Gillesland;" ob. 1313, s. p. m. Margaret, his
dau. and heir, married Ralph I.-1st Baron
Dacre, and carried the Barony of Multon of
Gillesland to that family, and which Barony
is now vested in Thomas, the present Baron
Dacre. Vide DACRE.

MULTON
OF EGREMONT.

BARONS BY TENURE.

I.   H.III. 1. Lambert de Multon, s. and h. of Thomas III.-
1st Baron ; he married Annabel, dau. and
coheir of Richard de Lucie of Egremont, and
acquired that Lordship; ob. 1247.

II.   H. III. 2. Thomas de Multon, son and heir; ob.1294.

BARONS BY WRIT.

1.   1299. 3. Thomas de Multon, s. and h. Summ. to Parl.
from 6 Feb. 27 Edward I. 1299, to 15 May,
14 Edward II. 1320; after the 1st Edward II.
with the addition of " de Egremund;" he
was also Summoned 26 Jan. 25 Edw. I.
1297; but it is doubtful if that Writ was
a regular Summons to Parliament; vide
" FITZ-JOHN;" ob. 1322.

II.   1322. 4. John de Multon, s and h. Summ. to Parl. from
27 Jan. 6 Edw. III. 1332, to 24 July, 8 Edw.
III. 1334, as "Johanni de Multon;" ob.
1334, s. p. leaving his three sisters his
heirs, viz. Joan, wife of Robert Baron Fitz-
Walter; Elizabeth, wife of Walter de Ber-
micham; and Margaret, wife of Thomas de
Lucie, who shared his inheritance ; and
among whose descendants and representatives this Barony is now in ABEYANCE.

MUNCHENSI.

BARONS BY TENURE.

I.   Will.I.   Hubert de Munchensi; living 1140.

II.   H. I.   Warine de Munchensi, son and heir; ob. ....

III. H. II.   Hubert de Munchensi, s. and h. living 1186;
the next mentioned is

IV.   Ric. I.   William de Munchensi; ob. circa 1204.

V.   John.   William de Munchensi, s. and heir; ob. circa
1213, s. p.

VI.   H. III.   Warine de Munchensi, uncle and heir; ob.
      BY WRIT. 1255.

I.   1264.   William de Munchensi, s. and h. Summ. to
Parl. 24 Dec. 49 Hen. III. 1264; ob. 1289,
s. p. m. Dyonisia, his sole dau. and heir,

married Hugh de Vere, younger son of Robert Earl of Oxford.

William de Munchensi, a younger brother of the last mentioned Warine, married Beatrix, dau. and coheir of William de Beauchamp, Baron of Bedford, and died 1286, leaving William his son and heir, who died 1302, leaving male issue; but none of this branch were ever Summoned to Parliament.

MUNCY.

BARON BY WRIT.

I. 1299. Walter de Muncy; Summ. to Parl. from 6 Feb. 27 Edw. I. 1299, to 22 Feb. 35 Edward I. 1307.

Dugdale gives no account of this Baron; nor is there any notice of him or his posterity by any other genealogical writer.

MURRAY.

BARONY, 8 August, 1786.

Vide STRANGE.

MUSARD.

BARONS BY TENURE.

I.   Will.I. 1. Hascoit Musard; held numerous Lordships at the General Survey.
II.   Hen.I. 2. Richard Musard, s. and h. ob. . . . .
III. H. II. 3. Hascoit Musard, s. and h. certified for several Knight's fees 1165; ob. ante 1187.
IV.   Ric. I. 4. Ralph Musard; s. and h.; ob. 1230.
V.   H.III. 5. Robert Musard, s. and h. ob. 1240, s. p.
VI.   H.III. 6. Ralph Musard, brother and heir; ob. 1265.
VII. H.III. 7. Ralph Musard, s. and h. ob. 1273.
VIII. Edw.I. 8. John Musard, s. and h. ob. 1289, s. p.
IX.   Edw.I. 9. Nicholas Musard, uncle and heir; ob. 1300, s. p. leaving his sisters his next heirs.

MUSCHAMP.

BARONS BY TENURE.

I.   Hen. I. 1. Robert de Muschamp; obtained divers Lord-
          ships from Henry I.
.II. H. II. 2. Thomas de Muschamp, s. and h. living 1172.
III. Ric. I. 3. Robert de Muschamp, s. and h. ob. .....
IV. H.III. 4. Robert de Muschamp, s. and h. ob. 1249, s.p.m.
          leaving his daughters his heirs.

MUSGRAVE.

BARON BY WRIT.

I.   1350.   Thomas Musgrave; Summ. to Parl. from 25
          Nov. 24 Edw. III. 1350, to 4 Oct. 47 Edw. III.
          1373, but never afterwards, nor any of his
          descendants, who continued in the male
          line when Dugdale wrote, and it is presumed
          are still extant,

NANSLADRON.

Vide LANSLADRON.

NELSON.

BARON.   VISC.
I. 1798.   I. 1801.   1. Sir Horatio Nelson, K. B. Created
BARONS,   Baron Nelson of the Nile and of
I. 1801.   Burnham Thorpe, co. Norfolk, Nov.
                       6, 1798 ; Created Viscount Nelson of
                       the Nile and Burnham Thorpe afore-
                       said, 22 May, 1801 ; Created Baron
                       Nelson of the Nile and of Hilbo-
                       rough, co. Norfolk, 4 August, 1801 ;
                       with remainder, failing his issue

male, to his father the Rev. Edmund
Nelson, Clerk, Rector of Burnham
Thorpe, and his issue male; failing
which, to the issue male severally
and successively of Susannah, wife of
Thomas Bolton, Esq. and of Catherine, wife of George Matcham, Esq.
sisters of the Viscount, Duke of
Bronté in Sicily; slain 1805; ob.
s. p. when the Barony of Nelson of
Burnham Thorpe and the Viscountry
became Extinct; but the Barony of
Nelson of Hilborough devolved,
agreeable to the above limitation, on

BARON.   EARL.

II. 1805.—I. 1805. 2. William Nelson, brother and heir;
Created Viscount Merton and Tra-
falgar of Merton, co. Surrey, and
Earl Nelson of Merton and Trafal-
gar, with remainder, failing his issue
male, to the issue male of his sisters
above mentioned, Nov. 20, 1805.
Present Earl and Baron Nelson and
Viscount Merton and Trafalgar; also
Duke of Bronté in Sicily.

NEREFORD.

William de Nereford; Summoned 8 June, 22 Edw. I.
1294, and 26 January, 25 Edward I. 1297; but it is
doubtful if either of these Writs can be considered as a
regular Summons to Parliament; vide " CLYVEDON" and
" FITZ-JOHN." He was never afterwards summoned; and
though he left male issue, they were never summoned to
Parliament, or considered as Barons of the Realm.

NEVILL
OF RABY.

BARONS BY TENURE.

I. H. II. 1. Geoffrey de Nevill (son and heir of Geoffrey,
eldest son of Gilbert de Nevill, supposed to

have been Admiral of William the Conqueror's fleet), having married Emma, dau.
and heir of Bertram de Bulmer, acquired her
lands; ob. 1194.

II.   John. 2. Henry de Nevill, s. and h. ob. 1227, s. p. leaving Isabel, his sister and heir, who married
Robert Fitz-Maldred, Lord of Raby, and left
issue,

III. H.III. 3. Geoffrey, who assumed the name of Nevill,
Lord of Raby; ob. ....

IV. H.III. 4. Robert de Nevill, s. and h. ob. 1282.

I.   1295. 5. Ralph de Nevill, grandson and heir, being son
and heir of Robert de Nevill (ob. v. p.) eldest
son of the last Baron; Summ. to Parl. from
23 June, 23 Edward I. 1295, to 18 February,
5 Edw. III. 1331; he was also Summoned 8
June, 22 Edw. I. 1294; but for the reasons
assigned under "CLYVEDON," it is very
doubtful if that Writ was a regular Summons
to Parliament; ob. 1331.

II. 1331. 6. Ralph de Nevill, s. and h. Summ. to Parl. from
20 Nov. 5 Edw. III. 1331, to 20 January, 39
Edward III. 1366; ob. 1367.

III. 1367. 7. John de Nevill, s. and h. Summ. to Parl. from
24 Feb. 42 Edward III. 1368, to 28 July, 12
Rich. II. 1388, as "Johanni de Nevill de
Raby," K. G.   His second wife was Elizabeth, dau. and heir of William IV.-4th Baron
Latimer, by whom he had one son John
Nevill, who succeeded as Baron Latimer,
jure matris, and a daughter Elizabeth, who
married Sir Thomas Willoughby, Knt.; ob.
1388.

IV. 1388. 8. Ralph de Nevill, s. and h. Summ. to Parl.
from 6 Dec. 13 Rich. II. 1389, to 30 Nov.
20 Rich. II. 1396, as " Ranulpho de Nevyll
de Raby;" Created Earl of Westmoreland
29 Sept. 1397.   Vide WESTMORELAND.

This Barony continued merged in the Earldom of
Westmoreland until 1570, when, with his other honors,
by the attainder of Charles VI.-6th and last Earl of Westmoreland, and IX.-13th Baron Nevill of Raby, it became
Forfeited.

NEVILL.

BARONS BY TENURE.

I. Hen. I.   Robert de Nevill; whether related or not to the above family is unknown; living 1101.

I. Hen. I.   Ralph de Nevill; living temp. Henry I.

I. Hen. I.   Gilbert de Nevill of Lincolnshire; liv. 1159.

I.   H. II. 1. Alan de Nevill, brother of the last Gilbert, Chief Justice of the Forests; ob. 1190.
II.   John. 2. Geoffrey de Nevill, s. and h. living 1221.
III. H. II. 3. John de Nevill, son and h. living 1265.

I.   H. II.   William de Nevill, Sheriff of Norfolk 1155; living 1224; he married Isabel, dau. and coheir of Walter de Walerand; ob. s. p. m. Joane, one of his daughters and coheirs, married Jordan St. Martin.

I.   H. II. 1. Ralph de Nevill; living 1175.   •
II. Ric. I. 2. Hugh de Nevill, s. and h. ob. circa 1199.
III. John. 3. Henry de Nevill, s. and h. ob. 1218.
IV. H. III. 4. Hugh de Nevill, s. and h.; ob. s. p. to whom succeeded
V.   H. III. 5. Johan de Nevill, brother and heir, who was a Justice Itinerant, and from whom the celebrated MS. in the Exchequer, "Testa de Nevill," takes its name.

I.   Ric. I.   Hugh de Nevill, Sheriff of Oxford, Essex, and Hertford 1198; living 1216; but of whom Dugdale says, "I have seen no more" than that he gave the manor of Lokeswold to the Knights Templars, and died 1222.

.

NEVILL
OF ESSEX.

BARONS BY TENURE.

I.   H. III. 1. Hugh de Nevill; founded Stoke Courcy Priory, in Devonshire; living 1229.
II. H. III. 2. John de Nevill, s. and h. ob. 1244.

BARON BY TENURE.

III. H.III. 3. Hugh de Nevill, s. and h. living 1265; from whom descended, as Dugdale supposes,

BARONS BY WRIT.

I. 1311. 1. Hugh de Nevill, who it is presumed was the Hugh de Nevill who was Summ. to Parl. from 19 December, 5 Edw. II. 1311, to 1 April, 9 Edw. III. 1335, though Dugdale takes no notice in his Baronage of any "Hugh de Nevill," having been summoned in those years, but merely states, that Hugh de Nevill was the father of

II. 1336. 2. John de Nevill; Summ. to Parl. from 23 Jan. 9 Edward III. 1336, to 10 March, 23 Edw. III. 1349, as "Johanni de Nevill de Essex;" ob. 1358, s. P. when if the Barony was created by the Writ of 23 Jan. 9 Edw. III. it became **Extinct**; but if the conjecture is correct, that Hugh the father of this John was Summoned to Parliament, and that the Writ of 23 Jan. 9 Edward III. was issued to his son on his death circa 9 Edward III. it became vested in the heirs of the body of the said Hugh de Nevill.

NEVILL
OF ——

BY WRIT.

I, 1342. Robert de Nevill; Summ. to Parl. 25 Feb. 16 Edward III. 1342, but never afterwards, and of whom nothing farther is known; ob. ...., when this Barony became **Extinct**.

NEVILL
OF HALLAMSHIRE.
Vide FURNIVAL.

NEVILL
OF FAUCONBERG.
Vide FAUCONBERG.

NEVILL
OF LATIMER.
Vide LATIMER.

NEVILL

OF MONTAGU.

Vide MONTAGU.

NEVILL

OF BERGAVENNY.

Vide ABERGAVENNY.

NEVILL

OF BERLING.

VISCOUNTCY, 17 May, 1784.

Vide ABERGAVENNY.

NEWARK.

VISCOUNTS.

I. 1627. 1. Robert Pierrepont ; Created Baron Pierrepont of Holme Pierrepont, co. Nottingham and Viscount Newark in the same county, 29 June, 1627; Created Earl of Kingston 25 July, 1628. Vide KINGSTON.

Extinct 1773.

VII. 1796. 1. Charles Meadows (assumed the name of) Pierrepont ; being son of Philip Meadows by Frances, sister and heir of Evelyn, last Duke of Kingston, and VI.-6th and last Baron Pierrepont of Holme Pierrepont, and Viscount Newark, K. G. Created Baron Pierrepont of Holme Pierrepont, co. Notts. and Viscount Newark, 23 July, 1796; Created Earl Manvers 9 April, 1806; ob. 1816.

VIII. 1816. 2. Charles Herbert Pierrepont, s. and h. Earl Manvers. Present Viscount Newark, Baron Pierrepont of Holme Pierrepont and Earl Manvers. ⚓

NEWBURGH.

BARONS.

I. 1716. 1. George Cholmondeley, 1st Baron of Newborough in Ireland ; Created Baron of Newburgh in the Isle of Anglesey, 2 July, 1716 ; succeeded as II.-2d Earl, and III.-3d Baron Cholmondeley in 1725. Vide CHOLMONDELEY.

George Horatio Cholmondeley, son and heir apparent
of George James, present Marquess of Cholmondeley,
K. G. and III.-3d Baron Newburgh; was Summ. to Parl.
in his father's Barony of Newburgh, 24 Dec. 1821.

NEWBURY.

BARONY, 10 September, 1674—€xtinct 1774.
Vide SOUTHAMPTON.

NEWCASTLE.

EARLS.

I.   1623.   Lodovick Stuart, 1st Earl of Richmond;
Created Earl of Newcastle-upon-Tyne and
Duke of Richmond 17 May, 1623, K. G.; ob.
1624, s. p. when this title became
€xtinct.

MARQ.   DUKES.

II. 1628.—I. 1643.—I. 1664. 1.William Cavendish (nephew
of William 1st Earl of De-
vonshire), 1st Baron Ogle
of Bolsover, and 1st Visc.
Mansfield; Created Baron
Cavendish of Bolsover, co.
Notts. and Earl of Newcastle-upon-Tyne 7 Mar. 1628;
Created Marquess of New-
castle*, co. Northumber-
land, 27 October, 1643;
Created Earl of Ogle and
Duke of Newcastle, both
co. Northumberland, 16
March, 1664; succeeded to
the ancient Barony of Ogle
on the death of his mother
in 1629, K. G.; ob. 1676.

---

* Beatson says he was at the same time created Baron of
Bothal and Hepple; whilst Heylin asserts he was created Baron
of Bertram and Marquess of Newcastle; Dugdale merely states
that he was then created Marquess of Newcastle.

BARONS. MARQ. DUKES.

III..... —II. .....—II. 1676. 2. Henry Çavendish s. and h.
K. G. ' ob. 1691, s. p. m.
when all his honors, excepting the ancient Barony of
Ogle, became

𝔈𝔵𝔱𝔦𝔫𝔠𝔱.

III. 1694. 1. John Holles, 4th Earl of
Clare, having married Mar-
garet, dau. and coheir of
Henry the last Duke, was
Created Marquess of Clare
and Duke of Newcastle 14
May, 1694, K. G.; ob.1711,
s. p. m. when his honors became

𝔈𝔵𝔱𝔦𝔫𝔠𝔱.

IV. 1715. ⎫ 1. Thomas Pelham (assumed
NEWCASTLE-UNDER-LYME. ⎬ the name of) Holles, 2d
DUKES. ⎨ Baron Pelham of Hough-
I. 1756. ⎭ ton, son and heir of Thomas 1st Baron Pelham by
Grace Holles, sister of the
last Duke; Created Viscount Pelham and
Earl of Clare 26 Oct. 1714; Created Marquess
of Clare and Duke of Newcastle, co. Northumberland, with remainder, failing his issue
male, to his brother Henry, 2 August, 1715.
His said brother having died s. p. m. he was
Created DUKE OF NEWCASTLE-UNDER-LYME, with
remainder, failing his issue male, to Henry
Earl of Lincoln and his issue male by Catherine his wife, niece of his Grace, 13 Nov.
1756; Created Baron Pelham of Stanmere,
with a special remainder, 4 May, 1762,
K. G.; ob. 1768, s. p. when the Dukedom of
• NEWCASTLE-UPON-TYNE, and all his honors,
excepting the Dukedom of NEWCASTLE-
UNDER-LYME, and Barony of Pelham of
Stanmere, became

𝔈𝔵𝔱𝔦𝔫𝔠𝔱.

DUKES.

II. 1768. 2. Henry Fiennes (assumed the name of Pelham) Clinton, XIX. 9th Earl of Lincoln, hus-

F 2

DUKES.

band of Catherine, 1st dau. and coheir of Henry Pelham, only brother of Thomas last Duke; succeeded to the Dukedom of NEW-CASTLE-UNDER-LYME, agreeable to the limitation before recited, 17 Nov. 1768, K. G.; ob. 1794.

III. 1794. 3. Thomas Pelham Clinton, s. and h. ob. 1795.

IV. 1795. 4. Henry Pelham Clinton, s. and h. Present Duke of Newcastle-under-Lyme, and Earl of Lincoln, K. G.

NEWMARCH.

BARONS BY TENURE.

1. Will. I. Bernard Newmarch; settled at Brecknock temp. Will. I.

I. Hen. I. Adam de Newmarch, gave three oxgangs of land in Halton to the Canons of Nostell, co. York.

I. H. II. William de Newmarch; living 1205, but becoming a leper, nothing farther is known of him.

I. H. II. 1. Henry de Newmarch; living 1166; ob. ...s.p.

II. John. 2. James de Newmarch, brother and heir; ob. circa 1232, s. p. m. leaving two daughters his heirs, viz. Isabel, wife of Ralph Russel, and Hawyse, who first married John de Botreaux, and 2dly, Nicholas de Moels.

BARON BY WRIT.

I. 1264. Adam de Newmarch, son of Robert de Newmarch; Summ. to Parl. 24 Dec. 49 Hen. III. 1264; ob. ...., leaving Roger his son and heir; but neither this Roger nor any of his descendants were ever Summoned to Parliament.

NEWPORT
OF THE ISLE OF WIGHT.

EARLS.

I. 1628. 1. Montjoy Blount, IX.-1st Baron Montjoy;

EARLS.

Created Earl of Newport in the Isle of Wight
3 Aug. 1628; ob. 1665.

II. 1665. 2. George Blount, s. and h. ob, 1676, s. p.
III. 1676. 3. Charles Blount, brother and heir; ob. 1676, s. p.
IV. 1676. 4. Henry Blount, brother and heir; ob. 1681,
s. p. when his titles became
Extinct.

NEWPORT
OF SHROPSHIRE.

VISCOUNTCY, 30 September, 1815.
Vide BRADFORD.

BARONS.

I. 1642.—1. Richard Newport; Created Baron Newport of
High Ercall, co. Salop 14 October, 1642; ob.
1650.

VISCOUNTS.

II. 1650.—I. 1675. 2. Francis Newport, s. and h. Created
Viscount Newport of Bradford, co.
Salop, 11 March, 1675, and Earl of
Bradford 11 May, 1694.

Extinct 1762. Vide BRADFORD.

NIDDRY.

BARON.

I. 1814. 1. John Hope, half-brother of James 3d Earl of
Hopetoun in Scotland, and 1st Baron Hopetoun in the Peerage of Great Britain; Created Baron Niddry of Niddry, co. Linlith-
gow, 3 May, 1814; succeeded as 2d Baron
Hopetoun, and as Earl of Hopetoun in
Scotland in 1816. Present Baron Hopetoun
and Baron Niddry; also Earl of Hopetoun,
&c. Scotland, G. C. B.

NOEL.

BARONS.

I. 1617. 1. Sir Edward Noel, 1st Bart. Created Baron
Noel of Ridlington, co. Rutland, 23 March,
1617, succeeded his father-in-law as II.-2d
Viscount Campden and Baron Hicks in 1629;
ob. 1643.

BARONS.

II. 1643. 2. Baptist Noel, s. and h. 3d Viscount Campden;
ob. 1682.

III. 1682. 3 } Edward Noel, son and heir apparent of Bap-
NOEL OF { tist 2d Viscount Campden; Created Baron
TITCHFIELD { Noel of Titchfield, co. Southampton, with
I. 1681.   } remainder, failing his issue male, to the
issue male of his father, 3 Feb. 1681; succeeded his father as 4th Viscount Campden,
4th Baron Hicks, and 3d Baron Noel of Ridlington, 1682; Created Earl of Gainsborough, with the same remainder, 1 Dec.
1682.   Vide GAINSBOROUGH.

Both these Baronies, on the death of Henry VI.-6th
Earl of Gainsborough, VI.-6th Baron Noel of Titchfield,
VIII.-8th Baron Noel of Ridlington, and IX.-9th Viscount
Campden in 1798, s. p. became

𝕰𝖝𝖙𝖎𝖓𝖈𝖙.

NONSUCH.

BARONY, 3 August, 1670—𝕰𝖝𝖙𝖎𝖓𝖈𝖙 1774.

Vide CLEVELAND.

NORFOLK.

EARLS.

I. Will. I. Ralph Waher or Guader; Created Earl of
Norfolk and Suffolk by William the Conqueror; 𝔉𝔬𝔯𝔣𝔢𝔦𝔱𝔢𝔡 his Earldoms for treason.

II. Steph. 1. Hugh Bigod, Steward to K. Henry I. Created
Earl of Norfolk by King Stephen, and like-
wise by King Henry II.; ob. 1177.

III. 1177. 2. Roger Bigod, s. and h. Created to, or rather
perhaps confirmed in, this Earldom by Rich.
I. 27 Nov. 1189; Steward of England. He
was one of the 25 celebrated Barons appoint-
pointed to enforce the observance of MAGNA
CHARTA; ob. 1220.

IV. 1220. 3. Hugh Bigod, s. and h.; he was also one of the
25 celebrated Barons appointed to enforce
the observance of MAGNA CHARTA; ob. 1225.

V. 1225. 4. Roger Bigod, s. and h. Marshal of England in
right of his mother Maud, the sister and coheir of Anselm Earl of Pembroke and Earl
Marshal; ob. 1270, s. p.

EARLS.

VI. 1270. 5. Roger Bigod, nephew and heir, being son and heir of Hugh Bigod, Justice of England, brother to the last Earl; Earl Marshal. Having no issue he surrendered this Earldom and the Marshal's Rod into the King's hands, which were re-granted to him and to the heirs of his body 1302; ob. 1307, s. p. leaving John his brother his next heir; but in consequence of the said surrender, his dignities became

Extinct.

VII. 1312. 1. Thomas Plantagenet, surnamed "De Brotherton," fifth son of King Edward I. Created Earl of Norfolk 16 December 1312, and Earl Marshal 10 Feb. 1335; ob. 1338, s. p. m. when the title became

DUCHESS.   Extinct.

I. 1397. Margaret Plantagenet, eldest dau. and eventually sole heir of the last Earl, styled Countess of Norfolk in the Rolls of Parliament 21 Ric. II. Created Duchess of Norfolk for life 29 Sept. 1397; she married, first, John Baron Segrave, and secondly, Sir Walter Manny, K. G.; ob. 1399, s. p. m. when the title again became

DUKES.   Extinct.

I. 1397. 1. Thomas VI.-12th Baron Mowbray, brother and heir of John V. 2d Baron Mowbray, and Earl of Nottingham, and 2d son of John IV.-10th Baron Mowbray by Elizabeth, dau. and heir of John Baron Segrave, by Margaret Plantagenet, the last Duchess of Norfolk; Created Earl of Nottingham 1383; constituted Earl Marshal of England for life 1383, with remainder to him and his heirs male 1396; Created Duke of Norfolk 29 Sept. 1397, K. G.; banished in the same year; ob. 1413.

II. 1424. 2. John Mowbray, 2d son, and heir to his brother Thomas, who never used this title, but simply that of Earl Marshal, and was beheaded (ob. s. p.) 1405; when his brother John succeeded him, and styled himself Earl of Nottingham and Earl Marshal until 1424, when

DUKES.

         he was restored * to the dignity of Duke of Norfolk. K. G.; ob. 1432.

III. 1432. 3. John Mowbray, s. and h. confirmed Duke of Norfolk 1444; Earl of Nottingham and Earl Marshal, K. G.; ob. 1461.

IV. 1461. 4. John Mowbray, s. and h. Earl of Nottingham; Created, vita patris, Earl of Warren and Surrey 29 March, 1451; Earl Marshal, K.G.; ob. 1475, s. p. m. Ann, his only dau. and heir, was contracted to Richard, 2d son of King Edward IV. but died before consummation. As this Duke died without male issue, his honors, with the exception of the Baronies of Mowbray and Segrave, became Extinct.

V. 1477. Richard Plantagenet, Duke of York, 2d son of King Edward IV. being betrothed to Ann, dau. and heir of John the last Duke, was Created Earl of Nottingham 12 June, 1476, and Earl Warren and Duke of Norfolk 7 February, 1477; murdered in the Tower with his brother King Edward V. 1483, then being only nine years of age, when all his honors became Extinct.

VI. 1483. 1. John Howard, s. and h. of Sir Robert Howard, by Margaret, dau. of Thomas Mowbray, I. 1st Duke of Norfolk, and cousin and ultimately coheir of John Mowbray IV.-4th and last Duke of Norfolk; Summ. to Parl. as Baron Howard 15 Oct. 10 Edward IV. 1470; Created Earl Marshal and Duke of Norfolk, 28 June, 1483, K. G.; slain at Bosworth-field 1485, and, being attainted, all his honors were Forfeited.

VII. 1514. 2. Thomas Howard, s. and h. Created, vita patris, Earl of Surrey 28 June, 1483; attainted 1485, when that Earldom became Forfeited; Restored to the Earldom of Surrey 1489; Created Duke of Norfolk 1 Feb. 1514; Lord Treasurer and Earl Marshal, K.G.; ob. 1524.

---

* Though his elder brother never assumed the title of Duke of Norfolk, and this Duke was *restored* to the dignity, it does not appear that the Act of Banishment of their father rendered them incapable by law of succeeding to his honors, as he was not thereby attainted, or his blood in any way corrupted.

DUKES.

VIII. 1524. 3. Thomas Howard. s. and h. attainted 1546, when his honors became **Forfeited** ; Restored 1553, K. G. ; ob. 1554.

IX. 1554. 4. Thomas Howard, grandson and heir, being son and heir of Henry Howard (eldest son of the last Duke), who was attainted and beheaded, vita patris, in 1547. Restored in blood and honors in 1553 ; succeeded to his grandfather's dignities 1554 ; he married Mary, daughter and ultimately sole heir of Henry Fitz-Alan, XXI.-18th Earl of Arundel, K. G. ; attainted and beheaded 1572, when all his dignities became

EARLS. **Forfeited.**

VIII. 1644. 5. Thomas Howard, son and heir of Philip Howard, XXII.-19th Earl of Arundel by descent and tenure (eldest son of Thomas the last Duke of Norfolk) ; which Philip was attainted in 1590 ; Restored in blood and to such honors as Philip Earl of Arundel his father enjoyed ; likewise as Earl of Surrey, "and to such dignities of Baronies as Thomas late Duke of Norfolk his grandfather lost by attainder" in 1603. By Act of Parl. 3 Car. 1. 1627, the Earldom of Arundel and the titles and dignities of the Baronies of Fitz-Alan, Clun and Oswaldestre, and Maltravers were annexed to the title, honor and dignity of Earl of Arundel, and, together with the Earldom of Arundel, were settled upon this Earl and upon the heirs male of his body ; in default of which, upon the heirs of his body ; with remainder to his uncle Lord William Howard * and the heirs

---

* It is a most singular fact, and which should have been stated in p. 28, that according to the limitation of the Earldom of Arundel and the Baronies of Fitz-Alan, Clun and Oswaldestre, and Maltravers, by the Act of 3 Car. I. the Earls of Suffolk who descend from Lord Thomas Howard (afterwards Lord Howard of Walden and Earl of Suffolk,) are postponed in the succession to these dignities to the Earls of Carlisle, notwithstanding that their ancestor, the above-mentioned Lord William Howard was a *younger* brother of Lord Thomas Howard the first Earl of Suffolk of this family. Vide the Pedigree in p. 475. It is thus

male of his body; failing which to the heirs of
his body; remainder to the said Thomas Earl
of Arundel and Surrey and his heirs for ever;
Created EARL OF NORFOLK 6th June, 1644,
K. G.; Earl Marshal; ob. 1646.

IX.   1646. 6. Henry Frederick Howard, s. and h. Summ. to
Parl. (v. p.) as Baron Mowbray; ob. 1652.

DUKES.

X. 1652.—X. 1660. 7. Thomas Howard, s. and h. Earl of
Arundel, Surrey, and Norfolk; Re-
stored to the Dukedom of Norfolk

with the original precedence of his ancestor, John Howard
VI.-1st Duke, by Act of Parl. 29 Dec. 1660, and confirmed by another Act 20 Dec. 1661, with limitation * to
him and the heirs male of his body; failing which, to
Henry Frederick Earl of Arundel, Surrey, and Norfolk,
his father, and his issue male; in default of which, to
Thomas Earl of Arundel, Surrey, and Norfolk his grandfather, and the heirs male of his body; failing which, to
Philip Earl of Arundel and Surrey, father of the said Thomas Earl of Arundel, Surrey, and Norfolk last mentioned,
and the heirs male of his body; failing which, to the heirs
male of the body of Thomas Earl of Suffolk, half-brother
of Philip Earl of Arundel and Surrey last mentioned; in
default of which, to the heirs male of the body of Lord
William Howard of Naworth, brother of the said Thomas Earl of Suffolk; failing which, to Charles Earl of
Nottingham, lineally descended from Thomas VII.-2d

---

manifest that the Suffolk line can never inherit the Earldom and
Baronies in question but under the last clause in the limitation,
viz. as heirs of the grantee. The cause of this strange omission
probably was, that Thomas Howard, 1st Earl of Suffolk, died
several years before the Act of Limitation passed, whilst Lord
William his brother survived until 1640; but it is nevertheless
extraordinary, that Theophilus 2d Earl of Suffolk, son and heir of
Thomas the 1st Earl, should have been so entirely passed over in
the succesion.

To avoid the possibility of error in stating the limitations of
these dignities and of the Dukedom of Norfolk under the Acts of
Restoration in 1650 and 1661, the official documents have in
both instances been consulted.

* In order more distinctly to shew the limitation of the Dukedom of Norfolk as settled by the Restoration of that dignity in
1660, the following slight Pedigree is inserted.

Duke of Norfolk, and the heirs male of his body; ob. 1677, s. p.

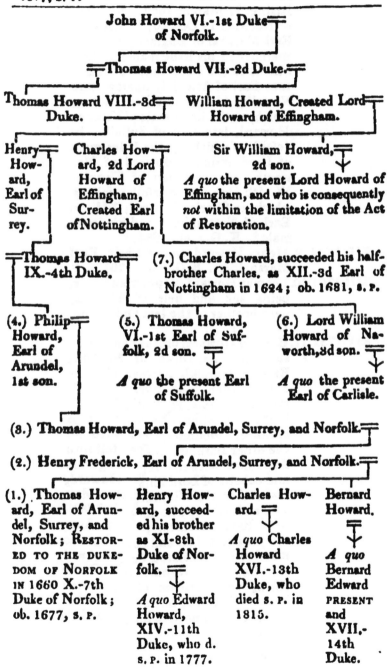

John Howard VI.-1st Duke of Norfolk.

Thomas Howard VII.-2d Duke.

Thomas Howard VIII.-3d Duke.

William Howard, Created Lord Howard of Effingham.

Henry Howard, Earl of Surrey.

Charles Howard, 2d Lord Howard of Effingham, Created Earl of Nottingham.

Sir William Howard, 2d son.
A quo the present Lord Howard of Effingham, and who is consequently *not* within the limitation of the Act of Restoration.

Thomas Howard IX.-4th Duke.

(7.) Charles Howard, succeeded his half-brother Charles. as XII.-3d Earl of Nottingham in 1624; ob. 1681, s. p.

(4.) Philip Howard, Earl of Arundel, 1st son.

(5.) Thomas Howard, VI.-1st Earl of Suffolk, 2d son.
A quo the present Earl of Suffolk.

(6.) Lord William Howard of Naworth, 3d son.
A quo the present Earl of Carlisle.

(3.) Thomas Howard, Earl of Arundel, Surrey, and Norfolk.

(2.) Henry Frederick, Earl of Arundel, Surrey, and Norfolk.

(1.) Thomas Howard, Earl of Arundel, Surrey, and Norfolk; RESTORED TO THE DUKEDOM OF NORFOLK IN 1660 X.-7th Duke of Norfolk; ob. 1677, s. p.

Henry Howard, succeeded his brother as XI.-8th Duke of Norfolk.
A quo Edward Howard, XIV.-11th Duke, who d. s. p. in 1777.

Charles Howard.
A quo Charles Howard XVI.-13th Duke, who died s. p. in 1815.

Bernard Howard.
A quo Bernard Edward PRESENT and XVII.-14th Duke.

LS.   DUKES.

.... —XI. 1677. 8. Henry Howard, brother and heir;
Created Baron Howard of Castle
Rising 27 March, 1669, and Earl
of Norwich 19 Oct. 1672; Created
Earl Marshal of England, with remainder to his issue male; failing
which, to the issue male of Thomas Earl of Arundel, Surrey, and
Norfolk, his grandfather; failing
which, to the heirs male of Thomas
Howard, late Earl of Suffolk; in
default of which, to the heirs male
of Lord William Howard of Naworth, youngest son of Thomas
IX.-4th Duke of Norfolk; failing
which, to Charles Howard, XII.-3d
Earl of Nottingham, and his issue
male *, K. G.; ob. 1684.

.... —XII. 1684. 9. Henry Howard, son and heir, Earl
Marshal, &c. K.G.; ob. 1701, s. p.

..... —XIII.1701.10.Thomas Howard, nephew and heir,
being son and heir of Thomas,
next brother of the last Duke, ob.
1732, s. p.

..... —XIV.1732.11. Edward Howard, brother and heir;
succeeded as Duke of Norfolk,
Earl of Arundel, Surrey, Norfolk
and Norwich, and Earl Marshal,
Baron Moubray, Howard, &c.; ob.
1777, s. p. when the Baronies of
Howard, Moubray, &c. with all
the other Baronies in fee, fell into
ABEYANCE between the daughters
and coheirs of Lord Philip Howard,
his brother, viz. Winifred, the eldest
dau. and coheir, who married William Baron Stourton; and Ann,
the youngest dau. and coheir, who
married Robert Baron Petre; and
the Barony of Howard of Castle
Rising and Earldom of Norwich
became Extinct; but all his other
dignities descended to his next heir
male,

* See the Pedigree in the preceding page.

EARLS. DUKES.

XV...... —XV. 1777. 12. Charles Howard, son and heir of Charles, eldest son of Charles Howard of Greystock, next brother of Henry XI.-8th Duke of Norfolk; succeeded as Duke of Norfolk, Earl of Arundel, Surrey, and Norfolk, Baron Fitz-Alan, Clun and Oswaldestre, and Maltravers; hereditary Earl Marshal of England; ob. 1786.

XVI. —XVI. 1786. 13. Charles Howard, s. and h. ob. 1815, s.p.

XVII.—XVII.1815. 14. Bernard Edward Howard, cousin and heir, being s. and h. of Henry, 2d, but eldest surviving son of Bernard, s. and h. of Bernard Howard, 8th son of Henry Frederick Earl of Arundel, Surrey, and Norfolk *. Present Duke of Norfolk, Earl of Arundel, Surrey, and Norfolk, Baron Fitz-Alan, Clun and Oswaldestre, and Maltravers, Earl Marshal, and Hereditary Earl Marshal of England.

NORMANBY.

MARQUESSES. DUKES.

1. 1694.—1. 1703. 1. John Sheffield, 3d Earl of Mulgrave; Created Marquess of Normanby, co. Lincoln, 10 May, 1694; Created Duke of Normanby 9 March, 1703, and Duke of Buckingham on the 23d of the same month, K. G.; ob. 1721.

II... ..—II. 1721. 2. Edmund Sheffield, s. and h. Duke of Buckingham, &c.; ob. 1735, s. p. when all his honors became Extinct.

VISCOUNTCY, 7 September, 1812.

Vide MULGRAVE.

NORRIS.

BARONS BY WRIT.

1. 1572. 1. Henry Norris; Summ. to Parl. from 8 May, 14 Eliz. 1572, to 24 Oct. 39 Eliz. 1597, as "Henrico Norris de Rycote, Chl'r;" he married Margery, dau. and coheir of John Lord

---

* Vide the pedigree, p. 475.

Williams of Thame, and one of the coheirs to the said Barony; ob. 1600.

II. 1600. 2. Francis Norris, grandson and heir, being s. and h. of William Norris (ob. v. p.) eldest son of the last Baron; Summ. to Parl. from 17 Oct. 43 Eliz. 1601, to 5 April, 12 Jaq. I. 1614; Created Viscount Thame and Earl of Berkshire Jan. 28, 1620; ob. 1620, s. p. m. Elizabeth, his sole dau. and heir, married Edward Wray, esq.; their only child, Bridget Wray, became the second wife of Montagu Bertie, 2d Earl of Lindsey, and

III. 1679. 3. James Bertie, s. and h. of the said Bridget by Montagu Earl of Lindsey, succeeded jure matris to this Barony; Summ. to Parl. as Baron Norris of Rycote, 17 Oct. 31 Car. II. 1679, and again 1 March, 32 Car. II. 1680; Created Earl of Abingdon 30 Nov. 1682. Vide ABINGDON, in which Earldom this Barony is merged.

NORTH.

I. 1554. 1. Edward North; Summ. to Parl. as "Edwardo North de Kirtling, Chev." from 17 Feb. 1 Philip and Mary, 1554, to 5 Nov. 5 and 6 Philip and Mary, 1558; ob. 1564.

II. 1564. 2. Roger North, s. and h. Summ. to Parl. from 30 Sept. 8 Eliz. 1566, to 24 Oct. 39 Eliz. 1597; ob. 1600.

III. 1600. 3. Dudley North, grandson and heir, being s and h. of John North (ob. v. p.) eldest son of the last Baron; Summ. to Parl. from 5 Nov. 3 Jaq. I. 1605, to 8 May, 3 Car. II. 1661; ob. 1666.

IV. 1666. 4. Dudley North, s. and h.; he was never Summ. to Parliament; K. B.; ob. 1677.

V. 1677. 5. Charles North, s. and h. Summ. to Parl. as Baron Grey of Rollestone, 17 Oct. 31 Car. II. 1673; ob. 1690.

VI. 1690. 6. William North, s. and h. Baron Grey of Rolleston; ob. 1734, s. p. when the Barony of Grey of Rolleston became Extinct; but that of North devolved on

BARONS BY WRIT.

VII. 1734. 7. Francis North, III.-3d Baron Guildford, being
s. and h. of Francis II.-2d Baron Guildford,
eldest son of Francis North I.-1st Baron
Guildford, 2d son of Dudley IV.-4th Baron
North; Created Earl of Guildford April 8,
1752; ob. 1790.

VIII. 1790. 8. Frederick North, s. and h. Earl of Guildford,
K. G.; ob. 1792.

IX. 1792. 9. George Augustus North, s. and h. Earl of
Guildford; ob. 1802, s. p. m. leaving three
daughters and coheirs, viz. Maria, who married John, present Marquess of Bute; Susan;
and Georgiana; between whom this Barony
is now in ABEYANCE.

NORTHALLERTON.

VISCOUNTCY, 9 November, 1706—Merged in the Crown 1727.
Vide CAMBRIDGE.

NORTHAMPTON.

EARLS.

I. WilL L 1. Waltheof Earl of Huntingdon, Northampton,
and Northumberland, being s. and h. of
Siward, Earl of those counties before the
Conquest; beheaded 1073; ob. s. p. m.

II. ....1. Simon de St. Liz, husband of Maud, eldest
dau. of the last Earl; obtained this Earldom
from William the Conqueror; living 1100.

III. H. I. 2. Simon de St. Liz, s. and h. Earl of Huntingdon; ob. 1153.

IV. 1153. 3. Simon de St. Liz, s. and h. Earl of Huntingdon;
ob. 1184, s. p. when the Earldom became
Extinct.

V. 1337. 1. William de Bohun, 3d son of Humphrey Earl
of Hereford and Essex, by Elizabeth Plantagenet, dau. of King Edward I.; Created Earl
of Northampton March 17, 1337, K. G.; ob.
1360.

VI. 1360. 2. Humphrey de Bohun, s. and h., succeeded
his uncle as Earl of Hereford and Essex, and
as Constable of England, in 1361: ob. 1372,
s. p. m. Eleanor, his eldest daughter and coheir, married Thomas Plantagenet, Duke of

Gloucester*; and Mary, his second dau. was
the wife of Henry Plantagenet, afterwards
King Henry IV. as this Earl died without
issue male, his honors became

MARQUESS.   Extinct.

I. 1547. ⎱ William Parr, 1st Baron Parr of Kendal, and
I. 1559. ⎰ XVII.-1st Earl of Essex, brother of Queen
Katherine, 6th and last wife of King Henry
VIII.; Created Marquess of Northampton
16 Feb. 1547; Lord Great Chamberlain,
K. G.; Attainted 1554, when his honors be-
came Forfeited; restored in blood, but not
in honors, the same year; again Created
Marquess of Northampton 13 Jan. 1559; ob.
1571, s. p. when this dignity became
Extinct.

VII. 1604.   Henry Howard, 2d son of Henry Earl of Surrey, and younger brother of Thomas IX.-
4th Duke of Norfolk, K. G. His father having been Attainted, he was restored in blood
1559; Created Baron Howard of Marnhill,
and Earl of Northampton 13 March, 1604,
K.G.; ob. 1614, s. p. when his honors became
Extinct.

VIII. 1618. 1. William Compton, II.-2d Baron Compton;
Created Earl of Northampton 2d Aug. 1618,
K. G.; ob. 1630.

IX.   1630. 2. Spenser Compton, s. and h. ob. 1642.
X.   1642. 3. James Compton, s. and h. ob. 1681.
XI.   1681. 4. George Compton, s. and h. ob. 1727.
XII. 1727. 5. James Compton, s. and h. He married Elizabeth Baroness de Ferrers of Chartley; ob.
1754, s. p. m. when the Barony of Compton
devolved on his only child, Charlotte Baron-

---

* Humphrey Stafford, Earl of Stafford, s. and h. of Edmund
Earl of Stafford, by Ann Plantagenet, dau. and heir of Thomas
Duke of Gloucester, by Eleanor eldest dau. and coheir of Humphrey de Bohun, Earl of Hereford, Essex, and Northampton,
styled himself, amongst other titles, in an Indenture dated London, 13 Feb. 1444, "Earl of Northampton," probably in consequence of the above-mentioned descent, but it does not appear
that he was ever formally created to that dignity.

EARLS.

ess de Ferrers of Chartley, Ijure matris, but this Earldom devolved on his brother and heir male,

XIII.1754. 6. George Compton, ob. 1758, s. P.

XIV.1758. 7. Charles Compton, nephew and heir, being s. and h. of Charles Compton, younger brother of George, last Earl; ob. 1763, s. P. M.

XV. 1763. 8. Spencer Compton, brother and heir; ob.1796.

MARQUESS.

XVI. 1796.—II. 1812. 9. Charles Compton, s. and h. Created Baron Wilmington of Wilmington, co. Sussex, Earl Compton of Compton, co. Warwick, and Marquess of the County of Northampton, 7 Sept. 1812. Present Marquess and Earl of Northampton, Earl Compton, and Baron Wilmington. ⊤

NORTHINGTON.

EARLS.

I. 1764. 1. Robert Henley, 1st Baron Henley; Created Viscount Henley and Earl of Northington, co. Hants, May 19, 1764, Lord Chancellor; ob. 1772.

II. 1772. 2. Robert Henley, s. and h.; Lord Lieut. of Ireland, K. T.; ob. 1786, s. P. when all his titles became **Extinct.**

NORTHUMBERLAND.

EARLS.

I. 1066. Morcar (younger son of Algar Earl of Chester), Earl of Northumberland before the Conquest; deprived of the Earldom for rebellion, when King William conferred it on

II. 1068. Copsi, who was slain a few weeks after he obtained that honor, and

III. 1068. Robert Comyn was constituted Earl of Northumberland 1068; slain 1069.

IV. 1069. Cospatrick, descended through his mother from Uctbred, Earl of this Province before the Conquest, obtained this Earldom from King William I. but was deprived of it for rebellion anno 1070; whereupon

EARLS.

V. 1070. Waltheof, son of Earl Siward, was appointed Earl of Northumberland; he married Judith, niece of William the Conqueror; beheaded 1075.

VI. 1076. Walcher, Bishop of Durham; appointed Earl of Northumberland 1076; murdered in 1080, when

VII. 1080. Alberic, a Norman, was constituted Earl of this County, but proving unfit for the dignity, he returned into Normandy about 1085, when Geoffrey Bishop of Constance had the government of this Earldom, and who styled himself, in the year 1088, "Eo tempore Northymbrorum Consulatum regebat;" but the next Earl was

VIII. 1090. Robert de Mowbray, nephew to the said Geoffery; deprived of the Earldom for treason circa 1095, and died 1106, s p.

IX. 1148. 1. Henry Prince of Scotland, s. and h. apparent of David King of Scotland (who, according to some writers, after the forfeiture of Robert the last Earl, also bore the title of Earl of Huntingdon), is generally considered to have been Earl of Northumberland; ob. vita patris, 1152.

X. 1152. 2. Malcolm, s. and h. who afterwards became King of Scotland; according to Dugdale, he surrendered the counties of Northumberland, Cumberland, and Westmoreland, to Hen. II. in 1154, in lieu whereof he obtained that of Huntingdon.

XI. 1192. Hugh de Pudsey, Bishop of Durham, called by some writers nephew of King Stephen, obtained the Earldom of Northumberland from Richard I. circa 1192, but voluntarily resigned it shortly afterwards; ob. 1195.

XII. 1377. 1. Henry Percy, IV.-13th Baron Percy; Created Earl of Northumberland 16 July, 1377, Earl Marshal; appointed Lord High Constable for life 1399; slain 1408; and being Attainted, his honors became
Forfeited.

III. 1414. 2. Henry Percy, grandson and heir, being s. and

h. of Sir Henry Percy, K. G. the renowned
"HOTSPUR," (ob. v. p.) eldest son of the last
Earl; restored to the Earldom Nov. 11, 1414,
and obtained a formal Charter of Creation to
that dignity in 1424; Lord High Constable;
slain 1455.

XIV. 1455. 3. Henry Percy, s. and h.; having married Eleanor, dau. and sole heir of Robert Baron Poynings, he was Summ. to Parl. vita patris, as
Baron Poynings; slain 1461; and being Attainted, his honors became
Forfeited.

XV. 1464. 1. John Nevill, Baron Montagu, brother of
Richard Earl of Warwick and Salisbury;
Created Earl of Northumberland May 27,
1464, which he RESIGNED in 1470, and was
Created Marquess of Montagu.

XVI. 1470. 4. Henry Percy, s. and h. of Henry XIV.-3d
Earl; restored in blood and honors circa
1470, although the reversal of his father's
Attainder does not appear on the Rolls of
Parliament until 12 and 13 Edward IV. K. G.;
ob. 1489.

XVII. 1489. 5. Henry Algernon Percy, s. and h. K. G. ob.
1527.

XVIII. 1527. 6. Henry Algernon Percy, s. and h. K. G. ob.
1537, s. p. and his brother, Sir Thomas Percy,
having been Attainted, his honors became
Extinct.

I. 1551. 1. John Dudley, Earl of Warwick; Created Duke
of Northumberland 11 Oct. 1551; Earl Marshal, K. G.; beheaded and attainted 1553,
when his dignities became
Forfeited.

XIX. 1557. 7. Thomas Percy, s. and h. of Sir Thomas Percy
(who was Attainted), next brother of Henry
Algernon Percy, XVIII.-6th and last Earl;
Created Baron Percy of Cockermouth and
Petworth, Baron Poynings, Lucy, Bryan, and
Fitz-Payne, with remainder, failing his issue
male, to his brother Henry and his issue male,
April 30, 1557; Created, May 1, 1557, Earl of
Northumberland, with the same remainder,

K. G.; beheaded 1572 (ob. s. p. m.) and having been attainted in 1571, his honors would have become forfeited but for the limitation before-mentioned, in virtue of which his titles devolved on

XX. 1572. 8. Henry Percy, his brother and heir male; he married Katherine, eldest dau. and coheir of John Nevill Baron Latimer; ob. 1585.

XXI. 1585. 9. Henry Percy, s. and h. K. G.; ob. 1632.

XXII. 1632. 10. Algernon Percy, s. and h.; Summ. to Parl. vita patris, as Baron Percy; K. G.; ob. 1668.

XXIII. 1668. 11. Josceline Percy, s. and h. ob. 1670, s. p. m. when the Earldom of Northumberland, together with the Baronies of Percy of Petworth and Cockermouth, Poynings, Lucy, Bryan, and Fitz-Payne, conferred by the Patent of Queen Mary, became
Extinct.

DUKE.

XXIV. 1674.—II. 1683. 1. George Fitz-Roy, natural son of King Charles II. Created Baron of Pontefract, co. York, Viscount Falmouth, co. Cornwall, and Earl of Northumberland, 1st Oct. 1674; Created Duke of Northumberland 6 April, 1683, K. G.; ob. 1716, s. p. when all his honors became
Extinct.

XXV. 1749. 1. Algernon Seymour, son and heir of Elizabeth Percy, dau. and sole heir of Joceline Percy, XXIII.-11th Earl, by Charles Seymour, Duke of Somerset. On the death of his mother in 1722 he was Summ. to Parliament as Baron Percy; succeeded his father as Duke of Somerset 2 Dec. 1748; Created Baron Warkworth of Warkworth Castle, co. Northumberland, and Earl of Northumberland 2 October, 1749, with remainder, failing his issue male, to his son-in-law, Sir Hugh Smithson, Bart. and to the heirs male of his body by Lady Elizabeth his wife; in default of which the dignities of Baroness Warkworth and Countess of Northumberland to the said Lady Elizabeth, and of Baron Warkworth and Earl of Northumber.

land to her heirs male; Created Baron
Cockermouth and Earl of Egremont, with a
special remainder, 3 October, 1749; ob.
1750, s. p. m.

DUKES.

XXVI. 1750.—III. 1766. 2. Sir Hugh Smithson, 4th Bart.
assumed the name of Percy,
husband of Lady Elizabeth,
only surviving child of Algernon Duke of Somerset, the last
Earl; succeeded agreeable to
the before-mentioned remainder as Baron Warkworth and
Earl of Northumberland; Created Earl Percy and Duke
of Northumberland 18 Oct.
1766, with remainder to his
issue male by Elizabeth his
wife; Created Baron Lou-
vaine of Alnwick, with a special remainder, 28 January,
1784, K. G.; ob. 1786.

XXVII. ....—IV. 1786. 3. Hugh Percy, s. and h. K. G.
Summ. to Parl. on the death
of his mother in 1777, as Baron Percy; ob. 1817.

XXVIII. ....—V. 1817. 4. Hugh Percy, s. and h. Summoned to Parliament, vita
patris, in the Barony of Percy.
Present Duke and Earl of
Northumberland, Earl Percy, Baron Percy,
Baron Warkworth, and a Baronet; also
eldest coheir of the Barony of Latimer, created by Writ 10 Hen. VI.; coheir of one
moiety of the Baronies of Scales and Plaitz,
and a representative of one of the coheirs of
the Barony of Badlesmere. K. G. ⸗

NORTHWICK.

BARONS.

I. 1797. 1. Sir John Rushout, 5th Bart.; Created Baron Northwick of Northwick Park, co. Worcester, 20 Oct. 1797; ob. 1800.

II. 1800. 2. John Rushout, s. and h. Present Baron Northwick.

NORTHWODE.

BARONS BY WRIT.

I. 1313. 1. John de Northwode; Summoned 8 June, 22 Edw. I. 1294; but it is very doubtful if that Writ was a regular Summons to Parliament, vide "CLYVEDON;" Summoned to Parl. from 8 Jan. 6 Edw. II. 1313, to 20 March, 12 Edw. II. 1319; ob. circa 1319.

II. 1319. 2. Roger de Northwode, grandson and heir, being son and heir of John de Northwode (ob. v. p.) eldest son of the last Baron; Summ. to Parl. 3 April, 34 Edw. III. 1360; ob. 1361.

III. 1361. 3. John de Northwode, s. and h. Summ. to Parl. from 1 June, 37 Edward III. 1363, to 20 Jan. 49 Edw. III. 1376; ob. 1379, leaving issue Roger, his son and heir, then 24 years of age, but who was never Summoned to Parliament, and appears to have died s. p. William, the brother of this Roger, died 7 Hen. IV. leaving John his son and heir, then ten years of age; which John died s. p. 4 Hen. V. 1416, being then just of age, leaving Elizabeth, wife of Peter Cat, and Eleanor the wife of John Adam, his sisters and coheirs. Of the issue of the said Elizabeth nothing is known; but Eleanor left a son and heir Thomas Adam, whose posterity in the male line have been traced for five descents, when Richard Adam, the representative of the family, was living, and who, though twice married, had no issue; Roger his brother then had five children, viz. Richard, John, and William; Bridget, wife of Adam Shepherd, Margery

wife of William Hawe, and Anne; and in the
representatives of the said Roger Adam this
Barony is probably vested.

NORWICH.

BARON BY WRIT.

I.   1342.   John de Norwich (s. and h. of Walter de Norwich, who being a Judge, was Summ. to
Parliament 8 Edw. II. and whom Dugdale,
vol. I. p. 90, erroneously considers a Baron
of Parliament); Summ. to Parl. 25 February,
16 Edw. III. 1342, and 3 April, 34 Edw. III.
1360; ob. 1362, leaving John de Norwich,
his grandson, viz. s. and h. of Walter de
Norwich (ob. v. p.) his eldest son, his next
heir, who was never Summoned to Parliament, and died 1374, s. p. leaving Katherine
de Brewz, dau. and heir of Thomas de Norwich his uncle, his heir; on whose death, s.
p. this Barony became
𝕰𝖗𝖙𝖎𝖓𝖈𝖙.

NORWICH.

EARLS.

I.   1626.   Edward Denney, 1st Baron Denney; Created
Earl of Norwich 24 Oct. 1626; ob. 1630,
s. p. m. when the Eardom became
𝕰𝖗𝖙𝖎𝖓𝖈𝖙.

II.   1645.   1. George Goring, 1st Baron Goring, s. and h. of
George Goring by Ann, sister and ultimately
coheir of Edward the last Earl; Created
Earl of Norwich 8 Nov. 1645; ob. 1662.

III.   1662.   2. Charles Goring, s. and h. ob. 1672, s. p. when
his honors became
𝕰𝖗𝖙𝖎𝖓𝖈𝖙.

IV.   1672.   1. Henry Howard, 1st Baron Howard of Castle
Rising, 2d son of Henry Frederick Earl of
Arundel, Surrey, and Norfolk; Created Earl
of Norwich 19 October, 1672; succeeded his
brother Thomas as X.-8th of Norfolk; and
also as Earl of Arundel, Surrey, and Norfolk,
&c.; Earl Marshal, K. G. ; ob. 1684.

EARLS,

V. 1684. 2. Henry Howard, s. and h. Duke of Norfolk,
&c. K. G.; ob. 1701, s. P.

VI. 1701. 3. Thomas Howard, nephew and heir, being son
and heir of Thomas Howard, next brother of
the last Earl; Duke of Norfolk, &c.; ob.
1732, s. P.

VII. 1732. 4. Edward Howard, brother and heir, Duke of
Norfolk, &c.; ob. 1777, s. P. when the Barony of Howard of Castle Rising and Earldom
of Norwich became

Extinct.

VIII. 1784. 1. Alexander Gordon, 4th Duke of Gordon in
Scotland; Created Earl of Norwich and
Baron Gordon of Huntly, co. Gloucester, 12
July, 1784. Present Earl of Norwich, Baron
Gordon of Huntly, Baron Mordaunt of Tur-
vey, and Baron Beauchamp of Bletsoe; also
Duke of Gordon, &c. in Scotland, K. T.

NOTTINGHAM.

Until the reign of King Richard II. no Charter or
Patent of Creation to the Earldom of this County is on
record. William Peverel, a natural son of William the
Conqueror, obtained the Lordship of Nottingham, which
passed by an heir female to the Ferrers, Earls of Derby,
who are sometimes, though erroneously, styled Earls of
Nottingham. John, afterwards King of England, received
a grant of the County and Castle of Nottingham, with
the whole honor of Peverel; but the first person who was
regularly created EARL of this County was,

EARLS.

I. 1377. John V.-11th Baron Mowbray, s. and h. of John
Baron Moubray, by Elizabeth, dau. and heir of
John Baron Segrave by Margaret Plantagenet,
Duchess of Norfolk, dau. and sole heir of
Thomas de Brotherton, Earl of Norfolk, and
Earl Marshal, younger son of King Edward I.
Created Earl of Nottingham, 16 July, 1377;

EARLS.

ob. 1383, infra æt. and s. p. when the Earldom became
Extinct.

II.   1383.   1. Thomas Baron Mowbray, brother and heir;
Created Earl of Nottingham in 1383, and
Duke of Norfolk 29 Sept. 1397; Earl Marshal, K. G.; ob. 1413. This Earldom continued merged in the Dukedom of Norfolk
until the death of John Mowbray, IV.-4th
Duke of Norfolk, and V.-6th Earl of Nottingham in 1475, when it became
Extinct.   Vide NORFOLK.

VI.   1476.   Richard Plantagenet, Duke of York, 2d son
of King Edward IV. being betrothed to Ann,
dau. and sole heir of John Mowbray IV.-4th
Duke of Norfolk and last Earl of Nottingham, was Created Earl of Nottingham 12
June, 1476, and Earl Warren and Duke of
Norfolk 7 February, 1477; murdered 1483,
æt. 9, when his honors became
Extinct.

VII.   1483.   William Baron Berkeley, s. and h. of James
Baron Berkeley by Isabel, dau. and at length
coheir of Thomas Mowbray, II.-1st Earl of
Nottingham, and I.-1st Duke of Norfolk;
Created Earl of Nottingham 28 June, 1483;
Created Marquess Berkeley 1488; Earl Mar-
shal; ob. 1491, s. p. when this Eardom again
became
Extinct.

IX.   1525.   Henry Fitz-Roy, natural son of King Henry
VIII. Created Earl of Nottingham and Duke
of Richmond 18 June, 1525, K. G. Lieut. of
Ireland; ob. 1536, infra æt. s. p. when all
his honors became
Extinct.

X.   1597.   1. Charles Howard, 2d Baron Howard of Effingham, descended from Sir Robert Howard and
Margaret his wife, dau. and ultimately coheir of Thomas Mowbray, II.-1st Earl of
Nottingham, and I.-1st Duke of Norfolk;

Created Earl of Nottingham 22 October, 1597; Lord High Admiral, K. G.; ob. 1624.

XI. 1624. 2. Charles Howard, 2d son and heir male; ob. 1642, s. p.

XII. 1642. 3. Charles Howard, half-brother and heir; ob. 1681, s. p. when the Earldom of Nottingham again became

Extinct.

XIII. 1681. 1. Heneage Finch, I.-1st Baron Finch of Daventry; Created Earl of Nottingham 12 May, 1681; Lord Chancellor; ob. 1682.

XIV. 1682. 2. Daniel Finch, s. and h. succeeded his cousin John V.-5th Earl of Winchilsea in 1729, to which dignity this Earldom has since been united.   Vide WINCHILSEA.

NOVANT.

I. Will. I. 1. Roger de Novant; obtained the inheritance of Juhell de Totneis from King William the Conqueror.

II. Will. II. 2. Hugh de Novant, s. and h. living 1104.

III. H. II. 3. Roger de Novant, s. and h. living 1167.

IV. H. II. 4. Henry de Novant, s. and h. of whom nothing farther is known, excepting that in the 9th of John he granted part of his lands to Roger de Valletort.

NUNEHAM.

VISCOUNTCY, 1 December, 1749.
       Vide HARCOURT.

OGLE.

I.   1461. 1. Robert Ogle ; Summ. to Parl. from 26 July, 1 Edward IV. 1461, to 7 Sept. 9 Edward IV. 1469, as " Roberto Ogle, Domino Ogle, Chl'r ;" ob. 1469.

II.   1469. 2. Owen Ogle, s. and h. Summ. to Parl. from 15 Nov. 22 Edw. IV. 1482, to 15 Sept. 1 Henry VII. 1485 ; ob. ...

III.   1509. 3. Ralph Ogle, s. and h. Summ. to Parl. 17 Oct. 1 Hen. VIII. 1509, and 28 Nov. 3 Hen. VIII. 1511 ; ob. 1512.

IV.   1512. 4. Robert Ogle, s. and h. Summ. to Parl. 23 Nov. 6 Hen. VIII. 1514, and 3 Nov. 21 Hen. VIII. 1529; ob. 1539.

V.   1539. 5. Robert Ogle, s. and h. ; he was never Summ. to Parl. ; ob. 1544.

VI.   1544. 6. Robert Ogle, s. and h. Summ. to Parl. from 14 Aug. 2 Ph. and Mary, 1553, to 5 Nov. 5 and 6 Ph. and Mary, 1558 ; ob. 1562.

VII. 1562. 7. Cuthbert Ogle, half-brother and heir ; Summ. to Parl. from 11 Jan. 5 Eliz. 1563, to 17 Oct. 43 Eliz. 1601 ; ob. 1597, s. P. M. when the Barony fell into ABEYANCE between his two daughters and coheirs, until the death, s. P. in 1627, of Joane, one of the said coheirs, wife of Edward Talbot, 7th Earl of Shrewsbury, on which event

. I. 1627. 8. Catherine, widow of Sir Charles Cavendish, and dau. and eventually sole heir of Cuthbert the last Baron, succeeded to the dignity, and by Letters Patent, dated 4 Dec. 1628, was declared Baroness Ogle, with a ratification of the honors to her and her heirs for ever ; ob. 1629.

BARONS.   EARLS.

VIII.1629.—I. 1664.   9. William Cavendish, son and heir of
OGLE OF BOTHAL.   Catherine Baroness Ogle; Created
I. 1620.   Baron Ogle of Bothal, co. ......,
and Viscount Mansfield, co. Nottingham, 3 Nov. 1620; Earl of
Newcastle 7 March, 1651; Marquess of Newcastle 27 Oct. 1643,
and Earl of Ogle and Duke of
Newcastle, both co. Northumberland, 16 March, 1664; succeeded
his mother in the Barony of Ogle,
created by the Writ of 1 Edw. IV.
1461, in 1629; K. G.; ob. 1676.

IX. 1676.—II.1676.   10.Henry Cavendish, s. and h. Duke
OGLE OF BOTHAL.   of Newcatle, &c. and Earl of Ogle,
II.   Baron Ogle, and Baron Ogle of
Bothal, K. G.; ob. 1691, s. P. M. when all his
honors, excepting the ancient Barony of
Ogle, became Extinct; which dignity fell
into ABEYANCE between his three daughters
and coheirs; of whom Elizabeth married,
first, Christopher Duke of Albemarle, and
secondly, Ralph Duke of Montagu, but died
s. P.; Frances was the wife of John, son and
heir apparent of the Earl of Breadalbane, and
likewise died s. P.; Margaret, married John
Holles, Earl of Clare (afterwards created
Duke of Newcastle); Catherine, married
Thomas Earl of Thanet; and Arabella was
the wife of Charles Earl of Sunderland;
and amongst the descendants and representatives of the said Margaret, Catherine, and
Arabella, this Barony is now in ABEYANCE.

OLDCASTLE.

BARON BY WRIT.

I.   1409.   John Oldcastle, having married Joane, grand-
daughter and heir of John II.-2d Baron Cob-
ham, he was Summ. to Parl. from 26 Oct.
11 Hen. IV. 1409, to 22 March, 1 Hen. V.
1413, as "Johanni Oldcastell, Chl'r;" though
he is generally considered to have been Baron Cobham jure uxoris, and in the proceedings in Parliament against him, anno 1417,

he is expressly called "Dominum Joh'em Oldcastell, Militem, Dominum de Cobham *;" ob. circa 1417, s. p. when the Barony created by the Writ of 11 Hen. IV. if a separate dignity from that of Cobham, became
Extinct.

ONSLOW.

BARONS.
I.   1716. 1. Sir Richard Onslow, 2d Bart. Created Baron Onslow of Onslow, co. Salop, and of West Clandon, eo. Surrey, 25 June, 1716, with remainder, failing his issue male, to his uncle Denzill Onslow and his issue male; failing which, to the issue male of his father Sir Arthur Onslow, 1st Bart.; ob. 1717.

II.   1717. 2. Thomas Onslow, s. and b. ob. 1740.

III. 1740. 3. Richard Onslow, s. and h. ob. 1776, s. p.

EARLS.
IV. 1776.—I. 1801. 4. George Onslow, 1st Baron Cranley, cousin and heir, being son and heir of Arthur, eldest son of Foot Onslow, next brother of Richard 1st Baron Onslow (Denzill Onslow, uncle to the said Richard Baron Onslow, having died s. p.); Created Viscount Cranley of Cranley, eo. Surrey, and Earl of Onslow, eo. Salop, 19 June, 1801; ob. 1814.

V. ..,.. —II. 1814. 5. Thomas Onslow, s. and b. Present Earl Onslow and Baron Onslow and Viscount and Baron Cranley. ⚲

ORFORD.

EARLS.
I.   1697. 1. Edward Russell, nephew of William VII.-5th Earl and IV. Duke of Bedford; Created Baron of Shingay, co. Cambridge, Viscount Barfleur in the Duchy of Normandy, and Earl of Orford, co. Suffolk, with remainder to his issue male; failing which, the dignity of Baron of Shingay to the issue male of Letitia his eldest

---

* Rot. Parl. vol. iv. p. 109[b].

sister, 7 May, 1697, ob. 1727, s. P. when all his honors (his said sister Letitia having died s. P. M.) became

Extinct.

II. 1742. 1. Sir Robert Walpole, K. G. Created Baron of Houghton and Viscount Walpole, co. Norfolk, and Earl of Orford, co. Suffolk, 6 Feb. 1742; ob. 1745.

III. 1745. 2. Robert Walpole, s. and h. Created Baron Walpole of Walpole, co. Norfolk, with a special remainder 1 June, 1723; he married Margaret Rolle, who in 1760 succeeded to the Barony of Clinton: K. B.; ob. 1751.

IV. 1751. 3. George Walpole, s. and h. ob. 1791, s. P.

V. 1791. 4. Horatio Walpole, uncle and heir, being next brother of Robert III.-2d Earl; ob. 1797, s. P. when the Barony of Houghton, Viscountcy of Walpole, and Earldom of Orford became

Extinct.

VI. 1806. 1. Horatio Walpole, 2d Baron Walpole of Woolterton, cousin and heir; succeeded as 4th Baron Walpole of Walpole in 1797; Created Earl of Orford 10 April, 1806; ob. 1809.

VII. 1809. 2. Horatio Walpole, s. and h. ob. 1822.

VIII.1822. 3. Horatio Walpole, s. and h. Present Earl of Orford, Baron Walpole of Walpole, and Baron Walpole of Woolterton. ⊤̵

ORIEL.

I. 1821. John Foster; Created Baron Oriel of Ferrard, co. Louth, 17 July, 1821. His Lordship married Margareta Amelia, who was Created Baroness Oriel and Viscountess Ferrard, both in the Peerage of Ireland. Present Baron Oriel. ⊤̵

ORMOND
OF ROCHFORD.

1495. Thomas Butler, 8th Earl of Carrick and 7th

Earl of Ormond in Ireland; Summoned to Parl. from 14 October, 1495, 11 Henry VII. to 23 Nov. 6 Hen. VIII. 1514, as "Thomas Ormond de Rochford, Chev.;" ob. 1515, s. P. M. leaving two daughters and coheirs, viz. Anne, wife of Sir John St. Leger, and Margaret, wife of Sir William Boleyn, between whose descendants and representatives this Barony is now in ABEYANCE.

ORMOND.

DUKES.

I. 1681. 1. James Butler, 1st Duke of Ormond in Ireland, and 1st Earl of Brecknock, &c. in England; Created Duke of Ormond 9 Nov. 1682, K. G.; ob. 1688.

II. 1688. 2. James Butler, grandson and heir, being s. and h. of Thomas Butler, 1st Baron Butler of More Park (ob. v. p.) eldest son of the last Duke, K. G.; attainted in 1715, when all his honors became

Forfeited.

ORMOND

OF LLANTHONY.

BARON.

I. 1821. 1. James Butler, 18th Earl of Ormond in Ireland; Created Baron Ormond of Llanthony, co. Monmouth, 17 July, 1821. Present Baron Ormond of Llanthony; also Earl of Ormond, &c. in Ireland, K. P.

ORREBY.

BARON BY WRIT.

I. 1309. John de Orreby; Summ. to Parl. from 4 March, 2 Edw. II. 1309, to 16 June, 4 Edw. II. 1311; ob. 1317, s. P. when the Barony became

Extinct.

OSBORNE.

BARONY, 15 August, 1673.

Vide LATIMER and LEEDS.

OSSULSTON.

BARONS.

I. 1682. 1. John Bennet; Created Baron Ossulston of Ossulston, co. Middlesex, 24 Nov. 1682; ob. 1688.

II. 1688. 2. Charles Bennet, s. and h. Created Earl of Tankerville, 19 Oct. 1714.

Vide TANKERVILLE.

OSWALDESTRE AND CLUN.

BARONIES, 1627.

Vide CLUN and NORFOLK.

OXFORD.

EARLS.

I. 1155. 1. Aubrey de Vere; Created Earl of Oxford by the Empress Maud, and confirmed by Hen. II. in 1155; Great Chamberlain of England; ob. 1194.

II. 1194. 2. Aubrey de Vere, s. and h. Lord Great Chamberlain; ob. 1214, s. p.

III. 1214. 3. Robert de Vere, brother and heir; he was one of the celebrated 25 Barons appointed to enforce the observance of MAGNA CHARTA; Lord Great Chamberlain; ob. 1221.

IV. 1221. 4. Hugh de Vere, s. and h. Lord Great Chamberlain; ob. 1263.

V. 1263. 5. Robert de Vere, s. and h. Lord Great Chamberlain; ob. 1296.

VI. 1296. 6. Robert de Vere, s. and h. Lord Great Chamberlain; ob. 1331, s. p.

VII. 1331. 7. John de Vere, nephew and heir, being son and heir of Alphonsus de Vere, next brother of the last Earl; L. G. Chamb.; he married Maud, daughter and coheir of Giles Baron Badlesmere; ob. 1360.

VIII. 1360. 8. Thomas de Vere, s. and h. Lord Great Chamberlain; ob. 1371.

IX. 1371. 9. Robert de Vere, s. and h. Created Marquess of Dublin 1386, and Summ. to Parl. by that title 8 Aug. in that year; Created Duke of

Ireland 18 March, 1387; L. G. Chamberlain, K. G.; ob. 1392, s. P.; but having been banished and attainted in 1388, all his honors were then

Forfeited.

X. 1392. 10.Aubrey de Vere, uncle and heir; obtained a grant of the Earldom to him and his heirs male 1392, and in 1397 the Attainder of his nephew, Robert the last Earl, was repealed and annulled; Lord Great Chamberlain, but shortly after his restoration he was deprived of that office; ob. 1400.

XI. 1400. 11.Richard de Vere, s. and h. K. G.; ob. 1417.

XII. 1417. 12.John de Vere, s. and h. He married Elizabeth, dau. and heir of Sir John Howard, and sole heir of the Barony of Plaitz; Attainted and beheaded 1461, when all his honors became

Forfeited.

XIII. 1464. 13.John de Vere, s. and h.; restored in blood and honors 1464; Attainted in 1474, when his dignities became **Forfeited**; restored to all his honors and possessions in 1485; obtained a confirmation of the office of Lord Great Chamberlain; L. H. Admiral; K. G., ob. 1513, s. P.

XIV. 1513. 14.John de Vere, nephew and heir, being s. and h. of Sir George Vere, next brother of the last Earl; L. G. Chamberlain; ob. 1526, s. P.

XV. 1526. 15.John de Vere, cousin and heir, being s. and h. of John, eldest son of Robert de Vere, next brother of John 12th Earl; L. G. Chamberlain; K. G.; ob. 1539.

XVI. 1539. 16.John de Vere, s. and h.; L. G. Chamberlain; ob. 1562.

XVII. 1562. 17.Edward de Vere, s. and h.; L. G. Chamberlain; ob. 1604.

XVIII. 1604. 18.Henry de Vere, s. and h.; L. G. Chamberlain; ob. 1625, s. P.

XIX. 1625. 19.Robert de Vere, cousin and heir, being s. and b. of Hugh, eldest son of Aubrey de Vere, brother of John 16th Earl; ob. 1632.

EARLS.

XX.   1632.20.Aubrey de Vere, s. and h. K.G.; ob. 1702,
     s. p. m. when this Earldom became
             Extinct.

XXI.   1711. 1.Robert Harley; Created Baron Harley of
     Wigmore, co. Hereford, Earl of Oxford and
     Earl Mortimer, 24 May, 1711, with remain-
     der, failing his issue male, to the issue male
     of Sir Robert Harley, K. B. his grandfather;
     Lord High Treasurer, K. G.; ob. 1724.

XXII. 1724. 2.Edward Harley, s. and h.; the FOUNDER of
     the celebrated HARLEIAN LIBRARY; ob. 1741,
     s. p. m.

XXIII.1741. 3.Edward Harley, 1st cousin and heir male,
     being eldest son of Edward Harley, next bro-
     ther of Robert XXI.-1st Earl; succeeded
     agreeable to the limitation recited above;
     ob. 1755.

XXIV. 1755. 4.Edward Harley, s. and h. ob. 1790, s. P.

XXV. 1790. 5.Edward Harley, nephew and heir, being s.
     and h. of the Hon. John Harley, Bishop of
     Hereford, next brother of the last Earl.
     Present Earl of Oxford and Earl Mortimer,
     and Baron Harley.

PAGANELL

OF DUDLEY.

BARONS BY TENURE.

I.   Will. I. 1. Ralph Paganell; held divers lordships at the
     General Survey; living 1089.

II. Will. II. 2. Fulk Paganell, s. and h. ob. ....

III. Steph. 3. Ralph Paganell, s. and h.; Lord of Dudley,
     co. Stafford; living 1140.

BARON BY TENURE.

IV. H. II. 4. Gervase Paganell, s. and h. living 1189; ob.
.... s.p.m. leaving Hawyse his dau. and heir,
who carried the Lordship of Dudley to her
first husband, John de Somery.

PAGANELL, or PAINELL,
OF BAHUNTUNE.

BARONS BY TENURE.

I.   H. II. 1. William Paganell, brother of Gervase above-
mentioned; he married Julian, dau. and
heir of Robert de Bahuntune, with whom he
acquired the Lordship of Bahuntune, co.
Devon; ob. ante 1180.

II. H. II. 2. Fulk Paganell, s. and h. ob. circa 1208.
III. John. 3. William Paganell, s. and h. ob. circa 1217.
IV. H. III. 4. William Painell, s. and h. ob. ....
V. H. III. 5. William Painell, s. and h. ob. 1294, s.p. leav-
ing Auda, the wife of John de Balun, his
sister and heir.

PAYNELL
OF DRAX.

BARON BY TENURE.

I.   John.   Hugh Painell, younger son of William 1st
Lord of Bahuntune, Lord of Drax, which he
obtained from King John; ob. 1244. Of this
line no further mention is made until 28
Edward I. when

BY WRIT.

I.   1299.   John Paynell of Drax was Summ. to Parl.
from 29 Dec. 28 Edw. I. 1299, to 25 Aug. 12
Edw. II. 1318; he is considered to have died
ante 1326. No account is given of his issue, nor does
Dugdale in his Baronage take any notice of him. From
the statement in Banks's Extinct Peerage, vol. i. p. 391,
it would appear there were two John Paynells Summoned to Parl. within the above period, but in all probability it was the same person; for though, in the Index
to the Lists of Summons, one John Paynell is described,
" de Drax," in the Writs themselves these words never
occur.

PAYNELL.

BARONS BY TENURE.

I. Rich. I. 1. Adam Painell, another son of William 1st
Lord of Babuntune; living 1215.

II. H. III. 2. Ralph Painell, s. and h. who in 1225 had
livery of the lands of his uncle, Robert Bardolph, but of whom nothing farther is recorded.

PAYNELL

OF CARLETON.

BARONS BY TENURE.

I. H. III. 1. Fulk Paynell; presumed to have been a
younger son of Fulke 2d Lord of Babuntune;
ob. ante 1260.

II. H. III. 2. William Paynell, s. and h.; living 1260; ob.
ante 1272.

III. Edw. I. 3. John Paynell, next heir to William the last
Baron; ob. 1284.

IV. Edw. I. 4. John Paynell, s. and h. ob. 1291, s. p.

V. Edw. I. 5. Philip Paynell, brother and heir; ob. 1324,
leaving John his son and heir; but as he was
not summoned to Parliament, this family
can no longer be considered as Barons of
the Realm.

PAYNELL.

BARON BY WRIT.

I. 1303.   William Paynell; presumed to have been of the
same family; Summ. to Parl. from 12 Nov. 32
Edw. I. 1303, to 6 Oct. 9 Edw. II. 1315; ob.
1317, s. p. when the Barony became
Extinct.

PAGET.

BARONS BY WRIT.

I. 1550. 1. Sir William Paget, K. G.; Summ. to Parl.
from 23 Jan. 5 Edw. VI. 1552, to 20 Jan. 4
and 5 Philip and Mary, 1558, as " Will. Paget de Beaudesert," co. Stafford, though it

is stated that he was first Summ. to Parl. 3 Dec. 4 Edward VI. 1550, and that he was created to that dignity 9 Jan. 1551; ob. 1563.

II. 1563. 2. Henry Paget, s. and h. Summ. to Parl. 30 Sept. 8 Eliz. 1566; ob. 1568, s. p. m. Elizabeth, his dau. and heir, died, according to Collins, June 29, 1571, aged about three years, though Dugdale states that she married Sir Henry Lee.

III. 1568. 3. Thomas Paget, brother of Henry the last Baron; Summ. to Parl. from 4 April, 13 Eliz. 1571*, to 6 Jan. 23 Eliz. 1581; Attainted 1581, when his honors became

Forfeited.

IV. 1603. 4. William Paget, s. and h.; restored to his father's honors 1st James I. and Summ. to Parl. from 5 Nov. 3 Jaq. I. 1605, to 7 March, 3 Car. I. 1628; ob. 1629.

V. 1629. 5. William Paget, s. and h.; Summ. to Parl. from 13 April, 15 Car. I. 1639, to 8 May, 13 Car. II. 1661; ob. 1678.

VI. 1678. 6. William Paget, s. and h.; Summ. to Parl. from 6 March, 31 Car. II. 1679; ob. 1713.

VII. 1713. 7. Henry Paget, s. and h. 1st Baron Burton; Created Earl of Uxbridge, co. Middlesex, 19 Oct. 1714; ob. 1743.

---

* It must be observed, that although this Barony has been considered a Barony in fee, as originating in a Writ of Summons, yet that, on the death of Henry second Lord, his brother Thomas third Lord, was apparently summoned to Parliament during the life-time of Elizabeth the dau. and heir of Henry 2d Lord; for, even admitting that Dugdale is erroneous in saying that she married Sir Henry Lee, it appears she survived her father about three years, and that her uncle was summoned to Parliament three months before the period when Collins (vol. vii. p. 12) says she died, viz. June 29, 1571, though in that Writer's "Baronies by Writ," p. 116, he says that Thomas 3d Baron did not succeed to the title until the death of the said Elizabeth, the date of which is not there given. In Dugdale's List of Summonses, the first mention of this Barony is 28 Jan. 5 Edw. VI. anno 1552, when "William Paget de Beaudesert" is stated to have been summoned to the Parliament begun at Westminster on that day.

VIII. 1743. 8. Henry Paget, grandson and heir, being s. and
h. of Thomas Catesby Paget (ob. v. p.) eldest
son of the last Baron; Baron Burton, and
Earl of Uxbridge; ob. 1769, s. P. when the
Barony of Burton and Earldom of Uxbridge
became Extinct; but the Barony of Paget
devolved on his cousin and heir,

IX. 1769. 9. Henry Bayley, who assumed the name of
Paget, being s. and h. of Sir Nicholas Bayley, Bart. by Caroline, dau. and heir of Thomas Paget, eldest son of Henry, next brother
of William 6th Baron Paget; Created Earl
of Uxbridge May 19, 1784; ob. 1812.

X. 1812. 10. Henry William Paget, s. and h. Earl of Uxbridge; Created Marquess of Anglesey 4
July, 1815. Present Baron Paget, Earl of
Uxbridge, Marquess of Anglesey, and a Baronet of Ireland, K. G., G. C. B.

PANTULF.

I. Will. I. William Pantulf; founded the Abbey of St.
Peter of Norum; living 1102.

II. H. I. Robert Pantulf, 2d son of the last Baron, succeeded to his father's Barony in England;
to whom succeeded

III. Steph. Hugh Pantulf; whose successor was

IV. H. II. Ivo Pantulf; who was succeeded by

V. John. William Pantulf, s. and h. of whom nothing
farther is recorded.

I. H. III. 1. Hugh Pantulf, brother of Ivo; living 1194.

II. H. III. 2. William Pantulf, s. and h. ob. 1233. Maud,
his dau. and heir, married Ralph Boteler, of
Oversley, to whom she carried the manor
of Wemme.

PARKER.

I. 1716.—I. 1721. 1. Thomas Parker; Created Baron Parker
of Macclesfield, co. Chester, 10 March,
1716; Created Viscount Parker of-

Ewelme, co. Oxford, and Earl of Macclesfied; with remainder, failing his issue male, of the dignity of Baroness Parker of Macclesfield, and Viscountess Parker of Ewelme aforesaid, and Countess of Macclesfield, to Elizabeth, his dau. wife of William Heathcote, Esq. and to the heirs male of her body, 5 Nov. 1721.   Vide MACCLESFIELD.

PARR

BARON.	OF KENDAL.
I. 1538.	William Parr; Created Baron Parr of Kendal 1538, and Summ. to Parl. from 28 April, 31 Henry VIII. 1539, to 4 June, 35 Henry VIII. 1543. His sister Katherine having married King Henry VIII. 12 July, 1543, he was Created Earl of Essex 23 Dec. in that year. Attainted 1553, when all his dignities became Forfeited.

PARR

BARON.	OF HORTON.
I. 1543.	William Parr, uncle to William Baron Parr of Kendal above-mentioned, and to Queen Katherine; Created Baron Parr of Horton, co. Northampton, 23 Dec. 1543; ob. 1546, S. P. M. when the title became Extinct.

PATESHULL.

BARON BY WRIT.	
I. 1342.	John de Pateshull; Summ. to Parl, 25 Feb. 16 Edw. III. 1342, but never afterwards; ob. 1349, leaving William his son and heir, who was never Summ. to Parl. and died in 1366, s. p. when his four sisters became his heirs, viz. Sybill, wife of Roger de Beauchamp; Alice, of Thomas Wake; Mabell, of Walter de Fauconberg; and Katherine, of Sir Robert de Tudenham, Knt. The Barony, however, on the death of John Baron Pateshull in consequence of only one Writ having been issued, and there being no proof of sitting, became Extinct.

I 2

PECHE

OF BRUNNE.

BARONS BY TENURE.

I.   H. II. 1. Hamon Peche, Lord of Brunne, co. Cambridge, in right of his wife, Alice, sister and coheir of Pain Peverell; living 1190; ob. ante 1195.

II. Rich.I. 2. Gilbert Peche, s. and h.; living 1212; ob. ante 1217.

III. H. III. 3. Hamon Peche, s. and h. ob. 1241.

IV. H. III. 4. Gilbert Peche, s. and h. ob. 1291; his successor was

BY WRIT.

I.   1299. 5. Gilbert Peche; Summ. to Parl. from 29 Dec. 28 Edw. I. 1299, to 3 Nov. 34 Edw. I. 1306, and again 14 March, 15 Edw. II. 1322; ob. circa 1323, leaving two sons, John and Edmund, who were never Summ. to Parl. but of whom, or of their descendants, Dugdale gives no account.

PECHE

OF WORMLEIGHTON.

BARONS BY TENURE.

I.   H. III. 1. Richard Peche, whose genealogy, as stated by Dugdale, is very confused, was Lord of Wormleighton, co. Warwick, jure matris, Petronill, dau. and heir of Richard Walshe; ob. . . . . .

BY WRIT.

I.   1321. 2. John Peche, s. and h.*; Summ. to Parl. from 15 May, 14 Edw. II. 1321, to 22 Jan. 9 Edw. III. 1336; ob. circa 1339, leaving John Peche, his grandson, his heir, who died in 1376, leaving John Peche, his son and heir, who died 1385, s. p. m. leaving Joan and Margaret

---

* If Dugdale is correct in saying this Baron was the son of Richard above mentioned, he must have died very aged, for he states that he continued loyal to Henry III. and in the 49th of that reign had the King's special letters of protection, and died about the 11th or 12th Edw. III. so that allowing him to have been only 21 in the 49th Henry III. 1244 he must have been above 95 years of age at his demise.

his daughters and coheirs; but neither of
these Johns were summoned to Parliament.
Joan, the eldest dau. and coheir of John Peche
last mentioned died s. p. leaving Margaret,
the wife of Sir William Montfort, her sister,
her heir, in whose descendants and representatives the Barony of Peche is vested.

PECHE.

OF ——

I. 1321. Robert Peche; Summ. to Parl. 15 May, 14
Edw. II. 1321, but never after, and of whom
Dugdale gives no account in his Baronage;
nor does he appear to be mentioned by any
other writer; on his death the Barony became
𝕰𝔵𝔱𝔦𝔫𝔠𝔱.

PELHAM.

BARONS.

I. 1706. 1. Sir Thomas Pelham, 5th Bart.; Created Baron Pelham of Laughton, co. Sussex, 29
Dec. 1706; ob. 1712.

VISC.

II. 1712. —I. 1714. 2. Thomas Pelham (assumed the
OF STANMERE.   name of) Holles, s. and h.; Cre-
I. 1672. 1.   ated, 26 Oct. 1714, Viscount Pelham of Houghton, co. Nottingham, and Earl
of Clare; with remainder, failing his issue
male, to Henry, his brother, and his issue
male; subsequently Created Marquess of
Clare, and Duke of Newcastle-upon-Tyne,
and in 1756 Duke of Newcastle-under Lyne,
with a special remainder; Created Baron
Pelham of Stanmere, co. Sussex, with remainder, failing his issue male, to his kinsman Thomas Pelham, of Stanmere, co. Sussex, Esq. 4 May, 1762, K.G.; ob. 1768, s. p.
when the Barony of Pelham of Laughton,
the Viscountcy of Pelham, the Earldom and
Marquisate of Clare, and Dukedom of Newcastle-upon-Tyne, became 𝕰𝔵𝔱𝔦𝔫𝔠𝔱; but the
Barony of Pelham of Stanmere, devolved,
agreeable to the above limitation, on

BARON.

II.   1768.   2. Thomas Pelham, of Stanmere, Esq. before
mentioned; he was s. and h. of Thomas,
eldest surviving son of Henry Pelham, younger
brother of Thomas 1st Baron Pelham of
Laughton; he also succeeded his cousin
Thomas 2d Baron Pelham of Laughton, and
1st Baron Pelham of Stanmere (Duke of
Newcastle, &c.) in the Baronetcy; Created
Earl of Chicester 23 June, 1801.

Vide CHICHESTER.

PEMBROKE.

EARLS.

I.   1138.   1. Gilbert de Clare; Created Earl of Pembroke
1138; ob. 1149.

II.   1149.   2. Richard de Clare, surnamed Strongbow, s.
and h.; Justice of Ireland; ob. 1176, s. p. m.

III.   1189.   1. William Marshal, having married Isabel de
Clare, dau. and heir of Richard the last Earl,
acquired the Earldom of Pembroke in 1189;
Marshal of England; ob. 1219.

IV.   1219.   2. William Marshal, s. and h.; was one of the
celebrated 25 Barons appointed to enforce
the observance of MAGNA CHARTA, being
then styled "Comes Mareschal Jun.;" Earl
Marshal; ob. 1231, s. p.

V.   1231.   3. Richard Marshal, brother and heir; Earl
Marshal; ob. 1234, s. p.

VI.   1234.   4. Gilbert Marshal, brother and heir; Earl Marshal; ob. 1241, s. p.

VII.   1241.   5. Walter Marshal, brother and heir; Earl Marshal; ob. 24 Nov. 1245, s. p.

VIII. 1245.   6. Anselm Marshal, brother and heir; Earl Marshal; ob. 5 Dec. 1245, s. p. when his honors
became

Extinct.

IX. H.III.   1. William de Valence, son of Hugh le Brun,
Earl of March, by Isabel, widow of King
John, and mother of King Henry III. said
to have been Created Earl of Pembroke in
1247; but Dugdale, speaking of the battle
of Lewes anno 1264, says this William was
"then called Earl of Pembroke, and not before, for aught I have seen;" ob. 1296.

X. 1296. 2. Aylmer de Valence, s. and h.; ob. 1323, s. p. when the title became
Extinct.

XI. 1339. 1. Laurence IV.-11th Baron Hastings, Lord of Abergavenny, grandson of John Baron Hastings, Lord of Abergavenny, by Isabel, dau. of William and sister and heir of Aymer de Valence, the last Earl; Created Earl of Pembroke 13 Oct. 1339; ob. 1348.

XII. 1348. 2. John Hastings, s. and h.; he married Anne, sole dau. and heir of Walter Baron Manny, ob. 1375.

XIII. 1375. 3. John Hastings, s. and h. K. G.; ob. 1389, s. p. when the Earldom again became
Extinct.

XIV. 1414. 1. Humphrey Plantagenet, youngest son of King Henry IV.; Summ. to Parl. as Duke of Gloucester and Earl of Pembroke 26 Sept. 1414, K. G.; ob. 1446, s. p. when his honors became
Extinct.

XV. 1446. 1. William de la Pole, VI.-4th Earl and I.-4th Marquess of Suffolk, obtained a reversionary grant of the Earldom of Pembroke 21 Feb. 1443, provided that Humphrey, at that time Earl of Pembroke and Duke of Gloucester, died without issue; Created Marquess of Suffolk 1444; succeeded to the Earldom of Pembroke 1446, and was Created Duke of Suffolk 2 June, 1448, K. G.; ob. 1450; and being attainted, all his dignities became
Forfeited.

XVI. 1452. 1. Jasper Tudor, surnamed of Hatfield, 2d son of Sir Owen Tudor, by Katherine, widow of King Henry V. and mother of King Henry VI.. Presumed to have been created Earl of Pembroke circa Nov. 1452, though Dugdale states, "there is no notice taken of it in the Roll of that time, nor in any other memorial of him that I have seen." By his attainder, in 1461, whatever honors he possessed became
Forfeited.

EARLS.

XVII. 1468. 1.William Herbert, 1st Baron Herbert of Chepstow ; Created Earl of Pembroke 27 May, 1468, K. G.; beheaded 1469.

XVIII.1469. 2.William Herbert, s. and h.; he surrendered this Earldom at the request of King Edward IV. and was created Earl of Huntingdon 4 July, 1472; ob. .....s. p. m.

XIX. 1469. Edward Plantagenet, Prince of Wales, son and heir apparent of King Edward IV.; Created Earl of March and Pembroke 8 July, 1479; succeeded his father as Edward V. when this title became merged in the Crown.

MARCHIONESS.

I. 1532. Ann Boleyn, dau. of Thomas Boleyn, Earl of Wiltshire ; Created Marchioness of Pembroke 1 Sept. 1532; became Queen of England as 2d wife to King Henry VIII. in January, 1533 ; beheaded 1536; Elizabeth, her only child, succeeded to the Throne, but the honor probably became merged in the Royal dignity on the Marchioness' marriage.

XX. 1551. 1.William Herbert, s. and h. of Sir Richard Herbert, natural son of William Herbert, XVII.-1st Earl ; Created Baron Herbert of Caerdiff 10 Oct. 1551, and Earl of Pembroke 11 October, 1551; he married Ann, sister and coheir of Thomas Parr, Marquess of Northampton, and sister of Queen Katherine Parr ; K. B. ; ob. 1569.

XXI. 1569. 2. Henry Herbert, s. and h. K. G.; ob. 1601.

XXII.1601. 3.William Herbert, s. and h. K.G. ; ob. 1630,s.p.

XXIII.1630.4.Philip Herbert, 1st Earl of Montgomery, and 1st Baron Herbert of Shurland; brother and heir, K. G. ; ob. 1650.

XXIV. 1650.5.Philip Herbert, s. and h. Earl of Montgomery ; ob. 1669.

XXV. 1669.6.William Herbert, s. and h. Earl of Montgomery; ob. 1674, s. p.

XXVI.1674. 7.Philip Herbert, half-brother and heir, Earl of Montgomery; ob. 1683, s. p. m.

XXVII.1683. 8.Thomas Herbert, brother and heir, Earl of Montgomery, L. H. Admiral, Lord Lieut. of Ireland, K. G. ; ob. 1733.

EARLS.

XXVIII.1733. 9. Henry Herbert, s. and h. Earl of Montgomery; ob. 1751.

XXIX.1751.10.Henry Herbert, s. and h. Earl of Montgomery; ob. 1794.

XXX.1794. 11.George Augustus Herbert, s. and h. 8th Earl of Montgomery, K. G. Present Earl of Pembroke and Montgomery, Baron Herbert of Caerdiff and Baron Herbert of Shurland. ⊤

PENSHURST.

BARON.

I. 1825. 1. Percy Clinton Sydney Smythe, 8th Viscount Strangford in Ireland; Created Baron Penshurst of Penshurst, co. Kent, January 1825. Present Baron Penshurst; also Viscount Strangford in Ireland; G. C. B. ⊤

PERCY.

BARONS BY TENURE.

I. Will. I. 1. William de Percy*, surnamed Algernon; obtained divers lands from William the Conqueror; ob. circa 1096.

II. Hen. I. 2. Alan de Percy, s. and h. living 1116; ob. . . . . .

III. Steph. 3. William de Percy, s. and h. living 1168; ob. . . . . . s. p. m.

IV. H. II. 4. Joscelaine de Louvaine, younger son of Godfrey Duke of Brabant, assumed the name of Percy on his marriage with Agnes de Percy, daughter and eventually sole heir of William the last Baron; ob. . . . . Agnes his wife survived him many years.

V. John. 5. Richard de Percy, youngest son of the said Josceline and Agnes de Percy; usurped the inheritance of his nephew William de Percy, and was chief of the family during his life; he was one of the celebrated 25 Barons appointed to enforce the observance of

---

* The early part of this account of the Barony of Percy is taken from Collins' Peerage, vol. ii. p. 280, who appears to have investigated the subject in the most laborious manner. His statement differs very materially from that given by Dugdale.

   Magna Charta; ob. circa 1244; his issue failed in his grandson.

VI. H. III. 6. William de Percy, s. and h. of Henry de Percy (ob. vita matris), eldest son of the said Josceline and Agnes; succeeded to his inheritance on the death of his uncle Richard; ob. 1245.

VII. 1245. 7. Henry de Percy, s. and h. ob. 1272.

VIII. 1272. 8. William de Percy, s. and h. ob. infans.

IX. Edw.I. 9. John de Percy, brother and heir; ob. infans.

I. 1299. 10. Henry de Percy, brother and heir; Summ. to Parl. from 6 February, 27 Edward I. 1299, to 29 July, 8 Edw. II. 1314; ob. 1315.

II. 1315. 11. Henry de Percy, s. and h. Summ. to Parl. from 14 March, 15 Edw. II. 1322, to 20 July, 26 Edw. III. 1352; ob. 1352.

III. 1352. 12. Henry de Percy, s. and h. Summ. to Parl. from 15 July, 27 Edw. 1353, to 20 January, 39 Edw. III. 1366; ob. 1368.

IV. 1368. 13. Henry de Percy, s. and h. Summ. to Parl. from 24 Feb. 42 Edw. III. 1368, to 20 January, 49 Edward III. 1376, as " Henrico de Percy de Piere," and 1 Dec. 50 Edward III. 1376, as " Henrico de Percy, Mareschallo Angliæ ;" Created Earl of Northumberland 16 July, 1377.   Vide Northumberland.

 The descent of the Barony of Percy has been the subject of considerable controversy; but the following statement it is presumed contains the facts of the case :

 In 1408 the Barony became Forfeited by the attainder of Henry Percy last mentioned, the XII.-1st Earl of Northumberland, but was restored in 1414 to his grandson Henry XIII.-2d Earl. It was however again Forfeited by the attainder of Henry XIV.-3d Earl, in 1461, but was restored to his son Henry XVI.-4th Earl, circa 1470, and continued merged in that Earldom until the death of Henry Algernon XVIII.-6th Earl in 1537, s. p. when, in consequence of the attainder of Sir Thomas Percy his brother and heir, it became Extinct. On the 30th April, 1557, Thomas Percy (son and heir of the said Sir Thomas, and nephew of Henry Algernon, the last Earl of Northumberland and Baron Percy) was Created, by Patent, Baron Percy of Cockermouth and Pet-

WORTH, Baron Poynings, Lucy, Bryan, and Fitz-Payne,
with remainder, *failing his issue male*, to his *brother Henry*
and *his issue male*, and was afterwards created Earl of
Northumberland with the same limitation. This creation
to the said Baronies must be considered as a creation
de Novo, and these honors would have become forfeited
in consequence of the attainder of the said Thomas
XIX-7th Earl, had it not been for the limitation recited
above, in virtue of which Henry his brother succeeded to
them and to the Earldom of Northumberland; in which
dignity the Baronies of Percy, Poynings, Lucy, Bryan
and Fitz-Payne, became merged. Henry his son, XXI.-9th
Earl of Northumberland, obtained a confirmation by
Patent 4 Car. I. anno 1628, " to him and the *heirs male
of his body* of the title and dignity of Baron Percy in such
manner as any of his ancestors had enjoyed the same ;"
but which Patent would decidedly be deemed illegal at
the present day, an Act of Parliament alone having the
power to give a precedency beyond the date of the Patent
of Creation : on the demise of Josceline Percy XXIII.-
11th Earl, s. p. m. in 1670, all the honors conferred by
the Patent of 30 April, 1557, and by that of 1628, as
well as the Earldom of Northumberland became 𝔈𝔵𝔱𝔦𝔫𝔠𝔱.
The Barony of Percy however was, notwithstanding, evidently considered to have been a Barony in fee, and as
such to have descended to Elizabeth, wife of Charles
Duke of Somerset, daughter and sole heir of the said
Earl Josceline; for on her Grace's death, 23 Nov. 1722,
her son and heir Algernon Seymour, was not only Summoned to Parliament as Baron Percy, but was placed in
the House of Peers in the precedency of the ancient Barony created by the Writ of Summons of 27 Edward I.
He succeeded as Duke of Somerset in 1748, and was
subsequently created Earl of Northumberland, &c.; he
died in 1750, and was unquestionably succeeded in the
Barony of Percy, created by the Writ of Summons of
1722, by his only child Elizabeth, on whose husband, Sir
Hugh Smithson, Bart. the Earldom of Northumberland
was limited, and who was created Duke of that county
in 1766. Her Grace died 5 Dec. 1776, when the Barony
devolved on her eldest son Hugh Percy, and who was accordingly Summoned to Parliament as Baron Percy in
1777 ; he succeeded his father in the Dukedom, &c. in
1786 ; and the Barony of Percy created by the Writ of
1722, together with his other honors, is now vested in his

grandson Hugh, the present Duke of Northumberland, and who was summoned to Parliament as Baron Percy, and placed in the precedency of the ancient Barony 12 March, 1812. From the preceding statement the following conlusions may be drawn:

1st. That, according to the fair deduction from modern decisions, the ancient Barony of Percy, created by the Writ of Summons of 6 Feb. 27 Edward I. 1299, became Extinct on the death of Henry Algernon, XVIII.-6th Earl, in 1537.

2d. That the Barony of Percy of Cockermouth and Petworth, with the Baronies of Poynings, Lucy, Bryan, and Fitz-Payne, created by the Patent of 30 April, 1557, became Extinct on the death, s. p. m. of Josceline XXIIL.-11th Earl, in 1670.

3d. That Algernon Seymour, afterwards Duke of Somerset, and XXV.-1st Earl of Northumberland, was erroneously placed in the precedency of the ancient Barony on being Summoned to Parliament in 1722.

4th. That Hugh Percy, grandson of the said Duke and Baron Percy jure matris, and Hugh the present Duke of Northumberland, were likewise erroneously placed in the precedency of the original Barony.

5th. That the only Barony of Percy, now vested in his Grace Hugh, present Duke of Northumberland, is the Barony in fee created by the Writ of Summons to his great-grandfather Algernon Seymour, in 1722.

EARLDOM.

I.   1766. 1. Hugh Smithson, husband of Elizabeth Baroness Percy, dau. and sole heir of Algernon Duke of Somerset, and XXV.-1st Earl of Northumberland, assumed the name of Percy, XXVI.-2d Earl of Northumberland; Created Earl Percy, and Duke of Northumberland 18 Oct. 1766.

Vide NORTHUMBERLAND.

PERCY

OF ALNWICK.

BARON.

I.   1643. 1. Henry Percy, younger son of Henry XXI.-9th Earl of Northumberland; Created Baron Percy of Alnwick, co. Northumberland, 28 June, 1643; ob. 1652, s. p. m. when the title became Extinct.

PERROT.

Ralph Perrot, Summoned 26 Jan. 25 Edward I. 1297;
but it is very doubtful if that Writ can be considered as a
regular Summons to Parliament; vide " FITZ-JOHN."
He was never afterwards summoned; and Dugdale gives
no account of him in his Baronage.

PERTH.

BARON.
1.   1797. 1. James Drummond, representative of the Earldom of Perth in Scotland, which dignity
his ancestor had forfeited in 1715; Created
Lord Perth, Baron Drummond of Stob-ball,
co. Perth, 26 October, 1797; ob. 1800, s.p.m.
when the title became
Extinct.

PETERBOROUGH.

EARLS.
I.   1628. 1. John Mordaunt, 5th Baron Mordaunt of Turvey; Created Earl of Peterborough 9 March,
1628; ob. 1642.
II.   1642. 2. Henry Mordaunt, s. and h. K.G.; ob. 1697,
s. p. m. when the Barony of Mordaunt de-
volved on Mary his dau. and sole heiress;
but he was succeeded in this Earldom by
III.   1697. 3. Charles Mordaunt, III.-1st Earl of Monmouth
and 2d Viscount Mordaunt of Avalon, his
nephew and heir male, being son and heir of
John 1st Viscount Mordaunt of Avalon, 2d
son of John 1st Earl of Peterborough; succeeded his cousin Mary Baroness Mordaunt
in that Barony and in the Barony of Beauchamp of Bletsho in 1705, K. G.; ob. 1735.
IV.   1735. 4. Charles Mordaunt, grandson and heir, being
s. and h. of John Mordaunt (ob. v. p.) eldest
son of the last Earl; Earl of Monmouth; ob.
1779.
V.   1779. 5. Charles Henry Mordaunt, s. and h. Earl of
Monmouth, ob. 1814, s. p. when the Earl-
doms of Peterborough and Monmouth, the

Viscountcy of Mordaunt of Avalon, and the Barony of Mordaunt of Ryegate became Extinct.

PETERSFIELD.

Barony, 19 August, 1673—Extinct 1734.

Vide Portsmouth.

PETERSHAM.

Barony, 25 June, 1674—Extinct 1682.

Vide Guildford.

Viscountcy, 9 February, 1742.

Vide Harrington.

PETRE.

BARONS.

I.   1603.   1. John Petre; Created Baron Petre of Writtle, co. Essex, 21 July, 1603; ob. 1613.

II.   1613.   2. William Petre, s. and h. ob. 1637.

III.   1637.   3. Robert Petre, s. and h. ob. 1638.

IV.   1638.   4. William Petre, s. and h. ob. 1683, s. p. m.

V.   1683.   5. John Petre, brother and heir; ob. 1684, s. p.

VI.   1684.   6. Thomas Petre, brother and heir; ob. 1707.

VII.   1707.   7. Robert Petre, s. and h. ob. 1713.

VIII.1713.   8. Robert James Petre, s. and h. ob. 1742.

IX.   1742.   9. Robert Edward Petre, s. and h.; he married Ann, dau. and coheir of Lord Philip Howard, brother of Edward XIV.-11th Duke of Norfolk; ob. 1801.

X.   1801.   10. Robert Edward Petre, s. and h. ob. 1809.

XI.   1809.   11. William Francis Henry Petre, s. and h.   Present Baron Petre; also in right of Ann his grandmother, youngest of the two daughters and coheirs of Lord Philip Howard, brother of Edward XIV.-11th Duke of Norfolk, coheir of the Baronies of Howard, Mowbray, Braose of Gower, Segrave, Dacre of Gillesland, Greystock, Ferrers of Wemme, Talbot, Strange of Blackmere, Furnival, Giffard of Brimmesfield, and Vernon, and probably also of the Barony of Arundel under the Writ of 1 Rich. II.*

* Vide p. 29.

PEVENSEY.

VISCOUNTCY, 14 May, 1730—Extinct 1743.
Vide WILMINGTON.

PEVEREL

OF NOTTINGHAM.

BARONS BY TENURE.

I. Will. I. Ranulph Peverell; held divers Lordships at the General Survey; he married Maud, dau. of Ingelric, and the concubine of William I.; the issue both by the said Ralph and by the King assumed the name of Peverell, of whom

II. Hen. I. William Peverell, obtained numerous Lordships from William the Conqueror, amongst others the Castle of Nottingham; living 1141.

III. Hen. II. William Peverell, s. and h. having poisoned Ralph Earl of Chester, fled from Justice. Margaret, his dau. and heir, carried his possessions to the family of Ferrers.

PEVEREL

OF ——

BARON BY TENURE.

I. Will. I. Hamon Peverel, eldest son of Ranulph Peverel, 1st Baron, of whom little is known.

PEVEREL

OF DOVER.

BARONS BY TENURE.

I. Will. I. 1. William Peverel of Dover (another son of Ranulph above mentioned), so called from being Castellan of that place; ob. . . . .

II. Hen. I. 2. William Peverell, s. and h. called "of Essex," who, with Maud his sister, having enfeoffed the posterity of Hugh Peverel of Sandford with divers Lordships, the Barony of the said William and Maud fell to the King.

K 2

PEVEREL

OF BRUNNE.

BARONS BY TENURE.

I. Hen. I. 1. Pain Peverel, 3d son of the said Ranulph; obtained the Barony of Brunne, co. Cambridge, from King Hen. I.; ob. circa 1112.

II. Hen. I. 2. William Peverel, s. and h. ob. .... s. p. leaving his four sisters his heirs, who shared his inheritance.

PEVRE.

BARON BY WRIT.

I.   1299.   John Pevre; Summoned 8 June, 22 Edw. I. 1294; but it is very doubtful if that Writ was a regular Summons to Parliament; vide "CLYVEDON;" Summ. to Parl. 6 Feb. 27 Edward I. 1299, but never afterwards. Dugdale gives no account of this Baron in his Baronage; nor is any thing recorded of his posterity by any other writer. The Barony on his death from the Writ of 27 Edward I. being the only regular Summons to Parliament ever directed to him, and there being no proof recorded of his having sat under it, probably became
𝕰𝖝𝖙𝖎𝖓𝖈𝖙.

PIERREPONT.

Simon de Pierrepont was summoned 8th June, 22 Edw. I. 1294; but it is very doubtful if that Writ can be deemed a regular Summons to Parliament; vide "CLYVEDON."

PIERREPONT

BARONS.   OF HOLME PIERREPONT.

I.   1627.   1. Robert Pierrepont; presumed to have been of the same family as the above Simon de Pierrepont; Created Baron Pierrepont of Holme Pierrepont, co. Nottingham, and Viscount Newark, 29 June, 1627; Created Earl of Kingston 25 July, 1628.
𝕰𝖝𝖙𝖎𝖓𝖈𝖙 1773.   Vide KINGSTON.

BARONY, 23 July, 1796.
Vide NEWARK.

PIERREPONT

OF HANSLAPE.

BARON.

I. 1714. Gervase Pierrepont, 1st Baron Pierrepont in Ireland, grandson of Robert 1st Earl of Kingston; Created Baron Pierrepont of Hanslape, co. Bucks, 19 Oct. 1714; ob. 1715, s.p. when his titles became
Extinct.

PINKNEY.

BARONS BY TENURE.

I. Hen.I. 1. Gilo de Pincheney.

II. Steph. 2. Ralph de Pincheney, s. and h. living 1140.

III. H. II. 3. Gilbert de Pincheney, s. and h. living 1165.

IV. Ric.I. 4. Henry de Pincheney, s. and h. living 1206.

V. John. 5. Robert de Pincheney, s. and h. ob. circa 1217.

VI. H.III. 6. Henry de Pincheney, s. and h. ob. 1254.

VII. H.III. 7. Henry de Pincheney, s. and h. living 1258.

VIII.Edw.I.8. Robert de Pincheney, s. and h. ob. circa 129ʻ.

BY WRIT.

I. 1299. 9. Henry de Pinkney, brother and heir; Summ. to Parl. 6 Feb. 27 Edw. I. 1299, and 29 Dec. 28 Edward I. 1299; he was likewise Summoned 26 January, 25 Edward I. 1297; but it is doubtful if that Writ can be deemed a regular Summons to Parliament; vide "FITZ-JOHN." He was present at the Parliament held at Lincoln 29 Edward I. when he was styled "Henricus de Pynkeney, Dominus de Wedone;" in 1301 he surrendered his lands to the King; ob. s. p. when the. Barony became **Extinct.**

PIPARD.

BARON BY WRIT.

I. 1299. Ralph Pipard; Summ. to Parl. from 6 Feb. 27 Edward I. 1299, to 24 July, 30 Edward I. 1302; he was likewise summoned 26 Jan. 25 Edw. I. 1297; but it is very doubtful if that

Writ can be deemed a regular Summons to
Parliament; vide " FITZ-JOHN;" ob. 1309,
leaving John his son and heir; but neither
he nor any of his descendants were ever
summoned to Parliament, and of whom
Dugdale gives no account.

PITT.

VISCOUNTCY, 4 August, 1756.

Vide CHATHAM.

PLAITZ.

BARONS BY WRIT.

Giles de Plaitz; Summoned 8 June, 22 Edw.
I. 1294; and 26 Jan. 25 Edward I. 1297; but
it is doubtful if either of these Writs can be
considered as a regular Summons to Parl.
vide "CLYVEDON" and "FITZ-JOHN;" ob. 1303.

I.   1317.   Richard de Plaitz, s. and h. Summ. to Parl.
from 20 Nov. 11 Edward II. 1317, to 14
March, 15 Edward II. 1322, ob. .... leaving
John his son and heir; he died in 1359,
leaving Sir John de Plaitz his son and heir,
neither of whom were ever summoned to Parliament.
Margaret, daughter and heir of the last mentioned Sir
John de Plaitz, was the first wife of Sir John Howard
(grandfather, by his second wife, of John Howard Duke
of Norfolk), by whom he had Sir John Howard, whose
daughter and heir, Elizabeth, married John Vere,
XII.-12th Earl of Oxford; in which title this Barony continued merged until the death of John XIV.-14th Earl, in
1526, when it fell into ABEYANCE between his three
sisters and coheirs, viz. Dorothy, who married John
Nevill Lord Latimer; Elizabeth, wife of Sir Anthony
Wingfield; and Ursula, who married, first, George Windsor, and secondly, Sir Edmund Knightly, but died s. p.
and who were also coheirs of one moiety of the Barony of
Scales, and the representatives of one of the coheirs of
the Barony of Badlesmere. The Barony of Plaitz is now
in ABEYANCE between Francis Dillon, Baron of the Holy
Roman Empire, as representative of the said Elizabeth

Wingfield, and the descendants and representatives of the above-mentioned Dorothy Lady Latimer; of which representatives his Grace the present Duke of Northumberland is the eldest, and who is consequently one of the coheirs of the moiety of this Barony possessed by Lady Latimer.

PLESSETIS.

BARONS BY TENURE.

I.   H. III.   1. John de Plessetis, husband of Margery, sister and sole heir of Thomas Earl of Warwick; styled Earl of Warwick by the King 1247; ob. 1263.

II. H.III.   2. Hugh de Plessetis, s. and h. but by a former wife; ob. 1291.

BY WRIT.

I.   1299.   3. Hugh de Plessetis, s. and h. Summoned 26 January, 25 Edw. I. 1297; but it is doubtful if that Writ can be deemed a regular Summons to Parliament; vide "FITZ-JOHN;" Summ. to Parl. 6 Feb. 27 Edward I. 1299, but never after, nor any of his descendants, and of whom Dugdale gives no account.

PLEYDELL BOUVERIE.

BARONY, 31 October, 1765.

Vide RADNOR.

PLUKENET.

BARON BY WRIT.

I.   1295.   Alan de Plukenet; Summ. to Parl. from 23 June, 23 Edw. I. 1295, to 29 Dec. 5 Edw. II. 1311; ob. circa 1312, s. p. when the Barony became

Extinct.

PLYMOUTH.

EARLS.

I.   1675.   Charles Fitz-Charles, natural son of King Charles II. Created Baron of Dartmouth, Viscount Totness, and Earl of Plymouth, all

EARLS.

co. Dévon. 29 July, 1675; ob. 1680, s. p. when all his titles became
Extinct.

II.   1682. 1. Thomas Hickman Windsor, VII-7th Baron Windsor; Created Earl of Plymouth 6 Dec. 1682; ob. 1687.

III. 1687. 2. Other Windsor, grandson and heir, being son and heir of Other Windsor (ob. v. p.) eldest son of the last Earl; ob. 1727.

IV. 1727. 3. Other Windsor, s. and h. ob. 1732.

V.   1732. 4. Other Lewis Windsor, s. and h. ob. 1771.

VI. 1771. 5. Other Hickman Windsor, s. and h.; ob. 1799.

VII. 1799. 6. Other Archer Windsor, s. and h.   Present Earl of Plymouth and 13th Baron Windsor. ==

POINTZ.

BARONS BY WRIT.

I.   1295. 1. Hugh Pointz; Summ. to Parl. from 23 June, 23 Edward I. 1295, to 26 August, 1 Edw. II. 1307; ob. 1307.

II.   1307. 2. Nicholas Pointz, s. and h. Summ. to Parl. from 4 March, 2 Edw. II. 1309, to 16 June, 4 Edw. II. 1311; ob. 1312.

III. 1312. 3. Hugh Pointz, s. and h. Summ. to Parl. from 20 November, 11 Edw. II. 1317, to 24 Feb. 17 Edw. III. 1343; though Dugdale in his account of this family, vol. I. p. 2, states, that this Hugh was only summoned to the 7th Edw. III. 1333, and that he died the 13th of October in that year, leaving Nicholas his son and heir, who did homage for his father's lands 14 Edw. III. but who was never summoned to Parliament, and left issue two daughters his coheirs, viz. Amicia, wife of John Barry, and Margaret, of John de Newburgh, between whose descendants and representatives this Barony is in ABEYANCE.

POMERAI.

BARONS BY TENURE.

I. Will.I. 1. Ralph de Pomerai; held divers Lordships at the Survey; to whom succeeded

II. Hen.I. 2. William de Pomerai; living 1102.

III. H. II. 3. Henry de Pomerai, s. and h. living 1204; ob. ante 1209.

IV. John. 4. Henry de Pomerai, s, and h. ob. 1222.

V. H.III. 5. Henry de Pomerai, s. and h. ob. 1237.

VI. H.III. 6. Henry de Pomerai, s. and h. ob. 1281.

VII. Edw.I. 7. Henry de Pomerai, s. aud h. ob. 1305; but as none of his descendants were ever summoned to Parliament, they ceased to be ranked among the Barons of the Realm until 1783, when Arthur Pomeroy, the heir male of this Henry de Pomerai, was created Baron Harberton in Ireland; whose son, Henry Pomeroy, present Viscount and Baron Harberton in Ireland, is the male representative of this ancient family.

POMFRET vel PONTEFRACT.

BARONY, 1 October, 1674—Extinct 1716.

Vide NOTRHUMBERLAND.

EARLS.

I. 1721. 1. Thomas Fermor, 2d Baron Lempster; Created Earl of Pomfret, co. York, 27 Dec. 1721,K.B.; ob. 1753.

II. 1753. 2. George Fermor, s. and h. ob. 1785.

III. 1785. 3. George Fermor, s. and h. Present Earl of Pomfret, Baron Lempster, and a Baronet. ≈

PONSONBY

OF SYSONBY.

BARONS.

I. 1749. 1. Brabazon Ponsonby, 1st Earl of Bessborough, and 2d Viscount Duncannon in Ireland; Created Baron Ponsonby of Sysonby, co. Leicester, 12 June, 1749; ob. 1758.

BARONS.

II.   1758. 2. William Ponsonby, s. and h. Earl of Besbo-
rough, &c. in Ireland; ob. 1793.

III. 1793. 3. Frederick Ponsonby, s. and h. Present Baron
Ponsonby of Sysonby; also Earl of Besbo-
rough, &c. in Ireland. ⸕

PONSONBY
OF IMOKILLY.

BARONS.

I.   1806. 1. William Ponsonby (s. and h. of John Ponsonby, next brother of William 2d Baron
Ponsonby of Sysonby, and Earl of Besbo-
rough in Ireland); Created Baron Ponsonby
of Imokilly, co. Cork, 13 March, 1806; ob.
1806.

II. 1806. 1. John Ponsonby, s. and h. Present Baron
Ponsonby of Imokilly. ══

PORCHESTER.

BARONS.

I.   1780. Henry Herbert, eldest son of William Herbert, 4th son of Thomas XXVII.-8th Earl of
Pembroke; Created Baron Porchester of
High Clere, co. Hants, 17 Oct. 1780; Created Earl of Carnarvon 3 July, 1793.

Vide CARNARVON.

PORT
OF BASING.

BARONS BY TENURE.

I.   Will.I. 1. Hugh de Port; held 55 Lordships at the
General Survey, among which was the Barony
of Basing; ob. ....

II. Will.II. 2. Henry de Port, s. and h. ob. ....

III. H. II. 3. John de Port, s. and h. living 1167; ob. ....

IV. Ric.I. 4. Adam de Port, s. and h. living 1213; he married Mabell, dau. of Reginald de Aurevalle
by Muriell, dau. and heir of Roger de St.
John; in consequence of which the posterity
of this Adam assumed the name of ST. JOHN.

Vide ST. JOHN.

PORT

OF HEREFORDSHIRE.

BARON BY TENURE.

Hen. II.   Adam de Port; held 21 Knight's fees, co. Hereford, anno 1165; living 1174. In 1194 William de Bravie, paid xxii*l*. xiii*s*. for these Knight's fees which belonged to this Adam; although it does not appear by what title he possessed them.

PORTLAND.

EARLS.

I.   1633. 1. Richard Weston, 1st Baron Weston, K. G. Created Earl of Portland 17 February, 1633; L. H. Treasurer; ob. 1634.

II.   1634. 2. Jerome Weston, s. and h. ob. 1662.

III.   1662. 3. Charles Weston, s. and h. ob. 1665, s. p.

IV.   1665. 4. Thomas Weston, uncle and heir, being 2d son of Richard 1st Earl; ob. circa 1688, s. p. when his titles became

Extinct.

V.   1689. 1. William Bentinck; Created Baron of Cirencester, co. Gloucester, Viscount Woodstock, co. Oxford, and Earl of Portland, co. Dorset, 9 April, 1689, K. G.; ob. 1709.

DUKES.

VI.   1709.—I. 1716. 2. Henry Bentinck, s. and h. Created Marquess of Titchfield, co. Southampton, and Duke of Portland, 6 July, 1716; ob. 1726.

VII.   1726.—II. 1726. 3. William Bentinck, s. and h. K. G.; ob. 1762.

VIII. 1762.—III. 1762. 4. William Henry Cavendish Bentinck, son and heir K. G.; ob. 1809.

IX.   1809.—IV. 1809. 5. William Henry Cavendish, assumed the name of Scott-Bentinck, s. and h. Present Duke and Earl of Portland, Marquess of Tichfield,

Viscount Woodstock and Baron
Cirencester. ⊤

PORTSMOUTH.

DUCHESS.

I. 1673. Louisa Renée de Puencovet de Queroualle,
mistress to Charles II. and by his Majesty
mother of Charles Lenox, Duke of Richmond ; Created Baroness Petersfield, co.
Southampton, Countess of Fareham, co.
Hants, and Duchess of Portsmouth for life,
19 August, 1673 ; ob. 1734, when her titles
became

EARLS. Extinct.

I. 1743. 1. John Wallop, 1st Viscount Lymington, and
1st Baron Wallop ; Created Earl of Portsmouth 11 April, 1743 ; ob. 1762.

II. 1762. 2. John Wallop, grandson and heir, being son
and heir of John Wallop (ob. v. p.) eldest son
of the last Earl ; ob. 1797.

III. 1797. 3. John Charles Wallop, s. and h. Present Earl
of Portsmouth, Viscount Lymington and
Baron Wallop.

POULETT.

BARONS.

I. 1627. 1. John Poulett ; Created Baron Poulett of
Hinton St. George, co. Somerset, 23 June,
1627 ; ob. 1649.

II. 1649. 2. John Poulett, s. and h. ob. 1665.

III. 1665. 3. John Poulett, s. and h. ob. 1680.

EARLS.

IV. 1680.—I. 1706. 4. John Poulett, s. and h. Created
Viscount Hinton of Hinton St.
George, co. Somerset, and Earl
Poulett, 29 Dec. 1706, K. G. ;
ob. 1743.

V. 1743.—II. 1743. 5. John Poulett, s. and h. ob. 1764, s.p.

VI. 1764.—III. 1764. 6. Vere Poulett, brother and heir ;
ob. 1788.

VII. 1788.—IV. 1788. 7. John Poulett, s. and h. K. T. ob.
1819.

BARON. EARL.

VIII.1819.—V. 1819. 8. John Poulett, s. and h. Present Earl and Baron Poulett and Viscount Hinton.

POWIS.

BARONS.

I. 1629. 1. Sir William Herbert, K. B. son and heir of Sir Edward Herbert, 2d son of William XX.-1st Earl of Pembroke; Created Baron Powis of Powis Castle, co. Montgomery, 2 April, 1629; ob. 1655.

II. 1655. 2. Sir Percy Herbert, s. and h.; he was created a Baronet vitâ patris; ob. 1666.

EARLS. MARQ.

III. 1666.—I. 1674.—I. 1687. 3. William Herbert, s. and h. Created Earl of Powis, co. Montgomery 4 April, 1674; Created Viscount Montgomery and Marquess of Powis 24 March, 1687 *; outlawed 1689; ob. 1696.

IV. 1696.—II. 1696.—II. 1696. 4. William Herbert, s. and h. Confirmed in his father's honprs in 1722; ob. 1745.

V. 1745.—III. 1745.—III. 1745. 5. William Herbert, s. and h. ob. 1748, s. p. when all his titles became

Extinct.

VI. 1748.—IV. 1748. 1. Henry Arthur Herbert, VII.-1st Baron Herbert of Cherbury, having married Barbara, dau. and heir of Edward Herbert, next brother of William the last Earl and Marquess, and being likewise descended from the common ancestor of the preceding Earls, was created Baron Powis of Powis Castle, Viscount

---

* He was Created Marquess of Montgomery and Duke of Powis by James II. after his abdication; but these titles were never allowed in England.

BARONS. EARLS.

Ludlow, co. Salop, and Earl of Powis aforesaid, 27 May, 1748; Created Baron Herbert of Cherbury and Ludlow, with a special remainder, 7 Oct. 1749; ob. 1772.

VII. .... —V. 1772. 2. George Edward Henry Arthur Herbert, s. and h. ob. 1801, s. p. when all his titles became

        Extinct.

VIII..... —VI.1804. 1. Edward Clive, 1st Baron Clive in England, and 2d Baron Clive in Ireland, having married Henrietta Antonia Herbert, daughter of Henry Arthur IV.-1st Earl, and sister and heiress of George Edward, the last Earl, was created Baron Powis of Powis Castle, co. Montgomery, Baron Herbert of Cherbury, co. Salop, Viscount Clive of Ludlow and Earl of Powis in the said county of Montgomery, 14 May, 1804. Present Earl and Baron Powis, Viscount Clive, Baron Clive, and Baron Herbert of Cherbury, also Baron Clive in Ireland. ⊤

POYNINGS.

BARONS BY WRIT.

I. 1337. 1. Thomas de Poynings (s. and h. of Michael de Poynings who was Summoned 8 June, 22 Edward I. 1294; but it is very doubtful if that Writ can be deemed a regular Summons to Parliament; vide "CLYVEDON"); Summ. to Parl. 23 April, 11 Edward III. 1337; ob. 1339.

II. 1329. 2. Michael de Poynings, s. and h. Summ. to Parl. from 25 Feb. 16 Edw. III. 1342, to 24 Feb. 42 Edward III. 1368; ob. 1369.

III. 1369. 3. Thomas de Poynings, s. and h.; he was never Summ. to Parl.; ob. 1375, s. p.

IV. 1375. 4. Richard de Poynings, brother and heir; Summ. to Parl. from 7 January, 6 Rich. II. 1383, to 3 Sept. 9 Rich. II. 1385; he married Isabel, dau. and heir of Robert Grey, who assumed the name of Fitz-Payne; ob. 1387.

BARONS BY WRIT.

V.   1387. 5. Robert de Poynings, s. and h. Summ. to Parl. from 25 August, 5 Hen. IV. 1404, to 13 Jan. 23 Hen. VI. 1445 ; ob. 1446, s. p. m. leaving Eleanor, dau. and heir of Richard de Poynings (ob. v. p.) his eldest son, his granddaughter and heir ; which Eleanor was then the wife of

VI. 1446.   Henry Percy, son and heir apparent of Henry XIII.-2d Earl of Northumberland ; he was Summ. to Parl. jure uxoris, as " Henrico de Percy, Chl'r, Domino de Poynings," from 14 Dec. 25 Hen. VI. 1446, to 26 May, 33 Hen. VI. 1455, when he succeeded his father as XIV.-3d Earl of Northumberland.

From this period the Barony of Poynings became merged in the dignity of Earl of Northumberland, and together with that title has been frequently forfeited and restored. As a full account of this Barony will be found under that of Percy in p. 510, it is only necessary in this place to give the following brief summary of its descent :
It was Forfeited, as well as the Earldom of Northumberland and Barony of Percy, in 1408, but was RESTORED in 1414 ; was again Forfeited in 1461, and RESTORED in 1417 ; but on the death of Henry Algernon, XVIII.-6th Earl of Northumberland, s. p. in 1537, it became Extinct in consequence of the attainder of his brother Sir Thomas Percy. On the 30th of April, 1557, Thomas Percy (son and heir of the said Sir Thomas Percy, and nephew of the last Earl, and last Baron Percy, and Poynings,) was *Created by Patent* Baron Percy of Cockermouth and Petworth, BARON POYNINGS, Lucy, Bryan, and Fitz-Payne, with remainder, failing his issue male, to his brother Henry and his issue male ; and shortly afterwards he was created Earl of Northumberland, with the same remainder. This Henry Percy succeeded to these honors, and they remained vested in his descendants until the demise of Josceline XXII.-11th Earl of Northumberland, s. p. m. in 1670, when all the honors conferred by the Patent of 30 April, 1557 (of course including the BARONY OF POYNINGS created by that instrument), became
Extinct.

POYNINGS

OF ———

BARON BY WRIT.

1.   1368.   Lucas de Poynings, younger brother of Michael
II.-2d Baron Poynings, having married Isa-
bel, widow of Henry de Burghersh, and sister
and ultimately sole heir of Edmond Baron
St. John of Basing, was Summ. to Parl.
from 24 Feb. 42 Edward III. 1368, to 20
Jan. 49 Edw. III. 1376, as " Lucie de Poynings ;" ob. circa 1385, leaving Thomas his
son and heir, who was styled Lord St. John,
but he was never summoned to Parliament.
Hugh de Poynings, his son, died v. p. leaving
three daughters his coheirs, viz. Constance,
wife of John Paulet, ancestor of the Marquess of Winchester; Alice, wife of John
Orrell, and Joane, who married Thomas
Bonville ; among whose descendants and
representatives this Barony, (as well as that
of St. John of Basing, unless, which is highly
probable, though no evidence of the fact
exists, that the above-mentioned Lucas de
Poynings was summoned in his wife's Barony
of St. John of Basing,) is in ABEYANCE.

POYNINGS.

BARON.

I.   1545.   Thomas Poynings (natural son of Sir Edward
Poynings, K. G. s. and h. of Robert Poyn-
ings, younger son of Robert 5th Baron
Poynings); Created Baron Poynings 30 Jan.
1545; ob. 1545, s. p. when the title became
Extinct.

PRUDHOE.

BARON.

I.   1816.   Algernon Percy, only brother of Hugh, present Duke of Northumberland; Created Ba-
ron Prudhoe of Prudhoe Castle, co. Northumberland, 27 Nov. 1816.   Present Baron
Prudhoe.

PULTENEY.

VISCOUNTCY, 14 July, 1742—Extinct 1764.

Vide BATH.

PURBECK.

VISCOUNT.

I.   1619.   John Villiers, son and heir of Sir George Villiers by Mary Duchess of Buckingham, and eldest brother of George Duke of Buckingham; Created Baron Villiers of Stoke, co. Bucks, and Viscount of Purbeck, co. Dorset, 19 June, 1619; ob. 1657, s. p. when his titles became
Extinct*.

---

* In 1678 Robert Villiers, son of Robert Wright, who took his wife's name of Danvers, claimed the titles of Baron Villiers, Viscount Purbeck, &c. and of Earl of Buckingham as heir-male of John Viscount Purbeck; but the House of Peers decided against him, on the ground that his father was illegitimate. These titles were afterwards claimed by the Rev. George Villiers, son of Edward, a younger son of the said Robert Wright, alias Danvers; but no proceedings were adopted, and on the death of George his son in 1774, s. p. the male line became extinct. The Earldom of Buckingham was claimed in consequence of a special remainder of that dignity when conferred on George Villiers, to his brothers John and Christopher and their heirs male. It was on the occasion of the claim of the above-mentioned Robert Villiers that the House of Peers, 18 June, 1678, came to the celebrated resolution, "that no fine now levied, nor at any time hereafter to be levied to the King, can bar such title of honor, or the right of any person claiming such title under him that levied, or shall levy such fine; thus confirming a similar decision in the case of the claim to the Barony of Grey de Ruthyn, 1 Feb. 1646.—Collins's Precedents, p. 256 and 306.

QUARENDON.

VISCOUNTCY, 5 June, 1674—Extinct 1776.

Vide LICHFIELD.

RABY.

BARONS.

I.   1640. 1. Thomas Wentworth, 1st Viscount Wentworth; Created Baron Raby of Raby Castle, co. Durham, with remainder, failing his issue male, to his younger brothers and their issue male, 12 Jan. 1640; Created Earl of Strafford, K. G.; beheaded and attainted 1641, when all his titles became

Forfeited.

II.   1665. 2. William Wentworth, s. and h. Restored to all his father's honors 1 Dec. 1665, K. G.; ob. 1695, s. P. when all his dignities, excepting the Barony of Raby and the Baronetcy, became Extinct; which dignities devolved, agreeably to the limitation, on

III.   1695. 3. Thomas Wentworth, his cousin and heir male, being s. and h. of Sir William, eldest son of Sir William, son and heir of Sir William Wentworth, next brother of Thomas 1st Baron Raby; Created Viscount Wentworth and Earl of Strafford 4 Sept. 1711.

Extinct 1799.   Vide STRAFFORD.

RADNOR.

EARLS.

I.   1679. 1. John Robartes, 2d Baron Robartes; Created Viscount Bodmin, co. Cornwall, and Earl of Radnor in Wales, 23 July, 1679; ob. 1685.

II. 1685. 2. Charles Bodville Robartes, grandson and heir, being s. and h. of Robert Robartes (ob. v. p.) eldest son of the last Earl; ob. 1723, s. p.

III. 1723. 3. Henry Robartes, nephew and heir, being son and heir of Russel Robartes, next brother of the last Earl; ob. 1741, s. p.

IV. 1741. 4. John Robartes, cousin and heir, being son and heir of Francis Robartes, younger son of John 1st Earl; ob. 1764, s. p. when all his titles became

Extinct.

V.   1765. 1. William Bouverie, 2d Viscount Folkestone; Created Baron Pleydell-Bouverie of Coleshill, co. Berks, and Earl of the County of Radnor in the Principality of Wales, with remainder of the Earldom, failing his issue male, to the heirs male of (his father) Jacob Bouverie, Viscount Folkestone, deceased, 31 Oct. 1765; ob. 1776.

VI. 1776. 2. Jacob Pleydell Bouverie, s. and h. Present Earl of Radnor, Viscount Folkestone, Baron Longford, Baron Pleydell Bouverie, and a Baronet. ⚲

RATCLIFFE AND LANGLEY.

VISCOUNTCY, 7 March, 1688—Forfeited 1716.

Vide DERWENTWATER.

RAVENSWORTH.

BARONS.

I.   1747. 1. Sir Henry Liddell, 4th Bart. Created Lord Ravensworth, Baron of Ravensworth, co. Durham, 29 June, 1747; ob. 1749, s. p. when the Barony became

Extinct.

II. 1821. 1. Sir Thomas Henry Liddell, 6th Bart. s. and h. of Sir Henry George Liddell, 5th Bart. eldest

son of Thomas Liddell (who died vita fratris),
next brother of the last Baron; Created
Baron Ravensworth of Ravensworth Castle,
co. Durham, 17 July, 1821. Present Baron
Ravensworth, and a Baronet. ⊤

RAWDON.

BARON.   EARL.

I. 1783.—I. 1816. 1. Hon. Francis Rawdon, assumed the
name of Hastings, s. and heir appa-
rent of John 1st Earl of Moira in
Ireland; Created Baron Rawdon of Rawdon,
co. York, 5 March, 1783; succeeded his father as Earl of Moira, &c. in Ireland 20
June, 1793; and his mother in the ancient
Baronies of Hastings, Hungerford, Botreaux,
and Molines, 12 April, 1808; Created Viscount Loudon, Earl of Rawdon, and Marquis
of Hastings, 7 Dec. 1816. Present Baron
and Earl Rawdon, Marquess of Hastings,
Baron Hastings, Botreaux, Molines, and
Hungerford; also sole heir of one moiety of
the Barony of Montagu, vide p. 434; and
sole heir of one moiety, and coheir of the
other moiety of the Barony of Moels; K. G.,
G. C. B. ⊤

RAYLEIGH.

BARONESS.

I.   1821. 1. Charlotte Mary Gertrude, wife of Joseph Holden Strutt, Esq. and daughter of James 1st
Duke of Leinster in Ireland; Created Baroness Rayleigh of Terling Place, co. Essex,
to hold to her and the heirs male of her
body by the said Joseph Holden Strutt,
18 July, 1821. Present Baroness Rayleigh. ⊤

RAYMOND.

BARONS.

I.   1731. 1. Robert Raymond; Created Lord Raymond,
Baron of Abbot's Langley, co. Hertford, 15
Jan. 1731; ob. 1732.

BARONS.

II. 1732. 1. Robert Raymond, s. and h.; ob. 1753, s. p. when the Title became

Extinct.

REDESDALE.

BARON.

I. 1802. 1. Sir John Freeman Mitford, Knt.; Created Baron Redesdale of Redesdale, co. Northumberland, 15 Feb. 1802; Lord Chancellor of Ireland. Present Baron Redesdale.

RENFREW,

Vide ROTHESAY.

RIALTON.

VISCOUNTCY, 29 December, 1706—**Extinct** 1766.

Vide GODOLPHIN.

RIBALD

OF MIDDLEHAM.

BARONS BY TENURE.

I. Will.I. 1. Ribald, brother of Alan 2d Earl of Brittany and Richmond, from whom he received the Lordship of Middleham, co. York.
II. H. II. 2. Ralph Fitz-Ribald, s. and h.; living 1168.
III. John. 3. Robert Fitz-Ralph, s. and h.; living 1206.
IV. John. 4. Ralph Fitz-Robert, s. and h.; ob. 1251.
V. H.III. 5. Ralph Fitz-Ralph, s. and h.; ob. 1270, s. p. m. leaving Mary, his eldest dau. the wife of Robert de Nevill; Joan, his 2d dau. the wife of Robert de Tatshall, and Anastatia, his youngest dau. who was then within age, his coheirs. The said Joan de Tatsall died s. p.

RIBBLESDALE.

BARONS.

I. 1797. 1. Thomas Lister; Created Baron Ribblesdale of Gisburne Park, in the West Riding of the County of York, 26 Oct. 1797. Present Baron Ribblesdale.

RICH.

BARONS.
I.   1547. 1. Richard Rich; Created Baron Rich of Leeze,
                  co. Essex, 16 Feb. 1547; Lord Chancellor;
                  ob. 1568.
II.   1568. 2. Robert Rich, s. and h. ob. 1581.
III.   1581. 3. Robert Rich, s. and h.; Created Earl of War-
                  wick 6 Aug. 1618.

𝕮𝖗𝖙𝖎𝖓𝖈𝖙 1759.

Vide WARWICK.

RICHMOND *.

EARLS.
I. Will.I. 1. Alan Fergaunt, Earl of Brittany, said to have
                been Created Earl of Richmond by William
                the Conqueror for his services at the battle
                of Hastings; ob. 1089, s. p.
II.   1089. 2. Alan Niger, brother of the last Earl; Earl of
                  Brittany; ob. 1093, s. p.
III.   1093. 3. Stephen, stated to have been the *brother*, but
                  he was more probably *the son* of the last
                  Earl; ob. 1137.
IV.   1137. 4. Alan, 2d son of the last Earl; Earl of Brit-
                  tany; ob. 1165.
V.   1165. 5. Conan le Petit, s. and h. Duke of Brittany;
                  ob. 1171, s. p. m. Constance, his sole dau. and
                  heir, married Geoffrey Plantagenet, 4th son
                  of King Henry II. by whom she had issue
                  Arthur and Eleanor, both of whom died s. p.
                  She married, secondly, Ralph de Blondville,
                  Earl of Chester, but from whom she was soon
                  afterwards divorced, when she married Guy
                  Viscount of Thouars. Each of her said hus-
                  bands have by most writers been styled Earls
                  of Brittany and Richmond *jure uxoris*, but
                  it is very questionable how far they were en-

---

* A very valuable account of the Earls of Richmond will be
found in the third General Report of the Lords' Committee on
the dignity of a Peer of the Realm, p. 96 et seq. from which the
statements of Dugdale, &c. have been corrected. There is,
however, still some obscurity on the subject, which it would be
hopeless to attempt to remove.

titled to the latter dignity. By her last husband Constance of Brittany had two daughters, of whom Alice, the eldest, married

VI. 1230. Peter de Dreux, who in 1219 had livery of all the lands of the Honor of Richmond; and, in a patent dated 14 Henry III. 1230, is styled Duke of Brittany and Earl of Richmond; ob. circa 1250 [*].

VII. 1268. 6. John de Dreux, s. and h. On the 6th July, 1268, he obtained a grant of the titles of Duke of Brittany and Earl of Richmond; ob. 1286.

VIII. 1286. 7. John de Dreux, s. and h. Duke of Brittany. He married Beatrix Plantagenet, dau. of King Henry III. and was summoned to be at Worcester with horse and arms, as " Joh'i de Britannia Com. Richem." 12 Dec. 5 Edw. I. 1276; ob. 1306.

IX. 1306. 8. John de Dreux, youngest son of the last Earl. He was Summ. to Parl. as " Johanni Britannia Juniori," in the 33d Edw. I.; Created Earl of Richmond 15 Oct. 34 Edw. I. 1306; and Summ. to Parl. as "Johanni de Britannia Comiti Richmond," 3d Nov. following, and in the 8th Edw. III. 1334; ob. circa 1334, s. P.

X, 1334. 9. John de Dreux, nephew and heir of the last Earl, being s. and h. of Arthur, his eldest brother, Duke of Brittany; Summ. to Parl. as "Johanni Duci Britanniæ and Comiti Richmund'," 1 April, 9 Edw. III. 1335, and 22 Jan. 9 Edw. III. 1336; ob. 1341, s. P. when the Earldom reverted to the Crown.

XI. 1342. John Plantagenet, surnamed of Gaunt, 4th son of King Edw. III.; Created Earl of Richmond 20 Sept. 1342, but he resigned that title in 46 Edw. III. 1372, when it was conferred upon

---

[*] Peter of Savoy, uncle of Queen Eleanor, is often included in the list of the Earls of Richmond, but it is evident that he only obtained a grant of the Honor of Richmond, and never used the title of Earl. Third General Report, p. 99.

EARLS.

XII. 1372. 10. John de Dreux, Earl of Montfort and Duke of Brittany, half-brother of John X.-9th Earl; Created Earl of Richmond 20 June, 46 Edw. III. 1372; ob. circa 1375.

XIII.1375. 11. John de Dreux, s. and h surnamed the Valiant. In the 7th Rich. II. Nov. 1383[*], the Earldom was adjudged to be 𝕱𝕠𝕣𝕗𝕖𝕚𝕥𝕖𝕕, for his adherence to the King of France. He is said to have been afterwards restored to it, with the proviso, that if he died without issue the Earldom and Honor should revert to the King[†]; in the 14th Rich. II. it was however again adjudged to have been 𝕱𝕠𝕣𝕗𝕖𝕚𝕥𝕖𝕕.

In the 1st Henry IV. 1399, Ralph Nevill, 1st Earl of Westmoreland, obtained a grant of "Castrum, Comitatum, Honorem, et Dominium de Richmond, h'end' p' termino vite sue, una cum omnimodis castris, honoribus, terris, &c. ac eciam cum feodis militum, &c. ac aliis possessionibus et p'tinenciis quibuscunq' ad d'c'u' Castru' Com' Honorem et Dominium qualit' cu'q' et ubicumq' spectantibus sive p'tinentibus, adeo libere et integre sicut Joh'es Dux Britann' seu aliquis antecessor' suor' ea melius et lib'ius h'uit et tenuit." Notwithstanding this grant, Ralph Nevill never assumed the title of Earl of Richmond[‡], and in the 2d Henry V. about eleven years before the death of the said Earl of Westmoreland

XIV. 1414. John Plantagenet, Duke of Bedford, was Created Earl of Richmond, with a reversion of the Castle, Earldom, Honor, and Lordship of Richmond, after the death of the said Ralph Earl of Westmoreland, to hold to him the said Duke, and the heirs male of his

---

[*] Rot. Parl. 14 Rich. II. n. 14. v. iii. p. 279.
[†] Third Peerage Report, p. 102.   [‡] Ibid. p. 102-3.

EARLS.

body, by patent * dated 6 May, 1414; and
which was afterwards enrolled in Parliament;
K. G.; ob. 1435, s.P. when this Earldom,
with his other honors, became €rtinct.

XV. 1452. 1. Edmund Tudor, surnamed of Hadham, son of
Sir Owen Tudor, by Katherine of France,
widow of King Henry V. and mother of King
Henry VI.; Created Earl of Richmond 23d
Nov. 1452, with precedence of all other
Earls; ob. 1456.

XVI. 1456. 2. Henry Tudor, s. and h.; succeeded to the
Throne as K. Hen. VII. 22 Aug. 1485, when
this Earldom became merged in the Crown.

XVII. 1525. 1. Henry Fitz-Roy, natural son of King Henry
VIII.; Created Earl of Nottingham and
Duke of Richmond and Somerset, 18 June,
1525, K. G. Admiral of England; ob. 1536,
s.P. when all his honors became
€rtinct.

DUKES.

XVIII. 1613.—I. 1623. 1. Lodovick Stuart, 2d Duke of Lenox in Scotland; Created Baron
of Setrington, co. York, and Earl
of Richmond, 6 Oct. 1613; Created
Earl of Newcastle-upon-Tyne and
Duke of Richmond, 17 May, 1623,

---

* In the third Report of the Lords' Committee just cited, it
is said that by this Patent "the Duke of Bedford was created
Earl of Richmond immediately, though he had the territorial
property only in reversion." P. 108. It is evident from the
same Report that the patent to Ralph Earl of Westmoreland is
considered to have created him *Earl* of Richmond, a fact denied by
the indefatigable Vincent; though the Editor will not presume
to give an opinion on the subject, he may be excused for alluding
to the singularity of the circumstance of creating the Duke of
Bedford, Earl of Richmond, if that title was then possessed by the
Earl of Westmoreland; and which strongly justifies the inference,
either that, if Ralph Nevill was then Earl of Richmond, the dignity, as well as possessions included in the grant to the Duke of
Bedford, were only intended to be in reversion; or that Vincent is
correct in supposing that the patent to the said Earl of Westmoreland merely gave him the Honor and not the Earldom of
Richmond.

K.G.; ob. 1624, s. p. when all his
titles became Extinct.

II. 1641. 1. **James Stuart**, 2d Earl of March in England,
and 3d Duke of Lenox in Scotland, s. and h.
of Esme Stuart, 1st Earl of March, and next
brother of the last Duke ; Created Duke of
Richmond, with remainder, failing his issue
male, to the issue male of his younger brothers, 8 Aug. 1641 ; K.G.; ob. 1655.

III. 1655. 2. **Esme Stuart**, s. and h. Duke of Lenox in
Scotland ; ob. 1660, s. p.

IV. 1660. 3. **Charles Stuart**, Earl of Litchfield, cousin and
heir, being s. and h. of George, next brother
of James II.-1st Duke ; Duke of Lenox in
Scotland; K.G.; ob. 1672, s.p. when all his
dignities became

Extinct.

V. 1675. 1. **Charles Lennox**, natural son of King Charles
II.; Created Baron of Setrington, Earl of
March, and Duke of Richmond, all co. York,
9 Aug. 1675 ; also, 9 Sept. following, Baron
Methuen of Torbolton, Earl of Darnley, and
Duke of Lennox in Scotland, K.G.; ob.
1723.

VI. 1723. 2. **Charles Lennox**, s. and h. Duke of Lennox
in Scotland, K.G.; ob. 1750.

VII. 1750. 3. **Charles Lennox**, s. and h. Duke of Lennox in
Scotland, K.G.; ob. 1806, s.p.

VIII. 1806. 4. **Charles Lennox**, nephew and heir, being s.
and h. of George Henry Lennox, youngest
son of Charles VI.-2d Duke ; Duke of Lennox in Scotland, K.G.; ob. 1819.

IX. 1819. 5. **Charles Lennox**, s. and h.; Present Duke,
of Richmond, Earl of March and Baron Setrington ; also Duke of Lennox, &c. in Scotland, and Duke of Aubigny in France.

RIDELL.

BARONS BY TENURE.

I. H. I.   Geoffrey Ridell, Justice of England temp.
Henry I. wrecked with Prince William anno
1119 ; ob. s. p. m. Maud, his dau. and heir,
married Richard Basset, afterwards Justice
of England; and his son,

BARONS BY TENURE.

II. H. III.   Geoffrey Basset, assumed the name of Ridell; living 1177.

III. H. II.   Hugh Ridell, 2d son; living 1184; to whom succeeded

IV. John.   Ralph Ridell; living 1204. In the 15th John, mention is made of a Geoffrey Ridell, and after him of Hugh Ridell, who is said to have died s. p.

RIE.

BARONS BY TENURE.

I. Will. I. 1. Eudo de Rie, obtained several Lordships from William the Conqueror; ob. 1120, s. p. m. Margaret, his dau. and heir, married William de Mandevil, father of Geoffrey Earl of Essex.

I. Steph. 1. Henry de Rie, living 1146; who was succeeded by

II. Hen. II. 2. Hubert de Rie; ob. 1172, s. p. m.

I. H. III.   John de Rye, presumed to have been of the same family, he joined the rebellious Barons temp. Henry III. and was living 1268.

John de Rye; Summoned 8 June, 22 Edw. II. 1294; but it is very doubtful if that Writ can be deemed a regular Summons to Parliament; vide " CLYVEDON." Dugdale gives no account of this personage, and nothing farther is recorded of him.

RIPARIIS, or RIVERS.

BARONS BY WRIT.

I.   1299. 1. John de Ripariis *; Summ. to Parl. from 6 Feb. 27 Edw. I. 1299, to 26 Aug. 1 Edw. II. 1307; ob. 1311.

II. 1313. 2. John de Ripariis, s. and h. Summ. to Parl. from 8 Jan. 6 Edw. II. 1313, to 16 Oct. 9 Edw. II. 1315; living 1339, but neither he

* He signed the celebrated letter to the Pope, 29 Edw. I. as " Johannes de Ripariis, Dominus de Angre."

nor any of his posterity (of whom nothing
farther is known) were ever again summoned
to Parliament.

Dugdale gives no account of this Baron in his Baronage; and the preceding account has been taken from the
List of Summonses to Parliament, and from Banks' Stemm-
mata Anglicana, p. 234. He was probably related to the
family of the Earls of Devon of that name.

RIPPON.

BARONY, 26 May, 1708—𝕮rtinct 1778.

Vide DOVER.

RITHRE.

BARON BY WRIT.

I.   1299.   William de Rithre; Summ. to Parl. from 29
             Dec. 28 Edw. I. 1299, to 26 Aug. 1 Edw. II.
             1307; to whom succeeded John de Rythre,
             his s. and h. who was Governor of Skypton
             Castle; but neither he nor any of his de-
             scendants were ever Summ. to Parl. and of
             whom Dugdale gives no farther account.

RIVERS.

Vide RIPARIIS.

RIVERS.

BARONS. EARLS.

I. 1448.—I. 1466. 1. Richard Widvile (father-in-law of
                       Edward IV.); Created Baron Rivers
                       29 May, 1448; Created Earl Rivers
                       24 May, 1466; Lord High Consta-
                       ble, K. G.; beheaded 1469.

II. 1469.—II. 1469. 2. Anthony Widvile, s. and h.; Baron
                       Scales jure uxoris; K. G.; beheaded
                       1483; ob. s. P.

III.1483.—III. 1483. 3. Richard Widvile, brother and heir;
                        ob. 1491, s. P. when his honors be-
                        came
                          𝕮rtinct.

        IV. 1626. 1. Thomas D'Arcy, 3d Baron D'Arcy
                       of Chiche, and 1st Viscount Col-
                       chester; Created Earl Rivers, with

remainder,. failing his issue male, to his son-
in-law, Sir Thomas Savage, and his heirs
male, 4 Nov. 1626; ob. 1639, s. p. m.

V. 1639. 2. John Savage, 2d Viscount Savage, grandson
and heir, being s. and h. of Sir Thomas Savage above mentioned, by Elizabeth his wife,
eldest dau. and coheir of the last Earl; succeeded his maternal grandfather in the Vis-
county of Colchester and Earldom of Rivers,
agreeable to the above limitation; ob. 1654.
He married Katherine Parker, dau. of William XII.-12th Baron Morley, Baron Mount-
eagle, and Baron Marshal.

VI. 1654. 3. Thomas Savage, s. and h.; in 1686 he became. in right of his mother, heir of one
moiety of the Baronies of Morley, Mount-
eagle, and Marshal; ob. 1694.

VII. 1694. 4. Richard Savage, 2d son and heir male; ob.
1712, s. p. m.

VIII.1712. 5. John Savage, cousin and heir, being s. and h.
of Richard Savage, next brother of Thomas
VI.-3d Earl; ob. 1728, s. p. when his titles
became Extinct.

I. 1641. 1. Elizabeth, dau. and coheir of Thomas Lord
D'Arcy, IV.-1st Earl Rivers, widow of Thomas 1st Viscount Savage, and mother of
Thomas Savage, 2d Viscount Savage, and
V.-2d Earl Rivers; Created Countess Rivers
for life, 21st April, 1641; ob. 1650, when
the title became Extinct.

RIVERS
OF STRATHFIELDSAY AND SUDELEY.

J. 1776. 1. George Pitt (descended from John Pitt, Esq.
OF SUDELEY   and Jane his wife, dau. of John V.-2d Earl
I. 1802.   Rivers, and widow of George Lord Chandos);
Created Baron Rivers of Strathfield Say, co.
Southampton, 20 May, 1776; Created Ba-
ron Rivers of Sudeley Castle, co. Gloucester,
1 April, 1802, with remainder, failing the
heirs male of his body, to his brother, Sir
William Augustus Pitt, K. B. and the heirs

BARONS.

male of his body; in default of which, to William Horace Beckford, Esq. son of Peter Beckford, of Stapleton, co. Dorset, Esq. by Louisa, his late wife, dau. of the said George Lord Rivers; ob. 1803.

II.   1803.   2. George Pitt, s. and h. Present Baron Rivers of Strathfieldsay, and Baron Rivers of Sudeley Castle.

ROBARTES.

BARONS.

I.   1625.   1. Sir Richard Robartes, 1st Bart.; Created Baron Robartes of Truro, co. Cornwall, 16 Jan. 1625; ob. 1634.

II.   1634.   2. John Robartes, s. and h.; Created Viscount Bodmin, co. Cornwall, and Earl of Radnor in Wales, 23 July, 1679.   Vide RADNOR. Extinct 1764.

ROBSERT.

Vide BOURCHIER.

ROCHE.

BARON BY WRIT.

I.   1299.   Thomas de la Roche; Summ. to Parl. from 29 Dec. 28 Edw. I. 1299, to 3 Nov. 34 Edw. I. 1306. Dugdale, in his Baronage, gives no account of this Baron; but in his "Index Baronum Summonitionibus," he says he was Summ. to Parl. from 28 to 35 Edw. I. and 8 Edw. II. The name, however, does not appear in the Summonses of the 8th Edw. II.

Banks, in his Stemmata Anglicana, p. 236, gives a pedigree of this family from Dugdale's Warwickshire, from which it appears that this Baron left male issue, which continued for four generations (none of whom, however, were ever Summ. to Parl.) when the representation vested in two coheirs, viz. Elena, who married, 1st. Edmund 5th Baron Ferrers of Chartley; and, 2dly, Philip Chetwynd; and Elizabeth, the wife of George Longville, and among whose descendants and representatives this Barony is probably now in ABEYANCE.

ROCHESTER.

VISCOUNT.

I.   1611.   1. Sir Robert Carr, K. B.; Created Viscount

Rochester 25 March, 1611; Created Baron
Brancepeth, co. Durham, and Earl of Somerset, 3 Nov. 1613; Lord Chamberlain; K.G.;
ob. 1645, s. p. m. when his honors became
Extinct.

I. 1652. 1. Henry Wilmot, 1st Baron Wilmot in England, and 2d Viscount Wilmot in Ireland;
ated Earl of Rochester 13 Dec. 1652; ob.1659.

II. 1659. 2. John Wilmot, s. and h. ob. 1680.

III. 1680. 3. Charles Wilmot, s. and h.; ob. 1681, s. p.
when his honors became
Extinct.

IV. 1682. 1. Lawrence Hyde, 1st Viscount Hyde of Kenil-
worth (2d son of Edward 1st Earl of Clarendon); Created Earl of Rochester 29 Nov.
1682; Lord Lieut. of Ireland; ob. 1711.

V. 1711. 2. Henry Hyde, s. and h.; succeeced his cousin
as 4th Earl of Clarendon in 1723; ob. 1753,
s. p. m. when the Earldoms of Clarendon and
Rochester, and all his other honors, became
Extinct.

ROCHFORD.

I. 1525. 1. Thomas Boleyn (father-in-law of King Henry VIII.); Created Viscount Rochford 18
June, 1525; Created, 8 Dec. 1529, Earl of
Wiltshire. with remainder to his heirs male,
and Earl of Ormond in Ireland, with limitation to his heirs general; K.G.; ob. 1538;
and his only son, George Boleyn, who was
Summ. to Parl. as "Georgio Bullen de Rochford," 5 Jan. 1533 (but never afterwards),
having been attainted and beheaded vita
patris, his honors, with the exception of the
Earldom of Ormond in Ireland, became
Extinct.

II. 1621. 1. Henry Carey, 4th Baron Hunsdon, great
grandson of Sir William Carey, by Mary Boleyn, his wife, dau. and (on the death of
Queen Elizabeth, niece of the said Mary)
sole heir of the last Viscount, created Viscount Rochford 6 July, 1621; Created Earl
of Dover 8 March, 1627.   Vide DOVER.
Extinct 1677.

EARLS.

I. 1695. 1. William Henry Nassau de Zuleistein, natural grandson of the Prince of Orange; Created Baron of Enfield, co. Middlesex, Viscount Tunbridge, co. Kent, and Earl of Rochford, co. Essex, 10 May, 1695; ob. 1708.

II. 1708. 2. William Henry Nassau, s. and h. ob. 1710, s. p.

III. 1710. 3. Frederick Nassau, brother and heir; ob.1738.

IV. 1738. 4. William Henry Nassau, s. and h. K.G.; ob. 1781, s. p.

V. 1781. 5. William Henry Nassau, nephew and heir, being s. and h. of Richard Savage Nassau, next brother of the last Earl. Present Earl of Rochford, Viscount Tunbridge, and Baron of Enfield.

ROCKINGHAM.

BARONS.

I. 1645. 1. Sir Lewis Watson, 1st Bart.; Created Baron Rockingham of Rockingham, co. Northampton, 29 Jan. 1645; ob. 1652.

II. 1652. 2. Edward Watson, s. and h. 1691.

EARLS.

III. 1691.—I. 1714. 3. Lewis Watson, s. and h.; Created Baron of Throwley and Viscount Sondes of Lee's Court, both co. Kent (which titles were borne by his father-in-law Sir George Sondes), and Earl of Rockingham, co. Northampton, 19 Oct. 1714; ob. 1724.

IV. 1714.—II. 1724. 4. Lewis Watson, grandson and heir, being s. and h. of Edward Watson, (ob. v. p.) eldest son of the last Earl; ob. 1745, s. p.

V. 1724.—III.1645. 5. Thomas Watson, brother and heir; ob. 1746, s. p. when the Barony of Throwley, Viscountcy of Sondes, and Earldom of Rockingham, became Extinct, but the Barony of Rockingham devolved on his cousin and heir male,

MARQUESSES.

VI. 1746.—I. 1746. 6. Thomas Wentworth, first Earl of

BARONS.   MARQ.

Malton, being s. and h. of Thomas Watson, who assumed the name of Wentworth, 2d son of Edward II.- 2d Baron; Created Marquess of Rockingham 19 April, 1746, K. B.; ob. 1750.

VII. 1750.—II. 1750. 7.Charles Watson Wentworth, s. and h.; Created Baron and Earl of Malton in Ireland, vita patris, 17 Sept. 1750, K. G.; ob. 1782, s. p. when all his dignities became
Extinct.

ROCKSAVAGE.

EARLDOM, September 1815.
Vide CHOLMONDELEY.

RODNEY.

BARONS.

I.   1782. 1. Sir George Brydges Rodney, 1st Bart.; Created Baron Rodney of Rodney Stoke, co. Somerset, 19 June, 1782, K. B.; ob. 1792.

II.   1792. 2. George Rodney, s. and h. ob. 1802.

III. 1802. 3. George Rodney, s. and h.   Present Baron Rodney, and a Baronet. ═══

ROLLE.

BARONS.

I.   1748. 1. Henry Rolle: Created Baron Rolle of Stevenstone, co. Devon, 8 Jan. 1748; ob. 1750, s. p. when the title became
Extinct.

II.   1796. 1. John Rolle, s. and h. of Dennis Rolle, next brother of the last Baron; Created Baron Rolle of Stevenstone, co. Devon, 20 June, 1796. Present Baron Rolle. ═══

ROMARE.

BARONS BY TENURE.

I.   H. I.   1. Roger, son of Gerold de Romare.

II.   H. II.   2. William de Romare, s. and h.; Governor of Newmarch 1118; living 1152.

III.   H. II.   3. William de Romare, grandson and heir, being s. and h. of William de Romare (ob. v. p.) eldest son of the last Baron; living 1182. His mother was Hawyse, dau. of Stephen Earl of Albemarle. Nothing farther is recorded of this family.

ROMNEY.

EARLS.

I.   1694.   1. Henry Sydney, 1st Viscount Sydney of the Isle of Shepey, and youngest son of Robert XIII.-2d Earl of Leicester; Created Earl of Romney, co. Kent, 25 April, 1694; ob. 1704, s. p. when all his honors became

         𝕰𝖝𝖙𝖎𝖓𝖈𝖙.

BARONS.

I.   1716.   1. Sir Robert Marsham, 4th Bart.; Created Baron of Romney, co. Kent, 25 June, 1716; ob. 1724.

II.   1724.   2. Robert Marsham, s. and h. ob. 1793.

         EARLS.

III.   1793.—II. 1801.   3. Charles Marsham, s. and h.; Created Viscount Marsham of the Mote, and Earl of Romney, 22 June, 1801; ob. 1811.

IV.   1811.—III. 1811.   4. Charles Marsham, s. and h. Present Earl and Baron Romney and Viscount Marsham, and a Baronet. ⚓

ROOS
OF HAMLAKE.

BARONS BY TENURE.

I.   Hen. I.   1. Peter de Roos, Lord of Roos in Holderness temp. Henry I.

II.   H. II.   2. Robert de Roos, s. and h. living 1156.

BARONS BY TENURE.

III. H. II. 3. Everard de Roos, s. and h. He married Rose, dau. and heir of William Trusbut, and died ante 1186.

IV. Ric.I. 4. Robert de Roos, s. and h. He was one of the celebrated 25 Barons appointed to enforce the observance of MAGNA CHARTA; and married Isabel, dau. of William the Lion, King of Scotland; ob. 1227.

V. 1227. 5. William de Roos, s. and h. ob. 1258.

BY WRIT.

I. 1264. 6. Robert de Roos, s. and h.; Summ. to Parl. 24 Dec. 49 Henry III. 1264. He married Isabel, dau. and heir of William de Albini, Lord of Belvoir Castle; ob. 1285.

II. 1295. 7. William de Roos, s. and h.; Summ. to Parl. from 23 June, 23 Edw. I. 1295*, to 6 Oct. 9 Edw. II. 1315. In 19 Edw. I. he was one of the competitors for the Crown of Scotland, in right of Isabel, his great-grandmother, above-mentioned; ob. 1316.

III. 1316. 8. William de Roos, s. and h.; Summ. to Parl. from 20 Nov. 10 Edw. II. 1317, to 12 Sept. 16 Edw. III. 1342; ob. 1343.

IV. 1343. 9. William de Roos, s. and h.; Summ. to Parl. 25 Nov. 24 Edw. III. 1350, and 20 Nov. 25 Edw. III. 1351; ob. 1352, s. p.

V. 1352. 10. Thomas de Roos, brother and heir; Summ. to Parl. from 24 Aug. 36 Edw. III. 1362, to 3 March, 7 Rich. II. 1384; ob. 1384.

VI. 1384. 11. John de Roos, s. and h.; Summ. to Parl. from 8 Aug. 10 Rich. II. 1386, to 13 Nov. 17 Rich. II. 1393; ob. 1393, s. p.

VII. 1393. 12. William de Roos, brother and heir; Summ. to Parl. from 20 Nov. 18 Rich. II. 1394, to 24 Dec. 1 Henry V. 1413; Lord Treasurer; ob. 1414.

---

* He was summoned 8 June, 22 Edw. I. 1294, as "Willielmo de Ros de Ingmanthorpe;" but it is very doubtful if that Writ can be considered as a regular Summons to Parliament; vide "CLYVE-DON." In the following year he was described "de Helmesley," and in 1299 as "de Hemelak," which last addition was frequently made to the names of these Barons in the Writs of Summons to Parliament.

BARONS BY WRIT.

VIII. 1414. 13. John de Roos, s. and h.; ob. 1421, infra ætatem, s. P.

IX. 1421. 14. Thomas de Roos, brother and heir; Summ. to Parl. 12 July and 3 Aug. 7 Henry VI. 1429; ob. 1431.

X. 1431. 15. Thomas de Roos, s. and h.; Summ. to Parl. from 2 Jan. 27 Henry VI. 1449, to 30 July, 38 Henry VI. 1460. Attainted 4 Nov. 1461, when his honors became

Forfeited.

XI. 1485. 16. Edmund de Roos, s. and b. obtained the reversal of his father's Attainder in 1485, but was never summoned to Parliament; ob. 1508, s. P. when the Barony fell into ABEYANCE between his sisters and coheirs, viz. Eleanor, who married Sir Robert Manners, Knt.; Isabel, who married Thomas Grey, and died s. P.; and Margaret, who is supposed to have died unmarried.

XII. 15... 17. George Manners, s. and h. of Sir Robert Manners, by Eleanor de Roos, sister and coheir of Edmund the last Baron. He is styled on his monument "Lord Roos," and succeeded to the Barony, jure matris, on the death of Isabel and Margaret s. P. the other coheirs, though he was never summoned to Parl. He married Ann, dau. and sole heir of Sir Thomas St. Leger, Knt. by Ann Plantagenet, sister of King Edward IV.; ob. 1513.

XIII. 1513. 18. Thomas Manners, s. and h.; Summ. to Parl. as "Thomæ Manners de Rosse, Chev'r. 12 Nov. 7 Henry VIII. 1515, and 15th April, 14 Henry VIII. 1523; Created Earl of Rutland 18 June, 1525, K. G.; ob. 1543.

XIV. 1543. 19. Henry Manners, s. and h.; Earl of Rutland, K. G.; ob. 1563.

XV. 1563. 20. Edward Manners, s. and h.; Earl of Rutland, K. G.; ob. 1587, s. P. M.

BARONESS.

I. 1587. 21. Elizabeth Manners, dau. and sole heiress of William Cecil, son and heir apparent of Thomas 1st Earl of Exeter; ob. 1591.

BARONS BY WRIT.

XVI. 1591.22.William Cecil, s. and h.; confirmed in the
Barony of Roos 22 July, 1616; ob. vita patris 1618, s. P.

XVII. 1618.23.Francis Manners, VII.-6th Earl of Rutland,
BARON BY cousin and h. being brother and heir of Roger
PATENT. VI. 5th Earl of Rutland, eldest son of John V.-
I. 1616. 4th Earl of Rutland, and next brother of Edward IV.-3d Earl of Rutland, and XVI.-20th
Baron Roos. In 1616 he claimed the Barony as
heir *male* of Henry XIV.-19th Baron, against
William Cecil, his heir *general*, to whom it was
allowed; but, by patent dated 22d July,
1616, he obtained a grant of the dignity of
Baron Roos of Hamlake to him and his issue
male, and succeeded to the ancient Barony
on the death of his cousin, the said William
Cecil, in 1618; K. G.; ob. 1632, s. P. M. when
the Barony created by the patent of 22 July,
1616, became Extinct, but the original Barony devolved on

BARONESS.

II. 1632. 24. Katherine Villiers, his sole dau. and heir;
widow of George Villiers, IV.-1st Duke of
BARON BY WRIT. Buckingham; ob. 1666.

XVIII.1666.25.George Villiers, s. and h. Duke of Buckingham, K. G.; ob. 1687, s. P. when the Barony
of Roos fell into ABEYANCE between the
heirs general of the sisters and heirs of George
Manners, VIII.-7th Earl of Rutland, brother
and heir male of Francis Manners, VII.-6th
Earl of Rutland, and XVIII.-23d Baron Roos,
and continued in abeyance until 1803, when

BARONESS.

III.1806. 26. Charlotte Fitzgerald (assumed the name of)
De Roos; wife of Lord Henry Fitz-Gerald,
(4th son of James 1st Duke of Leinster). Pe-
titioned the King to terminate the Abeyance of the Barony in her favour, she being one of
the coheirs of the said dignity, viz. dau. and sole heir
of the Hon. Robert Boyle Walsingham, by Charlotte,
youngest dau. and coheir of Sir Charles Hanbury Williams,
K. B. by Frances, dau. and at length only surviving child
of Thomas Earl of Coningsby, by his *second wife* Frances,

dau. and eventually sole heir, of Richard Earl of Ranelagh,
by Elizabeth, dau. and ultimately sole heir, of Francis 4th
Baron Willoughby of Parham, 4. and h. of Wiliam 3d Baron
Willoughby of Parham by Frances Manners his wife,
youngest sister and coheir of George Manners, VIII.-7th
Earl of Rutland, brother and heir male of Francis Manners, VII.-6th Earl of Rutland, and XVIII.-23d Baron
de Roos, whose heirs-general failed on the death of George
Duke of Buckingham, and XIX.-25th Baron de Roos in
1687. His Majesty was pleased to refer her Ladyship's
petition to the Attorney General, on whose report it was
referred to the House of Lords, who, 7th May, 1800, reported that the Barony was then in Abeyance between Sir
Henry Hunloke, Bart. (heir-general of Bridget Manners,
eldest sister and coheir of George VIII.-7th Earl of Rutland above mentioned); George Earl of Essex (as son and
heir of Frances, eldest daughter and coheir of Sir Charles
Hanbury Williams, K. B. before mentioned), and the
Petitioner; and on the 9th May, 1806, the King was
pleased to terminate the said Abeyance in her Ladyship's
favour*. Present Baroness de Roos.

ROOS

OF WERKE.

BARON BY WRIT.

I. 1295. Robert de Roos; obtained the Lordship of
Werke from his father Robert IV.-4th Baron
Roos of Hamlake; Summoned 8 June 22
Edw. I. 1294; but it is very doubtful if
that Writ can be deemed a regular Sum-

---

* It is worthy of remark, that her Ladyship was only youngest
coheir of one moiety of the Barony of Roos; the entire representation of the eldest coheir being vested in Sir Henry Hunloke, Bart.; and the Editor is not aware of any similar instance,
(excepting in the case of the Barony of Zouche of Haryngworth,
but which is not precisely in point, because, though Sir Cecil
Bishopp was only the eldest coheir of one moiety of that Barony,
no descendants could be traced of the coheir of the other moiety
after the time of the Commonwealth,) of the grace of the Crown
aving been exercised in favor of a coheir who did not wholly
resent one moiety of the dignity.

mons to Parliament; vide " CLYVEDON;"
Summ. to Parl. 24 June, 1 October, and 2
Nov. 23 Edward I. 1295, as " Roberto de
Roos de Werke," but never afterwards;
having been found guilty of treason, his lands
and honours became

Forfeited.

ROOS
OF KENDALL.

BARON BY TENURE.

1. Edw. I.   William de Roos, s. and h. of Robert de Roos
of Werke, by Margaret, sister and coheir of
Peter de Brus, who obtained from his mother
the Castle of Kendall; ob. 1339, leaving
issue Thomas, who was never Summ. to Parl.
and cannot therefore be considered among
the Barons of the Realm. John, s. and h. of
this Thomas, died s. p. in 1858, leaving Elizabeth his dau. and heir, who married Sir
William Parr, Knt. ancestor of the Parrs
of Kendall.

ROOS
OF ——

BARON BY WRIT.

I.   1332.   John de Roos, next brother of William III.-8th
Baron Roos of Hamlake; Summ. to Parl.
from 27 Jan. 6 Edward III. 1332, to 15 June,
12 Edward III. 1338; Admiral of the Fleet;
ob. 1338, s. p. when this Barony became

Extinct.

ROSCELYN.

Peter de Roscelyn was Summoned 8 June, 22 Edw. I.
1294; but it is very doubtful if that Writ can be considered as a regular Summons to Parliament; vide "CLYVE-
DON." Dugdale gives no account of him in his Baronage,
nor was he ever summoned to Parliament.

ROSS.

BARON.

I, 1815. George Boyle, 4th Earl of Glasgow in Scotland; Created Baron Ross of Hawkstead, co. Renfrew, 18 July, 1815. Present Baron Ross; also Earl of Glasgow, &c. in Scotland.

ROSSLYN.

EARLS.

I. 1801. 1. Alexander Wedderburn, 1st Baron Loughborough of Loughborough, co. Leicester, and 1st Baron Loughborough of Loughborough, co. Surrey; Created Earl of Rosslyn, co. Mid-Lothian, 21 April, 1801, with remainder, failing the heirs male of his body, to the heirs male of the body of Janet Erskine, his sister, widow of Sir Henry Erskine, of Alva, Bart.; Lord H. Chancellor; ob. 1805, s. p. when the Barony of Loughborough, co. Leicester, became Extinct; but his other honors devolved, agreeable to the above limitation, on

II. 1805. 2. Sir James St. Clair Erskine, Bart. his nephew and heir, being s. and h. of Sir Henry Erskine by Janet, sister of the last Earl. Present Earl of Rosslyn, and Baron Loughborough of Loughborough, co. Surrey, G. C. B.

ROTHESAY.

The heir apparent to the throne of Scotland has always been created Duke of Rothesay, Earl of Carrick, and Baron of Renfrew, and the descent of which will be found under the " PRINCES OF WALES;" since the union with Scotland, when these titles became dignities in the Peerage of the United Kingdom.

ROUS.

BARON.
I. 1796. 1. Sir John Rous, 6th Bart.; Created Baron Rous of Dennington, co. Suffolk, 14 June, 1796; Created Viscount Dunwich and Earl of Stradbroke, co. Suffolk, 18 July, 1821. Present Baron Rous, Viscount Dunwich, and Earl of Stradbroke.

ROYSTON.

VISCOUNTCY, 2 April, 1754.

Vide HARDWICKE.

RUSSELL.

BARONS.
I. 1539. 1. William Russell; Created Baron Russell of Cheneys, co. Buckingham, 9 March, 1539; Created Earl of Bedford 19 Jan. 1550, K. G.; Lord High Admiral.   Vide BEDFORD.

RUSSELL
OF THORNHAUGH.

BARONS.
I. 1603. 1. William Russell, younger son of Francis IV.-2d Earl of Bedford; Created Baron Russell of Thornhaugh, co. Northampton, 21 July, 1603; ob. 1613.

II. 1613. 2. Francis Russell, s. and h. succeeded his cousin Edward V.-3d Earl of Bedford in that Earldom, and as Baron Russell of Cheyneys, 3 May, 1627.   Vide BEDFORD.

RUSSELL
OF SHINGAY (OR SHINGAY).

BARONY, 7 May, 1697—Extinct 1727.

Vide SHINGAY.

RUTLAND.

I. 1390. 1. Edward Plantagenet, son and heir apparent of Edmund of Langley, Duke of York, 5th son of Edward III. Created Earl of Rutland 25 Feb. 1390, but with limitation of the title during his father's life only, " Habend, &c. durante vita dicti ducis patris sui ;" Created Duke of Albemarle 29 Sept. 1397 ; succeeded his father as Duke of York in 1402, when the Earldom of Rutland, agreeable to the limitation recited above, became **Extinct** *.

---

* This Earldom is by most writers attributed to Edmund Plantagenet, younger son of Richard Duke of York, who was murdered at Wakefield, aged about 12 years, and some authorities also attribute it to the said Richard Duke of York his father, as nephew and heir of Edward Duke of Albemarle, the first Earl ; but as the said Duke of. Albemarle was only so created until his father's decease, it of course became Extinct on that event in 1402. Brooke states, and in which he is not contradicted by Vincent, that Richard Duke of York above mentioned, was restored to be Duke of York, Earl of Cambridge and Rutland, and Lord of Tyndall, in the 4th Hen. VI. No Act of Restoration in that year, however, is to be found in the Rolls of Parliament ; but though he might have been restored to the Dukedom of York and Earldom of Cambridge, the former of 'which titles had been borne by his grandfather and uncle, and the latter by his father, it does not appear how he could have been *restored* to the Earldom of Rutland, as that title was first conferred on his uncle, and became extinct agreeable to the peculiar limitation cited in the text. The same writer calls Edmund Plantagenet (who was assassinated by Lord Clifford after the battle of Wakefield) third son of the said Richard Duke of York, the next Earl of Rutland, but he gives no account of the manner in which he became possessed of that title : the fact appears to be, that the younger branches of the House of York assumed the title of this Earldom ; but excepting to Edward, afterwards Duke of York, the 1st Earl, there was no regular creation to that dignity until it was conferred upon Thomas Manners, Lord Roos, by Henry VIII.

II. 1525. 1. Thomas Manners, XIV.-18th Baron Roos of Hamlake, s. and h. of George Baron Roos by Ann, sole dau. and heir of Sir Thomas St. Leger, Knt. by Ann Plantagenet, sister of King Edward IV. Created Earl of Rutland 18 June, 1525, K. G.; ob. 1543.

III. 1543. 2. Henry Manners, s. and h. Baron Roos, K. G.; ob. 1563.

IV. 1563. 3. Edward Manners, s. and h. Baron Roos, K. G.; ob. 1587, s. p. m. when the Barony of Roos devolved on Elizabeth his dau. and heir.

V. 1587. 4. John Manners, brother and heir male; ob.1588.

VI. 1588. 5. Roger Manners, s. and h. ob. 1612, s. p.

VII. 1612. 6. Francis Manners, brother and heir; succeeded to the Barony of Roos in 1618, K. G.; ob. 1632, s. p. m. when the Barony of Roos devolved on Katherine Duchess of Buckingham, his sole dau. and heir.

VIII. 1632. 7. George Manners, brother and heir; ob. 1641, s. p.

IX. 1641. 8. John Manners, cousin and heir male, being son and heir of George Manners, eldest son of Sir John Manners, 2d son of Thomas II.-1st Earl; ob. 1679.

DUKES.

X. 1679.—I. 1703. 9. John Manners, s. and h. 1st Baron Manners of Haddon; Created Marquess of Granby, co. Nottingham, and Duke of Rutland, 29 March, 1703; ob. 1711.

XI. 1711.—II. 1711. 10. John Manners, s. and h. K. G.; ob. 1721.

XII. 1721.—III. 1721. 11. John Manners, s. and h. K. G.; ob. 1779.

XIII. 1779.—IV. 1779. 12. Charles Manners, grandson and heir; being s. and h. of John Manners (ob. v. p.) eldest son of the last Duke; Lord Lieut. of Ireland, K. G.; ob. 1787.

XIV. 1787.—V. 1787. 13. John Henry Manners, s. and h. Present Duke and Earl of Rutland, Marquess of Granby, and Baron Manners of Haddon, K. G..

RYE. Vide RIE.

SACKVILLE.

VISCOUNTS.

I.   1782. 1. George Sackville (assumed the name of) Germain, younger son of Lionel 1st Duke of Dorset; Created Baron of Bolebrook, co. Sussex, and Viscount Sackville of Drayton, co. Northampton, 11 Feb. 1782; ob. 1785.

II.   1785. 2. Charles Sackville Germain, s. and h. succeeded his cousin George 4th Duke of Dorset in that Dukedom, and in his other honours, 14 February, 1815. Present Viscount Sackville, Baron Bolebrook, Duke and Earl of Dorset, and Earl of Middlesex, Viscount Germain, Baron Buckhurst, and Baron Cranfield.

ST. ALBANS.

VISCOUNT.

I.   1621.   Francis Bacon, the 1st and celebrated Baron Verulam; Created Viscount St. Albans, co. Herts, 27 Jan. 1621; Lord Chancellor; ob. 1626, s. p. when his honors became

EARLS.   **Extinct.**

I.   1628. 1. Richard de Burgh, 1st Viscount Tunbridge in England, and Earl of Clanrickard in Ireland; Created Earl of St. Albans 23 August, 1628; ob. 1636.

II.   1636. 2. Ulick de Burgh, s. and h. Created Marquess of Clanrickard in Ireland; ob. 1659, s. p. m. when his English honors and Irish Marquisate became

                Extinct.

III.   1660. 1. Henry Jermyn, 1st Baron Jermyn of St. Edmundsbury; Created Earl of St. Albans 27

April, 1660 , ob. 1683, s. p. when this Earldom again became

DUKES. **Extinct.**

I. 1684. 1. Charles Beauclerk, 1st Earl of Burford, natu-
ral son of King Charles II.; Created Duke
of St. Albans 10 January, 1684; he married
Diana, daughter and eventually sole heir of
Aubrey de Vere, XX.-20th and last Earl of
Oxford, K. G.; ob. 1726.

II. 1726. 2. Charles Beauclerk, s. and h. K. G. ; ob. 1751.

III. 1751. 3. George Beauclerk, s. and h. ob. 1786, s. p.

IV. 1786. 4. George Beauclerk, cousin and heir; being son
and heir of Charles, eldest son of William
Beauclerk, 2d son of Charles 1st Duke ; ob.
1787, s. p.

V. 1787. 5. Aubrey Beauclerk, 2d Baron Vere of Hanworth, cousin and heir, being son and heir
of Vere Beauclerk, 1st Baron Vere of Hanworth, 3d son of Charles 1st Duke; ob. 1802.

VI. 1802. 6. Aubrey Beauclerk, s. and h. ob. 1815.

VII. 1815. 7. Aubrey Beauclerk, s. and h. ob. 1816 infans.

VIII.1816. 8. William Beauclerk, uncle and heir, being 2d
son of Aubrey 5th Duke. Present Duke of
St. Albans, Earl of Burford, Baron of Hed-
dington, and Baron Vere of Hanworth.

ST. AMAND.

BARONS BY WRIT.

I. 1299. 1. Almaric de St. Amand ; Summ. to Parl. from
29 Dec. 28 Edward I. 1299, to 16 June, 4
Edward II. 1311; ob. 1312, s. p. when the
Barony became
Extinct.

II. 1313. 1. John de St. Amand, brother and heir of the
last Baron; Summ. to Parl. from 22 March,
6 Edward II. 1313, to 10 Oct. 19 Edward II.
1325 ; ob. 1326.

III. 1326. 2. Almaric de St. Amand, s. and h.; Summ. to
Parl. from 8 Jan. 44 Edward III. 1371, to 22
August, 5 Rich. II. 1381; ob. 1381.

IV. 1381. 3. Almaric de St. Amand, s. and h. Summ. to Parl.
from 9 August, 6 Rich. II. 1382, to 2 Dec.

3 Hen. IV. 1401 ; ob. 1403, s. p. m. leaving
Ida his dau. by his second wife, and Gerard
Braybroke his grandson (viz. son and heir of
Gerard Braybrooke by Alianore his dau. by
first wife) his heirs ; between whom the
Barony fell into ABEYANCE. The said Ida
married Sir Thomas West, but died s. p. ante
1426, when the three daughters and coheirs
of the above-mentioned Gerard Braybrooke
(grandson of the last Baron) became heirs to
the Barony. It continued in Abeyance until
1449, when

IV. 1449. William Beauchamp (grandson of John Baron
Beauchamp of Powyk), having married Elizabeth (who married secondly Roger Tuchet)
eldest dau. and coheir of the said Gerard
Braybrooke, grandson and ultimately sole
heir of the last Baron, was Summ. to Parl.
jure uxoris, as " Willielmo de Beauchamp,
Domino de St. Amand," from 2 Jan. 27
Henry VI. 1449, to 26 May, 32 Henry VI.
1455 ; ob. 1457.

V. 1457. 4. Richard Beauchamp, s. and h. attainted 1
Rich. III. when his honors became Forfeited,
but he was fully restored 1 Hen. VII. Summ.
to Parl. as " Richardo Beauchamp de S.
Amando," 16 January, 12 Henry VII. 1497;
ob. 1508, s. p. l. when the Barony is presumed
to have become vested in the descendants and
representatives of Isabella, sister of Almaric
II.-2d Baron (Maud and Alianore, the other
daughters and coheirs of the above mentioned
Gerard de Braybrooke having died s. p.) which
Isabella married, first, Richard Handlo, and
secondly, Robert de Ildesle *.

---

* Although no other issue is assigned to William, IV. Lord St.
Amand in either of the numerous pedigrees which the Editor has
consulted, than his son Richard, the last Baron, it is to be remarked, that in the will of the said Richard Lord St. Amand he
bequeathes a cup to *his niece Leverseye*. This expression was probably used to describe *his wife's niece ;* but it must be observed,
that if he had a sister of the whole blood who left issue, the Barony
n his demise, s. p. l. became vested in her or her descendants.

ST. ANDREWS.

DUKEDOM, 19 May, 1789.

Vide CLARENCE.

ST. ASAPH.

VISCOUNTCY, 14 May, 1730,

Vide ASHBURNHAM.

ST. GERMAINS.

EARLS.

I. 1815..1. John Craggs Eliot, 2d Baron Eliot; Created Earl of St. Germain's, co. Cornwall, 30 Sept. 1815, with remainder, failing the heirs male of his body, to his brother William; ob. 1823, s.p.

II. 1823. 2. William Eliot, brother and heir. Present Earl of St. Germains, and Baron Eliot. ⊤

ST. HELENS.

BARON.

I. 1801. 1. Alleyne Fitz-Herbert, 1st Baron Fitz-Helens in Ireland; Created Baron St. Helens in the Isle of Wight, co. Southampton, 15 July, 1801. Present Baron St. Helens, G. C. B.

ST. JOHN
OF BASING.

BARONS BY TENURE.

I. John. 1. William de St. John, s. and h. of Adam de Port of Basing (vide PORT) by Mabell, dau. of Reginald de Aurevalle by Muriell, dau. and heir of Roger de St. John and Cecily his wife, dau. and heir of Robert de Haya; living 1220.

II. H. III. 2. Robert de St. John, s. and h. ob. 1266.

III. H. III. 3. John de St. John, s. and h. ob. 1301.

I. 1299. 4. John de St. John, s. and h. Summ. to Parl. as " Jo. de Sancto Johanne, Juniori," 29 Dec. 28 Edward I. 1299; as " Johanni de Sancto Johanne," from 12 Nov. 31 Edw. I. 1303, to 5 Aug. 14 Edw. II. 1320, and as " Johanni de Sancto Johanne de Basyng," from 14 Mar. 15 Edward II. 1322, to 10 Oct. 19 Edward II. 1325 *; ob. 1329, leaving Hugh de St. John his son and heir, who died in 1337, and as Edmond de St. John, his only son, died infra ætatem, 21 Edw. III. Margaret and Isabel, the sisters of the said Edmund became his heirs. Margaret married John de St. Phillibert, but died s. p. s. 35 Edward III. and Isabel became the wife, first, of Henry de Burghersh, by whom she had no issue, and secondly, of Lucas Poynings, who was Summ. to Parl. from 42 to 49 Edw. III. probably in right of his wife, though he is only described in the Writs as " Luce de Poynings;" Thomas de Poynings their son and heir, was styled Lord St. John, and succeeded to his father's Barony, though he was never summoned to Parliament, and died in 1428, leaving his grand-daughters (the daughters and heirs of Hugh de Poynings his only son, who died vitâ patris) his heirs, viz. Constance, wife of John Paulet, Alice, wife of John Orrell, and Joane, the wife of Thomas Bonvill; among whose descendants and representatives the Baronies of St. John of Basing, and Poynings, (if Lucas de Poynings their great grandfather be not considered to have been

---

* John de St. John was also summoned 3 Dec. 1826; but as no local addition is affixed to his name, it is difficult to determine whether it was this Baron St. John, or Baron St. John of Lageham, though it is most probable it was the former. Dugdale cites an Escheat 3 Edw. III. to prove that this Baron died 14 May, 1319; but as he was regularly summoned until October 1325, it is presumed he died circa 3 Edw. III. viz. 1329.

BARON.

· summoned in his wife's Barony, but of which there is no evidence), are in ABEYANCE.

I. 1539, 1. William Paulet, great grandson and heir of John Paulet by Constance de Poynings above mentioned, and in her right coheir of the Baronies of St. John of Basing and Poynings, Created Baron St. John of Basing, with remainder to the heirs male of his body, 9 March, 1539; Created Earl of Wiltshire 19 January, 1550, and Marquess of Winchester 12 October, 1551, K. G.   Vide WINCHESTER.

ST. JOHN
OF BLETSHOE.

BARONS.

I. 1559. 1. Oliver St. John (presumed to have been descended from the family of St. John of Stantone), Baron Beauchamp of Bletshoe by descent; Created Baron St. John of Bletshoe, co. Bedford, 13 Jan. 1559; ob. 1582.

II. 1582. 2. John St. John, s. and h. ob. 1596, s. p. m. Ann, his sole dau. and heir, married William Lord Howard (son and heir apparent of Charles Earl of Nottingham), in whose descendants the Barony of Beauchamp of Bletshoe became vested.

III. 1596. 3. Oliver St. John, brother and heir male; ob. 1618.

IV. 1618. 4. Oliver St. John, s. and h. Created Earl of Bolingbroke 28 Dec. 1624; ob. 1646.

V. 1646. 5. Oliver St. John, grandson and heir, being son and heir of Sir Paulet St. John, K. B. (ob. v. p.) eldest surviving son of the last Baron; Earl of Bolingbroke; ob. 1688, s. p.

VI. 1688. 6. Paulet St. John, brother and heir, Earl of Bolingbroke; ob. 1711, s. p. when that Earldom became Extinct; but this Barony devolved on

VII. 1711. 7. Sir Paulet St. Andrew St. John, 4th Bart. cousin and heir male, being s. and h. of Sir An-

drew 3d Bart. eldest son of Sir St. Andrew
St. John, 2d Bart. son and heir of Sir Oliver
St. John, 1st Bart. only son of Rowland St.
John, younger son of Oliver, 3d Baron, ob.

BARONS.   1714, infans.

VIII. 1714. 8. William St. John, uncle and heir, being next
brother of Sir Andrew St. John, father of the
last Baron ; ob. 1720, s. p.

IX. 1720. 9. Rowland St. John, brother and heir; ob.
1722, s. p.

X. 1722. 10.John St. John, brother and heir; ob. 1757.

XI. 1757. 11.John St. John, s. and h. ob. 1767.

XII. 1767. 12.Henry Beauchamp St. John, s. and h. ob.1805,
s. p. m.

XIII.1805. 13.St. Andrew St. John, brother and heir; ob.
1817.

XIV. 1817. 14.St. Andrew St. John, s. and h. Present Baron
St. John of Bletshoe and a Baronet.

ST. JOHN

OF BATTERSEA.

BARONS. VISCOUNTS.

I. —I. 1716. 1.Sir Henry St. John, 4th Bart. descended
from Sir Oliver St. John, ancestor of the
Barons St. John of Bletshoe ; Created
Baron St. John of Battersea, co. Surrey,
and Viscount St. John 2d July, 1716, with
remainder to his issue male by Angelica
his second wife ; ob. 1742.

II. —II. 1742. 2. John St. John, s. and h. ob. 1749.

III.—III.1749. 3. Frederick St. John, s. and h. succeeded
his half uncle Henry Viscount Boling-
broke, who was attainted in 1714, but
restored in blood in 1725, as 2d Viscount
Bolingbroke and 2d Baron St. John of
Lydiard Tregoye in 1751 ; ob. 1787.

IV.—IV.1787. 4. George Richard St. John, s. and h. ob.
Nov. 1824.

V. —V. 1824. 5. Henry St. John, s. and h. Present Viscount Bolingbroke and Viscount St. John,

Baron St. John of Lydiard Tregose, Baron
St. John of Battersea, and a Baronet. ☥

ST. JOHN

OF LAGEHAM.

BARONS BY WRIT.

I.   1299. 1. John de St. John ; Summ. to Parl. from 21
Sept. 27 Edward I. 1299, to 6 Oct. 9 Edw. II.
1315; after the 6 Edw. II. occasionally with
the addition of " de Lageham ;" he was also
Summoned 26 Jan. 25 Edward I. 1297 ; but
it is doubtful if that Writ can be deemed a
regular Summons to Parliament ; " vide
" FITZ-JOHN;" ob. 1316.

II. 1316. 2. John de St. John, s. and h. Summ. to Parl.
from 20 Nov. 11 Edw. II. 1317, to 18 Sept.
16 Edward II. 1322, as " Johanni de S. Johanne de Lageham;" ob. 1322.

III. 1322. 3. John de St. John, s. and h. Summ. to Parl.
from 1st Aug. 1 Edward III. 1327, to 18 Feb.
5 Edward III. 1331, as " Johanni de S. Johanne ;" ob. 1349, leaving Roger his son
and heir, who died in 1353, s. p. when Peter
de St. John his kinsman was found to be his
heir ; but none of this family were ever
summoned to Parliament after 1331. The
Barony is now vested in the heirs-general of
John the first Baron.

ST. JOHN

OF LYDIARD TREGOZE.

BARONY, 7 July, 1712.

Vide BOLINGBROKE.

ST. JOHN

OF STANTON.

BARONS BY TENURE.

I.   Hen. I.   Thomas de St. John, Lord of Stanton, co.
Oxford ; living 1112 ; his successor was

II. Steph.   John de St. John ; living 1139.

III. Hen. II. Thomas de St. John, Lord of Stanton aforesaid 1166 ; he was succeeded by

BARONS BY TENURE.

IV. **John.**　Roger de St. John ; living 1175 ; ob. ante
　　　　　　　1215 ; his heir was

V. **Hen. III.** John de St. John ; living 1229 ; to whom
　　　　　　　succeeded

BY WRIT.

I.　**1264.**　Roger de St. John ; Summ. to Parl. 24 Dec.
　　　　　　　49 Henry III. 1264 ; slain at Evesham 1265 ;
　　　　　　　he left issue, John his son and heir ; but
　　　　　　　neither this John nor any of his descendants
　　　　　　　were ever summoned to Parliament ; and on
　　　　　　　the death of the said Roger the Barony be-
　　　　　　　came　　　Extinct.

ST. LIZ.

BARONS.

I.　**1664.**　1. Basil Fielding, 2d Earl of Denbigh ; Created
　　　　　　　Baron de St. Liz 2 Feb. 1664 (he being de-
　　　　　　　scended from Agnes, dau. and heir of John
　　　　　　　de Liz, the heir male of Simon de St. Liz,
　　　　　　　brother of Simon III.-2d Earl of Northamp-
　　　　　　　ton), with remainder, failing his issue male,
　　　　　　　to the heirs male of his father ; ob. 1675, s.p.

II.　**1675.**　2. William Fielding, Earl of Denbigh, nephew
　　　　　　　and heir, being son and heir of George Earl
　　　　　　　of Desmond in Ireland, next brother of the
　　　　　　　last Baron.　　　　　　　Vide DENBIGH.

ST. MAUR.

BARONS BY WRIT.

I.　**1314.**　1. Nicholas de St. Maur ; Summ. to Parl. 29
　　　　　　　July, 8 Edw. II. 1314, and 6 Oct. 9 Edw. II.
　　　　　　　1315 ; ob. 1316.

II.　**1316.**　2. Thomas de St. Maur, s. and h. ; he was never
　　　　　　　summoned to Parl. ; ob. .... s.p.

III.　**1351.**　3. Nicholas de St. Maur, brother and heir ; Summ.
　　　　　　　to Parl. from 15 Nov. 25 Edw. III. 1351, to
　　　　　　　20 Nov. 34 Edw. III. 1360 ; he married Mu-
　　　　　　　riel, grand-daughter and heir of Richard
　　　　　　　Baron Lovel of Kari ; ob. 1361.

IV.　**1361.**　4. Nicholas de St. Maur, s. and h. ob. infra æta-
　　　　　　　tem, s. p.

V.　**1380.**　5. Richard de St. Maur, brother and heir ;
　　　　　　　Summ. to Parl. from 26 August, 4 Rich. II.

1280, to 3 October 2 Henry IV. 1400, as
" Richardo Seymour;" ob. 1401.

VI. 1401. 6. Richard de St. Maur, s. and h. Summ. to Parl.
from 21 June, 3 Hen. IV. 1402, to 26 August,
8 Hen. IV. 1406, as " Richardo Seymour;"
ob. 1409, s. p. m. Alice, his sole daughter
and heir, married William IV.-5th Baron
Zouche of Haryngworth, in whose descendants, the Barons Zouche, it continued until
the demise of Edward XI.-12th Baron Zouche
in 1625, s. p. m. when, together with the
Baronies of ℤouche of Haryngworth and
Lovel of Kary, it fell into ABEYANCE between
his two daughters and coheirs, viz. Elizabeth,
wife of Sir William Tate, Knt. and Mary,
wife of Thomas Leighton, Esq. The Barony of
Zouche has been lately revived in the person of
Sir Cecil Bishopp, Bart. one of the coheirs of
that Barony, but the Baronies of St. Maur
and of Lovel of Kary are still in ABEYANCE
between the heirs-general of Edward XI.-
12th Baron Zouche, and XIII.-13th Baron of
St. Maur.

ST. MAUR

I. 1317. William de St. Maur; presumed to have been
of the same family; but of whom Dugdale in
his Baronage gives no account; Summ. to
Parl. from 20 Nov. 11 Edward II. 1317, to
14 March, 15 Edw. II. 1322.

ST. PHILIBERT.

I. 1299. Hugh de St. Philibert; Summ. to Parl. 6 Feb.
27 Edw. I. 1299, but never afterwards. Dugdale in his Baronage takes no notice of this
Hugh having been Summ. to Parl.; but he
appears to be the same Hugh de St. Philibert
who was in the Scottish wars 26 Edw. I. and
whose son and heir John had livery of his
lands 7 Edward II. and died 7 Edward III.
leaving his son and heir,

BARON BY WRIT.

II.   1348.   John de St. Philibert, who was Summ. to Parl.
20 Nov. 22 Edward III. 1348, 1 Jan. and 10
March, 23 Edw. III. 1349; ob. 1359, s. p. when
the Barony created by the Writ of 23 Edw.III.
unless issued to this Baron in consequence
of having succeeded Hugh de St. Philibert
before mentioned in the Barony created by
the Writ of 27 Edw. I. became Extinct; in
which case it would be vested in the descendants and representatives of the said Hugh de
St. Philibert.

ST. QUINTIN.

Herbert de St. Quintin was Summoned 8 June, 22
Edw. I. 1294, but never afterwards; and for the reasons
expressed under " CLYVEDON," it is presumed that that
Writ cannot be considered as a regular Summons to Parliament; and consequently that there never was such a
Barony, although the Earls of Pembroke, whose ancestor
married the heir-general of this Herbert de St. Quintin,
styled themselves Barons of St. Quintin.

ST. VINCENT.

VISCOUNTS. EARL.

I. 1801.—I. 1797. 1. Sir John Jervis, K. B. Created Baron
Jervis of Meaford, co. Stafford, and
Earl of St. Vincent, 27 May, 1797;
Created Viscount St. Vincent of Meaford, co. Stafford, 21 April, 1801, with remainder, failing his issue male, to his nephew William Henry Ricketts, Esq. Captain
in his Majesty's Navy, son of Mary Ricketts
his sister, by William Henry Ricketts of the
Island of Jamaica, and the heirs male of his
body; failing which, to Edward Jervis Ricketts, Esq. Barrister-at-law, son of the said
Mary and William Henry Ricketts, and the
heirs male of his body; failing which the dignity of Viscountess St. Vincent of Meaford
aforesaid to Mary, Countess of Northesk
(sister of the aforesaid William and Edward
Ricketts) and of Viscount St. Vincent to her
heirs male, G. C. B.; ob. 1823, s. p. when the
Barony of Jervis and Earldom of St. Vincent

became **Extinct**; but the Viscountcy devolved, agreeably to the above limitation, on

II. 1823. 2. William Jervis Ricketts (assumed the name of)
Jervis, as nephew and heir, he being son and
heir male (William Henry, his elder brother,
having died s. p. m.) of William Henry Ricketts, Esq. by Mary, the sister of the last
Viscount. Present Viscount St. Vincent. ⊤

ST. WALERIE.

BARONS BY TENURE.

I. Will. I.   Ranulph de St. Walerie, held divers Lordships
at the General Survey co. Lincoln.

———

I. Steph.   1. Reginald de St. Walerie, Lord of Haseldene,
co. Gloucester; living 1164.
I. H. II.   2. Bernard de St. Walerie, s. and h.; ob. 1190.
III. Rich. I. 3. Thomas de St. Walerie, s. and h.; ob. 1219,
s. p. m. Annora, his sole dau. and heir, married, 1st, Robert de Dreux, and, 2dly, Henry,
Lord of Suilly.

———

Richard de St. Walerico, probably the nephew of the
last Baron, was summoned 8 June, 22 Edw. I. 1294, but
it is very doubtful if that Writ can be considered a regular Summons to Parl. Vide "CLIVEDON." He was
never afterwards Summoned to Parliament.

SALISBURY.

EARLS.

I. Steph.   1. Patrick D'Evereux; Created Earl of Salisbury
by the Empress Maud; ob. 1167.
II. 1167.   2. William D'Evereux, s. and h.; ob. 1196, s.p.m.
Ela, his dau. and heir, married
III. Ric. I.   William de Longespee, natural son of Hen. II.
who became Earl of Salisbury jure uxoris;
ob. 1226. William de Longespee, his son and
heir, claimed the Earldom, but Dugdale expressly says he was never allowed it. He
died in 1250, leaving a son William, who
died in 1256, s. p. m. and whose dau. and coheir, Margaret, commonly called Countess of
Salisbury, married Henry de Lacy, Earl of
Lincoln.

EARLS.

IV. 1337. 1. William de Montacute, III.-4th Baron Montacute ; Created Earl of Salisbury 16 March, 1337 ; ob. 1343.

V. 1343. 2. William de Montacute, s. and h. K. G. ; ob. 1397, s. p. s.

VI. 1397. 3. John de Montacute, Baron Montacute and Monthermer, nephew and heir, being s. and h. of John Baron Montacute, second son of William IV.-1st Earl ; Marshal of England ; beheaded and attainted anno 1400, when his honors became

Forfeited.

VII. 1409. 4. Thomas de Montacute, s. and h. ; he appears to have been restored to the Earldom as early as 11th of Henry IV. for on the 26th October in that year (1409) he was Summ. to Parl. as "Thomæ Comiti Sarum"; K. G. ; ob. 1428, s. p. m. Alice, his sole dau. and heir, having married

VIII. 1442. 1. Richard Nevill, 3d son of Ralph I.-1st Earl of Westmoreland, he was created Earl of Salisbury 4th May, 1442; Attainted in 1459, when his honors became Forfeited, but he appears to have been restored in 1460 ; Lord High Chamberlain ; K. G.; beheaded 1460.

IX. 1460. 2. Richard Nevill, Earl of Warwick, s. and h. K. G.; slain 1471, s. p. m. and being Attainted, his honors became

Forfeited.

X. 1472. 1. George Plantagenet, Duke of Clarence, brother of Edward IV. having married Isabel, eldest dau. and coheir of the last Earl, was created Earl of Warwick and Salisbury 25 March, 1472; executed and attainted 1477, when all his honors became

Forfeited.

XI. 1477. 1. Edward Plantagenet, son and heir apparent of Richard Duke of York (afterwards King Richard III.) by Ann Nevill, youngest dau. of Richard IX.-2d Earl of Salisbury, and Earl of Warwick ; Created Earl of Salisbury 1477 ; Created Prince of Wales and Earl of of Chester 1483 ; ob. 1484, s. p. when all his dignities became

𝔈𝔵𝔱𝔦𝔫𝔠𝔱.

COUNTESS.

1. 1513. Margaret Plantagenet, dau. and eventually sole heir, of George Duke of Clarence, the X.-1st Earl of Salisbury; Created Countess of Salisbury 14 Oct. 1513; she married Sir Richard Pole, K. G. by whom she had several children. Attainted 1539, and beheaded in 1541, when the title again became

𝔉𝔬𝔯𝔣𝔢𝔦𝔱𝔢𝔡.

EARLS.

XII. 1605. 1. Robert Cecil, 1st Viscount Cranborne; Created Earl of Salisbury 4 May, 1605, K. G.; Lord High Treasurer; ob. 1612.

XIII. 1612. 2. William Cecil, s. and h. K. G. ob. 1668.

XIV. 1668. 3. James Cecil, grandson and heir, being s. and h. of Charles Cecil (ob. v. p.) eldest son of the last Earl; K. G.; ob. 1683.

XV. 1683. 4. James Cecil, s. and h. ob. 1694.

XVI. 1694. 5. James Cecil, s. and h. ob. 1728.

XVII. 1728. 6. James Cecil, s. and h. ob. 1780.

MARQUESSES.

XVIII. 1780.—I. 1789. 7. James Cecil, s. and h.; Created Marquess of Salisbury Aug. 10, 1789, K. G.; ob. 1823.

XIX. 1823.—II. 1823. 8. James Brownlow William Cecil, s. and h. Present Marquess and Earl of Salisbury, Viscount Cranbourne, and Baron Cecil of Essingdon. ⟂

SALTERSFORD.

BARONS.

I. 1796. 1. James Stopford, 2d Earl of Courtown in Ireland; Created Baron Saltersford of Saltersford, co. Palatine of Chester, 7 June, 1796, K. P.; ob. 1810.

II. 1810. 2. James George Stopford, s. and h. Present Baron Saltersford; also Earl of Courtown, &c. in Ireland; K. P. ⟂

SAMPSON.

BARON BY WRIT.
I.   1299.   William Sampson; Summ. to Parl. from 29
Dec. 28 Edw. I. 1299, to 3 Nov. 34 Edw. I.
1306.   Dugdale gives no account of this Baron in his Baronage.

SANDON.

VISCOUNTCY, 19 July, 1809.

Vide HARROWBY.

SANDWICH.

EARLS.
I.   1660.   1. Sir Edward Montagu, K. G. (s. and h. of Sir
Sydney Montagu, younger brother of Henry
1st Earl of Manchester;) Created Baron Mon-
tagu of St. Neot's, Viscount Hinchinbroke,
both co. Huntingdon, and Earl of Sandwich,
co. Kent, 12 July, 1660; slain 1672.
II.   1672.   2. Edward Montagu, s. and h. ob. 1689.
III.   1689.   3. Edward Montagu, s. and h ob. 1729.
IV.   1729.   4. John Montagu, grandson and heir, being s.
and h. of Edward Richard Montagu (ob. v. p.)
eldest son of the last Earl; ob. 1792.
V.   1792.   5. John Montagu, s. and h. ob. 1814.
VI.   1814.   6. George John Montagu, s. and h. ob. 1818.
VII.   1818.   7. John William Montagu, s. and h.   Present
Earl of Sandwich, Viscount Hinchinbroke,
and Baron Montagu of St. Neot's. His Lordship is likewise one of the coheirs of the Baronies of St. John of Basing and of Poynings
created by the Writ of 42 Edw. III. *

SANDYS
OF OMBERSLEY.

BARONS.
I.   1743.   1. Samuel Sandys; Created Lord Sandys, Baron
of Ombersley, co. Worcester, 20 Dec. 1743;
ob. 1770.

---

* Vide p. 528.

BARONS.

II. 1770. 2. Edwin Sandys, s. and h.; ob. 1797, s. p. when the title became

Extinct.

BARONESS.

I. 1802. 1. Mary Hill, dau. and heir of the Hon. Martin Sandys, next brother of the last Baron, and widow of Arthur Hill, 2d Marquess of Downshire in Ireland, and 2d Earl of Hillsborough in England; Created Baroness Sandys of Ombersley, co. Worcester, June 15, 1802, with remainder to her second son, Arthur Moyes William Hill, and his younger brothers, and their heirs male successively; failing which, to her eldest son Arthur, present Marquess of Downshire, &c. and his heirs male. Present Baroness Sandys of Ombersley. ♉

SANDYS

OF THE VINE.

BARONS BY WRIT.

I. 1529. 1. William Sandys; Summ. to Parl. from 3 Nov. 21 Henry VIII. 1529, to 16 Jan. 33 Hen. VIII. 1542; Dugdale states that he was " advanced to the degree of a Baron of the Realm by the title of Lord Sands, 27 April, 1523," though there is no patent on record; K. G.; ob. 1542.

II. 1542. 2. Thomas Sandys, s. and h.; Summ. to Parl. from 14 June, 35 Henry VIII. 1543, to 5 Nov. 5 and 6 Philip and Mary, 1558; ob. ..

III. 15... 3. William Sandys, grandson and h. being s. and h. of Henry Sandys (ob. v. p.) eldest son of the last Baron; Summ. to Parl. from 8 May, 14 Eliz. 1572, to 14 Nov. 19 Jaq. I. 1621; ob. 1623.

IV. 1623. 4. William Sandys, s. and h.; he was never Summ. to Parl.; ob. 1629, s. p. when the Barony devolved on

V. 1629. 5. Henry Sandys, his half nephew and heir, being son and heir of Sir Edwin Sandys by Elizabeth Sandys, only daughter of William 3d Baron, and half sister of William the last Baron; he was never Summ. to Parl.; ob. 1644.

BARONS BY WRIT.

VI. 1644. 6. William Sandys, s. and h. Summ. to Parl. 8 May, 13 Car. II. 1661 ; ob. 1668, s. p.

VII. 1668. 7. Henry Sandys, brother and heir ; Summ. to Parl. 6 March, 31 Car. II. 1679, and 21 March, 32 Car. II. 1680 ; ob. .... s. p.

VIII. 167 . 8. Edwin Sandys, brother and heir ; he was never summoned to Parliament ; ob. circa 1700, s. p. leaving his six sisters his heirs, viz. Hester, wife of Humphrey Noy, whose heir general is Davies Giddy Gilbert, Esq. M. P. and who is consequently eldest coheir of this Barony ; Alathea, wife of Francis Goston, Esq. ; Mary, wife of Dr. Henry Savage ; Jane, wife of John Harris, Esq. ; Margaret, wife of Sir John Mill, Bart. ; and Margery, who married Sir Edmund Fortescue ; amongst whose descendants and representatives the Barony is now in ABEYANCE.

SARESBURIE.

BARONS BY TENURE.

I. Will. I. 1. Edward de Saresburie, son of Walter de Euris, or D'Evereux, Earl of Rosmar in Normandy, held divers Lordships at the Survey ; living 1119.

II. Steph. 2. Walter de Saresburie, s. and h. ob. ....

III. Steph. 3. Patric de Saresburie, or D'Evereux, s. and h. : Created Earl of Salisbury.

　　　　　　　　　　　Vide SALISBURY.

SAUNDERSON.

BARONS.

I. 1714. James Saunderson, Viscount Castleton in Ireland ; Created Baron Saunderson of Saxby, co. Lincoln, ... 1714 ; Created Viscount Castleton in 1716.　Vide CASTLETON.

　　　　Extinct 1723.

SAUNZAVER.

Ralph Saunzaver was summoned 8 June, 22 Edw. I. 1294; but, for the reasons assigned under "CLYVEDON," it is very doubtful if that Writ can be considered as a regular Summons to Parliament. Neither this Ralph, nor any of his descendants were ever summoned to Parliament.

SAVAGE.

VISCOUNTS.

I. 1626. 1. Sir Thomas Savage, 2d Bart.; Created Viscount Savage of Rocksavage, co. Chester, 6 Nov. 1626 ; ob. 1635.

II. 1635. 2. John Savage, s. and h.; succeeded his maternal grandfather as Viscount Colchester and Earl Rivers in 1639.   Vide RIVERS.
Extinct 1728.

SAVERNAKE.

VISCOUNTCY, 17 July, 1821.
Vide AILESBURY.

SAVILE.

BARONS.

I. 1628. 1. John Savile; Created Baron Savile of Pontefract, co. York ; 21 July, 1628 ; ob. 1630.

II. 1630. 2. Thomas Savile, s. and h.; Created Viscount Savile in Ireland 25 May, 1644; Created Earl of Sussex.   Vide SUSSEX.
Extinct 1671.

SAVILE
OF ELANDE.

BARONY, 13 January, 1668. Vide HALIFAX.
Extinct 1700.

SAY.

BARONS BY TENURE.

I. Will. I.   1. Picot de Say, living 1088; the next who occurs is

II. Will.II.   2. Ingelram de Say, living 1138; he was succeeded by

III. Steph.   3. William de Say; he married Beatrix, sister and heir of Geoffrey de Mandeville, Earl. of Essex; ob. ....

IV. Rich.I.   4. Geoffrey de Say, 2d son and heir male (William the eldest having died v. p. s. p. m.); ob. 1214.

V. John.   5. Geoffrey de Say, s. and h. He was one of the celebrated 25 Barons appointed to enforce the observance of MAGNA CHARTA; ob. 1230.

VI. H.III.   6. William de Say, s. and h. ob. 1272.

VII. Edw.I.   7. William de Say, s. and h. Summoned 8th June, 22 Edw. I. 1294; but it is very doubtful if that Writ can be considered as a regular Summons to Parliament; vide "CLYVEDON;" ob. 1295.

BY WRIT.

I.. 1313.   8. Geoffrey de Say, s. and h.; Summ. to Parl. from 26 July, 7 Edw. II. 1313, to 14 May, 14 Edw. II. 1321; ob. 1322.

II. 1322.   9. Geoffrey de Say, s. and h.; Summ. to Parl. from 25 Feb. 16 Edw. III. 1342, to 15 July, 27 Edw. III. 1353; ob. 1359.

III. 1359.   10. William de Say, s. and h.; Summ. to Parl. from 14 Aug. 36 Edw. III. 1362, to 4 Oct. 47 Edw. III. 1373; ob. circa ....

IV. 1375.   11. John de Say, s. and h.; ob. infra ætatem 1382, s. p. leaving Elizabeth his sister and heir; she married, 1st, John de Falvesley, who was Summ. to Parl. from 20 Aug. 1383, to 8 Sept. 1392, and died s. p. m. in that year; and, 2dly, Sir William Heron, who was Summ. to Parl. from 13 Nov. 1393, to 25 Aug. 1404, when he died s. p. Although it is evident both her husbands were summoned jure uxoris, yet as they were never styled Barons Say in the Writs of Summons, they are not placed under this title. Elizabeth Lady

Say died in 1399 s.p. leaving the descendants of her aunts,
viz. Idonea,* who married Sir John Clinton, and whose
heir-general, the present Lord Clinton is the eldest coheir
of this Barony, and Joan, the wife of Sir William Fienes,
sisters of William III.-10th Baron her heirs, among whose
descendants and representatives this Barony is in ABEYANCE.

SAY AND SELE.

BARONS BY WRIT.

I.   1447. 1. James Fienes, 2d son of Sir William Fienes,
BY PATENT. son and heir of Sir William Fienes, by
I. 1447. Joan de Say above-mentioned, youngest sister,
        of William III.-10th Baron Say; Summ. to
        Parl. as "Jacobo de Fynes, Militi, Domino de
        Say and Sele," from 3 March, 27 Henry VI.
        1447, to 23 Sept. 28 Henry VI. 1449; Created
        Lord Baron Say and Sele 6 March, 1447,
        by Patent, with remainder to the heirs male
        of his body; Lord High Treas.; ob. 1450.

II. 1450. 2. William Fienes, s. and h.; Summ. to Parl. as
        "Willielmo Fenys, Militi, Domino Say," or
        as "Willielmo Fenys de Say," from 13 April,
        29 Henry VI. 1451, to 7 Sept. 9 Edw. IV.
        1469; slain 1471.

III. 1471. 3. Henry Fienes, s. and h.; he was never Summ.
        to Parl.; ob. 1476.

IV. 1476. 4. Richard Fienes, son and heir; he was never
        Summ. to Parl.; ob. infra ætatem, 14..

V. 14... 5. Edward Fienes, s. and h.; he was never Summ.
        to Parl. or used the title; ob. 1529.

VI. 1529. 6. Richard Fienes, s. and h.; he was never Summ.
        to Parl.; ob. 1573.

VII. 1573. 7. Richard Fienes, s. and h.; he obtained a con-
        firmation of the title of Baron Say and Sele

---

* On the creation of Sir James Fienes, to the title of Lord
Say and Sele in 1447, John Lord Clinton, the representative of
Idonea de Say, the other sister and coheir of William III.-10th
Baron Say, relinquished all claim to the Barony and Arms of
Say. How far this resignation affects the right of his representatives to the moiety of this Barony has not been determined; but
the decisions relative to the surrender of dignities cited in p. 529,
render it almost certain, that the act of the said Lord Clinton
does not affect the interest of his representative in this dignity.

BARONS BY WRIT
AND PATENT. to him and the heirs male of his body 9 Aug.
1603; ob. 1613.

VISCOUNTS.

VIII. 1613.—I. 1624. 8. William Fienes, s. and h.; Created
Viscount Say and Sele 7 July, 1624;
ob. 1662.

IX. 1662.—II. 1662. 9. James Fienes, s. and h.; ob. 1674,
s. p. m. when the Barony created
by the Writ of Summons of 3d
March, 1447, fell into ABEYANCE
between his two daughters and
coheirs, viz. Elizabeth, wife of Sir
John Twisleton; and Frances, wife
of Andrew Ellis, Esq. (vide infra);
but the Viscountcy, and the Barony
created by Patent 6 March, 1447,

BARONS BY   and confirmed by the patent of 9
PATENT.   Aug. 1603*, devolved on

X.   1674.—III. 1674. 10. William Fienes, as nephew and
heir male, being s. and h. of Na-
thaniel Fienes (ob. vita fratris),
next brother of the last Viscount;
ob. 1696.

XI.   1696.—IV. 1696. 11. Nathaniel Fienes, s. and h. ob.
1710, s. p.

XII. 1710.—V. 1710. 12. Laurence Fienes, cousin and heir,
being s. and h. of John Fienes, 3d
son of William 1st Viscount; ob.
1742, s. p.

XIII. 1742.—VI. 1742. 13. Richard Fienes, cousin and heir
male, being s. and h. of Richard,
eldest son of Richard Fienes, 4th
son of William 1st Viscount; ob.
1781, s. p. when the Viscountcy
and the Barony being both limited
to heirs male became
Extinct.

---

* The precedency of this Barony was manifestly 6th March,
1447, as James Fienes, 1st Baron Say and Sele, is stated by
Dugdale, vol. ii. p. 245, to have been summoned to Parl. on the
3d of March, 1447; and three days afterwards "he was advanced
to the degree and dignity of a Baron of this Realm, by the same
itle of Lord Say and Sele, *and to the heirs male of his body.*"
'ollins, however, does not mention such a remainder.

THE BARONY CREATED BY THE WRIT OF SUMMONS OF 3D
MARCH, 27 HEN. VI. 1447, WAS IN 1781 CLAIMED BY
BARONS BY WRIT.

X. 1781. 10. Thomas Twisleton, as heir general of James
IX.-9th Baron Say and Sele, the 2d Viscount;
being s. and h. of John Twisleton, eldest son
of Fienes Twisleton, s. and h. of Geo. Twisleton, by Cecil his wife, dau. and heir of Sir John
Twisleton, of Barley, co. York, by Elizabeth
Fienes, his wife, eldest dau. and coheir, and
the only daughter whose issue then survived
(the issue of Frances, the other dau. and coheir, having failed in 1715) of James Fienes,
IX.-9th Baron Say and Sele, and 2d Viscount, which claim being allowed by the
House of Peers, he was Summ. to Parl. 29
June, 1781, as Baron Say and Sele; ob.
1788.

XI. 1788. 11. Gregory William Twisleton, s. and h. Present
Baron Say and Sele, and youngest coheir of
one moiety of the Barony of Say created by
the Writ of 7 Edward II. ⊤

SAY

OF RICHARD'S CASTLE.

BARON BY TENURE.
I. H. II. Hugh de Say, son of Hugh Fitz-Osborn, presumed to have assumed the name of Say
from Eustatia de Say, his mother; Lord of
Richard's Castle, co. Hereford, as heir to his
brother, Osbert Fitz-Hugh, temp. Henry II.
ob. circa 1195, s. p. m. His dau. and sole
heir, married Hugh de Ferrers.

SAY

BARON BY TENURE.   OF CLUN.
h Steph. Helyas de Say, or the same family as the
above Baron; Lord of Clun, co. Salop; ob.
s. p. m. Isabel, his sole dau. and heir, married, first, William Boterell, and, 2dly, William Fitz-Alan, to whom she conveyed the
Lordship of Clun.

P 3

SCALES.

BARONS BY TENURE.

I. Steph. 1. Hugh de Scales, Lord of Berkhampsted.
II. H. II. 2. Henry de Scales, s. and h. living 1167.
III. Ric. I. 3. Hugh de Scales, s. and b. ob.....
IV. John. 4. Henry de Scales, s. and h. ob. circa 1220, s. p.
V. H. III. 5. Geoffrey de Scales, brother and heir; ob. 1266,
of whom Dugdale says, "I have seen no
than than that Alianore, his widow, had the
wardship of his heir."

I. H. II. 1. Stephen de Scales, nephew of Hugh 1st Baron;
living 1165; to whom succeeded
II. Ric. I. 2. William de Scales, ob. circa 1207.
III. John. 3. Richard de Scales, s. and h.; ob. 1230, s. p. m.
leaving Lucia his daughter and heir.

I. H. III. John de Scales, of the same family as the
preceding Barons, Sheriff of Cambridgeshire
and Huntingdonshire in 1248 and 1259.

I. H. III. 1. Robert de Scales, the principal remaining
branch; ob. 1266.

BY WRIT.

I. 1299. 2. Robert de Scales, s. and h.; Summ. to Parl.
from 6 Feb. 27 Edw. I. 1299, to 22 Jan. 33
Edw. I. 1305; ob. 1305.
II. 1305. 3. Robert de Scales, s. and h.; Summ. to Parl.
from 3 Nov. 34 Edw. I. 1306, to 14 March,
15 Edw. II. 1322; ob. 1322.
III. 1322. 4. Robert de Scales, s. and h. Summ. to Parl.
from 25 Feb. 16 Edw. III. 1342, to 6 April,
43 Edw. III. 1369; ob. 1369.
IV. 1369. 5. Roger de Scales, s. and h. Summ. to Parl. from
28 Dec. 49 Edw. III. 1375, to 3 Sept. 9 Rich.
II. 1385; ob. 1386.
V. 1386. 6. Robert de Scales, s. and h. Summ. to Parl.
from 30 Nov. 20 Richard II. 1326, to 3 Oct.
2 Henry IV. 1400; ob. 1402.
VI. 1402. 7. Robert de Scales, s. and h. he was never Summ.
to Parl.; ob. 1418, s. p.
VII. 1418. 8. Thomas de Scales, brother and heir; Summ.
to Parl. from 13 Jan. 23 Hen. VI. 1445, to 9

Oct. 38 Henry VI. 1459; ob. 1460, s. p. m.
Elizabeth, his sole dau. and heir, married
first, Henry Bourchier, 2d son of Henry Earl
of Essex, who died s. p. and secondly,

BARON BY WRIT.

VIII. 1462. Anthony Widvile, son and heir apparent of
Richard 1st Earl Rivers; he was Summ. to
Parl. jure uxoris, as " Domino Scales," 22
Dec. 2 Edw. IV. 1462, 23 Feb. 2 Edw. IV.
1463, and 28 Feb. 5 Edw. IV. 1466, K. G.;
succeeded his father as 2d Earl Rivers in 1469;
beheaded 1483; ob. s. p.   Elizabeth Lady
Scales, his wife, having died before him, the
descendants of Margaret, wife of Sir Robert
Howard (ancestor, by his *second* wife, of the
Dukes of Norfolk); and of Elizabeth, who
married Sir Roger de Felbrigge, the sisters of
Roger IV.–5th Baron Scales became her heirs,
and among their descendants and representatives the Barony has since been in ABEY-
ANCE.

SCARBOROUGH.

EARLS.

I. 1690. 1. Richard Lumley, 1st Viscount Lumley; Created Earl of Scarborough 15 April, 1690;
ob. 1721.

II. 1721. 2. Richard Lumley, s. and h. K. G.; ob.1740,s.p.

III. 1740. 3. Thomas Lumley (assumed the name of)
Saunderson, brother and heir, K. B.; ob.
1752.

IV. 1752. 4. Richard Lumley Saunderson, s. and h. ob.
1782.

V. 1782. 5. George Augusta Lumley Saunderson, s. and
h. ob. 1807, s.p.

VI. 1807. 6. Richard Lumley Saunderson, brother and heir.
Present Earl of Scarborough, Viscount and
Baron Lumley, also Viscount Lumley in
Ireland. ═══

SCARSDALE.

EARLS.

I.　1645. 1. Francis Leke, 1st Baron Deincourt of Sutton; Created Earl of Scarsdale 11 Nov. 1645; ob. 1655.

II.　1655. 2. Nicholas Leke, s. and h. ob. 1680.

III.　1680. 3. Robert Leke, s. and h. ob. 1707, s. p.

IV.　1707. 4. Nicholas Leke, nephew and heir, being son and heir of Richard Leke, next brother of the last Earl; ob. 1736, s. p. when all his honors became

BARONS.　　　𝖤xtinct.

I.　1761. 1. Sir Nathaniel Curzon, 5th Bart; Created Baron Scarsdale, co. Derby, 9 April, 1761; ob. 1804.

II.　1804. 2. Nathaniel Curzon, s. and h. Present Baron Scarsdale and a Baronet. ⊤

SCHOMBERG.

DUKES.

I.　1689. 1. Frederick de Schomberg; Created Baron Teyes and Earl of Brentford, co. Middlesex, Marquess of Harwich, co. Essex, and Duke of Schomberg, 10 April, 1689, with remainder to his second son Charles de Schomberg, and his issue male; failing which, to Memhardt de Schomberg his eldest son, and his issue male, K. G.; ob. 1690.

II.　1690. 2. Charles de Schomberg, 2d son and heir to the above titles agreeable to the said limitation; ob. 1693, s. p.

III.　1693. 3. Meinhardt Schomberg, 1st Duke of Leinster in Ireland, brother and heir, being son and heir of Frederick 1st Duke. K. G.; ob. 1719, s. p. m. when all his titles became

𝖤xtinct.

SCOTENI.

BARONS BY TENURE.

I. Hen. II. 1. Lambert de Scoteni; held ten Knight's fees 1168; ob. circa 1195, s. p. m. leaving Berta and Aumirais his sisters and heirs.

II. John. 2. William de Scoteni, son of Berta, dau. of the last Baron; gave LX marks for that portion of the lands of the said Lambert, which belonged to him jure matris; living 1212; ob. s. p. m. leaving his three daughters his heirs.

I. John. 1. Thomas de Scoteni, descended from Aumirais, the other sister of Lambert the first Baron; held divers Knight's fees with the above William in 1212; ob. 1246.

II. H. III. 2. Peter de Scoteni, s. and h. ob. 1277, and of whom nothing farther is known.

SCROPE

OF BOLTON.

BARONS BY TENURE.

I. H. II. 1. Robert le Scrope; certified three Knight's fees, co. Gloucester, 1165.

II. John. 2. Henry le Scrope, s. and h. living 1217.

III. H. III. 3. William le Scrope, son and heir; living 1295. Henry le Scrope, his son and heir, was appointed Justice of the Common Pleas 17 Nov. 3 Edw. II. 1309, and was Summ. to Parl. *ex officio*, from 8 to 19 Edw. II.; he died circa 1336, leaving William le Scrope his son and heir, who was never summoned to Parl. and died s. p. 1345, when he was succeeded in

BY WRIT. his lands by his brother and heir

I. 1371. 1. Richard le Scrope; who was Summ. to Parl. from 8 Jan. 44 Edw. III. 1371, to 14 August, 3 Hen. IV. 1402; ob. 1403.

II. 1403. 2. Roger le Scrope, s. and h. Summ. to Parl. 20 Oct. and 23 Nov. 5 Hen. IV. 1403; he married Margaret, dau. and coheir of Robert Baron Tiptoft, ob. 1404.

BARONS BY WRIT.

III. 1404. 3. Richard le Scrope, s. and h.; he was never
Summ. to Parl.; ob. 1420.

IV. 1420. 4. Henry le Scrope, s. and h. Summ. to Parl. from
3 Dec. 18 Hen. VI. 1441, to 26 May, 33 Hen.
VI. 1455, as " Henrico le Scrope de Bolton,
Chev^r;" ob. 1459.

V. 1459. 5. John le Scrope, s. and h. Summ. to Parl. from
30 July, 38 Hen. VI. 1460, to 16 Jan. 12
Hen. VII. 1497, K. G. though according to
Dugdale he died 12 July, 1494.

VI. 1494. 6. Henry le Scrope, s. and h.; he was never
Summ. to Parl.; ob. 1506.

VII. 1506. 7. Henry le Scrope, s. and h. Summ. to Parl.
from 23 Nov. 6 Hen. VIII 1514 *, to 9 Aug.
31 Hen. VIII. 1529; ob. circa 1532.

VIII.1532. 8. John le Scrope, s. and h. Summ. to Parl. from
5 Jan. 25 Hen. VIII. 1533, to 5 Jan. 6 Edw.
VI. 1553; ob. circa 1554.

IX. 1554. 9. Henry le Scrope, s. and h. Summ. to Parl.
from 21 Oct. 2 and 3 Ph. and M. 1555, to 4
Feb. 31 Eliz. 1589; ob. 1592.

X. 1592. 10. Thomas le Scrope, s. and h. Summ. to Parl.
from 19 Feb. 35 Eliz. 1593, to 6 Oct. 8 Jac. I.
1610, K. G.; ob. circa 1612.

XI. 1612. 11. Emanuel le Scrope, s. and h. Summ. to Parl.
from 5 April, 12 Jac. I. 1614, to 17 May,
1 Car. I. 1625; Created Earl of Sunderland
19 June, 1627; ob. 1627, s. p. l. when the
Barony devolved on the issue and representatives of Mary, only dau. of Henry IX Baron;
she married William Bowes, Esq. and it continued vested in her descendants until 1815,
when the issue of all the other coheirs having failed, the Barony devolved on Charles
Jones, Esq. he being heir-general of the body
of Henry IX. Baron, though he has never
urged his claim to the dignity.   Mr. Jones

---

* In Dugdale's Lists of Summons he is described as *Richard*
le Scrope in the 6th and 7th Hen. VIII.; but probably this is an
error in transcribing the List from the Rolls of those years.

is likewise eldest coheir of the Barony of Tiptoft, created by the Writ of 10 March, 1 Edw. II. 1308; and coheir of one moiety of the Barony of Badlesmere.

SCROPE

OF MASHAM AND UPSAL.

BARONS BY WRIT.

I. 1342. 1. Henry le Scrope, first cousin of Richard I.-1st Baron Scrope of Bolton; Summ. to Parl. from 25 Feb. 16 Edw. III. 1342, to 7 Sept. 15 Rich. II. 1391, as " Henrico le Scrope;" ob. 1391.

II. 1391. 2. Stephen le Scrope, s. and h. Summ. to Parl. from 23 Nov. 16 Rich. II. 1392, to 1 Jan. 7 Hen. IV. 1406; ob. 1406.

III. 1406. 3. Henry le Scrope, s. and h. Summ. to Parl. from 26 Aug. 8 Henry IV. 1408, to 26 Sept. 2 Hen. V. 1414, as " Henrico le Scrope de Masham;" beheaded and attainted (ob. s. p.) 1415, when his honors became

𝕱𝖔𝖗𝖋𝖊𝖎𝖙𝖊𝖉.

IV. 1421. 4. John le Scrope, brother and heir. He appears to have obtained a restoration to his brother's honors and inheritance in 1421; Summoned to Parl. from 7 January, 4 Henry VI. 1426, to 26 May, 33 Hen. VI. 1455, as " Johanni le Scrope de Masham;" ob. 1455.

V. 1455. 5. Thomas le Scrope, s. and h. Summ. to Parl. from 9 Oct. 38 Hen. VI. 1459, to 19 August, 12 Edw. IV. 1472, as " Thomæ le Scrope de Masham;" ob. 1475.

VI. 1475. 6. Thomas le Scrope, s. and h. Summ. to Parl. from 15 Nov. 22 Edw. IV. 1482, to 12 Aug. 7 Hen. VII. 1492, as " Thomæ le Scrope de Masham;" ob. 1494, leaving Alice his dau. and heir, then 13 years of age; she became the second wife of Henry Lord Scrope of Bolton; but died s. p. s. 1501, when this Barony devolved on her uncle and heir,

VII. 1501. 7. Henry le Scrope, next brother of the last Baron; Summ to Parliament as " Henrico

BARONS BY WRIT.

    Scroope de Scroope et Upsall, Chl'r ;" 28 Nov.
3 Hen. VIII. 1511 ; ob. circa 1512, s.p.

VIII. 1512. 8. Ralph de Scrope, brother and heir ; he was
never Summ. to Parl. though he is errone-
ously said by Dugdale in his Baronage to
have been so summoned 6 Hen. VIII. ; ob.
1515, s. p.

IX. 1515. 9. Geoffrey le Scrope, brother and heir ; he was
never Summ. to Parliament ; ob. 1517, s. p.
leaving his three sisters, viz. Alice, wife of
Thomas Strangways ; Mary, wife of Sir
Cristopher Danby, Knt.; and Elizabeth, wife
of Sir Ralph Fitz-Randolph, Knt. or their
issue his next heirs ; among whose descendants and representatives this Barony is in
ABEYANCE.

SEAFORTH.

BARON.

I.   1797. 1. Francis Humberstone Mackenzie (descended
from Kenneth 3d Earl of Seaforth in Scotland, whose title was forfeited in 1715) ;
Created Lord of Seaforth, Baron Mackenzie
of Kintail, co. Ross, 26 Oct. 1797 ; ob. 1814,
s. p. m. when the title became
        Extinct.

SEAHAM.

Viscountcy, 8 July, 1823.

                    Vide VANE.

SEGRAVE.

BARONS BY TENURE.

I. H. II. 1. Gilbert de Segrave, Lord of Segrave, co. Leicester, temp. Hen. II.; living 1198.

II. John. 2. Stephen de Segrave, s. and h. ob. 1241.

III. H.III. 3. Gilbert de Segrave, s. and h. ob. circa 1254.

BY WRIT.

I.   1264. 4 Nicholas de Segrave, s. and h. Summ. to Parl.
24 Dec. 49 Henry III. 1264, and 24 June, 23
Edw. I. 1295 ; ob. 1295.

BARONS BY WRIT.

II.   1295. 5. John de Segrave, s. and h. Summ. to Parl.
from 26 August, 24 Edw. I. 1296, to 6 May,
18 Edw. II. 1325; ob. 1325.

III. 1325. 6. John de Segrave, grandson and heir, being son
and heir of Stephen de Segrave (ob. v. p.)
eldest son of the last Baron; Summ. to Parl.
from 29 Nov. 10 Edward III. 1336, to 15 Nov.
25 Edw. III.1351; he married Margaret Plantagenet, dau.
and eventually sole heir of Thomas de Brotherton, Earl
of Norfolk, younger son of King Edward I.; ob. 1353,
s. p. m. Elizabeth, his sole daughter and heir married
John IV.-10 Baron Mowbray, whose son Thomas was
created Duke of Norfolk, in which title this Barony,
together with that of Mowbray, continued merged until
the death of John IV.-4th Duke of Norfolk, when they
devolved on his daughter and heir, Ann, on whose death,
s. p. the descendants of Margaret and Isabel, sisters of
John II.-2d Duke of Norfolk, became her heirs, between
whose representatives (viz. the present Earl of Berkeley,
as heir of the said Isabel, and the Barons Petre and
Stourton as heirs-general of the said Margaret) this Barony is now in ABEYANCE.   Vide MOWBRAY.

SEGRAVE

OF ——

BARON BY WRIT.

I.   1295.   Nicholas de Segrave, 2d son of Nicholas I.-4th
Baron Segrave; Summoned to Parliament
as " Nicholao de Segrave, Juniori," from 24
June, 23 Edw. I. 1295, to 26 Jan. 25 Edw.
I. 1297, and as "Nicholao de Segrave" from thence to
25 May, 14 Edward I. 1321; ob. 1322, s. p. m. Maud, his
only daughter and heir married Edmund de Bohun; in
whose descendants and representatives this Barony is now
vested.

SELSEY.

BARONS.

I.   1790. 1. Sir James Peachey, 4th Bart.; Created Baron
Selsey of Selsey, co. Sussex, 13 August, 1790;
ob. 1808.

II. 1808. 2. Henry John Peachey, s. and h. Present Baron
Selsey, and a Baronet. ═

SETRINGTON.

BARONY, 6 October, 1613—Extinct 1624.
BARONY, 9 August, 1675.
　　　　　Vide RICHMOND.

SEYMOUR.

BARONS.
I.　1547.　1. Edward Seymour. IX.-1st Earl of Hertford;
Created 15 Feb. 1547, Baron Seymour, with
remainder to the heirs male of his body by
Ann his second wife; remainder to Edward
Seymour his son by Catherine his first wife *,
,"whereby," as the King declares in the Patent, the name of that family " from which
his most beloved mother Jane, late Queen
of England, drew her beginning, might not
be clouded by any higher title or colour
of dignity;" Created Duke of Somerset, with
the same remainder the next day; K. G.;
Lord Protector ; beheaded and att ainted
1552, when all his honors became
　　　　　Forfeited.

II.　1660.　2. William Seymour, 1st Marquess of Herfford,
and heir agreeable to the above limitation of
the Barony of Seymour and Dukedom of
Somerset, was restored to those titles by Act
of Parliament in 1660; and this Barony has
since been merged in the Dukedom of Somerset.　　　　　　Vide SOMERSET.

SEYMOUR
OF SUDLEY.

BARON.
I.　1547.　Thomas Seymour, younger brother of the Protector; Created Baron Seymour of Sudley,
co. Gloucester, 16 Feb. 1547; Lord High

---

* Vide a Note on the effect of this singular limitation under
HERTFORD, p. 321.

Admiral; K. G.; attainted and beheaded 1549 (ob. s. p.) when his honors became
Forfeited.

SEYMOUR

BARONS.   OF TROUBRIDGE.

I.   1641. 1. Francis Seymour, next brother of William I. Marquess of Hertford, and VII.-2d Duke of Somerset; Created Baron Seymour of Troubridge, co. Wilts, 19 Feb. 1641; ob. 1664.

II. 1664. 2. Charles Seymour, s. and h. ob. 1665.

III. 1665. 3. Francis Seymour, s. and h. succeeded his kinsman, John Seymour, as XIV.-5th Earl of Hertford and X.-5th Duke of Somerset in 1675. This Barony continued merged in the Dukedom of Somerset until the death of Algernon Seymour, XII.-7th Duke of Somerset, and 5th Baron Seymour of Troubridge, s. p. in 1750, when it became
Extinct.

SHAFTESBURY.

EARLS.

I.   1672. 1. Anthony Ashley Cooper, 1st Baron Ashley; Created Baron Cooper of Pawlett, co. Somerset, and Earl of Shaftesbury, 23 April, 1672; Lord Chancellor; ob. 1683.

II. 1683. 2. Anthony Ashley Cooper, s. and h. ob. 1699.

III. 1699. 3. Anthony Ashley Cooper, s. and h ob. 1713.

IV. 1713. 4. Anthony Ashley Cooper, s. and h. ob. 1771.

V.   1771. 5. Anthony Ashley Cooper, s. and h. ob. 1811, s. p. m.

VI. 1811. 6. Cropley Ashley Cooper, brother and heir. Present Earl of Shaftesbury, Baron Ashley, Baron Cooper, and a Baronet. ⚓

SHEFFIELD

OF BUTTERWIKE.

BARONS.

1.   1547. 1. Edmund Sheffield; Created Baron Sheffield of Butterwike, co. Lincoln, 16 Feb. 1547; ob. 1548.

BARONS.

II.   1548. 2. John Sheffield, s. and h. ob. 1569.

III. 1569. 3. Edmund Sheffield, s. and h. Created Earl of
               Mulgrave 7 Feb. 1626, K. G.

                                        Vide MULGRAVE.

                   𝕰𝖝𝖙𝖎𝖓𝖈𝖙 1735.

SHEFFIELD

OF SHEFFIELD.

BARONS.

I.   1802. 1. John Baker Holroyd, 1st Baron Sheffield in
               Ireland; Created Baron Sheffield of Sheffield,
               co. York, 29 July, 1802; Created Earl of Shef-
               field in Ireland 1816; ob. 1821.

II.   1821. 2. George Augustus Frederick Charles Holroyd,
               s. and h. Present Baron Sheffield ; also Earl
               of Sheffield, &c. in Ireland,

SHEPEY.

COUNTESS.

I.   1680.   Elizabeth Bayning, sister and at length co-
       •   heir of Paul Viscount Bayning, and widow of
              Francis Lennard, XIII.-13th Baron Dacre.,
              Created Countess of Shepey for life, 6 Sept.
              1680; ob. 1690, when the title became
                   𝕰𝖝𝖙𝖎𝖓𝖈𝖙.

SHERARD.

VISCOUNT.

I.   1718.   Bennet Sherard, 1st Baron Harborough in
              England, and 3d Baron Sherard in Ireland ;
              Created Viscount Sherard of Stapleford, co.
              Leicester, 31st Oct. 1718, with remainder to
              his issue male ; Created Earl of Harborough,
              with a special remainder, 8 May, 1719; ob.
              1732, s. P. when this Viscountcy became
                   𝕰𝖝𝖙𝖎𝖓𝖈𝖙.

SHERBORNE.

BARONS.

I. 1784. 1. James Dutton; Created Baron Sherborne of Sherborne, co. Gloucester, 20 May, 1784; ob. 1820.

II. 1820. 2. John Dutton, s. and h. Present Baron Sherborne. ⚓

SHINGAY.

BARON.

I. 1697. Edward Russell, nephew of William VII.-5th Earl, and IV.-5th Duke of Bedford; Created Baron of Shingay (or Baron Russell of Shingay), co. Cambridge, Viscount Barfleur, and Earl of Orford, 7th May, 1697, with remainder to his issue male; failing which, of the dignity of Baron Shingay (or Russell of Shingay) to the issue male of Letitia, his eldest sister; ob. 1727, s. p. when all his honors (his said sister Letitia having died s.p. m.) became

𝔈𝔵𝔱𝔦𝔫𝔠𝔱.

SHREWSBURY.

EARLS

I. 1066. 1. Roger de Montgomery; Created Earl of Shrewsbury and Arundel, &c. by William the Conqueror; ob. 1094.

II. 1094. 2. Hugh de Montgomery, 2d son; succeeded to the Earldom; ob. 1098, s. p.

III. 1098. 3. Robert de Belesme, brother and heir, and eldest son of Roger 1st Earl; divested of the Earldom circa 1102.

IV. 1442. 1. John Talbot, VI.-12th Baron Talbot; also Baron Strange of Blackmere by descent, and Baron Furnival jure uxoris; Created Earl of Shrewsbury 20 May, 1442; Created Earl of Wexford and Earl of Waterford in Ireland 17 July, 1446; Lord Lieut. of Ireland 1446, K. G.; ob. 1453.

V. 1453. 2. John Talbot, s. and h. Lord Treasurer, K. G.; ob. 1460.

Q 3

EARLS.

VI. 1460. 3. John Talbot, s. and h. ob. 1473.

VII. 1473. 4. George Talbot, s.and h. K. G.; ob. 1541.

VIII. 1541. 5. Francis Talbot, s. and b. K. G.; ob. 1560.

IX. 1560. 6. George Talbot, s. and h. Earl Marshal, K. G.; ob. 1590.

X. 1590. 7. Gilbert Talbot, s. and b. K. G.; ob. 1616, s. p. m. when the Baronies of Talbot, Furnival, and Strange of Blackmere, fell into ABEYANCE between his three daughters and co-heirs; but the Earldoms of Shrewsbury, Wexford, and Waterford devolved on

XI. 1616. 8. Edward Talbot, his brother and heir male; ob. 1618, s. p.

XII. 1618. 9. George Talbot, cousin and heir male, being son and heir of John, eldest son of John, son and heir of John, son of Sir Gilbert Talbot of Grafton, 2d son of John V.-2d Earl; ob. 1630, s. p.

XIII. 1630. 10. John Talbot, nephew and heir, being son and heir of John Talbot, next brother of the last Earl; ob. 1653.

XIV. 1653. 11. Francis Talbot, s. and b. ob. 1667.

DUKE.

XV. 1667.—I. 1694. 12. Charles Talbot, s. and h. Created Marquess of Alton, co. Stafford, and Duke of Shrewsbury 30 April, 1694; Lord High Treasurer; K.G.; ob. 1718, s. p. when the Marquisate of Alton and this Dukedom became Extinct; but the Earldoms of Shrewsbury, and of Waterford and Wexford in Ireland, devolved on

XVI. 1718. 13. Gilbert Talbot, his first cousin and heir male, being son and heir of Gilbert Talbot, younger son of John XIII.-10th Earl; ob. 1743.

XVII. 1743. 14. George Talbot, nephew and heir, being son and heir of George, next brother of the last Earl; ob. 1787, s. p.

XVIII. 1787. 15. Charles Talbot, nephew and heir, being son and heir of Charles, next brother of George last Earl. Present Earl of Shrewsbury, also Earl of Wexford and Waterford in Ireland. ═

SIDMOUTH.

VISCOUNT.

I. 1805. 1. Henry Addington ; Created Viscount Sidmouth of Sidmouth, co. Devon. 12 Jan. 1805. Present Viscount Sidmouth. ⊤

SILCHESTER.

BARON.

1. 1821. 1. Thomas Pakenham, 1st Earl of Longford in Ireland ; Created Baron Silchester, co. Southampton, 17 July, 1821. Present Baron Silchester ; also Earl of Longford, &c. in Ireland, K. P. ⊤

SNAWDON.

BARONY, 15 July, 1726—Merged in the Crown 1760.
Vide EDINBURGH.

SOMERHILL.

BARONY, 3d April, 1624—Extinct 1659.
Vide TUNBRIDGE AND ST. ALBANS.

SOMERIE.

BARONS BY TENURE.

I. Steph. 1. Roger de Somerie; living 1189. The next mentioned is

II. H. II. 2. John de Someri, who acquired the Barony of Dudley by marrying Hawyse, sister and heir of Gervase Paganell. Vide DUDLEY.

SOMERS.

BARONS.

I. 1697. 1. John Somers, created Lord Somers, Baron of Evesham, co. Worcester, 2 Dec. 1697 ; Lord Chancellor ; ob. 1716, s. p. when the title became

Extinct.

II. 1784. 1. Sir Charles Cocks, 1st Baronet, s. and h. of John Cocks, eldest surviving son of Charles

Cocks, by Mary, eldest sister and coheir of
the last Baron ; Created Lord Somers, Baron
of Evesham, co. Worcester, 17 May, 1784 ;
ob. 1806.

EARL.

1806.—I. 1821. 2. John Sommers Cocks, s. and h. Created
Viscount Eastnor, of Eastnor Cas-
tle, co. Hereford, and Earl Sommers,
17 July 1821.   Present Earl and
Baron Sommers, Viscount Eastnor,
and a Baronet. ⸤

SOMERSET.

EARLS.   MARQUESS.
I.   1397.—I.   1397. 1. John de Beaufort, eldest natural
son of John of Gaunt, Duke of
Lancaster (but legitimated by Act
of Parliament, with an exception against
any claim to the throne); Created Earl of
Somerset 1397, and Marquess of Dorset 29
Sept. 1397, which title he soon afterwards resigned ; and the same day, i. e. 29th Sept.
was Created Marquess of Somerset ; but he
always was styled Marquess of Dorset until
1st Hen. IV. when he was deprived of that
title, and was only considered as Earl of Somerset.   Restored to the Marquisate of Dorset 4 Hen. IV. but he was never styled Marquess of Somerset, which dignity was probably considered to have been cancelled. K.G.
Lord High Admiral ; ob. 1410.

II.   1410. 2. Henry de Beaufort, s. and h. ; ob. 1418, s. p.
DUKES.

III.   1418 —I.   1443. 3. John de Beaufort, brother and heir;
Created Earl of Kendal and Duke
of Somerset 1443; K. G.; ob. 1444,
s. p. m. (Margaret, his only daughter and heir, married Edmund
Earl of Richmond, and was by
him mother of King Henry VII.)
when the Dukedom of Somerset
and Earldom of Kendal became
Extinct, but the Earldom of Somerset devolved on

EARLS. DUKES.

IV. 1444.—II. 1448. 4. Edmund de Beaufort, Marquis of Dorset, as brother and heir male; Created Duke of Somerset 31 March 1448 ; Regent of France ; Lord High Constable; K. G. ; ob. 1455.

V. 1455.—III. 1455. 5. Henry de Beaufort, s. and h. beheaded 1463, (ob. s. P. L.) and being attainted, all his honours became 𝕱𝖔𝖗𝖋𝖊𝖎𝖙𝖊𝖉.

Edmund de Beaufort, brother and heir, is said to have been restored to his brother's honours in the 49th Henry VI. and to have attended that parliament; but his name does not appear in the list of summonses in that year, and his restoration is too doubtful a point to allow of his being considered to have possessed his brother's dignities ; beheaded 1471 ; ob. s. P. when, if the said honours had been restored to him, they would have become 𝕰𝖝𝖙𝖎𝖓𝖈𝖙; and being attainted, would again have been 𝕱𝖔𝖗𝖋𝖊𝖎𝖙𝖊𝖉, even had he left issue.

IV. 1496. 1. Edmund Tudor, 3d son of King Henry VII.; Created Duke of Somerset 1496 ; ob. 1499, infans, when the title became 𝕰𝖝𝖙𝖎𝖓𝖈𝖙.

V. 1525. 1. Henry Fits Roy, natural son of King Henry VIII.; Created Earl of Nottingham and Duke of Richmond and Somerset 18 June,1525; Admiral of England, K.G.; ob. 1536, s. P. when all his dignities became 𝕰𝖝𝖙𝖎𝖓𝖈𝖙.

VI. 1547. 1. Edward Seymour IX.-1st Earl of Hertford, brother-in-law of King Henry VIII. and uncle of King Edward VI.; Created Duke of Somerset 15th Feb. 1547, with remainder to his issue male by his second wife; failing which, to his issue male by his first wife; Lord Protector, K. G.; beheaded 1552; and being attainted, all his honors became 𝔣𝔬𝔯𝔣𝔢𝔦𝔱𝔢𝔡.

EARL.

VI. 1613. 1. Robert Carr, 1st Viscount Rochester; Created Baron of Brancepeth, co. Durham, and Earl of Somerset, 3d November, 1613; Lord Chamberlain, K. G.; ob. 1645, s. p. m. when his titles became 𝔈𝔵𝔱𝔦𝔫𝔠𝔱.

DUKES.

VII. 1660. 2. William Seymour, 1st Marquess, and XI.-2d Earl of Hertford; Restored to the Dukedom of Somerset and Barony of Seymour, by the reversal of the attainder of Edward VII.-1st. Duke, the Protector, 13 Sept. 1660, and confirmed by another Act, 20 Dec. 1661; he being eldest son of Edward Seymour (ob. v. p.) s. and h. of Edward X.-1st Earl of Hertford, eldest son of the said Duke by his *second* wife, and, agreeable to the Patent of creation of the Barony of Seymour and Dukedom of Somerset, heir to those dignities; K. G.; ob. 1660.

. VIII. 1660. 3. William Seymour, grandson and heir; being s. and h. of Henry Seymour (ob. v. p.) eldest son of the last Duke; ob. 1671, s. p.

IX. 1671. 4. John Seymour, uncle and heir, being 2d son of William VII.-2d Duke; ob. 1675, s. p.

X. 1675. 5. Francis Seymour, 3d Baron Seymour of Troubridge, cousin and heir, being s. and h. of Charles, 2d Baron, eldest son of Francis, 1st Baron Seymour of Troubridge, younger brother of William VII.-2d Duke of Somerset; ob. 1678, s. p.

XI. 1678. 6. Charles Seymour, brother and heir; he married Elizabeth, sole daughter and heir of Josceline, Earl of Northumberland; K. G.; ob. 1748.

XII. 1748. 7. Algernon Seymour, s. and h.; Created Earl of Northumberland, Egremont, &c.; ob. 1750, s. p. m. when the Earldom of Hertford, Viscountcy of Beauchamp, and Barony of Sey-

DUKES.

mour, of Troubridge, became **Extinct**; but the Barony of Seymour and Dukedom of Somerset devolved on,

XIII. 1750. 8. Sir Edward Seymour, 6th Baronet, he being heir male of Sir Edward Seymour, son and heir, by his *first* wife (all the male descendants of the *second* wife having failed), of Edward VI.-1st Duke the Protector; ob. 1757.

XIV. 1757. 9. Edward Seymour, s. and h.; ob. 1792, s. p.

XV. 1792. 10. Webb Seymour, brother and heir; ob. 1793.

XVI. 1793. 11. Edward Adolphus Seymour, s. and h.; present Duke of Somerset, Baron Seymour, and a Baronet. ☥

SONDES,

OF THROWLEY.

BARONY, 8th April 1676—**Extinct** 1709.

Vide FEVERSHAM.

SONDES,

OF LEES COURT.

VISCOUNTCY, 8 April 1676—**Extinct** 1709.

Vide FEVERSHAM.

VISCOUNTCY, 19th Oct. 1714—**Extinct** 1746.

Vide ROCKINGHAM.

BARONS.

I.   1760. 1. Lewis Monson, assumed the name of Watson, 2d son of John, 1st Baron Monson, by Margaret, dau. of Lewis, Earl of Rockingham, and III.-1st Viscount Sondes, and aunt of Thomas, 3d Earl of Rockingham, and last Viscount Sondes, of Lees Court, co. Kent; Created Baron Sondes, of Lees Court, co. Kent, 20th May 1760; ob. 1795.

II.   1795. 2. Lewis Thomas Watson, s. and h.; ob. 1806.

III.   1806. 3. Lewis Richard Watson, s. and h.; present Baron Sondes, of Lees Court.

SOUTHAMPTON.

EARLS.

I.   1537. 1. William Fitzwilliam (descended from the common ancestor of the present Earl Fitz-William); Created Earl of Southampton 18th

Oct. 1537 ; Admiral of England, K. G.; ob.
1543, s. p. when the title became

EARLS.   Extinct.

II.   1547. 1. Thomas Wriothesley, 1st Baron Wriothesley ;
          created Earl of Southampton 16th February,
          1547 ; Lord Chancellor, K. G. ; ob. 1550.

III. 1550. 2. Henry Wriothesley, s. and h. ; ob. 1581.

IV. 1581. 3. Henry Wriothesley, s. and b. attainted in 1598,
          when all his honors became forfeited ; re-
          stored in 1603 ; Created, by a new patent,
          dated 21st July, 1603, Earl of Southampton,
          with the same rights and privileges as he for-
          merly enjoyed, K. G. ; ob. 1624.

V.   1624. 4. Thomas Wriothesley, s. and b. K. G. ; ob
          1667, s. p. m. when all his titles became

                 Extinct.

COUNTESS.

1. 1670. 1. Barbara Villiers, dau. and heir of William Vis-
         count Grandison, and mistress of King Charles
         II.; Created Baroness Nonsuch, co. Surrey,
         Countess of Southampton, and Duchess of
         Cleveland, with remainder to Charles and
         George Fitz-Roy, her natural sons by the
         King, 3d August, 1670; ob. 1709.

EARLS.   DUKES.

VI. 1709.—I. 1674. 1. Charles Fitz-Roy, natural son of
                  King Charles II.; Created Baron of
                  Newbury, co. Berks, Earl of Chi-
                  chester, co. Sussex, and Duke of
                  Southampton, 10 Sept. 1674 ; suc-
                  ceeded his mother in the Duke-
                  dom of Cleveland and Earldom of
                  Southampton 1709; K. G. ; ob. 1730.

VII. 1730.—II. 1730. 2. William Fitzroy, s. and h. Duke of
                  Cleveland, and Duke and Earl of
                  Southampton; ob. 1774, s. p. when
                  all his honours became

BARONS.   Extinct.

I.   1780. 1. Charles Fitzroy, next brother of Augustus, 3d
         Duke of Grafton, and grandson of Henry
         Fitz-Roy, 1st Duke of Grafton, natural bro-
         ther of Charles, 1st Duke of Southampton ;

BARONS.

Created Baron of Southampton, co. Hants, 17 Oct. 1780; ob. 1797.

II. 1797. 2. George Ferdinand Fitz-Roy, s. and h.; ob. 1810.

III. 1810. 3. Charles Fitz-Roy, s. and h.; present Baron Southampton.

SPELLESBURY.

BARONY, 5 June, 1674—Extinct 1776.

Vide LITCHFIELD.

LE SPENCER.

Vide DESPENCER.

SPENCER

OF WORMLEIGHTON.

BARONS.

I. 1603. 1. Robert Spencer (said by some authorities to have been descended from a younger branch of the ancient Barons Despencer); Created Baron Spencer of Wormleighton, co. Warwick, 21 July 1603; ob. 1627.

II. 1627. 2. William Spencer, s. and h.; ob. 1636.

III. 1636. 3. Henry Spencer, s. and h.; Created Earl of Sunderland, 8 June, 1643.

Vide SUNDERLAND and MARLBOROUGH.

SPENCER

OF ALTHORP.

BARONS. VISCOUNTS. EARLS.

I. 1761.—I. 1761.—I. 1765. 1. John Spencer, eldest son of John Spencer, 3d son of Charles, 3d Earl of Sunderland, and 5th Baron Spencer of Wormleighton; Created Baron Spencer, of Althorp, co. Northampton, and Viscount Spencer of Althorp aforesaid, 3 April 1761; Created Viscount Althorp, co. Northampton, and Earl Spencer, 1 Nov. 1765; ob. 1783.

BARONS. VISCOUNTS. EARLS.

II. 1783.—II. 1783.—II 1783 2. George John Spencer, s. and
        h. ; present Baron, Vis-
        count and Earl Spencer, and
        Viscount Althorp, K.G.

STAFFORD.

BARONS BY TENURE.

L Will.I. 1.Robert de Stafford ; held numerous Lordships
   at the General Survey.

II. Hen.I. 2.Nicholas de Stafford, s. and h. ob. ....

III. H. II. 3.Robert de Stafford, s. and h. ob. circa 1176.

IV. H. II. 4.Robert de Stafford, s. and h. ob. s. p. leaving
    Milisent his sister and heir, who married
    Hervey Bagot ; their son

V. H.III. 5. Hervey, assumed the name of Stafford ; ob.1237.

VI. H.III. 6. Hervey de Stafford, s. and h. ; ob. 1241, s. p.

VII. H.III. 7. Robert de Stafford, brother and heir ; ob.1282.

VIII.Edw.I.8. Nicholas de Stafford, s. and h. ; ob. 1287.

BY WRIT.

I. 1299. 9. Edmund de Stafford, s. and h. Summ. to
    to Parl. from 6 Feb. 27 Edw. I. 1299, to 26
    Aug. 1 Edw. II. 1307, as " Edmundo Baroni
    Stafford ;" ob. 1308.

EARLS.

II. 1308—I. 1351. 10.Ralph de Stafford, s. and h. Summ.
       to Parl. from 14 Jan. 10 Edw. III.
       1337, to 25 Nov. 24 Edw. III.
       1350 ; Created Earl of Stafford
       5 March, 1351. He married
       Margaret, dau. and heir of Hugh
       de Audley II. Baron Audley, by
       Writ *, and (jure uxoris) Earl of
       Gloucester, by Elizabeth de Clare,
       grand-daughter of King Edw. I. ;
       K. G. ; ob. 1372.

III. 1372.—II. 1372. 11.Hugh de Stafford, s. and h. K. G. ;
       ob, 1386.

IV. 1386.—III. 1386. 12. Thomas de Stafford, s. and h. ; ob.
       1392, s. p.

V. 1392.—IV. 1392. 13. William de Stafford, brother and
       heir ; ob. 1395, s. p.

VI. 1385.—V. 1385. 14. Edmund de Stafford, brother and

---

* Vide p. 36.

heir, K. G. He married Ann
Plantagenet, dau. and heir of
Thomas of Woodstock, Duke of
Gloucester, younger son of King
Edw. III.; and was slain 1403.

VII. 1403.—VI. 1403. 15. Humphrey de Stafford, son and
heir; Created Duke of Bucking-
ham 14 Sept. 1444, K.G.; slain 1460.

VIII. 1460.—VII. 1460 16. Henry de Stafford, grandson and
heir; being s. and h. of Hum-
phrey (ob. v. p.) eldest son of the
last Earl; Duke of Buckingham;
Lord High Constable, K.G. beheaded 1483.

IX. 1483.—VIII.—1483. 17. Edward de Stafford, s. and h.
Duke of Buckingham, Lord High
Constable, K. G., beheaded 1521;
and, being attainted, all his ho-
BARONS. nours became 𝔉𝔬𝔯𝔣𝔢𝔦𝔱𝔢𝔡.

I. 1547. 1. Henry Stafford, s. and h. of Edward, the last
Baron and Earl of Stafford, and Duke of
Buckingham in 1547; it was enacted by Act of
Parliament 1 Edw. VI. " that the said Henry
Lord Stafford, and the heirs male of his body
coming, may be taken, and reputed as Lord
Stafford, with a seat and voice in Parliament as
a Baron; and further that the said Henry * be
restored in blood as son and heir of Edward late
Duke of Buckingham," &c. Summoned to
Parliament from 24 Nov. 2 Edw VI. 1548, to
5th Nov. 5 and VI. Ph. and Mary, 1558. He
married Ursula, dau. of Sir Richard Pole,
K. G. by Margaret Plantagenet, Countess of
Salisbury, dau. and heir of George, Duke of
Clarence, brother of King Edward IV. and
King Richard III.; ob. 1562.

---

* Dugdale states that he was restored in blood in 1522; but on
a reference to the authorised Collection of the Statutes it appears,
that, in 14 and 15 Hen. VIII. the Act in question was passed,
and which merely enabled the said Henry and Ursula his wife, and
the heirs of their bodies, to hold and enjoy certain estates granted
them by Letters Patent dated 20 Dec. 14 Hen. VIII. 1522.

BARONS.

II.   1562. 2. Edward Stafford, son and heir*; ob. 1603.

III. 1603. 3. Edward Stafford, s. and h.; ob. 1625.

IV.   1771. 4. Henry Stafford, grandson and heir, being s.
              and h. of Edward Stafford (ob. v. p.) eldest
              son of the last Baron; ob. 1637, infra ætatem,
              s. p. when the barony being limited to the
              heirs male of Henry Baron Stafford, in 1547,
              devolved on

V.   1637. 5. Roger Stafford, s. and h. of Richard, younger
              son of the said Henry, and who accordingly
              claimed it, but was unjustly denied the dig-
              nity on the ground of his poverty. He after-
              wards formally surrendered the Barony into
              the King's hands, and dying unmarried circa
              1640, the male line of the said Henry Baron

---

* The printed case of the Stafford Barony, in contradiction to Dugdale's statement, vol. I. p. 171, and that of most
other writers, places one Baron too many in the descent of the
title; as it asserts that Henry, who was restored, or rather
created to the dignity, in 1547, was succeeded by his son
HENRY, an error which is supported by Dugdale stating, in his
Lists of Summons, that Henry Stafford was summoned to Parliament from 2 Edw. VI. to 18 Eliz. On examination it appears that
no such Henry ever succeeded to the dignity; for in Cole's Escheats,
in the Harl. MSS. the Inquisition on the death of Edward II.-2
Baron, in 1603, is abstracted; whence it appears, that the said
Edward succeeded Lord Stafford, his father, who was the son of the
attainted Duke of Buckingham: and in a valuable collection of
pedigrees of Peers, compiled in 1587 (Harl. MSS. 806), no
notice whatever is taken of Edward Stafford, the Baron then
living, having succeeded his brother Henry, nor is the name of
Henry to be found in that generation. Moreover, a MS note of
the late Francis Townsend, Esq. Windsor Herald (the result of
whose learning and industry being liberally placed at the disposi-
tion of the Editor, by his son Francis Townsend, Esq. Rouge Dra-
gon, has conferred important advantages on this Work), states,
that the Writ of 8 Eliz. was directed to *Edward* Stafford, and
that the said *Edward* was found heir to his mother in the 12
Eliz. No Inquisition on the death of Henry Lord Stafford (the
son of the Duke of Buckingham) has been found; but the preceding facts, it is presumed, are decisive of the point at issue.

Stafford, is presumed to have terminated, when the Barony created by the Act of 1547, became **Extinct.**

VISCOUNT.

I. 1640.—1. 1640. 1. Sir William Howard, K.B. (younger son of Thomas, XXIII.-20 Earl of Arundel) having married Mary, sister and sole heir of Henry IV.-4th Baron; they were created Baron and Baroness Stafford, with remainder to the heirs male of their bodies; failing which, to the heirs of their bodies*, 12 Sept. 1640. The

---

* The precedency given by this Patent is the same as that which was possessed by Henry Stafford, IV.-4th Baron, viz. 1547; but a new creation giving precedence beyond the date of the Patent, without an Act of Parliament, is illegal. As the public have heard a good deal of the claims of a Mr. Richard Stafford Cooke to the ancient Barony of Stafford, a few words on his pretensions may possibly be expected. That gentleman is said to be the heir-general of Dorothy, daughter of Henry, who was created Baron Stafford in 1547, which Dorothy married Sir William Stafford, of Grafton. Admitting this descent, it is difficult to find any real claim which it affords to the Barony of Stafford. The ancient Barony undoubtedly became FORFEITED on the attainder of Edward, Duke of Buckingham, in 1521, and which attainder has never been reversed. Henry Stafford, his son and heir, was created Baron Stafford *de novo*, with an express limitation to " the *heirs male* of his body coming," by Act of Parl. 1 Edward VI. 1547, and which dignity became EXTINCT on the termination of the male descendants of the said Henry, about the year 1640

It is thus clear, that after the attainder of Edward, Duke of Buckingham, in 1521, a Barony of Stafford in fee, and as such descendible to heirs general, never existed, until that created to Sir William Stafford, and Mary his wife, in 1640; when, in default of issue male, the Barony was limited to the HEIRS OF THEIR BODIES. The attainder of William Viscount Stafford, prevented his issue from inheriting his dignities; and though it did not affect his wife's honours during her life, it in effect produced their extinction on her demise, as it prevented her descendants from succeeding to them until the reversal of the said

R 3

said Sir William Howard was created Visc. Stafford, with remainder
to his heirs male, Nov. 11, 1640.
Beheaded 1678; and being attainted, all his honors became
𝔉𝔬𝔯𝔣𝔢𝔦𝔱𝔢𝔡.

---

attainder in 1824; but as Mr. Cooke does not descend from the
first Viscount and Viscountess Stafford, he, of course, can derive
no benefit from the said creation; nor could the attainder, which
impeded the descent of their dignities, in any shape afford him
a pretension to any part of the honors of the House of
Stafford. The reversal of the iniquitous attainder of Sir William
Howard, Viscount Stafford, however, renders Sir George Jerningham Baron Stafford under the Creation of 1640; and he is
also heir-general of the body of Henry Baron Stafford (son of the
attainted Duke of Buckingham), who was restored in blood, and
consequently heir in blood of Edward Duke of Buckingham, the
last person possessed of the ancient Barony. Notwithstanding
that the descent of the different titles of Stafford are, it is
hoped, tolerably clearly shewn in the text, the following brief
summary may prove acceptable.

1st. The ancient Barony created by the Writ of Summons of
5th Feb. 27 Edw. I. 1299, and the Earldom created by the Patent
of 5th March, 1351, were both FORFEITED by the attainder of
Edward Duke of Buckingham, IX. Baron and VIII. Earl of Stafford, in 1521.

2ndly. The Barony created by the Act of Parliament 1st Edward VI. 1547, to Henry Stafford, son of Edward last Duke of
Buckingham, &c. became EXTINCT on the death of his last male
descendant, about the year 1640.

3dly. The Barony of Stafford, created to William Howard 12th
Sept. 1640, became FORFEITED on his attainder in 1678, but is
now vested in Sir George Jerningham, as his heir-general, in consequence of the reversal of the said attainder a few months since.

4thly. The Viscountcy created to the said William Stafford
by Patent 11 Nov. 1640, became FORFEITED by his attainder;
but though the said attainder is reversed, the Viscountcy is now
EXTINCT from default of the heirs male of the said Viscount.

5thly. The Barony created to Mary, wife of the said William Stafford, Viscount and Baron Stafford, by Patent 12th Sept.
1640, did not on her death descend to her issue, in consequence
of the attainder of her husband preventing his children inheriting;
and the dignity of Countess of Stafford became extinct on the
same occasion, agreeably to the limitation.

BARONESS. COUNTESS.

I. 1640.—I. 1688. 1. Mary Howard, sister and sole heir of Henry IV.-4th Baron Stafford, and wife of Sir William Howard, K. B ; Created Baroness Stafford, as is before stated in p. 601, 12th Sept. 1640; Created Countess of Stafford, for life, 5th Oct. 1688; ob. 1693, when the dignity of Countess became Extinct, and her husband having been attainted, his issue by her could not succeed to the Barony.

EARLS.

IX. 1688. 1. Henry Stafford Howard, eldest son of William Howard, 1st Viscount Stafford, and Mary, Baroness Stafford, his wife, was Created Earl of Stafford, with remainder, failing his issue male, to John and Francis, his brothers and their issue male, 5 Oct. 1688 ; ob. 1719, s. p.

X. 1719. 2. William Stafford Howard, nephew and heir, being s. and h. of John, next brother of the last Earl ; ob. 1734.

XI. 1734 3. William Mathias Stafford Howard, s. and h.; ob. 1751, s. p.

XII. 1751. 4. John Paul Stafford Howard, uncle and heir, being next brother of William X.-2d Earl ; ob. 1762, s. p. when the Earldom became Extinct.

BARON.

II. 1824. 2. Sir George Jerningham, 7th Bart. (s. and b. of Sir William Jerningham, eldest son of Sir George Jerningham, by Mary, dau. and sole

---

6thly. The Earldom of Stafford, created to Henry Stafford Howard by Patent 5 Oct. 1688, became EXTINCT on the termination of the issue male of the brothers of the said Henry, in 1762.

7thly. Sir George Jerningham, by the reversal of the attainder of William Howard, 1st Viscount Stafford, has succeeded to the Barony of Stafford, created by Patent 12th Sept. 1640, as heir-general of the bodies of the said William Howard, Viscount Stafford, and of Mary his wife, Baron and Baroness Stafford.

heir of Francis Plowden by Mary Stafford his wife, sister and eventually sole heir of John Paul, XII.-4th and last Earl of Stafford, and heir-general of Sir William Howard, K. B. 1640, I.-1st Baron, and I.-1st Viscount Howard, and of Mary Stafford his wife), succeeded to the Barony of Stafford, created by the Patent of 12 Sept. 1640, the reversal of the attainder of the said William Howard, Viscount and Baron Stafford having been passed by the Crown in 1824, as heir-general of the bodies of the said William Howard and Mary his wife, Baron and Baroness Stafford. No act of recognition of the Barony being vested in his Lordship has however as yet taken place. ☥

STAFFORD
OF CLIFTON.

BARON BY WRIT.
1. 1371. Richard de Stafford, s. and h. of Richard Stafford (younger brother of Ralph 1st Earl of Stafford), who acquired the Lordship of Clifton, co. Stafford, by marrying Maud, dau. and heir of Richard de Camvill; Summ. to Parl. from 8 Jan. 44 Edward III. 1371, to 20 Oct. 3 Rich. II. 1379; ob. 1381, leaving Edmund, afterwards Bishop of Exeter, his son and heir, and Thomas his 2d son; which Thomas left issue Thomas Stafford, who died s. p. leaving Katherine his sister and heir, who married Sir John Arden, Knt. Maud Arden, their only child, married Sir Thomas Stanley; but none of the descendants of this Baron were ever summoned to Parliament. The Barony is however vested in the descendants and representatives of the said Maud, wife of Sir Thomas Stanley.

STAFFORD
OF ———

BARON BY WRIT.
I. 1371. Hugh de Stafford; Summ. to Parl. 8 January, 44 Edward III. 1371. Dugdale in his Baronage gives no account of a Hugh de Stafford having been summoned in that year. It is probable it was Hugh, the son and heir apparent of Ralph 1st Earl of Stafford, and who became 2d Earl in August, 1372.

STAFFORD
OF SUTHWYCK.

BARON BY WRIT.

I. 1461. Humphry Stafford (descended from Sir John
Stafford of Hooke, the lineal descendant of
Hervey Bagot and Milisent Stafford his wife,
the common ancestors of the Barons and
Earls of Stafford); Summ. to Parl. from 26
July, 1 Edw. IV. 1461, to 28 Feb. 3 Edw. IV.
1463, as " Humfrido Stafford de Sutbwyk
Chev.;" Created by Patent Lord Stafford of
Suthwyck, 24 April, 1464; Created Earl of
Devon, 7 May, 1469; beheaded 1469; ob. s.p.
when all his honors became

Extinct.

STAFFORD BARON BOURCHIER.

Vide BOURCHIER.

STAFFORD.

MARQUESSES.

I.   1786. 1. Granville Leveson Gower, 2d Earl Gower;
Created Marquess of the County of Stafford
28 Feb. 1786; K. G.; ob. 1803.
II. 1803. 2. George Granville Leveson Gower, s. and h.
Present Marquess of Stafford; Earl and Baron
Gower, Viscount Trentham, and a Baronet,
K. G. ⊤

STAMFORD.

EARLS.

I.   1628. 1. Henry Grey, 2d Baron Grey of Groby; Created Earl of Stamford, co. Lincoln, 26 Mar.
1628; ob. 1673.
II.   1673. 2. Thomas Grey, grandson and heir; being son
and heir of Thomas Grey (ob. v. p.) eldest
son of the last Earl; ob. 1720, s. P.
III. 1720. 3. Harry Grey, cousin and heir, being son and

heir of John Grey, 2d son of Henry 1st Earl;
ob. 1739.

IV.　1739.　4. Harry Grey, s. and h.　He married Mary, sole
dau. and heir of George Booth, last Earl of
Warrington, and Baron Delamere; ob. 1768.

V.　1768.　5. George Harry Grey, s. and h. Created Baron
De la Mere, and Earl of Warrington 22
April, 1796; ob. 1819.

VI.　1819.　6. George Harry Grey, s. and h.　Present Earl of
Stamford, Earl of Warrington, Baron Grey
of Groby, and Baron Delamere. ⟱

STANHOPE

OF HARRINGTON.

BARONS.

I.　1605.　1. John Stanhope; Created Baron Stanhope of
Harrington, co. Northampton, 4 May, 1605;
ob. 1620.

II.　1620.　2. Charles Stanhope, s. and h. ob. 1675, s. p.
when the title became
Extinct.

STANHOPE

OF SHELFORD.

BARONS.

I.　1616.　1. Philip Stanhope (great-grandson of Sir Michael
Stanhope, father of John 1st Baron Stan-
hope of Harrington); Created Baron Stanhope of Shelford, co. Nottingham, 7 Nov.
1616; Created Earl of Chesterfield 4 August,
1628.　　　　　　　Vide CHESTERFIELD.

STANHOPE

OF ELVASTON AND MAHON.

BARONS.　　VISC.　　EARLS.

I. 1717.—I. 1717.—I. 1718.　1. James Stanhope (son and
heir of Alexander Stanhope,
younger son of Philip 1st
Baron Stanhope of Shelford,
and 1st Earl of Chester-
field); Created Baron Stan-

hope of Elvaston, co. Derby, and Viscount Stanhope of Mahon in the Island of Minorca, 12 July. 1717, with remainder, failing his issue male, to his kinsman Thomas Stanhope of Elvaston, Esq. and his brothersCharles, andWilliam (afterwards Earl of Harrington), descended from Sir John Stanhope, great-grandfather of the Viscount, and to their issue male respectively; Created Earl Stanhope, with remainder to the heirs male of his body, 14 April, 1718; ob. 1721.

II. 1721.—II. 1721.—II. 1721. 2. Philip Stanhope, s. and h. ob. 1786.

III.1786.—III.1786.—III.1786.3.Charles Stanhope, s. and h. ob. 1816.

IV.1816.—IV.1816.—IV.1816. 4. Philip Henry Stanhope, son and heir. Present Earl, Viscount, and Baron Stanhope.

STANLEY.

I. 1456. 1. Thomas Stanley; Summ, to Parl. from 20 Jan. 34 Hen. VI. 1456, to 9 Dec. 1 Rich. III. 1483; Created Earl of Derby 27 Oct. 1485. This Barony continued merged in the Earldom of Derby until the demise of Ferdinand XV.-5th Earl of Derby in 1594, s. p. m. when it fell into Abeyance between his three daughters and coheirs, among whose representatives this Barony, together with that of Strange of Knokyn, is now in ABEYANCE.

Vide STRANGE OF KNOKYN.

STAPLETON.

BARONS BY WRIT.

I.   1313.   1. Miles de Stapleton; Summ. to Parl. 8 Jan. and 22 May, 6 Edward II. 1313, and 26 July, 7 Edw. II. 1313; ob. 1314.

II.   1342.   2. Nicholas de Stapleton, s. and h. Summ. to Parl. 25 Feb. 16 Edward III. 1342; ob. 1343, leaving Miles his son and heir, whose only son Thomas died s. p. leaving Elizabeth his sister, wife of Thomas Metham, his heir; in whose descendants and representatives this Barony is vested.

STAVORDALE.

Vide ILCHESTER.

STAWEL.

BARONS.

I.   1813.   1. Ralph Stawel; Created Baron Stawel of Somerton, co. Somerset, 15 Jan. 1683; ob. 1689.

II.   1689.   2. John Stawel, s. and h. ob. 1692, s. p. m.

III.   1692.   3. William Stawel, half-brother and heir; ob. 1742, s. p. m.

IV.   1742.   4. Edward Stawel, brother and heir; ob. 1755, s. p. m. when the title became

BARONESS.   Extinct.

I. 1760.   1. Mary Legge, dau. and sole heir of Edward the last Baron, and wife of the Right Hon. Henry Bilson Legge; Created Baroness Stawel of Somerton, co. Somerset, with remainder of the dignity of Baron Stawel of Somerton aforesaid to the heirs male of her body by her said husband, 20 May, 1760; ob. 1780.

BARON.

V.   1780.   2. Henry Stawel Bilson Legge, s. and h. ob. 1820, s. p. m. when the title again became

Extinct.

STEWART
OF GARLIES.

BARONS.
I. 1796. 1. John Stewart, 8th Earl of Galloway in Scotland; Created Baron Stewart of Garlies, co. Wigtown, 6 June, 1796, K. T.; ob. 1806.

II. 1806. 2. George Stewart, s. and h. Present Baron Stewart of Garlies; also Earl of Galloway, &c. in Scotland, K. T. ⚓

STEWART
OF STEWART'S COURT.

BARON.
I. 1814. 1. Charles William (assumed the name of) Vane-Stewart, 2d son of Robert 1st Marquess of Londonderry in Ireland; Created Baron Stewart of Stewart's Court and Ballilawn, co. Donegal, in the Peerage of the United Kingdom, 1st July, 1814; succeeded his brother Robert as 3d Marquess of Londonderry in Ireland in 1822; Created Earl Vane and Viscount Seaham, with a special remainder, 8 July, 1823. Present Baron Stewart of Stewart's Court, Viscount Seaham and Earl Vane; also Marquess of Londonderry, &c. in Ireland, G. C. B. ⚓

STEYNGREVE.

John de Steyngreve was Summoned 8 June, 22 Edw. I. 1294; but for the reasons assigned under "CLYVEDON," it is very doubtful if that Writ was a regular Summons to Parliament. Neither he, nor any of his descendants, were ever summoned to Parliament.

STOURTON.

BARONS.
I. 1448. 1. John Stourton; Created Baron Stourton of Stourton, co. Wilts, 13 May, 1448; ob. 1462.

II. 1462. 2. William Stourton, s. and h. ob. 1478.

III. 1478. 3. John Stourton, s. and h. ob. 1484, s. p.

IV. 1484. 4. William Stourton, brother and heir; ob. 1522, s. p.

V. 1522. 5. Edward Stourton, brother and heir; ob. 1536.

VI. 1536. 6. William Stourton, s. and h. ob. 1548.

VII. 1548. 7. Charles Stourton, s. and h.; executed 1557, when his honors became

Forfeited.

VIII. 1575. 8. John Stourton, s. and h.; Restored in blood and honors by Act of Parliament 1575; ob. 1588, s. p.

IX. 1588. 9. Edward Stourton, brother and heir; ob. 1632.

X. 1632. 10. William Stourton, s. and h. ob. circa 1672.

XI. 1672. 11. William Stourton, grandson and heir, being s. and h. of Edward Stourton (ob. v p.) eldest son of the last Baron; ob. 1685.

XII. 1685. 12. Edward Stourton, s. and h. ob. 1720, s. p.

XIII. 1720. 13. Thomas Stourton, brother and heir; ob. 1744, s. p.

XIV. 1744. 14. Charles Stourton, nephew and heir, being son and heir of Charles Stourton, next brother of the last Baron; ob. 1753, s. p.

XV. 1753. 15. William Stourton, brother and heir. He married Winifred, daughter and coheir of Philip Howard, brother of Edward XIV.-11th Duke of Norfolk; ob. 1781.

XVI. 1781. 16. Charles Philip Stourton, s. and h. ob. 1816.

XVII. 1816. 17. William Stourton, s. and h. Present Baron Stourton; also in right of Winifred his grandmother (eldest of the two daughters and coheirs of Philip Howard, brother of Edward XIV.-11th Duke of Norfolk), coheir of the Baronies of Howard, Mowbray, Braose of Gower, Segrave, Dacre of Gillesland, Greystock, Ferrers of Wemme, Talbot, Strange of Blackmere, Furnival, Giffard of Brimmesfield, and Verdon, and probably also of the Barony of Arundel under the Writ of 1 Richard II. *; also coheir of one moiety of the Barony of Fitz Payne. ⊤

* Vide p. 29.

STOWELL.

BARONS.

I. 1821. 1. William Scott, elder brother of John 1st Baron
and 1st Earl of Eldon; Created Baron Stowell
of Stowell Park, co. Gloucester, 17 July,
1821. Present Baron Stowell.

STRABOLGI.

BARONS BY WRIT.

I. 1322. 1. David de Strabolgi, Earl of Athol in Scotland;
Summ. to Parl. from 14 March, 15 Edw. II.
1322, to 3 Dec. 39 Edw. II. 1826; ob. 1327.

II. 1327. 2. David de Strabolgi, s. and h. Earl of Athol in
Scotland; Summ. to Parl. from 25 January,
4 Edw. III. 1330, to 24 July, 8 Edw. III.
1334; ob. 1335.

III. 1335. 3. David de Strabolgi, s. and h. Earl of Athol in
Scotland; Summ. to Parl. from 20 Jan. 9 Edw.
III. 1366, to 6 April, 9 Edward III. 1369; ob.
1375, s. P. M. leaving his daughters Elizabeth
and Philippa his heirs. Eli beth marr. first,
Sir Thomas Percy, K   and, secondly, Sir
John Scrope, Knt.   and Phillippa was first
the wife of Sir   ph Percy (brother of the
aforesaid Sir T   omas Percy), and secondly of
Sir John Hal   am; and among the descend-
ants and re   resentatives of these coheirs this
Barony is i ABEYANCE.

RADBROKE.

EARLS.

I. 1821. John R
Du   us, 1st Baron Rous; Created Viscount
Suf   wich, and Earl of Stradbroke, both co.
St: olk, 18 July, 1821. Present Earl of
ar   adbroke, Viscount Dunwich, Baron Rous,
 l   d a Baronet.
or
.l.
ir
.ra   s 2

STRAFFORD.

EARLS.

I.　1640. 1. Thomas Wentworth, 1st Viscount Wentworth;
Created Baron Raby of Raby Castle, with a
special remainder, and Earl of Strafford, co.
York, 12 Jan. 1640; Lord Lieut. of Ireland,
K. G.; beheaded 1641, and being attainted,
all his honors became

Forfeited.

II.　1665. 2. William Wentworth, s. and h. Restored to all
his father's honors in December, 1665, K. G.;
ob. 1695, s. p. when all his titles, excepting
the Barony of Raby and the Baronetcy,
became

Extinct.

III. 1711. 1. Thomas Wentworth, 3d Baron Raby (great-
grandson of Sir William Wentworth, next brother of Thomas 1st Earl); Created Viscount
Wentworth of Wentworth Woodhouse, and
of Stainborough, co. York, and Earl of Strafford, with remainder of these dignities, failing his issue male, to his brother Peter
Wentworth and his issue male, 4 Sept. 1711,
K. G.; ob. 1739.

IV.　1739. 2. William Wentworth, s. and h. ob. 1791, s. p.

V.　1791. 3. Frederick Thomas Wentworth, cousin and
heir, being son and heir of William, eldest
son of Peter Wentworth, next brother of
Thomas III. 1st Earl; ob. 1799, s. p. when
all his dignities became

Extinct.

STRANGE

BARONS BY TENURE.

I.　H. II. 1. Guy le Strange, Lord of Weston and Alvithele,
co. Salop; ob. circa 1195.

II. John. 2. Ralph le Strange, s. and h. ob. . . . . . , s. p. leaving his three sisters his heirs.

I.　Hen. II.　Hamon le Strange, Lord of Wrockwurdine,
brother of Guy above mentioned, but of
whom nothing farther is known.

STRANGE

BARONS BY TENURE.   OF KNOKYN.

I. H. II. 1. John le Strange, Lord of Nesse and Chese-wurdine, co. Salop, brother of Hamon and Guy before mentioned; ob. circa 1217.

II. H III. 2. John le Strange, s. and h. ob. 1269.

III. H.III. 3. John le Strange, s. and h. Lord of Knokyn; he married Joan, daughter and coheir of Roger de Somery, Baron of Dudley; ob. 1276.

BARONS BY WRIT.

I. 1299. 4. John le Strange, s. and h. Summ. to Parl. as "Jobanni Extraneo" from 29 Dec. 28 Edw. I. 1299, and as "Jobanni Lestrange de Knokin," from 4 March, 2 Edward II. 1309, to 12 Dec. 3 Edward II. 1309; ob. 1310.

II. 1310. 5. John le Strange, s. and h. Summ. to Parl. 16 June, 4 Edw. II. 1311 ; ob. 1311.

III. 1311. 6. John le Strange, s. and h. Summ. to Parl. 8 Jan. 12 May, 6 Edward II. 1313, and 26 July, 7 Edw. II. 1313; ob. 1324, s. P.

IV. 1324. 7. Roger le Strange, brother and heir; Summ. to Parl. from 25 Feb. 16 Edw. III. 1342, to 10 March, 23 Edw. III. 1349; ob. 1349.

V. 1349. 8. Roger le Strange, s. and h. Summ. to Parl. from 20 Sept. 29 Edward III. 1355, to 9 Aug. 6 Rich. II. 1382; ob. 1382.

VI. 1382. 9. John le Strange, s. and h. Summ. to Parl. from 20 August, 7 Rich. II. 1383, to 18 July, 21 Rich. II. 1397; ob. circa 1398.

VII. 1398. 10. Richard le Strange, s. and h. Summ. to Parl. from 25 August, 5 Henry IV. 1404, to 2 Jan. 27 Hen. VI. 1449; ob. 1449.

VIII. 1449. 11. John le Strange, s. and h. Summ. to Parl. from 28 Feb. 6 Edward IV. 1466, to 19 August, 12 Edw. IV. 1472. He married Jaquetta, dau. of Richard Earl Rivers, and sister-in-law of King Edward IV.; ob. 1477, s. P. M. Johanna, sole dau. and heir, married

IX. 1482. George Stanley, s. and h. apparent of Thomas XI.-1st Earl of Derby, and was Summ. to Parl. jure uxoris, as "Georgio Stanley de la Strange," from 15 Nov. 22 Edw. IV. 1482, to 16 Jan. 12 Henry VIII. 1497, K. G.; ob. 1497.

X. 1497. 12. Thomas Stanley, son and heir; succeeded his grandfather in 1504, as XII.-2d Earl of Derby, when this Barony became merged in the Earldom of Derby until the death of Ferdinando Stanley, XV.-5th Earl of Derby in 1594, s. p. m. (during which period several of the eldest sons of the said Earls were Summoned to Parliament vita patris as Barons Strange), when, together with the Barony of Stanley, it fell into Abeyance between his three daughters and coheirs, viz. Ann, who married, first, Grey 5th Lord Chandos, and secondly, Mervin Earl of Castlehaven; Frances, wife of John Earl of Bridgewater; and Elizabeth, who married Henry Earl of Huntingdon; between whose descendants and representatives the Baronies of Strange of Knokyn, and Stanley, are in ABEYANCE.

STRANGE

I. 1308. 1. Fulk le Strange (brother and heir of John le Strange, Lord of Whitchurch, and son of Robert, next brother of John III.-3d Baron le Strange of Knokyn); Summ. to Parl. from 13 Jan. 2 Edw. II. 1308, to 13 Sept. 18 Edw. II. 1324, as "Fulcy le Strange;" ob. 1324.

II. 1324. 2. John le Strange, s. and h. Summ. to Parl. from 6 Sept. 4 Edward III. 1330, to 20 April, 17 Edw. III. 1343, as "Johanni le Strange," and to 10 March, 23 Edw. III. 1349, as "Johanni le Strange de Blackmere;" ob. 1349.

III. 1349. 3. Fulk le Strange, s. and h.; he was never Summ. to Parl.; ob. 1349, s. p.

IV. 1349. 4. John le Strange, brother and heir; Summ. to Parl. 3 April, 34 Edw. III. 1360 *; ob. 1361.

V. 1361. 5. John le Strange, s. and h. ob. infra ætatem, 1375, s. p. m. leaving Elizabeth his dau. and heir, then an infant. She married Thomas Mowbray, Earl of Nottingham; but died s. p.

---

* Though Dugdale, in his Baronage, does not mention any ROGER Baron Strange of Blackmere, it is to be observed, that writs were issued to " *Rogero* le Straunge de Blakemere" from 9 January, 44 Edw. III. 1371, to 4 October, 47 Edw. III. 1373.

23 August, 1383, leaving her aunt Ankaret, sister of John her father, the IV. Baron, her heir, who married

VI. 1384. Richard Talbot, son and heir apparent of Gilbert Baron Talbot ; he was Summoned to Parl. from 3 March, 7 Rich. II. 1384, to 17 Dec. 11 Rich. II. 1387, as " Ricardo Talbot de Blackmere," when he succeeded his father as Baron Talbot ; ob. 1396.

VII. 1396. 6. Gilbert Talbot, s. and h. Baron Talbot ; ob. 1419, leaving Ankaret his dau. and sole heir, who died an infant in 1421, when this Barony, together with that of Talbot, devolved on her uncle and heir,

VIII. 1421. 7. John Talbot ; Created Earl of Shrewsbury 20 May, 1442, in which title this Barony, together with the Baronies of Talbot and Furnival, continued merged until the death of Gilbert X.-7th Earl of Shrewsbury, s. p. m. in 1616, when they fell into ABEYANCE between his three daughters and coheirs, viz. Mary, who became the wife of William XXII.-3d Earl of Pembroke, and died 25 Feb 1649-50 ; Elizabeth, who married Henry XIX.-8th Earl of Kent, and died 7 Dec. 1651 ; and Althea, who married Thomas Howard XXIII.-20th Earl of Arundel, Surrey, and Norfolk. On the death of the said Mary and Elizabeth the Abeyance of this Barony, and of the Baronies of Talbot and Furnival terminated, and those dignities are presumed to have become vested in Althea Countess of Arundel, Surrey, and Norfolk above mentioned, as she is supposed to have survived her sisters * ; and her descendants the Earls of Arundel and Surrey, and Dukes and Earls of Norfolk inherited the said Baronies until the demise of Edward Howard, XIV.-11th Duke of Norfolk, and Baron Talbot, Furnival, and Strange of Blackmere, in 1777, s. p. when they again fell into ABEYANCE betweenthe two daughters and coheirs of Philip Howard, brother of the said Edward Duke of Norfolk ; between whose representatives, viz. William, present Baron Stourton, and William Francis Henry, present Baron Petre, they are now in ABEYANCE.

---

* She was living 16 April, 1649. Vide a letter from her in Harl. MSS. 287, fol. 282, dated at Amsterdam, on that day : the date of her demise could not be ascertained, though much trouble was taken on the subject.

STRANGE

OF ELLESMERE.

BARONS BY TENURE.

1. H. III. 1. Hamon le Strange, presumed to have been a younger son of John II.-2d Baron Strange of Knokyn, Lord of Ellesmere and Stretton,
BY WRIT.   1267; ob. ....., s. P.
I.   1295. 2. Roger le Strange, brother and heir; presumed to have been the " Rogero Extraneo" who was Summ. to Parl. 24 June, 3 Sept. and 2 Nov. 23 Edward I. 1295, and 26 August. 24 Edw. I. 1296 ; he was also Summoned 26 Jan. 25 Edward I. 1297 ; but it is doubtful if the latter Writ was a regular Summons to Parliament ; vide " FITZ-JOHN." Dugdale states that he was living 1303, but that " farther he cannot say of him ;" and is silent about his having been summoned to Parliament. He probably died s. P.

STRANGE

OF ——

BARON BY WRIT.

I.   1326. 1. Eubolo le Strange, younger son of John I.-4th Baron Strange of Knokyn, having married Alice, dau. and at length heir of Thomas de Lacy, Earl of Lincoln, was Summ. to Parl. from 3 Dec. 20 Edward II. 1326, to 1 April, 9 Edward III. 1335 ; ob. 1335, s. P. when the Barony became
                    Extinct.

STRANGE

OF ——

BARONS BY WRIT.

I.   1628. 1. James Stanley, son and heir apparent of William Stanley, XVI.-6th Earl of Derby ; Summ. to Parl. as " Jacobo Stanley de

BARONS BY WRIT.

Strange, Chl'r," 7 March, 3 Car. I. 1628, 20 Jan. 4 Car. I. 1629, and in the next Parliaments, viz. 13 April and 3 Nov. 15 Car. I. 1639; succeeded as XVII.-7th Earl of Derby in 1642, K. G.; beheaded 1651.

II. 1651. 2. Charles Stanley, s. and h. XVIII.-8th Earl of Derby; ob. 1672.

III. 1672. 3. William George Richard Stanley, s. and h. XVIII.-9th Earl of Derby; ob. 1702, s. p. m. when the Barony fell into ABEYANCE between Henrietta and Elizabeth his two daughters and coheirs. Elizabeth died unmarried in 1714, when the Barony devolved on

BARONESSES.

I. 1714. 4. Henrietta, her sister and heir; she was twice married, but by her 2d husband only, John Lord Ashburnham, had surviving issue; ob. 1718.

II. 1718. 5. Anne Ashburnham, dau. and heir; ob. unmarried in 1732, when this Barony devolved on her uncle,

BARONS BY WRIT.

IV. 1732. 6. James Stanley, XX.-10th Earl of Derby, he being her heir ex parte materna; ob. 1736, s. p. when the Barony devolved on

V. 1736. 7. James Murray, 2d Duke of Atholl in Scotland, he being son and heir of John 1st Duke of Atholl, eldest son of John 1st Marquess of Atholl by Amelia Sophia, daughter of James Stanley, XVII.-7th of Derby, and 1st Baron Strange; claimed and was allowed the Barony as heir-general of the said Earl of Derby and Baron Strange, 14 March, 1737; ob. 1764, s. p. m.

BARONESS.

III. 1764. 8. Charlotte Murray, daughter and sole heir, wife of her cousin John Murray, 3d Duke of Atholl; ob. 1805.

BARON BY WRIT. EARL.

VI. 1805.—I. 1786. 9. John Murray, s. and h. succeeded his father as 4th Duke of Atholl in Scotland in 1774; Created Earl

Strange and Baron Murray of Stanley, co.
Gloucester, 8 August, 1786; succeeded his
mother in the Barony of Strange 13 October,
1805. Present Earl and Baron Strange, and
Baron Murray of Stanley; also Duke of
Atholl, &c. in Scotland, K. T.

STRATHEARN.

DUKEDOM, 18 October, 1766—Extinct 1790.

Vide CUMBERLAND.

DUKEDOM, 23 April, 1799—Extinct 1820.

Vide KENT.

STRIVELYN.

BARON BY WRIT.

I.   1371.   John de Strivelyn; Summ. to Parl. from 25
Feb. 16 Edw. III. 1342, to 8 Jan. 44 Edw.III.
1371; ob. . . . . ; but "farther," says Dugdale, "I shall not say of him, none of his
posterity having been so summoned:" other
writers state, that Christian his daughter,
who married Sir John Middleton, was eventually his heir. If this statement be correct,
this Barony is vested in her descendants and
representatives.

STUART
OF LEIGHTON BROMSWOLD.

BARONY, 7 June, 1619—Extinct 1672.

Vide MARCH.

STUART
OF NEWBURY.

BARONY, 10 December, 1645—Extinct 1672.

Vide LITCHFIELD.

STUART

OF CASTLE STUART.

BARONS.

I. 1796. 1. Francis Stuart, 8th Earl of Moray, in Scotland; Created Baron Stuart of Castle Stuart, co. Inverness, 4th June, 1796; ob. 1810.

II. 1810. 2. Francis Stuart, s. and h. Present Baron Stuart of Castle Stuart; also Earl of Moray, &c. in Scotland.

STUTEVILLE.

BARONS BY TENURE.

I. Will. I. 1. Robert de Stuteville, called also Fronteboef, a Baron temp. William I. and living 1106; ob. ....

II. Steph. 2. Robert de Stuteville, s. and h.; living 1176.

III. H. I. 3. Robert de Stuteville, s. and h.; ob. ....

IV. H. II. 4. William de Stuteville, s. and h.; ob. 1203.

V. John. 5. Robert de Stuteville, s. and h.; ob. 1205, s. p.

VI. H.III. 6. Nicholas de Stuteville, brother and heir; ob..

VII. H.III. 7. Nicholas de Stuteville, s. and h.; ob 1232, s.p.m. leaving Johanna, wife of Hugh de Wake, and Margaret, who married William Mastoc, and died s. p. his daughters and co-heirs.

I. H. III. 1. Eustace de Stuteville, half-brother of William 4th Baron above-mentioned; ob. ante 1242.

II. H. III. 2. Robert de Stuteville, s. and h. In 26 H. III. anno 1242, Joan, wife of Hugh de Wake mentioned above, obtained livery of the lands of this Robert.

I. H. III. 1. Henry de Stuteville, of the same family, had his lands seized in 1225.

I. H. III. 1. William de Stuteville, son of Osmund, brother of Robert 3d Baron; ob. 1259.

II. H. III. 2. Robert de Stuteville, s. and h.; living 1266, when the King restored to him his manor of Witheresfield, of which he had been deprived.

STUTEVILLE.

BARONS BY TENURE.

I. H. III. 1. John de Stuteville, possessor of the manors of Kirkby, Hekington, &c.; living 1264, when he had his lands seized.

II. Edw.I. 2. Robert de Stuteville, s. and h.; ob. 1305, leaving a son John; but neither he nor his descendants being ever summoned to Parliament, this family ceased to be Barons of the Realm.

SUDBURY.

BARONY, 11 September, 1675.

Vide EUSTON.

SUDLEY.

BARONS BY TENURE.

I. Will. I. 1. Harold, according to some authorities son of Ralph Earl of Hereford, but, according to other writers, natural son of King Harold, held several Lordships at the General Survey, among others that of Sudley; his son and heir,

II. Hen. I. 2. John, assumed the name of Sudley.

III. H. III. 3. Ralph de Sudley, s. and h.; living 1165.

IV. Ric. I. 4. Otwell de Sudley, s. and h.; ob. circa 1195, s.p.

V. John. 5. Ralph de Sudley, s. and h.; ob. circa 1204.

VI. H. III. 6. Ralph de Sudley, s. and h.; ob. ....

VII.H. III. 7. Bartholomew de Sudley, s. and h.; ob. 1274.

BY WRIT.

I. 1299. 8. John de Sudley, s. and h.; Summ. to Parl. from 29 Dec. 28 Edw. I. 1299, to 15 May, 14 Edw. II. 1321; ob. 1336, s. p. according to Dugdale, vol. i. p. 428; but in his History of Warwickshire, he states that John (the son of Bartholomew de Sudley) was his *grandson* and heir. Joane, wife of William de Boteler, of Wemme, and Margery, wife of Sir Robert Massey, were the daughters, and eventually coheirs, of the John de Sudley (son of Bartholomew) last mentioned; and (if this statement be authentic), among whose descendants and representatives this Barony is in ABEYANCE.

SUFFIELD.

BARONS.

I. 1786. 1. Sir Harbord Harbord, 2d Bart.; Created Baron Suffield of Suffield, co. Norfolk, 8th August, 1786; ob. 1810.

II. 1810. 2. William Asheton Harbord, s. and h.; ob. 1821, s. p.

III. 1821. 3. Edward Harbord, brother and heir. Present Baron Suffield, and a Baronet. ⊤

SUFFOLK.

EARLS.

I. 1337. 1. Robert de Ufford, 2d Baron de Ufford; Created Earl of Suffolk 16 March, 1337, K. G.; ob. 1369.

II. 1369. 2. William de Ufford, son and heir; Admiral of the King's Fleet, K. G.; ob. 1382, s. p. when the Earldom became
𝔈𝔵𝔱𝔦𝔫𝔠𝔱.

III. 1385. 1. Michael de la Pole, 1st Baron de la Pole; Created Earl of Suffolk 6th Aug. 1385; Lord Chancellor; outlawed circa 1388, when his honors were
𝔉𝔬𝔯𝔣𝔢𝔦𝔱𝔢𝔡.

IV. 1397. 2. Michael de la Pole, s. and h.; restored to his father's dignities 1397; ob. 1415.

V. 1415. 3. Michael de la Pole, s. and h.; slain 1415; ob. s. p. m.

MARQ.   DUKE.

VI. 1415.—I. 1444.—I. 1448. 4. William de la Pole, uncle and heir male, being next brother of Michael IV.-2d Earl; Created Marquess of Suffolk 14 Sept. 1444; succeeded as Earl of Pembroke, according to an express limitation, in 1446; Created Duke of Suffolk 2 June, 1448; Lord Chancellor; Lord High Admiral; K. G.; he married Alice, grand-dau. of Geoffrey Chaucer, the poet; beheaded 1450, and having been attainted, his honors became
𝔉𝔬𝔯𝔣𝔢𝔦𝔱𝔢𝔡.

SUFFOLK.

II. 1463. 1. John de la Pole, s. and h. ; Created Duke of Suffolk 23 March, 1463; he married Elizabeth Plantagenet, sister of King Edward IV. K. G. ; ob. 1491.

III. 1491. 2. Edmund de la Pole, s. and h. K.G.; beheaded 1513 (ob. s. p. m.) * and being attainted, his honors became

Forfeited.

IV. 1514. 1. Charles Brandon, V.-1st Viscount L'Isle; Created Duke of Suffolk 1st Feb. 1514, he married to his third wife Mary Tudor, daughter of King Henry VII. by whom he had three daughters, K. G.; ob. 1545; he was succeeded in his honors by

V. 1545. 2. Henry Brandon, his s. and h. by his last wife, Katherine, dau. of William Lord Willoughby of Eresby; ob. 1551, s. p. when the Dukedom became

Extinct.

VI. 1551. 1. Henry Grey, VI.-3d Marquess of Dorset, having married Frances, dau. of Charles IV.-1st Duke, by Mary, sister of King Henry VIII. (by whom he had the unfortunate Lady Jane Grey), was Created Duke of Suffolk 10 Oct. 1551, K. G. beheaded 1554; and being attainted, all his honors became

Forfeited.

VI. 1603. 1. Thomas Howard, first Baron Howard de Walden (younger son of Thomas IX.-4th Duke of Norfolk); Created Earl of Suffolk 21 July, 1603; Lord High Treasurer; K. G.; ob. 1626.

VII. 1626. 2. Theophilus Howard, s. and h. K.G. ob. 1640.

VIII. 1640. 3. James Howard, s. and h.; ob. 1688, s. p. m. when the Barony of Howard de Walden fell into Abeyance between his daughters and coheirs.

---

* Richard, his brother, is said to have assumed the title of Duke of Suffolk. He was slain in 1525, and died s. p.

EARLS.

IX. 1688. 4. George Howard, brother and heir male; ob. 1691, s. p. m.

X. 1691. 5. Henry Howard, brother and heir; ob. 1709.

XI. 1709. 6. Henry Howard, s. and h.; 1st Baron Chesterford, and Earl of Bindon, having been so created vitâ patris; ob. 1718.

XII. 1718. 7. Charles William Howard, s. and h.; Earl of Bindon and Baron Chesterford; ob. 1722, s. p. when these titles became Extinct; but the Earldom of Suffolk devolved on

XIII. 1722. 8. Edward Howard, uncle and heir, being next brother of Henry XI.-6th Earl; ob. 1731, s. p.

XIV. 1731. 9. Charles Howard, brother and heir; ob. 1733.

XV. 1733. 10. Henry Howard, s. and h. ob. 1745, s. p.

XVI. 1745. 11. Henry Bowes Howard, V.-4th Earl of Berkshire, cousin and heir, being descended from Thomas Howard, 1st Earl of Berkshire, 2d son of Thomas Howard, VI.-1st Earl of Suffolk; ob. 1757.

XVII. 1757. 12. Henry Howard, grandson and heir, being s. and h. of William Howard (ob. v. p.) eldest son of the last Earl; Earl of Berkshire; ob. 1779.

XVIII. 1779. 13. Henry Howard, s. and h. Earl of Berkshire; ob. 1779, infans.

XIX. 1779. 14. Thomas Howard, grand uncle and heir, being younger son of Henry Bowes, XVI.-11th Earl; Earl of Berkshire; ob. 1783, s. p.

XX. 1783. 15. John Howard, cousin and heir male, being lineally descended from Philip Howard, younger son of Thomas 1st Earl of Berkshire, second son of Thomas VI.-1st Earl of Suffolk; Earl of Berkshire; ob. 1820.

XXI. 1820. 16. Thomas Howard, s. and h. Present Earl of Suffolk, Earl of Berkshire, Viscount Andover, and Baron Howard of Charleton. ☿

SUNBURY.

VISCOUNTCY, 14 October, 1714—Extinct 1715.

VISCOUNTCY 14 June, 1715—Extinct 1772.

Vide HALIFAX.

SUNDERLAND.

EARLS.

I.   1627.   Emanuel Scrope, 11th Baron Scrope of Bolton; Created Earl of Sunderland 19 June, 1627; ob. 1640, s. p. when the Earldom became

𝔈𝔵𝔱𝔦𝔫𝔠𝔱.

II.   .1643. 1. Henry Spencer, 3d Baron Spencer of Wormleighton; Created Earl of Sunderland 8 June, 1643; ob. 1643.

III. 1643. 2. Robert Spencer, s. and h. K. G. ob. 1702.

IV. .1702. 3. Charles Spencer, s. and h.; Lord Lieutenant of Ireland, K. G.; ob. 1722.

V.   1722. 4. Robert Spencer, s. and h. ob. 1729, s. p.

VI. 1729. 5. Charles Spencer, brother and heir; succeeded as Marquess of Blandford and Duke of Marlborough in 1733.

Vide MARLBOROUGH.

SUNDRIDGE.

BARONS.

I.   1766.   1. John Campbell (commonly called Marquess of Lorn), son and heir apparent of John, 4th Duke of Argyle in Scotland; Created Baron Sundridge of Coombank, co. Kent, with remainder, failing his issue male, to his brothers Frederick and William, and their issue male respectively, 22 Dec. 1766; succeeded as 5th Duke of Argyle in 1770; ob. 1806.

II. 1806.   2. George William Campbell, s. and h.   Present Baron Sundridge and Baron Hamilton; also Duke of Argyle, &c. in Scotland. ═

SURREY.

EARLS.

I. Will. II. 1. William de Warren, Earl Warren in Normandy; Created Earl of Surrey by William Rufus; he married Gunnora, dau. of William the Conqueror; ob. 1089.

II.   1089. 2. William de Warren, s. and h.; ob. 1135.

III. 1135. 3. William de Warren, son and heir; ob. 1148,

s. p. m. Isabel, his sole dau. and heir, having married

IV. 1148. William de Blois, natural son of King Stephen, he became Earl of Surrey jure uxoris; ob. 1160, s. p. Isabel, his widow, having married, secondly, in 1163,

V. 1163. Hameline Plantagenet, natural son of Geoffrey Earl of Aujou, father of King Henry II. he obtained the Earldom of Surrey in that year; ob. 1202.

VI. 1202. 4. William Plantagenet, s. and h.; ob. 1240.

VII. 1240. 5. John Plantagenet, s. and h.; ob. 1304.

VIII. 1304. 6. John Plantagenet, grandson and heir, being s. and h. of John Plantagenet (ob. v. p.) eldest son of the last Earl; ob. 1347, s. p. leaving Alice, wife of Edmund Earl of Arundel, his sister and heir.

IX. 1347. 7. Richard Fitz-Alan, XIII.-11th Earl of Arundel, s. and h. of Edmund Earl of Arundel, by Alice, his wife, sister and heir of the last Earl, is considered to have succeeded to the Earldom of Surrey, and so styled himself; but it is doubtful if he was ever formally invested with that Earldom; K. G.; ob. 1375.

X. 1375. 8 Richard Fitz-Alan, s. and h.; Earl of Arundel and Surrey, K. G.; beheaded 1397, and being Attainted, his honors became

Forfeited.

DUKE.

1. 1397. Thomas Holland, IX.-3d Earl of Kent; Created Duke of Surrey 29 Sept. 1397; Earl Marshal; K. G.; and being Attainted in 1400, his honors became

Forfeited.

XI. 1400. 9. Thomas Fitz-Alan, son and heir of Richard X.-8th Earl; restored as Earl of Arundel and Surrey, 1400; K. G.; ob. 1415, s. p. leaving his sisters his heirs, of whom Elizabeth married Thomas Mowbray, I.-1st Duke of Norfolk

T 3

EARLS.

XII. 1451.   John Mowbray, son and heir apparent of
John III.-3d Duke of Norfolk, and great-
grandson of John 1st Duke of Norfolk, by
Elizabeth, sister and heir of Thomas the last
Earl of Surrey; Created Earl of Warren and
Surrey 29 March, 1451, vitâ patris; suc-
ceeded as IV.-4th Duke of Norfolk in 1461;
Earl Marshal; K. G.; ob. 1475, s. p. m. when
the titles of Norfolk, Surrey and Warren,
became

Extinct.*

XIII. 1483.   1. Thomas Howard; Created Earl of Surrey 28
June, 1483; Attainted 1485, when his ho-
nors became Forfeited, but was restored to
the Earldom in 1489; Created Duke of Norfolk (his father, John VI.-1st Duke having
been Attainted) 1st Feb. 1514, K. G. ob. 1524.

XIV. 1524.   2. Thomas Howard, s. and h. Duke of Norfolk;
Attainted 1546, when his dignities became
Forfeited.; restored 1553; K. G. ob. 1554.

XV. 1554.   3. Thomas Howard, Duke of Norfolk, grandson
and heir, being s. and h. of Henry Howard,
K. G. the Poet, who is generally styled Earl
of Surrey (eldest son of the last Duke,) who
was Attainted and beheaded 1547; restored in
blood and honors 1553; Attainted and beheaded 1572, when all his honors became
Forfeited.

XVI. 1603.   4. Thomas Howard, s. and h. of Philip Howard,
Earl of Arundel (eldest son of Thomas the

---

* Brooke considers (and in which he is not contradicted by
his severe commentator Vincent) that Richard Plantagenet,
Duke of York, 2d son of King Edward IV. who was betrothed to
Ann Moubray, the dau. and heir of John Duke of Norfolk, and
last Earl of Surrey, was created Earl of Surrey, and which title is
likewise attributed to him by most other writers. Dugdale and
Vincent however cite his patents of creation to the Earldoms of
Nottingham and Warrren, and to the Dukedom of Norfolk, but takes
no notice of any patent creating him *Earl of Surrey*, though 20*l.*
a year was assigned him out of the counties of Surrey and Sussex
to support his other dignities. It is consequently very doubtful if
he really ever possessed that Earldom.

EARLS.

last Duke), which Philip was Attainted in
1590. Restored in blood, and to such honours as his father enjoyed, likewise as Earl
of Surrey, in 1603; Created Earl of Norfolk
6 June 1644, K.G.; ob. 1646.

XVII. 1646.5.Henry Frederick Howard, s. and h. Earl of
Arundel, Norfolk, and Surrey; ob. 1652.

XVIII. 1652.6.Thomas Howard, s. and h. Earl of Arundel,
Norfolk, and Surrey. Restored to the Dukedom of Norfolk 8th May, 1644; since which
period the Earldom of Surrey has been merged
in that dignity.

Vide NORFOLK.

SUSSEX.

EARLS.

I.   Will.I.1.Roger de Montgomery; Created Earl of Sussex * by William the Conqueror; ob. 1094.

II.   1094. 2.Hugh de Montgomery, 2d son; ob. 1098.

III. 1098. 3. Robert de Belesme, eldest brother and heir,
being s. and h. of Roger, 1st Earl; deprived
of the Earldom for treason, 1102.

IV.   Hen.I.1.William de Albini, s. and h. of William de Al-
bini Pinerna, by his marriage with Adeliza
Queen of England, widow of King Henry I.
acquired the castle of Arundel and the
County of Sussex†, and was styled Earl of
Arundel; ob. 1176.

V.   1176. 2. William de Albini, s. and h.; ob. 1222.

---

* Vide Dugdale, vol. I. p. 26. It is to be observed, that this
family is not included in the catalogue of the Earls of this County,
either by Brooke or Vincent.

† Dugdale, speaking of this Earl, vol. I. p. 119, says:—" In
the reign of Henry he did not only obtain the castle and honor of
Arundel to himself and his heirs, but a confirmation of the Earldom of Sussex (for though the title of Earl was most known by
Arundel and Chichester, at which places his chief residence used
to be, yet it was of the County of Sussex that he was really Earl)
by the *Tertium Denarium* of the Pleas of Sussex granted to him,

EARLS.

VI.　1222. 3. William de Albini, s. and h.; ob. ....

VII.　12... 4. William de Albini, s. and h.; ob. 1233, s. p.

VIII.1233. 5. Hugh de Albini, brother and heir, ob. 1243,
s. p. after which the Earldom of Sussex terminated, probably in consequence of his great
possessions being divided amongst his four
sisters and heirs.

IX.　1529. 1. Robert Ratcliffe IX.-13th Baron and I. Viscount Fitzwalter; Created Earl of Sussex
28th December, 1529, K. G. Lord High
Chamberlain; ob. 1542.

X.　1542. 2. Henry Ratcliffe, s. and h. K. G.; ob. 1556.

XI.　1556. 3. Thomas Ratcliffe, s. and h. K. G.; ob. 1583,
s. p.

XII.　1583. 4. Henry Ratcliffe, brother and heir, K. G.; ob.
1593.

XIII.1593. 5. Robert Ratcliffe, s. and h. K. G.; ob. 1629, s.p.

XIV.1629. 6. Edward Ratcliffe, cousin and heir, being s.
and h. of Humphrey, 2d son of Robert, 1st
Earl, succeeded as Viscount Fitzwalter and
Earl of Sussex; ob. 1641, s. p. when these
titles became
Extinct.

XV.　1644. 1. Thomas Savile, 2d Baron Savile in England,
and 1st Viscount Castlebar in Ireland; Created Earl of Sussex 25 May, 1644; ob. 1646.

XVI.1646. 2. James Savile, s. and h.; ob. 1671, s. p. when
his honors became
Extinct.

XVII. 1674. 1. Thomas Lennard XIV.-14th Baron Dacre;
Created Earl of Sussex 5th October, 1674;
ob. 1715, s. p. m. when the Earldom again
became
Extinct.

XVIII.1717. 1.Talbot Yelverton XV.-16th Baron Grey of
Ruthyn, and 2d Viscount Longueville; Cre-

which was the usual way of investing such great men (in ancient
times) with the possession of any Earldom, after those ceremonies
of girding with the sword, and putting on the robes, performed,
which have ever, till of late, been thought essential to their
creation."

ated Earl of Sussex 26 Sept. 1717, with remainder, failing his issue male, to his brother, Henry Yelverton, and his issue male.
EARLS. K. B.; ob. 1731.

XIX. 1731. 2. George Augustus Yelverton, s. and h.; ob.
1758, s. p.

XX. 1758. 3. Henry Yelverton, brother and heir; ob. 1799,
s. p. m. when the Viscountcy of Longueville
and Earldom of Sussex became

Extinct.

DUKE.

I. 1801. 1. H. R. H. Augustus Frederick, 6th son of His
Majesty King George III. and brother of His
present Most Gracious Majesty; Created Baron of Arklow in Ireland, Earl of Inverness
in North Britain, and Duke of Sussex, 7th
November 1801. Present Duke of Sussex
and Earl of Inverness; also Baron Arklow, in
Ireland, K. G.

SUTTON.

BARON BY WRIT.

1. 1323. 1. John de Sutton, Summ. to Parl. from 26th
Dec. 17 Edw. II. 1323, to 30 December,
18 Edw. II. 1324, as "Johanni de Sutton,"
and is presumed to be the same person who
was summoned from 20 July, 6 Edw. III.
1332, to 20 April, 17 Edw. III. 1343, as "Jobanni de Sutton de Holdernesse."

It is difficult to ascertain who this John de Sutton was,
unless he was the John de Sutton who married Margaret,
sister and coheir of John de Somerie, I.-8th Baron of Dudley,
whose son and heir, John de Sutton, was Summ. to Parl.
as John de Sutton de Dudley, 25 Feb. 16 Edw. III. 1342,
and died in 1359. Dugdale gives no account, in his
Baronage, of any person called Sutton being summoned
before 1342, but his statement relative to this family is
very obscure and unsatisfactory. There was also a

BARON BY WRIT.

I. 1360. John de Sutton, Summ. to Parl. as "Johanni
de Sutton de Essex," 3 April, 34 Edw. III.
1360, but nothing more is said of him.

SWILLINGTON.

BARONS BY WRIT.

1.   1326. 1. Adam de Swillington, Summ. to Parl. from 3d
          December, 20 Edw. II. 1326, to 5 March, 2
          Edw. III. 1328, but never afterwards, nor any
          of his posterity, and of whom Dugdale gives
          no further account.

SWYNERTON.

BARON BY WRIT.

1.   1337. 1. Roger de Swynerton, Summ. to Parl. 23 April,
          11 Edw. III. 1337, but never afterwards, nor
          any of his posterity, which continued in the
          male line for several generations.

SYDNEY
OF PENSHURST.

BARONS.

1.   1603. 1. Robert Sydney (son of Sir Henry Sydney, K. G.
          by Mary, sister of Robert Dudley, Earl of Lei-
          cester) ; Created Baron Sydney of Penshurst,
          co. Kent, 13th May, 1603; Created Viscount
          L'Isle May 4, 1605, and on 2 August, 1618,
          Earl of Leicester, in which dignity this Ba-
          rony, and the Viscountcy of L'Isle, continued
          merged until the death of Josceline Sydney,
          XVIII.-18th Earl of Leicester, in 1743, when
          they became
          𝕰𝖝𝖙𝖎𝖓𝖈𝖙.

This Barony was claimed in May, 1782, by Elizabeth,
widow of William Perry, Esq. and daughter, and eventually sole heir of Thomas Sydney, next brother of Josceline, last Earl of Leicester and Baron Sydney, under the
presumption that Robert Sydney (the Petitioner's grandfather) the son and heir apparent of Philip XIV.-3d Earl
of Leicester, having been summoned to Parliament, vita
patris, in his father's Barony, a Barony IN FEE was
thereby created ; but the House of Lords resolved, 17 June
1782, " That Robert Sydney, commonly called Viscount
L'isle, the Petitioner's grandfather, under whom she de-

rives her claim, acquired no new Barony; but being the eldest son of his father, the Earl of Leicester, was summoned into his father's Barony in tail male; therefore the Petitioner has no right in consequence of her grandfather's summons and sitting."

SYDNEY

OF MILTON AND SHEPPEY.

BARON. VISCOUNT.

I. 1689.—I. 1689. Henry Sydney, brother of Philip, XIV.-3d Earl of Leicester; Created Baron Sydney of Milton, and Viscount Sydney of Sheppey, both co. Kent, 9 April, 1689; Created Earl of Romney 14th May, 1694; ob. 1700, s. p. when all his titles became

𝕰𝔵𝔱𝔦𝔫𝔠𝔱

SYDNEY

OF CHISLEHURST, AND ST. LEONARDS.

BARONS.   VISCOUNTS.

I. 1783.—I. 1789. 1. Thomas Townshend, eldest son of Thomas Townshend, 2d son of Charles 2d Viscount Townshend, K. G. by Elizabeth, dau. of Thomas, 1st Baron Pelham, son of Sir John Pelham, Bart. by Lucy Sydney, his wife, sister of Philip XIV.-3d Earl of Leicester, and 3d Baron Sydney of Penshurst, and of Henry Sydney, last Baron Sydney of Milton, and Viscount Sydney of Sheppey; Created Baron Sydney of Chislehurst, co. Kent, 6 March 1783, and on the 11th June, 1789, Viscount Sydney of St. Leonard's, co. Gloucester; ob. 1800.

II. 1800.—II. 1800. 2. John Thomas Townshend, s. and h. Present Viscount and Baron Sydney.

TADCASTER.

VISCOUNT.

I.   1714. 1. Henry O'Bryen, Earl of Thomond in Ireland ;
              Created Viscount Tadcaster, co. York, 19th
              Oct. 1714; ob. 1741, s. p. when the Viscountcy
              became
                          𝕰𝖝𝖙𝖎𝖓𝖈𝖙.

TALBOT.

BARON BY TENURE.

1. Hen. I.   Geoffrey Talbot, s. and h: of Richard Talbot.
              He held divers knight's fees, temp. Hen. I.
              but Dugdale gives no farther account of him
              than that he was living in 1138 : in the reign
              of Henry II. the above knight's fees were
              possessed by Walter de Meduana.

TALBOT

OF ——

BARONS BY TENURE.

I.   Hen. I. 1. Hugh Talbot, presumed to have been brother
                ther to the above Geoffrey ; ob. ....
II. Steph. 2. Richard Talbot, s. and h. living 1153.
III. H. II. 3. Gilbert Talbot, s. and h. living 1205.
IV. H. III. 4. Richard Talbot, s. and h.; ob. ....
V.   Edw. I. 5. Gilbert Talbot, s. and h.   He married Guen-
                lian, dau. and at length heir, of Rhese ap
                Griffiths, Prince of South Wales ; ob. 1274.
VI. Edw. I. 6. Richard Talbot *, s. and h. Though never sum-
                moned to Parliament, it is evident, from his
                being present at the Parliament held at Lin-

---

 * This Baron relinquished his paternal coat-armour, of bendy of
ten Argent and Gules, and assumed that of his mother, viz. Gules,
a lion rampant within a bordure Or, and which has been retained
as the ensigns of his illustrious descendants.

coln 29 Edw. I. and signing the letter to the
Pope as "Ricardus Talebot, Dominus de Eck-
leswell," that he ranked among the Barons
of his times; ob. 1306.

I. 1331. 7. Gilbert Talbot, s. and h. Summ. to Parl. from
5th June, 4 Edw. III. 1331, to 20th April,
17 Edw. III. 1343; ob. 1346.

II. 1331. 8. Richard Talbot, s. and h. Summ. to Parl.
from 5 June, 4 Edw. III. 1331, to 22 Oct. 29
Edw. III. 1355; ob. 1356.

III. 1356. 9. Gilbert Talbot, s. and h. Summ. to Parl. from
14 Aug. 36 Edw. III. 1362, to 8 Aug. 10 Rich.
II. 1386; ob. 1387.

IV. 1387. 10. Richard Talbot, s. and h. having married Ankaret, sister, and eventually sole heir of
John, Baron Strange of Blackmere; he was
Summ. to Parl. vitâ patris, from 3 March,
7 Rich. II. 1384, to 17 Dec. 11 Rich. II. 1387,
as "Richardo Talbot de Blackmere." Succeeded his father in the Barony of Talbot in
1387; and it appears that, on 17 Dec.11 Ric. II.
1387, in the same writ in which he was summoned as "Richard Talbot of Blackmere," he
was likewise summoned as "Ricardo Talbot
de Godricke Castell," and from that time to
13th Nov. 17 Rich. II. 1393, by the same designation; ob. 1396.

V. 1396. 11. Gilbert Talbot, s. and h. Summ. to Parl. as
"Gilberto Talbot," from 25 Aug. 5 Hen. IV.
1404, to 5 Oct. 5 Hen. V. 1417, K.G.; ob. 1419,
leaving Ankaret, his sole daughter and heir;
who dying an infant in 1431, this Barony,
together with that of Strange of Blackmere,
devolved on her uncle and heir,

VI. 1421. 12. John Talbot, next brother of Gilbert the last
Baron, who having married Maud de Ne-
vill, eldest dau. and coheir of Thomas V.
Baron Furnival, was Summ. to Parl. from 26
Oct. 11 Hen. IV. 1409, to 26 Nov. 8 Hen. V.
1421, as "Johanni Talbot de Furnyvall." Summoned
as "Johanni Talbot Militi," from 19 Feb. 3 Hen. VI.
1425, to 5 July, 13 Hen. VI. 1435; Created Earl of
Shrewsbury 20 March 1442, K.G. This Barony, together

.. with those of Furnival and Strange of Blackmere, con-
. tinued vested in the Earls of Shrewsbury until the death
of Gilbert, X-7th Earl, in 1626, s.p.m. when they fell
into ABEYANCE between, his three daughters and coheirs.
· On the demise of two of the said coheirs, s. p. the Abeyance of the Baronies of Talbot, Furnival, and Strange of
Blackmere, terminated, and they are presumed to have
become vested in Althea, widow of Thomas .Howard
XXIII.-20 Earl of Arundel, the third daughter and coheir;
and her descendants, the Earls of Arundel and Surrey, and
Dukes of Norfolk, inherited these Baronies until the death
. of Edward Howard XIV.-11th Duke of Norfolk, in 1777,
s. p. when they again fell into ABEYANCE between the two
daughters and coheirs of Philip Howard, brother of the
said Edward Duke of Norfolk,·Baron Talbot, Strange of
Blackmere, Furnival, &c. between whose representatives,
viz. William, present Baron Stourton, and William
. Francis .Henry, present Baron Petre, they are now in
ABEYANCE.   Vide STRANGE of BLACKMERE.

TALBOT

· OP HENSOL.

BARONS.
I.   1733. 1. Charles Talbot, lineally descended from Sir
            . Gilbert Talbot of Grafton, 3d son of John,
            V-2d Earl of Shrewsbury; Created Baron Tal-
            bot of Hensol, co. Glamorgan, 5 Dec. 1733.
            Lord Chancellor; ob. 1737.

    EARLS.
II. 1737.—I. 1761. 2. William Talbot, son and heir; Created
                    Earl Talbot 10 Mar. 1761; Cre-
                    ted Baron Dynevor, with a spe-
                    cial remainder 17 Oct. 1780; ob.
                    1782, s. p. m. when the Earldom
                    of Talbot became Extinct; but
                    the Barony of Talbot devolved on
III. 1782.—II. 1784. 3. John Chetwynd Talbot, nephew
                    and heir male, being son and
                    heir of John Talbot, 2d son of
                    Charles 1st Baron; Created Vis-
                    count Ingestrie, co. Stafford and
                    Earl Talbot of Hensol, co. Gla-
                    morgan, 3 July, 1784; ob. 1793.
IV. 1793.—III. 1793. 4. Charles Chetwynd Talbot, s. and

h. Present Earl and Baron Talbot, and Viscount Ingestrie, Lord
Lieut. of Ireland in 1819, K. P.

TALBOT

OF RICHARD'S CASTLE.

Richard Talbot, next brother of Gilbert I.-7th Baron
Talbot, having married Joan, dau. and coheir of Hugh Mortimer of Castle Richard, co. Hertford, acquired that ter-
ritory about the end of the reign of Edward II. to whom
succeeded John his son and heir, whose daughters, or according to Dugdale, grand-daughters and heirs Elizabeth
and Philippa (the former the wife of Sir Warine Arch-
dekne, Knt. and the latter of Sir Matthew Gournay, Knt.)
shared the inheritance; but none of this branch of the
Talbot family were ever summoned to Parliament; and
as they did not acquire this Barony until the reign of
Edward II. they cannot be considered to have been
BARONS of the Realm, as feudal honors rarely, if ever existed after the 23d of Edw. I.

TALBOYS.

BARON BY WRIT.
I. 1529. 1. Gilbert Talboys, lineally descended from Henry
Talboys by Elizabeth his wife, dau. and heir
of Gilbert Burdon by Elizabeth his wife,
sister and heir of Gilbert Earl of Angos, son
and heir of Gilbert Earl of Angos by Lucie de
Kyme his wife, sister and heir of William
II.-8th Baron Kyme; Summ. to Parl. 21
Hen. VIII. anno 1529, as "Gilbert Talboys
de Kyme," and sat by that title in the Parliament held 28 Hen. VIII. anno 1536; ob.

BARONESS. 15.., S. P. M.
I. 15.. 2. Elizabeth, his sole dau. and heir, is presumed
to have succeeded to the Barony, as Mr.
Wimbish her husband, claimed the dignity
jure uxoris, when it was solemnly decided in
the presence of King Henry VIII. " that no
man, husband of a Baroness, should use the

U 2

title of her dignity until he had a child by her, whereby he should become tenant by courtesie of her Barony." She married, secondly, Ambrose Dudley, Earl of Warwick, but died s. p. when the title became

𝕰𝔵𝔱𝔦𝔫𝔠𝔱.

TAMWORTH.

Viscountcy, 3 September, 1711.

Vide FERRERS.

TANI.

BARONS BY TENURE.

I.   Will.I. 1. Robert de Tani, temp. William I. to whom succeeded

II. Hen.I. 2. Haseulf de Tani; living 1139; his successor was

III. Steph. 3. Rainald de Tani; ob. .... s. p.

IV. H. II. 4. Gruel de Tani, brother and heir; living 1165; ob. 1179.

V.   H. II. 5. Hasculf de Tani; presumed to have been son and heir; living 1190; to whom succeeded

VI. Ric. I. 6. Gilbert de Tani; ob. 1221, s. p.

I.   H. III. 1. Peter de Thani; presumed to have been of the same family; living 1236.

II. H. III. 2. John de Thani, son and heir; ob. ante 1246.

III. H. III. 3. Richard de Thani, s. and h. ob. 1271.

IV. Edw.I. 4. Richard de Thani, s. and h. ob. 1296, leaving Roger his son and heir; but as neither he nor his posterity were ever summoned to Parliament, they can no longer be ranked among the Barons of the Realm.

. TANKERVILLE *.

EARLS.

I.   1695. 1. Forde Grey, 3d Baron Grey of Werke; Created Viscount Grey of Glendale, and Earl of

----

* Sir John Grey, ancestor of the Barons Grey of Powis, was created Earl of Tankerville in NORMANDY, 6 Hen. VI. which dignity his grandson forfeited the 38 Hen. VI.

BARONS BY TENURE.

Tankerville, co. Northumberland, 11 May, 1695; ob. 1701, S. P. M. when the Viscountcy and Earldom became

Extinct.

II. 1714. 1. Charles Bennet, 2d Baron Ossulston, having married Mary, sole dau. and heir of the last Earl, was created Earl of Tankerville 19 October, 1714, K. T.; ob. 1722.

III. 1722. 2. Charles Bennet, s. and h. K. T.; ob. 1753.

IV. 1753. 3. Charles Bennet, s. and h. ob. 1767.

V. 1767. 4. Charles Bennet, s. and h. ob. 1822.

VI. 1822. 5. Charles Augustus Bennet, s. and h. Present Earl of Tankerville and Baron Ossulston. 🜨

TATSHALL.

BARONS BY TENURE.

I. Will.I. 1. Eudo, Lord of Tatshall, temp. Will. I. ob.....

II. Steph. 2. Hugh Fitz-Eudo, s. and h. Lord of Tatshall; living 1139.

III. H. II. 3. Robert Fitz-Hugh, s. and h. living 1167.

IV. Ric. I. 4. Philip Fitz-Robert, s. and h. Lord of Tatshall, ob. circa 1199.

V. John. 5. Robert de Tatshall, s. and h. ob. 1213.

VI. H.III. 6. Robert de Tatshall, s. and h.; he married Amabill, eldest dau. and coheir of William de
BY WRIT. Albini, Earl of Arundel; ob. 1249.

I. 1295. 7. Robert de Tatshall, s. and h. Summ. to Parl. from 24 June, 23 Edward I. 1295, to 26 Aug. 24 Edward I. 1296; he was likewise Summoned 26 Jan. 25 Edw. I. 1297; but for the reasons assigned under "FITZ-JOHN," it is doubtful if that Writ can be considered as a regular Summons to Parliament; ob. 1297.

II. 1299. 8. Robert de Tatshall, s. and h. Summ. to Parl. from 6 February, 27 Edward I. 1299, to 13 September, 30 Edward I. 1302; ob. 1303, leaving Robert his son and heir, who died in 1306, s. P. and in his minority, when his aunts, the sisters of Robert his father, or their issue, became his heirs; among whose descendants and representatives this Barony,

if the above statement be correct*, is in
ABEYANCE.

TAVISTOCK.

MARQUESATE, 11 May, 1694.
        Vide BEDFORD.

TEMPLE.

COUNTESS.		
I.	1749.	1. Hester Granville, Viscountess and Baroness Cobbam, wife of Richard Grenville, Esq. Created Countess Temple, with remainder of the dignity of Earl Temple to her issue male,
EARLS.		18 Oct. 1749; ob. 1752.
I.	1752.	2. Richard Grenville (assumed the name of) Temple, s. and h. K. G.; ob. 1779, s. p.
II.	1779.	3. George Grenville (assumed the names of) Nugent-Temple, nephew and heir, being son and heir of George Grenville, next brother of the last Earl; Created Marquess of Buckingham 30 Nov. 1784; ob. 1813.
III.	1813.	4. Richard Temple Nugent Grenville (assumed
OF STOWE.		the names of) Brydges-Chandos, s. and h.;
I.	1822.	Created Duke of Buckingham and Chandos, Marquess of Chandos and Earl Temple of Stowe, with remainder of the said Earldom, failing the heirs male under the former patent to Anne Eliza, his Grace's granddaughter, and the heirs male of her body; 12 Jan. 1822. Present Earl Temple, and Earl Temple of Stowe, Viscount and Baron Cob-

---

* It is to be observed, that neither Dugdale, Collins, nor Banks
state that any of this family were ever summoned to Parl. From
the Lists of Summonses, however, a Robert de Tateshall appears
to have been summoned the 23th, 24th, 25th, 27th, 28th,
and 30th of Edward I. and the only ground which the Editor has
for asserting, that *both* the last Barons were summoned, is the
years assigned by Dugdale for their deaths. Robert the last
Baron summoned, was born about the year 1274; hence it is
possible that *all* the Writs were directed to him, though the
above statement is the most probable.

ham, Duke of Buckingham and Chandos, Marquess of Buckingham and Marquess of Chandos, also Earl Nugent in Ireland, K.G.

TEWKSBURY.

BARONY, 9 November, 1706—Merged in the Crown 11 June, 1727.   Vide CAMBRIDGE.

TEYES.

BARONY, 7 July, 1660—Extinct 1688.
       Vide ALBEMARLE.

BARONY, 10 April, 1689—Extinct 1719.
       Vide SCHOMBERG.

TEYNHAM.

BARONS.

I. 1611. 1. John Roper ; Created Baron Teynham of Teynham, co. Kent, 9 July, 1616 ; ob. 1618.

II. 1618. 2. Christopher Roper, s. and h. ob. 1622.

III. 1622. 3. John Roper, s. and h. ob. 1627.

IV. 1627. 4. Christopher Roper, s. and h. ob. 1673.

V. 1673. 5. Christopher Roper, s. and h. ob. 1688.

VI. 1688. 6. John Roper, s. and h. ob. 1689, s. p.

VII. 1689. 7. Christopher Roper, brother and heir ; ob. 1697, s. p.

VIII.1697. 8. Henry Roper. brother and heir ; ob. 1723.

IX. 1723. 9. Philip Roper, s. and h. ob. 1727, s. p.

X. 1727. 10.Henry Roper, brother and heir ; ob. 1781.

XI. 1781. 11.Henry Roper, s. and h. ob. 1786.

XII. 1786. 12 Henry Roper, s. and h. ob. 1800, s. p.

XIII.1800. 13.John Roper, brother and heir ; ob. 1824, s. p.

XIV.1824. 14.Henry Francis Roper (assumed the name of) Curzon, 1st cousin and heir, being son and heir of Francis Roper, brother of Henry X.-10th Baron. Present Baron Teynham.

THAME.

VISCOUNTCY, 28 January, 1620—Extinct 1620.
       Vide BERKSHIRE.

THANET.

EARLS.

I.   1628. 1. Nicholas Tufton, 1st Baron Tufton; Created Earl of Thanet, co. Kent, 5 August, 1628; ob. 1632.

II.   1632. 2. John Tufton, s. and h.; he married Margaret, dau. and coheir of Richard Earl of Dorset by Ann Baroness Clifford; ob. 1664.

III. 1664. 3. Nicholas Tufton, s. and h. ob. 1679, s. p.

IV. 1679. 4. John Tufton, brother and heir; ob. 1680, s. p.

V.   1680. 5. Richard Tufton, brother and heir; ob. 1684, s. p.

VI. 1684. 6. Thomas Tufton, brother and heir; claimed and was allowed the ancient Barony of Clifford in 1691; ob. 1729, s. p. m. when the Barony of Clifford fell into ABEYANCE between his daughters and coheirs; his other honors devolved on

VII. 1729. 7. Sackville Tufton, nephew and heir male, being s. and h. of Sackville Tufton, next brother of the last Earl; ob. 1753.

VIII.1753. 8. Sackville Tufton, s. and h. ob. 1786.

IX. 1786. 9. Sackville Tufton, s. and h.; ob. 1825.

X.   1825.10. Charles Tufton, brother and heir. Present Earl of Thanet, Baron Tufton, and a Baronet.

THETFORD.

VISCOUNTCY, 12 April, 1672.

Vide ARLINGTON.

THOMOND.

BARON.

I.   1801. Murrough O'Bryen, 1st Marquess of Thomond in Ireland; Created Baron Thomond of Taplow, co. Bucks, 2 Oct. 1801, K.P.; ob. 1808, s. p. when the Barony became
𝔈𝔵𝔱𝔦𝔫𝔠𝔱.

THORPE.

BARONS BY WRIT.

I.   1309.   John de Thorpe; Summ. to Parl. from 11 June, 2 Edward II. 1309, to 10 Oct. 19 Edw. II. 1325.

THORPE.

OF ——

I.   1381.   William de Thorpe; Summ. to Parl. from 16 July, 5 Rich. II. 1381, to 12 Sept. 14 Rich. II. 1390.

It is singular that neither Dugdale, nor Collins give any account of these Barons. Beatson says that John de Thorp was Lord of Creke, co. Norfolk, in right of his grandmother Margaret, eldest sister and coheir of Bartholomew, Lord of Creke; he is however silent with respect to William de Thorpe. Banks, in his Stemmata Anglicana (though he has omitted to notice them in his Extinct Baronage) states, John Baron Thorpe died in 17 Edw. II. and deduces the pedigree to Sir Edmund Thorpe, who died in 1417, leaving two daughters his coheirs, viz. Isabel, who married Philip Tylney, and Joan, who married first Sir Robert Echingham, and secondly Sir John Clifton: if this pedigree be correct, the Barony created by the Writ of 2 Edw. II. is vested in the descendants and representatives of the said Joan and Isabel. None of the descendants of John de Thorpe were however summoned to Parliament. Nothing appears to be recorded of the descendants of William Baron Thorpe.

THROWLEY.

BARONY, 8 April, 1676—Extinct 1709.

Vide FEVERSHAM.

BARONY, 19 October, 1714—Extinct 1746.

Vide ROCKINGHAM.

THURLOW.

BARONS.

I.   1778. 1. Edward Thurlow; Created Baron Thurlow of
OF THURLOW.   Ashfield, co. Suffolk, 3 June, 1778; Created
I.   1792.   Baron Thurlow of Thurlow, co. Suffolk, with remainder, failing his male issue, to his brothers and their issue male, 12 June, 1792; Lord High Chancellor; ob. 1806, s. p. when

the Barony of Thurlow of Ashfield became **Extinct**; but the Barony of Thurlow of Thurlow·devolved, agreeably to the limitation, on

II. 1806. 2. Edward Hovell Thurlow, nephew and heir, being son and heir of Thomas Thurlow, Bishop of Durham, next brother of the last Baron.   Present Baron Thurlow of Thurlow. ⊤

THWENG.

I.   1307. 1. Marmaduke de Thweng ; Summ. to Parl. 8 June, 22 Edward I. 1294; but it is very doubtful if that Writ can be considered as a regular Summons to Parl. vide " CLYVE-DON ; Summ. to Parl. from 22 Feb. 35 Edw.I. 1307, to 18 Sept. 16 Edw. II. 1322 ; ob.1323.

II.   1323. 2. William de Thweng, s. and h. Summ. to Parl. 30 Dec. 18 Edw. II. 1324, but never after ; ob. 1341, s. p. leaving his brother Robert his heir, a Priest, who died 1344, s. p. to whom succeeded Thomas his brother, also a Priest, and who died s. p. 1374, leaving the descendants of his three sisters, viz. Lucia, who married Sir Robert Lumley; Margaret, who married Sir Robert Hilton; and Katherine, who married Sir Rauf Daubenie, his heirs; between whose descendants and representatives this Barony is in ABEYANCE.

THYNNE.

BARONY, 11 December, 1682.
                              Vide WEYMOUTH.

TIBETOT.

I.   1308. 1. Pain de Tibetot; Summoned to Parl. from 10 March, 1 Edward II. 1308, to 26 Nov. 7 Edw. II. 1310 ; ob. 1314.

II.   1314. 2. John de Tibetot, s. and h. Summ. to Parl.

- - from 1 April, 9 Edw. III. 1335, to 20 Jan. 39 Edward III. 1366; he married Margaret, sister and coheir of Giles Lord Badlesmere; ob. 1367.

III. 1367. 3. Robert de Tibetot, s. and h. Summ. to Parl. 24 Feb. 42 Edward III. 1368, and 8 Jan. 44 Edward III. 1371; ob. 1372, s. P. M. leaving Margaret, Milisent, and Elizabeth, his daughters and coheirs; Margaret married Roger 2d Lord Scrope of Bolton; Milisent became the wife of Stephen le Scrope; and Elizabeth married Philip le Despencer; between whose descendants and representatives this Barony is in ABEYANCE.

Margaret, the eldest coheir of this Barony is now represented by Charles Jones, Esq. the heir-general of the body of the said Margaret, and of her husband Roger Lord Scrope. Vide SCROPE OF BOLTON.

TIBETOT VEL TIPTOFT.

I. 1426. 1. John de Tiptoft, s. and h. of Pain de Tibetot, next brother of Robert 3d Baron; Summ. to Parl. from 7 Jan. 4 Hen. VI. 1426, to 3 Dec. 20 Hen. VI. 1441, probably from having married Joyce, the daughter and coheir of Edward Baron Cherleton. Dugdale says he bore the title of Lord Tiptoft and Powys; but he was never summoned by any other designation than "Johanni Tiptoft, Chl'r;" ob. 1443.

II. 1443. 2. John de Tiptoft, s. and h. Created Earl of Worcester 16 July, 1449, being then just of age; beheaded and attainted 1470, when his honors became

Forfeited.

III. 1471. 3. Edward de Tiptoft, s. and h. Restored in blood; Earl of Worcester; ob. 1485, s. P. infra ætatem, leaving his aunts, sisters of John 2d Baron, and 1st Earl of Worcester, his heirs, viz. Philippa, wife of Thomas Roos; Joan, wife of Sir Edmund Inglethorpe; and

Joice, who married Edmund Dudley; between whose descendants and representatives
this Barony is in ABEYANCE.

TINDALE.

BARONS BY TENURE.

I.   Hen. I. 1. .... de Tindale; held the Barony of Lange-
ley, co. Northumberland, temp. Henry I. to
whom succeeded

II. Ric. I. 2. Adam de Tindale; living 1194; ob. s. p. m.
leaving Philippa, who married Adam de Bol-
teby, and .... his daughters and coheirs.

TINMOUTH.

EARLDOM, 19 March, 1687—Forfeited 1695.

Vide BERWICK.

TIPTOFT.   Vide TIBETOT.

TITCHFIELD.

MARQUISATE, 6 July, 1716.

Vide PORTLANLD.

TIVIOTDALE.

DUKEDOM, 23 April, 1799.

Vide CUMBERLAND.

TODENI.

BARONS BY TENURE.

I.   Will. I. 1. Robert de Todeni; Lord of Belvoir, co. Lincoln; ob. 1088.

II. Will. II. 2. William de Todeni, s. and h.   He assumed the
name of Albini.   Vide ALBINI.

TONI.

BARONS BY TENURE.

I.   Will.I. 1. Ralph de Toni ; Standard Bearer to William the Conqueror, from whom he obtained divers Lordships ; ob. 1102.

II. Hen.I. 2. Ralph de Toni, s. and h. ob. .. ...

III. Steph. 3. Roger de Toni, s. and h. ob. 1162.

IV. Ric. I. 4. Roger de Toni, s. and h. living 1199.

V.   John. 5. Ralph de Toni ; presumed to have been son and heir of the last Baron ; ob. 1239.

VI. H.III. 6. Roger de Toni, s. and h. ; ob. 1277.

VII.Edw.I. 7. Ralph de Toni, s. and h. living 1294.

BY WRIT.

I.   1299. 8. Robert de Toni, s. and h. Summ. to Parl. from 10 April, 27 Edward I. 1299, to 16 June, 4 Edw. II. 1311 ; ob. circa 1311, s. p. when this Barony became
Extinct.

Dugdale says nothing of any of this family having ever been summoned to Parliament, and states that this Robert died 3 Edw. II. 1310.

TORBAY.

BARONY, 29 May, 1689—Extinct 1716.

Vide TORRINGTON.

TORRINGTON.

EARLDOM, 7 July, 1660—Extinct 1688.

Vide ALBEMARLE.

EARLS.

III. 1689. 1. Arthur Herbert, descended from the common ancestor of the Earls of Pembroke, Barons Herbert of Chirbury, &c. ; Created Baron of Torbay and Earl of Torrington, both co. Devon, with remainder, failing his issue male, to Charles Herbert his brother, May 29, 1689 ; ob. 1716, s. p. ; and his brother having died vitâ fratis, s. p. his honors became

BARON.   -   ### Extinct.

I.   1716.   Thomas Newport, 2d son of Francis I.-1st Earl of Bradford ; Created Baron of Torrington, co.

Devon. 25 June, 1716; ob. 1719, s. p. when
the title again became

Extinct.

VISCOUNTS.
I. 1721. 1. Sir George Byng, 1st Bart.; Created Baron
Byng of Southill, co. Bedford, and Viscount
Torrington, co. Devon. 9 Sept. 1721, K. B.;
ob. 1733.
II. 1733. 2. Pattee Byng, s. and h. ob. 1747, s. p.
III. 1747. 3. George Byng, brother and heir; ob. 1750.
IV. 1750. 4. George Byng, s. and h. ob. 1812, s. p. m.
V. 1812. 5. John Byng, brother and heir; ob. 1813.
VI. 1813. 6. George Byng, s. and h. Present Viscount
Torrington, Baron Byng, and a Baronet. ⊤

TOTNESS.

EARLS.
I. 1626. George Carew, 1st Baron Carew of Clopton;
Created Earl of Totness, co. Devon. 5 Feb.
1626; ob. 1629, s. p. m. when his honors
became

Extinct.

VISCOUNTCY, 29 July, 1675—Extinct 1680.

Vide PLYMOUTH.

TOWNSHEND.

BARONS.   VISCOUNTS.
I. 1661.—I. 1682. 1. Sir Horatio Townshend, 3d Bart.;
Created Baron Townshend of Lynn
Regis, co. Norfolk, 20 April, 1661;
Created Viscount Townshend of
Raynham, co. Norfolk, 11th Dec.
1682; ob. 1687.
II. 1687.—II. 1687. 2. Charles Townshend, s. and h. K. G.;
Lord Lieut. of Ireland 1717; ob.
1738.
III. 1738.—III. 1738. 3. Charles Townshend, s. and h. ob.
1764.
MARQUESSES.
·86.—IV. 1786.—I. 1786. 4. George Townshend, s. and
h. Created Marquess Towns-
hend of Raynham, co. Nor-

BARONS.   VISC.   MARQ.

folk, 27 Oct. 1786; Lord Lieut. of Ireland. He married Charlotte Baroness Ferrers de Chartley; ob. 1807.

V.1807.—V.1807.—II. 1807. 5. George Townshend, s. and h. Baron Ferrers de Chartley jure matris; Created Earl of Leicester, vitâ patris, 18 May, 1784; ob. 1811.

VI.1811—VI.1811—III. 1811. 6. George Ferrers Townshend, s. and h. Present Marquess, Viscount, and Baron Townshend; Earl of Leicester, Baron Ferrers de Chartley, Baron Compton, and coheir of the Barony of Bourchier*. ═══

TRACI.

BARONS BY TENURE.

I. Steph. 1. Henry de Traci ; held the Honor of Barnstaple, co. Devon. by gift of King Stephen ; living 1146.

II. H. II. 2. Oliver de Traci, s. and h. ob. circa 1184.

III. Ric. I. 3. Oliver de Traci, s. and h. ob. 1210.

IV. John. 4. Henry de Traci, s. and h. ob. circa, 1274, s. p. m. Eve, his sole daughter, having married Guy de Bryan, left issue, Maud, wife of Geoffry de Camville, who was found to be his next heir.

———

I. H. II. 1. William de Traci ; held 26 Knight's fees in 1165 ; Steward of Normandy. He was one of the murderers of the celebrated Thomas à Becket; living 1223, " but further," says Dugdale, " I have not seen of him." Banks states, that John Viscount Tracy in Ireland was descended from this family.

———

* Vide Note to p. 369, et seq.

TRAFALGAR.

VISCOUNTCY, 20 November, 1805.

Vide NELSON.

TRAILLI.

BARONS BY TENURE.

I.   S'eph. 1. Geoffrey de Trailli ; living 1175.
II. H. II. 2. Walter de Trailli, s. and h. living 1212, of whom Dugdale gives no further account.

TREGOZ.

BARONS BY TENURE.

I.   H. II.   1. Geoffrey de Tregoz ; ob. circa 1174.
II.   John.   2. William de Tregoz, s. and h.; ob. 1208.
III. H. II.   3. Robert de Tregoz, s. and h. living 1236 ; to whom succeeded
IV.   H. III. 4. Robert de Tregoz, son of Geoffrey ; ob. 1265.

BY WRIT.

I.   1299. 5. John de Tregoz, son and heir; Summoned 26 Jan. 25 Edw. I. 1297; but it is very doubtful if that Writ can be considered as a regular Summons to Parl.; vide " FITZ-JOHN ;" Summ. to Parl. 6 Feb. and 10 April, 27 Edward I. 1299; ob. 1300.   His grandson John, son of Roger la Warre by Clarice de Tregoz, his eldest daughter; and Sybil his second dau. wife of Sir William de Grandison, Knt. being his heirs ; among whose descendants and representatives this Barony is in ABEYANCE.

TREGOZ

BARON BY WRIT.   OF ——

I.   1305.   Henry de Tregoz, presumed to have been of the above family; Summ. 8 June, 22 Edw. I. 1294; but it is very doubtful if that Writ can be deemed a regular Summons to Parliament ; vide " CLYVEDON ;" Summ. to Parl. from 22 January, 33 Edward I. 1305, to 14 March, 15 Edw. II. 1322; " but further," observes Dugdale, I cannot say of him."

TREGOZ

BARON BY WRIT. OF ——

I. 1378. Thomas de Tregoz; Summoned to Parliament 4 January, 11 Edward II. 1318, and from 20 October, 6 Edward III. 1332, to 1 April, 9 Edward III. 1335; but of whom Dugdale in his Baronage gives no account.

TREGOZ

OF HIGHWORTH.

BARON.

I. 1626. 1. Oliver St. John, 1st Viscount Grandison in Ireland (descended from John I.-5th Baron Tregoz, and uncle of Sir John St. John, Bart. whose grandson, Sir Henry St. John was created Viscount St. John) ; Created Baron Tregoz of Highworth, co. Wilts, 21 May, 1626; ob. 1629, s. p. when this Barony became

Extinct.

TREMATON.

VISCOUNTCY, 27 July, 1726—Extinct 1765.

Vide CUMBERLAND.

TRENCH.

BARON.

I. 1815. 1. Richard le Poer Trench, 2d Earl of Clancarty in Ireland; Created Baron Trench of Garbally, co. Galway, 15 July, 1815; Created Viscount Clancarty, of the County of Cork, 17 Nov. 1823.

Vide CLANCARTY.

TRENTHAM.

VISCOUNTCY, 8 July, 1746.

Vide GOWER.

TREVOR.

BARONS.

I. 1711. 1. Thomas Trevor ; Created Baron Trevor of Bromham, co. Bedford, 31 Dec. 1711 ; ob. 1730.

x 3

BARONS.

II. 1730. 2. Thomas Trevor, s. and h. ob. 1753, s. p. m.

III. 1753. 3. John Trevor, brother and heir; ob. 1764, s. p. m.

IV. 1764. 4. Robert Trevor (assumed the name of) Hampden, half-brother and heir; Created Viscount Hampden 14 June, 1776.

𝕰𝖗𝖙𝖎𝖓𝖈𝖙 1824.   Vide HAMPDEN.

TRUSBUT.

BARON BY TENURE.

I. Hen. I. William de Trusbut; raised from a low condition to eminence by King Hen. I; living 1139; ob. .... leaving three sons, Richard, Geoffrey, and Robert, who all died s. p. when their three sisters became their heirs; of whom, Rose married Everard de Roos, Hillaria was the wife of Robert Budlers, but died s. p. and Agatha married William de Albini.

TRUSSEL.

BARON BY WRIT.

I. 1342. 1. William Trussel (whose ancestor, William Trussel, was summoned 8 June, 22 Edw. I. 1294; but for the reasons assigned under "CLYVEDON," it is doubtful if that Writ can be considered as a regular Summons to Parliament); Summ. to Parl. 25 Feb. 16 Edw. III. 1342, but never afterwards, nor any of his posterity; Admiral of the King's Fleet; ob. ..... when the Barony became

𝕰𝖗𝖙𝖎𝖓𝖈𝖙.

TUCHET.

BARON BY WRIT.

I. 1299. William Tuchet; Summ. to Parl. from 29 Dec. 28 Edw. I. 1299, to 3 Nov. 34 Edw. I. 1306; but of whom Dugdale gives no further account; he is presumed to have been related to the ancestor of John Touchet, who acquired the Barony of Audley, temp. Hen. IV.

TUFTON.

BARONS.

I. 1626. 1. Sir Nicholas Tufton, 2d Bart. Created Baron Tufton of Tufton, co. Sussex, 1 Nov. 1626; Created Earl of Thanet 5 Aug. 1628.

Vide THANET.

TUNBRIDGE.

VISCOUNTS.

I. 1624. 1. Richard Burgh, Earl of Clanrickard in Ireland; Created Baron Somerhill and Viscount Tunbridge, co. Kent, 3 April, 1624; Created Earl of St. Albans 23 Aug. 1628.

𝕰𝖝𝖙𝖎𝖓𝖈𝖙 1659. Vide ST. ALBANS.

VISCOUNTCY, 10 May, 1695.

Vide ROCHFORD.

TURNHAM.

BARONS BY TENURE.

I. Hen. II 1. Robert de Turnham; held large possessions in Kent. temp. Hen. II.

II. Ric. I. 2. Robert de Turnham, s. and h. ob. 1211, s.p.m. Isabel his daughter being his heir.

←——

I. Hen. II. 1. Stephen de Turnham, brother of the last Baron; Seneschal of Anjou 1186; ob. ante 1214; and in 1219 several persons shared his inheritance, but by what right is not recorded.

TYES.

BARONS BY WRIT.

I. 1299. 1. Henry de Tyes *; Summoned to Parl. from 6 Feb. 27 Edw. I. 1299, to 26 Aug. 1 Edw. II. 1307; ob. 1308.

---

* Dugdale in his account of this family merely says, that Henry (the 2d Baron) son of this Henry, was summoned to Parliament from 28 Edward I. to 14 Edward II.; but as a "Henry de Tyes," received a Summons 8 June, 22 Edw. I. 1294 (though probably not to Parliament); and as from the 1st of Edward II.

BARONS BY WRIT.

II.   1308. 2. Henry de Tyes, s. and h. Summ. to Parl. from
        8 Jan. 6 Edward II. 1313, to 15 May, 14
        Edw. II. 1321; beheaded 1321; ob. s. p. leav-
        ing Alice, his sister, wife of Warine de L'isle,
        his heir ; in whose descendants and represen-
        tatives (if her father was summoned to Par-
        liament as is here stated) this Barony is vested.

TYES

BARONS BY WRIT.   OF ⸺

I.   1299. 1. Walter de Tyes *, probably of the same family
        as the preceding Barons ; Summ. to Parl.
        from 6 Feb. 27 Edw. I. 1299, to 26 August, 1
        Edw. II. 1307; ob. 1324, s. p. when his honors
        became

Extinct.

TYNDALE.

BARONY, 14 February, 1663—Forfeited 1685.
Restored 23 March, 1743.

Vide DONCASTER.

TYNDALE.

BARONY, 7 March, 1688—Forfeited 1716.

Vide DERWENTWATER.

TYRONE.

BARONS.

I.   1786. 1. George de la Poer Beresford, 2d Earl of
        Tyrone in Ireland ; Created Baron Tyrone of
        Haverford West, co. Pembroke, 8 August,
        1786 ; Created Marquess of Waterford in
        Ireland, August, 1789 ; ob. 1800.

II.   1800. 2. Henry de la Poer Beresford, s. and h.   Present
        Baron Tyrone ; also Marquess of Waterford,
        &c. in Ireland, K. P.

---

when the first Henry died, no Henry Tyes was summoned for five
years, viz. until the 6th of Edward II. it is most probable that
both were summoned to Parliament as is stated in the text.

 * Dugdale says nothing of this Walter having been summoned
to Parl.   Vide tome II. p. 21.

UFFINGTON.

VISCOUNTCY, 13 June, 1801.

Vide CRAVEN.

UFFORD.

BARONS BY WRIT.

I.　1308.　1. Robert de Ufford; Summ. to Parl. from 13 Jan. 2 Edw. II. 1308, to 19 Dec. 5 Edw. II. 1311; ob. 1316.

II.　1316.　2. Robert de Ufford, s. and h.; Summ. to Parl. from 27 Jan. 6 Edw. III. 1332, to 14 Jan. 10 Edw. III. 1337; Created Earl of Suffolk 16 March, 1337, K. G.; ob. 1369.

III.　1342.　3. Robert de Ufford, son and heir apparent of Robert Earl of Suffolk, the last Baron, was Summ. to Parl. as "Roberto de Ufford le Fitz," 25 Feb. 16 Edw. III. 1342; ob. .... vita patris, s. P. when the Barony created by that Writ (unless it is considered that he was merely summoned in his father's Barony) became 𝔈𝔵𝔱𝔦𝔫𝔠𝔱.

IV. 1364.　4. William de Ufford, brother and heir of Robert the last Baron, and 2d son of Robert Earl of Suffolk; Summ. to Parl. 4 Dec. 48 Edw. III. 1364, and 20 Jan. 39 Edw. III. 1366; succeeded his father in the Earldom of Suffolk in 1369, K. G.; ob. 1382, s. P. when, if the Writ of 4 Dec. 1364, be considered as a distinct Barony, it became 𝔈𝔵𝔱𝔦𝔫𝔠𝔱; but the Barony created by the Writ to his grandfather, Robert 1st Baron, who was summoned 13 Jan. 2 Edw. II. 1308, as is stated above, fell into ABEYANCE between his sisters and heirs; viz. Cecily, wife of William Lord

Willoughby of Eresby, Katherine, who married Robert Lord Scales; and Margaret, wife of Robert Lord Ferrers of Groby, between whose descendants and representatives this Barony is now in ABEYANCE.

UFFORD

BARON BY WRIT.   OF ——

I.   1360.   John de Ufford, son and heir of Ralph de Ufford (brother of Robert 2d Baron, and 1st Earl of Suffolk), by Eve, dau. and heir of John de Clavering, his first wife; Summ. to Parl. 3 April, 34 Edw. III. 1360; ob. 1361, when the dignity became
Extinct.

UGHTRED.

BARON BY WRIT.

I.   1343.   Thomas de Ughtred; Summ. to Parl. from 30 April, 17 Edw. III. 1343, to 4 Dec. 38 Edw. III. 1364; ob. 1365, leaving Thomas his son and heir, then a Knight, and of full age; but neither he nor any of his descendants were ever summoned to Parliament. The Barony is however vested in his descendants and representatives.

UMFRAVILLE.

BARONS BY TENURE.

I.   Will. I.   Robert de Umfravill, Lord of Toures, Kinsman of William I. obtained a grant of the Lordship of Kiddesdale, co. Northumberland, in 1076. The next mentioned is

II.   Hen. I.   Gilbert de Umfravill; living in the reign of Henry the First; and after him

III.   Steph.   Robert de Umfravill; living 1139; and in 1161 of

IV.   Hen. II.   Odonell de Umfravill, who died 1182, being then Lord of Prudhow.

V.   Hen. II.   Robert de Umfravill, s. and h.; ob. ....

VI.   Rich. I.   Richard de Umfravill, s. and h.; Lord of Prudhow; ob. 1226.

VII. Hen. III.   Gilbert de Umfravill, s. and h.; ob. 1244.

BARONS BY WRIT.

I. 1295. Gilbert de Umfravill, s. and h. Earl of Angos in Scotland; Summ. to Parl. 24 June, 1 Oct. and 2 Nov. 23 Edw. I. 1295, and 26 Aug. 24 Edw. I. 1296, as "Gilberto de Umfravill," and from 26 Jan. 25 Edw. I. 1297, to 19 Jan. 1 Edw. II. 1308, as "Gilberto de Umfravill, Comiti de Anggos;" ob. 1308.

II. 1308. Robert de Umfravill; s. and h.; Summ. to Parl. as Earl of Angos, from 4 March, 2 Edw. II. 1309, to 30 Dec. 18 Edw. II. 1324; ob. 1325.

III. 1325. Gilbert de Umfravill, s. and h.; Summ. to Parl. as Earl of Angos, from 27 Jan. 6 Edw. II. 1332, to 26 Aug. 4 Ric. II. 1380; ob. 1381, s. p. s. leaving Eleanor, his niece, wife of Henry Talboys, and dau. and heir of Elizabeth, his sister, who married Gilbert Burton, his heir of the whole blood; and Thomas, his brother of the half-blood, his next heir male, but none of this family were ever afterwards summoned to Parliament. The Barony created by the Writ of Summons of 23 Edw. I. is vested in the descendants and representatives of Thomas de Umfraville, the half-brother and heir male of Gilbert, Earl of Angos, the last Baron.

UPPER OSSORY.

BARON.

I. 1794. 1. John Fitz-Patrick, 2d Earl of Upper Ossory in Ireland; Created Baron of Upper Ossory of Amphill, co. Bedford, 12 Aug. 1794; ob. 1818, s. p. m. when his honors became
𝕰𝔵𝔱𝔦𝔫𝔠𝔱.

DE URTIACO.
Vide L'ORTI.

UVEDALE.

BARON BY WRIT.

I. 1332. Peter de Uvedale; Summ. to Parl. from 27 Jan. 6 Edw. III. 1332, to 22 Jan. 9 Edw. III. 1336.

Dugdale gives no account of this Baron in his Baronage; but Banks, in his Stemmata Anglicana, p. 267, states that he died s. p. in which case this Barony became
𝕰𝔵𝔱𝔦𝔫𝔠𝔱.

UXBRIDGE.

EARLS.

I.   1714. 1. Henry Paget, 7th Baron Paget, and 1st Baron Burton; Created Earl of Uxbridge, co. Middlesex, 19 Oct. 1714; ob. 1743.

II.   1743. 2. Henry Paget, grandson and heir; being s. and h. of Thomas Catesby Paget (ob. v. p.) eldest son of the last Earl; ob. 1769, s. p. when the Barony of Burton and Earldom of Uxbridge became
                        Extinct.

III. 1784. 1. Henry Bayley-Paget, 9th Baron Paget, cousin and heir of the last Earl; Created Earl of Uxbridge, co. Middlesex, 19 May, 1784; ob. 1812.

IV. 1812. 2. Henry William Paget, s. and h.; Created Marquess of Anglesey 4 July, 1815. Present Earl of Uxbridge, Marquess of Anglesey, Baron Paget, and a Baronet of Ireland, K. G. G. C. B.

VALENCE.

BARON BY TENURE.

I. H. III. 1. William de Valence, son of Hugh le Brun, Earl of Marche, in Poictou, by Isabel, widow of King John, and mother of Henry III.; he married Joan, sister and heir of William Baron de Montchensy; Created Earl of Pembroke; ob. 1296.

BY WRIT.

I.   1299. 2. Aymer de Valence, s. and h.; Summ. to Parl. from 6 Feb. 27 Edw. I. 1299, to 3 Nov. 34 Edward I. 1306, "Adomarus de Valencia" only, though he succeeded his father as Earl of Pembroke in 1296; he is first styled Earl of Pembroke in Writs of Summons on 19 Jan. 1 Edward II. 1308. He was also summoned 26 Jan. 25 Edw. I. 1297; but, for the reasons assigned under " FITZ JOHN," it is doubtful if that Writ was a regular Summons to Parliament; ob. 1323, s. p. when all his dignities became
                        Extinct.

VALLETORT.

BARONS BY TENURE.

I. Hen. II. Ralph de Valletort held one knight's fee, co. Devon 1165; the next mentioned is

II. John. Roger de Valletort, who in 1186 held the honor of Tremeton, in Cornwall; living 1203; to whom succeeded

III. H. III. Reginald de Valletort; ob. 1246, s. p.

IV. H. III. Ralph de Valletort, brother and heir; ob. 1259.

V. H. III. Reginald de Valletort, s. and h.; ob. 1270, s. p.

VI. Edw. I. Roger de Valletort, uncle and heir; ob. 1290, s. p. leaving Henry de Pomerai and Peter Corbet his next heirs.

MOUNT EDGCUMB AND VALLETORT.

VISCOUNTCY, 5th March, 1781.

Vide MOUNT EDGCUMBE.

VALOINS.

BARONS BY TENURE.

I. Will. I. 1. Peter de Valoines held several Lordships temp. William I.

II. Hen. II. 2. Roger de Valoines, s. and h.; ob. 1184, s. p. m. Gunnora, his dau. and sole heir, married Robert Baron Fitz-Walter.

I. H. II. 1. Alan de Valoines, of the same family as the above Barons; ob. ante 1194, s. p.

II. John. 2. Robert de Valoines, brother and heir; living 1210.

III. H. III. 3. Robert de Valoines, s. and h.; ob.... s. p. leaving his two daughters his heirs, viz. Roese, wife of Sir Edward de Pakenham, and Cicely, who married Robert de Ufford, Earl of Suffolk.

I. H I. Robert de Valoines; ob. 1282, seised of a moiety of the manor of Ixworth, which he held in capite by Barony, and of several other manors.

I. Ric. I. 1. Theobald de Valoines, "another branch of this stock;" ob. 1209.

II. John. 2. Thomas de Valoines, s. and h.; living 1217; but of whom Dugdale gives no further account.

I. Ric. I. 1. Philip de Valoines, "another branch of this family," brother and heir of Geoffrey de Valoines in 1190; ob. circa 1195, leaving Sybilla his daughter and heir.

VANE.

I. 1823. 1. Charles William Stewart (assumed the name of) Vane, 1st Baron Stewart of Stewart's Court in England, and 3d Marquess of Londonderry in Ireland; Created Viscount Seaham, co. Durham, and Earl Vane, with remainder to the issue male of his body, by Frances, his present wife*, 8 July, 1823. Present Earl Vane, Viscount Seaham, and Baron Stewart of Stewart's Court; also Marquess of Londonderry, &c. in Ireland; G. C. B.

VAUGHAN.

I. 1643. 1. Richard Vaughan, 2d Earl of Carberry, in Ireland; Created Baron Vaughan of Emlyn, co. Caermarthen, 25 Oct. 1643; ob. 1687.

II. 1687. 2. John Vaughan, s. and h. Earl of Carberry, in Ireland; ob. 1713, s.p.m. when the Barony became Extinct.

VAUX.

I. Steph. 1. Hugh de Vallibus, or Vaux, obtained the Barony of Gillesland; ob. ....

II. Hen. II. 2. Robert de Vaux, s. and h. living 1176.

III. John. 3. Robert de Vaux, s. and h. living 1215; ob. s.p.

---

* His Lordship married, first, Katherine, dau. of John Earl of Darnley, by whom he had Frederick Viscount Castlereagh, and who is heir apparent to the Barony of Stewart of Stewart's Court, and to the Irish Honors.

BARONS BY WRIT.

IV. John.   4. Ranulph de Vaux, brother and heir, ob. ....

V. H. III. 5. Robert de Vaux, s. and h. living 1234.

VI. H. III. 6. Hubert de Vaux, s. and h.; ob. ..... s. p. m.
        Maud, his sole daughter and heir, married
        Thomas de Multon, to whom she brought the
        Barony of Gillesland.

———

I. Steph. 1. Robert de Vallibus, or Vaux, younger brother
        of Hubert, 1st Baron of Gillesland.

II. Hen. II. 2. William de Vaux, s. and h.

III. Hen. II. 3. Robert de Vaux, s. and h.

IV. Rich. I. 4. Robert de Vaux, s. and h.; ob. ante 1211. s.p.

V. John.   5. Oliver de Vaux, brother and heir, living 1244.

VI. H. III. 6. William de Vaux, s. and h. of Robert (who is
        presumed to have died v. p.) eldest son of the
        last Baron; ob. ante 1253, s. p.

VII. H. III. 7. John de Vaux, brother and heir. Steward
        of Acquitaine 1283; ob. 1288, s. p. m. Pe-
        tronilla, who married William de Nerford,
        and Maud, the wife of William de Roos, being
        his daughters and heirs.

VAUX

BARONS.   OF HARROWDEN.

I.   1523. 1. Nicholas Vaux (descended from a younger
        branch of the preceding family); Created
        Baron Vaux of Harrodon, co. Northampton,
        27th April, 1523; ob. 1523.

II. 1523. 2. Thomas Vaux, s. and h. living 1558; ob.
        ante 1562.

III. 1562. 3. William Vaux *, s. and h.; ob. 1595.

———

* It appears, from the list of Summonses, that this William
was summoned to Parliament from 11th January, 5 Eliz. 1563,
to 4th February, 31 Eliz. 1589, and that in the next Parliament,
viz. 19th Feb. 35 Eliz. 1593, " *Thomæ* Vaux de Harrowden
Chel'r," was summoned. The name of Vaux does not occur
again among the Barons summoned, until 18 James I. viz. 3 January, 1621, when *Edward* Vaux was summoned. Dugdale, in
his account of this family, vol. II. p. 304, takes no notice of
there having been a *Thomas* Vaux, who succeeded to the title,
and it is possible that the entry in the list of summonses was erroneously transcribed from the Roll.

BARON.

IV. 1595. 4. Edward Vaux, grandson and heir, being s. and
h. of George Vaux, ob. V. P.), eldest son of the
last Baron ; ob. 1661, s. P. L. when the Barony
became Extinct *.

VAVASOUR.

BARON BY WRIT.

I. 1299. 1. William le Vavasour. Summoned to Parliament from 6th Feb. 27 Edw. I. 1299, to 7th
Jan. 6 Edw. II. 1313, but of whom nothing
further is known.

VAVASOUR

OF ——

BARON BY WRIT.

I. 1313. 2. Walter le Vavasour, presumed to have been
nearly related to the preceding Baron. Summ.
to Parl. 26 July, 7 Edw. II. 1313, but never
afterwards, " nor any other of his family.
Kimber states that he died s. p. and that Eli-
sabeth, his daughter and heir, married Sir
Robert Strelly, of Nottinghamshire †. On
the death of this Baron the dignity probably
became Extinct.

---

* Mr. Banks, in his Stemmata Anglicana, cites the following
monumental inscription in the church of Eye in Suffolk, to
prove, that on the death of Edward Baron Vaux in 1661, the
title devolved on his brother Henry, who, he conjectures, to have
been poor, and therefore that he did not claim the dignity :—
" Exiit ultimus Baronu' de Harrowden, Henricus Vaux, Septemb.
20, Anno D'ni MDCLXIII."

† Kimber erroneously calls this Baron *Robert*. In the able cri-
tique on the first volume of Banks' Dormant and Extinct Baronage, in the Monthly Review, vol. 54, p. 48, it is stated that this
Barony still exists in the heirs of the said Sir Robert Strelley ; if,
however, the above Walter le Vavasour was not immediately descended from William le Vavasour, the first Baron of that family,
and summoned, in consequence of that descent, this statement is
probably incorrect, as it has been held that a *single* Writ of Summons unaccompanied by a sitting in Parliament does not constitute a Barony in fee.

VEEL.

BARON BY WRIT.

I. 1342. Peter le Veel. Summ. to Parl. 25 Feb. 16 Edw. III. 1342, but never afterwards, nor any of his descendants.

Dugdale gives no account of this Baron in his Baronage; on his death the Barony became Extinct.

VERDON.

BARONS BY TENURE.

I. Will. I. 1. Bertram de Verdon, Lord of Farneham Royal at the General Survey. His successor was

II. Hen. I. 2. Norman de Verdon, living 1140.

III. H. III. 3. Bertram de Verdon, s. and h.; ob. 1192.

IV. Rich. I. 4. Thomas de Verdon, s. and h.; ob. 1199, s. p.

V. John. 5. Nicholas de Verdon, brother and heir; ob. 1231, s. p. m. leaving Robese his daughter and heir, who married Theobald le Butiler, but retained her own name. She died in 1247, leaving

VI. H. III. 6. John de Verdon, her son and heir, who bore his mother's name; ob. 1274.

BY WRIT.

I. 1295. 7. Theobald de Verdon, s. and h. Summ. to Parl. from 24 June, 23 Edw. I. 1295, to 3 Nov. 34 Edw. I. 1306; after 27 Edw. I. with the addition of "Seniori;" ob. 1309.

II. 1299. 8. Theobald de Verdon, s. and h. Summ. to Parl. from 29 Dec. 28 Edw. I. 1299, to 22 Feb. 35 Edw. I. 1307, as "Theobaldo de Verdon Juniori." Summ. to Parl. as "Theobaldo de Verdon" from 4 March, 2 Edw. II. 1309, to 24 Oct. 8 Edw. II. 1314. He married, 2dly, Elizabeth, daughter, and eventually coheir, of Gilbert de Clare, Earl of Gloucester, by Joan Plantagenet, daughter of King Edw. I.; ob. 1316, s. p. m. leaving, by his first wife (Maud, dau. of Edmund Lord Mortimer) Joan, Elizabeth, and Margaret; and by his second wife a posthumous daughter, Isabel, who married Henry Baron Ferrers of Groby. Joan de Verdon, his eldest daughter, became the wife of Thomas Baron Furnival, and died in childbed in 1334; Elizabeth married Bartholomew Baron Burghersh; and Margaret, his other daughter, married first William Le Blunt, secondly Marcus Husee, and lastly John Crophull; and

Y 3

between the descendants and representatives of these four daughters the Barony of Verdon is in ABEYANCE.

VERDON

OF ——

BARON BY WRIT.

I. 1332. 1. John de Verdon. Summ. to Parl. from 27 27 Jan. 6 Edw. III. 1332, to 22 Jan. 9 Edw. III. 1336, and again the 25th Feb. 16 Edw. III. 1342, but never afterwards, and of whom nothing more is recorded.

Dugdale gives no account of him in his Baronage. Banks, in his Stemmata Anglicana, p. 272, conjectures that he was the John de Verdon noticed in Blomefield's History of Norfolk, vol. I. p. 50, and which is not improbable.

VERE.

BARONS BY TENURE.

I. Will. I. 1. Alberic de Vere held numerous Lordships at the General Survey.

II. Hen. I. 2. Alberic de Vere, s. and h.; Created Lord Great Chamberlain of England by King Henry I. to him and his heirs; ob. 1140.

III. Steph. 3. Alberic de Vere, s. and h.; Created Earl of Oxford in 1155. Vide OXFORD.

VERE

BARON BY WRIT. OF ——

I. 1299. 1. Hugh de Vere, supposed to have been a younger son of Robert 5th Earl, and brother of Robert, 6th Earl of Oxford. Summ. to Parl. from 21 Sept. 27 Edw. I. 1299, to 3d March, 11 Edw. II. 1318. It appears that he married Dionysia, dau. and heir of William, son of Warine de Montchensy, which Dionysia died s. p. 1313. Though Dugdale gives a long account of this Hugh, it is singular that he does not notice his having been summoned to Parliament; and this omission has likewise been made by some recent writers, who have seldom taken the trouble to seek for information beyond what the pages of that admirable (though occasionally incorrect) writer afforded them: This Hugh de Vere is presumed to have died s. p. when the Barony became Extinct.

VERE
OF TILBURY.

BARON.
I. 1625. Horatio Vere, youngest son of Geoffry Vere, brother of John 16th Earl of Oxford; Created Baron Vere of Tilbury, co. Essex, 25th July, 1625; ob. 1635, s. p. m. when the title became

Extinct.

VERE
OF HANWORTH.

BARONS.
I. 1750. 1. Vere Beauclerk, third son of Charles 1st Duke of St. Alban's, by Diana, daughter, and eventually sole heir of Aubrey de Vere, 20th and last Earl of Oxford; Created Baron Vere of Hanworth, co. Middlesex, 28th March, 1750; ob. 1781.

II. 1781. 2. Aubrey Beauclerk, s. and h. succeeded as 4th Duke of St. Alban's, in 1787, in which dignity this Barony is merged.
Vide ST. ALBAN's.

VERNON.

BARONS.
I. 1762. 1. George Venables-Vernon; Created Lord Vernon, Baron of Kinderton, co. Chester, 12 May, 1762; ob. 1780.

II. 1780. 2. George Venables Vernon, son and heir; ob. 1813.

III. 1813. 3. Henry Venables-Vernon, s. and h. Present Baron Vernon.

VERULAM.

BARON.
1. 1618. 1. Francis Bacon, the celebrated Philosopher; Created Baron Verulam of Verulam, co. Herts, 11th July 1618; Created Viscount St. Alban's 27 Jan. 1621. Lord Chancellor; ob. 1626, s. p. when his titles became

Extinct.

VERULAM
OF GORHAMBURY.

BARONS.

I.   1790. 1. James Bucknall Grimston, 3d Viscount Grimston in Ireland; Created Baron Verulam of Gorhambury, co. Herts, 9 July 1790; ob 1808.

EARL.

II. 1808.—I.   1815. 2. James Walter Grimston, s. and h.; Created Viscount Grimston and Earl Verulam 24 Nov. 1815. Present Earl and Baron Verulam and Viscount Grimston in ENGLAND; Viscount Grimston and Baron Dunboyne in IRELAND; and Baron Forrester, *jure matris*, in SCOTLAND. ☿

VESCI.

BARONS BY TENURE.

I.   Will.I. 1. Yvo de Vesci held numerous lordships at the General Survey, in right of his wife Alda, dau. and sole heir of William Tyson, Lord of Alnwick. Beatrix, his dau. and sole heir, married Eustachius Fitz-John; their son and heir

II. Hen.II. 3. William assumed his mother's name of De Vesci; ob. 1184.

III. John. 4. Eustace de Vesci, s. and h.; he was one of the 25 celebrated Barons appointed to enforce the observance of MAGNA CHARTA; and married Margaret, daughter of William, and sister of Alexander, Kings of Scotland; ob. circa 1216.

IV. H. III. 5. William de Vesci, s. and h.; ob. 1253.

BY WRIT.

I.   1264. 6. John de Vesci, s. and h. Summ. to Parl, 24 Dec. 49 Hen. III. 1264; ob. 1289, s. P.

II. 1295. 7. William de Vesci, brother and heir, summoned to Parliament 24 June, 1 Oct. and 2 Nov. 23 Edw. I. 1295. He was one of the competitors for the Crown of Scotland, temp. Edw. I.; ob. 1297, s. P. L. when the Barony became Extinct.

VESCI.

BARON BY TENURE.

I.   1313.   William de Vesci, natural son of William the
last Baron. Summ. to Parl. from 8 Jan. 6
Edw. II. 1313, to 29 July, 8 Edw. II. 1314;
ob. 1315, s. p. when this Barony also became
Extinct.

The lands of which William, the last Baron, died seized,
devolved on the heir of his putative father, viz. the descendant of Margery, dau. and heir of Warine de Vesci,
brother of Eustace III. Baron; which Margery married
Gilbert de Aton. In 28 Hen. VI. Henry de Bromflete,
being descended from a coheir of the said Gilbert de Aton,
was summoned to Parliament as " Henry Bromflete de
Vesci."   **Vide BROMFLETE**

VESCI.

BARON BY TENURE.

I. Will I. 1. Robert de Vesci, brother of Yvo I.-1 Baron,
held numerous Lordships at the General Sur-
vey, but of whom, or his descendants, no
account is given.

VICOUNT.

BARONS BY TENURE.

I. Hen. II. John le Vicount (son of Odoard Baron of
Emesdon, in Northumberland), living 1162:
his successor was,

II. Rich. I. John le Vicount, living 1196.

III. Hen. III. John le Vicount, s. and h.; ob. 1214, s. p. m.
leaving Ramet, the wife of Everard Tyes, or
Teutonic, his daughter and heir: she married, secondly, Hereward de Marisco.

VILLIERS.

VISCOUNTS.

I.   1616. 1. George Villiers, 1st Baron Whaddon; Created
Viscount Villiers Aug. ... 1616; Created Earl
of Buckingham 5 Jan. 1617.
                        Extinct 1687.   **Vide BUCKINGHAM.**

VILLIERS
OF DARTFORD AND HOO.

BARONS.   VISCOUNTS.

I.   1691.—I.   1690. 1. Edward Villiers, son of Sir Edward, 2d son of Sir George Villiers (whose second wife was created Duchess of Buckingham) by his first wife; Created Baron Villiers of Hoo, and Viscount Villiers of Dartford, both co. Kent, 20 March, 1691 ; Created Earl of Jersey, 13th Oct. 1697.

Vide JERSEY.

VILLIERS
OF DAVENTRY.

BARONY, 18 April 1623.

𝕮rtinct 1659.   Vide ANGLESEY.

VILLIERS
OF STOKE.

BARONY, 19 June 1619.

𝕮rtinct 1657.   Vide PURBECK.

VIPOUNT.

BARONS BY TENURE.

I.   Will. I.   Robert de Vipount, slain in 1085. The next mentioned is,

II. Hen. I.   Robert de Vipount, who was living 1107 ; and after him,

III. Steph.   William de Vipount, who was living 1203.

IV. Hen. II. Robert de Vipount, brother of the said William, held the honour of Totneys 1165 ; ob. 1227.

V.   Hen. III.John de Vipount, s. and h. ; ob. 1242.

VI. Hen. III.Robert de Vipount, s. and h.; ob. circa 1265, s. p. m. leaving Isabel, wife of Roger de Clifford, and Idonea, who married, first, Roger de Leyburne, and 2dly, John de Cromwell, his daughters and heirs.

———

John.   Yvo de Vipount, brother of Robert IV. Baron, had his lands seized 1216.

WAHULL.

I. Hen. I. Simon de Wahull, living circa the reigns o
Henry I. or Stephen; to whom succeeded,

II. Hen. II. Walter de Wahull, living 1172. His successor was,

III. Rich. I. Simon de Wahull; ob. 1196.

IV. John. John de Wahull, ... and heir; ob. 1216,
s. p. leaving his sisters his heirs, but the
honour of Wahull devolved on

V. H. III. Saiher de Wahull; ob. 1250.

VI. H. III. Walter de Wahull, s. and h.; ob. 1269.

VII. Edw. I. John de Wahuil, s. and h.; ob. 1295.

VIII. Edw. I. Thomas de Wahull, s. and h. summoned 26
Jan. 25 Edw. I. 1297; but for the reasons
assigned under " FITZ-JOHN," it is very
doubtful if that Writ can be considered as a
regular summons to Parliament; ob. 1304,
leaving John, his son and heir; but neither
this John, nor any of his posterity, were ever
summoned to Parliament.

In the reign of James I. Sir Richard Chetwode, the heir-
general of Thomas Baron Wahull last mentioned, possessing the manor and castle of Odell, claimed the dignity of a Baron, which claim was referred to the Duke
of Lenox, the Lord Howard, and the Earl of Nottingham, as exercising the office of Earl Marshal, whose
certificate, as given by Banks, stated that the aver-
ments in his petition, that his ancestors were Barons in
their own right before the usual calling of Barons by

Writs, and were also summoned to Parliament *, were
true; and on these, and other grounds, but which had
nothing to do with his claim to the dignity in question,
reported that they held him worthy the honour of a Baron, if his Majesty thought meet.

Nothing was done in consequence of this certificate,
which, it must be remembered, by no means admitted
his right to the Barony, but merely recommended him
to the notice of the Crown, as a proper person to receive
the dignity of the Peerage.

WAITH.

BARONY, 19th Nov. 1734.

Extinct, 1782.   Vide MALTON.

WAKE.

BARONS BY TENURE.
I.   Hen. I. 1. Hugh Wac, Lord of Wilesford, &c. Lincoln,
                    ob. . . . .
II. H. II.   2. Baldwin Wake, s. and h.; ob. 1201.
III. John.   3. Baldwin Wake, s. and h.; ob. 1206.
IV. John.   4. Baldwin Weke, s. and h.; ob. circ. 1213.
V.   H. III. 5. Hugh Wake, s. and h.; ob. 1241.
VI. H. III. 6. Baldwin Wake, s. and h.; ob. 1282.
BY WRIT.
I.   1295.   1. John Wake, s. and h. Summ. to Parl. from
                    4 Octr. 23 Edw. I. 1295, to 29 Dec. 28 Edw. I.
                    1299, ob. 1300.
II. 1300.   2. John Wake, s. and h.; he was never summoned
                    to Parliament; ob. . . . . ., s. p.
III. 1317.   3. Thomas Wake, brother and heir, Summoned
                    to Parliament from 20 Nov. 11 Edw. II. 1317,
                    to 20 Nov. 22 Edw. III. 1348, generally as
                    "Thomæ Wake," but sometimes as "Thomæ
                    Wake de Lydell," He married Blanch,

* From this expression it would be inferred, that repeated
Writs of Summons had been issued to his ancestors, but, as is
stated in the last page, there is but one instance recorded of a
Writ of Summons to Parliament having been directed to this family, and that instance is the doubtful Writ of the 25th Edw. I.

daughter of Henry Plantagenet, Earl of Lancaster; ob. 1349, s. p. leaving Margaret Countess of Kent, widow of Edmund Plantagenet, Earl of Kent, younger son of King Edward 1. his sister and heir, who succeeded to the Barony, and which on her death devolved on Joan Plantagenet, her daughter and heir, which Joan styled herself " Lady of Wake." She married, first, Sir Thomas Holland, K. G. and secondly, Edward the Black Prince, and by the latter was mother of King Richard II. By her first husband Sir Thomas Holland, this Joan (who from her extraordinary beauty was called the fair maid of Kent) had Thomas Holland, Earl of Kent, who inherited this Barony, and which became merged in that dignity until the attainder of Thomas Holland Duke of Surrey, and IX. 3d Earl of Kent in 1400, when; with all his other honors, it became forfeited. Dugdale states, that Edmund, brother of the said Thomas Holland, succeeded to the Earldom of Kent, in which case the Attainder probably was reversed (though no notice of such a circumstance is mentioned by that author, or in the Rolls of Parliament), when he likewise became possessed of this Barony: he died in 1407, s. p. and if he be considered to have been legally seised of the Barony of Wake, it then fell into ABEYANCE between his sisters and coheirs, and is now vested in their descendants and representatives.　　　　Vide HOLLAND *.

WALDEGRAVE.

BARONS.

I.　1686.　1. Sir Henry Waldegrave, 4th Bart.; Created Baron Waldegrave of Chewton, co. Somerset, 20 Jan. 1686; ob. 1689.

EARLS.

II.　1689.—I.　1729. 2. James Waldegrave, s. and h. Created Viscount Chewton of Chewton, co. Somerset, and Earl Waldegrave, co. Northampton, 13 Sept. 1729; K. G.; ob. 1741.

III. 1741.—II.　1741. 3. James Waldegrave, s. and h. K.G.; ob. 1763, s. p. m.

IV. 1763.—III. 1763. 4. John Waldegrave, brother and heir; ob. 1784.

* P. 327.

BARONS.   EARLS.

V.   1784.—IV. 1784. 5. George Waldegrave, s. and h. ob.
1789.

VI. 1789.—V. 1789. 6. George Waldegrave, s. and h. ob.
1794, s. P.

VII. 1794.—VI. 1794. 7. John James Waldegrave, brother
and heir. Present Earl and Ba-
ron Waldegrave, Viscount Chewton, and a Baronet. �ᵻ

WALERAN.

BARONS BY TENURE.

I. Hen. II.   Walter Waleran; held 25 Knight's fees in 1165;
he married Isabel, dau. of William, son and
heir of William Longespee, Earl of Salisbury;
ob. 1200, s. p. m. leaving his three daughters
his heirs, viz. Cecily, wife of John de Monmouth; Aubrey, who married John de Inge-
ham; and Isabel, wife of William de Nevill.

I. H. III. 1. Robert Waleran; presumed to have been of
the same family; ob. 1273, s. p. leaving Robert
Waleran his nephew and heir, but who was
never considered as a Baron of the Realm.

WALEYS.

BARON BY WRIT.

I.   1321.   Richard Waleys; Summ. to Parl. 15 May, 14
Edw. II. 1321; but never afterwards. Dugdale gives no account of this Baron in his
Baronage, nor are there any particulars recorded of him : on his death the Barony became   Extinct.

WALLINGFORD.

VISCOUNT.

I. 1616. 1. William Knollys, 1st Baron Knollys; Cre-
ated Viscount Wallingford, co. Berks, 14
Nov. 1616; Created Earl of Banbury 18
Aug. 1626, K. G.

Extinct 1632.   Vide BANBURY.

WALLOP.

BARONY, 11 June, 1720.

Vide LYMINGTON.

WALPOLE

OF WALPOLE.

BARONS.

I. 1723. 1. Robert Walpole, son and heir apparent of Sir Robert Walpole, K. G. (afterwards Earl of Orford) ; Created vitâ patris 10 June, 1723, Baron Walpole of Walpole, co. Norfolk, with remainder, failing his issue male, to his brothers Edward and Horatio, and to their issue male respectively; in default of which, to their father the said Sir Robert Walpole, K. G. and his issue male; failing which, to the issue male of Robert Walpole, Esq. father of the said Sir Robert, and grandfather of this Baron; succeeded his father as Earl of Orford, Viscount Walpole, and Baron Houghton in 1745, K. B.; ob. 1751.

II. 1751. 2. George Walpole, s. and h. Viscount and Earl of Orford; ob. 1791, s. p.

III. 1791. 3. Horatio Walpole, uncle and heir, being brother of Robert 1st Baron, and younger son of Sir Robert Walpole, K. G. 1st Earl of Orford, &c.; Earl of Orford; ob. 1797, s. p. when all his honors, excepting the Barony of Walpole, became Extinct. ; which Barony, agreeable to the limitation, devolved on

IV. 1797. 4. Horatio Walpole, 2d Baron Walpole of Woolterton (vide infra), cousin and heir, he being eldest son of Horatio 1st Baron Walpole of Woolterton, next brother of Robert 1st Earl of Orford, K. G. and uncle of Robert 1st Baron above mentioned ; Created Earl of Orford 10 April, 1806; in which dignity the Baronies of Walpole of Walpole, and Walpole of Woolterton are merged.

Vide ORFORD.

z 2

WALPOLE
OF HOUGHTON.

VISCOUNTS.

I.   1742. 1. Sir Robert Walpole, K. G. father of Robert
            1st Baron Walpole of Walpole ; Created
            Baron of Houghton, Viscount Walpole of
            Houghton, both co. Norfolk, and Earl of
            Orford 6 Feb. 1742 ; ob. 1745.
                    Extinct, 1797.
                                Vide ORFORD.

WALPOLE
OF WOOLTERTON.

BARONS.

I.   1756. 1. Horatio Walpole, brother of Robert 1st Earl
            of Orford and Viscount Walpole, &c.; Cre-
            ated Baron Walpole of Woolterton, co. Nor-
            folk, 4 June, 1756 ; ob. 1757.

II.   1757. 2. Horatio Walpole, s. and h. succeeded to the
            Barony of Walpole of Walpole on the demise
            of Horatio Walpole, 3d Baron Walpole of
            Walpole, and 4th Earl of Orford in 1797 ;
            Created Earl of Orford 10 April, 1806.
                                Vide ORFORD.

WALSINGHAM.

COUNTESS.

I.   1722.   Melesina de Schulemberg, niece of the
            Duchess of Kendal ; Created Baroness of
            Aldborough, co. Suffolk, and Countess of Wal-
            singham, co. Norfolk, for life, 7 April, 1722;
            she married Philip Dormer, Earl of Chester-
            field, K. G.; ob. 1778, when her honors be-
            came
                    Extinct.

BARONS.

I.   1780. 1. Sir William de Grey, Knt.; Created Baron
            Walsingham of Walsingham, co. Norfolk, 17
            Oct. 1780 ; ob. 1781.

II.   1781. 2. Thomas de Grey, s. and h. ob. 1818.

III. 1818. 3. George de Grey, s. and h. Present Baron
            Walsingham.

WALTER.

BARONS BY TENURE.

I. H. II. 1. Hervey, son of Hubert Walter.

II. Ric. I. 2. Theobald Walter, s. and h. Butler of Ireland; ob. 1209.

III. John. 3. Theobald Walter, s. and h. He assumed the name of Boteler, and was progenitor of the noble House of Butler, Earls, Marquesses, and Dukes of Ormond.

WARD.

BARONS.

I. 1644. 1. Humble Ward; Created Baron Ward of Birmingham, co. Warwick, 23 March, 1644; he married Frances Baroness Dudley; ob. 1670.

II. 1670. 2. Edward Ward, s. and h. succeeded his mother in the ancient Barony of Dudley in 1697. This Barony became merged in that of Dudley until the death of William XVI.-22d Baron Dudley, and 5th Baron Ward in 1740, s. p. when the Barony of Ward devolved on his next heir male, viz.

VI. 1740. 6. John Ward, he being son and heir of William Ward, eldest son of William Ward, 2d son of Humble 1st Baron Ward; Created Viscount Dudley and Ward 21 April, 1763; ob. 1774.

VII. 1774. 7. John Ward, s. and h. Viscount Dudley and Ward; ob. 1788, s. p.

VIII. 1788. 8. William Ward, half-brother and heir; Viscount Dudley and Ward; ob. 1823.

IX. 1823. 9. John William Ward, s. and h. Present Baron Ward and Viscount Dudley and Ward.

WARDE.

Vide DE LA WARDE.

WARKWORTH.

BARONY, 2 October, 1749.

Vide NORTHUMBERLAND.

WARR.

Vide DE LA WARR.

WARREN.

William de Warren, who was created Earl of Surrey
by William Rufus, is considered to have been Earl
Warren in Normandy; and his descendants, who inherited the Earldom of Surrey, styled themselves " Earls
Warren *;" but it does not appear that it was ever considered as a regular Earldom in this country until 1451,
when

EARLS.

I. 1454. 1. John Mowbray, son and heir apparent of
John III.-3d Duke of Norfolk, and great
grandson of John I. Duke of Norfolk by Elizabeth, sister and heir of Thomas Fitz-Alan,
XI.-9th Earl of Surrey and Arundel; and
who, like all his predecessors in the former
Earldom, styled himself " Earl Warren;"
was Created Earl Warren and Surrey 29
March, 1451, but (probably from being a minor) he was never summoned to Parliament
by those titles; he succeeded his father as
IV.-4th Duke of Norfolk in 1461; K. G.;
ob. 1475, s. p. m. when the Earldoms of Warren and Surrey, became

Extinct.

II. 1477. 1. Richard Plantagenet, Duke of York, 2d son
of King Edward IV. being betrothed to
Ann Mowbray, dau. and sole heir of John
Mowbray, Duke of Norfolk, and last Earl
Warren and Surrey, was created Earl War-

---

* Vide SURREY.

ren and Duke of Norfolk 7 Feb. 1477; murdered in the Tower in 1483, when all his honors became

Extinct.

WARREN
OF WIRMGAY.

BARONS BY TENURE.

I. H. II. 1. Reginald de Warren, a younger son of William II.-2d Earl Warren and Earl of Surrey, Lord of Wirmgay, co. Norfolk, in right of Alice, dau. and heir of William de Wirmgay; living 1171, ob. ante 1184.

II. Ric. I. 2. William de Warren, s. and h. ob. 1208, s. p. m. leaving Beatrix, widow of Dodo Bardulf, his dau. and heir; which Beatrix afterwards married Robert de Burgh, Earl of Kent.

WARRINGTON.

EARLS.

I. 1690. 1. Henry Booth, 2d Baron Delamere; Created Earl of Warrington, co. Lancaster, 17 April, 1690; ob. 1693.

II. 1698. 2. George Booth, s. and h. ob. 1758, s. p. m. when this Earldom became,

Extinct.

III. 1796. 1. George Harry Grey, 5th Earl of Stamford, son and heir of Harry 4th Earl of Stamford by Mary, sole dau. and heir of George the last Earl; Created Baron Delamere of Dunham Massey, co. Chester, and Earl of Warrington 22 April, 1796; ob. 1819.

IV. 1819. 2. George Harry Grey, s. and h. 6th Earl of Stamford. Present Earl of Warrington, Earl of Stamford, Baron Grey of Groby, and Baron de la Mere of Dunham Massey.

WARWICK.

I.   Will.I. 1. Henry de Newburgh, younger son of Roger de Bellomont, Earl of Mellent in Normandy ; Created Earl of Warwick by William the Conqueror ; ob. 1123.

II.   1123. 2. Roger de Newburgh, s. and h.; ob. 1153.

III.   1153. 3. William de Newburgh, s. and h. ob. 1184, s.p.

IV.   1184. 4. Waleran de Newburgh, brother and heir; ob. 1205.

V.   1205. 5. Henry de Newburgh, s. and h.; ob. 1229.

VI.   1229. 6. Thomas de Newburgh, s. and h. ob. 1242, s. p. leaving Margery his half-sister his heir, who married first

VII.   1242.   John Mareschall, of the family of the Earls of Pembroke, who is styled Earl of Warwick by most authorities jure uxoris ; ob. 1243, s. P. Margery his widow having remarried

VIII.   1246.   John de Plessets; he styled himself in her right, Earl of Warwick circa 1246 ; ob. 1263, without issue by Margery his second wife, who soon afterwards died s. p. when her inheritance devolved on her first cousin and heir,

IX.   1263. 7. William Mauduit, s. and h. of William Mauduit, Baron of Hanslape by Alice, half-sister of Henry V.-5th Earl, and aunt of the half-blood to the said Margery, and who consequently became Earl of Warwick, and by that title was Summoned to attend the King at Worcester in 1263 ; ob. 1267, s. P. when his nephew,

X.   1267. 8. William de Beauchamp, Baron of Elmley, succeed to the inheritance of this Earldom, he being son and heir of William de Beauchamp by Isabel de Mauduit, sister and heir of the last Earl. It is evident from the will of William, father of this Earl, that he assumed the title of Earl of Warwick during his mother's life-time, his right to do so being very questionable; ob. 1298.

XI.   1298. 9. Guy de Beauchamp, s. and h.; ob. 1315.

EARLS.

XII. 1315. 10. Thomas de Beauchamp, s. and h. K. G.; ob. 1369.

XIII. 1369. 11. Thomas de Beauchamp, 2d son and heir male (Guy the eldest son having died vitâ patris, s. p. m.); attainted 1397, when his honors were forfeited, but restored in blood and honors in 1399; K. G.; ob. 1401.

XIV. 1401. 12. Richard de Beauchamp, s. and h. Created Earl of Aumarle for life 1417; K. G.; ob. 1439.

DUKE.

XV. 1439.—I. 1444, 13. Henry de Beauchamp, s. and h. Created Premier Earl of England, with the special privilege of wearing a gold coronet, 2 April, 1444; Created Duke of Warwick 5 April following; Crowned King of the Isle of Wight by the King's own hand circa 1445; K. G.; ob. 1445, s. p. m. when the Dukedom became

COUNTESS. Extinct.

I. 1445. 14. Ann de Beauchamp, dau. and sole heir of Henry the last Earl and Duke of Warwick, styled Countess of Warwick; ob. 1449, s. p. when the Earldom also became

Extinct.

XVI. 1449. Richard Nevill (son and heir apparent of Richard Earl of Salisbury), having married Ann de Beauchamp, sister of Henry XV.-13th Earl and I. Duke of Warwick, and heir to her niece Ann Countess of Warwick above mentioned, was created Earl of Warwick, to him and the heirs of his said wife, "with all pre-eminences that any of their ancestors before the creation of Henry Duke of Warwick used;" succeeded as Earl of Salisbury in 1462, K. G., slain 1471, (ob. s. p. m.) and being attainted, his honors became

Forfeited.

XVII. 1472. 1. George Plantagenet, Duke of Clarence, brother of King Edward IV. having married

Isabel Nevill, eldest daughter and coheir of Richard the last Earl, was created Earl of Warwick and Salisbury 25 March, 1472; murdered and attainted in 1477, when his dignities became

Forfeited.

XVIII.14... 2. Edward Plantagenet, s. and h. of George Duke of Clarence, the last Earl; bore the title of Earl of Warwick, though it does not appear that his father's attainder was reversed; beheaded 1499, and being attainted, by whatever right he was possessed of this Earldom, it again became

Forfeited.

XIX. 1547. 1. John Dudley, VII.-1st Viscount L'isle, being son and heir of Edmond Dudley, by Elizabeth, dau. and eventually coheir of Edward Grey, III.-1st Viscount L'isle, by Elizabeth, daughter and ultimately coheir of John Talbot, I.-1st Viscount L'isle, younger son of John Earl of Shrewsbury by Margaret Beauchamp, daughter of Richard XIV.-12th Earl of Warwick, and half-sister of Henry XV.-13th Earl and I. Duke of Warwick; was created Earl of Warwick 17 February, 1547; Created Duke of Northumberland 11 Oct. 1551, K. G.; attainted and beheaded 1553, when all his honors became

Forfeited.

XX. 1567. 1. Ambrose Dudley, s. and h. being restored in blood, was created Baron L'isle 25 Dec. 1561; Created Earl of Warwick 26 Sept. 1567; K. G.; ob. 1589, s. p. when his honors became

Extinct.

XXI. 1618. 1.Robert Rich, 3d Baron Rich of Leeze; Created Earl of Warwick 6 Aug. 1618; ob. 1618.

XXII. 1618.2.Robert Rich, s. and h. ob. 1658.

XXIII.1658.3.Robert Rich, s. and h. ob. 1659, s. p. m.

XXIV.1659.4.Charles Rich, brother and heir; ob. 1673, s.p.

EARLS.

XXV. 1673.5. Robert Rich, II.-2d Earl of Holland, cousin and heir male, being son and heir of Henry 1st Earl of Holland, 2d son of Robert Rich, XXI.-1st Earl of Warwick ; ob. 1675.

XXVI. 1675.6. Robert Rich, s. and h. Earl of Holland; ob. 1701.

XXVII. 1701.7. Edward Henry Rich, s. and h. Earl of Holland; ob. 1721, s. p.

XXVIII. 1721.8. Edward Rich, cousin and heir male, being son and heir of Cope Rich, eldest son of Cope Rich, next brother of Robert II. Earl of Holland and XXV.-5th Earl of Warwick ; Earl of Holland ; ob. 1759, s. p. m. when all his honors became

Extinct.

XXIX. 1759.1. Francis Greville, I. Earl Brooke (descended from Walter Beauchamp, Baron of Alcester and Powyck, brother of William Beauchamp, X.-8th Earl of Warwick); Created Earl of Warwick 21 Nov. 1759 ; K. T.; ob. 1773.

XXX. 1773.2. George Greville, s. and h. Earl Brooke ; ob. 1816.

XXXI. 1816.3. Henry Richard Greville, s. and h. Present Earl and Baron Brooke, and Earl of Warwick. ⊤

WATEVYLL.

BARON BY WRIT.

I. 1326. Robert de Watevyll; Summ. to Parl. from 3 Dec. 20 Edward II. 1326, to 25 Jan. 4 Edw. III. 1330.

Dugdale gives no account of this Baron in his Baronage.

WELLES.

BARONS BY WRIT.

I. 1299. 1. Adam de Welles ; Summ. to Parl. from 6 Feb. 27 Edw. I. 1299, to 16 June, 4 Edw. II. 1311 ; ob. 1311.

II. 1311. 2. Robert de Welles, son and heir ; he was never Summ. to Parl.; ob. 1320, s. p.

BARONS BY WRIT.

III. 1320. 3. Adam de Welles, brother and heir; Summ. to
Parl. from 20 July, 6 Edward III. 1332, to 20
April, 17 Edw. III. 1343 f ob. 1345.

IV. 1345. 4. John de Welles, s. and h. Summ. to Parl. 15
Dec. 31 Edward III. 1357, and 20 Nov. 34
Edw. III. 1360 ; ob. 1361.

V. 1361. 5. John de Welles, s. and h. Summ. to Parl. from
20 Jan. 49 Edward III. 1376, to 26 Feb. 8
Hen. V. 1421 ; ob. 1421 *.

VI. 1421. 6. Leo de Welles, grandson and heir, being son
and heir of Eudo de Welles (ob. v. p.) eldest
son of the last Baron ; Summ. to Parl. from
25 February 10 Hen. VI. 1432, to 30 July, 38
Henry VI. 1640 ; slain 1461, and being attainted, his honors became

Forfeited.

VII. 1468. 7. Richard de Welles, son and heir of Leo the
last Baron, having married Joan, dau. and
heir of Robert VI. 6th Baron Willoughby of
Eresby was Summ. to Parl. from 26 May, 33
Hen. VI. 1455, to 28 Feb. 6 Edw. IV. 1466, as
" Ricbardo Welles, Domino Willoughby, Militi ;" obtained a full Restoration in blood
and honors 8 Edward IV. 1468 ; beheaded in
1469. Robert de Welles, his only and heir,
was beheaded in the same year ; and in the
14th Edward IV. 1474, they were both attainted, when their honors again became Forfeited. This Robert dying s. p. Joane his
sister became his heir, who married Richard
Hastings ; and though it does not appear

---

* Though Dugdale's statement relative to this Baron has been
followed in the text, it must be observed, that a " John de
Welles" (and apparently the same personage) was regularly summoned to Parliament from 29 September, 1 Hen. VI. 1422, to 8
August, 7 Hen. VI. 1429. Many instances are to be found of
Writs of Summons being directed to Barons several years after
their deaths, probably from ignorance of their demises : of which
that of Maurice Lord Berkeley is a singular example, who
though dead in 1868 was regularly summoned until 1380, viz.
twelve years after his decease. Vide p. 60.

either that the Attainder of Robert her brother, or of Richard her father the VII.-7th
Baron, was ever reversed *, the said

VIII. 1482. Richard Hastings was Summ. to Parl. 15
Nov. 22 Edw. IV. 1482, and 9 December, 23
Edw. IV. 1483, as "Richardo Hastinges de
Welles, Chl'r;" ob. 1503, s. P. s. and Joane
his wife died in 1505, s. P. when, if the original Barony be
considered to have been revived so as not to be affected
by the Attainders above mentioned, it fell into ABEYANCE
between the descendants of the four daughters of Leo VI.
Baron Welles, viz. of Alianore, who married Thomas
Lord Hoo and Hastings; Margaret, who was the wife of
Sir Thomas Dymocke; Cecily, who married Sir Robert
Willoughby; and Katherine, who was the wife of Sir
Thomas de la Launde; among whose representatives this
Barony would now be in ABEYANCE: but if the Writ to
Richard Hastings as Lord Welles be considered as a crea-
tion *de novo*, and which is most probable, it became
Extinct on his demise in 1503, s. P. s.

WELLES
OF ——

VISCOUNT.

I. 1487. John Welles, 2d son of Leo VI.-6th Baron
Welles (by his second wife); Created Viscount Welles, by which title he was first summoned to Parliament 1 Sept. 1487, though
the precise date of his Patent does not appear. He married Cecily Plantagenet, dau.
of King Edward IV.; K. G.; ob. 1498, s. P. M.
(Ann, his sole daughter and heir, died an infant shortly after her father's death), when
his title became
Extinct.

---

* In the Act of Attainder in question, special provision is
made, that Richard Hastings should enjoy certain manors which
belonged to the attainted Barons, in consideration that he had
married Joan, sister and heir of the said Robert de Welles, and
also of his loyalty and services. Rot. Parl. anno 14 Edw. IV.

WELLESLEY.

BARON.

I. 1797.   1. Richard Colley Wellesley, 2d Earl of Morning-
ton in Ireland; Created Baron Wellesley of
Wellesley, co. Somerset, 20 Oct. 1797; Created Marquess of Wellesley in Ireland 2 December, 1799.   Present Baron Wellesley;
also Marquess of Wellesley, &c. in Ireland,
K. G. $=$

WELLINGTON.

VISC.   EARL.   MARQ.   DUKE.

I.1809.—I.1812.—I.1812.—I.1814. 1. Sir Arthur Wellesley,
K.B. brother of Richard
1st Marquess of Welles-
ley in Ireland, and 1st Baron Wellesley in England;
Created Baron Douro of Wellesley, co. Somerset, and
Viscount Wellington of Talavera, and of Wellington, co.
Somerset, 4 Sept. 1809; Created Earl of Wellington, co.
Somerset, 28 Feb. 1812; Created Marquess of Wellington
aforesaid, 18 Aug. 1812; Created Marquess of Douro aforesaid, and Duke of Wellington 3 May, 1814. Present Duke,
Marquess, Earl, and Viscount Wellington, and Marquess
and Baron of Douro; also Prince of Waterloo in the Netherlands; Duke of Ciudad Rodrigo in Spain, and a
Grandee of the First Class; Duke of Vittoria, Marquess
of Torres Vedras, and Count of Vimiera in Portugal;
K. G., G. C. B., G. C. H. and Knight Grand Cross of every
illustrious Order in Europe. $=$

WEMYSS.

BARON.

I. 1821.   1. Francis Wemyss Charteris Douglas, 6th Earl
of Wemyss, in Scotland; Created Baron
Wemyss of Wemyss, co. Fife, 17 July, 1821.
Present Baron Wemyss; also Earl of Wemyss,
&c. in Scotland. $=$

WENLOK or WENLOCK.

BARON.

I. 1461. John Wenlok; Created Baron Wenlok of Wenlok, co. Salop, ..., 1461; and was Summ. to Parl. as "Johanni Wenlok de Wenlok, Milite," 26 July, 1 Edw. IV. 1461; K.G.; ob.1471, s. p. when his honors became **Extinct.**

WENTWORTH.

BARONS BY WRIT.

I. 1529. 1. Thomas Wentworth; Summ. to Parl. from 2 Dec. 21 Hen. VIII. 1529, to 4 Nov. 2 Edward VI. 1548; ob. 1551.

II. 1551. 2. Thomas Wentworth, s. and h. Summ. to Parl. from 23 Jan. 5 Edward VI. 1552, to 4 Feb. 31 Eliz. 1589; ob.1590.

III. 1590. 3. Henry Wentworth, s. and h. Summ. to Parl. 19 Feb. 35 Eliz. 1593; ob. 1594.

IV. 1594. 4. Thomas Wentworth, s. and h. Summ. to Parl. from 30 Jan. 18 Jac. I. 1621, to 17 May, 1 Car. I. 1625; Created Earl of Cleveland, co. York, 5 Feb. 1626; ob. 1667, s. p. m. when that Earldom became **Extinct;** but the Barony of Wentworth devolved on

BARONESSES.

I. 1667. 5. Henrietta Maria Wentworth, his granddaughter and heir, being dau. and sole heir of Thomas Wentworth (ob. v. p. in 1664), who was Summ. to Parliament in his father's Barony, eldest son of the last Baron; ob. 1686, s. p.

II. 1686. 6. Ann Wentworth, aunt and heir, being only surviving child of Thomas IV. Baron, grandfather of the last Baroness; she married John Lord Lovelace; ob. 1697.

III.1697. 7. Martha Lovelace, grand-daughter and heir, being dau. and sole heir of John Lord Lovelace (ob. vita matris), eldest son of the last Baroness; she married Sir Henry Johnson, Knt.; ob. 1745, s. p.

BARON BY WRIT. VISC.

V. 1745.—I. 1762. 8. Sir Edward Noel, 4th Bart. cousin and heir, being son and heir of Sir

Clobery Noel, eldest son of Sir John Noel, brother and heir of Sir Thomas Noel, son and heir of Sir William Noel by Margaret Lovelace, 2d daughter of Ann II.-6th Baroness; Created Viscount Wentworth of Wellesborough, co. Leicester, 4 May, 1762; ob. 1774.

BARON
BY WRIT. VISC.
VI. 1774.—II. 1774. 9. Thomas Noel, s. and h. ob. 1815, s. p. when the Viscountcy became Extinct; but the Barony fell into Abeyance between his eldest sister, Judith, wife of Sir Ralph Milbank, Bart. and his nephew Nathaniel Curzon, son and heir apparent of Nathaniel, present Lord Scarsdale by Sophia Susannah, his second sister. The Barony of Wentworth is now in Abeyance between the said Hon. Nathaniel Curzon, and the Right Hon. Ann Isabella, widow of the late George Gordon Byron Noel Lord Byron, she being the only child of Judith, late wife of Sir Ralph Milbank (who afterwards assumed the name of) Noel, above mentioned.

WENTWORTH
OF WENTWORTH WOODHOUSE.

BARONS. VISCOUNTS.
I. 1628.—I. 1628. 1. Sir Thomas Wentworth, 2d Bart.; Created Baron Wentworth of Wentworth Woodhouse, co. York, 22 July, 1628; Created Viscount Wentworth 10 Dec. following; Created Earl of Strafford 12 Jan. 1640, K. G.

Forfeited 1641—Restored 1665—Extinct 1695.
Vide Strafford.

Viscountcy, 4 September, 1711—Extinct 1799.
Vide Strafford.

WEST.

BARONS BY WRIT.
I. 1342. 1. Thomas West; Summ. to Parl. 25 Feb. 16 Edw. III. 1342; ob. 1343.

BARONS BY WRIT.

II.   1343, 2. Thomas West, s. and h.; he was never Summ.
to Parl.; ob. 1386.

III. 1402. 3. Thomas West, s. and h. Summ. to Parl. 21
June, 3 Henry IV. 1402, and 25 August, 4
Henry IV. 1404; he married Joan, daughter
of Roger Baron la Warr; ob. 1405.

IV. 1405. 4. Thomas West, s. and h.; he married Ida,
daughter and coheir of Almaric, Baron St.
Amand, but was never Summ. to Parl.; ob.
1415, s. p.

V. 1414. 5. Reginald West, s. and h. Summ. to Parl. as
" Baron de la Warr," in 1426, jure matris;
in which Barony that of West became
merged.

This Barony, together with the *ancient* Barony of De
la Warr, is now vested in the descendants and representatives of Sir Owen West, half-brother of Thomas West,
IX.-9th Baron de la Warr.   Vide DE LA WARR, p. 184.

WESTON.

BARONS.

I.   1628. 1. Richard Weston; Created Baron Weston, of
Neyland, co. Essex, 13 April, 1628; Created
Earl of Portland 17 Feb. 1633.
           𝕰xtinct 1688.   Vide PORTLAND.

WESTMORELAND.

EARLS.

I.   1397. 1. Ralph Nevill, IV.-8th Baron Nevill of Raby;
Created Earl of Westmoreland 29 September,
1397; K. G. Earl Marshal; ob. 1425.

II. 1425. 2. Ralph Nevill, grandson and heir, being son
and heir of John Nevill (ob. v. p.) eldest son
of the last Earl; ob. 1485, s. p. s.

III. 1485. 3. Ralph Nevill, nephew and heir, being son and
heir of John Nevill next brother of the last
Earl; ob. 1523.

IV. 1523. 4. Ralph Nevill, grandson and heir, being son
A A 3

and heir of Ralph Nevill (ob. v. p.) eldest son of the last Earl; K. G.; ob. 1549.

V. 1549. 5. Henry Nevill, s. and h. K. G.; ob. 1563.

VI. 1563. 6. Charles Nevill, s. and h. Attainted in 1570, when all his honors became

forfeited*.

VII. 1624. 1. Francis Fane, son and heir apparent of Sir Thomas Fane by Mary Nevill, Baroness Despencer and Burghersh, dau. and sole heir of Henry Nevill, XIII,-4th Baron Bergavenny, lineally descended from Edward Nevill, younger son of Ralph 1st Earl of Westmoreland; Created Baron Burghersh and Earl of Westmoreland, with remainder to his heirs male, 29 Dec. 1624; succeeded his mother in the ancient Baronies of Despencer and Burghersh in 1626: ob. 1628.

VIII. 1628. 2. Mildmay Fane, s. and h. ob. 1665.

IX. 1665. 3. Charles Fane, s. and h. ob. 1691, s. p.

X. 1691. 4. Vere Fane, brother and heir; ob. 1693.

XI. 1693. 5. Vere Fane, s. and h. ob. 1699, s. p.

XII. 1699. 6. Thomas Fane, brother and heir; ob. 1736, s.p.

XIII. 1736. 7. John Fane, brother and heir; Created Baron Catherlough in Ireland 4 Oct. 1733; ob. 1762, s. p. when the Baronies of Despencer and Burghersh (by Writ) fell into Abeyance, and his Irish Barony became Extinct; but the Barony of Burghersh (by Patent) and the Earldom of Westmoreland, devolved on

XIV. 1762. 8. Thomas Fane, as next heir male, being son and heir of Henry, eldest son of Sir Francis Fane, K. B. s. and h. of Sir Francis Fane, K.B. 2d son of Francis VII.-1st Earl; ob. 1771.

---

* In the reign of James I. Edmond Nevill, the lineal descendant of George Nevill, younger son of Ralph 1st Earl, and next heir male of Charles the last Earl, claimed the Earldom of Westmoreland; but it was decided against him, on the ground that the Attainder had caused all the honors possessed by the said Charles to be FORFEITED to the Crown as an estate of inheritance. A copy of Edmond Nevill's claim, which is a curious document, may be found in Landsdowne MSS. 254, p. 376.

EARLS.

XV. 1771. 9. John Fane, s. and h. ob. 1774.

XVI. 1774. 10. John Fane, and h. Present Earl of Westmoreland and Baron Burghersh, K. G. ⊤

WEYMOUTH.

VISCOUNTS.

I. 1682. 1. Sir Thomas Thynne, 2d Bart. Created Baron
Thynne of Warminster, co. Wilts, and Viscount Weymouth, co. Dorset, 11 Dec. 1682,
with remainder, failing his issue male, to his
brothers and their issue male respectively;
ob. 1714, s. p. m.

II. 1714. 2. Thomas Thynne, grand-nephew and heir male,
being son and heir of Thomas, eldest son of
Henry Thynne, next brother of Thomas 1st
Viscount; ob. 1751.

III. 1751. 3. Thomas Thynne, s. and h. Created Marquess
of Bath, 18 August, 1789; K. G.; ob. 1796.

IV. 1796. 4. Thomas Thynne, s. and h. Present Marquess
of Bath, Viscount Weymouth, Baron Thynne,
and a Baronet, K. G. ⊤

WHARTON.

BARONS BY WRIT.

I. 1545. 1. Thomas Wharton; Summ. to Parl. from 30
Jan. 36 Hen. VIII. 1545, to 30 Sept. 8 Eliz.
1566; ob. 1568.

II. 1568. 2. Thomas Wharton, s. and h. Summ. to Parl.
2 April, 13 Eliz. 1571, and 8 May, 14 Eliz.
1572; ob. 1572.

III. 1572. 3. Philip Wharton, s. and h. Summ. to Parl.
from 6 Jan. 23 Eliz. 1581, to 17 May, 1 Car.
I. 1625; ob. 1625.

IV. 1625. 4. Philip Wharton, grandson and heir, being son
and heir of Thomas Wharton (ob. v. p.)
eldest son of the last Baron; Summ. to
Parl. from 3 Nov. 15 Car. I. 1639, to 19 May,
1 Jac. II. 1685; ob. 1696.

EARLS. MARQUESS.

V. 1696.—I. 1706.—I. 1715, 5. Thomas Wharton, s. and h.
Created Viscount Winchen-
don, co. Bucks, and Earl of

Wharton, co. Westmore-
land, 24 Dec. 1706; Cre-
ated Marquess of Malmes-
bury, co. Wilts. and Mar-
quess of Wharton, co.West-
moreland, 1 January, 1715,
and on the same day Baron
of Trim, Earl of Rathfar-
num, and Marquess of Ca-
therlogh in Ireland ;   ob.
1715.

BARONS. EARLS. MARQUESS. DUKE.
VI.1715.—II.1715.—II.1715.—I.1718.6. Philip Wharton, son
and heir ; Created
Duke of Wharton, co. Westmoreland, 20
Jan. 1718; Attainted in 1728, when all his
honors became
𝔉orfeited.

It does not appear that his Attainder has been reversed; but should his heirs ever be rendered capable of
inheriting his honors, the Barony would become vested in
the descendants and representatives of Lucy and Jane,
his sisters and cobeirs *; but as he died s. p. in 1731, all
his other honors, if he had not forfeited them in 1728,
would then have become 𝔈xtinct.

WHITTINGTON.

John de Whittington ; Summoned 26 January, 25
Edward I. 1297; but for the reasons assigned under
" FITZ-JOHN," it is doubtful if that Writ can be considered as a regular Summons to Parliament. Dugdale
gives no account of such a Baron, nor does he appear
ever afterwards to have been summoned.

---

* Banks' Stemmata Anglicana, states, that these ladies died s.p.
and that the representation of the Barony is vested in the present
Marchioness of Cholmondeley, and her sister Lady Willoughby
of Eresby, as the heirs of Elizabeth, dau. of Philip the 4th Baron, who married Robert 3d Earl of Lindsey; in Charles Kemeys
Kemeys Tynte, Esq. the representative of Mary, another dau.
of the said Baron, who married first, Edward Thomas, Esq. and
secondly, Sir Charles Kemeys, Bart.; and in the issue, if any exists,
of Philadelphia (who married, first, Sir George Lockhart, and
secondly, Captain John Ramsay), another daughter of the said
Philip 4th Baron.

WIDDRINGTON.

BARONS.

I. 1643. 1. Sir William Widdrington, 1st Bart.; Created Baron Widdrington, of Blankney, co. Lincoln, 10 Nov. 1643; ob. 1651.

II. 1651. 2. William Widdrington, s. and h. ob. 1676.

III. 1676. 3. William Widdrington, s. and h. ob. 1695.

IV. 1695. 4. William Widdrington, s. and h.; Attainted in 1716, when his honors became
𝔉𝔬𝔯𝔣𝔢𝔦𝔱𝔢𝔡.

WILINGTON.

BARONS BY WRIT.

I. 1329. 1. John de Wilington; Summoned to Parliament from 14 June, 3 Edw. III. 1329, to 15 Nov. 12 Edward III. 1338. Dugdale in his Baronage omits to notice, that a John de Wilington was ever summoned to Parliament; but it is pretty evident it was this John whom he states had his lands seised 15 Edw. II. but which were restored to him by Edward III. and who was father of

II. 1342. 2. Ralph de Wilington; Summ. to Parl. 25 Feb. 16 Edward III. 1342, but never afterwards; ob. 1348, s. p. leaving Ralph de Wylington his uncle his heir, when this Barony became
𝔈𝔵𝔱𝔦𝔫𝔠𝔱.

WILLIAMS

OF THAME.

BARON BY WRIT.

I. 1554. 1. John Williams; Summ. to Parl. from 2 April, 1 Philip and Mary, 1554, to 5 Nov. 5 and 6 Philip and Mary, 1558, as " Johanni Williams de Thame;" ob. 1559, s. p. m. leaving his two daughters, Isabel, who married Sir Richard Wenman, and Margery, the wife of Henry Lord Norris, his heirs, and between whose descendants and representatives (of whom the Earl of Abingdon is the heir-general of Margery), this Barony is now in ABEYANCE.

WILLOUGHBY

OF ERESBY. ·

I. 1313. 1. Robert Willoughby; Summoned to Parliament 26 July, and 26 Nov. 7 Edw. II. 1313 ; he married Alice, sister and cobeir of Walter, Baron Beke; ob. 1316.

II. 1316. 2. John Willoughby, s. and h.; Summ. to Parl. from 27 Jan. 6 Edw. III. 1332, to 10 March, 23 Edw. III. 1349; ob. 1349.

III. 1349. 3. John Willoughby, s. and h.; Summ. to Parl. from 25 Nov. 24 Edw. III. 1350, to 8 Jan. 44 Edw. III. 1371, as "Johanni de Wilughby de Eresby ;" ob. 1372.

IV. 1372. 4. Robert Willoughby, s. and h.; Summ. to Parl. from 20 Jan. 49 Edw. III. 1376, to 20 Nov. 18 Rich. II. 1394; ob. 1396.

V. 1396. 5. William Willoughby, s. and h. ; Summ. to Parl. from 30 Nov. 20 Rich. II. 1396, to 26 Oct. 11 Hen. IV. 1409 ; ob. 1409.

VI. 1409. 6. Robert Willoughby, s. and h.; Summ. to Parl. from 21 Sept. 12 Hen. IV. 1411, to 5 Sept. 29 Hen. VI. 1450.; ob. 1452, s. p. m.; Joane his sole daughter and beir having married

VII. 1455. Richard Welles, son and heir apparent of Leo VI. Baron Welles; he was Summ. to Parl. *jure uxoris*, as "Ricbardo de Welles, Domino Willoughby Militi," from 26 May, 33 Hen. VI. 1455, to 28 February 6 Edward IV. 1466 ; beheaded, together with his only son, Robert Welles, in 1469 ; and were both Attainted in 1472. Joane, his only sister and beir, married Richard Hastings; who was Summ. to Parl. in 1482, as Baron Welles ; he died s. p. in 1503, and his said wife Joane in 1505, likewise without issue; when this Barony devolved upon her next heir, jure matris, viz.

VIII. 1508. 7. William Willoughby, he being son and heir of Christopher, brother and heir of Robert, eldest son of Robert, son and heir of Thomas Willoughby, next brother of Robert VI. Baron; Summ. to Parl. from 17 Oct. 1 Hen.

VIII. 1509, to 15 April, 14 Hen. VIII. 1523 ;
ob. 1525, s. p. m.

BARONESS.

I. 1525. 8. Katherine Willoughby, dau. and heir ; she
married first, Charles Brandon, Duke of
Suffolk, and by him had two sons, who died
in their infancy ; her second husband was
Richard Bertie, Esq. ; ob. 1580.

BARONS BY WRIT.

IX. 1580. 9. Peregrine Bertie, s. and h. ; claimed and was
allowed the Barony, and was Summ. to Parl.
from 16 Jan. 23 Eliz. 1581, to 24 Oct. 39
Eliz. 1597 ; ob. 1601.

X. 1601. 10. Robert Bertie, s. and h.; Summ. to Parl.
from 5 Nov. 3 Jaq. I. 1605, to 17 May,
1 Car. I. 1625 ; Created Earl of Lindsey 22
Nov. 1626. This Barony continued merged
in the Earldom of Lindsey and Dukedom
of Ancaster until the demise of Robert IV.
Duke of Ancaster, VII. Earl and II. Marquess
of Lindsey, and XVI. Baron Willoughby of
Eresby, in 1779, s. p. when it fell into ABEY-
ANCE between his two sisters and heirs, viz.
Priscilla Barbara Elizabeth Bertie, the present Baroness, and Georgiana Charlotte
Bertie, since married to the present Marquess of Cholmondeley. On the 18th March,
1780, his Majesty was pleased to terminate
the Abeyance in favour of

II. 1780. 11. Priscilla Barbara Elizabeth Burrell, wife of
Peter, 1st Baron Gwydir, and eldest sister
and coheir of Robert, Duke of Ancaster, &c.
the last Baron Willoughby of Eresby. Present Baroness Willoughby of Eresby, eldest
coheir of one moiey of the Barony of Beke,
and joint Great Chamberlain of England. ⚎
Ƴ

WILLOUGHBY DE BROKE.

BARONS BY WRIT.

I. 1492. 1. Robert Willoughby, grandson of Sir Thomas
Willoughby, 2d son of Robert IV. Baron
Willoughby of Eresby ; Summoned to Par-
liament from 12 Aug. 7 Hen. VII. 1492, to

BARONS BY WRIT.

　　　　16 Jan. 12 Hen. VII. 1497, as "Roberto
　　　　Willoughby de Brooke, Chev.;" ob. 1503.

II.　1503.　2. Robert Willoughby, s. and h.;　Summ. to
　　　　Parl. from 28 Nov. 3 Hen. VIII 1511, to 12
　　　　Nov. 7 Hen. VIII. 1515; ob. 1522, s. p. m.
　　　　Edward, his eldest son, died vitâ patris,
　　　　s. p. m. between whose daughters, Elizabeth,
　　　　who married Sir Fulke Greville, and Blanch,
　　　　who became the wife of Sir Francis Dawtrey,
　　　　the Barony fell into ABEYANCE.　In 1606 it
　　　　was claimed by, and allowed to,

III.　1696.　3. Richard Verney, he being 2d son, and eventu-
　　　　ally heir of Sir Greville Verney, son and heir
　　　　of Sir Richard Verney, by Margaret, sister
　　　　and sole heir of Fulke Greville, I. Baron
　　　　Brooke, son and heir of Sir Fulke Greville,
　　　　eldest son of Sir Fulke Greville, by Elizabeth
　　　　Willoughby above mentioned, dau. and ulti-
　　　　mately sole heir (her sister Blanch, Lady
　　　　Dawtrey, having died s. p.), of Edward Wil-
　　　　loughby, who died vitâ patris, eldest son of
　　　　Robert, II. Baron; allowed the Barony, 13
　　　　Feb. 1696; ob. 1711.

IV.　1711.　4. George Verney, s. and h.; ob. 1728.

V.　1728.　5. Richard Verney, s. and h.; ob. 1752, s. p.

VI.　1752.　6. John Peyto Verney, nephew and heir; being
　　　　s. and h. of John Verney, next brother of the
　　　　last Baron; ob. 1816.

VII.　1816.　7. John Peyto Verney, s. and h.; ob. 1820, s. p.

VIII.　1820.　8. Henry Peyto Verney, brother and heir; pre-
　　　　sent Baron Willoughby de Broke; and being
　　　　heir general of the Barony of Latimer,
　　　　created by Writ of Summons of 20 Dec. 28
　　　　Edw. I. 1299, also Baron Latimer.

WILLOUGHBY
OF PARHAM.

BARONS.

I.　1547.　1. William Willoughby, s. and h. of Christopher.
　　　　Willoughby, next bro. of William VIII.-7th Ba-
　　　　ron Willoughby of Eresby; Created Baron Wil-

BARONS.

loughby of Parham, eo. Suffolk, 16 Feb. 1547; ob. 1574.

II. 1574. 2. Charles Willoughby, s. and h.; ob. 1603.

III. 1603. 3. William Willoughby, grandson and heir; being s. and h. of William Willoughby (ob. v. P.), eldest son of the last Baron; ob. 1617.

IV. 1617. 4. Henry Willoughby, s. and h.; ob. 16..., infans.

V. 16—. 5. Francis Willoughby, brother and heir; ob. 1666, s. P. M.

VI. 1666. 6. William Willoughby, brother and heir; ob. 1673.

VII. 1673. 7. George Willoughby, s. and h.; ob. 1674.

VIII. 1674. 8. John Willoughby, s. and h.; ob. 1678, s. P.

IX. 1678. 9. John Willoughby, uncle and heir; being next brother of George, VIII. Baron; ob. 1678, s. P.

X. 1678. 10. Charles Willoughby, brother and heir; ob. 1679, s. P.

XI. 1679. 11. Thomas Willoughby, s. and h. of Thomas Willoughby, *third* son of Charles, II. Baron, was erroneously allowed the Barony, on the presumption that the issue male of his elder brother, Ambrose Willoughby, *second* son of Charles, II. Baron, was extinct; and was summoned to Parliament by Writ directed "Thomæ Willoughby de Parham, Chl'r." 19 May, 1 Jaq. II. 1685; ob. 1692.

XII. 1692. 12. Hugh Willoughby, s. and h.; ob. 1712, s. P.

XIII. 1712. 13. Edward Willoughby, nephew and heir; being s. and h. of Francis Willoughby, next brother of the last Baron; ob. 1713.

XIV. 1713. 14. Charles Willoughby, brother and heir; ob. 1715.

XV. 1715. 15. Hugh Willoughby, s. and h.; ob. 1765, s. P. when the Barony was allowed to

XVI. 1765. 16. Henry Willoughby, s. and h. of Henry, eldest son of Henry, son and heir of Edward, only son of Sir Ambrose Willoughby, *second* son of Charles, II. Baron, whose issue male, when the Barony was allowed to Thomas, XI. Baron, was supposed to be extinct; ob. 1776, s. P. M. .

XVII. 1776. 17. George Willoughby, nephew and heir; being
s. and h. of Fortune Willoughby, next brother
of the last Baron; ob. 1779, s. P. when the
Barony created by the Patent of 1547 became
Extinct.

WILMINGTON.

BARON.   EARL.
I. 1728. — I. 1730. Sir Spencer Compton, K. B. 2d son of
James X.-3d Earl of Northamp-
ton; Created Baron Wilmington,
co. Sussex, Jan. 11, 1728; Created
Viscount Pevensey and Earl of
Wilmington, both co. Sussex, 14
May, 1730, K. G.; ob. 1743, s. P.
when all his honours became

Extinct.

BARONY, 7 Sept. 1812.
Vide NORTHAMPTON.

WILMOT.

BARONS.
I.   1643. 1. Henry Wilmot, 2d Viscount Wilmot in Ireland; Created Baron Wilmot of Adderbury,
co. Oxford, 29 June, 1643; Created Earl of
Rochester, 13 Dec. 1652.

Extinct 1681.
Vide ROCHESTER.

WILTON.

VISCOUNTCY, 19 Oct. 1714.—Extinct 1789.
Vide CARNARVON and CHANDOS.

WILTON.

EARLS.
I.   1801. 1. Thomas Egerton I.-1st Baron Grey de Wilton
of Wilton Castle; Created 26 June, 1801,
Viscount Grey de Wilton and Earl of Wilton,
of Wilton Castle, co. Hereford, with remainder, failing his issue male, to his grandson
Thomas Grosvenor, 2d son of his daughter

Eleanor, wife of Robert Viscount Belgrave (now Earl Grosvenor), and his heirs male, failing which to the third, fourth, and every other son of the said Eleanor, by her present or any future husband, and to their heirs male respectively; ob. 1814, s. p. m. when he was succeeded in the Earldom, agreeable to the limitation, by his grandson,

EARL.

II. 1814. 2. Thomas Grosvenor (assumed the name of), Egerton. Present Earl of Wilton, and Viscount Grey de Wilton. ⚌

WILTSHIRE.

EARLS.

I. 1397. 1. William le Scrope, brother of Stephen, 2d Baron Scrope of Masham; Created Earl of Wiltshire, 29 Sept. 1397; K.G.; beheaded and attainted 1399, when his honours became
Forfeited.

II. 1449. 1. James Butler, son and heir apparent of James 4th Earl of Ormond in Ireland; Created Earl of Wiltshire, 8 July, 1449. Succeeded as 5th Earl of Ormond in Ireland, in 1452, Lord Treasurer; K. G.; beheaded 1461; ob. s. p. when this Earldom became
Extinct.

III. 1470. 1. John Stafford, a younger son of Humphrey, I. Duke of Buckingham, and VI. Earl of Stafford; Created Earl of Wiltshire, 5 Jan. 1470; K. G.; ob. 1473.

IV. 1473. 2. Edward Stafford, s. and h. ob. 1499, s. p. when the Earldom again became
Extinct.

V. 1509. 1. Henry Stafford (younger son of Henry, II. Duke of Buckingham, and VII. Earl of Stafford, and cousin of Edward the last Earl); Created Earl of Wiltshire 1509; K. G.; ob. 1523, s. p. when the Earldom again became
Extinct.

VI. 1529. 1. Thomas Boylen, 1st Viscount Rochford (afterwards father-in-law to King Henry VIII. and

grandfather of Queen Elizabeth); Created
Earl of Wiltshire, with remainder to his heirs
male, and Earl of Ormond in Ireland, with
remainder to his heirs-general, 8 Dec. 1529;
K. G.; ob. 1538; and his only son, George
Bolyen (who was Summoned to Parliament
as "Georgio Bullen de Rochford," 5 Jan.
1533), having been beheaded and attainted
vita patris, the Earldom of Ormond fell into
ABEYANCE between the issue of his two
daughters and coheirs *, but the Earldom of
Wiltshire again became
Extinct.

VII. 1550. 1. William Paulet I.-1st Baron St. John of
Basing; Created Earl of Wiltshire, 19 Jan.
1550; Created Marquess of Winchester
12 Oct. 1551, in which dignity this Earldom
is now MERGED.
Vide WINCHESTER.

WIMBLEDON.

VISCOUNT.

1.   1626. 1. Edward Cecil, 1st Baron Cecil of Putney,
Created Viscount Wimbledon, co. Surrey,
July 25, 1626; ob. 1638, s. p. when his
titles became
Extinct.

WINCHENDON.

VISCOUNTCY, 23 Dec. 1706—Forfeited 1728.
Vide WHARTON.

---

* On the death of Queen Elizabeth, the only issue of Ann
Boleyn, the eldest coheir became EXTINCT, when it is presumed
that the Abeyance of the Earldom of Ormond, agreeably to the
limitation, terminated, and consequently, that dignity reverted
to the representative of the other coheir, the heir-general of
whom is the present Earl of Berkeley; and who, under the said
limitation, must probably. be considered as Earl of Ormond in
Ireland.

WINCHELSEA.

COUNTESS.

I.   1628. 1. Elizabeth, 1st Viscountess Maidstone, widow
of Sir Moyle Finch, Bart.; Created Countess
of Winchelsea, with remainder to her issue
male, 12 July, 1628 ; ob. 1633.

EARLS.

I.   1633. 2. Sir Thomas Finch, 2d Bart. s. and h. ob.
1639.

II. 1639. 3. Heneage Finch, s. and h.; Created Baron
Fitz-Herbert 26 June, 1660; ob. 1689.

III. 1689. 4. Charles Finch, grandson and heir, being s. and
h. of William Finch (ob. v. p.), eldest son of
the last Earl ; ob. 1712. s. p.

IV. 1712. 5. Heneage Finch, uncle and heir, being 2d son
of Heneage, II. Earl; ob. 1726, s p.

V.   1726. 6. John Finch, brother and heir ; ob. 1729, s. p.
when the Barony of Fitz-Herbert became
Extinct ; but his other honours devolved on
his next heir male.

VI. 1729. 7. Daniel Finch, XIV.-2d Earl of Nottingham;
s. and h. of Heneage XIII.-1st Earl of Nottingham, eldest son of Heneage Finch, younger
son of Sir Moyle Finch and Elizabeth I.
Countess of Winchelsea ; ob. 1730.

VII. 1730. 8. Daniel Finch, s. and h. Earl of Nottingham ;
K. G. ; ob. 1769, s. p. m.

VIII.1769. 9. George Finch, nephew and heir, being s. and
h. of William Finch, next brother of the last
Earl. Present Earl of Winchelsea, and XVI.-
4th Earl of Nottingham, Viscount Maidstone, Baron Finch of Daventry, and a Baronet ; K. G. ⚌

WINCHESTER.

EARLS.

I.   1210. 1. Saier de Quincy ; Created Earl of Winchester
circa 1210. He was one of the celebrated
twenty-five Barons who were appointed to
enforce the observance of MAGNA CHARTA ;
ob. 1219.

II. 1219. 2. Roger de Quincy, 2d son succeeded to the

EARLS.

Earldom ; ob.1264, s. p. m. when the Earldom became
Extinct.

III. 1322. 1. Hugb II.-3d Baron Despencer ; Created Earl
of Winchester 10 May, 1322; bebeaded
1326, and having been attainted the Earldom became
Forfeited.

IV. 1472. 1. Lewes de Bruges, Prince of Steenbuse, &c.
in Germany ; Created Earl of Winehester
13 Oct. 1472. SURRENDERED the Earldom in
1499.

MARQUESSES.

I.   1551. 1. William Paulet, VII.-1st Earl of Wiltsbire;
Created Marquess of Winchester 12 Oct. 1551,
Lord High Treasurer ; K. G. ; ob. 1572.

II.   1572. 2. John Paulet, s. and b.; ob. 1576.

III. 1576. 3. William Paulet, s. and b.; ob. 1598.

IV.   1598. 4. William Paulet, s. and b.; ob. 1628.

V.   1628. 5. John Paulet, s. and b.; ob. 1674,

VI.   1674. 6. Charles Paulet, s. and b. ; Created Duke of
Bolton 9 April, 1689; in which Dukedom
this Marquisate continued merged until the
death of Harry Paulet VI. Duke of Bolton
and XI. Marquess of Winchester, &c.; s.
p. m. in 1794, when the latter dignity devolved on his next beir male, viz.

XII. 1794. 12. George Paulet, eighth but only surviving son
of Norton Paulet, s. and h. of Francis, eldest
son of Henry Paulet, 2d son of William, IV.
Marquess ; ob. 1800.

XIII.1800. 13. Charles Ingoldesby Paulet, s. and b. Present
Baron St. John of Basing, Earl of Wiltsbire,
and Marquess of Winchester. ⊥

WINDSORE.

BARONS BY TENURE.

I. Will. I. 1. William Fitz-Other, held several Lordships
at the General Survey, and being Castellan
of Windsore, assumed that surname; ob.....

II. Hen. I. 2. William de Windsore, s. and h.; living, 1135.

III. Hen. II. 3. William de Windsore, s. and h.; living, 1194.

IV. John 4. Walter de Windsore, s. and h.; ob. circa 1205, S. P. M. leaving Christian, his dau. and heir, who married Duncan de Lascells, and inherited her father's lands; but, in 1212, William de Windsore, a younger brother of Walter, the last Baron, obtained livery of part of the said lands, which dwindling the Barony, none of this family were afterwards considered as Barons until

BARON BY WRIT.

I. 1381. William de Windsore, the lineal descendant of William de Windsore above mentioned, was Summoned to Parl. from 22 Aug. 5 Rich. II. 1381, to 3 March, 7 Rich. II. 1384; he married the celebrated Alice Piers; Lieutenant of Ireland; ob. 1384 *, when the dignity is presumed to have become

Extinct.

---

* Collins, vol. IV. p. 67, cites the Inquisition taken on the death of this Baron, by which it appears that his three sisters were his heirs; hence it has been concluded that he died s. P; but Dugdale, in his Warwickshire, p. 431 (cited in Banks' Stemmata Anglicana), states, that he left his *daughters* his heirs, of whom Joane, the eldest, married Robert Skerne. The noncupative will of Lord Windsore supports the opinion that he died without issue; but Alice his widow, in her testament, dated in 1400, speaks of three daughters, Joane, Jane, and another Joane: to the latter (whom she describes as her youngest daughter) she gives her manor of Gaines in Upminster, and bequeaths to her two other daughters all her manors, &c. which John Windsore, or others by his consent, had usurped, and orders her executors to recover them; for she emphatically adds, " I say on the pain of my soul he hath no right there, nor never had." It is consequently somewhat doubtful whether this Baron left legitimate issue or not; but should he have done so, the Barony of course became vested in his descendants.

OF STANWELL.

BARONS BY WRIT.

I.   1529. 1. Andrews Windsor, descended from Sir Miles
Windsor, who is said to have been brother of
William the last Baron; Summoned to Parliament from 3 Nov. 21 Hen. VIII. 1529,
to 8 June, 28 Hen. VIII. 1536, as " Andræ
Windsor de Stanwell;" ob. 1543.

II.   1543. 2. William Windsor, s. and h.; Summ. to Parl.
from 28 April, 31 Hen. VIII. 1539*, to 5
Nov. 6 Ph. and M. 1558; ob. 1558.

III.   1558. 3. Edward Windsor, 5th, but eldest surviving son
and heir †; Summ. to Parl. from 11 Jan.
5 Eliz. 1563, to 8 May, 18 Eliz. 1576; ob. 1575.

IV.   1575. 4. Frederick Windsor, s. and h.; Summ. to Parl.
6 Jan. 23 Eliz. 1581; ob. 1585, s. p.

V.   1585. 5. Henry Windsor, brother and heir; Summ. to
Parl. from 15 Oct. 28 Eliz. 1586, to 19 March,
1 Jaq. 1603; ob. 1605.

VI.   1605. 6. Thomas Windsor, s. and h.; Summ. to Parl.
from 30 Jan. 18 Jaq. 1621, to 13 April, 15
Car. I. 1639; ob. 1642, s. p. leaving his two
sisters, Elizabeth, wife of Dixie Hickman,
Esq. and Elizabeth (the younger), who married first, Andrew Windsor, and secondly,
Sir James Ware, his heirs, between whom
this Barony fell into ABEYANCE, until 16 June,
1660, when it was terminated by the Crown
in favour of

VII. 1660. 7. Thomas Hickman (assumed the name of)
Windsor, nephew of the last Baron, being

---

* So in the Summonses in that year, and in the two following
Parliaments; but as it is evident his father was then living, it is
probable that "*Willielmo*" is erroneously substituted for "*Andræ*
de Windsore*," in Dugdale's Summonses to the Parliaments of
the 31st, 33d, and 35th, Hen. VIII, as Andrew the first Baron
did not die until the 35th year of that reign.

† Thomas his elder brother, who died in 1552, left a daughter,
Ann, but she is presumed to have died before her grandfather, as
he does not mention her in his will.

son and heir of the above mentioned Dixie
Hickman and Elizabeth his wife; Summoned to Parl. from 8 May, 13 Car. II.
1661, to 21 March, 32 Car. II. 1680; Created
Earl of Plymouth, 6 Dec. 1682, in which title
this Barony is now merged.

Vide PLYMOUTH.

A Thomas *Windsor* is included in Dugdale's List of
Summonses 5 Nov. 5 & 6 Ph. & Mary, 1558, but neither
he nor Collins give any account of such a Baron; and as
only *one* Lord Windsor is mentioned in the Journals of
the House of Lords as having been Summoned in that
year, the insertion of his name on that occasion is probably
an error of the person who transcribed the List from the
Roll.

WINDSOR.

EARLDOM, 20 Feb. 1796.

Vide BUTE.

WODEHOUSE.

BARONS.

I.   1797. 1. Sir John Wodehouse, 7th Bart.; Created
              Baron Wodehouse of Kimberley, co. Norfolk,
              26 Oct. 1797. Present Baron Wodehouse,
              and a Baronet.

WOKINGHAM.

BARONY, 9th April, 1689.—Extinct 1708.

Vide CUMBERLAND.

WOLVERTON.

BARONS BY TENURE.

I.   Hen. I. 1. Hamon, son of Menfelin, Lord of Wolverton,
              co. Bucks; ob. circa 1176.
II.   H. II. 2. Hamon de Wolverton, s. and h. living 1184.
III. Rich. I. 3. William de Wolverton, s. and h.; ob. 1246,
              s. p.

BARONS BY WRIT.

IV. H. III. 4. Alan de Wolverton, brother and heir; ob. circa 1249.

V. H. III. 5. John de Wolverton, s. and h. living 1249; to whom succeeded,

VI. Edw. I. 6. John de Wolverton ; but neither he, nor any of his descendants, having been summoned to Parliament, they ceased to be ranked among the Barons of the Realm.

WOODSTOCK.

BARON BY WRIT.

I. 1320. 1. Edmund Plantagenet, youngest son of King Edw. I. Summ. to Parl. as " Edmundo de Wodestok" 5 Aug. 14 Edw. II. 1320, about two years before he became of age ; but he was not included in the next list of Summonses, viz. 15 May, 14 Edw. II. 1321, and was created Earl of Kent in that year, when he was summoned by that title, viz. on the 14 March, 15 Edw. II. 1322.

As it appears that the Earl of Kent *sat in Parliament* as a *Baron* under the Writ of 14 Edw. II,* a Barony in fee was thereby created, and which dignity, with his other honors, became FORFEITED on his attainder in 1330. Edmund Plantagenet, his son and heir, was however fully restored, but died in 1333, leaving John his brother his heir, who likewise died s. P. in 1352, when Joan his sister (surnamed the Fair Maid of Kent) became his heir, and who succeeded to this Barony, and (*jure matris*) to that of WAKE.

From that period the Baronies of Wake and Woodstock have been vested in the same individuals; and as the account of the descent of the former in p. 669 necessarily explains that of the latter, it is only necessary to refer to that article.

---

* Vide page 470.

WOODSTOCK.

VISCOUNTCY, 9 April, 1689.

Vide PORTLAND.

WORCESTER.

Urso d'Abitot is said to have been Created Earl of Worcester in 1076, but it is most probable that he was nothing more than Sheriff of Worcestershire. He died s. P. M.

EARLS.

I. 1144. Waleran de Bellomont, son of Robert Earl of Mellent in Normandy, stated, by many writers of authority, to have been Created Earl of Worcester in 1144. He died in 1166, leaving issue male, but none of his descendants ever bore this title.

II. 1397. Thomas Percy, 2d son of Henry I. Earl of Northumberland; Created Earl of Worcester 29 Sept. 1397; K. G. beheaded 1402; ob. s. P. when the title became

Extinct.

III. 1420. Richard Beauchamp II.-2 Baron Abergavenny; Created Earl of Worcester in 1420; ob. 1431, s. P. M. when this Earldom became

Extinct.

IV. 1449. 1. John Tiptoft, II.-2. Baron Tiptoft; Created Earl of Worcester 16 July 1449; K. G.; beheaded and attainted 1470, when all his honors became

Forfeited.

V. 14... 2. Edward Tiptoft, s. and h. is considered by most writers of authority to have been restored to his father's honors, but no notice of the reversal of the last Earl's attainder is to be found in the Rolls of Parliament; ob. 1485, s. P. when this Earldom became

Extinct.

VI. 1514. 1. Charles Somerset, L. Baron Herbert of Chepstow, Ragland, and Gower, and, jure uxoris,

, EARLS.

Baron Herbert of Chepstow; Created Earl
of Worcester 2 Feb. 1514, Lord Chamb. K. G.
ob. 1526.

VII. 1526. 2. Henry Somerset, s. and h.; ob. 1549.

VIII. 1549. 3. William Somerset, s. and h. K. G.; ob. 1589.

IX. 1589. 4. Edward Somerset, s. and h. K. G.; ob. 1628.

MARQUESSES.

X. 1628.—I. 1642. 5. Henry Somerset, s. and h.; Created Marquess of Worcester 2 Nov.
1642; ob. 1646.

XI. 1646.—II. 1646. 6. Edward Somerset (he was *intended*
to have been created Earl of Gla-
morgan and Baron Beaufort of
Caldecot Castle, vitâ patris, *vide*
Glamorgan); ob. 1667.

XII. 1667.—III. 1667. 7. Henry Somerset, s. and h.; Created Duke of Beaufort, 3d Dec.
1682.   Vide BEAUFORT.

WOTTON

OF MABERLY.

BARONS.

I. 1603. 1. Edward Wotton; Created Baron Wotton of
Maberly, co. Kent, the 13th May, 1603;
ob. 16....

II. 16.. 2. Thomas Wotton, s. and h.; ob 1630, S. P. M.
when his honors became

Extinct.

WOTTON

OF WOTTON.

BARON.

I. 1650. 1. Charles Henry Kirkhoven *, (s. and h. of John
Poliander Kirkhoven, Lord of Hemfleet in
Holland, by Katherine, eldest dau. and co-
heir of Thomas the last Baron, and widow of
Sir Henry Stanhope, s. and h. of Philip, 1st

---

* Dugdale states that this Baron was the *husband* instead of
the *son* of Katherine, Countess of Chesterfield, but all other authorities assert the latter to have been the fact.

Earl of Chesterfeld ; which Henry dying
v. P. the said Katherine was, in 1660, created
Countess of Chesterfield for life) ; Created
Baron Wotton of Wotton, co. Kent, 31 Aug.
1650 ; Created Earl of Bellomont in Ireland
in 1677 ; ob. 1682, s. P. when his dignities
became

𝕰𝔵𝔱𝔦𝔫𝔠𝔱.

WRIOTHESLEY.

BARONS.

I.   1544. 1. Thomas Wriothesley; Created Baron Wriothesley of Titchfield, co. Hants, Jan. 1,
1544, K.G, ; Created Earl of Southampton
16 Feb. 1547.

𝕰𝔵𝔱𝔦𝔫𝔠𝔱 1667.   Vide SOUTHAMPTON.

WYCOMBE.

BARONS.

I.   1760. 1. John Fitzmaurice Petty, 1st Earl of Shelburne in Ireland; Created Baron Wycombe
of Chipping Wycombe, co. Bucks, 17 May,
1760 ; ob. 1761.

EARLS.

II. 1761.—I.   1784. 2. William Petty, s. and h. ; Earl of
Shelburne in Ireland; Created
Viscount Calne and Calston, Earl
of Wycomb, co. Bucks, and
Marquess of Lansdowne, co. Somerset, 6 Dec. 1784; K.G.; ob.
1805.

III. 1805.—II. 1805. 3. John Henry Petty, s. and h. Marquess of Lansdowne, &c.; ob.
1809, s. P.

IV. 1809.—III. 1809. 4. Henry Fitz Maurice Petty, half
brother and heir. Present Mar-
quess of Lansdowne, Earl and
Baron Wycombe, and Viscount
Calne and Calston; also Earl
of Kerry and Shelburn in Ireland. ⚓

YARMOUTH.

1. 1673.—I. 1679. 1. Sir Robert Paston, 1st Bart. ; Created Baron Paston of Paston, and Viscount Yarmouth, both co. Norfolk, 19 Aug. 1673 ; Created Earl of Yarmouth 30 July 1679; ob. 1682.
II. 1682.—II. 1682. 2. William Paston, s. and h.; ob. 1732, s. p. m. when his honors became
Extinct.

BARONESS. COUNTESS.
I. 1740. — I. 1740. 1. Amelia Sophia de Walmoden, presumed to have been mistress of King George II. ; Created Baroness and Countess of Yarmouth, co. Norfolk, for life, 24 March, 1740 , ob. 1675, when these titles became
Extinct.

EARLDOM, 5 July 1793.

Vide HERTFORD.

YARBOROUGH.

BARONS.
I. 1794. 1. Charles Anderson Pelham ; Created Baron Yarborough of Yarborough, co. Lincoln, 13 Aug. 1794 ; ob. 1824.
II. 1824. 2. Charles Anderson Pelham, s. and h.   Present Baron Yarborough.

YORK.

EARL.

I. **Rich. I.** Otho, son of Henry Duke of Bavaria, by
Maud, dau. of Hen. II. is said to have been
created Earl of York by King Richard I.
and he is stated afterwards to have exchanged
that Earldom for that of Poictou. He was
afterwards Emperor of Germany.

DUKES.

I.   1385. 1. Edmund Plantagenet, surnamed De Langley,
Earl of Cambridge, fifth son of King Edw.
III.; Created Duke of York 6th Aug. 1385;
K.G.; ob. 1402.

II.   1406. 2. Edward Plantagenet, s. and h. who was Created Duke of Albemarle 29 Sept. 1397, and
was restored to the dignity of Duke of York
in 1406, which he had been previously rendered incapable of inheriting; K.G. slain at
Agincourt 1415; ob. s. p.

III. 1415. 3. Richard Plantagenet, nephew and heir, s. and
h. of Richard Earl of Cambridge, brother to
the last Duke, by Anne, daughter of Roger
Mortimer, Earl of March, through which
alliance the house of York derived their
right to the Crown; K.G.; slain 1460.

IV. 1460. 4. Edward Plantagenet, s. and h. Ascended the
Throne as King Edw. IV. 4 March 1461,
when this Dukedom became merged in the
Crown.

V.   1474. 5. Richard Plantagenet, 2d son of King Edw.
IV.; Created Duke of York 28 May 1474;
Created Earl of Nottingham, Duke of Nor-
folk, and Earl Warren; K.G. Murdered in
the Tower 1483, when his honors became
Extinct.

VI. 1491. 1. Henry Tudor, 2d son of King Henry VII.;
Created Duke of York 1 Nov. 1491; Created
Prince of Wales (after the death of his brother Arthur) 18 Feb. 1503. Ascended the
Throne as King Henry VIII. 21 April 1509,
when this Dukedom again became merged in
the Crown.

DUKES.

VII. 1604. 1. Charles Stuart, 2d son of King James I.; Created Duke of York 6 Jan. 1604. On the death of his elder brother Henry, in 1612, he succeeded as Duke of Cornwall, and on the 4th Nov. 1616, was Created Prince of Wales. Ascended the throne as King Charles I. 27 March, 1625, when this Dukedom again became merged in the Royal dignity.

VIII. 1643. 1. James Stuart, 2d son of King Charles I. declared Duke of York at his birth, but not so Created until 27 Jan. 1643. Ascended the Throne as King James II. 6 Feb. 1685, when this Dukedom again became merged in the Crown.

IX. 1716. 1. Ernest Augustus, brother of King George I.; Created Duke of York and Albany in Great Britain, and Earl of Ulster in Ireland, 29 June, 1716; K. G.; ob. 1728, s. p. when his honors became
Extinct.

X. 1760. 1. Edward Augustus, brother of King George III. ; Created Duke of York and Albany, in Great Britain, and Earl of Ulster in Ireland, 1 April 1760; K. G. ; ob. 1767, s. p. when his dignities became
Extinct.

XI. 1784. 1. H. R. H. Frederick, next brother of his present Majesty ; Created Duke of York and Albany in Great Britain, and Earl of Ulster, in Ireland, 27 Nov. 1784. Present Duke of York and Albany, and Earl of Ulster in Ireland, K. G. G. C. B. HEIR PRESUMPTIVE TO THE THRONE.

ZOUCHE
OF ASHBY.

BARONS BY TENURE.

I.   Rich. I. 1. William le Zouche, descended from the Earls of Brittany; ob. 1199, s. p.

II. John. 2. Roger le Zouche, brother and heir, living 1229; ob. ....

III. H. III. 3. Alan le Zouche, s. and h.; ob. 1269.

IV. Edw. I. 4. Roger le Zouche, s. and h.; ob. 1285.

BY WRIT.

I.   1299. 5. Alan le Zouche, s. and h. Summ. to Parl. from 6 Feb. 27 Edw. I. 1299, to 26 Nov. 7 Edw. II. 1313. He was also summoned 26 Jan. 25 Edw. I. 1297, but it is doubtful if that Writ was a regular Summons to Parliament. Vide "FITZ-JOHN;" ob. 1314, s. p. m. leaving his three daughters his heirs, viz. Elene, who married, first, Nicholas de St. Maur, and 2dly, Alan de Charlton; Maud, who was the wife of Robert de Holland; and Elizabeth, a nun; and between the descendants and representatives of the said Elene and Maud this Barony is in ABEYANCE.

ZOUCHE
OF HARYNGWORTH.

BARONS BY TENURE.

I. Edw. I. 1. Eudo le Zouche, younger brother of Roger IV. Baron Zouche of Ashby. He married Milisent, widow of John de Montalt, and sister and coheir of George de Cantilupe, Baron of Bergavenny; ob. ....

c c 3

BARONS BY WRIT.

I.   1308. 2. William le Zouche, s. and h. Lord of Haryng-
      worth, co. Northampton, Summoned to Par-
      liament from 13 Jan. 2 Edw. II. 1308, to 14
      Feb. 22 Edw. III. 1348; ob. 1352.

II.   1348. 3. William le Zouche, grandson and heir, being
      s. and h. of Eudo le Zouche (ob. v. p.) eldest
      son of the last Baron, Summ. to Parl. from
      20 Nov. 22 Edw. III. 1348 (vita avi), to 15
      Noy. 25 Edw. III. 1351*, as "Willielmo la
      Zousche de Haryngworth Juniori," and as
      "Willielmo la Zousche de Haryngworth,"
      from 20 July, 26 Edward III. 1352, to 24
      March, 5 Rich. II. 1382; ob. 1382.

III. 1382. 4. William le Zouche, s. and h. Summ. to Parl.
      from 7 Jan. 6 Rich. II. 1383, to 20 Nov. 18
      Rich. II. 1394; ob. 1396.

IV.   1396. 5. William le Zouche, s. and h. Summ. to Parl.
      from 30th Nov. 20 Rich. II. 1396, to 26 Sept.
      2 Hen. V. 1414; ob. 1415.

V.   1415. 6. William le Zouche, s. and h. Summ. to Parl.
      from 7 Jan. 4 Hen. VI. 1426, to 28 Feb. 2
      Edw. IV. 1463. He married Alice, daughter
      and sole heir of Richard VI. Baron de St.
      Maur, and Baron Lovel of Kary; ob. 1463.

VI.   1463. 7. William le Zouche, s. and h. Summ. to Parl
      28 Feb. 6 Edw. IV. 1466. Baron St. Maur
      jure matris; ob. 1467.

VII. 1467. 8 John le Zouche, s. and h. Summ. to Parl. 22
      Jan. 22 Edw. IV. 1482, and 9 Dec. 1 Rich.
      III. 1483; attainted 1485, when his honors
      became forfeited; but his attainder being
      reversed in 1495, he was restored to his
      former honors, and was again Summ. to
      Parl. from 17 Oct. 1 Hen. VIII. 1509, to 12
      Nov. 7 Hen. VIII. 1515; ob. 1526.

---

* On the 10 March, 23d Edw. III. 1349, the Writ was addressed to "Willielmo la Zouche de Haryngworth", without
the addition of "Juniori;" and as his grandfather was then living,
it is doubtful to which of these Barons it was directed; but as
the II.-3. Baron was not summoned on that occasion by his usual
designation, it is most probable it was to him instead of his
grandfather.

BARONS BY WRIT.

VIII. 1526. 9. John le Zouche, s. and h. Summ. to Parl. from 3 Nov. 21 Hen. VIII. 1529, to 4 Nov. 2 Edw. VI. 1548 ; ob. 1550.

IX. 1550. 10. Richard le Zouche, s. and h. Summ. to Parl. 23 Jan. 5 Edw. VI. 1552; ob. 1552.

X. 1552. 11. George le Zouche, s. and h. Summ. to Parl. from 5 Jan. 6 Edw. VI. 1553, to 30 Sept. 8. Eliz. 1566; ob. 1569.

XI. 1569. 12. Edward le Zouch, s. and h. Summ. to Parl. from 2 April, 13 Eliz. 1571, to 17 May, 1 Car. I. 1625 ; ob. 1625 s. p. m. when the Baronies of Zouch of Haryngworth, and St. Maur fell into ABEYANCE between his two daughters and coheirs, viz. Elizabeth, wife of Sir William Tate, and Mary, who married first Thomas Leighton, Esq. and secondly, William Connard, Esq. among whose representatives they continued in that state, until 27th Aug. 1815, when his Majesty was pleased to terminate the Abeyance of the Barony of ZOUCHE in favor of

XII. 1815. 13. Sir Cecil Bishopp, 7th Baronet, the eldest coheir of one moiety* of the said Barony, he being s. and h. of Sir Cecil Bishopp, by Susannah, daughter, and eventually sole heir of Charles Hedges, Esq. by Catherine, eldest daughter and coheir of Bartholomew Tate, Esq. son and heir of William Tate, eldest son of Zouche Tate, son and heir of the above-mentioned Sir William Tate, by Elizabeth Zouche, eldest daughter and coheir of Edward, the last Baron. Present Baron Zouche of Haryngworth, and eldest coheir of the Baronies of St. Maur and of Lovel of Kari, and coheir of one moiety of the Barony of Grey of Codnor. ☿

---

* No descendants of the coheir of the other moiety of the Barony could be traced after the time of the Commonwealth. Vide note to p. 550.

ZOUCHE
OF MORTIMER.

I.   1323. 1. William, son of Robert III.-3 Baron Mortimer of Richard's Castle, by Joice, daughter and heir of William le Zouche, 2d son of Roger II.-2 Baron Zouche of Ashby, assumed his mother's name of Zouche. Summoned to Parliament from 26 Dec. 17 Edw. II. 1323, to 14 Jan. 10 Edw. III. 1337, at first only as " Willielmo la Zouche," but afterwards as "Willielmo le Zouche de Mortimer," or " de Mortuomari;" ob. .... leaving Alan le Zouche his son and heir. But none of his descendants were ever summoned to Parliament ; though, among the descendants and representatives of this William Baron Zouche of Mortimer, the Barony is presumed now to be in ABEYANCE.

REFERENCES

TO SUCH PROOFS OF

BARONS' SITTINGS 'IN PARLIAMENT

AS OCCUR ON

THE ROLLS OF PARLIAMENT.

REFERENCES

TO

PROOFS OF BARONS' SITTINGS, &c.

ANNO 1277.—Vol. I. p. 224.—Claus. 6 Edw. I. m. 5. dorso.
Memorandum quod in Parliamento Regis Edwardi apud
Westm' in festo Sancti Mich'is anno regni ejusdem Regis
sexto in presenciâ Episcoporum Wynton', Dunelm', Here-
ford', Norwic', Prioris Provincial' Ordinis Fratrum Predi-
catorum in Angliâ, Decani Sarum, Magistri Thome Bek,
Willielmi de Valencia, Avunculi Regis, Comitum Cornub',
Glouc', Waren, Warr, & de Karrik,

Roberti de Tybetot	Galfridi de Neubaud
Antonij Bek	Johannis de Cobbeham
Magistri Roberti de Scarde-	Willielmi de Brompton
burgh	Philippi de Wyleby
Radulphi de Sandwico	Thome de Weyland
Johannis de Lovetot	Walteri de Helyun
Walteri de Hopton	Ricardi de Holebroke
Magistri Galfridi de Aspale	Bartholomei de Sudleye
Walteri de Wynbourne	Hugonis filij Ottonis
Nicholai de Stapelton	Patricij de Cadurcis
Radulphi de Hengham	Roberti filij Walteri

& aliorum multorum; venit Alexander Rex Scocie, filius
Alexandri quondam Regis Scocie, ad predictum Edwardum
Regum Angliæ, apud Westm' in Camerâ ejusdem Regis,
& ibidem optulit idem Rex Scocie eidem Regi Anglie
devenire Hominem suum ligeum, & facere ei homagium
suum, & illud ei fecit in hec verba, &c.

Anno 1290.—Vol. I. p. 25.—18 Edw. I. Memorand' quod
in crastino Sancto Trinitatis, anno regni Regis decimo
octavo in pleno Parliamento ipsius Domini Regis, Robertus Bathon' et Wellens' (&c.) Episcopi, Edmundus frater
Domini Regis, Will'us de Valenc'-Comes Penebrok, &c.

Robertus de Tipetot	Rogerus de Monte alto
Reginaldus de Grey	Will'us de Brewose
Johannes de Hastinges	Theobaldus de Verdun
Johannes de Sancto Johanne	Wal terusde Huntercumb
Ricardus filius Johannis	Nich'us de Segrave
Will'us le Latymer	

& ceteri magnates & proceres tunc in Parliamento exist-
entes, pro se & communitate totius regni, quantum in
ipsis est, concesseruut Domino Regi ad filiam suam pri-
mogenitam maritand', quod ipse Dominus Rex percipiat &
habeat tale auxilium, & tantum quale & quantum Dominus
Henricus Rex Pater suus percepit & habuit de Regno, &c.

Note. The earliest List of Summonses to Parliament
now extant, except that of 49 Hen. III. is in the 22d
Edw. I. or rather, perhaps, the 23d, as it may be ques-
tioned whether the Summons of 22d of that King was to
a *Parliament*, although it has been admitted as such
at the Bar of the House of Lords*. It is consequently
impossible to prove that any of the individuals mentioned
in the two foregoing extracts were Barons, by shewing
that they were summoned as such to the Parliaments
held in the 6th and 18th Edw. I. respectively. But it is
not unreasonable to conclude, that such of them as appear
to have been summoned, either in the 22d or 23d Edw. I.,
or soon after, and continued to be so summoned during
their lives, were Barons of Parliament in the 6th and
18th. In the List of persons present when the King of
Scotland performed his homage anno 6 Edw. I. there is
only one who answers this description, viz. Robert Fitz-
Walter, who was summoned to Parliament 23 Edward I.
and from that time regularly until his death. But of
those who were consenting to the Aid granted to the King
anno 18 Edward I. all except Robert Tibetot and William
de Brewose were summoned to Parliament in subsequent
years of that reign, and continued to be so summoned
until their deaths, viz. Theobald de Verdon in the 22d,
Reginald de Grey, John de Hastinges, Richard Fitz-
John, Roger de Montalt, Walter de Huntercombe, and
Nicholas de Segrave in the 23d, John de St. John in the
25th, and William de Latymer not till the 28th; but he
appears to have been actively employed in the 22d and

---

* In the case of the Barony of Roos. Vide "Clyvedon," p. 141.

25th Edward I. in the Wars of Gascony; and in the 26th and 27th in those of Scotland, where the King left him in the latter year to superintend the fortifying of Castles, which may account for his not having a Summons to Parliament before the 28th *.

Robert de Tibetot, whose name occurs in both Lists, lived till the 26th Edw. I. without being summoned; but he appears also to have been much engaged in the wars of France or Scotland. His son, Payn Tibetot, was summoned to Parliament in 1 Edw. II.; as were his descendants down to the 44th Edw. III.

William de Brewose died before 22 Edw. I. viz. anno 19, leaving a son and heir William, who was summoned anno 23, and continued to be so summoned to the period of his death.

The List in 6 Edw. I. with the exception of Tibetot and Fitz-Walter, consists of the Judges of the several Courts, and probably the Officers of the Palaces. Neubaud was Chancellor†, and Cobbeham and Wyleby Barons of the Exchequer; Hopton one of the Justices Itinerant; Weyland Chief Justice, and Lovetot, Brompton, and Heylun, Puisne Justices of the Common Pleas; Hengham Chief Justice, and Wynborne and Stapleton, Puisne Justices of the King's Bench‡. Sandwich appears to have been Keeper of the Wardrobe 49 Hen. III. and possibly retained that office; in the 18th Edw. I. he was Constable of the Tower of London §. The remaining seven, viz. Bek, Scardeburgh, Aspale, Holebroke,

---

* In the Summonses of the 11th Edward III. thirteen Barons were omitted, because they were in Scotland, or beyond seas. In 46 Edw. III. and in divers years of King Henry V. few Earls and Barons were summoned, the King being then making war in France; and such omissions were thought to be no disparagement to their honour. Cruise, on Dignities, 2d Ed. § 42. p. 97.

In the Claus. Roll of 10 Edward III. m. 1. dorso. is a memorandum, that the Writs of Summons directed to the Earl of Angus, Robert de Morley, Ralph de Stafford, and Anthony Lucy, were not sent, because they were in Scotland in obsequio Regis.

† Madox's History of the Exchequer, vol. II. p. 321.

‡ For all these see Dugd. Orig. Jud.

§ Madox's History of the Exchequer, vol. I. p. 70.

Sudleye, Fitz-Otes, and de Cadurcis *, are not sufficiently identified.

Anno 1303.—Vol. I. p.159. 33 Edw. I. TRIER OF PETITIONS:
Sire Aymer de Valence.

Anno 1304.—Vol. II. p. 267. 33 Edw. I. Claus. m. 13.
dorso. " Ordinatio facta per D'n'm Regem super stabi-
litate terre Scocie;" reciting that the King had made
known by the Bishop of Glagu, the Earl of Carrik, and
others, that the Commonalty of Scotland should be
assembled, and that a certain number of persons on the
part of Scotland should come to the Parliament which
the King had ordained to hold at Westminster, in Lent,
within three weeks of the Nativity of St. John the Baptist then next ensuing, and which was held after two
prorogations on the feast of the Nativity of Our Lady‡;
that certain Bishops, and others therein named, did appear at the said Parliament on behalf of the Commonalty
of Scotland, and that certain English persons therein
mentioned, were appointed to treat with them, &c.
Amongst those persons summoned as Barons to that Parliament, were the following, viz.

> Mons'r Hugh le Despens'
> Mons'r Henry de Percy
> Mons'r Johan de Hastinggs, mes il ne poiet
>   venir p' la maladie
> Mons'r Johan Boteturt
> Mons'r William Martyn.

Anno 1306.—Vol. I. p. 188. 35 Edw. I. A List of Persons
summoned to the Parliament held at Carlisle in the
Octaves of St. Hilary, touching the State of Scotland and
other affairs. The following Barons are distinguished by
the word *hic* in the margin as present.

Hugo le Despenser	Walt'us de Muncy
Hugo de Curtenay	Will's de Grandisono
Rog'us de Mortuomari	Joh'es de Sudle
Will's de Rithre	Walt'us de Teye

---

* *Query.* If it was not this Patrick de Cadurcis, or Chaworth,
who is mentioned as a Baron by Tenure in p. 119, and whose
dau. and heir married Henry Plantagenet Earl of Lancaster. This
Patrick de Cadurcis died in 1282, thirteen years before Writs of
Summons (excepting that of 49 Hen. III.) appear on record.
† 8 Sept. 1305.

Two, viz. Philip de Kyme and Geffry de Camuill, are said to be excused by the King; three, Peter de Mauley, Edmund Deyncurt, and William Martyn, by the Judges; one, Simon de Montacute, because he was in Scotland. Against the name of Robert Fitz-Walter is entered, " Veniet cum Card'," and against that of Reginald de Grey, " Ven' pro Thom' de Wytnesham attorn'."

Anno 1314.—Vol. I. p. 450, 8 Edw. II. Pat. p. 1, m. 26. A Commission from the King under the Privy Seal, " W. Exoniensi Episcopo, Adomaro de Valencia, Comiti Pembrok, &

Henrico de Bello Monte,"

to open the Parliament to be held on Monday, the Eve of the Nativity of the Virgin.

Ibid. p. 359 b. 8 Edw. II. In a record of the proceedings between the Council of the King and the Delegates of the Earl of Flanders on the discussion of certain Differences, it appears that in the Parliament at Westminster, it was agreed, &c.

And afterwards reciting the insurrection of the Flemings against the King of France, &c. that " prefati Arnaldus & Thomas, Attornati Perrote & Joh'is predicor' coram venerabilibus Patribus W. Cant' Archie'po, &c. Thoma Comite Lanc', &c.

Barth'o de Badlesm'e,

& aliis *Baronibus* & D'ni Regis Fidelibus apud Westm' super quibusdam negotijs statum D'ni Regis & regni tangentibus tractandis convocatis; supplicarunt, quod D'nus n'r Rex, &c.

Anno 1315.—Vol. I. p. 350, 9 Edw. II. Among the TRIERS OF PETITIONS in a Parliament held at Lincoln:

Edwardus * Deyncourt
Phillippus de Kyme †.

---

* *Qu.* If not Edmundus?

† His name does not occur in the Summonses after 7 Edw. II. but he lived until the 16th.

Anno 1320.—Vol. I. p. 365. 14 Edward II. Amongst the Peers present in a Parliament held at Westminster was,

> Edmundo de Woodstok, f'ris ipsius D'ni Regis*.

Ibid. TRIERS OF PETITIONS :
> Joh'es de Som'ry
> Ric'us de Grey
>
> Hugo de Curteney
> Will'us Martyn.

Anno 1331.—Vol. II. p. 61 b. Art. 2, 5 Edw. III. In the record of the occurrences of this Parliament held at Westminster, are the names of Nobles appointed by the King to treat with certain Nobles of France. Amongst them are the following, who were summoned as Barons to this Parliament :
> Mons'r Henr' de Beaumont
> Mons'r Henr' de Percy
> Mons'r Hugh de Courtenay.

Anno 1331.—Vol. II. p. 61b. Art. 7. 5 Edw. III. Amongst the names of the MAINPERNORS of Hugh le Despencer, are those of

> Mons'r Eble Lestrange
> Mons'r Rauf Basset
> Mons'r Rauf de Nevill

who were among the Barons † summoned to this Parliament, and also

John de Roos, who was Summ. 6, 7, 8, and until 12 Edw. III.

Richard Talbot, Summ. 4, 6, 8, &c. until 29 Edw. III.

Robert de Colevill, Summ. 16 to 39 Edw. III.

John de Verdon, Summ. 6, 7, 8, 9, and 16 Edw. III.

John Darcy, Summ. 6, 7, and 16 Edw. III.

Anno 1332.—Vol. II. p. 68. Art. 2. 6 Edw. III. TRIERS OF PETITIONS in a Parliament held at York :
> Mons'r Hugh de Courtenay

---

* Vide p. 702.

† A John de Rythre was another of the said Mainpernors, who was probably son of William Baron de Rythre, who was Summoned temp. Edw. I. Vide p. 540. This John de Rythre was Governor of Skypton Castle, but was never Summoned to Parl. There was likewise a John de *Rivers*, or *Ripariis*, living at that riod, who was Sum. to Parl. from 6 to 9 Edw. II. but of whom hing further is known. Vide p. 539.

> Mons'r Will. la Zousch de Assheby
> Mons'r Rauf Basset de Drayton
> Mons'r Richard de Grey—BARONS.

Anno 1332.—Vol. II. p. 69 ^{b}. Art. 6.—And in the same Parliament amongst the Lords appointed to treat of the affairs of Scotland are,

> Le Seign' de Percy
> Mons'r Henri de Beaumont
> Mons'r Hugh de Courteney, and
> Mons'r William de Clynton—BARONS.

Anno 1339.—Vol. II. p. 103 ^{b}. 13 Edw. III. Among the Peers who grant an Aid to the King in a Parliament at Westminster are,

Le Seignur de Wake	Le Seignur de Morle
—————— de Moubray	Le Seignur de Bardolf
—————— de Segrave	De Mons'r Gilbert Talebot
—————— de Berkele	Mons'r Robert de l'Isle.
De Mons'r Hugh le Despenser	

Anno 1340.—Vol. II. p. 112 ^{b}. 14 Edw. III. Art. 4. contains a list of some of each rank PRESENT the second day of the Parliament held at Westminster, and among them four Barons, viz.

> Le Seign' de Wake
> —————— de Wylughby
> Le Baron de Stafford
> Mons'r Rauf Basset.

Ibid. p. 113 ^{b}. Art. 21. And in the same Parliament amongst the TRIERS OF PETITIONS,

> Le Seignur de Wake
> Le Seign'r de Berkele
> Mons'r Nicol de Cantelu
>
> Mons'r Rauf Basset de Drayton
> Mons'r Roger de Grey
> Le Seignur de Wylughby
> Mons'r Antoigne de Lucy.

Ibid. p. 118 ^{b}. Art. 10. And in the same year, upon granting an Aid to the King, the following Barons were PRESENT in Parliament:

> Mons'r le Wak
> Mons'r Rauf Basset de Drayton

Mons'r Bertlemeu de Burghassh'
Mons'r Thomas de Berkele.

Anno 1341.—Vol. II. p. 126 b. Art. 3. 15 Edw. III. TRIERS OF PETITIONS in the Parliament held at Westminster :

Le Seign' de Wake
Mons'r Thomas de Berkele
Mons'r Johan de Cherleton.

Ibid. Art. 4. The following Barons * are mentioned as PRESENT when the causes of calling the Parliament were declared :

Le Seignurs de Percy
———————— de Wake
Mons'r Hugh le Despenser
Mons'r Nichol de Cantelou
Le Seign' de Segrave.

Anno 1341.—Vol. II. p. 129. Art. 17. 15 Edw. III. The King appoints four Bishops, four Earls, four Barons, and others learned in the law, to consider of, and report to him concerning certain Petitions ; the Barons are,

Le Seignurs de Wake,
———————— de Percy
Monsieur Rauf de Nevill &
Mons'r Rauf Basset de Drayton.

Anno 1343.—Vol. II. p. 135 b. Art. 5. 17 Edw. III. TRIERS OF PETITIONS :

Le S. de Percy
Mons'r Thomas de Berkele } Ou l'un de eux.

Mons'r Rauf de Nevil
Mons'r Antoigne de Lucy.

Ibid. Art. 6. 17 Edw. III. Barons PRESENT when the causes of calling the Parliament were declared :

Le Seign' de Percy
Le Seign' de Wak
Mons'r Rauf de Nevill
Mons'r Hugh le Despens'r
Mons'r Thomas Berkele.

---

* It is worthy of observtaion, that amongst the Prelates "& autres Grantz" then present was "Mons'r Robert d'Artoys," who possessed no dignity in this country ; his name occurs immediately vfore all the Earls.

Anno 1344.—Vol. II. p. 146ᵇ. Art. 3. 18 Edw. III.   Triers of Petitions :

  Le Seign' de Wake
  Le Seign' de Percy
  Le Seign' de Berkele
  Mons'r Nicol de Cantelowe.

Ibid. p. 147. Art. 6. 18 Edward III. Barons present when the causes of Summoning the Parliament were declared :

  Le Seign' de Wake
  Le Seign' de Percy
  Le Seign' de Berkele
  Mons'r Hugb le Despenser
  Mons'r Rauf de Nevill.

Anno 1346.—Vol. II. p. 157ᵇ. Art. 3. 20 Edw. III.   Triers of Petitions :

  Le Seign' de Wake
  Mons'r Thomas de Berkele.

Anno 1347.—Vol. II. p. 164. Art. 2. 21 Edw. III.   Triers of Petitions :

  Le Seign' de Wake
  Le Seign' de Percy
  Le Seign' de Berkeley
  Mons'r Rauf de Nevill.

Ibid. Art 3.

  Le Baroun de Stafford
  Mons'r Richard Talebot
  Mons'r Wauter de Manny.

Anno 1348.—Vol. II. p. 158. Art. 6. 20 Edw. III.   Letters Patent from the King, dated near Calais, 8 Sept. Anno 20 Edw. III. 1348, nominating

  Bartholomew de Burghersb,

and others * (not Barons), to open the Parliament, and

---

* One of these Commissioners was "Mons'r Johan Darcy, le Chaumberleyn," but no person of that name being summoned to that Parliament, he is not placed among the Barons in the list in the text ; but a John Darcy was summoned to Parliament from 6 Edw. III. 1332, to 7 Edw. III. 1334, and again in the 16 Edw. III. 1342, and died in 1347, when he was succeeded by his son

declare the causes of its being summoned; who accordingly do so in the PRESENCE of divers Prelates, &c. and
the following Barons:

> Le Seignur de Wake *
> Le Seignur de Segrave
> Le Seignur de Berkele.

In the 22 Edw. III. there were no Triers of Petitions,
nor any proof of sittings.

Anno 1351-2.—Vol. II. p. 236. Art. 3. 25 Edw. III. TRIERS
OF PETITIONS :

> Le Seign' de Percy
> Mons'r Rauf de Nevill
> Mons'r Richard Talbot.

Anno 1354.—Vol. II. p. 254 ᵇ. Art. 6. 28 Edw. III. TRIERS
OF PETITIONS :

> Le Seign' de Percy
> Mons'r Rauf de Nevill.

Ibid. Art. 7.

> Mons'r Guy de Bryan.

Anno 1355.—Vol. II. p. 264. 29 Edw. III. The causes of
calling this Parliament were declared by

> Mons'r Wauter de Manny ;

but there is no list of Triers of Petitions, nor any Barons
named as present on the occasion †.

Anno 1362.—Vol. II. p. 268 ᵇ. Art. 4. 36 Edw. III. TRIERS
OF PETITIONS :

> Le Sire de Nevill.

John Darcy, who was likewise summoned to Parliament from the
22 to the 28 Edw. III. one of which persons was probably the
Commissioner on this occasion.

  * Neither the names of Burghersh nor Wake appear on the
Roll as being summoned to this Parliament. Vide second and third
Report of the Lords' Committee on the dignity of a Peer of the
Realm, p. 318. and Appendix thereto, No. I. p. 559.

  † It is worthy of observation, that among the Earls then present
was the "Count de Ormount," the names of all the other Earls
mentioned occur in the Writs of Summonses issued in that year,
but Ormond was an Irish Earldom.

Anno 1362.—Vol. II. p. 268ᵇ. Art. 5. 36 Edw. III. TRIERS OF PETITIONS :

> Le Sire de Manny
> Mons'r Henry le Scrop' *
> Mons'r Johan Moubray.

Anno 1363.—Vol. II. p. 275ᵇ. Art. 5. 37 Edw. III. TRIERS OF PETITIONS :

> Le Sire de Moubray
> Le Sire de Percy
> Le Sire de Beaumont
> Le Sire de Clifford
> Mons'r Rauf de Nevill
> Mons'r Guy Brian.

Ibid. Art. 6.

> Le Sire le Despenser †
> Le Sire de Roos
> Mons'r Waut'r de Manny
> Mons'r Henri le Scrop' *
> Mons'r Rog'r de Beauchamp.
> Mons'r Johan Moubray.

Anno 1364-5.—Vol. II. p. 283ᵇ. Art. 5. 38 Edw. III. TRIERS OF PETITIONS :

> Le Sire de Perey
> Mons'r Rauf de Nevill
> Mons'r Guy de Brian.

Ibid. Art. 6.

> Le Sire le Despenser
> Mons'r Waut'r de Manny
> Mons'r Henri le Scrop ‡

---

* His name does not appear in the Lists of Summons lately printed by the House of Lords among the Barons summoned to this Parliament, though he was summoned to the preceding Parliament, viz. 34 Edw. III. as well as to several before and subsequent to it.

† His name is not in the List of Summonses before cited to this Parliament, but he was summoned in the 31, 34, 38, 39, and 46 Edw. III.

‡ He is not included in the Lists of Summons to either of these Parliaments.

> Mons'r Rog'r de Beauchamp
> Mons'r Johan Moubray.

Anno 1366.—Vol. II. p. 289 b. Art. 5. 40 Edw. III. TRIERS
OF PETITIONS:

> Le Sire de Percy
> Mons'r Rauf de Nevill
> Mons'r Guy Brian.

Ibid. Art. 6.

> Le Sire le Despenser
> Mons'r Wauter de Manny
> Mons'r Roger de Beauchamp
> Mons'r Johan Moubray.

Anno 1368.—Vol. II. p. 294 b. Art. 5. 42 Edw. III. TRIERS
OF PETITIONS:

> Le Sire de Percy
> Mons'r Rauf de Nevill *
> Mons'r Guy Brian.

Ibid. Art. 6.

> Mons'r Wauter de Manny
> Mons'r Roger de Beauchamp
> Mons'r Johan Moubray.

Anno 1369.—Vol. II. p. 299 b. Art. 6. 43 Edw. III. TRIERS
OF PETITIONS:

> Le Sire de Percy
> Mons'r Johan de Nevill
> Mons'r Guy Brian.

Ibid. p. 300. Art. 7.

> Mons'r Roger de Beauchamp
> Mons'r Johan de Moubray.

Anno 1371.— Vol. II. p. 303 b. Art. 4. 45 Edw. III. TRIERS
OF PETITIONS:

> Le Sire de Latymer
> Mons'r John de Nevill
> Mons'r Guy Brian
> Mons'r Roger Beauchamp.

---

* There appears to be an error here in the christian name,
Ralph Nevill of Raby having died in the preceding year, as appears by the Esc. 41 Edw. III. No. 47; his son John was summoned to this Parliament.

Anno 1371.—Vol. II. p. 303 ᵇ. Art. 5. 45 Edw. III. TRIERS OF PETITIONS:

> Mons'r. Wauter de Manny
> Mons'r Rauf Basset de Drayton.
> Mons'r Joh'n de Moubray.

Anno 1372.—Vol. II. p. 309 ᵇ. Art. 5. 46 Edw. III. TRIERS OF PETITIONS.

> Le S'r Despenser
> Le S'r de Roos
> Mons'r Guy de Briane.

Ibid. Art. 6.

> Mons'r Johan de Charleton de Powys
> Mons'r Rauf Basset de Drayton
> Mons'r Joh'n Moubray.

Anno 1373.—Vol. II. p. 317. Art. 10. 47 Edw. III. TRIERS OF PETITIONS:

> Mons'r William la Zouche de Haryngworth
> Mons'r Guy de Brian
> Mons'r Henry le Scrop.

Ibid. Art. 11.

> Le S'r de Clyfford
> Mons'r Amary Seint Amand
> Mons'r Richard de Stafford.

Anno 1376.—Vol. II. p. 321. Art. 6. 50 Edw. III. TRIERS OF PETITIONS:

> Le S'r de Percy
> Le S'r de Roos
> Le S'r de la Zouche de Haryngworth
> Mons'r Guy de Bryan.

Ibid. p. 322. Art. 7.
> Le S'r de Basset de Drayton *
> Le S'r de Bardolf

---

* Lord Basset of Drayton does not appear to have been summoned to Parliament between the 46 Edw. III. and 1 R. II. In the List of the Mainpernors, vol. II. p. 326 of the Lord Latymer in this year, his name again occurs, with that of three Earls and twelve Barons, who were summoned to this Parliament *(Vide Infra)*; as well as several others, who, though undoubtedly

Le S'r de Clifford
Mons'r Guy de Bryene
Mons'r Amory de Seint Amande
Mons'r Henry le Scrop
Mons'r Richard de Stafford.

Anno 1376.—Vol. II. p. 326ᵇ. Art. 39. 50 Edw. III. MAIN-
PERNORS of Le S'r de Latymer *:

Le Counte de Stafford, ⎱ s'il plest au Roi.
Le Sire de Percy, ⎰

Le Sire de Darcy
Le Sire de Nevill
Le Sire de Roos
Le Sire de Basset
Le Sire de Clifford, s'il plest
　au Roi
Le Sire la Zousche, pur atant
　come sa terre vaut pur un
　an
Le Sire Filz Wauter
Le Sire L'Estrange

Le Sire de Bardolf, s'il plest
　au Roi
Le Sire de Buttetourt
Mons'r Johan d'Arundell
Mons'r Johan de Montagu
Mons'r Robert de Ferrers
Mons'r Johan Lovell
Mons'r Rauf Crumwell
Le Sire de Berkele
Mons'r Michell de la Pole.

Anno 1376-7.—Vol. II. p. 363ᵇ. Art. 16. 51 Edw. III. TRIERS
OF PETITIONS :

Le Seign'r de Percy
Le Seign'r de Latymer
Le Seign'r de Nevill
Le Seign'r de Fitz Wauter
Mons'r Guy de Bryane.

Ibid. Art. 17.

Le Seign' de Roos
Le Seign' de Basset de Drayton †

Barons, and summoned as such in other years, do not appear in
the list of persons summoned to this Parliament, viz. Le Sire
L'Estrange, Le Sire de Darcy, Mons'r Johan Montagu, Mons'r
Johan Arundel, and le Sire de Berkele.

　* In this List the following persons are also included, but
neither of whom were ever summoned to Parliament as Barons,
viz. Mons'r William Beauchamp, Mons'r William de Nevill,
Mons'r Rauf de Ferrers, Mons'r Johan de Burele, Mons'r Johan
Clanvowe, Le Sire de Gomerriz, Mons'r Thomas Morrieux, and
Mons'r Philip de la Vache; and of those inserted in the text
five were not summoned the 50 of Edw. III.—Vide the preceding
note

　† See Note on the Triers of Petitions, Anno 1376, 50 Edw. III.

Le S'r de Clifford
Mons'r Johan de Montagu *
Mons'r Henr' Le Scrop
Mons'r Richard de Stafford.

Anno 1377.—Vol. III. p. 4ᵇ. Art. 9. 1 Ric. II. TRIERS OF PETITIONS:

Le S'r de Latymer
Le S'r de Nevill
Le S'r de Cobham
Le S'r de Fitz Wauter
Mons'r Roger Beauchamp.

Ibid. Art. 10.

Le Sire de Roos
Le Sire de Basset
Le Sire de Clifford
Le Sire de Bardolf
Mons'r Richard de Stafford.

Ibid. p. 5. Art. 12. 1 Ric. II. C'est assavoir le Roy de Castell & de Leon Duc de Lancastre, l'Evesq' de Loudres, l'Evesq' d'Ely, l'Evesq' de Roucestre, l'Evesq' Karduill, le Conte de la Marche, le Conte d'Arondell, le Conte de Warrewyk, le Conte de Angos, &

Le S'r de Nevill
Mons'r Henr' le Scrop
Mons'r Ric' le Scrop, &
Mons'r Ric' le Stafford;

et ce lour estoit grantez de par le Roy en PARLEMENT.

Anno 1378.—Vol. III. p. 34. Art. 13. 2 Ric. II. TRIERS OF PETITIONS:

Le S'r de Latymer
Le S'r de Cobham
Mons'r Henry le Scrop
Mons'r Roger Beauchamp
Mons'd Ric' de Stafford.

---

* He was not summoned to Parliament between 50 Edw. III. and 5 R. II. though he was so on several occasions both before and after that period.

Anno 1378.—Vol. III. p. 34. Art. 14. 2 Ric. II.

> Le S'r Lestraunge de Knokyn
> Le S'r Fitz-Wauter
> Mons'r Johan Montagu *
> Mons'r Johan d'Arondell, Mareschal d'Engl'.

Anno 1379.—Vol. III. p. 56 b. Art. 10. 2 Ric. II.   TRIERS OF PETITIONS :

> Le S'r de Latymer
> Mons'r Johan d'Arondell, Mareschal d'Engl'
> Le S'r de Cobbam
> Mons'r Roger Beauchamp
> Mons'r Ric' de Staff'.

Ibid. p. 57. Art. 11.

> Le S'r Lestrange de Knoykn
> Le S'r de Bardolf
> Mons'r Johan Montagu.

Anno 1379-80.—Vol. III. p. 72. Art. 8. 3 Ric. II †.   TRIERS OF PETITIONS :

> Le S'r de Latymer
> Le S'r de Cobbam
> Mons'r Richard Staff'.

Ibid. p. 72 b. Art. 9.

> Le S'r Lestrange de Knokyn
> Le S'r de Bardolf
> Mons'r Johan Montagu.

Anno 1380.—Vol. III. p. 89. Art. 7. 4 Ric. II.   TRIERS OF PETITIONS :

> Le S'r de la Zouche
> Le S'r de Bardolf.

---

* Vide note to the last page.

† Anno 1379-80.—Vol. III. p. 78 b. Art. 15. 3 Ric. II. Among the Commissioners appointed by the King " ad scrutiniu' faciend' in Hospic' & Cur' Reg'." are,

> Will'o de Latymer
> Guydoni de Briene, &
> Joh' de Monte-acuto, Banerettis.

But it is doubtful whether this record be a proof of sitting in Parliament.

Anno 1380.—Vol. III. p. 89. Art. 8. 4 Ric. II.

    Le S'r Lestrange de Knokyn
    Le S'r de Scales
    Mons'r Guy de Bryen
    Mons'r Johan Montagu.

Anno 1381.—Vol. III. p. 99. Art. 5. 5 Ric. II. Pt. 1. TRIERS OF PETITIONS:

    Mons'r Johan Cobham
    Mons'r Richard le Scrop
    Mons'r Guy de Bryen.

  Ibid. Art. 6.

    Le S'r la Souch
    Le S'r Fitz-Wautier
    Mons'r Henry le Scrop
    Le S'r de Wilughby.

Anno 1381.—Vol. III. p. 100. Art. 14. 5 Ric. II. Among the Lords appointed to confer with the Commons were,

Le S'r de Nevill	Le S'r de Wilughby
Le S'r de Clifford	Johan de Cobham
Le S'r Fitz-Wauter	Richard le Scrop
Le S'r la Zouche de Haryng-worth	Guy de Bryan, BANERETTZ.

Anno 1382.—Vol. III. p. 123. Art. 7. 5 Ric. II. TRIERS OF PETITIONS:

    Le S'r de Nevill
    Mons'r Johan Cobham
    Mons'r Guy de Bryen.

  Ibid. Art. 8.

    Le S'r Fitz-Wautier
    Le S'r de Wilughby.

Anno 1382.—Vol. III. p. 133. Art. 6. 6 Ric. II. TRIERS OF PETITIONS:

    Le S'r de Nevill
    Mons'r Johan Cobham
    Mons'r Guy de Bryene.

  Ibid. Art. 7.

    Le S'r de Fitz Wauter
    Le S'r de Wylughby.

Anno 1382.—Vol. III. p. 145. Art. 6. 6 Ric. II. TRIERS OF
  PETITIONS:

> Le S'r de Nevill
> Mons'r Guy de Bryene.

  Ibid. Art. 7.

> Le S'r Fitz-Wauter
> Mons'r Richard Le Scrop.
> Mons'r Johan de Cobham de Kent.

Anno 1383.—Vol. III. p. 151. Art. 9. 7 Ric. II. TRIERS OF
  PETITIONS:

> Le S'r de Nevill
> Mons'r Ric' le Scrop
> Mons'r Guy de Bryen.

  Ibid. Art. 10.

> Le S'r Fitz Wauter
> Mons'r Johan de Cobham de Kent.

Anno 1384.—Vol. III. p. 167. Art. 7. 7 Ric. II. TRIERS OF
  PETITIONS:

> Le S'r le Zouche
> Le S'r de Nevill
> Mons'r Guy Bryen.

  Ibid. Art. 8.

> Le S'r de Cobham.

Anno 1384.—Vol. III. p. 185. Art. 8. 8 Ric. II. TRIERS OF
  PETITIONS:

> Le S'r de Nevill
> Mons'r Richard le Scrop
> Mons'r Guy de Brien.

  Ibid. Art. 9.

> Le S'r Fitz Wauter
> Mons'r Johan de Cobham de Kent.

Anno 1385.—Vol. III. p. 204. Art. 8. 9 Ric.   . TRIERS OF
  PETITIONS:

> Le Sire de Nevill
> Mons. Richard le Scrop
> Mons'r Guy de Brien.

Anno 1385.—Vol. III. p. 204. Art.9. 9 Ric. II.

> Le S'r Fits-Wauter
> Mons'r John de Cobham de Kent.

Anno 1385.—Vol. III. p. 205 b. 206 b. 207 b. Art. 14, 15, and 16. 9 Ric. II. Witnesses to the creations of the Duke of York, the Duke of Gloucester, and the Earl of Suffolk in full Parliament:

> Joh'e de Nevill de Raby
> Joh'e Lovell
> Waltero Fitz Wauter
> Hugones Segrave *, Thesaurario n'ro
> Joh'e de Monte-Acuto, Senescallo Hospicii n'ri.

Anno 1385.—Vol. III. p. 399. No. 26. 9 Ric. II. Barons appointed by the King to hear the suit of Thomas Lovell:

> Will'o de Morley †
> Joh'ni de Nevyll de Raby
> Joh'ni de Cobeham
> Walto' fitz Wautier &
> Ric'o le Scrop.

Anno 1386.—Vol. III. p. 215 b. Art. 4. 10 Ric. II. TRIERS OF PETITIONS:

> Le Sire de Nevill
> Mons'r Richard le Scrop
> Mons'r Guy de Brien.

Ibid. p. 216. Art. 5.

> Mons'r Johan de Cobeham de Kent.

Anno 1387-8.—Vol. III. p. 228. Art. 4. 11 Ric. II. TRIERS OF PETITIONS:

> Le Sire de Nevill
> Mons'r Richard le Scrop.

---

* It does not appear that this Hugh de Segrave was ever summoned to Parliament.

† There is probably an error in the Christian name of this Baron; as in the Summonses for this year a *Thomas* de Morley appears, but no *William*. William de Morley, who was summoned from 35 Edw. III. till 2 R. II. died in the latter year (Esc. 2 R. II. No. 34.), and was succeeded by his son, Thomas Morley, who was summoned from 5 R. II. until his death, 4 H. V.

Anno 1387-8.—Vol. III. p. 229, Art. 5. 14 Ric .II.

         Mons'r Johan de Cobeham de Kent.

Anno 1389.—Vol. III. p. 257 ᵇ. Art. 4. 13 R. II. TRIERS OF PETITIONS:

         Le S'r de Wilughby
         Mons'r Richard le Scrop.

    Ibid. p. 258. Art. 5.

         Le S'r de Lovell
         Mons'r Johan de Cobeham de Kent.

Anno 1389.—p. 261. Art. 16. 13 Ric. II. MAINPERNORS of John De Aske :

         Johan S'r de Nevill &
         Mons'r Johan Lovell, " PRESENTZ EN PAR-
         LIAMENT."

Anno 1390.—Vol. III. p. 277 ᵇ. Art. 4. 14 Ric. II. TRIERS OF PETITIONS:

         Le S'r de Wylughby
         Mons'r Richard le Scrop.

    Ibid p . 278. Art. 5.

         Le Sire de Lovell
         Mons'r Johan de Cobeham de Kent.

Anno 1391.—Vol. III. p. 284 ᵇ. Art. 5. 15 Ric. II. TRIERS OF PETITIONS :

         Le S'r de Wylughby
         Mons'r Richard le Scrop.

    Ibid. p. 285. Art. 6.

         Mons'r Johan Lovell.

Anno 1393.—Vol. III. p. 300 ᵇ. Art. 4. 16 Ric. II. TRIERS OF PETITIONS :

         Le S'r de Willughby
         Mons'r Richard le Scrop
         Mons'r Philipp Spenser.

    Ibid. Art. 5.

         Le S'r de Grey de Ruthyn
         Mons'r Johan Lovell.

Anno 1394.—Vol. III. p. 309 b. Art. 4, 17 Ric. II. Triers
of Petitions :

> Le S'r de Wilughby
> Mons'r Richard le Scrop
> Mons'r Philipp Spenser.

Ibid. p. 310. Art. 5.

> Le S'r de Grey de Ruthyn
> Le S'r de Cobbeham.

Anno 1395.—Vol. III. p. 329 b. Art. 4, 18 Ric. II. Triers of
Petitions :

> Le S'r de Wilughby
> Mons'r Richard le Scrop
> Mons'r Philipp Spenser.

Ibid. p. 330. Art. 5.

> Le S'r de Zouche
> Le S'r de Cobeham.

Anno 1397.—Vol. III. p. 337 b. Art. 5. 20 Ric. II. Triers of
Petitions :

> Le Sire de Nevill.
> Mons'r Richard le Scrop
> Mons'r Philipp Spenser.

Ibid. p. 338. Art. 6.

> Le Sire Despenser
> Le Sire de Grey de Ruthyn.

Anno 1397.—Vol. III. p. 343 b. and 344 b. Art. 32, and 33.
20 Ric. II. Witnesses to the creation of the Earl of Somerset, " per ipsum Regem in Parliamento," and to a
charter granting the office of Earl Marshal of England to
the Earl of Nottingham .

> Reginaldo de Grey
> Radulpho de Nevill
> Joh'e de Lovell, MILITIBUS.

Anno 1397.—Vol. III. p. 348. Art. 6. 21 Ric. II. Triers of
Petitions :

> Le Sire de Nevill
> Le Sire de Grey de Codnore
> Le Sire de Lovell.

Anno 1397.—Vol. III. p. 348. b. Art. 7.

> Le Sire le Dispenser
> Le Sire de Grey de Ruthyn.

Anno 1397.—Vol. III. p. 356. Art. 39. 21 Ric. II. Barons who swore to observe and keep the statutes made in this Parliament " en presence du Roy :"

Le Sire de Camoys	Le Sire de Seint Amand
Le Sire de Burghchier	Le Sire de Furnyvall *
Le Sire de Powys	Le Sire de Ferrers
Le Sire Fitz Wauter	Le Sire de Seymour
Le Sire de Roos	Le Sire de Lovell
Le Sire de Haryngton	Le Sire de Bardolf
Le Sire de Burnell	Le Sire de Morley
Le Sire de Berkelee	William Beauchamp, S'r de
Le Sire de Darcy	Bergeveny
Le Sire de Wilugbby	Rauf de Cromwell
Le Sire de Grey de Codnore	Rauf de Lomley
Le Sire de Grey de Ruthyn	Phelipp le Despenser
Le Sire de Scales	

Anno 1398.—Vol. III. p. 373 b. Art. 89. 21 Ric. II. Barons sworn at the Cross at Canterbury in the presence of the King, 18 March, Anno 21 R. II. 1398, to observe the statutes made in that Parliament :

> Le Sire de Grey de Ruthyn
> Le Sire de Ferrers de Groby
> Le Sire de Lovell'
> Le Sire de Camoys.

Anno 1399.—Vol. III. p. 416. Art. 8. 1 Hen. IV. TRIERS OF PETITIONS :

> Le Sire de Roos
> Le Sire de Cobham.

Ibid. Art. 9.

> Le Sire de Berkeleye
> Le Sire de Wilughby.

---

* This personage was Thomas Nevill Baron Furnivall, jure uxoris, though he is uniformly called " Thomas Nevyll de Halumshire," in the Writs: he was summoned from 7 R. II. 14 H. IV. Vide " FURNIVALL," p. 259.

Anno 1399.—Vol. III. p. 427. Art. 74. On the question relating to the safe custody of the late King (Richard II.) Thursday, 23 Oct. 1399. " les nouns des Seign'rs demandez & assentuz sur la question suis dite cy ensuent c'est assavoir :"

Le S'r de Roos	Le S'r de Burnell
Le S'r de Grey de Ruthyn	Le S'r de Lovell
Le S'r de Cherlton	Le S'r de Camoys
Le S'r de Bardolf	Le S'r de Seymour
Le S'r de Wilughby	Le S'r de Crombwell
Le S'r de Furnyvall	Le S'r de Cobham
Le S'r de Ferrers	Mons'r Henry Percy ‡
Le S'r de Beaumont *	Mons'r Richard Scrop
Le S'r de Berkeley	Le S'r Fitz Hugh
Le S'r Fitz Wautier	Le S'r de Bergeveny
Le S'r de Manley †	Le S'r de Lomley
Le S'r de Scales	Le Baron de Greystok
Le S'r de Morley	Le Baron de Hilton.

Anno 1401.—Vol. III. p. 455. Art. 6. 2 Hen. IV. TRIERS OF PETITIONS :

Le Sire de Roos
Le Sire de Cobham.

Ibid. Art. 7.

Le Sire de Berkeley
Le Sire de Wilughby.

---

* Apparently Henry Lord Beaumont, though his name does not appear in the Lists of Summons in this year. John, his father, was summoned from 7 to 17 Ric. II. and died in 1396; but this Henry is not recorded to have been summoned until the 5th Hen. IV. Vide BEAUMONT, p. 54.

† Evidently a misprint for Mauley.

‡ The renowned " Hotspur," eldest son of Henry Earl of Northumberland ; it does not appear that he was ever summoned to Parliament, but it is evident from the above record, that he was present in Parliament, and ranked as a Baron of the realm.

Anno 1401.—Vol. III. p. 459 ᵇ. Art. 31. 2 Hen. IV.   Barons PRESENT at the declaration made in Parliament relative to the Forfeiture of Thomas Holland Earl of Kent, and others:

Richard Sire de Grey de Co-
  denore
Thomas Sire de Berkeley
Johan Sire de Charleton
Reynald Sire de Grey de Ru-
  thyn
Thomas Sire de Camoys
Thomas Sire de Furnyvall
Roberd Sire de Scales

Johan Sire de Beaumond
William Sire de Wilughby
Hugh Sire de Burnell
William Sire de Ferrers de
  Groby
William Sire de Bergeveny
Johan Sire de Lovell
Roberd Sire de Haryngton.

Richard Le Scrop.

Anno 1402.—Vol. III. p. 486. Art. 7. 4 Hen. IV *.   TRIERS OF PETITIONS:

  Le Sire de Roos
  Le Sire de Lovell.

Ibid. Art. 8.

  Le Sire de Berkeley
  Le Sire de Wilughby.

Ibid. p. 486 ᵇ. Art. 10.   Barons appointed to confer with the Commons, Tuesday, 10 Oct.:

  Le S'r de Roos
  Le S'r de Berkeley
  Le S'r de Bergeveny
  Le Sire de Lovell.

Anno 1404.—Vol. III. p. 523. Art. 6. 5 Hen. IV.   TRIERS OF PETITIONS:

  Le Sire de Burnell
  Le Sire de Lovell.

Ibid Art. 7.

  Le Sire de Berkeley
  Le Sire de Wilughby.

---

* The Writs for this Parliament are dated 13 Aug. 3 Hen. IV. 402.

Anno 1404.—Vol. III. p. 545 b. Art. 6. 6 Hen. IV *. Triers of Petitions :

      Le Sire de Burnell
      Le Sire de Lovell.

Ibid. p. 546. Art. 7.

      Le Sire de Berkeley
      Le Sire de Wylughby.

Anno 1405-6.—Vol. III. p. 567 b 7 & 8 Hen. IV. Triers of Petitions :

      Le Sire de Burnell
      Le Sire de Lovell.

Ibid p. 568. Art. 7.

      Le Sire de Roos
      Le Sire de Berkeley.

Anno 1406.—Vol. III. p. 582. and p. 583. Art. 60. 8 Hen. IV.—Among the witnesses PRESENT in Parliament to two Patents for the Settlement of the Crown, dated 22 Dec. 8 Hen. IV. 1406, are the following Barons :

Will'mi Domini de Roos	Reginaldi Domini de Grey
Ric'i Domini de Grey de Co-denore	de Ruthyn
	Will'mi Domini de Ferrers
Hen' Domini de Beaumont	Thome Domini de Furnyvale

---

* Anno 1404.—Vol. III. p. 530. Art. 37. Among the Lords and others named by the King in Parliament to be " de son grant & continuel Conseil," are the following Barons ; but it is somewhat doubtful if this record be a proof of sitting in Parliament.

      Le Sire de Roos, Tresorer d'Engleterre
      Le Gardéin du Prive Seal
      Le Sire de Berkeley
      Le Sire de Wilughby
      Le Sire de Furnyval
      Le Sire de Lovell.

On Friday, the last day of this Parliament (Vol. III. p. 552b. Art. 32.), the Earl of Arundell & " les Sires de Powys & de Furnyvall," were appointed to observe a certain ordinance ; but as it is not certain that this record can be deemed a proof of sitting, it is not placed in the text.

Will'mi Domini de Wylugbby
Hugonis Domini de Burnell
Will'mi Domini de Clynton
Thome Domini de Morley
Joh'is Domini de Darcy
Joh'is Domini de Lovell
Bartholomei Domini de Burghcbier
Gilb'ti Domini de Talbot
Will'mi Domini la Zouche
Thome Domini de Camoys
Ric' Domini de Seymour
Henrici Fitz-Hugh
Henrici le Scrop de Masham
Joh'is de Welles

Joh'is Cobbam
Petri de Malolacu
Joh'is de Latymer
Edwardi de Charleton de Powys
Mag'ri Thome de la Warre
Thome Berkeley de Berkeley
Rad'i de Crumwell
Rad'i de Greistok
Will'mi Beauchamp de Berge-venny
Joh'is Tochet
Rob'ti Ponynges
Joh'is de Haryngton *, &
Ric'i Lestrange

Anno 1407.—Vol. III. p. 609. Art. 10. 9 Hen. IV. TRIERS OF PETITIONS :

Le Sire de Burnell
Le Sire de Lovell.

Ibid. Art. 11.

Le Sire de Roos
Le Sire de Berkeley.

Anno 1410.—Vol. III. p. 623. Art. 8. 11 Hen. IV. TRIERS OF PETITIONS :

Le S'r de Burnell
Le Sire de Morley.

Ibid. Art. 9.

Le S'r de Roos
Le S'r de Berkeley.

Anno 1411.—Vol. III. p. 648. Art. 7. 13 Hen. IV. TRIERS OF PETITIONS :

Le Sire de Burnell
Le Sire de Morley.

---

* He appears to have been constantly summoned by the name of *Robert*, but his real name was, as is stated in the Rolls of Parliament, *John*. His father, Robert de Haryngton, died anno 7 Hen. IV.

Anno 1411.—Vol. III. p. 648. Art. 8.

>Le Sire de Roos
>Le Sire de Berkeley.

Anno 1413.—Vol. IV. p. 4. Art. 5. 1 Hen. V. TRIERS OF PETITIONS:

>Le S're de Burnell
>Le S're de Ferrerys.

Ibid. Art. 6.

>Le S're de Roos
>Le S're de Berkeley.

Anno 1414.—Vol. IV. p. 16. Art. 4. 2 Hen. V. TRIERS OF PETITIONS:

>Le Sire de Roos
>Le Sire de Berkeleye.

Ibid. p. 16^b. Art. 5.

>Le Sire de Clifford
>Le Sire de Maule *.

Anno 1414.—Vol. IV. p. 35. Art. 8. 2 Hen. V. TRIERS OF PETITIONS:

>Le S'r de Berkeley
>Le S'r de Morley
>Le S'r de Powys †.

Ibid. Art. 9.

>Le S'r de Grey de Ruthyn
>Le S'r Lescrop
>Le S'r de Haryngton.

Anno 1415.—Vol. IV. p. 63. Art. 2. 3 Hen. V. TRIERS OF PETITIONS:

>Le Sire de Grey de Ruthyn
>Le Sire de Powys
>
>Le Sire de Talbot
>Le Sire de Ponynges.

---

* Apparently Peter Baron Mauley.
† Edward de Cherleton. Vide p. 122.

Anno 1415.—Vol. IV. p. 71. Art. 7. 3 Hen. V. TRIERS OF PETITIONS:

> Le S'r de Gray de Ruthyn
> Le S'r de Berkeley.

Ibid. Art. 8.

> Le S'r de Ponynges.

Anno 1416.—Vol. IV. p. 95. Art. 6. 4 Hen. V. TRIERS OF PETITIONS:

> Le Sire de Gray de Ruthyn
> Le Sire de Berkeley.

Ibid. Art. 7.

> Le Sire de Ponynges.

Ibid. p. 96. Art. 11. 4 Hen. V. The King, several Spiritual Peers, Dukes, and Earls, and the following Barons PRESENT in Parliament:

> Le S'r de Grey de Ruthyn
> Le S'r de Bourcer *
> Le S'r de Haryngton
> Le S'r de Clynton
> Le S'r de Camoys
> Le S'r de Ponynges
> Le S'r Fitz-Hugh.

Anno 1417.—Vol. IV. p. 107. Art. 6. 5 Hen. V. TRIERS OF PETITIONS:

> Le S'r de Gray de Ruthyn.

Ibid. Art 7.

> Le S'r de Ponynges.

---

* Apparently Hugh Stafford, who was summoned to Parliament in right of his wife, Elizabeth, daughter and heir of Bartholomew Lord Bourchier, anno 12 and 14 Henry IV. and 1 Hen. V. He lived till the 9th Hen. V.; but his name does not appear in the Lists of Summons after the 1st Henry V. Under "BOURCHIER," p. 77, he is erroneously said to have been summoned in the 3d Hen. V.

Anno 1419.—Vol. IV. p. 116ᵇ. Art. 5. 7 Hen. V. TRIERS OF PETITIONS :

  Le Sire de Camoys.
 Ibid. p. 117. Art. 6.

  Le Sire de Ponynges.

Anno 1419.—Vol. IV. p. 118. Art. 10. 7 Hen. V. The following Barons were PRESENT in Parliament :

  Le Sire de Grey de Ruthyn
  Le Sire de Ferreres de Groby
  Le Sire de Camoys
  Le Sire de Clynton *
  Le Sire de Ponynges
  Le Sire de Botreaux.

Anno 1420.—Vol. IV. p. 123ᵇ. Art. 4. 8 Hen. V. TRIERS OF PETITIONS :

  Le Sire de Gray de Ruthyn.

 Ibid. Art. 5.

  Le Sire de Ponynges.

Anno 1421.—Vol. IV. p. 129. Art. 4. 9 Hen. V. TRIERS OF PETITIONS :

  Le S'r de Gray de Ruthyn.

 Ibid. p. 130. Art. 5.

  Le S'r de Ponynges.

Anno 1421.—Vol. IV. p. 150ᵇ. Art. 7. 9 Hen. V. TRIERS OF PETITIONS :

  Le S'r de Gray du Ruthyn.

 Ibid. p. 151. Art. 8.

  Le Sire de Clynton.

---

 * His name does not appear in the List of Summonses in this year, though he was summoned in the 5th of Henry V. and again in the 8th of Henry V. It is to be remarked, that according to the Lists lately printed by the House of Lords, only 18 Barons were summoned this year, and 13 the next; but all the Barons mentioned as present in the 7th of Henry V. are recorded to have been summoned in that year, excepting Lord Clinton.

Anno 1422.—Vol. IV. p. 170. Art. 10. 1 Hen. VI. Triers
Petitions :

> Le Sire de Crumbewell
> Le Sire de Ponynges.

Ibid. p. 170ᵇ. Art. 13. 1 Hen. VI. Among the Peers
in whose PRESENCE in Parliament the Bishop of Durham
Lord High Chancellor to King Henry V. delivered up the
Great Seal and received it again, are the following Barons

> Johanne D'no de Talbot & de Furnyvale
> Willielmo D'no de Clynton
> Roberto D'no de Ponynges.

Anno 1422.—Vol. IV. p. 175ᵇ. Art. 26. 1 Hen. VI. Among
the "Persones d' estate," appointed to be of the Council
to Humphry Duke of Gloucester are the following
Barons: " les nons des queux persones escriptz en une
petit Cedule lueez overtement en ceste Parlement ci
ensuent."

> Le Sire Fitz-Hugh
> Mons'r Rauf Crumbwell
> Mons'r Wauter Hungerford *
> Mons'r John Tiptoft *.

---

* Neither of these names appear in the Lists of Summons
printed by order of the House of Lords until the 4 Henry VI. ;
although they are noticed in the Rolls as present in Parliament
in the 2d and 3d years of that reign. *(Vide infra.)* After the
name of Mons'r John Tiptoft that of " Mons'r Wauter Beauchamp" occurs ; but he does not appear ever to have been summoned to Parliament. It should be particularly observed, that the
lists of persons summoned in the latter years of Henry V. and
the 1st, 2d, and 3d of Henry VI. contain, comparatively with
other years, very few names, and certainly do not comprise the
whole of the then existing Peerage. The following is an abstract from the 1st Henry V. to 4 Henry VI. :

Anno 1 Hen. V. By Writs tested 22 March, 6 Earls, 32 Ba-
              rons ; by Writs tested 1 Dec. 2 Dukes,
              9 Earls, 29 Barons ; by Writs tested 24 Dec.
              2 Dukes, 9 Earls, 29 Barons.
  2 Hen. V. 4 Dukes, 11 Earls, 28 Barons.
  3 Hen. V. By Writs tested 12 Aug. 2 Earls, 17 Barons ;
              by Writs tested 29 Sept. 3 Earls, 16 Barons ;

Hen. VI. anno 1423.—Vol. IV. p. 198. Art. 6, 2 Hen. VI. TRIERS OF PETITIONS:

> Le Sire de Grey.

Ibid. Art. 7.

> Le Sire de Crumwell.

V. *ibid.* anno 1423.—Vol. IV. p. 201. Art. 15. 2 Hen. VI. Among the Council appointed by the Parliament to assist the Duke of Gloucester are the following Barons:

> Le Sire de Crumwell
> Le Sire Fitz Hugh
> Le Sire de Bourghchier*
> Le Sire de Scrop *
> Mons'r Walter Hungreford †
> Mons'r John Tiptoft †.

---

	by Writs tested 21 Jan. 3 Dukes, 6 Earls, 19 Barons.
4 Hen. V.	3 Dukes, 9 Earls, 24 Barons.
5 Hen. V.	1 Duke, 3 Earls, 14 Barons.
6 Hen. V.	Nullæ Summonitiones apparent.
7 Hen. V.	3 Earls, 13 Barons.
8 Hen. V.	By Writs tested 21 Oct. 3 Earls, 13 Barons by Writs tested 26 Feb. 2 Dukes, 6 Earls, 20 Barons.
9 Hen. V.	3 Earls, 12 Barons.
10 Hen. V.	Nullæ Summonitiones apparent.
1 Hen. VI.	2 Dukes, 5 Earls, 16 Barons.
2 Hen. VI.	2 Dukes, 5 Earls, 19 Barons.
3 Hen. VI.	2 Dukes, 5 Earls, 18 Barons.
4 Hen. VI.	4 Dukes, 2 Earls, 23 Barons.

* Neither of these Barons was summoned to Parliament in the 2d of Hen. VI. but Sir Lewis Robsert, K. G. was summoned to Parliament, jure uxoris, as Baron Bourchier in the following year, and until the 7 Henry VI. The Sire de Scrop was probably John 4th Lord Scrope of Masham, brother and heir of Henry Lord Scrope of Masham, who was attainted in 1415: the said John appears to have been restored to his brother's honors and inheritance in 1421, although he is not recorded to have been summoned to Parliament until the 4th Henry VI.

† Vide a Note in the last page relative to these Barons.

Anno 1425.—Vol. IV. p. 261. b. Art. 7. 3 Hen. VI. TRIERS OF PETITIONS :

>Le Sire de Crumwell.

Ibid. p. 262. Art. 8.

>. Le Sire de Bourghchier
>Le Sire de Scrope *.

Anno 1425.—Vol. IV. p. 262 b. Art. 10. 3 Hen. VI. Among the Peers PRESENT in Parliament on the 14th May, are the following Barons :

Johanne de Grey	Will'o de Botreaux
Will'o de Ferrariis de Groby	Will'o de Haryngton, &
Jacobo de Audeley	Joh'e de Dacre ‡, ac
Lodovico de Bourghchier	Joh'e de Roos §, infra ætatem
Radulpho de Crumwell	existen'.
Johanne Lecrop †	Waltro Hungerford ‖
Willielmo de Clynton	Johanne Tiptoft ‖
Robert de Ponynges	

Anno 1426.—Vol. IV. p. 295 b. Art. 6. 4 Hen. VI. TRIERS OF PETITIONS :

>Le S'r de Crumwell
>Le S'r de Scrop.

Ibid. p. 296. Art. 7.

>Le Sire de Bourchier
>Le Sire de Ferrers de Groby.

---

* Vide Note * in preceding page.

† The name of John le Scrope was originally inserted in the Writ to this Parliament; but according to the copy printed by order of the House of Lords, it was afterwards erased. Vide Appendix to Report I. and II. p. 861.

‡ The Christian name of Baron Dacre was *Thomas;* he was summoned to the Parliament then sitting as " Thome de Dacre de Gyllesland, Chivaler."

§ This Baron was not summoned in the 3d Hen. VI.; and as he was under age the cause of his being omitted is satisfactorily accounted for.

‖ Vide Note * to p. 744.

Anno 1426.—Vol. IV. p. 297. Art. 12. 4 Hen. VI. Among the personages appointed in Parliament, Tuesday, 12th March, to act as Arbitrators of the disputes between the Duke of Gloucester and the Bishop of Winchester was,

Ralph de Cromewell.

Anno 1427.—Vol. IV. p. 316 b. Art. 8. 6 Hen. VI. 'TRIERS OF PETITIONS :

Le Sire de Bourchier
Le Sire de Tiptoft.

Ibid. p. 317. Art. 9.

Le Sire de Crumwell.

Anno 1428.—Vol. IV. p. 327 b. Art. 27. 6 Hen. VI. Among the " Lordes Spirituell and Temporell, assembled by the commandement of the Kyng oure soverain Lord in yis his present Parlement" who signed a Declaration and Answer relative to the Powers of the Protector, the Barons were,

Jacobus de Audeley
Lodowicus de Bourghchier
Reginaldus le Warr'
Johannes l'Escrop
Radulphus de Cromwell

Walterus Hungerford Thesaurarius Anglie
Johannes de Tiptost
Robertus de Ponynges.

Anno 1429.—Vol. IV. p. 336. Art. 7. 8 Hen. VI. TRIERS OF PETITIONS :

Le Sire de Cromwell
Le Sire de Tiptoft.

Ibid. Art. 8.

Le Sire de Roos
Le Sire le Scrop.

Anno 1430.—Vol. IV. p. 344 b. Art. 28. 8 Hen. VI. Among the Lords who " IN PLENO PARLIAMENTO" subscribed a Schedule of Ordinances for the observance of the Dukes of Gloucester and Bedford, and other Lords of the King's Council, were,

> Lodowicus Robessart
> Radulphus Cromwell
> Johannes le Scrop
> Walterus Hungreford Thesaurarius Anglie
> Johannes Tiptoft.

Anno 1431.—Vol. IV. p. 368. Art. 8. 9 Hen. VI. TRIERS OF PETITIONS:

> Mons'r John Tiptoft.

Ibid. Art. 9.

> Le Sire de Scrop
> Le Sire de Ponynges.

Anno 1432.—Vol. IV. p. 388ᵇ. Art. 7. 10 Hen. VI. TRIERS OF PETITIONS:

> Le Sire de Beaumont
> Le Sire de Hungerford.

Ibid. p. 389. Art. 8.

> Le Sire de Ponynges.

Anno 1433.—Vol. IV. p. 419ᵇ. Art. 7. 11 Hen. VI. TRIERS OF PETITIONS:

> Le Sir de Cromwell
> Le Sir de Hungreford.

Ibid. p. 420. Art. 8.

> Le Sir de Lovell
> Le Sir de Tiptoft.

Ibid. p. 422ᵇ. Art. 15. 11 Hen. VI. Among the Peers who swore to observe certain articles agreed on in this Parliament against Riots, Treasons, &c. are the following Barons:

> de Beaumont, Chivaler *
> Willielmus de Ferrariis de Groby, Chivaler

---

* *John* de Beaumont, by which name he was summoned to this Parliament.

Willielmus le Zouch, Chivaler
Thomas de Morley, Chivaler
Radulphus Cromwell, Thesaurarius Anglie
Jacobus de Berkeley, Chivaler
Henricus de Grey de Codenore, Chivaler
Henricus le Bourchier, Chivaler *
Johannes de Latymer, Chivaler †
Robertus de Ponynges, Chivaler
Thomas de Dacre, Chivaler
Johannes de Welles, Chivaler ‡
     de Fauconberg, Chivaler §
Willielmus de Lovell, Chivaler
Walterus Hungerford, Chivaler
Johannes de Tiptoft, Chivaler
ᴅ. Johannes Cornewayll de Faunhope, Chivaler
Johannes le Scrop de Masham, Chivaler, pro-
     misit in Camera sua propria, quia infirmus, in
     manus Cancellar' Quinto die Decembris."

Anno 1435.—Vol. IV. p. 482. Art. 6. 14 Hen. VI. Triers
of Petitions :
     Le Sir de Tiptoft
     ᴅ. Le Sir de Faunhope.

Ibid. Vol. IV. p. 482. Art. 7. 14 Hen. VI. Triers of
Petitions :
     Le Sire de Ponynges.

---

* His name does not occur in the Summonses for this year;
but it is possible that he was summoned subsequent to the general Summonses which were dated 24th May, as he did not succeed
to the Barony until 1st of July following, but of which no record
appears.

† There appears to be an error in the Christian name of this
Baron in the Rolls of Parliament. John Nevill Lord Latimer
died in the 9th Hen. VI. and was succeeded by his son George,
who was summoned from 10 Henry VI. to 9 Edw. VI.; in the
Writs his name properly stands *George*.

‡ There appears to be an error in the Christian name of this
Baron also. John de Welles died in the 9th Hen. VI. and was
succeeded by his grandson Leo de Welles, who was summoned
from 10 to 38 Hen. VI. by Writs directed " Leoni Wellis, Ch'r."

§ William de Nevill, who was summoned to this Parliament,
though not with the designation of Lord Fauconberg. Vide p.
228.

Anno 1435.—Vol. IV. p. 484 b. 14 Henry VI.   Among the
Peers PRESENT in Parliament were,

Dominis de Audeley	Dominis de Crumwell, Thes'
Ponynges	Hungerford
Fauconberge*	Tiptoft &
Fitz-Hugh	₱. de Faunhope.

Anno 1436—Vol. IV. p. 496. Art. 8. 15 Hen. VI.   TRIERS
OF PETITIONS:

     Le Sire de Tiptot.

Ibid. Art. 9.

     Le Sire de Scrop
     Le Sire de Ponynges.

Anno 1439.—Vol. V. p. 4. Art. 7. 18 Hen. VI.   TRIERS OF
PETITIONS :

     Le S'r de Beaumont
     Le S'r de Audeley.

Ibid. Art. 8.

     Le S'r de Berkeley
     Le S'r de Scroop
₱. Le S'r de Faunhope.

Anno 1442.—Vol. V. p. 36 b. Art. 3. 20 Hen. VI.   TRIERS
OF PETITIONS :

     Le S'r Gray de Ruthyn
     Le S'r Scrop de Bolton
     Le S'r de Hungerford
₱. Le S'r de Faunhope
     Le S'r de Dudley

     Le S'r de Morley
     Le S'r de Scroop de Masham.

Anno 1444.—Vol. V. p. 66 b. Art. 6. 23 Hen. VI.   TRIERS
OF PETITIONS:

     Le Sire Grey de Ruthyn
     Le Sire de Dudley
     Le Sire de Fauconberge.

---

* Vide Note § to the last page.

Anno 1444.—Vol. V. p. 67. Art. 7. 23 Hen. VI. TRIERS OF PETITIONS:

> Le Sire de Cromwell
> Le Sire de Latymer.

Anno 1447.—Vol. V. p. 129. Art. 7. 25 Hen. VI. TRIERS OF PETITIONS:

> Le Sire de Scrope de Masham
> Le Sire de Dudley.

Ibid. Art. 8.

> Le Sire de Cromwell
> ℞.* Le Sire de Sudley.

Anno 1449.—Vol. V. p. 141 b. Art. 4. 27 Hen. VI. TRIERS OF PETITIONS:

> Le S'r de Cromwell
> Le S'r de Moleyns
> Le S'r de Grey.

Ibid. Art. 5.

> Le S'r de Dudley
> ℞. Le S'r de Sudeley.

Anno 1449.—Vol. V. p. 171 b. Art. 4. 28 Hen. VI. TRIERS OF PETITIONS:

> ℞. Le S'r de Lisle
> Le S'r de Fitz-Hugh
> ℞. Le S'r de Sudeley.

Ibid. Art. 5.

> Le S'r de Cromwell
> Le S'r de Say de Sele.

Anno 1450.—Vol. V. p. 182. Art. 50. 28 Hen. VI. " Memorand', that on Tuesday the xviith day of Marche, the Kyng sent for all his Lordes both Spirituell and Temporell thenne beyng in towne, that is for to sey: (after Bishops, Earls, and Abbots),

Barons Roos	Barons Wellys
Grey de Ruthyn	Scales

---

* Those Barons to whose names this letter is prefixed, derived their dignities under a *Patent.* " Le Sire de Sudley" was Ralph Boteler, who was created by Patent 10 Sept. 1441, Baron Sudley of Sudley, co. Gloucester, under which title the article in p. 73 ought perhaps to have been placed.

Barons Cromwell	Barons Say
𝔭. Lisle	Seint Amond
Ferrers de Groby	𝔭. Hastynges *
Cobham	Moleyns
Dudley	𝔭. Stourton
𝔭. Sudeley	𝔭. Ryvers and
𝔭. Beauchamp	𝔭. Vessy,

into his innest chambre, with a gavill wyndowe over a cloyster, within his paleys of Westm.; and whence they were all assembled," &c.

Anno 1450.—Vol. V. p. 210 b. Art. 4. 29 H. VI. TRIERS OF PETITIONS:

> Le S'r de Cromwell
> Le S'r de Ferrers de Groby.

Ibid. Art. 5.

> Le S'r de Welles
> Le S'r de Roos
> Le S'r de Lisle.

Anno 1453.—Vol. V. p. 227 b. Art. 4. 31 H. VI. TRIERS OF PETITIONS:

> Le S'r de Grey de Ruthyn
> Le S'r de Graystok
> Le S'r Fitz Hugh †.

---

* No Baron was included in the List of Summonses of this year by the name of Hastings; but it was probably Thomas Lord Hoo and Hastings, so created by Patent 26 Henry VI. and who was summoned to this Parliament by the title of "Thomas Hoo, Chivaler;" he died in 1453, and the Lord Hastings mentioned on the Rolls after 1 Edw. IV. was William Baron Hastings of Ashby de la Zouch.   Vide p. 309.

† Lord Fitz Hugh was not summoned to Parliament in the 31st Hen. VI.   William IV.-12th Lord Fitz-Hugh was summoned from 7 to 29 Hen. VI. and died in the 31st of that reign. Henry his son was not summoned until 26 May, 33 Hen. VI. 1455 (erroneously printed in p. 241, "26 May, *twenty*-third Hen. VI 1455)."   In the 30th Hen. VI. no Writs of Summons appear to have been issued.

Anno 1453.—Vol. V. p. 227ᵇ. Art. 5.

>Le Sᵗr de Cromwell
>Le Sᵗr de Duddeley
>Le Sᵗr de Seint Amond.

Anno 1454.—Vol. V. p. 249ᵇ. Art. 48. 32 Hen. VI. Among the Peers PRESENT in Parliament 15 March, 12 Hen. VI. 1454, when the King created Prince Edward, Prince of Wales and Earl of Chester, were the following Barons:

>Fauconbergh ⎫
>Wyllughby ⎬ Milites.
>𝔭.Stourton ⎭

Anno 1455.—Vol. V. p. 278ᵇ. Art. 5. 33 Hen. VI. TRIERS OF. PETITIONS :

>Le Sᵗr de Faukenbrigge
>Le Sᵗr de Cromwell.

Ibid. p. 279. Art. 6.

>Le Sᵗr de Bonvyle
>Le Sᵗr de Berners.

Anno 1455.—Vol. V. p. 279ᵇ. Art. 16. 33 Hen. VI. On Thursday the second day of the Parliament, after the Chancellor, by command of the King, had declared the causes for which they were assembled, " prefati Domini inter se concordarunt," on the articles then exhibited, certain Lords as well Spiritual as Temporal were appointed to consider and treat of the said matters, among whom were the following Barons:

>Dominus de Cromwell
>𝔭. Dominus de Sudeley .
>
>Dominus de Faucomberge
>𝔭. Dominus de Stourton.
>
>Dominus de Scales
>Dominus Fitzwareyn
>Dominus de Bonevyle.

Anno 1453.—Vol. V. p. 282ᵇ. & 283. Art. 25. 33 Hen. VI. " The xxII day of July, the xxxIIIᵗⁱ yere of our Soveraine Lord Kyng Henry the VIᵗᵉ. at Westm' in the grete Counsaill Chambre, tyme of Parlement, in the presence of oure said Soveraine Lord, the Lords Spirituell and

Temporell, in shewing theire trouth, feith, and love that they have and bere to his Highnesse, every Lord Spirituell leiyng his hond uppon his brest, and every Temporell Lord takying oure saide Soveraine Lord by the hande, frely sware and promitted in manere and forme that folowith. I" &c.—Among the names of the said Peers are the following Barons :

Dominus de Gray de Ruthyn'	Dominus Clynton
Dominus de Faukenberge	Dominus Say
Dominus de Scales	Dominus Fitz Wareyn
Dominus de Cromwell	Dominus Bonvyle
Dominus Ferrers de Groby	Dominus de Ruggemond
⅌. Dominus de Sudeley	Gray
⅌. Dominus de Beauchamp	Dominus de Berners
Dominus de Scrop de Bolton	Dominus de Clifford *
⅌. Dominus Stourton	Dominus de Powes †.

Anno 1459.—Vol. V. p. 345 b. Art. 4. 38 Hen. VI. TRIERS OF
PETITIONS :

> Le S'r de Clyfford
> Le S'r Fitz Hugh
> Le S'r de Lovell.

Ibid. Art. 5.

> Le S'r de Dacre de Gilleslond
> Le S'r de Dudley.
> ⅌. Le S'r de Beauchamp
> Le S'r de Berners.

Anno 1459.—Vol. V. p. 351 b, & p. 352. Art. 26. 38 Hen. VI.
Among the Peers who took the oath of allegiance to the

---

* Lord Clifford was not summoned to this Parliament ; no Writs of Summons appear on record between the 31st and 38th Hen. VI. (to both of which Parliaments he was summoned), excepting in the 33 Hen. VI. the Parliament referred to in the text, in which he was present.

† Vide p. 284, relative to the presence of this Baron in Parliament. He is there presumed to have been Richard de Grey, father of John 1st Lord Grey of Powis, but which Richard was never summoned to Parliament.

King, in the Parliament Chamber at Coventry, 11 Dec. this year, were the following Barons:

Dominus Clyfford	P. Dominus Sudeley
Dominus Grey de Rutbyn	P. Dominus Beauchamp
Dominus Grey	Dominus Rugemond Grey
Dominus Wellys	Dominus Bonvyle
Dominus Greystok	Dominus Scroupe de Ma-
Dominus Fitz Hugh	sham
Dominus Dacre	P. Dominus Stourton
Dominus Dacre de Gyl-	P. Dominus Egremond'
leslond	Dominus Berners
Dominus Scales	Dominus Wyllughby
Dominus Bergavenny	Dominus Stanley
Dominus Dudley	Dominus Nevill.

Anno 1460.—Vol. V. p. 373 b. Art. 4. 39 Hen. VI. TRIERS OF PETITIONS:

> Le S'r Grey de Rutbyn
> Le S'r de Dacre
> Le S'r Fitz Waryn.

Ibid. Art. 5.

> Le S'r de Scrop' *
> Le S'r de Bonevyle
> Le S'r de Berners
> Le S'r de Rugemond Grey.

Anno 1461.—Vol. V. p. 461 b. Art. 4. 1 Edw. IV. TRIERS OF PETITIONS:

Le S'r de Audeley	Le S'r de Scrop'
Le S'r de Grey Rutbyn	P. Le S'r de Stourton
Le S'r de Greystok	Le S'r de Hastynges
Le S'r de Clynton	Le S'r de Suthwyk †.

---

* Thomas Lord Scrope of Masham, and John Lord Scrope of Bolton, were both summoned this year, and it is consequently difficult to decide which Baron was the person appointed a Trier of Petitions on the above occasion.

† Evidently Humphry Stafford, who was summoned to Parl. as "Humphrido Stafford de Suthwyck Chev'r," from 26 July, 1 Edw. IV. to 28 Feb. 2 Edw. IV. He was created Lord Stafford of Suthwyck by Patent, 24 April, 1464, and subsequently Earl of Devon. Vide p. 605.

Anno. 1461.—Vol. V. p. 462. Art. 5.

>Le S'r Fitz Hugh
>Le S'r de Scrop de Upsale
>Le S'r de Cobham *
>Le S'r de Dacre.

Anno 1463.—Vol. V. p. 496ᵇ. Art. 4. 3 Edw. IV.   TRIERS OF PETITIONS:

>Le S'r de Berners
>Le S'r de Audeley
>Le S'r de Hastynges
>Le S'r de Wenlok
>Le S'r de Suthwyk.

Ibid. Art. 5.

>Le S'r de Wyllughby
>Le S'r de Mountegue
>Le S'r de Herberd
>Le S'r de Dacre.

Anno 1467.—Vol. V. p. 571ᵇ. Art. 4. 7 Edw. IV.†   TRIERS OF PETITIONS :

>Le S'r de Berners
>Le S'r de Audeley
>Le S'r de Hastynges.

Ibid. Art. 5.

>Le S'r de Scales
>Le S'r de Dudeley
>Le S'r de Dacres.

---

* On the authority of Dugdale's "Index Baronum Summonitionibus," Edward Broke Lord Cobham, is stated, in p. 142, only to have been summoned to Parliament to the 38 Hen. VI. but on referring to the Lists lately printed by order of the House of Lords, it appears that he was also summoned 23 May, and 13 June, 1 Edw. IV. 1461, the 22 Dec. 2 Edw. IV. 1462, and on the 28 Feb. 2 Edw. IV. 1463.

† The Summonses for this Parliament were issued anno 6 Edw. IV. to meet at Westminster on the 3d of June following, which day was in the 7th of Edw. IV. No Writs of Summons are on record for the 3d, 4th, 7th, or 8th Edw. IV.

Anno 1471.—Vol. VI. p. 234ᵇ. 11 Edw. IV. Among the Peers who took the oath of allegiance to Edward Prince of Wales, as son and heir apparent of Edward IV. at Westminster "IN CAMERA PARLIAMENTI," 3 July, 11 Edw. IV. 1471, were,

E. Arundell Mautravers *	P. Mountejoye
A. Grey	Dynham
J. Duddeley	Howard
J. Audeley	Duras †
Dacre	J. Fenys
Ed. Bergevenny	P. R. Beauchamp
J. Straunge	Sir Robᵗ Fenys
J. Scrop	Bourgchier
W. Ferrers	T. Bourgchier, and several
Berners	Knights.
Hastyngs	

Anno 1472.—Vol. VI. p. 3ᵇ. Art. 4. 12 Edw. IV. TRIERS OF PETITIONS :

P. Le Sʳr de Stourton
Le Sʳr de Hastynges
P. Le Sʳr de Mountjoye.

Ibid Art. 5.

Le Sʳr de Straunge
Le Sʳr de Dacre.

---

* It would appear that this Baron was Thomas Fitz Alan, alias Arundel, the eldest son of William Fitz Alan XVIII.-15th Earl of Arundel and Baron Maltravers, but no record exists of the said Thomas having been summoned to any Parliament as a Baron. The initial of the christian name is probably an error, for the baptismal name of no person who could possibly use the title of "Maltravers," ever commenced with the letter E.

† Although this and the following names are inserted above, it does not appear that either of them were Barons of the realm, excepting the signature of "Bourgchier," who was probably Fulk Lord Fitz Waryn, no Writ of Summons to a Temporal Peers is on record either in the 10 or 11 Edw. IV. "R. Beauchamp," might be an error for John Lord Beauchamp of Powyk, who was summoned in the 12 Edward IV.

Anno 1478.—Vol. VI. p. 167 ᵇ. Art. 6. 17 Edw. IV*.   TRIERS OF PETITIONS :

> Le S'r de Stanley.
> Le S'r de Hastynges
> Le S'r de Dynham.

Ibid Art. 7.

> ꝓ. Le S'r de Beauchamp
> Le S'r de Ferrers.

Anno 1482.—Vol. VI. p. 196 ᵇ. Art. 4. 22 Edw. IV.   TRIERS OF PETITIONS :

> Le S'r de Stanley
> Le S'r Hastynges
> Le S'r de Dacre.

Ibid. Àrt. 5.

> Le S'r de Dudley
> Le S'r de Fitz Hugh
> Le S'r de Scrope.

Anno 1484.—Vol. VI. p. 238. Art. 1. 1 Ric. III.   TRIERS OF PETITIONS :

> Le S'r de Grey †
> Le S'r de Awdeley
> ꝓ. Le S'r de Powyk ‡.

Anno 1485.—Vol. VI. p. 268. 1 Hen. VII.   TRIERS OF PETITIONS :

> Le S'r de Bergevenny

---

* No Writs of Summons to Parliament appear on record between 12 & 22 Edw. IV. Each of these five Barons was summoned 12 Edw. IV. and likewise in 22 Edw. IV. excepting Lord Beauchamp, who died in 1475, and was succeeded by his son Richard, who was summoned 22 Edw. IV.

† Three Barons Grey were summoned to this Parliament, viz. Reginald Grey de Wilton, " Henry Grey, Ch'r;" and " John Grey de Powes;" but there are no means of ascertaining which of them was the Trier of Petitions on the above occasion.

‡ Richard Lord Beauchamp of Powyck.

Le S'r de Cobham
𝔓. Le S'r de Beauchamp.

Le S'r Fitzwater
Le S'r de Dudley.

Anno 1485.—Vol. VI. p. 288. Art. 15. 1 Hen. VII. Among the Peers who took an oath in Parliament against abetting treason, felonies, &c. were the following Barons, viz.

> Grey
> Dudley
> Bergeveny
> Fitzwalter
> Grey de Wylton
> 𝔓. Beauchamp, &
> Hastings *.

Anno 1487.—Vol. VI. p. 386. 3 Hen. VII. TRIERS OF PETITIONS :

> Le S'r de Audely †
> Le S'r de Bergevenny
> Le S'r Gray.
>
> Le Sire Fitzwater
> Le Sire Straunge.

Anno 1488.—Vol. VI. p. 410. 4 H. VII. TRIERS OF PETITIONS :

> Le Sire de Bergevenny
> Le Sire d' Audeley ‡
> Le Sire d' Ormond §.

---

* In the List of Summonses to this Parliament, the names of Richard de Welles and of Edward Hastings de Hungerford are included; the latter was likewise Baron Hastings of Ashby de la Zouche. Hence it is difficult to determine which of these individuals was the Baron then present in Parliament.

† Apparently John Touchet VI.-13th Baron Audley, who is recorded to have been summoned to Parliament from 1 Edw. IV. to 1 Ric. III. and to have died in 1491, but although his name does not occur in the Lists of Summons published by Dugdale, of the 3 & 4 Hen. VII. it is evident he was present in Parliament in those years.

‡ Vide the preceding note.

§ The earliest notice of an English Baron of this title is the 14 October, 11 Hen. VII. 1495, when Thomas Butler, 7th

Le S'r Dynham
Le Sy'r de la Warre
Le Sire Dudley.

Anno 1491.—Vol. VI. p. 441. Art. 1.7 Hen. VII.   TRIERS OF
PETITIONS :

D'nus Dynham, Miles

D'nus Scrop de Bolton
D'nus Audeley *.

Anno 1495.—Vol. VI. p. 458 b. 11 H. VII.   TRIERS OF PE-
TITIONS :

D'nus de Ormond
D'nus de la Warre
D'nus Dudley
℗. D'nus Daubeney.

D'nus Bergevenny
D'nus Straunge
D'nus Audeley.

Anno 1496.—Vol. VI. p. 509 b. 12 H. VII.   TRIERS OF PE-
TITIONS :

Le Sn'r Beauchamp
℗. Le Sn'r Daubeney
Le Sn'r Broke.

Ibid. p. 510.

Le Sn'r Dynham
Le Sn'r Hastynges.

Earl of Ormond in Ireland was summoned to Parliament by the
style of "Thomas Ormond de Rochford, Chev'." From the
above record it is evident, however, that he sat in Parliament
about seven years before he was summoned, unless, as it is not
improbable, the Lists published by Dugdale are imperfect;
those printed by order of the House of Lords terminate with the
end of Edward IV.

* James Touchet Lord Audley, son and heir of John Lord
Audley noticed in the note to the last page ; he was summoned
from 12 August in this year to 12 Hen. VII.

Anno 1503.—Vol. VI. p. 521. 19 H. VII. Triers of Petitions:

    🐋 Le S'r Daubeney
    Le S'r Hastinges
    Le S'r Herberd

    Le S'r Burgavenney
    Le S'r Dacre de Dacre
  🐋. Le S'r Mountjoye.

The preceding proofs of Barons' Sittings in Parliament
have been extracted solely from the Rolls of Parliament;
but the following copy of the celebrated Letter from the
Barons assembled in the Parliament held at Lincoln in February, 29 Edw. I. anno 1301, to Pope Boniface VIII. on
behalf of themselves and the whole community of England,
would have been inserted in its proper place according to
chronological order, as an unquestionable proof that those
Peers whose names occur therein sat in Parliament on
that occasion, had not the Editor been aware that some
doubt exists in the minds of many individuals who are
highly competent to judge of the subject, as to the authenticity of the document itself *. Under these circumstances,
he has thought it advisable to place the letter after the extracts from the Rolls of Parliament, and also to enter, at
some length, into the consideration of the question. With
this object, first, notes are added to the name of each person who was not included in the Writ to the Parliament
ordered to be held at Lincoln, containing such facts as are
recorded of him, in order that some judgment may be formed
of the cause of his then acting as a Baron of Parliament; 2dly,
correct lists are inserted of the Barons who were summoned
to the said Parliament, but whose names do not occur in
the letter; of such Barons whose names are inserted in
the letter, but who were not summoned to that Parliament, distinguishing those who had been summoned to
previous Parliaments (and particularly marking such as received Writs to the Parliament *immediately* preceding, and

---

* Cruise's Treatise on Dignities, 2d edit. and I. and II. Report of the Lords' Committee on the Dignity of a Peer of the
Realm, p. 240, et seq. cited hereafter.

such as were only summoned on the doubtful occasions of
the 22d and 25th Edw. I.) from those who were either not
summoned for several years afterwards, and the latter,
from those to whom no Writs of Summons to Parliament are
recorded ever to have been issued; and, lastly, such observations in support of the authenticity of the letter are submitted, as an attentive examination of the subject has
produced.

The importance of the document, not merely in an historical point of view, for as such its discussion would not
belong to this work, but as evidence of many Barons having
sat in Parliament under the Writs directed to them at a
period when such proofs of the fact cannot, from the lamentable deficiency of parliamentary records, otherwise be
found, and consequently establishing the existence of many
Baronies in their descendants, which, if this evidence be
rejected, must be deemed extinct, will, it is hoped, apolo-
gize for the space appropriated to its consideration. It is,
the Editor trusts, needless for him to assert that his remarks are offered with unfeigned diffidence; and as the
question, in itself one of great difficulty, is rendered extremely embarrassing, from his having to contend against
an opinion, the reasons for which have never, he believes,
been publicly expressed, he is confident he may rely on that
indulgence, which the consideration, for the first time of a
subject no less obscure than important, so obviously requires.

S'c'issimo in Xp'o p'ri D'no B. divina p'videncia S'c'e Romane ac univ'salis eccl'ie sum'o pontifici sui devoti filii.

¶ Joh'es, Com' Warenn' *
¶ Thom' Com' Lancastrie
¶ Rad'us de Monte H'meri, Com' Glouc' & Herf' †

¶ Those persons to whose names this mark is prefixed, were
duly summoned to the Parliament in which this letter was se.
* Earl of Surrey, by which title he was summoned to
Parliament.
† Earl of Hertford and Gloucester, jure uxoris, from 27 Ed.
I. 1299, to her death in 1307, after which he was summoned
Parliament as a Baron only.

¶ Humfr' de Bohun, Com' Hereford et Essex, & Contab' Angl' *

¶ Rog's Bigod, Com' Norf' & Maresch' Angl.

¶ Guido, Com' Warr'

¶ Ric', Com' Arundell'

¶ Adomar' de Valenc', D'n's de Montiniaco †

¶ Henr' de Lancastr', D'n's de Munemue

¶ Joh'es de Hastyng', D'nus de Bergeveny ‡

¶ Henr' de Percy, D'n'us de Topclive §

¶ Edmu'dus de Mortuo Mari, D'n's de Wigemor'

¶ Rob'tus, fil' Walteri, D'n's de Wodeham

Joh'es de S'c'o Joh'e, D'n'us de Hannak ||

---

* It is a fact worth stating, in this place, though not immediately connected with the object of the insertion of this letter, that on each side of the arms of Bohun, on the seal of this Earl, is a shield, suspended from what would appear to be a trefoil, charged with the arms of Fitz-Piers, Earls of Essex, which Earldom was acquired by the Bohuns in consequence of the marriage of Humphrey de Bohun, Earl of Hereford, (the grandfather of the Earl whose seal is affixed to this document,) with Maud, sister and heir of William Fitz-Piers, the last Earl of Essex of that family. This is perhaps the earliest instance of any approach to the system of quartering arms, which was not regularly adopted in this country, though examples somewhat earlier are to be found on the continent, until the reign of Edw. III.

† He succeeded his father as Earl of Pembroke in 1296, though he never used that title until 1 Edw. II. 1308, when he was summoned to Parliament by that appellation.

‡ The arms of the family of Hastings, of Bergavenny, afterwards Earls of Pembroke, are always described as, Or, a maunch gules; but those on the seal of this Baron differ materially thereon, as, on the one side is a cross between four fleurs de lis, charged with five fleurs de lis, and on the other side a cross charged with five fleur de lis, between, in the first and fourth quarters, a lion passant gardant, and in the 2d and 3d quarters a lion rampant.

§ Henry Percy, sealed with the arms of Brabant solely.

|| Possibly the same person who was summoned to this Parliament as " John de St. John de Lageham;" but his designation, Lord of Hannak, would rather admit the inference that it, John de St. John (son and heir apparent of John de St. John, of Basing), who was not summoned to the Parliament at Lincoln, but was summoned to the previous Parliament by Writ

¶ Hug' de Veer, D'n's de Swansechaumpis
¶ Will's de Breouse, D'n's de Gower
¶ Rob'tus de Monte Alto, D'n's Hawardyn
¶ Rob'tus de Tatteshale, D'n's de Bokeham
¶ Reginaldus de Grey, D'n's de Ruthyn
   Henr' de Grey, D'n's de Codenore *
¶ Hugo de Bardolf, D'n's de Wirmegeye
¶ Rob'tus de Tony, D'n's de castro Matill'
   Will' de Ros, D'n's de Hamelak †
¶ Rob'tus de Clifford, castellanus de Appelby
   Petr' de Malo Lacu, D'n's de Mulgreve ‡
¶ Ph's, D'n's de Kyme
¶ Rob'tus, fil' Rog'i, D'n's de Clav'yng'
¶ Joh'es de Mohun, D'n's de Dunsterre
¶ Almaricus de S'c'o Amando, D'n's de Wydehay
¶ Alanus la Zouch, D'n's de Assheby
¶ Will' de Ferar', D'n's de Groby
   Theobald de Verdun, D'n's de Webbele §

---

tested at Berwick, December, 28, 1299, and directed " Joh'i
de S'c'o Joh'i, juniori," from the circumstance that the St.
John's of Basing possessed the manor of *Halnac*, afterwards
Halnakerd, in Sussex ; and no place at all similar in name appears
among the possessions of which John St. John of Lageham, or
any of his family, died seized. The arms on his seal, viz. on a
chief two mullets, allow of no conclusion, as both the families of
St. John alluded to bore nearly the same coat.—Vide Dugdale,
vol. II. p. 9 ; and vol. I. p 464.

   * He was not summoned to this Parliament, although he was
summoned on the 22d, and twice in the 27th Edw. I. but not
again, for nearly nine years, viz. in the 1st and 2d Edw. II. and
died in the year last mentioned.

   † This Baron likewise was not summoned to this Parliament,
though he was summoned in the 23d, 27th, and 30th Edw. I.
and from the 1st to the 9th Edw. II.

   ‡ Though not summoned to this Parliament, he was summoned
to the Parliament immediately preceding, viz. on the 29th Dec.;
and also from the 23d Edw. I. to 3d Edw. II.

   § Theobald de Verdon was summoned to the Parliament immediately preceding, viz. on the 29th Dec. 28 Edw. I. as well as to
several Parliaments both before and after, but his name does not
appear in the Writs of Summons to this Parliament. There is
some difficulty in deciding whether the Theobald de Verdon present on this occasion was the person usually summoned as Theo-

¶ Thom' de Furnivall, D'n's de Sheffeld
¶ Thom' de Molton', D'n's de Egremont
¶ Will's le Latim', D'n's de Corby
¶ Thom' D'n's de Berkely
¶ Fulco fil' Warini, D'n's de Whitington
¶ Joh's D'n's de Seg'ave
¶ Edm'us de Eyncourt, D'n's de Thurgeriton
¶ Pet'r Corbet, D'n's de Caus
¶ Will's de Cantilup', D'n's de Ravenesthorp'
¶ Joh's de Bellocampo, D'n's de Hacche
¶ Rog'us de Mortuo Mari, D'n's de Pentkellyn
¶ Joh's fil' Regin', D'n's de Blekeneny
Ranulphus de Nevill', D'n's de Raby *
¶ Brianus fil Alani, D'n's de Bedale
Will'us Mareschall, D'n's de Hengh'am †

---

bald de Verdon, senior, or his son, who was designated in the Writs of Summons as Theobald de Verdon, junior; for both were summoned to the Parliament immediately preceding. The Castle of Webbeley, in the county of Hereford, was acquired by the marriage of John de Verdon (father of Theobald de Verdon, *senior*) with his first wife, Margery, dau. of Gilbert de Laci, and might have been assigned to Theobald de Verdon, *junior*, by his father, for his residence and support.

* He was regularly summoned to Parliament from 23 to 27 Edw. I. but not again until the 5th Edw II.; nor is his name to be found in the Writs of service within that period. It would be difficult, if not impossible, to account for this long interruption, unless he was absent from the kingdom on the King's service: from the 5th Edw. II. he was summoned until the 5th Edw. III. in which year he died.

† This Baron does not appear to have been summoned to Parliament until the 2d Edw. II. (and from thence to the 7th Edw. II. and died in the following year) though, in 1284, he succeeded his father John Marshall, who was a Baron by Tenure. His seal contains two batons, one on each side of his arms, which were probably indicative of his hereditary office of Mar-

¶ Walt'us D'n's de Hunt'cumbe
¶ Will'us Martin, D'n's de Cameiso
¶ Henr' de Tyes, D'n's de Chilton
¶ Rog'us le Ware, D'n's de Isefeld
¶ Joh's de Ripar', D'n's de Angre
¶ Joh's de Lancastr', D'n's de Grisdale
¶ Rob's fil' Pagani, D'n's de Lammer
　Henr' Tregoz, D'n's de Garinges *
. ¶ Rad's Pipard, D'n's de Linford
¶ Walt'us D'n's de Faucumb'ge
　Rog'us le Estr'ange de Ellesm'e †
¶ Johannes Lestr'ange de Cknokyn
　Thom' de Chaurces, D'n's de Norton ‡

---

shall of Ireland, which was granted in fee to John Marshall his great great grandfather, by King John. At the time when this Parliament assembled he was barely of age, as he was but five years old at the death of his father in 1284; and though possible just twenty-one when the Writs for it were issued, yet as he could scarcely have had time to obtain livery of his inheritance, his not having been *summoned* to this or to previous Parliaments is accounted for. His attendance, however, may be attributed to his official situation; and possibly in the interval between the issuing of the Writs, 26 Sept. 1300, and the February following, when the Parliament met, he might have done his homage, and been admitted to his lands.

* *Henry* de Tregoz was not summoned to Parliament until the 32d Edw. I. though he was summoned in the 22d Edw. I. to a council (on which Writ see some observations under "CLYVEDON," p. 141). In the same year in which he was present at this Parliament he obtained the King's license for a market and fair at *Gatinges*, in Sussex: from the 32d he was summoned until the 15th Edw. II.; after which period nothing is known of him.

† This Baron is recorded to have been three times summoned to Parliament in the 23d Edw. I. and again in the 24th and 25th of that reign, but never afterwards, though it is certain that he lived until the 31st Edw. I. 1303.

‡ Thomas de Chaworth was summoned to Parliament 22d and 25th and 27th Edw. I. but never afterwards, nor were any of his posterity.

Walt'us de Bellocampo, D'n's Alecestr' *
Ri'eus Talebot, D'n's de Ekleswell †
Joh'es Bettetourte, D'n's de Mendesham ‡

---

* No person of this family is recorded to have been summoned to Parliament until his descendant, John Beauchamp, was created, by Patent, Baron Beauchamp of Powyck, in 1447. This Walter de Beauchamp was, in the 24 Edw. I. Steward of the King's household, and attended him into Flanders in the 25th, and into Scotland in the 26th year of his reign: in the 28th Edw. I. he obtained a grant of free warren in all his demesne lands at Alcester, in the county of Warwick, as also at Powyck, and other places in Gloucestershire. From three documents printed in the edition of the Fœdera, published by order of the Record Commission in 1816 (Vol. 1. Part II. p. 944, et ante,) the first dated 30 Oct. 28 Edw. I. the second 12 July, 30 Edw. I. and the third 8 Oct. 30 Edw. I. it is certain that he was Seneschal to the King in those years, and, as it has just been observed, on the authority of Dugdale, that he held that office in the 24th Edw. I. it can scarcely be doubted that he was possessed of it when the Parliament met at Lincoln, the importance of which satisfactorily explains the cause of his being present in Parliament, and being considered as a Baron of the realm. In the Writ of Service, tested Stayvinagg, 26 Sept. 26 Edw. I. the names of the persons summoned are divided into two classes; against the first division the word "Comit'" occurs, and opposite to the second class is the word "Baron';" and in the latter list Walter de Beauchamp's name is inserted. This circumstance is deserving of some attention; for, with the exception of the "Conte Patrik," this Walter de Beauchamp, John Hoddelston (who, as it will be noticed hereafter, was also present in the Parliament at Lincoln), John de Cantilupe, Simon Fresel, and Richard Syward, every person, amounting altogether to one hundred and eighteen, whose name is inserted in that list, was regularly summoned to Parliament some time in that reign.

† Notwithstanding that he succeeded in 1274 to a Barony by Tenure, and was evidently a personage of considerable importance, he is not recorded to have been summoned to Parliament. He died in 1306, leaving Gilbert his son and heir, who was summoned to Parl. from 4 to 17 Edw. III.

‡ This Baron is not stated to have been summoned to Parliament until the 1st Edw. II. but during the greatest part of the

¶ Joh's Engayn, D'n's de Columb
¶ Hugo Pointz, D'n's de Corimalet
¶ Ad' D'n's de Welle
¶ Simon D'n's de Monte Acuto
¶ Joh'es D'n's de Sulleye
   Joh'o de Moeles, D'n's de Caudebir' *
¶ Edm'us Baro Staff'
¶ Joh's Lovel, D'n's de Dakkyng †
¶ Edmu's de Hasting' D'n's de Enchimeholmok
¶ Rad's fil' Will'i, D'n's de Grinthorp
¶ Rob'tus de Skales, D'n's de Neuseles
¶ Will'us Thouchet, D'n's de Levenbales
¶ Joh's ab Adam, D'n's de Bev'iston
   Joh's de Hav'ingges, D'n's de Grafton ‡

---

reign of Edw. I. he held some distinguished office : in 1294 he
was Admiral of the King's Fleet, and attended that monarch into
Gascoign, and into Scotland in 1297, 1298, 1299, and 1304.
From the 1st he was regularly summoned to the 18th of Edw. II.
in which year he died.

* John de Moels was summoned to Parliament the 25th and
27th of Edw. I. and 2d, 3d, and 4th Edw. II. though omitted
in the 28th of Edw. I.; like nearly every other Baron who was
in the Parliament at Lincoln, he was summoned to be at Carlisle, with horse and arms, on 24 June, 28 Edw. I.; and if he
obeyed the Writ, he was probably out of the kingdom when
the Writs for the Parliament to be held at Lincoln were issued;
but as this observation applies to the majority of those included in that Writ of Service, no deduction can be made therefrom, unless it be presumed either that few actually assembled at
Carlisle on the day appointed, and that they who did so were
those whose names were omitted; or that all, excepting the persons not summoned on the 26 Sept. 28 Edw. I. returned before
the issuing of the said Writs.

† He was summoned to this Parliament as John Lovel of
Tichmersh; but Dugdale states that he died seized of certain
lands in *Docking,* in Norfolk, which probably were those of
which he described himself as Lord.

‡ There is considerable difficulty in identifying this Baron.   In
the 27th of Edw. I. two Writs of Summons to Parliament were
issued to a *John de Hav'ing',* and to this very Parliament, as well
as to that immediately preceding, it appears that among the Judges

¶ Rob'tus la Warde, D'n's de Alba Aula
¶ Nich's de Seg'ave, D'n's de Stowe *

---

and Clerks of the Council, a " John de Hav'ing'," who is described
as Joh'i de Hav'ing, Justic' Northwall," was summoned.—
Among the Barons to whom Writs were issued on this occasion,
was a *John de Clavering*, but who was not *present* at Lincoln,
and some writers have considered that the name of *Havering* was
erroneously placed on the Rolls of 27 Edw. I. for Clavering,
from the circumstance of a John de *Clavering* having been
summoned from 10 April, 28 Edw. I. to 5 April, 5 Edw. III.
In two records printed in the Fœdera, the name of John de
Havering occurs; the first is dated in the 25th Edw. I. in which
he was appointed, among others Knights and Sheriffs, to inquire
into the cause of certain disturbances, and the department assigned him was " Norwales;" and in the second document alluded
to, dated 14 Dec. 26 Edw. I. he is addressed as Justice of North
Wales.   The arms on the seal of this Baron, as affixed to the
letter to the Pope, are decidedly different from those of the
family of Clavering, the former being a lion rampant, double
quevée, and the latter quarterly, Or and Gules, over all a bend
Sable; and which. fact confirms the opinion that the " *John de
Havering, Dominus de Grafton*," was a distinct person from *John
de Clavering* above mentioned; but the next questions which
present themselves are, was the individual summoned in the 27
Edw. I. and who, in the 28 Edw. I. was described as " Justic'
Northwall," and who unquestionably was the individual named in
the records just cited from the Fœdera, the same person? and if
not, which of them was the one who sat in the Parliament at
Lincoln?   These points it is almost impossible to decide, but
the facts just stated afford a sufficient explanation of the name of
a *John* de Havering appearing among the persons then present.
In the Rolls of the Parliament held at Westminster 30 Edw I. (vol.
I. p. 150.) a John de Havering, with William Inge, one of the
Judges, and others, are noticed in some proceedings relative to
William de Braos; and in the 33 Edw. I. a " Sire Johan de
Haveryng" was appointed, with the Bishop of Chester, the Earl
of Lincoln, and some other nobles, a *trier* of Petitions, and it is
highly probable that it was this John de Havering, who sat in
the Parliament at Lincoln.

    * Though summoned to this Parliament, and a party to the
letter, his seal was not affixed.

Walt'us de Teye, D'n's de Stangreve *
¶ Joh'es de Lisle, D'n's de Wodeton'
¶ Eustacbius D'n's de Hacch'
¶ Gilb'tus de Pecche, D'n's de Corby
Will's Paynel, D'n's de Fracyngtou †
¶ Bugo de Knovill, D'n's de Albo Monast'io
Fulco Lestrange, D'n's de Corsh'm ‡
Henr' de Pinkeny, D'n's de Wedon §

---

* He was summoned to Parliament from 27th Edw. I. to 1st
Edw. II. and though not summoned to this Parliament, he was
so to that immediately preceding it, viz. on the 29th Dec. 28
Edw. I. from which time he was not summoned to Parliament
until the 32d Edw. I. Dugdale does not mention his having
been so summoned, but states, that in the 27th, 28th, 31st, and
34th Edw. I. he was in the wars of Scotland, and died in 18
Edw. II.

† This Baron is not recorded to have been summoned to
Parliament until the 32d Edw. I. from which time he continued
to be summoned until the 9th Edw. II. and died in the following year. In the Rolls of Parliament, Vol. I. p. 146, this
William Paynell and Elizabeth his wife presented a petition in
Parliament for certain lands which belonged to her first husband; and in the proceedings on which is the following proof
that he was present in this Parliament: "Postea ad proximum
Parliamentum sequens, videlicet, ad Parliamentum ipsius Domini
Regis apud Linc', in octab' San'ti Hillar', anno regni sui vicesimo
nono, *venit predictus Will's,* et Margareta per attornatum suum
venit, &c."

‡ Fulk le Strange, here described as Lord of Corsham, was summoned to Parliament from the 2d to 18th Edw. II. In the 26th,
29th, and 34th Edw. I. he appears to have been in the wars of
Scotland; and though not summoned to this or to any previous
Parliament, he was evidently a personage of importance.

§ He was summoned to Parliament the 25th and 27th Edw. I.
and to the Parliament immediately preceding that which was held
at Lincoln, to which however he was not summoned: seven
months after he was present in that assembly he surrendered
his lands to the King, after which surrender he was never summoned to Parliament, nor is there any thing farther recorded of
him by Dugdale.

Joh's de Hodelleston, D'n's de Aneys *
Rog'us de Huntingfeld, D'n's de Bradinham †
Hugo fil. Henr', D'n's de Ravenewath ‡
Joh's le Breton, D'n's de Sporle §

---

* That this John de Hodelleston, though never summoned to Parliament, ranked among the Barons of his time, is manifest from his having been so described in the Writ of Service tested 26 Edw. I. and which is cited in a note to p. 767. Mr. Banks, in his Stemmata Anglicana, asserts that he was Lord of Aneys in Cumberland, and that he died unmarried.

† He was a Baron by tenure, and was summoned in the 22d and 25th Edw. I. but it is somewhat doubtful if either of these assemblies was a regular Parliament. Vide notes under CLYVEDON and FITZ-JOHN, pp. 141 & 242. No other Summons to Parliament appears to have been issued to him, and he died in 1801.

‡ Hugh Fitz-Henry was a Baron by Tenure, and the father of Henry 1st Baron Fitz-Hugh. He appears to have been summoned in the 22 Edw. I. to the Council noticed under "CLYVEDON;" but on no other occasion was he ever summoned to Parliament.

§ Lord of Sporle in Norfolk; of this name was John le Breton, who was appointed a Puisne Judge of the Common Pleas in 1269, and was removed to the same situation in the Court of King's Bench in November in the same year; and John Breton, who was consecrated Bishop of Hereford 3 June, 1269, and died in 1275. The Fœdera contains an Ordinance, dated in the 30th of Edw. I. by which a John le Breton and the Sheriff of Norfolk were appointed to levy the aid for the marriage of the King's eldest daughter in that county; and in the Rolls of Parliament Vol. I. p. 218, is another Ordinance of the King, dated 18 Feb. 35 Edw. I. 1307, appointing a John le Breton, with a Judge, and three other persons, on a judicial commission in the counties of Norfolk and Surrey. As two of these persons, if not the third, were considerable landholders in those counties, it is extremely probable that this John le Breton was the same person who was appointed to levy the aid in the 30 Edw. I., and that he styled himself " Dominus de Sporle" in the letter to the Pope. In the 1st of Edw. II. the name of John le Bretton, and who apparently was the same individual, occurs among the Judges and Clerks of the Council summoned to Parliament in that year, and on this authority Bishop Nicholson not only considers him to have been a Judge, but the author of the well known legal treatise entitled " Bretton." In the List of Judges, &c. in Chronica Juridicialia, only one John

Nicb's de Carru D'nus de Muleford *
¶ Thome D'n's de la Roche
¶ Walt'us de Moncy, D'n's de Thornton
Joh's fil' Mermeduci, D'n's de Hordene†

---

le Breton occurs, who certainly might be living in 1308; for
allowing him to have been thirty when appointed in 1269, he
would not then have been above seventy years of age. If, however, John le Breton, who was so appointed in 1269, lived until
1308, it is very singular that his name is not to be found in any
Writ *before* that year; he was only so summoned in the four
following Writs, the last of which was tested 10 March, 2 Edw.
II. 1309. The arms with which John le Breton, Dominus de
Sporle, sealed, were, quarterly, within a bordure; but it is
somewhat doubtful whether he was the same personage who was
summoned in the 1st and 2d of Edw. II. among the Judges, &c. and
still more so whether he was the individual who was appointed a
Justice of the Common Pleas in 1269, and who was shortly afterwards removed to the King's Bench. It should also be noticed,
that a "John le Bretun," or le Breton, was Mayor of London
in the 25th Edw. I.; though it is scarcely possible that he could
have been the individual in question.

* Nicholas de Carew was never summoned to Parliament,
though frequently included in Writs of Service after this period.
He was unquestionably a person of much consequence, and died in
1308, leaving issue; but none of his descendants enjoyed the
dignity of the Peerage, until George Carew was created Baron
Carew of Clopton, in 1625. There does not appear to be any
cause to which his being present in this Parliament can be attributed, unless he was then a Knight of the Shire.

† This personage, from the local description added to his
name, as well as from the arms on his seal, was evidently Marmaduke de Thweng. Dugdale states, that *his father*, Marmaduke
de Thweng, was summoned in the 22 Edw. I. and that he left two
sons, viz. Robert the eldest, who died s. p. m. and this Baron.
He was summoned to Parliament from the 35th Edw. I. to the
18th Edw. II.: in the 25th, 29th, and 32d Edw. I. he was in
the wars of Scotland, and particularly distinguished himself at
the battle of Strivelyn. On his death, in 1323, he was succeeded
by his son William, who was summoned to Parliament 18 Edw. II.
but never afterwards, and died s. p.

Joh's D'n's Kyngeston *
Rob'tus Hastang, D'n's de la Desiree †
Radulphus D'n's de Grendon ‡
Will's D'nus de Leyburne
Joh's de Greystok, D'n's Morpath §

---

* Banks, in his Stemmata Anglicana, conjectures, with much
probability, that this Baron was the same person as the John de
Kingeston, who, as a Knight Banneret, had an allowance for
Robes in the 28th Edw. I. and who in the 33 Edw. I. was appointed one of the Custodes of the Kingdom of Scotland, and
who, according to the Rolls of Parliament in that year, vol. I.
p. 268, was constituted Constable and Keeper of the Castle of
Edinburgh; but it appears that he filled that situation some time
before; for in a letter printed in the last edition of the Fœdera,
vol. I. part II. p. 934, dated 12 May, 29 Edw. I. 1301, he was
then addressed as Constable of the Castle of Edinburgh. These circumstances prove him to have been of considerable importance,
and his presence at the Parliament at Lincoln possibly arose from
his official situation.

† The only Writ of Summons to Parliament which is on
record as having been issued to this Baron, is tested 19 Dec. 5
Edw. II. Dugdale's account of him is very unsatisfactory;
for he merely informs us, that his father, Robert Hastang, was
living in the 49th Hen. III.; that this Robert was his successor
(but he does not state in what year), and that he was summoned
to Parliament in the 5th Edw. II. Banks repeats this statement,
but adds, that in the 2d Edw. I. he was one of the Justices for
Goal Delivery at Warwick.

‡ This Baron, though not summoned to the Parliament at
Lincoln, was however (for the first time) summoned to the Parliament which immediately preceeded it, viz. on the 29th Dec.
28 Edw. I. 1299; he was not again summoned till the 32d Edw.
I. and notwithstanding that he lived until the year 1321, he was
never afterwards summoned to Parliament.

§ John de Greystock was summoned to most Parliaments
between the 24th and 33d Edw. I. and although he was omitted
in the Writ to the Parliament at Lincoln, he was included in that
to the previous Parliament which assembled in London. He
was not summoned in the 30th or 31st; but his name again
occurs in the Writs of the 32d of Edw. I.

Matt's fil. Joh'is, D'n's de Stokeham *
Nich's de Meynhyl, D'n's de Wherleton †, &
¶ Joh's Paynel, D'n's de Otteleye.

devota pedu' oscula beator'. S'c'a Romana Mat' Ecc'a,
p' cuj' minist'ium fides catholica gub'natur in suis act:!',
eum ea, sicut firmit' credim' et tenem', mat'itate p'·· d.:
q'd nulli p'judicare s', singulo' jura non minus in al''s
q' in se ip'a tanq' mat' alma cons'vari velit illesa, sane
co'vocato nup' p' serenissimu' d'n'm n'r'm Edwardum Dei

---

* The only Writ on record to this Baron which can ve
deemed a Writ of Summons to Parliament, is that of the 25th
Edw. I. on which some remarks are submitted in p. 242, et seq.
Dugdale, vol. I. p. 625, states, that in the 16 Edw. I. he was
Governor of the Castle of Exeter, and in that year, as well as 22d
Edw. I. Sheriff of Devonshire. In the 29th Edw. I. the custody
of the Forests of Melkesham and Chippeham, which had been
seized into the King's hands, were restored to him, he having
been Warden of them as pertaining to the Castle of Devizes;
from which it appears, that about the period in question he was
Governor of that place. From these facts it is evident, that in
the very year in which he was present in the Parliament at Lincoln, he was possessed of the King's favour, and was in the
exercise of an office of great trust and importance; circumstances which, when the uncertainty of proof as to what at that
time constituted a right to a seat in Parliament be considered,
may be deemed as sufficiently explanatory of his presence on that
occasion.

† This Nicholas de Meynill appears to have been the natural
son of a Baron of the same name, who was summoned to Parlia-
ment from the 23d to 27th Edw. I. and died in that year s. p. l.
The Nicholas de Meynill who was present at the Parliament at
Lincoln, succeeded, in consequence of a settlement, to divers
lands of his putative father, of which the manor of Wherleton or
Quereleton, in the county of York, formed part. In the 28th
Edw. I. he was in the wars of Scotland, and again in the 34th Edw.
I. and 4 Edw. II. and was not summoned to Parliament until the
6th Edw. II. from which year he continued to be summoned until
the 15th of that reign, when he died s. p. No cause presents
itself to which his being present as a Baron in this Parliament
can be attributed.

gr'a regem Angl' illustrem p'liamento apud Lincoln' g'n'ali,
item D'n's n'r quasdam l'ras ap'licas quas sup' c'tis
negociis condic'onem & statum regni Scoc' tangent' ex
p'te v'ra recep'at, in medio exhiberi et seriose fecit nob'
exponi; quibus auditis & diligencius intellectis tam n'ris
sensib' admiranda q' hacten' inaudita in eisdem audivim'
contin'i. Scim' eni' pat' s'c'issime et notorium est in
p'tib' Angl' & nonnullis aliis non ignotum q'd a
prima insti'c'oe regni Angl', reges ej'd' regni tam
temp'ib' Brettonu' q' Anglo' sup'ius & directum d'nium
regni Scoc' h'uerunt & in possessionem vel q'si sup'io-
ritatis & directi d'nii ip'ius regni Scoc' successivis tem-
p'ib's extit'unt. Nec ullis temp'ib's ip'm regnu' in tem-
p'ib's p'tinuit v'l p'tinet quovis jure ad ecc'm sup'd'c'am,
quinimo idem regnum Scoc' p'genitorib' p'd'ci d'm'ni
n'ri regib' Angl' atq' sibi feodale extit't ab antiquo.
Nec eciam reges Scoto' et regnum alii' q' regib' Angl'
s'bfuerunt vel subj'ci consuev'unt; neq' reges Angl' sup'
jurib' suis in regno p'd'c'o aut aliis suis temp' alib' cor'
aliquo judice ecc'astico v'l seculari, ex lib'ra p'minencia
status sue regie & dignitatis & consuetudinis cunctis
temp'ib' irref'gabil'r obs'vate, responderunt aut respondere
debebant. Unde, h'ito t'actatu & delib'ac'one diligenti
sup' contentis in v'ris li'ris memoratis, is concors &
unanimis o'nium n'r'm & singulor' consensus fuit est & erit
inconcusse Deo p'pitio in futurum q'd p'fatus d'n's n'r
rex sup' jurib' regni sui Scoc' aut aliis suis temp'alib'
nullaten' judicialit' respondeat coram vob' nec jud'm
subeat quoquomodo aut jura sua p'd'c'a in dubiu' ip'ius
deducat nec ad p'sent' v'ram p'cur' aut nunc' ad hoc
mittat. Precipue cum p'missa cederent manifeste in
exh'ed'ac'om juris corone regni Angl' & regie dignitatis
ac subv'sione' status ejusdem regni notoriam n'non in
p'judicium lib'tatum consuetudinu' & legum pat'na' ad
qua' obs'vac'onem & defensionem ex debito p'stiti jura-
menti astringimur &● que manutenebim' toto posse
totisq' virib' cum Dei auxilio defendem'. Nec etiam
p'mittim' aut aliq'ten' p'mittem' sicut nec possum' nec
debem' p'missa tam insolita indebita p'judicialia & alias
inaudita p'libatu' d'm'm n'r'm regem eciam si vellet fac'e
seu quomodolibet attemptare. Quocirca sanctitati v'r'
reve'nt' & humilit' supplicam' q'ten' eund'm d'n'm

a'r'm regem qui int' alios p'cipes orbis t're catholicu' se
exhibet & ecc'e Romane devotu' jura sua lib'tates con-
suetudi'es & leges p'd'ca' absq' diminuc'one & inquietu-
dine pacifice possidere & ea illibata p'sist'e benigne
p'mittat'. In cujus rei testimoniu' sigilla n'ra tam p'
nob' q' p' tota com'unitate p'd'c'i regni Angl' p'sentib'
sunt appensa. Dat' apud Lincoln' xij die Febr' anno d'ni
M°.CCC°. *

The following Peers were summoned to the Parliament
which met at Lincoln, but their names do not occur among
the persons mentioned in the preceding Letter†.

Robert de Vere, Earl of Ox- ford	John de Ferrers
	John de la Mare
Gilbert, Earl of Angos	Hugh de Courtenay

---

* 1300-1, 29 Edw. I. This copy is taken from that printed
in the Appendix to the first Report of the Lords' Committees
on the dignity of a Peer of the Realm.

† A List of the Barons who were summoned to this Parliament, but who did not attend, as well as of those whose seals
are affixed to the preceding Letter, but who were not summoned
on that occasion, is given in Dugdale's List of Summonses, and
reprinted in the Appendix to the first Report of the Lords'
Committees on the dignity of a Peer of the Realm, with the observation, that " the *original* is not now to be found." The Lists
in the text have been made from a careful collation of the Writs,
with the signatures given to the Letter, as printed in the said
Appendix, for, as the Committees have remarked, in p. 127 of
their first and second report, Dugdale's lists are very erroneous.
For the following reason it appears, however, that he compiled them,
and consequently that no original besides his own manuscript ever
existed : in the list of the names of Barons who sealed the Letter,
as given by Dugdale, that of Roger Bigod, Earl of Norfolk and
Earl Marshal, is omitted ; and we accordingly find, that in his
list of persons summoned, but who did not seal is the name of
that Earl. It is presumed, from Dugdale's citing the original

John de St. John de Lage-
  ham *
Peter de Chaumpvent
Ralph Basset, of Drayton
Alexander de Baliol
William de Ryther
John de Clavering

William de Grandison
Philip Darcy
Thomas le Latimer
William le Vavasour
Elias Daubeney
Andrew de Astley.

The seals of the following persons are affixed to the said Letter, but neither of them were summoned to that Parliament.

Henry de Grey of Codnor
William de Roos
Peter de Malolacu
Theobald de Verdon
John de St. John
Ralph de Nevill
Roger le Strange
Thomas de Chaworth
John de Moeles

John de Haveringes.
Walter de Teyes
Henry de Pinkney
‖ § Roger de Huntingfield
‖ Hugh Fitz Henry
Ralph de Grendon
John de Greystock
§ Matthew Fitz John.

All of the above Barons, though there is no record of either of them having been summoned to the Parliament at Lincoln, were summoned to previous, and the greatest part of them also to subsequent Parliaments. Those whose names are printed in Italics, were summoned to the Parliament *immediately* preceding, and to whom, if the Parliament at Lincoln was an *adjourned Parliament*, it was not necessary that Writs should have been issued to enable them to attend on that occasion. The only Writ on record to the Barons with this mark ‖, is the doubtful one of the 22d Edw. I. and to those thus marked §, that of the 25th Edw. I. Vide "CLYVEDON" and "FITZ-JOHN," pp. 141 and 242.

---

in the Chapter House, that his copy was taken therefrom; if so, the error in the omission of the Earl of Norfolk, as well as several mistakes in the Letter itself, arose either from the carelessness of the transcriber or compositor.

* There is, however, some doubt whether this John de St. John was summoned to this Parliament or not. Vide note ‖, p. 768; but, in the following list, he is considered *not* to have been so.

There is no record of either of the following personages having been summoned to Parliament, until some years after, they were present in the Parliament at Lincoln, in 29 Edw. I.

William Marshall	Fulk le Strange
Henry Tregoz	John Fitz Marmaduke
John Botetourt	Robert Hastang
William Paynel	Nicholas de Meynill.

It does not appear that either of the following persons were ever summoned to Parliament as a Peer of the realm.

Walter de Beauchamp	John le Breton
Richard Talbot	Nicholas Carew
John de Hodeleston	John de Kingeston.

The Seals of the following Barons were not affixed to the Letter when the copy of it was taken by command of Thomas Earl of Arundel in 1629, though they are named as parties to it, and all of them were summoned to the Parliament at Lincoln.

Robert Fitz Roger	John Engagne
Roger la Warre	John ap Adam
John de Ripariis	Nicholas de Segrave
Ralph Pipard	John de l'Isle.

Although the battle of Falkirk had nearly subjected Scotland to the power of King Edward the First, the native courage of its inhabitants was far from subdued ; but, sensible of the weakness of their own forces, they sought for assistance from foreign courts. Their applications were, however, little attended to by any other sovereign than the reigning Pontiff, Pope Boniface the Eighth, who eagerly embraced that opportunity to exert his authority ; and on the 5th of the Kalends of June, in the fifth year of his pontificate, he issued a Bull, directed to Edward, in which, after stating numerous arguments against the claim which that Monarch had urged to Scotland, he concluded by asserting that he himself was the liege lord of that kingdom ! *

---

* Printed in the Fœdera, Edit. 1816, vol. I. part II. p. 907-8.

This claim, though never before heard of, was urged in too confident a manner not to receive the utmost attention: Edward consequently summoned a Parliament to meet at Lincoln, for the consideration of the question, and in which the letter which is the subject of these remarks, is said to have been written. In order the more satisfactorily to investigate the point, it is necessary, in the first instance, to examine what positive evidence is extant that the Parliament in which the letter is said to have been dated was then assembled, and still more, what proof exists that one of the objects, if not the sole object, for which it was convened, was the discussion of the pretensions urged by Boniface to the kingdom of Scotland. On this point the evidence which will be cited is, it is confidently presumed, complete, and such as, from the remoteness of the period when the transaction took place, could scarcely have been expected. As Pope Boniface's Bull was dated 5th of the Kalends June (28 May), in the Vth year of his Pontificate, and as he is generally stated to have attained that dignity on the 24th December, 1294, it would appear, according to the calculation adopted relative to the years of the reigns of the Kings of England, that the 5th year of his Pontificate was in 1299; though Lord Hailes * expressly states that Rymer, in assigning that year as the date of the Bull, had committed a mistake. If the Bull was dated on the 28 May, 1299, it can scarcely be explained why Edward deferred summoning a Parliament to take it into consideration until the 26th of September in the *following* year: this circumstance, therefore, strengthens the observation of Lord Hailes; and the actual date of the Bull was, in all probability, the 28 May, 1300, which would allow three months for its dispatch from Rome, and for the discussion by the King and his council, as to the measures to be adopted in consequence of its receipt; and which appear to have terminated in a resolution to submit the important document to the legislative assembly of the nation.

On the 26th of September, 1300, 28 Edw. I. we accord-

---

* Annals of Scotland, cited by Dr. Lingard in his valuable History of the Reign of Edw. I.

ingly find that Writs were issued to the Spiritual and
Temporal Peers usually summoned, to attend a Parliament
at Lincoln in the Octaves of St. Hillary next ensuing.
These Writs were tested at "La Rose;" and although
no evidence is to be found in them bearing on the subject of the Pontiff's Bull, a copy of them is perhaps necessary
in this place.

"R.' ven'abili in xp'o R.' eadem gr'a archiep'o
Cantuar' tocius Angl' primati sal't'm. Cum nup' p' eo
utilitate pop'li regni n'ri concesserim' q'd carta de foresta
in sing'lis suis artic'lis firmit' observaret'r assignando
quosdam de fidelib' n'ris in sing'lis com' ejusdem regni
in quib' foreste n're existunt ad p'ambulaco'em in
eisdem forestis faciendam. Ita q'd p'ambulaco'em illam
distincte & ap'te f'cam ad nos anteq'a' aliqua execucio
vel aliquid aliud inde fieret rep'tarent et q'd jura-
mentu' n'r'm jus corone Angl' ro'nes & calumpnie
n're nec jus ro'nes & calumpnie alio' om'i' salva forent.
Nos, licet d'ci fideles n'ri [nu'c] p'mo ad nos detulerint
quod fecer[u]'t in negocio memora[to], quia tamen prelati,
comites, barones, & cet'i magnate[s] d'ci regni in quor'
p'sentia n'ras & alior' p'poni & audi[ri] volum' ro'nes & de
quo' consilio in eodem negocio p'ut alia[s] dixim' intendim'
op'ari: maxime cu' ip'i ad observand' & manutenend'
jura regni & corone p'd'ce una nob'cum [j]uramenti vin-
culo sint ast'cti juxta latus n'r'm tu'c tempo[re]... ne' fuer[i]'t
ac p' eo similit' q'd illi qui suas r'ones q'a[s]... illud negociu' eos tangit p'pon'e h'ebant inde p'mu[...] no' era't
eidem negocio sine ip'o' conailio finem i[...]pon'e non
potuim' bono modo: et quia negociu' il[...]d q'ntum
possum' cupim' maturari, ita q'd p' nos no'[...]et, quia
absq' ult'ioris dil' onis incom'odu eff'o'm debita[...] sereiat'r
volentes cu' prelatis, comitib', baronib', & [...] agnatib'
sup'd'cis, ac aliis de co'itate d'ci regni sup' h[...] quib'-
dam aliis arduis negociis, nos & statu' regni [...] ci tan-
gentib' h'ere colloquiu' & t'actata'; vob' mandat[...] n fide &
dilecc'o'e quib's nob' tenemini firmit' injungent [...] q'd sitis
ad nos ad p'liamentu' n'r'm apud Lincoln' in [...] b' S'e'i
Hillar' p'xi'o futur', nob'um ibidem unà cu' [...] is prelatis & p'cerib' p'd'c'is sup' p'missis t'ctaturi [...] aq' consiliu' impensuri. Et hoc sicut nos & co'modu' [...] p'd'c'i

diligitis nullaten' omittatis. T. R'. apud la Rose, xxvi die Septembr' *.

"Consimiles l're dirigunt'r T. Archiep'o Ebor' Angl'. primati, & ep'is & abbatib' subsc'ptis, videl't : &c.

To the Earls and Barons the following Writ was issued.

"R. dil'co & fideli suo Joh'i de Warenna comiti Surr' sal't'm. Cum nup' p' c'oi utilitate &c. (ut sup'a usq' ibi'.) Vob mandam' in fide & homagio quib' nob' tenemini firmit' injungentes, q'd sitis ad nos ad p'liamentu' n'r'm apud Lincoln' in octab' S'c'i Hillar' p'xi'o futur' nob'cum ibidem una cu' prelatis & p'cerib' p'd'cis sup' p'missis tractaturi v'r'mq' consiliu' impensuri. Et hoc sicut nos & co'modu' regni p'd'c'i diligitis nullaten' omittatis. T.R. apud la Rose xxvi die Septembr'.

"Consimiles l're dirigunt'r comitib', baronib', & militib' subsc'iptis, videl't," &c. †

Writs of a similar tendency were likewise issued to the the Bishops, and Abbots; to nine Earls, and eighty Barons, to the Sheriffs of Cumberland and of thirty-five other counties, commanding each Sheriff to return the *same* Knights from each county, the *same* citizens from each city, and from each borough the *same* burgesses, "qui ad p'd'c'm p'liamentu' n'r'm alias sic venerunt," to the Parliament to be held at the same time and place ‡.

In these Writs no mention is made of the subject of Pope Boniface's Bull, nor is any inference to be drawn therefrom that it was to form the subject of deliberation by the Parliament which they were commanded to attend; but the following Writs most clearly establish that that Parliament was summoned for the express purpose of canvassing the question. The first here cited is to the Clerks of the Council, who on former occasions were summoned by Writs similar to those issued to the Judges.

"R. dil'co cl'ico suo mag'ro Reginaldo de Braundon sal't'm. Quia sup' jure & d'nio que nob' in regno Scocie competu't & que antecessores n'ri reges Angl' in eodem regno Scocie h'uerunt temporib' retroactis cu' jurisp'itis & cet'is de consilio n'ro sp'ale colloquiu' h'ere volum' & t'actatu'; vob' mandam' firmit' injungentes q'd modis omnib' sitis ad nos apud Lincoln' in Octab' S'ci Hillar'

---

* Appendix to I. & II. Peerage Reports, p. 122.
† Ibid. p. 123.   ‡ Ibid.

p'ximo futur' nob'cum & cn' cet'is de consillo n'ro sup'
p'missis t'actaturi v'r'mq' consiliu' impensuri. Et hæc, sicut
nos & honore' ac co'modu' regni n'ri diligitis, nullaten'
omittatis. T. R. apud la Rose xxvi die Septembr'.

Consimiles l're dir' subscriptis, videl't,

The Dean of Chichester, the Dean of St. Paul's, Mag'ro
de Sandene, offic' Cantuar', the Archdeacon of Chester, the
Dean of Wells, the Dean of Litchfield, the Archdeacon of
the East Riding of Yorkshire, Magistro Pho' Martel,
Mag'ro Will'o de Pykering, and to six other persons simi-
larly described *.

The Writs to the Judges were in the usual words: but as
a proof of the care taken to have the attendance not only
of learned men at the deliberation, but also that every
document in the kingdom likely to contain information on
the subject to be there discussed, should be produced,
Writs bearing the same test, of which copies are subjoined,
were likewise issued to each University, commanding
them to send from two to five persons " de discretorib' &
in jure scripto magis exp'tis univ'sitatis p'd'ce," to the
Parliament at Lincoln; and to all the Abbeys and Convents, and other repositories of manuscripts in the realm,
commanding that all chronicles and archives which in any
degree related to the kingdom of Scotland, should be sent
to the Parliament at Lincoln in the octaves of St. Hillary.

The following is a copy of the Writ to the Chancellor
and University of Oxford:—

" Rex dilectis sibi in Christo Cancellario & Universitati
Oxon' salutem.

" Quia super jure & dominio que nobis in Regno Scocie
competunt, & que antecessores nostri Reges Anglie in
eodem regni Scocie habuerunt temporibus retroactis, cum
jurisperitis & ceteris de consilio nostro speciale colloquium
habere volumus & tractatum; Vobis mandamus firmiter
injungentes, quod quatuor vel quinque de discretoribus
& in jure scripto magis expertis universitatis predicte, ad
Parliamentum nostrum apud Lincoln' mittatis; ita quod
sint ibidem in octabis Sancti Hillarii proximò futuris ad
ultimum, nobiscum & cum ceteris de consilio nostro super
premissis tractaturi, suumque consilium impensuri. Et
hoc, sicut nos & honorem ac commodum regni nostri dili-

---

* Appendix to I. & II. Peerage Reports, p. 124.

gitis, nullatenus omittatis. T. R'. apud la Rose xxvi die Septembris *."

The Writ of the same date, to the Chancellor and University of Cambridge, commanded them, in similar terms, to send to the said Parliament " duos vel tres de discrecioribus & magis in jure scripto expertis *."

The Writs to the different Convents and Abbey were in the following words:

" Rex dilectis sibi in Christo Abbati & Conventui Westm' salutem.

" Quia super jure & dominio que nobis in regno Scocie competunt, & que antecessores nostri Reges Anglie in eodem regno Scocie habuerunt temporious retroactis, cum jurisperitis & ceteris de concilio nostro, speciale colloquium habere volumus & tractatum; Vobis mandamus firmiter injungentes, quod scrutatis diligenter omnibus cronicis, archivis, & secretis domûs vestre, quicquid invenire poteritis, quod tangat dictum regnum Scocie quoquo modo; nobis ad Parliamentum apud Lincoln' in octabis Sancti Hillarii proximo futuris, per aliquem de vestris, de quo confidenciam habueritis, & qui in hujusmodi negocio majorem noticiam habuerit, transmittatis. Et hoc, sicut nos & honorem ac commodum regni nostri diligitis, nullatenus omittatis. T. R. apud la Rose, xxvi die Septembris †."

Similar letters were sent to,

The Abbot of Waltham	Abbot of Bardenaye
———— St. Augustine's,	——— Barlings
Canterbury	——— St. Peter of Gloucester
The Prior & Convent of the Church of Christ's Church	——— Furneys
The Abbot of St. Edmond's	——— Holmcoltram
———— St. Alban's	——— Cirencester
———— Evesham	——— Jervault
———— St. Wergburge, Chester	——— Fontibus
	——— Reading
Prior & Convent, Durham	——— Glastonbury
———— Carlisle	——— Wynchecumbe
Abbot of Malmesbury	——— Ramesey
Prior & Convent of Rochester	——— St. Mary of York

* Fœdera, Edition 1816, vol. I. part II. p. 924, and Appendix to I. & II. Peerage Report, p. 125, from rot. claus. 28 Edw. I.

† Fœdera, Edition 1816, vol. I. part II.

Abbot of St. Peter	Abbot of Thorney
————— St. Augustine's,	Prior & Convent of St.
Bristol	Swithin, Winchester.

Also to the

Dean and Chapter of the Church of St. Paul, London
————————————————— St. Mary, Sarum
————————————————— Chichester

Dean & Bishop of Exeter	Prior & Convent of Norwich
————————— Wells	Dean and Chapter of York
Prior & Convent of Bath	Abbot & Convent of Oseneie
Dean & Chapter of Hereford	————————— of Abing-
Prior & Convent of Coventry	don
Dean & Chapter of Litchfield	————————— Alnwyck
————————— Lincoln	————————— New Min-
Prior & Convent of Ely	ster.

These Writs must, it is presumed, be deemed satisfactory
evidence that the Pope's pretensions to Scotland, was to
form the chief object for which the Parliament at Lincoln
was to be assembled; and from the unusual, and as far
as records are extant, unprecedented Writs to the Abbeys
and Universities, it is no less manifest that extraordinary
pains were taken that the subject should be investigated
with the aid of all the muniments and learning which the
kingdom afforded.

From the defective state of the Rolls of Parliament no
account is preserved of the proceedings in Parliament on
this affair, for, excepting a notice * of two proceedings in
the Parliament held at Lincoln in the octaves of St. Hillary, 29 Edw. I. no other record of this Parliament is to be
found on the Rolls. These notices, however, are additional
proofs that the Parliament summoned by the Writs tested
26 Sept. 28 Edw. I. actually assembled; but the only evidence of the result of its deliberations relative to Boniface's
claim, is the letter from the Barons to that Pontiff, which
is the subject of these remarks : and however extraordinary this fact may appear, when contrasted with the manner in which the proceedings of some subsequent Parliaments are recorded, other instances may be adduced to
prove that this omission is by no means a solitary one. It

---

* Rot. Parl. vol. I. p. 145.

is impossible to imagine that the Parliament which sat at Lincoln transacted no other business than what is noticed on the Rolls in that year; and it is no less incredible that the important and extensive preparations made in September, to be discussed by the Parliament at Lincoln early in the February following, were totally abandoned when that Parliament assembled. But these inferences must be drawn, if no other evidence is admitted of the proceedings of that Parliament, than the imperfect record on the Rolls.

It may here be observed, that besides the answer returned to Pope Boniface's claim by the Barons, King Edward himself, shortly after the date of that document, addressed his Holiness in a very long letter, a copy of which is also printed in the Fœdera, in which he entered more fully into the question at issue between them; and from which, as a judicious historian * has well remarked, it would appear, that though, as a judge, neither he nor the nation would admit of his interference in any transaction relating to this kingdom, yet as a friend he willingly offered him every possible explanation.

Having stated what evidence is extant that the Parliament, in which the letter of the Barons is supposed to have been written, was duly summoned, as well as what proofs can be adduced that the subject on which that letter treats, formed part of the deliberations on that occasion; and having, it is hoped, established the fact, that the Parliament was expressly summoned for the discussion of that very subject, it is now necessary to allude to the contents of the letter itself, the persons by whom it was signed, and, in short, to inquire what internal evidence of authenticity it contains. The internal evidence of the document which will be noticed in this part of these remarks, are, the contents of the letter, and the names of the persons whose seals were attached to it. The letter is dated at Lincoln, on the 12th of February, 1300 †, and the Parliament was ordered to assemble in the octaves of St. Hillary, next ensuing to the 26 September, 28 Edw. I. that is to say, within eight days after the feast of St. Hillary,

---

* Dr. Lingard.   † 1300-1.

the 13th of the following January. If the Parliament met on the first day of the eight within which it was commanded to assemble, twenty-eight days elapsed before the letter was written; but if, as is more likely, it did not commence business until the last day of the octaves of St. Hillary, only twenty-one days elapsed before the Barons expressed the result of their deliberation on Boniface's pretensions, in the letter addressed to him. Either of these periods is what would probably occur before the subject could be determined; hence the date of the letter strongly corroborates its authenticity. The Barons express in firm language the validity of Edward's claim, and consequently the fallacy of that urged by Boniface; and whilst they adduce arguments in support of their Sovereign's right, they take care to assure the Pontiff that they did not mean thereby to acknowledge him as their judge; and conclude by asserting that the crown of England was free and sovereign; that they had sworn to maintain its prerogatives; and that they would not consent that the King himself, were he willing, should relinquish its independency. These sentiments are such as the historians of the times have on numerous occasions imputed to the Baronage of this country, and several instances might be cited in which their conduct was strictly in unison with the resolutions contained in their letter on that occasion. It is thus certain, that no inference against the authenticity of the letter is to be drawn from its contents, whilst a very strong one in support of it is supplied by the fact that not one of the Spiritual Peers, all of whom were summoned to the Parliament at Lincoln, appear as parties to it. This circumstance may, without hesitation, be imputed to the determination so strongly expressed by the Barons to keep the kingdom entirely independent of the Holy See in secular affairs; for though the letter is couched in language consonant to the respect which, as faithful sons of the church, they owed, and probably felt, to the Pontiff, still the general tenor of its contents was too rebellious to his will for it to obtain the avowed approbation of any member of the clerical body. The letter is therefore sealed only by the Temporal Peers who were then present in Parliament, not only as their sentiments, but likewise as the sentiments of the whole community of England; and it now becomes requisite to inquire by what right the per-

sons who appear as parties to that instrument, sat in the
Parliament in which the affair was transacted. It has been
already observed that *nine* Earls and *eighty* Barons were,
by the Writs tested on the 26th of September, 28 Edw. 1.
1300, commanded to attend a Parliament to be held at
Lincoln in the octaves of the feast of St. Hillary next
ensuing, although *seven* Earls and *ninety-six* Barons (or
rather *ninety-six* to whose names the word " *Dominus*" is
appended,) are recorded as parties to the letter to the
Pope. Of the *nine* Earls and *eighty* Barons summoned, it
appears either that *two* Earls and *fifteen* Barons declined
becoming parties to that document, or, which is much
more likely, that they did not attend that Parliament:
thus the letter appears as the act of only *seven* of the Earls
and *sixty-five* of the Barons who were duly summoned to
the Parliament at Lincoln. *Thirty-one* persons, therefore,
were parties to the letter who are not recorded to have
been duly authorised to be present on that occasion: of
this number *eighteen* had been summoned to former, and
many of them likewise to subsequent Parliaments; *eight*
are not recorded to have been summoned to Parliament
until some years after the date of the letter to the Pope;
and *six* do not appear ever to have received a Writ of
Summons to Parliament. On these *six* some remarks will
be offered, but it must first be observed, that the eighteen
persons who, though not summoned to the Parliament at
Lincoln, had on former occasions received Writs to Parliament, were, at the time when the letter was written,
undoubtedly, even according to the acceptation of the word
at the present day, BARONS of the realm. The cause of
their names not appearing in the Writs tested 26 September
cannot satisfactorily be explained, but it is obvious that
omissions of this sort were by no means uncommon; and
three reasons may be submitted why names which occur in
Writs to Parliament are not to be found in subsequent
Writs, or if they are to be found in some subsequent Writ,
why an interval of greater or less time occured in the
issuing of such Writs; though in the case in question the
omission may be imputed to a different cause, and which
will afterwards be stated.

The first cause to which omissions of this nature may be
imputed, is the defective state of records; for although most
of the names of persons to whom Writs were directed at the

general issuing of such Writs may be recorded, still Writs to individuals may afterwards have been sent, and of which either no record was made, or such record, from its being of a more isolated nature, and less likely to have been preserved, may not now be extant [*].

Secondly, persons who, though indubitably entitled to Writs to Parliament, may at the time when the general Writs were issued, have been absent from the kingdom, and it is in this case, or in cases of Summonses for the first time (now termed a new creation), that Writs to individuals are supposed to have been issued between the time when the Writs were generally issued and the meetings of Parliament.

Thirdly, the Will of the Sovereign; for it cannot be doubted that Writs of Summons, in the reign of Edward the First, and indeed in a few successive reigns, depended on the pleasure of the Crown, which, in numerous cases, suspended the issuing of Writs to persons summoned to former Parliaments; and in many instances Writs, though issued to a person for several years, were never again issued to him or to his posterity.

If either of these causes apply to the eighteen Barons here alluded to, the first is the most probable one; but it is necessary to advert to Writs of Service tested on the

---

[*] In illustration of this assertion, the following instance is given:—

The general Writs to the Parliament of 11 Henry VI. were tested on the 24th May in that year, viz. 1433. At that time the Barony of Bourchier was vested in Elizabeth, widow of Sir Lewis Robsert, K. G. who was summoned to and sat in Parliament as Baron Bourchier, *jure uxoris*. The said Lady Bourchier died on the 1st of July, 1433, leaving her cousin Henry Bourchier, Earl of Ewe in Normandy, her next heir, and who was also heir to the Barony of Bourchier. The earliest Writ of Summons to Parliament recorded to have been issued to this Henry Bourchier, was dated 5th July, 13 Hen. VI. 1435; but from the Rolls of Parliament it appears that he was present in Parliament on the 3d November, 1433, four months after he succeeded his cousin in the Barony of Bourchier, and above nineteen months before any notice of a Writ of Summons having been issued to him is to be found. It must therefore be inferred, that a special Writ was directed to him, though no record of it has been preserved. Vide p. 77 and 749.

30 Dec. 28 Edw. I. 1299, commanding those to whom they were addressed to be at Carlisle on the feast of the Nativity of St. John the Baptist, i. e. the 24th June next ensuing. By these Writs all those who by Writs tested on the 26th of the following September were summoned to the Parliament at Lincoln, were included, though the Writs of Service only included four * of those who were not summoned to that Parliament: this fact is material, as it allows the inference, that of those eighteen Barons, all, excepting the four just alluded to were not in the kingdom in the 28th Edward I. or that they were otherwise engaged on the King's service, which would equally account for his not requiring their attendance in Parliament; for notwithstanding the omission of their names in the Writ of Summons to Parliament tested the 26 Sept. 1300 might *possibly* have arisen from the King's intention to divest them of Baronial rank, their not being included in the Writ of Service can only be attributed to their being otherwise employed, as however much the intention was to degrade them, the Crown was not likely to lose the military service which they owed it.

Thus of eighteen of these personages, out of thirty-one whose attendance in Parliament cannot be traced to Writs of Summons, it is presumed that their presence on that occasion may be rationally accounted for, as we have decided proof that they were at that time BARONS of the realm: only one remark therefore on the subject of any part of this number remains to be offered. From the Placita it may be doubted whether such of the Barons as were summoned to the Parliament at Westminster immediately preceding that at Lincoln, required (even according to existing practice) to have been summoned to the latter; for it appears that some of the proceedings in the former were *adjourned* to the *next* Parliament, and it might perhaps be argued that this fact (notwithstanding the Writs of the 26th Sept.) rendered the Parliament which met at Lincoln an *adjourned* Parliament, that Parliament being the *next* to the one in which the proceedings were so adjourned; in which case the Barons

---

* Verdon, Pinkney, Teyes, and Mauley.

included in the Writ to the Parliament at Westminster would have had a right to attend the Parliament at Lincoln, though not specially summoned thereto. * In corroboration of the opinion that the Parliament which met at Lincoln was an *adjourned* Parliament, it must also be observed, that the Writs to the Sheriffs commanded them to return to that Parliament *the same* Knights, Citizens, and Burgesses as were returned to the last Parliament.

No record, as has before been noticed, is to be found of a Writ of Summons to Parliament having ever been issued to *eight* of the Barons whose seals are affixed to the letter to the Pope, antecedent to the meeting of the Parliament at Lincoln, though they were summoned to several subsequent Parliaments. Hence, according to present opinions, they were not at that time entitled to be considered as BARONS of the realm. Whether either or all of them had received Writs to that or to previous Parliaments, though no record of them is to be found, can only be conjectured; but it is proper to remark, that one of them was not only a Baron by Tenure, but he was at that very moment Marshal of Ireland†, another was Admiral of the King's Fleet‡, and that the father of a third §, and the putative father of the fourth ‖, whom he succeeded in his lands, had been summoned to Parliament. It is thus certain, that notwithstanding neither of these persons are ever recorded to have been summoned to Parliament when they sat in the Parliament at Lincoln, the majority of them were persons of high rank, that two of them then held important offices, and that each was on subsequent occasions regularly summoned to Parliament among the other Barons of the kingdom, though it must be admitted that we have no evidence of their possessing that dignity at the period in question. Of the personages whose seals appear to the letter to the Pope *six* still remain to be accounted for, and as only one of them, viz. Richard Talbot, who, having succeeded to his

---

* Vide also I. and II. Report of the Lords' Committees, p. 242.
† William Marshall, vide note §, p. 765.
‡ John de Botetourt, *ibid.* note ‡, p. 767.
§ John Fitz Marmaduke, *ibid.* note †, p. 772.
‖ Nicholas de Meynill, *ibid.* note †, p. 774.

father's lands in 1274, was unquestionably a Baron by Tenure, appears to have been possessed of Baronial rank, it is almost impossible satisfactorily (unless a conjecture which will presently be submitted be correct), to explain the cause of their presence in Parliament. Walter de Beauchamp, however, who was one of the six, was at that time Steward of the King's Household, and his official situation may explain the reason of his attendance ; and there is some doubt whether John le Breton, another of that number, was not, in some degree at least, present in a judicial character, though his description in the letter to the Pope is similar to that of the Barons. Nicholas de Carew, John de Kyngeston, and John de Hodelestone, whose names complete the six here stated never to have been summoned to Parliament, were persons of considerable landed property and local consequence, but had no pretensions to rank among the Barons of the Realm. In one Writ of Service, however, in which the names are divided into "Comites" and "Barones," Hodelstone's name is inserted among the latter. Many other circumstances tending in some degree to account for the names of each of the persons not recorded to have been summoned to the Parliament at Lincoln, being parties to the letter to the Pope, will be found in the notes added to their names in the copy of the letter inserted in this Work, and to which it is only necessary in this place to refer.

As Writs are extant for the attendance of Knights of the shires and Burgesses to this Parliament, and as the letter expressly states, that it was sealed by the persons whose names are recited in the body of it, on the behalf of the whole community of England, " tam p' nob' q' p' totâ com'unitate p'd'ci regni Angl'," it is worthy of consideration whether many of the persons who were not at that time Barons of the realm, nor held any high official situation, whose names occur as parties to the document, were Knights of Shires : for if this suggestion be well founded it would account for the words just quoted, as such of them as affixed their seals to the letter may have been deputed by the rest of the commons, or, which is more probable, that even so small a part of that body doing so, may have been deemed sufficient to evince the consent of the whole.

The names of parties appearing to this letter, whose presence in Parliament cannot be attributed to a Writ of
Summons, even if no other causes can at this distance
of time be assigned for it, cannot however invalidate the
authenticity of that instrument, without the same argument
being applied against the authority of the Rolls themselves; for numerous instances occur where Barons are
stated to have been present in Parliament who are not
recorded to have been summoned to *that* particular Parliament *; and more than one, where individuals are
stated to have been present, who are never once recorded
to have been summoned to Parliament †. If this then was
the fact at comparatively modern periods, when the records of Parliament are infinitely more perfect, how
much more strongly does the argument apply to a period of Parliamentary History of which but little certain is known: and though to the investigation of it the
talent, research, and zeal of the Lords' Committees was de-
voted, no satisfactory account could be given. Nor is it too
much to contend, in the absence of a cause which, according to our slight knowledge of the constitution of the legislative assemblies of that period, would explain the circumstance of persons sitting as Barons of the Realm who are not
recorded to have been summoned as such, that each of the
individuals in question had a legal right to that dignity,
notwithstanding the source in which the dignity originated
cannot now be traced.

These observations are far from intended to support the
opinion, that the proof afforded by this letter of the presence
of persons as Barons to whom Writs of Summons to Parliament had not previously been issued, should establish an
hereditary dignity; but it is submitted, that with respect to
such persons as are recorded to have been summoned to
that Parliament (if not to any previous Parliament), the
proof which this letter affords of their presence on that occasion, is the most satisfactory evidence which is extant of a
proof of a sitting in Parliament.

---

* Vide notes to p. 719, 724, 725, *ter.* 722, 729, 730, 737,
742, 743, 744, 745, 746, 749, 752, 754, 758, 759.
    † Vide notes, p. 722, 724, 733, 737, 754, 757, 759.

·Having thus stated such arguments in support of the evidence which the letter would establish, and alluded to points which might be objected against it, it is necessary in the next place to notice the important fact, that a document, supposed to be either the original letter, or a duplicate of it made at the same time and sealed by each of the Barons, is preserved in the Chapter House at Westminster; and it is essential to inquire, whether *that document* would be received as an authentic instrument; for as the *original* letter was addressed to the Pope, it may fairly be supposed, that any similar document not found in the archives of the Holy See, or which could not be positively traced once to have been deposited in those archives, would not be deemed the *original.* Whether the original document does or does not exist among the records of that State, has not, it is presumed been ascertained; but if it be clearly established, that no such letter is extant, and that no record of its ever having been deposited there is to be found, it will then become a question whether the letter was ever forwarded, and consequently whether the document at the Chapter House is not the *original.* That it is a MS. of that period the most competent judges admit, and from the seals and other marks of authenticity, a rational doubt can scarcely be entertained, that if it be not the ORIGINAL LETTER, it is an OFFICIAL DUPLICATE of it. Nor can it possibly be a matter of surprise that a duplicate of so important an instrument, expressing as it did the opinion of the legislative assembly of the kingdom on a subject of the highest political interest, should have been made.

Excepting as a point of historical curiosity, the only object for inquiring whether the document in the Chapter House at Westminster is the original or a duplicate, is the possibility of its being offered as evidence of a sitting in Parliament. The *Custos* is therefore necessarily an object of attention; but as it is impossible to enter properly into a question which could only be discussed with advantage after an investigation into the nature of the records contained in the Chapter House, a point which the Editor has not the means of ascertaining in a manner satisfactory to himself, this subject must be dismissed with merely alluding to a circumstance which will be more fully noticed,

that there is proof that the document was among the
archives of the Treasury of the Receipt of the Exchequer in
the reign of James the First: and with observing, that if
the most competent persons were to be examined as to
which they would deem the proper depository for a record
written and sealed in a Parliament held in the 29th
Edw. I. to be discovered in, it is presumed, from the state of
the records in this country, that considerable difference of
opinion would be found to exist; and if the letter in
the Chapter House be deemed, as it is here strenuously
contended, a DUPLICATE of the ORIGINAL, made for the purpose of being preserved among the public muniments of the
kingdom, it would perhaps be difficult to assign to it a more
proper *Custos* than that in which it is now, and for above
two centuries at least, has been preserved.

At the commencement of these remarks it was stated,
that no reason has ever been publicly assigned against the
authenticity of the document preserved among the records
in the Treasury of the Receipt of the Exchequer; and it is
now proper that reference should be made to the only
notice of it which the Editor believes has been printed.
The first copies printed were those inserted in ' the
early editions of the Fœdera; the next, that published in
Dugdale's "Copy of all Summons of the Nobility to the
Great Councils and Parliaments of this Realm, from the
XLIX of King Henry III. until these present Times," London, 1685: on both these copies some observations will be
made.   In 1729 the Society of Antiquaries published in the
first volume of the Vetusta Monumenta, engravings of the
seals attached to the letter, and of the letter itself (though
it is to be regretted, that the engraving of the letter was
not a fac simile of the MS. of the document in the Chapter
House), taken from a transcript and drawing made in
1624 by Augustine Vincent, Windsor Herald, by command
of the Earl Marshal; to which is attached a certificate, that
it had been carefully collated " cum *originali Instrumento*
in Thesauro D'ni Regis Caroli Westmonasterij remanente ;
verbatim concordare vidit Job'es Bradshaw in eodem Thesauro Procamerarius; omniaq' prælibata sigilla, prout in au-
tographo se conspicienda præbent, exactè delineari curavit
idem Job'es, Windsor Heraldus, mense Novembris, 1629."
From this transcript two conclusions of importance may

be drawn; the one, that above two centuries ago the document now preserved in the Chapter House was in that repository; and the other, that it was then considered the ORIGINAL LETTER. Upon the word *original*, as applied to the record in question, it must be remarked, that it was in all probability meant to express that it was written and sealed in the Parliament at Lincoln; but whether a duplicate made for the purpose of being preserved among the muniments of this kingdom, or the document executed for the purpose of being forwarded to Rome, was not a point which by the words " Original Instrument" was intended to be determined. On two other occasions only has this document been noticed, by Mr. Cruise in his Treatise on Dignities, and by the Lords' Committees appointed to Search the Journals of the House, Rolls of Parliament, and other records and documents for all matters touching the dignity of a Peer of the Realm. The manner in which the document is alluded to by the Lords' Committees demands the utmost attention; but as in the comments which will be offered on the Committees' observations, the copy in the Fœdera, as well as that given by Dugdale, will be noticed, and as the remarks of Mr. Cruise on the subject are unconnected, they will first be quoted. In the first edition, 1810, of his valuable treatise on Dignities, the Letter to the Pope is thus spoken of :—

" The most ancient proof of a sitting in Parliament is the letter written by the Nobles in Parliament in 29 Edw. I. to the Pope, respecting the sovereignty of Scotland," p. 239. But in the second and last edition, published in 1823, this opinion is most materially changed; for he observes,

" It is said that the most ancient proof of a sitting in Parliament extant, is the letter written by the Nobles in Parliament in 29 Edw. I. to the Pope, respecting the sovereignty he claimed in Scotland; which may be seen in Rymer's Fœdera, under that year; and also in Dugdale's Summonses to Parliament. But this is a mistake; for there are two records of a prior date to that letter published in the Rolls of Parliament, vol. I. p. 25, No. 15, and p. 224, No. 2, in which the names of several persons who then sat in Parliament are mentioned; *and the letter to the Pope is not now held to be authentic*." P. 263.

On these extracts it must be observed, that the words,

" It is said," can only apply to what Mr. Cruise *himself* said in the first edition of his work, and some reason for the change in the opinion which he then expressed in so unqualified a manner, might perhaps have been expected: none however is assigned, and consequently it is merely necessary to state, lest the words of that distinguished writer should be misunderstood, that not only has no judicial decision been pronounced on the document in question, but that it has never been tendered in Evidence.

. To the observations of the Lords' Committees, the greatest deference is due; and much diffidence is consequently felt in contending against the impression which the slight notice taken of the record in the Chapter House, in their first and second Report, is calculated to produce.

· The Committees commence their remarks in a manner which at once proves the opinion they entertain of the document in the Chapter House:

· " There is," the report states, " in the treasury of the receipt of the Exchequer, a *copy* of a letter *supposed* to have been addressed by the Earls and Barons assembled in this Parliament to the Pope, in consequence of a Papal Bull, in which it was asserted that Scotland was a fee of the Romish Church. *If this copy can be considered as evidence of the existence of such an instrument*, perhaps the contents may be deemed material to the subject of the enquiries of the Committee, in many points of view *."

, It is evident, from this passage, not only that the Committees consider the document alluded to a *copy*, but that they have some doubt whether such a letter ever was written. That question has however been already noticed; but as not one cause for the opinion is expressed, it would be useless to contend against mere conjecture, however exalted in talent and reputation the persons may be from whom it emanates; especially when arguments, which, from the evidence on which they are founded, must be admitted to be of considerable weight, have been used in favour of a conclusion immediately opposed to the hypothesis which the words of the Committees tend to establish. The next paragragh is, however, more important:—

· " Some of the persons whose names are inserted in the

---

* First and Second Report, p. 240.

letter do not appear, by the Roll, to have been summoned to the Parliament at Lincoln, and some persons whose names are not in the letter were summoned. But perhaps the most important circumstances in this transaction are, that the Parliament assembled at Lincoln is called in the letter a General Parliament, and that those whose names were inserted in, and seals affixed to the letter, assumed the power to address the Pope for themselves and the whole community of the kingdom, without any apparent authority from the knights, citizens, and burgesses, if they attended that Parliament *."

On the first part of this extract, it is not requisite to make any observation, because the subject has already been noticed at considerable length; but, with relation to the latter part, that though expressly called a GENERAL Parliament, the parties to the letter had no *apparent* authority from the Knights, Citizens, and Burgesses, to assert that it was written on the behalf of the whole community of the Kingdom, it is necessary to refer to a conjecture hazarded in a former part of these observations, that some, if not the majority, of the persons whose names appear in the letter, and who were not summoned to *that* Parliament, or to *previous* Parliaments, as Barons, were Knights of the Shires, returned under the Writs commanding their election, which Writs have been before cited; and though the Editor had not the means of ascertaining who were the persons returned under those Writs to the Parliament at Lincoln, the Lords' Committee have doubtless access to records which would supply that information. If, however, it could be established, that not a single individual whose name is recited in that letter was either a Knight of the Shire, Citizen, or Burgess of Parliament, it may be confidently asked, is it any argument against the authenticity of the document, that no *apparent* authority exists by which the persons who were parties to the instrument stated, that they did so in a General Parliament, and on the behalf of the whole community of the realm, when not only individuals, but even the Committees themselves, have candidly recorded, that no satisfactory conclusion can be drawn as to the forms and customs of the Parliaments of that period? The words "GENERAL PAR-

---

* First and Second Report, p. 241.

LIAMENT" probably meant either a Parliament consisting of the three estates of the kingdom, or of persons not always summoned, but whose presence was necessary to render the assembly what was deemed a GENERAL Parliament. We have evidence that each estate was duly summoned to be present at the Parliament which met at Lincoln, and from the following abstract of the number of persons recorded to have been summoned to Parliament, from the 23d Edw. I. to the 5 Edw. II. inclusive, it is positive that the number named in the letter to the Pope considerably exceeded the usual number summoned to Parliament as Barons; the presence of which additional number in that Parliament may possibly account for the expression "General Parliament," and the statement that the letter was attested by those whose names appear in it, "Tam pro nobis quàm pro totâ communitate predicti Regni Angliæ."

DATES OF WRITS.		EARLS.	BARONS.
23 Edw. I.	24 June, 1295	11	53
————	1 Oct. 1295	9	41
————	11 Nov. 1295	8	38
24 Edw. I.	26 Aug. 1296	6	37
25 Edw. I.	26 Jan. 1297	6	75
Edw. I.	6 Feb. 1299	10	80
————	10 April, 1299	10	47
————	21 Sept. 1299	4	5
28 Edw. I.	29 Dec. 1299	11	99
————	26 Sept. 1300 *	9	80
30 Edw. I.	2 June, 1302	10	83
————	24 July, 1302	10	82
————	13 Sept. 1302	10	73
32 Edw. I.	12 Nov. 1304	9	94
33 Edw. I.	22 Jan. 1305	8	93
————	13 July, 1305	6	8
34 Edw. I.	3 Nov. 1306	12	86
1 Edw. II.	26 Aug. 1307	9	71
————	18 Jan. 1308†	11	60

* The Parliament which met at Lincoln.
† To attend the King's Coronation.

DATES OF WRITS.		EARLS.	BARONS.
————	19 Jan. 1308	11	46
————	10 March, 1308	10	47
2 Edw. II.	16 Aug. 1308	9	57
————	8 Jan. 1309	9	42
————	4 March, 1309	9	81
————	11 June, 1309	8	69
3 Edw. II.	26 Oct. 1309	12	84
————	12 Dec. 1309	12	68
5 Edw. II.	8 Oct. 1311	7	38
————	19 Dec. 1311	8	60
————	At York	9	42

This abstract also proves, that on no occasion, from
the 23d Edw. I. to the 5th Edw. II. both years inclusive,
were so many persons summoned to Parliament as to the
Parliament immediately preceding that at Lincoln; and
if, as has been supposed *, the Parliament which met at
Lincoln was an *adjourned* Parliament, all the persons who
were summoned to attend the previous Parliament would
have had a right to attend it, and the extraordinary number of Writs then issued may have caused the Parliament
that assembled at Lincoln to have been considered a GENE-
RAL Parliament. The number of Barons generally summoned, it appears, was from seventy to eighty-five; and,
on two occasions, they amounted to ninety-three or ninety-
four, but they sometimes did not exceed fifty. It is therefore far from unlikely, though perhaps it would be difficult
to establish the fact, that both the Parliaments to which
the unusual number of ninety-three Barons were summoned, were likewise styled GENERAL PARLIAMENTS, of the
precise meaning of which term we have, as has been
before remarked, no precise information.

The Committees, however, admit that

" It seems probable, from the existence of the document
in the Exchequer, that a letter to the same effect, was written to the Pope;" and the Report proceeds to observe :—

"In the copy given in the Foedera, the name of " Wil-
lelmus, Dominus de Molyns is inserted, which is not in the

---

* Pages 789, 790.

Record in the Exchequer. In the copy given by Dugdale
there is added a note, in which it is stated that several
persons named, twenty-eight in number, whose seals are
affixed to the letter, were not summoned to the Parliament,
&c. A list is added of fifteen persons, whose seals were not
affixed to the letter, and who are represented in the same
note as having been summoned; but, on examination of
the Roll, neither of these lists appear to have been correct.
It is therefore difficult to conceive from which document
the copy in Dugdale was transcribed, or from what document the name of Lord Molyns was introduced in the copy
given in the Fœdera."

With respect to the copy in the last edition of the Fœdera, to that given by Dugdale, and to the copies in earlier
editions of the Fœdera, one authority only is named as that
from which the copy in each of these works was taken, viz.
the document in the Chapter House at Westminster. Hence
it may be inferred, that any deviation from that document must be considered as the error of the transcriber.
All these copies have been collated with each other, and
with the copy lately printed by the Lords' Committees, in
the Appendix to their first and second Report, the latter
being considered the verbatim et literatim transcript from
the document itself. The result of this examination was,
that the Copy inserted in the last edition of the Fœdera proved to be a verbatim copy from that in former
editions of that work, and that those copies not only differ
from that printed by the Lords' Committees, in having the
name of "Willielmus Dominus Molyns," but that many
other variations exist between them, the most material of
which are inserted in the note below *. Dugdale's copy of

---

* In the list of Barons in the copy in the Fœdera, edit. 1705,
London, and edit. 1737, Hague, and also in the edition, pub-
lished by order of the Commission for the preservation of the
Records in 1816 the Earl of Norfolk is merely styled " Comes
Norfolk," whilst, in the original, the words " et Maresch
Angl' " are added to his name.

John Lovel is called " Dominus de *Berekingg*, instead of
" *Dakkyng*."

" Robertus *la* Warde" stands as " Robertus *de* Warde."

" Nich's *de* Meynhull," as " Nich's Meynhyll."

" Joh'es *de Lisle*, D'n's de Wodeton, as John *de Insula*, D'n's
de Wodeton."

the Letter itself, varies in a slight degree both from the copy printed by the Lords' Committees, and from that published in the different editions of the Fœdera just cited; and

" Gilbertus de Pecche, as " *Gilbertus Pecche*."

" Rob'tus Hastang, D'n's de *la Désirée*," as D'n's *de* Désirée.

" Will's Paynel, D'n's de *Fracyngton*," as " D'n's de *Tracyngton*.

" Fulco le Strange, D'n's de Corsh'm," as " D'n's de *Corfham*."

" John' de *Hodelleston*," as " Johannes de *Hudleston*."

" John' de Greystok, D'n's *Morpath*," as "D'n'us *de* Morpath."

In the Letter itself the following are the chief variations between the copies in the Fœdera and that printed by the Lords' Committees.

In the first line, instead of

" p'videncia S'c'e Romane *ac univ'salis* eccl'ie sum'o," &c.

the copies in the Fœdera stand,

" p'videncia *S'c'e Romane eccl'ie*, sum'o," &c.

Line 5, p. 774, " velit illesa sane co'vocato *nup'* p' serenissimo," &c. stands in the Fœdera,

" velit illesa *sane convocato* per serenissimo," &c.

Line 25, p. 775, " et unanimis o'nium *n'r'm* & singulor'," &c. In the copies in the Fœdera the word *nostrorum* is omitted.

Line 30, *Ibid.* " in dubiu' *ipsius* denicat," *ipsius* is omitted in the Fœdera.

Line 3, p. 776, " & leges p'd'cæ absq' dim'uc'one, &c. in the Fœdera, the word *predictæ* is omitted.

The date assigned to the letter in the Fœdera is M.CCCI. whilst that given in the copy published by the Lords' Committees is M.CCC. The year was, in fact, 1300-1; and in the original record the date, 1300, is written in words at length.

These variations and omissions, though not otherwise of moment, are nevertheless important, as they prove that the copies printed in the editions of the Fœdera here cited, were not, as they profess to be, copied from the original, and hence are undeserving of any notice which can at all militate against the document from which they are said to have been taken.

The chief difference between Dugdale's copy and that printed by the Lords' Committees, besides the omission of the Earl of Norfolk's name, and many, though not all the variations which distinguish the copies in the Fœdera, consists in the omission of the words: " *Angl. & regie dignitatis ac subv'sione status ejusdem regni*," in line 32, p. 775.

though the list of names in Dugdale's transcript does not contain that of Lord Molines, it omits that of "Roger Bigot, Earl of Norfolk and Earl Marshal." Thus the number of persons, parties to the Letter, are stated in the Fœdera to have been 104, in Dugdale to have been 102, and in the copy inserted in the Appendix to the Report of the Lords' Committees, to have been 103; the latter of which is correct.

The difficulty, therefore, which the Report expresses of conceiving from what document the copy in Dugdale was transcribed, may perhaps be entirely removed, by attributing it to the Fœdera; and that writer appears to have omitted the name of Lord Molines because he was aware, from having previously compiled the account of that family, which is inserted in his Baronage*, that no "William Lord Molines" existed at the period when the Letter was written; a fact which will be more fully commented upon. The omission of the name of the Earl of Norfolk cannot be imputed to that cause, and must be attributed to precisely the same cause as that to which the introduction of the name of Lord Molines, in the early editions of the Fœdera, may be assigned, namely, the carelessness of the person appointed to transcribe the copy from the document in the Chapter House. That this error should not have been detected by those to whose care the new edition of the Fœdera was entrusted, may excite surprise, so far as regards its learned Editors; but surely it can create no prejudice against the authenticity of a document which is cited as the authority for every copy which is known to exist, however much those copies may vary from the original, or from each other.

That no William Lord Molines could have been a party to the letter to the Pope in 29 Edw. I. may be inferred from, if it be not decidedly proved by, the following circumstances. The family of Molines did not attain to any rank or importance in this country until the reign of Edw. III. In Dug-

---

It is consequently manifest that the copy in the three editions of the Fœdera just cited, as well as that given by Dugdale, were not *correctly* copied from the record to which references are made, as the authority for their insertion in those works.

* The second volume of Dugdale's Baronage, in which his account of the Molines' family is given, was printed in 1676; and his Lists of Summons, in which the copy of the Barons' Letter is inserted, in 1685.

-dale's history of that family he says * : " That this family of Molins, whereof I am now to speak, was originally of French extraction, from that town in Bourbonnois so called, is not at all to be doubted : howbeit, until the beginning of King Edward the Third's reign, that John de Molins became a person not a little eminent, as well for his esteem with that King, as his large possessions in several counties, especially Buckinghamshire, *I have not seen any thing of note thereof*, from our public records." The concluding part of this statement is corroborated by there not being even a solitary reference to the name in the Index to that part of the last edition of the Fœdera, which contains documents contemporary with the period when this William, Lord Molines, must have lived; nor do there appear to be any Inquisitions Post Mortem of any person of the name of Molines until the reign of Edw. III. One fact on the subject, but which is of a convincing nature, only remains to be stated : in the most authentic pedigrees of Molines recorded in the College of Arms, among Vincent's collections, no " *William* de Molines" occurs, until a William de Molines, who is styled " Chevalier Valectus Regis," temp. Edw. III. and who was the son of John de Molines, the first baron of the family; which John, Baron Molines, died in the 45th Edw. III. 1371, and the said William, his son, appears to have deceased in 1380!

The important question, whether the document preserved in the Chapter House at Westminster is the original, or a duplicate of the original, made at the same time and place, must chiefly depend upon the existence of a document of the same nature in the archives of the Holy See. If such a document be deposited in those archives, the one in question may, it is confidentlv concluded, be deemed a duplicate, and which it would be desirable should be collated with that which is supposed to exist at Rome. If, however, no such instrument be extant among the pontifical records, this document may possibly be the original, which, for various political reasons, was not forwarded to the personage to whom it is addressed.

Whatever may be the decision on the question as to whether it is the original or a duplicate, cannot, it is

---

* Tome II. p. 145.

contended, affect its character as evidence that the persons whose seals are affixed to it were then present in Parliament. Lord Coke's *dictum*, which has uniformly been acted upon by the House of Lords, that "the proofs of a sitting in Parliament, by virtue of a Writ of Summons, must be by the records of Parliament," strongly argues for the admission of this document. Nothing, until the commencement of the Journals in 1509, but the Rolls of Parliament, is extant, which can be deemed the Records of Parliament; and the latter have been received as proof that Peers mentioned therein as having been appointed Triers of Petitions, or Witnesses to certain transactions in Parliament, were then present*; the correctness of which notices must, of course, depend upon others than the Peers themselves. Is it possible, then, to imagine that a document containing the solemn decision of the Legislative Assembly of the Realm upon a subject which, it is indisputably proved, that assembly was specially convened to discuss, and to which *each* Baron placed his *own* seal, will not be received as part of the Records of Parliament, because from the imperfect state of the Rolls of the period when it was written, it is not, as it undoubtedly ought, to be found thereon? Were the ordinary records of Parliament of that period as perfect and minute as it is notorious they are scanty and incomplete, and no notice of the affair alluded to in the Letter was to be found on them, there might be some ground for suspicion; but when a page contains all the account recorded of the proceedings of a Parliament for which more than ordinary preparations for business were made, it is impossible to anticipate, whenever the Letter may be tendered as a proof of sitting in Parliament of those Barons who were summoned to the Parliament in which that document was written, and who are named as parties to it, that it will not be received as incontrovertible evidence of the fact which it would be produced to establish.

---

* The first instance in which the Rolls of Parliament are positively known to have been received as proofs of Sitting in Parliament, was in the case of the Barony of Botetourt, in 1764, when the following records were cited to prove that the Barons of Botetourt were present in Parliament. To shew that John Botetourt, the first Baron, sat in Parliament, the Rolls of Parliament in the 33d Edw. I. (*Vide* p. 718.) were adduced; and the sitting of John de Botetourt, his grandson, the second Baron, was proved by his having been one of the Mainpernors of Lord

If the Letter be received as evidence of the sitting in Parliament of these persons who were summoned to that Parliament, and whose names occur as parties to it, it would still

---

Latymer, in the 50th Edw. III. (*Vide* p. 728.) In the case of the Barony of Zouche, on which the House of Lords reported in 1807, Mr. Cruise states, in p. 267 of his Treatise on Dignities, " That several proofs of Sitting in Parliament, from the printed Rolls were produced, and which were admitted as evidence ;" and moreover, the Baronies of Grey of Ruthyn in 1640, Mowbray in 1639, Le Despencer in 1603 and 1763, as well as that of Percy in 1722, were allowed, though no proof of Sitting, in either case, could be proved after the year 1509, when the Journals of the House of Lords commenced, and which proofs could consequently only be found on the Rolls of Parliament. *Ibid.* p. 266.

The proofs of Sitting which were read, in the Zouche case, were those which are referred to in pp. 727, 728, 730, 731, 732, 735, 740, and 749, of this work.

· It is also to be observed, that in the case of the Barony of Botetourt, a proof of John de Botetourt, the first Baron, having sat in Parliament, was cited from the Close Roll, on which his name occurs among several Barons who were appointed in that Parliament to make certain ordinances for the better regulation of the King's household, but of which circumstance not the slightest notice is to be found in the printed Rolls of Parliament; nor is any account there given of a Parliament having been held between the 2d and 5th Edw. II. though a Parliament certainly met at Stamford in the 3d Edw. II. In the Botetourt case, however, the Lords' Committee refused to allow the extract from the Rolls of Parliament of the 33 Edw. I. (*Vide* p. 718.) to be read in evidence, it not being written upon the Clause Roll, but affixed or tacked to it, and from its being in a different hand-writing from that of the Roll; it was therefore decided that the record in question was not a record of Parliament in such a sense of the term as would entitle it to be read in evidence; nor was the extract from the Clause Roll of the 3 Edw. II. read in evidence, as Mr. York, the counsel for the claimant, contented himself with proving the sitting of John the last Baron, by the Rolls of Parliament of the 50 Edw. III. (*Vide* p. 728.) which record was admitted as evidence. The question of the admissibility of the extract from the Clause Roll of the 3 Edw. II. was consequently not decided.

Notwithstanding that John de Botetourt, the first Baron, was a

be a subject for decision, how far it was a proof of sitting of
such Barons, who, though parties to the Letter, were not
summoned to that Parliament, though frequently summoned
to previous Parliaments. In the present state of the question, however, any discussion on the point would be useless.

Since the preceding remarks on the letter to Pope Boniface VIII. were written, the Editor has been enabled, through
the kindness of John Caley, Esq. F. R. S. F. S. A. the Keeper
of the Records in the Chapter House, to examine the document which is there preserved; and the result of an attentive
examination of it has not only tended powerfully to confirm
his previous opinion of its authenticity, but some facts
have been ascertained which it is material to the proper
consideration of the question should be stated. It has
already been said, that in 1624, Augustine Vincent, Windsor Herald, made a transcript of the letter and drawings of
the seals attached to it, which copy and drawings were,
in 1629, collated by John Bradshaw, Windsor Herald, and
from which the plates engraved by the Society of Antiquaries in 1729, were taken. These plates, as Vincent's transcript has been lost, it was important should be compared
with the original, because they may fairly be deemed to be
evidence of the state of the document when seen by Bradshaw in 1629. The trifling variations which on this collation were found to exist between the drawings and the seals
it is not material to point out; but the state of the record
at this moment necessarily merits a particular notice. If
the certificate of Vincent and Bradshaw be correct, it is a
lamentable fact, that in the last two centuries the record has
received more injury than in the *three preceding* ones, not
only in those parts which unavoidably would be affected by
time, but proof exists of wilful spoliation. The engraving
affords us evidence that in 1629 there were *ninety-five* seals
attached to the letter, and Vincent informs us, that " all
these seals were fastened to the said charter or letter with
silk strings, with divers seals upon one string; and upon
the back of the writing, right over against every label or
string were written the names of those whose seals depended thereupon." At this moment, independent of three

---

party to the letter to the Pope, that circumstance does not appear
to have been cited as a proof of Sitting in Parliament, probably because no record is extant of his having been summoned to Parliament
until three years afterwards, viz. on 13th July, 38 Edw. I. 1305.

duplicates which will be again alluded to, only EIGHTY-TWO seals are to be found, neither of which is now attached to the letter;* and though from two to six seals occur on the same string, not the slightest remains exist of the labels or names noticed by Vincent. It is thus certain, that *thirteen seals** have been lost, and it is no less positive, that many of those which are extant have been much mutilated since the drawings of them were taken. In a former part of these observations it has been presumed, that the copy of the letter published in the Appendix to the I. and II. Peerage Report was a verbatim et literatim copy from the original in the Chapter House; such however is not the case, for although the sense appears to have been strictly preserved, several words are abbreviated which in the original are written at length, and in a few instances the names both of persons and places are differently spelt. Moreover it is impossible to give so perfect a copy as is there printed, for many parts of the letter are so much torn, that an hiatus in several places, especially towards the end, would be unavoidable. This fact is not otherwise important than as it tends to prove, that no verbatim et literatim copy of the original has as yet been published. Why the variations which are to be found in the copy printed in the Appendix to the Peerage Report were made, it would be useless to inquire, nor can the object even be guessed at which pro-

---

* The thirteen seals which are not now to be found, are those of Humphrey de Bohun, Earl of Hereford and Essex; Ralph de Monthermer, Earl of Gloucester and Hertford; Henry of Lancaster, William de Roos, Henry de Grey, Henry de Percy, Edmond de Mortimer, Robert Fitz-Payne, John Fitz-Reginald, Fulk Fitz-Warine, Ralph Fitz-William, Nicholas de Meynhill, and Walter de Mouncy. Whilst this loss, together with the manifest injury which the record has sustained since 1624, cannot be too much regretted, it is at the same time very satisfactory to reflect, that the zeal of the gentlemen to whose custody that document is now so judiciously entrusted, no less than the exertions of the Commission for the Preservation of the Public Records, may be confidently relied on to prevent any further deterioration in a muniment of so interesting and important a nature; and hence it cannot be doubted, that such measures will speedily be adopted as must ensure its better preservation. For many reasons an accurate transcript of the document in its present state, by the authority of the Commission, would be highly desirable.

duced abbreviations and contractions in a copy which do not exist in the original. Vincent expressly asserts, that eight Barons, whose names will be found in p. 778 never affixed their seals to the letter, and the state in which he describes the document in 1624 perhaps rendered it positive that they did not do so; but at this moment it would be impossible to say, whether those whose seals are not to be found ever sealed, or whether the seals of the Barons in question have been lost; however, as we have proof that thirteen seals existed in that year, of which no vestige is now to be found, the conclusion from the existing state of the record would be, that they were originally affixed to it, but that they have since been destroyed or taken away. It has been just noticed, that duplicates of three seals are now extant, namely, those of the Earl of Arundel, of Aymer de Valence, and of William de Leyburne. To what cause this curious fact is to be attributed we have no evidence by which to decide; conjecture may therefore be offered, and the most natural suggestion appears to be, if Vincent's statement is correct that eight Barons named as parties to the letter never affixed their seals to it, that one of them was represented by the Earl of Arundel, and two others by Valence and Leyburne, who consequently were their proxies; nor is it improbable that the remaining five who did not seal, were represented by five other Barons in a similar manner; for notwithstanding that no other duplicates are to be found, they might not only have been originally attached to the letter, but even have existed when Vincent copied the record, for he takes no notice of the duplicate seals above mentioned. This is however an hypothesis which has no other foundation that the absence of a more satisfactory cause, and the circumstance of there being nothing which can be urged in contradiction to it.

Before these observations are concluded, a record which is printed in the Fœdera *, and alluded to in the 1st and 2d Report † of the Lords' Committees, before cited, requires a slight notice. It appears that in the 2d of Edw. II. Writs tested at Westminster on the 21th of June were issued to the Bishops and Abbots, to eight Earls, and 69 Barons, and to the Judges, commanding them to meet at Stamford, on

---

* Edition 1816, tome II. p. 84.　　† P. 258.

the Sunday next after the feast of St. James the Apostle*,
"tractatu'& colloq'ium v'ituri no'r'mque co'silin' impe'su'ri."
But, in the margin, the word Parliament does not occur, as
it is only noted, "Summonitio de veniendo ad tractandum
cum rege." It is doubtful, the Report observes, " whether
this meeting was properly a Common Council of the Realm
assembled in Parliament, or only a great Council;" but as,
in subsequent writs the meeting is expressly styled a PAR-
LIAMENT, as the Writs by which the Nobility were summoned are similar to former writs, marked in the margin as
Summonses to Parliaments, and still more as a statute
called the Statute of Stamford, appears in the authorised
Collection of the Statutes of the Realm, it is presumed that
that meeting was a regular Parliament. At this assembly
a Letter was agreed to be sent to the Pope for remedy of the
grievances and oppressions to which the kingdom was subject; and to this Letter, the King issued a Writ †, tested on
the 6th of August, 3 Edw. II. 1309, fourteen days after that
on which the Peers were ordered to meet at Stamford, commanding *the Earls and Barons to affix their seals.*

The cause of this notice being taken of the circumstance
is the impression created in the Editor's mind, that this
Letter, of which not even a copy appears to be extant in
this country, is probably preserved · among the records of
the Holy See; in which case it would perhaps be worthy of
inquiry, whether the seals of the Barons who were sum-
moned· by Writs tested on the 11th June were affixed to
that document; and if so, whether that circumstance is
not evidence of their having on that occasion *sat* in *Parliament.*

No notice of the Meeting at Stamford occurs on the
Rolls of Parliament, nor are any Writs·extant to the Commons; but notwithstanding these facts, it is submitted that
the express designation of the assembly as a PARLIAMENT in
the Writ just alluded to, as well as in another Writ cited in
the Report from the Close Roll of the 3d Edw. II. m. 1
dorso ‡, together with the circumstance of a Statute having
been enacted by that assembly, would tend to establish that
the meeting at Stamford in the 3d Edw. II. and in which the
Letter alluded to is said·to have been written, was a regular
PARLIAMENT.

---

* 27 July, 1309, *third* Edw. II.
† Fœdera. II. p. 84.   ‡ Vide note to p. 805.

INDEX

TO THE

PROOFS OF BARONS' SITTINGS, &c.

———◆———

₊ The Names printed in Italics occur on the Rolls of Parliament before Writs of Summons are recorded (with the exception of that of the 49 Hen. III.) to have been issued; and those in the Roman type are only to be found in the Barons' Letter to the Pope, anno 29 Edw. I. 1301.

————

————

* Vide a note to p. 805.

* Vide a note to p. 805.

---

* Vide a note to p. 805.

* Vide a note to p. 805.

SUCCESSION

OF

ARCHBISHOPS AND BISHOPS

FROM THE

CONQUEST TO THE PRESENT TIME.

M M 2

SUCCESSION

OF

ARCHBISHOPS AND BISHOPS

OF THE

PROVINCE OF CANTERBURY.

CANTERBURY.

YEAR.

1138 Theobald, Abbot of Becco. Elected in Dec. 1138; ob. 1160.

THE SEE VACANT TWO YEARS.

1162 Thomas à Becket. Consecrated 27 May, 1162. Murdered 28 Dec. 1170.

1171 Richard. Succeeded in 1171, and died 16 Feb. 1183, or 17 Feb. 1184.

1184 Baldwin. Translated from Worcester towards the end of 1184; died at Acre, in Palestine, circa 1191.

1191 Reginald Fitz Joceline. Translated from Wells in 1191; ob. 25 Dec. 1191.

THE SEE VACANT TWO YEARS.

1193 Hubert Walter. Succeeded 1193; Lord Chancellor; ob. 29 June, 1205.

     Reginald, the Sub Prior, was chosen by the monks ; but afterwards, at their own request set aside by the King. They then chose

     John Grey, Bishop of Norwich, but the Pope set him aside in favour of

1206 Stephen Langton. Consecrated 17 June, 1206 or 1207. A CARDINAL; ob. 9 July, 1228.

     Walter de Hempsham was then elected, but set aside both by the King and Pope.

1229 Richard Weathershed. Consecrated 10 June, 1229; ob. circa 1231.

     Ralph Nevil, Bishop of Chichester, was elected and approved by the King, but set aside by the Pope, when

     John, the Sub Prior, was elected, but set aside by the Pope, after which

     Richard Blundy was elected, but he was also set aside by the Pope.

1234 Edmund. Consecrated 2 April, 1234; ob. 16 Nov. 1242.

1244. Boniface of Savoy. Consecrated 15 Jan. 1244; ob. 18 July, 1270.

William Chillenden elected, but set aside by the Pope.

1272 Robert Kilwarby. Consecrated 26 Feb. 1272. Was made a CARDINAL in 1278, when he resigned this See.

Robert Burnel, Bishop of Bath and Wells, elected, but set aside by the Pope.

1278 John Peckham. Consecrated 6 March, 1278; ob. 8 Dec. 1292.

1293 Robert Winchelsey. Elected 13 Feb. 1293; confirmed 4 Sept. 1294 ; ob. 11 May, 1313.

Thomas Cobham, Precentor of York, elected, but never confirmed by the Pope.

1313 Walter Reynolds. Translated from Winchester 1 Oct. 1313, Lord Chancellor and Lord Treasurer; ob. 16 Nov. 1327.

1327 Simon Mepham. Elected 11 Dec. 1327; ob. 12 Oct. 1333.

1333 John Stratford. Translated from Winchester 3 Nov. 1333; Lord Chancellor ; ob. 23 Aug. 1348.

1348 John de Ufford, Dean of Lincoln, nominated to this See by Bull, dated 24 Sept. 1348, ob. June 7, 1349, before he was consecrated, or received the Pall, for which reason Godwin does not include him in succession. Lord Chancellor.

1349 Thomas Bredewardin. Nominated by Bull, dated 19 June, 1349; ob. 26 Aug. 1349.

1349 Simon Islip. Nominated by Bull dated 7 Oct. 1349; ob. 26 April, 1366.

William Edington, Bishop of Winchester, was elected to this See 10 May, 1366, but he refused to accept the dignity.

1366 Simon Langham. Translated from Ely by Bull dated 23 July, 1366. Lord Chancellor. Made a CARDINAL 22 Sept. 1368, and resigned this See 27 Nov. 1368; ob. 22 July, 1376.

1369 William Whittlesey. Translated from Worcester 15 Jan. 1369; ob. 5 June, 1374.

A Cardinal of Rome was elected, who, according to the Canterbury Register, was Simon Langham, apparently the same personage

who resigned this See in 1368; but Godwin
states that his name was Adam Easton. The
election was, however, set aside by the Pope
in favor of

1375 Simon Sudbury, alias Tibold, who was translated from
London 26 May 1375. Lord Chancellor. Beheaded
by the rebels 14 June, 1381.

1381 William Courtenay, translated from London 23 Oct.
1381; ob. 31 July, 1396.

1396 Thomas Fitz-Alan, alias Arundel. Translated from
the Archbishoprick of York 25 Sept. 1396. Lord
Chancellor. In 1398 he was charged with high-
treason; and having left the kingdom, Roger Walden, Dean of York, was consecrated, and exercised
the Archiepiscopal functions; but on the accession
of Henry IV. in 1399, this Roger being pronounced
an intruder, Thomas Arundel was restored to the
possession of this dignity; ob. 19 or 20 Feb. 1413.

1414 Henry Chicheley. Translated from St. David's 4
March 1413; ob. 12 April, 1443.

1443 John Stafford. Translated from Bath and Wells by
Bull dated 15 May, 1443. CARDINAL and Lord
Chancellor; ob. May 25, or July 6, 1452.

1452 John Kemp. Translated from the Archbishoprick of
York by Bull, dated at Rome 21 July 1452. CAR-
DINAL and Lord Chancellor; ob. 22 March 1454.

1454 Thomas Bourchier. Translated from Ely 22 April
1454. CARDINAL and Lord Chancellor; ob. 30
March, 1486.

1486 John Morton. Translated from Ely 13 June, 1486.
CARDINAL and Lord Chancellor; ob. 15 Sept. 1500.

Thomas Langton, Bishop of Winchester, was
elected to this See 22 Jan. 1501, but died on
the 27th of that month, before his translation
could be perfected.

1501 Henry Deane. Translated from Salisbury 26 April,
1501; ob. 15 or 16 Feb. 1502.

1504 William Warham. Translated from London 29 Nov.
1504 *. Lord Chancellor; ob. 23 Aug. 1532.

---

* If this date be correct the See must have been vacant above
two years, but which is not noticed by Le Neve or Heylyn.

YEAR.

1533 Thomas Cranmer. Nominated by Bull dated 22 Feb. 1533. Burnt 21 March, 1555.

1555 Reginald Pole. Consecrated 22 March, 1555. CAR-DINAL; ob. 17 Nov. 1558, æt. 58.

1559 Matthew Parker. Elected 1 Aug. 1559; ob. 17 May, 1575.

1575 Edmund Grindal. Translated from York 10 Jan. 1576; ob. 6 July, 1583, æt. 63.

1583 John Whitgift. Translated from Worcester 14 Aug. 1583; ob. 29 Feb. 1604.

1604 Richard Bancroft. Translated from London 9 Oct.1604; ob. 2 Nov. 1610, æt. 67.

1611 George Abbot. Translated from London 4 March, 1611; ob. 4 Aug. 1633, æt. 71.

1633 William Laud. Translated from London 6 Aug. 1633; beheaded 10 Jan. 1644.

THE SEE VACANT SIXTEEN YEARS.

1660 William Juxon. Translated from London 3 Sept.1660; ob. 4 June 1663.

1663 Gilbert Sheldon. Translated from London 14 July, 1663; ob. 9 Nov. 1677.

1678 William Sancroft. Consecrated 27 Jan. 1678. De-prived 1 Feb. 1691; ob. 24 Nov. 1693, æt. 77.

1691 John Tillotson. Nominated 23 April, 1691; ob. 22 Nov. 1694.

1694 Thomas Tenison. Translated from Lincoln, 6 Dec. 1694; ob. 1715.

1715 William Wake. Translated from Lincoln 1715; ob. 1737.

1737 John Potter. Translated from Oxford 1737; ob. 1747.

1747 Thomas Herring. Translated from York 1747; ob.1757.

1757 Matthew Hutton. Translated from York 1757; ob. 1758.

1758 Thomas Secker. Translated from Oxford 1758; ob. 1768.

1768 Honourable Frederick Cornwallis. Translated from Litchfield and Coventry 1768; ob. 1783.

1783 John Moore. Translated from Bangor 1783; ob. 1805.

1804 Charles Manners Sutton. Translated from Norwich in 1805. PRESENT Lord Archbishop of Canterbury, and Primate of All England.

ST. ASAPH.

1148 Gilbertus.
1152 Geoffrey of Monmouth. Consecrated 24 Feb. 1152;
    ob. 1154.
1154 Richard, presumed to have been consecrated in 1154,
    and to have died in 1155.
1155 Godfrey. Quitted this See in 1175.
1175 Adam, a Welchman, Canon of Paris. Consecrated 18
    Oct. 1175; ob. 1181.
1183 John I. Consecrated 25 June, 1183; ob. circa 1186.
1186 Reyner. Consecrated 1186; ob. 1224.
1225 Abraham. Consecrated 1225; ob. 1234.
1235 Hugh. Consecrated 17 June, 1235; ob. 1240.
1240 Howel ap Ednevet. Consecrated Aug. or Sept. 1240;
    ob. 1247.

THE SEE VACANT TWO YEARS.

1249 Anian, or Enion I. Consecrated Nov. 1249; ob.
    Sept. 1266.
1267 John II. Consecrated 1267.
1268 Anian II. Consecrated 21 Oct. 1268; ob. 5 Feb. 1293.
1293 Leoline de Bromfeld, Canon of St. Asaph. Elected
    6 April, 1293; ob. 1313.
1314 David ap Blethin I. Consecrated 12 Jan. 1314.
1352 John Trevour I. Consecrated 24 March, 1352; ob.
    1357.
1357 Leoline ap Madoc, Dean of St. Asaph. Appointed 19
    Aug. 1357; ob. 1375.
1376 William de Springlington, Dean of St. Asaph. Appoint-
    ed 4 Feb. 1376; ob. 9 April 1382.
1382 Lawrence Child. Nominated 18 June, 1382; ob. 27
    Dec. 1389 [*].
1390 Alexander Bache. Appointed 28 Feb. 1390; ob. 1395.
1395 John Trevour II. Prebendary of Hereford. Ap-
    pointed 6 July 1395. Deprived in 1402, but living
    May 16, 1409.

---

[*] Le Neve here inserts the following query, " Who was that
who was styled ' I. Episcopus Assaven. 20 Oct. 1384 ?' Rymer,
Vol. VII. p. 445."

YEAR.

1402 David II. said to have succeeded in 1402, and to have enjoyed this See until 1411.—*Sed Quere de hoc.* Le Neve.

1411 Robert de Lancaster. Consecrated 28 June, 1411; ob. 1433.

1433 John Lowe. Appointed 17 Aug. 1433; translated to Rochester in 1444.

1444 Reginald Peacock. Appointed 22 April, 1444; translated to Chichester 23 March, 1449.

1450 Thomas I. Succeeded 27 Jan. 1450; ob. circa 1461.

1461 Thomas II.; ob. in 1471.

1471 Richard Redman. Consecrated about the middle of 1472, translated to Exeter in 1495.

1495 Michael Dyacon. Consecrated Jan. 1496; ob. 1500.

1499 David III. Consecrated 26 April, 1500; ob. 1503.

1503 David ap Owen, Abbot of Conway. Appointed 18 Dec. 1503; ob. 11 or 12 Feb. 1512.

1513 Edmund Birkhead. Appointed 15 April, 1513; ob. April 1518.

1518 Henry Standish. Consecrated 11 July, 1518; ob. 9 July, 1535.

1536 William Barlow, Prior of Bisham. Elected 16 Jan. 1535; translated to St. David's in the same year.

1536 Robert Warton or Parfew, Abbot of Bermondsey. Elected 8 June, 1536; translated to Hereford 1554.

1555 Thomas Goldwell. Appointed 12 May 1555, and was intended to have been translated to Oxford; but on Queen Elizabeth's accession he went into voluntary exile.

1559 Richard Davies. Consecrated 21 Jan. 1559; translated to St. David's 21 May, 1561.

1562 Thomas Davies. Appointed 2 April 1562; ob. Sept. 1573.

1573 William Hughes. Appointed 11 Dec. 1573; ob. 18 Nov. 1600.

1601 William Morgan. Translated from Landaff 17 Sept. 1601; ob. 10 Sept. 1604.

1602 Richard Parry, Dean of Bangor. Consecrated 30 Dec. 1604; ob. 26 Sept. 1623.

1624 John Hanmer, Prebendary of Worcester. Elected 20 Jan. 1624; ob. 23 July, 1629.

1629 John Owen, Archdeacon of St. Asaph. Consecrated 20 Sept. 1629; ob. 15 Oct. 1651.

THE SEE VACANT NINE YEARS.

YEAR.

1660 George Griffith, Archdeacon of St. Asaph. Consecrated 28 Oct. 1660 ; ob. 28 Nov. 1666.

1667 Henry Glenham, Dean of Bristol. Consecrated 13 Oct. 1667 ; ob. 17 Jan. 1669.

1669 Isaac Barrow. Translated from Sodor and Man, 21 March, 1669; ob. 24 June, 1680.

1680 William Lloyd, Dean of Bangor. Consecrated 3 Oct. 1680; translated to Litchfield and Coventry in 1692.

1692 Edward Jones. Translated from Cloyne, in Ireland, 13 Dec. 1692; ob. May, 1703.

1703 George Hooper, Dean of Canterbury. Consecrated 31 Oct. 1703 ; translated to Bath and Wells in 1704.

1704 William Beveridge, Archdeacon of Colchester. Consecrated 16 July, 1704 ; ob. 5 March, 1708.

1708 William Fleetwood, Canon of Windsor. Elected 13 May, 1708 ; translated to Ely in Nov. 1714.

1714 John Wynne, Principal of Jesus College, Oxford. Elected 11 Jan. 1714; translated to Bath and Wells in 1727.

1728 Francis Hare, Dean of Worcester, and Dean of St. Paul's. Translated to Chichester in 1731.

1731 Thomas Tanner, Canon of Christ Church, Oxford. Elected 1731 ; ob. 1735.

1736 Isaac Maddox, Dean of Wells. Translated to Worcester in 1743.

1743 John Thomas, Dean of Peterborough. Elected 1743, but not consecrated; translated to Lincoln in the same year.

1743 Samuel Lisle, Archdeacon of Canterbury. Elected 1743; translated to Norwich in 1748.

1748 Robert H. Drummond, Prebendary of Westminster. Elected 1748; translated to Salisbury in 1761.

1761 Richard Newcombe. Translated from Landaff in 1761 ; ob. 1769.

1769 Jonathan Shipley. Translated from Landaff in 1769; ob. 1788.

1789 Samuel Halifax. Translated from Gloucester in 1789; ob. 1790.

1790 Lewis Bagot. Translated from Norwich in 1790; ob. 1802.

YEAR.

1802 Samuel Horsley, translated from Rochester in 1802;
 ob. 1806.

1806 William Cleaver. Elected 1806; ob. 1815.

1815 John Luxmore. Elected 1815. PRESENT Lord Bishop
 of St. Asaph.

BISHOPS OF BANGOR.

1105 Hervey. Translated to Ely in 1109.

THE SEE VACANT ABOUT ELEVEN YEARS.

1120 David, a Scot. Consecrated about 1120.

1139 Mauritius, or Meuric. Succeeded in 1139; ob. 1161.

.... William, Prior of St. Austin's, in Bristol. No date of
 his election or death is recorded.

1177 Guy, or Guianus. Consecrated 22 May, 1177; ob.
 circa 1190.

THE SEE VACANT ABOUT FOUR YEARS.

1195 Alban, Prior of St. John of Jerusalem. Consecrated
 16 April, 1195; ob. 1196.

1197 Robert de Shrewsbury. Consecrated 17 March, 1197;
 ob. 1213.

1215 Martin, apparently consecrated 16 July, 1215. He is
 omitted by Godwin; and, if he was ever possessed
 of this See, he held it a short time; for, in the
 same year, 1215, Caducan I. was consecrated. He
 quitted his Bishoprick some years before his death,
 which occurred 11 April, 1241.

1236 Howel I. Consecrated 1236.

1240 Richard. Consecrated, according to Godwin, in 1240;
 but other authorities assert, in 1241; ob. 1268.

1267 Anian, Archdeacon of Anglesey. Appointed 12 Dec.
 1268; ob. circa 1300.

1303 Caducan II. Succeeded in 1303 or 1306.

1306 Griffith, or Griffin ap Yerward. Consecrated 26 March,
 1307; ob. 1309.

1309 Anian Seys. Consecrated 9 Nov. 1309; ob. 26 Jan.
 1327.

YEAR.

1337 Matthew de Englefeld*. Elected 25 Feb. 1337; ob.
25 April, 1357.

1357 Thomas de Ringstede. Succeeded 16 Dec. 1357; ob.
8 Jan. 1365.

1366 Gervase de Castro. Appointed 17 Feb. 1366; ob.
Sept. 1370.

1370 Howel II. Succeeded in Jan. 1370; ob. Feb. 1371.

1371 John Gilbert. Appointed 16 Nov. 1372; translated
to Hereford 12 Sept. 1375.

1376 John Swaffham †, Bishop of Clogher in Ireland. Translated to this See 28 Oct. 1376.

1400 Richard Young. Appointed 20 May, 1400; translated
to Rochester in 1404.

.... Lewis is the next mentioned by Godwin and other
writers, but Le Neve observes there is great uncertainty on the subject.

1408 Benedict Nichols. Appointed 22 July, 1408; translated to St. David's in 1417.

1418 William Barrow, Canon of Lincoln. Appointed 16
April, 1418; translated to Carlisle in 1423.

1424 John Clederow. Appointed 20 March, 1425; ob.
1435. Will proved 23 Dec. in that year.

1436 Thomas Cheryton. Appointed 6 Feb. 1436.

1448 John Stanbery, Confessor to King Henry VI. the first
Provost of Eton. Appointed 4 May, 1448. Translated to Hereford in 1452.

1454 James Blakedon, Bishop of ——, in Ireland. Translated to this See 26 March, 1452; ob. Sept. 1464‡.

---

* Beatson and Heylyn make Lewis I. to have succeeded Bishop
Griffith in 1320, but he is omitted by Le Neve; whilst, on the
other hand, the two writers above cited take no notice of Bishop
Seys.

† Beatson and Heylyn call Jo. Clovensis Suffragan to the Archbishop of Cashell, the successor of Bishop Gilbert, and state
that he was succeeded by Bishop Swaffham in 1383. Le Neve
has, however, been followed in the text.

‡ Heylyn says he was Bishop of Achad-Fobhair, in Ireland; an ancient Bishoprick, now only a parish-church, and
head of a rural deanery, in the diocese of Tuam and county of
Mayo.

YEAR.

1464 Thomas Ednam, alias Richard Evynden. Appointed 18 March, 1464; living 1485.

1496 Henry Deane, Prior of St. Lanthony, and Lord Chancellor of Ireland. Appointed 6 Oct. 1496. Translated to Salisbury in 1500.

1500 Thomas Pigot. Succeeded in 1500; ob. 15 Aug. 1504.

1504 John Penny. Succeeded in 1504; translated to Carlisle in 1509.

1509 John Skeffington, Abbot of Waverley. Consecrated 17 June, 1509; ob. June, 1533.

1534 John Salcot, alias Capon, Abbot of Hyde. Consecrated 19 April, 1534; translated to Salisbury 14 Aug. 1539.

1539 John Bird (the last provincial of the Carmelites). Elected 24 July, 1539; translated to Chester in 1541.

1541 Arthur Bulkeley. Consecrated 19 Feb. 1541; ob. 14 March, 1552.

THE SEE VACANT TWO YEARS.

1555 William Glynn, Master of Queen's College, Cambridge. Consecrated 8 Sept. 1555; ob. 21 May 1558.

1559 Rowland Merrick, Chancellor and Residentiary of St. David's. Consecrated 21 Dec. 1559; ob. 24 Jan. 1566.

1566 Nicholas Robinson. Consecrated Oct. 20, 1566; ob. 13 Feb. 1584.

1585 Hugh Bellot. Consecrated 25 Jan. 1585; translated to Chester in 1595.

1595 Richard Vaughan, Archdeacon of Middlesex. Elected 22 Nov. 1595; translated to Chester in 1597.

1598 Henry Rowlands. Elected 16 Sept. 1598; ob. 6 July 1616.

1616 Lewis Baily. Elected 28 Aug. 1616; ob Oct. 1631.

1632 David Dolben, Vicar of Hackney. Elected 18 Nov. 1631; ob. 27 Nov. 1633.

1633 Edmund Griffith, Dean of Bangor. Elected 31 Dec. 1633; ob. 26 May, 1637.

1637 William Roberts, Sub-dean of Wells. Appointed 24 Sept. 1637; ob. 1665.

1666 Robert Morgan, Archdeacon of Merioneth. Elected 8 June, 1666; ob. 1 Sept. 1673, æt. 65.

YEAR.

1673 Humphrey Lloyd, Dean of St. Asaph. Elected 11 Oct. 1673 ; ob. 18 Jan. 1688, æt. 78.

1689 Humphrey Humphreys, Dean of Bangor. Consecrated 30 June, 1689; translated to Hereford in 1701.

1701 John Evans. Consecrated 4 Jan. 1701 ; translated to Meath, in Ireland, in 1715.

1715 Benjamin Hoadley. Elected 1715; translated to Hereford in 1721.

1721 Richard Reynolds, Dean of Peterborough. Elected 1721; translated to Lincoln in 1723.

1723 William Baker, Warden of Wadham College, Oxford. Elected in 1723; translated to Norwich in 1728.

1728 Thomas Sherlock, Dean of Chichester. Elected in 1728; translated to Salisbury in 1734.

1734 Charles Cecil. Translated from Bristol in 1734; ob. 1737.

1737 Thomas Herring, Dean of Rochester. Elected 1737; translated to York in 1743.

1743 Matthew Hutton. Elected 1743; translated to York in 1748.

1748 Zachariah Pearce, Dean of Winchester. Elected in 1748; translated to Rochester in 1756.

1756 John Egerton, Dean of Hereford. Elected in 1756; translated to Litchfield and Coventry in 1769.

1769 John Ewer. Translated from Landaff in 1769 ; ob. 1774.

1774 John Moore, Dean of Canterbury. Elected 1774; translated to Canterbury in 1783.

1783 John Warren. Translated from St. David's in 1783; ob. 1800.

1800 William Cleaver. Translated from Chester in 1800; translated to St. Asaph in 1807.

1807 John Randolph. Translated from Oxford in 1807; translated to London in 1809.

1809. Henry William Majendie. Translated from Chester in 1809. PRESENT Lord Bishop of Bangor.

BISHOPS OF BATH AND WELLS.

YEAR.

1088 John de Villula, a Frenchman. Succeeded in 1088; ob. 29 Dec. 1122.

1123 Godfrey Chancellor to the Queen. Consecrated 26 Aug. 1123; ob. 16 Aug. 1135.

1136 Robert, Monk of Lewes, in Sussex. Succeeded in 1135, or 1136; ob. 1165.

THE SEE VACANT EIGHT YEARS AND EIGHT MONTHS.

1174 Reginald Fitz Joceline. Consecrated in 1174. Translated to Canterbury in 1191, but died before his translation could be perfected.

1192 Savaricus, Archdeacon of Northampton, and Abbot of Glastonbury; whither he removed the Bishoprick. Consecrated 29 Sept. 1192; ob. 8 Aug. 1205.

1205 Josceline, Canon of Wells, called Josceline de Welles, Consecrated 28 May, 1206; ob. 19 Nov. 1242.

THE SEE VACANT TWO YEARS.

1244 Roger, Chaunter of Salisbury. Consecrated 11 Sept. 1244; ob. 13 Jan. 1247.

1247 William Bitton, or Button I. Archdeacon of Wells. Elected 4 May, 1247; ob. 1264.

1264 Walter Giffard, Canon of Wells, Lord Chancellor. Elected 22 May, 1264. Translated to York in 1266.

1267 William Bitton, or Button II. Archdeacon of Wells. Appointed 4 March, 1266; ob. Nov. 1274.

1274 Robert Burnell, Archdeacon of York, Lord Chancellor, and Lord Treasurer. Elected 23 Jan. 1274; ob. 25 Oct. 1292.

1293 William de Marchia, Dean of St. Martin's, Lord Treasurer. Elected 30 Jan. 1293; ob. June, 1302.

1302 Walter Haselshaw, Dean of Wells. Appointed 12 Sept. 1302; ob. 1309.

1310 John de Drokenesford, Keeper of the King's Wardrobe, and Deputy to the Lord Treasurer. Appointed 15 May, 1309; ob. 8 May, 1329.

N N 3

YEAR

1329 Ralph de Shrewsbury. Elected 2 June, 1329; ob. 14 Aug. 1363.

1363 John Barnet. Translated from Worcester, 24 Nov. 1363; Lord Treasurer. Translated to Ely in 1366.

1366 John Harewell, Chancellor of Gascoigne, Chaplain to the Black Prince. Consecrated 7 May, 1566; ob. July, 1386.

1386 Walter Skirlaw. Translated from Litchfield and Coventry in 1386; translated to Durham in 1388.

1388 Ralph Erghum. Translated from Salisbury 14 Sept. 1388; ob. 10 April, 1401.

1401 Richard Clifford, was elected to this See, but before consecration was removed to Worcester.

1402 Henry Bowet, Canon of Wells. Appointed 19 Aug. 1401; translated to York 1 Dec. 1407.

1408 Nicholas Bubbewith. Translated from Salisbury 1 April, 1408; ob. 27 Oct. 1424.

1425 John Stafford, Dean of Wells, Lord Treasurer. Appointed 12 May, 1425; translated to Canterbury 23 Aug. 1443.

1443 Thomas Beckyngton, Warden of New College, Oxford, Keeper of the Privy Seal. Appointed 24 Sept. 1443; ob. 14 Jan. 1464.

Jo Phreas elected, but died before consecration.

1466 Robert Stillington, Archdeacon of Taunton, Lord Chancellor. Appointed 26 Jan. 1466; ob. May, 1491.

1491 Richard Fox. Translated from Exeter 8 Feb. 1491; translated to Durham in 1495.

1495 Oliver King. Translated from Exeter 6 Nov. 1495; ob. Sept. 1503.

1505 Adrian de Castello, CARDINAL. Translated from Hereford 13 Oct. 1504. Deposed by Pope Leo for a conspiracy in 1518.

1518 Thomas Wolsey, CARDINAL, Archbishop of York. Nominated 28 Aug. 1518, but was never consecrated; he appears to have held this See *in commendam;* Lord Chancellor; resigned this Bishoprick in 1522.

1523 John Clerk, Master of the Rolls, Dean of Windsor. Nominated 2 May, 1523; ob. 3 Jan. 1540.

1541 William Knight, Secretary of State, Prebendary of St.

YEAR.

Paul's. Consecrated 29 May, 1541; ob. 29 Sept. 1547.

1548 William Barlow. Translated from St. David's 3 Feb. 1548; deprived by Queen Mary in 1553. Vide Chichester.

1554 Gilbert Bourn, Prebendary of St. Paul's, Lord President of Wales. Elected 28 March, 1554; ob. 10 Sept. 1560.

1559 Gilbert Berkeley. Elected 29 Jan. 1560; ob. 2 Nov. 1581.

THE SEE VACANT NEARLY THREE YEARS.

1584 Thomas Godwin, Dean of Canterbury. Elected 10 Aug. 1584; ob. 19 Nov. 1590, æt. 73.

THE SEE VACANT TWO YEARS.

1592 John Still, Master of Trinity College, Cambridge, and Prebend of Westminster. Elected 23 Jan. 1592; ob. 26 Feb. 1607.

1608 James Montague, Dean of Worcester. Elected 29 March, 1608; translated to Winchester 4 Oct. 1616.

1616 Arthur Lake, Dean of Worcester, and Master of St. Cross. Elected 17 Oct. 1616; ob. 4 May, 1626.

1626 William Laud. Translated from St. David's, 20 June, 1626; translated to London in July, 1628.

1628 Leonard Mawe, Master of Trinity College, Cambridge. Elected 24 July, 1628; ob. 3 Sept. 1629.

1629 Walter Curle. Translated from Rochester 29 Oct. 1629; translated to Winchester in 1632.

1632 William Pierce. Translated from Peterborough 26 Nov. 1632; ob. April, 1670.

1670 Robert Creighton, Dean of Wells. Elected 25 May, 1670; ob. 21 Nov. 1672, æt. 79.

1672 Peter Mew, Dean of Rochester. Elected 19 Dec. 1672; translated to Winchester 22 Nov. 1684.

1685 Thomas Kenn, Prebend of Winchester. Consecrated 25 Jan. 1685; deprived for not taking the oaths to King William and Queen Mary, 1 Feb. 1691.

YEAR.

1691 Richard Kidder, Dean of Peterborough. Nominated 13 June, 1691; ob. 26 Nov. 1703.

1703 George Hooper. Translated from St. Asaph, 14 March, 1703; ob. 1727.

1727 John Wynne. Translated from St. Asaph, 1727; ob. 1743.

1743 Edward Willes. Translated from St. David's in 1744; ob. 1774.

1774 Charles Moss. Translated from St. David's, 1774; ob. 1802.

1802 Richard Beadon. Translated from Gloucester, 1802; ob. 1824.

1824 George Henry Law. Translated from Chester, 1824, PRESENT Lord Bishop of Bath and Wells.

BISHOPS OF BRISTOL.

This Diocese was one of the six Sees erected by Henry VIII. out of the spoils of the Monasteries and other religious houses which that monarch dissolved.

YEAR.

1542 Paul Bushe, Provincial of the Bonhommes. Appointed 16 June, 1542; resigned the See on the Accession of Mary in 1553; ob. 11 Oct. 1558, æt. 68.

1554 John Holyman, Monk of Reading. Elected 10 Nov. 1554; ob. 20 Dec. 1558.

THE SEE VACANT ABOVE THREE YEARS.

1562 Richard Cheney, Archdeacon of Hereford. Appointed 29 April, 1562. He held the See of Gloucester, by dispensation, with this See; ob. 1578.

THE SEE VACANT ABOVE TWO YEARS.

1581 John Bullingham, Prebendary of Worcester and St. Paul's. Succeeded to this See and that of Glouces-

YEAR.

ter, which he held by dispensation, in 1581; he resigned the See of Bristol in 1589.

1589 Richard Fletcher, Dean of Peterborough. Elected 13 Nov. 1589, translated to Worcester in 1593.

THE SEE VACANT TEN YEARS.

1603 John Thornborough. Translated from Limerick in Ireland, 30 May, 1603; translated to Worcester 8 Dec. 1616.

1617 Nicholas Felton, Prebendary of St. Paul's. Elected 4 March, 1617; translated to Ely in 1618.

1619 Rowland Searchfield, Vicar of Charlbury in Oxfordshire. Elected 18 March, 1619; ob. 11 Oct. 1622.

1622 Robert Wright, Canon of Wells. Elected 28 Jan. 1623; translated to Litchfield and Coventry in 1632.

1632 George Coke. Elected 28 Nov. 1632; translated to Hereford in 1636.

1636 Robert Skinner. Elected 26 July, 1636; translated to Oxford in 1641.

1641 Thomas Westfield, Archdeacon of St. Albans. Succeeded in 1641; ob. 28 June, 1644.

1644 Thomas Howell, Canon of Windsor. Nominated in July, 1644; ob. 1646.

THE SEE VACANT SIXTEEN YEARS *.

1660 Gilbert Ironside, Prebendary of York. Elected 14 Dec. 1660; ob. 19 Sept. 1671.

1671 Guy Carleton, Dean of Carlisle. Elected 20 Dec. 1671; translated to Chichester 8 Jan. 1678.

1678 William Gulston, Rector of Symondsbury, Dorsetshire. Elected 16 Jan. 1678; ob. 4 April, 1684.

1684 John Lake. Translated from Sodor and Man, 12 Aug. 1684; translated to Chichester in Oct. 1685.

1685 Sir Jonathan Trelawny, Bart. Consecrated 8 Nov. 1685; translated to Exeter 13 April 1689.

* *Quere*, de Samuele Collins, 1651 ? Vide Fuller's Worthies, p. 137.

YEAR.

1689 Gilbert Ironside, Warden of Wadham College, Oxford. Consecrated 13 Oct. 1689; translated to Hereford 29 July, 1691.

1691 John Hall, Master of Pembroke College, Oxford. Consecrated 30 Aug. 1691; ob. 4 Feb. 1709.

1710 John Robinson, Dean of Windsor, Lord Privy Seal. Consecrated 19 Nov. 1710; translated to London in 1713.

1714 George Smallridge, Dean of Christ Church, Oxford Consecrated 14 April, 1714; ob. 1719.

1719 Hugh Boulter, Archdeacon of Surrey. Elected 1719; translated to Armagh in Ireland, 1724; ob. 1742.

1724 William Bradshaw, Dean of Christ Church, Oxford. Elected 1724; ob. 1732.

1732 Charles Cecil. Elected 1732; translated to Bangor in 1734.

1734 Thomas Secker, Prebendary of Durham. Elected 1734; translated to Oxford 1737.

1737 Thomas Gooch, Prebendary of Canterbury. Elected 1737; translated to Norwich in 1738.

1738 Joseph Butler, Prebendary of Rochester. Elected 1738; translated to Durham 1750.

1750 John Coneybeare, Dean of Christ Church, Oxford. Elected 1750; ob. 1758.

1758 John Hume, Residentiary of St. Paul's. Elected 1758; translated to Oxford the same year.

1758 Philip Yonge, Residentiary of St. Paul's. Elected 1758; translated to Norwich 1761.

1761 Thomas Newton, Prebendary of Westminster, and Dean of St. Paul's. Elected 1761; ob. 1782.

1782 Lewis Bagot, Dean of Christ Church, Oxford. Elected 1782; translated to Norwich 1785.

1785 Christopher Wilson, Prebendary of Westminster. Elected 1785; ob. 1792.

1792 Spencer Madan, Canon Residentiary of Litchfield. Elected 1792; translated to Peterborough 1794.

1794 Henry Reginald Courtenay, Prebendary of Rochester. Elected 1794; translated to Exeter in 1797.

1797 Folliot Herbert Walker Cornwall, Dean of Canterbury. Elected 1797; translated to Hereford 1802.

1802 Hon. George Pelham. Elected 1803; translated to Exeter 1807.

YEAR.

1808 William Lort Mansel. Elected 1808; ob. 1820.
1820 John Kaye. Elected 1820. PRESENT Lord Bishop of
Bristol.

BISHOPS OF CHICHESTER.

YEAR.

1082 Stigand was appointed Bishop of Selsey by William the
Conqueror 23 May, 1070; and was translated to
the See of Chichester circa 1082; ob. 1087.

1087 Godfrey, by some improperly called William. Consecrated 1087; ob. 1088.

1091 Ralph became Bishop of this See in 1091; ob.
1123.

1125 Seffridus I. Abbot of Glastonbury. Consecrated 12
April, 1125; ob. 1150.

11.. Hilary. It is uncertain when he obtained this See,
some authorities state in 1133, but others assert
that he was consecrated 3 Aug. 1147; if either be
correct his predecessor must have been deprived or
resigned; ob. 1169.

THE SEE VACANT FOR ABOUT FOUR YEARS.

1173 John de Greenford, Dean of Chichester. Elected
1173; ob. 1180.

1180 Seffridus II. Consecrated 17 Oct. 1180; ob. 1204.

1199 Simon de Welles. Obtained this See 11 July, 1204;
ob. 1207.

1209 Nicholas de Aquila. Succeeded in 1209; ob. or resigned in 1215.

1215 Richard Poor, Dean of Salisbury. Consecrated 25
Jan. 1215; translated to Salisbury in 1217.

1217 Ralph de Warham, Prior of Norwich. Elected 17
Dec. 1218; ob. 14 Sept. 1222.

1223 Ralph Nevill, Lord Chancellor. Elected 1 Nov. 1222;
elected to Canterbury, but rejected by the Pope;
ob. 1 Feb. 1244.

Robert Papelew was elected next Bishop, but
the election was made void.

1245 St. Richard, surnamed de la Wich. Consecrated 1245;
ob. 2 or 3 April 1253, æt. 56.

1258 John Clipping, Dean of Chichester.   Consecrated
    1258; ob. 1261.

1261 Stephen de Berksteed.   Appointed 20 June, 1261;
    ob. 21 Oct. 1287.

1288 St. Gilbert de Sancto Leofardo, Treasurer of Chiches-
    ter; styled "father to orphans, comforter to wi-
    dows, visitor to the sick, and refresher to the poor."
    Elected 30 Jan. 1288; ob. 12 Feb. 1305.

1306 John Langton, Lord Chancellor.   Elected 5 April,
    1305; ob. 1337.

1338 Robert Stratford, Archdeacon of Canterbury, Lord
    Chancellor, and Chancellor of Oxford.   Appointed
    21 Sept. 1337; ob. 9 April, 1362.

1362 William de Lenne, or Lullimore.   Consecrated about
    June 1362; translated to Worcester in Oct. 1368.

1369 William Reade.   Appointed 11 Oct. 1369; ob. 1385.

1385 Thomas Rushooke.   Translated from Landaff 6 Dec.
    1385; deprived in 1388.

1389 Richard Mitford, Lord Treasurer of Ireland.   Ap-
    pointed 7 May, 1389; translated to Salisbury in
    1395.

1395 Robert Waldby, Archbishop * of Dublin.   Translated
    to this See in 1395; removed to York in 1396.

1396 Robert Reade.   Translated from Carlisle, 12 May,
    1396; ob. 1417.

1417 Stephen Partington.   Translated from St. David's in
    Dec. 1417, but died before his translation could be
    perfected.

1418 Henry Ware, Official to the Archbishop of Canter-
    bury, and Prebend of St. Paul's.   Appointed 13
    May, 1418.

1421 John Kemp.   Translated from Rochester 28 Feb.
    1421; translated to London 17 Nov. following.

1423 Thomas Poldon.   Translated from Hereford 17 Nov.
    1421; translated to Worcester in March 1425.

1426 John Rickingale, Chancellor of York.   Appointed 1
    May, 1426; ob. July, 1429.

1430 John Sidenham, Dean of Salisbury.   Appointed 24
    Jan. 1430; ob. Feb. 1437.

---

* Heylin and Beatson call him *Archdeacon* of Dublin, but as in
the text in Le Neve.

YEAR.

1438 Richard Praty, Chancellor of Oxford. Appointed 14 July, 1438; ob. July, 1445.

1445 Adam Molins, Dean of Salisbury, Lord Privy Seal. Appointed 3 Dec. 1445; murdered at Portsmouth 9 June, 1449.

1450 Reginald Peacock. Translated from St. Asaph 23 March, 1450; deprived for opposing the Romish tenets in 1457.

1459 John Arundel, Prebendary of St. Paul's. Appointed 26 March, 1459.

1478 Edward Story. Translated from Carlisle 27 March, 1478; ob. 1503.

1504 Richard Fitz-James. Translated from Rochester 29 Jan. 1504; translated to London in 1506.

1508 Robert Sherburn. Translated from St. David's 18 Sept. 1508; resigned this See a little before his death, which occurred 21 Aug. 1536, æt. 96.

1536 Richard Sampson, Dean of Litchfield; and in 1536 appointed Dean of St. Paul's. Consecrated 9 June 1536; translated to Litchfield and Coventry in March, 1543.

1543 George Day, Provost of King's College, Cambridge. Elected 24 April, 1543; deprived 10 Oct. 1551, and imprisoned; restored by Queen Mary in 1553; ob. 2 Aug. 1556.

1552 John Scory. Translated from Rochester 23 May, 1552; deprived by Queen Mary in 1553; and in 1559 made Bishop of Hereford by Queen Elizabeth.

1557 John Christopherson, Dean of Norwich. Consecrated 21 Nov. 1557; deprived in 1558, and died in Dec. the same year.

1559 William Barlow, the deprived Bishop of Bath and Wells. Appointed to this See 20 Dec. 1559; ob. Aug. 1568.

1570 Richard Curteys. Confirmed 26 April, 1570; ob. Aug. 1582.

THE SEE VACANT THREE YEARS.

1585 Thomas Bickley, Warden of Merton College, Oxford. Elected 30 Dec. 1585; ob. 30 April, 1596, æt. 90.

1596 Anthony Watson, Dean of Bristol, Bishop Almoner. Nominated 1 June, 1596; ob. 10 Sept. 1605.

1605 Launcelot Andrews, Dean of Westminster. Elected
　　　16 Oct. 1605 ; translated to Ely in 1609.

1609 Samuel Harsnet, Archdeacon of Essex, Elected 13
　　　Nov. 1609; translated to Norwich in 1619.

1619 George Carleton. Translated from Landaff, 8 Sept.
　　　1619; ob. May, 1628.

1628 Richard Montague, Canon of Windsor. Elected 14
　　　July, 1628 ; translated to Norwich in 1638.

1638 Brian Duppa, Dean of Christ Church, Oxford, Tutor
　　　to the Prince. Appointed 12 June, 1638; trans-
　　　lated to Salisbury in 1641.

1641 Henry King, Dean of Rochester. Consecrated 19
　　　Dec. 1641 ; ob. Sept. or Oct. 1669.

1670 Peter Gunning, Master of St. John's College, Cam-
　　　bridge. Elected 17 Feb. 1670; translated to Ely 4
　　　March, 1675.

1675 Ralph Brideoke, Dean of Salisbury. Elected 9 March,
　　　1675 ; ob. 6 July, 1678, æt. 74.

1679 Guy Carleton. Translated from Bristol 8 Jan. 1679;
　　　ob. 6 July, 1685.

1685 John Lake. Translated from Bristol 19 Oct. 1685;
　　　deprived for not taking the oaths; ob. Aug. 1689.

1689 Simon Patrick, Dean of Peterborough. Consecrated
　　　13 Oct. 1689; translated to Ely 2 July, 1691.

1691 Robert Grove, Archdeacon of Middlesex. Consecrated
　　　30 Aug. 1691.

1696 John Williams, Prebendary of Canterbury. Conse-
　　　crated 13 Dec. 1696.

1709 Thomas Manningham, Dean of Windsor. Confirmed
　　　10 Nov. 1709; ob. 1722.

1722 Thomas Bowers, Archdeacon of Canterbury. Elected
　　　1722; ob. 1724.

1724 Edward Waddington. Elected 1724; ob. 1731.

1731 Francis Hare. Translated from St. Asaph 1731 ; ob.
　　　1740.

1740 Matthias Mawson. Translated from Landaff 1740;
　　　translated to Ely 1754.

1754 Sir William Ashburnham, Bart. Dean of Chichester.
　　　Elected 1754 ; ob. 1797.

1797 John Buckner. Elected 1797 ; ob. 1824.

1824 Robert James Carr. Elected 1824. PRESENT Lord
　　　Bishop of Chichester.

COVENTRY.—Vide Litchfield.

BISHOPS OF ST. DAVID'S,

WITH ARCHIEPISCOPAL POWER.

YEAR.

1061 Bleitbud, or Bledud; ob. circa 1070.

1070 Sulgheyn. He resigned in 1076.

1076 Abraham. Slain in 1078.

1078 Sulgheyn resumed the Bishoprick in 1078, and again resigned it in 1085; ob. 1088.

1085 Rythmark, or Rithmarch. Succeeded in 1085, and died in 1096 or 1100.

1100 Wilfridus, or Griffry; ob. 1115.

1115 Bernard, Chancellor to Queen Adeliza; he submited himself and his church to the See of Canterbury. Consecrated in 1115; ob. 1147.

BISHOPS OF ST. DAVID'S,

SUFFRAGANS TO THE SEE OF CANTERBURY.

YEAR.

1147 David Fitz Gerald, Archdeacon of Cardigan. Consecrated 19 Dec. 1147; ob. May, 1176.

1176 Peter de Leia, Prior of Wenlock. Consecrated 7 Nov. 1176; ob. 16 July, 1198.

1199 Giraldus Cambrensis, alias Barry. Elected 1199; resigned 10 Nov. 1203.

1203 Geoffrey. Elected 10 Nov. 1203; ob. 1214.

1214 Gervase. Consecrated 1214; ob. 1229.

1230 Anselm le Gros. Consecrated in March, 1230; ob. 1247.

1248 Thomas Wallensis. Consecrated 26 July, 1248, according to Wikes, and 25 July, 1259, according to Wharton; ob. 11 July, 1255.

1256 Richard de Carew. Consecrated in 1256; ob. 1 April, 1280.

1280 Thomas Beck, Archdeacon of Dorset. Elected 3 June, 1280; Lord Treasurer; ob. 14 April, 1293.

YEAR.

1293 David Martyn. Elected June, 1293; ob. 9 March, 1328.

1328 Henry Gower. Elected 21 April, 1328; ob. 1347.

1347 John Thoresby. Consecrated 23 Sept. 1347; Lord Chancellor; translated to Worcester in 1349.

1350 Reginald Brian. Appointed 18 Jan. 1350; translated to Worcester in 1352.

1353 Thomas Falstóffe. Appointed 29 March, 1353; ob. June, 1361.

1361 Adam Houghton. Appointed 20 Sept. 1361; Lord Chancellor; ob. 13 Feb. 1389.

Richard Metford was Elected, but set aside by the Pope.

1389 John Gilbert. Translated from Hereford, 6 May, 1389; Lord Treasurer; ob. 28 July, 1397.

THE SEE VACANT FOUR YEARS.

1401 Guy de Mona. Appointed 9 Oct. 1401; Lord Treasurer; ob. 31 Aug. 1407.

1408 Henry Chicheley, Archdeacon of Salisbury. Appointed 8 April, 1408; translated to Canterbury in 1414.

1414 John Ketterich, alias Catryk, Archdeacon of Surrey. Appointed 27 April, 1414; translated to Litchfield and Coventry 1 Feb. 1415.[1]

1415 Stephen Patryngton. Appointed 6 April, 1415; translated to Chichester in 1417.

1417 Benedict Nicholls. Translated from Bangor 15 Dec. 1417; ob. 1433.

1433 Thomas Rodeburn. Appointed 5 Oct. 1433; ob. circa 1442.

1442 William Lynwood. Appointed 14 Aug. 1442; Lord Privy Seal; ob. 21 Oct. 1446.

1447 John Langton, Chancellor of Cambridge. Appointed 23 Jan. 1447; ob. May, 1447.

1447 John Delabere, Dean of Wells. Appointed 15 Sept. 1447; living 1460 *.

1460 Robert Tully. Appointed 20 Oct. 1460; ob. 1481.

---

* Vide a note in Le Neve's *Fasti Ecclesiæ Anglicanæ*, relative to this prelate.

YEAR.

1482 Richard Martin, Privy Counsellor to King Edward IV. Appointed 26 April, 1482 ; ob. circa 1483.

1483 Thomas Langton, Prebendary of Wells. Appointed 21 May, 1483; translated to Salisbury, 9 Feb. 1485.

1484 Andrew ————; his surname does not appear, nor is he noticed by Godwin, Isaacson, Heylyn, or Beatson ; Le Neve, however, states that he subscribed his name as a witness to a deed given in Rymer, dated 25 June, 1484.

1485 Hugh Pavy, alias Parry, Archdeacon of Wilts. Appointed 19 Sept. 1485; ob. ......

1496 John Morgan, alias Young, Dean of Windsor. Appointed 23 Nov. 1496; ob. May 1504.

1505 Robert Sherborne, Dean of St. Paul. Appointed 12 April, 1505: translated to Chichester 18 Sept. 1508.

1509 Edward Vaughan, Treasurer and Prebendary of St. Paul's. Appointed 13 June, 1509 ; ob. Nov. 1522.

1523 Richard Rawlins, Prebendary of St. Paul's. Appointed 11 March, 1523 ; ob. 18 Feb. 1536.

1536 William Barlow. Translated from St. Asaph 10 April, 1536; translated to Bath and Wells 3 Feb. 1548.

1548 Robert Ferrar. Appointed 1 July, 1548 ; deprived by Queen Mary 20 March, 1554, and burnt 30 March, 1555.

1553 Henry Morgan, Principal of St. Edward Hall, Oxford. Consecrated 1 April, 1553 ; deprived by Queen Elizabeth June, 1559.

1559 Thomas Young, Chancellor of St. David's. Elected 6 Dec. 1559; translated to York 25 Feb. 1561.

1561 Richard Davies. Translated from St. Asaph 21 May, 1561 ; ob. Oct. 1581, æt. 80.

1582 Marmaduke Middleton. Translated from Waterford, in Ireland, 6 Dec. 1582 ; deprived in 1590 for publishing a forged will ; ob. 30 Nov. 1592.

THE SEE VACANT TWO YEARS.

1594 Anthony Rudd, Dean of Gloucester. Elected 8 March, 1594; ob. 7 March, 1615.

YEAR.

1615 Richard Milbourne, Dean of Rochester. Elected 20 April, 1615 ; translated to Carlisle in June 1631.

1621 William Laud, Dean of Gloucester. Elected 10 Oct. 1621 ; translated to Bath and Wells 18 Sept. 1626.

1627 Theophilus Field. Translated from Landaff 12 July, 1627; translated to Hereford in 1635.

1636 Roger Manwaring, Dean of Worcester. Elected 19 Jan. 1636; ob. July 1, 1653.

THE SEE VACANT ABOVE SEVEN YEARS.

1660 William Lucy. Elected 11 Oct. 1660; ob. 4 Oct. 1677.

1677 William Thomas, Dean of Worcester. Elected 19 Nov. 1677; translated to Worcester in 1683.

1683 Lawrence Womack, Archdeacon of Suffolk. Consecrated 11 Nov. 1683; ob. 12 March, 1686, æt. 73.

1686 John Lloyd, Principal of Jesus College, Oxford. Consecrated 17 Oct. 1686; ob. 13. Feb. 1687.

1687 Thomas Watson. Consecrated 26 June, 1687 ; deprived for Simony and other crimes 3 August, 1699.

THE SEE VACANT FIVE YEARS AND EIGHT MONTHS.

1705 George Bull, Archdeacon of Landaff. Elected 23 March, 1705; ob. 18 Feb. 1710.

1710 Philip Bisse. Consecrated 19 Nov. 1710 ; translated to Hereford 16 Feb. 1712.

1712 Adam Ottley, Archdeacon of Salop, and Prebendary of Hereford. Elected 28 Feb. 1712; ob. 1723.

1723 Richard Smalbroke, Treasurer of Landaff. Elected 1723 ; translated to Litchfield and Coventry 1730.

1730 Elias Sydall, Dean of Canterbury. Elected 1730; translated to Gloucester 1731.

1731 Nicholas Clagett, Dean of Rochester. Elected 1731 ; translated to Exeter 1743.

1743 Edward Willes, Dean of Lincoln. Elected 1743 ; translated to Bath and Wells 1744.

1744 Hon. Richard Trevor, Canon of Windsor. Elected 1744 ; translated to Durham 1752.

1752 Anthony Ellis, Prebendary of Gloucester. Elected 1752; ob. 1761.

1761 Samuel Squire, Dean of Bristol. Elected 1761 ; ob. 1766.

YEAR.

1766 Robert Lowth, Prebendary of Durham; Elected 1766 ; translated to Oxford the same year.

1766 Charles Moss, Archdeacon of Colchester. Elected 1766 ; translated to Bath and Wells 1774.

1774 Hon. James York, Dean of Lincoln. Elected 1774 ; translated to Gloucester 1779.

1779 John Warren, Archdeacon of Worcester. Elected 1779 ; translated to Bangor 1783.

1783 Edward Smallwell. Elected 1783 ; translated to Oxford 1788.

1788 Samuel Horsley, Prebendary of Gloucester. Elected 1788 ; translated to Rochester 1793.

1793 Hon. William Stuart. Elected 1793 ; translated to Armagh 1800.

1800 Lord George Murray. Elected 1800; ob. 1803.

1803 Thomas Burgess, Prebendary of Durham. Elected 1803. PRESENT Lord Bishop of St. David's.

BISHOPS of ELY.

YEAR.

1109 Hervey, translated from Bangor in 1109; ob. 30 Aug. 1131.

THE SEE VACANT TWO YEARS.

1133 Nigellus, Prebendary of St. Paul's. Consecrated 1 Oct. 1133 ; Lord Treasurer; ob. 3 June, 1169.

THE SEE VACANT FIVE YEARS.

1174 Geoffrey Ridel, a Baron of the Exchequer, Lord Treasurer. Consecrated 6 Oct. 1174; ob. 21 Aug. 1189.

1189 William Longchamp, Lord Chancellor, Legate. Consecrated 31 Dec. 1189; ob. 31 Jan. 1198.

1198 Eustace, Dean of Salisbury. Consecrated 1 March, 1198 ; Lord Chancellor; ob. 2 or 3 Feb. 1215.

THE SEE VACANT FIVE YEARS.

YEAR.

1220 John de Fontibus, Abbot of Fountains in Yorkshire. Consecrated 8 March, 1220; ob. 6 May, 1225.

1225 Geoffrey de Burgh, or Burrough, Archdeacon of Norwich. Consecrated 29 June, 1225; ob. 17 May, 1229.

1229 Hugh Northwold, or Norwold, Abbot of St. Edmundsbury. Consecrated 10 June, 1229; ob. 6 Aug. 1254.

1255 William de Kilkenny, Archdeacon of Coventry. Consecrated 15 Aug. 1255; Lord Chancellor; ob. 21 Sept. 1256.

1257 Hugh Balsam, Sub-Prior of Ely. Consecrated 14 Oct. 1257; ob. June, 1286.

1286 John de Kirkeby, Canon of Wells and York. Elected 26 July, 1286; Lord Treasurer; ob. 26 March, 1290.

1290 William de Luda, Archdeacon of Durham. Elected 4 May, 1290; Lord Chancellor; ob. 25 March, 1298.

1299 Ralph Walpole. Translated from Norwich 15 July 1299; ob. 22 March, 1302.

1302 Robert Orford, Prior of Ely. Elected 14 April, 1302; ob. 21 Jan. 1310

1310 John de Ketene or Keeton, Almoner of Ely. Elected 10 July, 1310; ob. 14 May, 1316.

1316 John Hotham, Prebendary of York. Appointed 20 July 1316; Lord Chancellor and Lord Treasurer; ob. 25 Jan. 1337.

1337 Simon de Montacute. Translated from Worcester in March, 1337; ob. 20 June, 1344.

1344 Thomas Lisle or Lylde, Prior of Winchester. Consecrated July, 1344; died in exile 23 June, 1361.

1362 Simon Langham, Abbot of Westminster. Appointed 10 Jan. 1362; Lord Treasurer, and afterwards Lord Chancellor; translated to Canterbury 25 July, 1366.

1366 John Barnet. Translated from Bath and Wells 15 Dec. 1366; Lord Treasurer; ob. 7 June, 1373.

1374 Thomas de Arundel, alias Fitz-Alan, Archdeacon of Taunton. Appointed 9 April, 1374; Lord Chancellor; translated to York 3 April, 1388.

1388 John Fordham. Translated from Durham, 3 April, 1388; ob. 19 Nov. 1425.

1426 Philip Morgan. Translated from Worcester 22 April, 1426; ob. 25 Oct. 1434.

1438 Louis de Luxemburgh, called by Le Neve, Lewis Lushborough, Archbishop of Rouen in France. A Cardinal. Appointed 3 April, 1438; ob. 18 Sept. 1443.

1443 Thomas Bourchier. Translated from Worcester 20 Dec. 1443; translated to Canterbury in 1454.

1454 William Grey, Archdeacon of Northampton. Appointed 6 Sept. 1454; Lord Treasurer; ob. 4 Aug. 1478.

1478 John Morton, Prebendary of Salisbury, Lincoln, St. Paul's, and York. Elected 9 Aug. 1478; Master of the Rolls, Lord Chancellor; translated to Canterbury in 1486. A Cardinal.

1486 John Alcock. Translated from Worcester 7 Dec. 1486; Lord Chancellor; ob. 1 Oct. 1500.

1501 Richard Redman. Translated from Exeter 26 Sept. 1501; ob. 25 Aug. 1505.

1506 James Stanley, Warden of Manchester and Dean of St. Martin's. Appointed 5 Nov. 1506; ob. 23 Mar. 1515.

1515 Nicholas West, Dean of Windsor. Appointed 18 May, 1515; ob. April, 1533.

1534 Thomas Goodrich, Canon of St. Stephen's, Westminster. Elected 17 March, 1534; Lord Chancellor; ob. 10 May, 1554.

1554 Thomas Thirlby. Translated from Norwich 15 Sept. 1554; deprived 1558; ob. 26 Aug. 1570.

1559 Richard Cox, Dean of Christ Church, Oxford. Elected 28 July, 1559; ob. July, 1581.

THE SEE VACANT ABOVE EIGHTEEN YEARS.

1599 Martin Heton, Dean of Winchester. Elected 20 Dec. 1599; ob. 12 July, 1609.

1609 Lancelot Andrews. Translated from Chichester 22 Sept. 1609; translated to Winchester, March, 1619.

1619 Nicholas Felton. Translated from Bristol 2 March, 1619; ob. 5 Oct. 1626.

1628 John Buckeridge. Translated from Rochester 17 April, 1628; ob. 23 May, 1631.

1631 Francis White. Translated from Norwich 15 Nov. 1631; ob. Feb. 1638.

1638 Matthew Wren. Translated from Norwich 5 May, 1638; ob. 24 April, 1667.

YEAR.

1667 Benjamin Laney. Translated from Lincoln, 24 May, 1667 ; ob. 24 Jan. 1675.

1675 Peter Gunning. Translated from Chichester, 13 Feb. 1675 ; ob. 6 July, 1684, æt. 71.

1684 Francis Turner. Translated from Rochester 23 Aug. 1684; deprived for not taking the oaths 1 Feb. 1690.

1691 Simon Patrick. Translated from Chichester 23 April, 1691 ; ob. 31 May, 1707.

1707 John Moore. Translated from Norwich 31 July, 1707 ; ob. 31 July, 1714.

1714 William Fleetwood. Translated from St. Asaph 18 Dec. 1714; ob. 1723.

1723 Thomas Green. Translated from Norwich 1723; ob. 1738.

1738 Robert Butts. Translated from Norwich 1738; ob. 1748.

1748 Sir Thomas Gooch, Bart. Translated from Norwich 1748; ob. 1754.

1754 Matthias Mawson. Translated from Chichester 1754; ob. 1770.

1770 Edmund Keene. Translated from Chester 1770; ob. 1781.

1781 Hon. James Yorke. Translated from Gloucester 1781; ob. 1808.

1808 Thomas Dampier. Translated from Rochester 1808; ob. 1812.

1812 Bowyer Edward Sparke. Translated from Chester 1812. PRESENT Lord Bishop of Ely.

BISHOPS OF EXETER.

YEAR.

1050 Leofric Bishop of Devonshire and Cornwall. Settled both those Sees at Exeter anno 1050; ob. 10 Feb. 1074.

1074 Osbert. Consecrated 28 May, 1074; ob. 1103.

THE SEE VACANT NINE YEARS.

1107 William Warlewast. Said by some writers to have

.been Consecrated in 1112, and to have died in 1127 ; but according to others he was Consecrated 11 August, 1107, resigned his See in 1127, and died 1st Oct. 1137.

1128 Robert Chichester. Succeeded in 1128 or 1138; ob. 1150.

1150 Robert Warlewast. Succeeded in 1150; ob. 1159.

1161 Bartholomew Iscan. Consecrated in 1161 ; ob. 15 Dec. 1184.

1185 John. Elected in 1185 ; ob. 1 June, 1191.

THE SEE VACANT ABOVE TWO YEARS.

1193 Henry Marshall. Elected in 1193; ob. Oct. 1206.

THE SEE VACANT ABOVE SEVEN YEARS.

1214 Simon de Apulia. Consecrated 1 Oct. 1214; ob. 1223 or 1224.

1224 William Brewer, Privy Counsellor to King III. Consecrated 14 April, 1224; ob. 24 Oct. 1244.

1245 Richard Blondy. Consecrated 22 Oct. 1245; ob. 26 Dec. 1257.

1258 Walter Bronescombe, Archdeacon of Surrey. Elected 25 Feb. 1258; ob. 22 July, 1280.

1280 Peter Quiril, Canon of Exeter. Consecrated 1280; ob. 6 Oct. 1291.

1292 Thomas de Button, Dean of Wells. Elected 30 Nov. 1292; ob. Sept. or Oct. 1307.

1307 Walter Stapleton. Elected Nov. 1307; Lord Treasurer; beheaded by the mob in London 15 Oct. 1326.

1326 James de Berkeley. Elected 12 Dec. 1326 ; ob. 24 June, 1327.

John Godeleigh was Elected, and had the Royal assent 31 July, 1327; but before Consecration he was set aside by the Pope.

1327 John Grandison. Appointed 28 Aug. 1327; ob. July, 1369.

1370 Thomas Brentingham, Lord Treasurer. Appointed 4 March, 1370; ob. 3 Dec. 1394.

YEAR.

1395 Edmund Stafford. Appointed 15 Jan. 1395; Lord
　　　Chancellor; ob. Aug. 1419.

1419 John Ketterich. Translated from Litchfield and Co-
　　　ventry 20 Nov. 1419; ob. 1420.

　　　　　James Cary, Bishop of Litchfield and Coventry,
　　　　　　is called by Godwin the next Bishop of this
　　　　　　See; but he died before he took possession
　　　　　　of the dignity.

1420 Edmund Lacy. Translated from Hereford 3 July,
　　　1420; ob. 18 Sept. 1455.

　　　　　John Halls was next offered this See, but he
　　　　　　refused it.

1456 George Nevill, Prebendary of Lincoln. Appointed
　　　21 March, 1456; Lord Chancellor, and Chancellor
　　　of Oxford; translated to York 15 March, 1465.

1465 John Booth, Prebendary of St. Paul's. Appointed 12
　　　June 1465; ob. 1 April, 1478.

1478 Peter Courtenay, Archdeacon of Exeter. Appointed
　　　5 Sept. 1478; translated to Winchester 29 Jan.
　　　1487.

1487 Richard Fox, Prebendary of Salisbury. Appointed
　　　2 April, 1487; Lord Privy Seal; translated to Bath
　　　and Wells 8 Feb. 1492.

1492 Oliver King, Prebendary of St. Paul's. Appointed 1
　　　Oct. 1492; translated to Bath and Wells in 1495.

1496 Richard Redman. Translated from St. Asaph 7 Jan.
　　　1496; translated to Ely in Sept. 1501.

1502 John Arundel. Translated from Litchfield and Co-
　　　ventry 29 June, 1502; ob. 15 March, 1504.

1504 Hugh Oldham, Prebendary of York and Litchfield.
　　　Appointed 27 Nov. 1504; ob. 25 June, 1519.

1519 John Voysey, alias Harman, Dean of Windsor. Ap-
　　　pointed 31 Aug. 1519. He resigned this See in 1551.

1551 Miles Coverdale. Appointed 14 Aug. 1551. De-
　　　prived and banished by Queen Mary in 1553;
　　　and, after her death, he refused to return to his
　　　Bishoprick, and lived privately until he attained the
　　　81st year of his age.

1553 John Voysey. Restored to the Bishoprick 28 Sept.
　　　1553; ob. 23 Oct. 1554.

1555 James Turberville. Consecrated 8 Sept. 1555; de-
　　　prived in Jan. 1560.

YEAR.

1560 William Alley, Prebendary of St. Paul's. Elected 20 May, 1560; ob. April, 1570.

1571 William Bradbridge, Dean of Salisbury. Elected 1 March, 1571; ob. 27 June, 1578.

1579 John Wolton, Canon-residentiary of Exeter. Elected 2 July, 1579; ob. 13 March, 1594.

1594 Gervase Babington. Translated from Landaff, 4 Feb. 1594; translated to Worcester 4 Oct. 1597.

1598 William Cotton, Canon-residentiary of St. Paul's. Elected 6 Sept. 1598; ob. 26 Aug. 1621.

1621 Valentine Carey, Dean of St. Paul's. Elected 27 Sept. 1621; ob. 10 June, 1626.

1627 Joseph Hall, Dean of Worcester. Elected 5 Nov. 1627; translated to Norwich in 1641.

1642 Ralph Brownrigg, Prebendary of Durham. Elected 31 March, 1642; ob. 7 Dec. 1659.

1660 John Gauden, Master of the Temple. Elected 3 Nov. 1660; translated to Worcester in 1661.

1662 Seth Ward, Dean of Exeter. Elected 8 July, 1662; translated to Salisbury in 1667.

1667 Anthony Sparrow, Archdeacon of Sudbury. Elected 14 Oct. 1667; translated to Norwich in 1676.

1676 Thomas Lamplugh, Dean of Rochester. Elected 3 Oct. 1676; translated to York, 8 Dec. 1688.

1689 Sir Jonathan Trelawney, Bart. Translated from Bristol 13 April, 1689; translated to Winchester in 1707.

1707 Offspring Blackhall. Elected 23 Jan. 1707; ob. 1716.

1716 Lancelot Blackburn, Dean of Exeter. Elected 1716; translated to York 1724.

1724 Stephen Weston. Elected 1724; ob. 1743.

1743 Nicholas Clagget. Translated from St. David's 1743; ob. 1746.

1746 George Lavington, Canon-residentiary of St. Paul's. Elected 1746; ob. 1762, æt. 79.

1762 Hon. Frederick Keppel, Canon and Dean of Windsor. Elected 1762; ob. 1777.

1778 John Ross, Prebendary of Durham. Elected 1778; ob. 1792.

1792 William Buller, Dean of Canterbury. Elected 1792; ob. 1796.

1797 Henry Reginald Courtenay. Translated from Bristol 1797; ob. 1803.

YEAR.

1803 John Fisher, Archdeacon of Exeter. Elected 1803; translated to Salisbury 1807.

1807 Hon. George Pelham. Translated from Bristol 1807; translated to Lincoln 1820.

1820 William Carey. Elected 1820. PRESENT Lord Bishop of Exeter.

BISHOPS OF GLOUCESTER.

This See was one of the six erected by King Henry the Eighth in the year 1541, and was formerly part of the Diocese of Worcester.

YEAR.

1541 John Wakeman, the last Abbot of Tewkesbury. Consecrated 20 Sept. 1541; ob. Dec. 1549.

1550 John Hooper. Nominated 15 May, 1550; deprived in 1553; and burnt 9 Feb. 1555.

1554 James Brookes, Master of Baliol College, Oxford. Consecrated 1 April, 1554; ob. 7 Sept. 1558.

THE SEE VACANT ABOVE THREE YEARS.

1562 Richard Cheyney, also Bishop of Bristol. Consecrated 19 April, 1562; ob. 25 April, 1579.

THE SEE VACANT ABOVE TWO YEARS.

1581 John Bullingham, also Bishop of Bristol. Elected 15 Aug. 1581; ob. 20 May, 1598.

1598 Godfrey Goldsborough, Prebendary of Worcester Elected 28 Aug. 1598; ob. 26 May, 1604.

1605 Thomas Ravis, Dean of Christ Church, Oxford. Consecrated 19 March, 1605; translated to London 18 May, 1607.

1607 Henry Parry, Dean of Chester. Consecrated 12 July, 1607; translated to Worcester in 1610.

1611 Giles Thompson, Dean of Windsor. Elected 15 Mar. 1611; ob. June 1612.

1612 Miles Smith, Canon-residentiary of Hereford. Elected 15 July, 1612; ob. 20 Oct. 1624.

1624 Godfrey Goodman, Dean of Rochester. Elected 26 Nov. 1624. His Bishoprick was sequestered in 1640, and he died 16 Jan. 1655.

YEAR.

THE SEE VACANT UNTIL THE RESTORATION.

1660 William Nicholson, Archdean of Brecknock. Elected
26 Nov. 1660; ob. 5 Feb. 1672.

1672 John Pritchet or Pritchard. Elected 10 Oct. 1672;
ob. 1 Jan. 1680.

1681 Robert Frampton, Dean of Gloucester. Consecrated
27 March, 1681; deprived for not taking the oaths;
1 Feb. 1691.

1691 Edward Fowler, Prebendary of Gloucester. Nominated
23 April, 1691; ob. 26 Aug. 1714.

1715 Richard Willis, Dean of Lincoln. Appointed 15 Jan.
1715; translated to Salisbury, 1721.

1721 Joseph Wilcocks, Prebendary of Westminster. Elected
1721; translated to Rochester 1731.

1731 Elias Sydall. Translated from St. David's 1731; ob.
1734.

1734 Martin Benson, Prebendary of Durham. Elected
1734; ob. 1752.

1752 James Johnson, Canon-residentiary of St. Paul's.
Elected 1752; translated to Worcester 1760.

1760 William Warburton, Dean of Bristol. Elected 1760;
ob. 1779.

1779 Hon. James Yorke. Translated from St. David's 1779;
translated to Ely 1781.

1781 Samuel Halifax. Elected 1781; translated to St.
Asaph 1789.

1789 Richard Beadon, Archdeacon of London. Elected
1789; translated to Bath and Wells 1802.

1802 George Isaac Huntingford, Warden of Winchester.
Elected 1802; translated to Hereford in 1815.

1815 Hon. Henry Ryder. Elected 1815; translated to
Litchfield and Coventry 1824.

1824 Christopher Bethell. Elected 1824. PRESENT Lord
Bishop of Gloucester.

BISHOPS OF HEREFORD.

YEAR.
1060 Walter, Chaplain to the Queen. Consecrated 1060;
ob. 1079.

1079 Robert Losing, Prebendary of St. Paul's. Consecrated
29 Dec. 1079; ob. 26 June, 1095.

1095 Gerard, Chancellor to King William the Conquerer.
Appointed circa 1095; translated to York in 1100.

Roger, nominated by the King; but died before Consecration.

1101 Rainelm, Chancellor to the Queen. Appointed 1101;
ob. 1115.

1115 Geoffrey de Clyve, Chaplain to the King. Consecrated 26 Dec. 1115; ob. 3 Feb. 1119.

1120 Richard de Cappella, Clerk to the Seal. Consecrated
16 Jan. 1120; ob. 15 Aug. 1127.

1131 Robert de Bethun, Prior of Lanthony. Consecrated
19 June, 1131, or 30 May, 1133; ob. April,
1148.

1148 Gilbert Foliot, Abbot of Gloucester. Consecrated 5
Sept. 1148; translated to London in 1168.

1164 Robert de Melun, Prior of Lanthony. Consecrated
22 May, 1164; ob. 27 Feb. 1166.

THE SEE VACANT SEVEN YEARS.

1174 Robert Foliot, Archdeacon of Oxford. Consecrated
6 Oct. 1174; ob. 9 May, 1186.

1186 William de Vere, Prebendary of St. Paul's. Consecrated 10 Aug. 1186; ob. 24 Dec. 1199.

1200 Giles Bruce, alias de Braose. Consecrated 24 Sept.
1200; ob. 17 Nov. 1215.

1216 Hugh de Mapenore, Dean of Hereford. Consecrated
6 Dec. 1216; ob. April, 1219.

1219 Hugh Foliot, Archdeacon of Salop. Consecrated 1
Nov. 1219; ob. July, 1234.

1234 Ralph de Maydenstune, or Maidstone, Dean of Hereford. Appointed 30 Sept. 1234; he resigned 17
Dec. 1239; ob. 1244.

1240 Peter de Egueblank, or Egeblaunch, a Savoyard.
Elected 24 Aug. 1240; ob. 27 Nov. 1268.

1268 John Breton. Appointed 6 Dec. 1268; ob. April or
May, 1275.

1275 Thomas de Cantilupe, Archdeacon of Stafford. Elected 20 June, 1275; Lord Chancellor, and Chancellor
of Oxford; ob. 25 Aug. 1282, and was CANONISED.

1282 Richard de Swinefeld. Elected 1 Dec. 1282; ob. 15
March, 1317.

YEAR.

1317 Adam de Orleton. Appointed 7 April, 1317; Lord Treasurer; translated to Worcester Oct. 1327.

1327 Thomas Charlton, Canon of York. Consecrated 18 Oct. 1327; Lord Chancellor of Ireland; ob. 11 Jan. 1344.

1344 John Trilleck. Elected 23 Feb. 1344; ob. Jan. or Feb. 1360.

1361 Lewis de Charleton, Canon of Hereford, Chancellor of Oxford. Appointed 10 Sept. 1361; ob. 23 May, 1369.

1369 William Courtenay, Canon of York. Appointed 17 Aug. 1369; translated to London 12 Sept. 1375.

1375 John Gilbert. Translated from Bangor 12 Sept. 1375; Lord Treasurer; translated to St. David's in 1389.

1389 John Trevenant, or Treffnant, Canon of St. Asaph and Lincoln. Appointed 6 May, 1389; or March or April, 1404.

1404 Robert Mascall, Confessor to the King. Appointed 2 July, 1404; ob. 22 Dec. 1416.

1417 Edmund Lacy, Canon of Windsor. Consecrated 18 April, 1417. Translated to Exeter in 1420.

1420 Thomas Polton, Dean of York. Appointed 15 July, 1420. Translated to Chichester in 1422.

1422 Thomas Spofford, Abbot of St. Mary's, York, Bishop elect of Rochester, but was removed to this See before Consecration, 17 Nov. 1422. He resigned in 1448.

1448 Richard Beauchamp, Archdeacon of Suffolk. Appointed 4 Dec. 1448; translated to Salisbury in 1450.

1450 Reginald Butler, alias Boulers, Abbot of Gloucester. Appointed 23 Dec. 1450; translated to Litchfield and Coventry 3 April, 1453.

1453 John Stanbury. Translated from Bangor 7 Feb. 1453; ob. 11 May, 1474.

1474 Thomas Milling, Abbot of Westminster. Appointed 15 Aug. 1474; ob. 1492.

1492 Edmund Audley. Translated from Rochester 22 June, 1492; translated to Salisbury in 1502.

1502 Adrian de Castello, Prebendary of St. Paul's. Consecrated 1502; translated to Bath and Wells in 1504.

1504 Richard Mayhew, or Mayo, President of Magdalen College, Oxford. Appointed 9 Aug. 1504; ob. 18 April, 1516.

YEAR.

1516 Charles Booth, Prebendary of Lincoln. Appointed 21 July, 1516; ob. 5 May, 1535.

1535 Edward Fox, Provost of King's College, Cambridge. Elected 2 Sept. 1535; ob. 8 May, 1538.

1538 Edmund Bonner, Archdeacon of Leicester. Elected 27 Nov. 1538; but, before Consecration, he was translated to Lincoln.

1539 John Skyp, Archdeacon of Dorset. Elected 24 Oct. 1539; ob. 30 March, 1552.

1553 John Harley, Prebendary of Worcester. Consecrated 26 May, 1553. Deprived in 1554.

1554 Robert Warton, alias Parfew, alias Purfoy. Translated from St. Asaph 24 April, 1554; ob. 22 Sept. 1557.

> Thomas Reynolds was nominated by Queen Mary; but, on her death, he was set aside by her successor.

1559 John Scory, the deprived Bishop of Chichester. Elected 15 July, 1559; ob. 26 June, 1585.

1585 Herbert Westfaling, Canon of Windsor. Nominated 17 Nov. 1585; ob. 1 March, 1602.

1602 Robert Bennet, Dean of Windsor. Nominated 7 Jan. 1602; ob. 25 Oct. 1617.

1617 Francis Godwin. Translated from Landaff 10 Nov. 1617; ob. April, 1633.

> William Juxon, Dean of Worcester, was elected, but before Consecration he was translated to London, when
>
> Godfrey Goodman, Bishop of Gloucester, was elected, but he resigned his pretensions.

1634 Augustin Lindsell, translated from Peterborough 7 March, 1634; ob. 6 Nov. 1634.

1634 Matthew Wren, Dean of Windsor. Elected 5 Dec. 1634; translated to Norwich in 1635.

1635 Theophilus Field. Translated from St. David's 15 Dec. 1635; ob. 2 June, 1636.

1636 George Coke. Translated from Bristol 18 June, 1636; ob. 10 Dec. 1646.

THE SEE VACANT ABOUT FOURTEEN YEARS.

1660 Nicholas Monk, Provost of Eton College. Elected 1 Dec. 1660; ob. 17 Dec. 1661.

YEAR.

1662 Herbert Croft, Dean of Hereford. Elected 21 Jan. 1662; ob. 18 May, 1691.

1691 Gilbert Ironside. Translated from Bristol 27 May, 1691; ob. 27 Aug. 1701, æt. 69.

1701 Humphrey Humphreys. Translated from Bangor 2 Dec. 1701; ob. 20 Nov. 1712, æt. 63.

1713 Philip Bisse. Translated from St. David's 6 Feb. 1713; ob. 1721.

1721 Benjamin Hoadly. Translated from Bangor 1721; translated to Salisbury 1723.

1723 Hon. Henry Egerton. Elected 1723; ob. 1746.

1746 Lord James Beauclerk, Canon of Windsor. Elected 1746; ob. 1787, æt. 85.

1787 Hon. John Harley, Dean of Windsor. Elected 1787; ob. 1788, æt. 60.

1788 John Butler. Translated from Oxford 1788; ob. 1802.

1802 Folliot Herbert Walker Cornewall. Translated from Bristol 1802; translated to Worcester 1808.

1808 John Luxmore. Translated from Bristol 1808; translated to St. Asaph 1815.

1815 George Isaac Huntingford. Translated from Gloucester 1815. PRESENT Lord Bishop of Hereford.

BISHOPS OF LANDAFF.

1059 Herewald. Consecrated 1059; ob. 6 March, 1103.

THE SEE VACANT ABOVE FOUR YEARS.

1108 Urban, Archdeacon of Landaff. Consecrated 10 Aug. 1108; ob. 1133.

THE SEE VACANT SIX YEARS.

1139 Uhtred. Consecrated 1139; ob. 1148.
1148 Galfrid; ob. 1153.
1153 Nicholas ap Gwrgant; ob. 1183.

THE SEE VACANT ABOUT TWO YEARS.

1185 William de Salso Marisco, or Saltmarsh. Consecrated 1185; ob. circa 1191.

119. Henry, Prior of Abergavenny. Consecrated ante 1196; ob. Nov. 1218.

1219 William, Prior of Godcliffe. Consecrated Oct. 1219; ob. 1229.

1230 Elias de Radnor. Elected 1230; ob. 13 May, 1240.

THE SEE VACANT ABOUT FOUR YEARS.

1244 William De Burgh, Chaplain to the King. Consecrated 1244; ob. 1253.

1253 John de la Warr. Elected 26 July, 1253; ob. 30 June, 1256.

1256 William de Radnor. Elected 30 July, 1256; ob. 1265.

1266 William de Braose, Prebendary of Landaff. Elected March, 1266; ob. 19 March, 1287.

The See is generally considered to have been vacant from 1287 to 1296; but Le Neve, on the authority of Prynne, states, that

1287 Philip de Staunton, succeeded in Sept. 1287.

1296 John de Monmouth. Nominated March, 1295; consecrated Feb. 1296; ob. 8 April, 1323.

1323 John de Eglescliffe. Translated from Connor, in Ireland, in Sept. 1323: ob. 2 Jan. 1346.

John Coventre was Elected, but set aside by the Pope.

1347 John Paschall. Appointed 3 June, 1347; ob. 11 Oct. 1361.

1361 Roger Cradock. Translated from Waterford, in Ireland, 15 Dec. 1361; ob. 1382.

1383 Thomas Rushooke, Confessor to the King. Appointed 16 Jan. 1383. Translated to Chichester in 1386.

1386 William de Bottlesham, Titular Bishop of Bethlehem. Appointed in 1386; translated to Rochester in 1389.

1389 Edmund de Brumfeld. Appointed 17 Dec. 1389; ob. 1391.

1393 Tideman de Winchecomb, Abbot of Beauly. Appointed 5 July, 1393; translated to Worcester in 1395.

1395 Andrew Barret. Appointed 25 Aug. 1395; ob. May, 1396.

1396 John Burghill, alias Bruehilla, Confessor to the King. Appointed 15 June, 1396; translated to Litchfield and Coventry in 1398.

1398 Thomas Peverel. Translated from Ossory, in Ireland, 16 Nov. 1398; translated to Worcester in 1407.

1408 John la Zouche. Appointed 7 June, 1408; ob. . . . .

Le Neve says—" Quære, de Johanne Fulford."

1425 John Wells. Appointed 9 July, 1425; ob. 1440.

1441 Nicholas Ashby, Prior of Westminster. Appointed 18 Feb. 1441; ob. 1458.

1458 John Hunden, Prior of King's Langley, Hertfordshire. Appointed 25 Aug. 1458. He resigned his See some time before his death.

1476 John Smith. Appointed July 1476; ob. 1478.

1478 John Marshal. Appointed 18 Sept. 1478; ob. . . . . .

1496 John Ingleby, Prior of Shene. Appointed 2 Sept. 1496.

1500 Miles Salley, or Sawley. Appointed May 12, 1500; ob. 1516.

1516 George Athequa, De Attica, or Attien, a Spaniard, he was Chaplain to Queen Katherine of Arragon, whom he attended to this country. Appointed 11 Feb. 1517; ob. . . . . .

1537 Robert Holgate, Prior of Wotton. Appointed 29 March, 1537; translated to York, 10 Jan. 1545.

1545 Anthony Kitchin, or Dunstan. Elected 26 March, 1545; ob. 31 Oct. 1566.

1567 Hugh Jones. Elected 17 April, 1567; ob. Nov. 1574, æt. 66.

1575 William Blethyn, Prebendary of York. Elected 13 April, 1575; ob. 15 Oct. 1590.

1591 Gervase Babington, Prebendary of Hereford. Elected 7 Aug. 1591; translated to Exeter in 1595.

1595 William Morgan. Elected 30 June, 1595; translated to St. Asaph 17 Sept. 1601.

1601 Francis Godwin, Canon of Wells. Elected 14 Oct. 1601; translated to Hereford in 1617.

1617 George Carleton. Elected 23 Dec. 1617; translated to Chichester in 1619.

1619 Theophilus Field. Elected 25 Sept. 1619; translated to St. David's in 1627.

YEAR.

1627 William Murray. Translated from Kilfenora, in Ireland, 28 Nov. 1627.

1639 Morgan Owen. Elected March, 1639, ob. 1645.

THE SEE VACANT ABOUT SIXTEEN YEARS.

1660 Hugh Lloyd, Archdeacon of St. David's. Elected 16 Oct. 1660; ob. June or July, 1667.

1667 Francis Davies, Archdeacon of Landaff. Elected 29 July, 1667; ob. 15 March, 1674.

1675 William Lloyd, Prebendary of St. Paul's. Elected 6 April, 1675; translated to Peterborough in 1679.

1679 William Beaw. Consecrated 22 June, 1679; ob. 1707.

1707 John Tyler, Dean of Hereford. Elected 1707; ob. 1724.

1724 Robert Clavering, Canon of Christ Church, Oxford. Elected 1724; translated to Peterborough in 1728.

1728 John Harris, Prebendary of Canterbury. Elected 1728; ob. 1738.

1738 Matthias Mawson. Elected 1738; translated to Chichester 1740.

1740 John Gilbert, Dean of Exeter. Elected 1740; translated to Salisbury 1748.

1748 Edward Cresset, Dean of Hereford. Elected 1748; ob. 1755.

1755 Richard Newcome, Canon of Windsor. Elected 1755; translated to St. Asaph 1761.

1761 John Ewer, Canon of Windsor. Elected 1761; translated to Bangor 1769.

1769 Jonathan Shipley, Dean of Winchester. Elected 1769; translated to St. Asaph the same year.

1769 Hon. Shute Barrington, Canon of St. Paul's. Elected 1769; translated to Salisbury 1782.

1782 Richard Watson, Archdeacon of Ely. Elected 1782; ob. 1816.

1816 Herbert Marsh. Elected 1816; translated to Peterborough 1819.

1819 William Van Mildert. Elected 1819. PRESENT Lord Bishop of Landaff.

BISHOPS OF LINCOLN.

YEAR.

1072 Remigius de Feschamp. Translated from Dorchester
in 1072; ob. May, 1092 ; CANONIZED.

1093 Robert Blovet. Succeeded in 1093; Lord Chancellor;
ob. 10 Jan. 1123.

1123 Alexander, Archdeacon of Salisbury. Nominated 15
April, 1123; Lord Chancellor; ob. 1147.

1147 Robert de Querceto, alias de Katineto, alias de Cheney. Consecrated Sept. 1147 ; ob. 1166.

THE SEE VACANT SEVEN YEARS.

1173 Geoffrey Plantagenet. Elected 1173; resigned in
1182.

1183 Walter de Constantiis, Archdeacon of Oxford. Consecrated 25 June, 1183; Lord Chancellor; translated to Rouen, 1184.

THE SEE VACANT TWO YEARS.

1186 Hugh, Prior of the Carthusians at Witham, in Somer-
shire *. Elected 10 Aug. 1186; ob. 1200. CANON-
IZED.

THE SEE VACANT ALMOST THREE YEARS.

1203 William de Blois, or Bleys, Prebendary of Lincoln.
Consecrated 24 Aug. 1203; ob. May, 1206.

THE SEE VACANT ALMOST THREE YEARS.

1209 Hugo Wallys, Archdeacon of Wells, Lord Chancellor.
Consecrated Dec. 1209; ob. 8 Feb. 1234.

1234 Robert Grosthead, or Grouthed, Archdeacon of Leicester. Elected 1234 ; ob. 4 Oct. 1253.

1253 Henry Lexington, Dean of Lincoln. Elected 30 Dec.
1253; ob. 8 Aug. 1258.

---

* Vide Rapin, Vol.I. p. 354.

YEAR.

1258 Richard Gravesend, Dean of Lincoln. Nominated 24
        Aug. 1258; ob. 18 Dec. 1279.

1280 Oliver Sutton, Dean of Lincoln. Elected 1 March,
        1280; ob. 13 Nov. 1299.

1300 John D'Aldreby. Elected 20 Jan. 1300; ob. 5 Jan.
        1319.

1319 Thomas Beke, Chancellor of Lincoln. Elected 27
        Jan. 1319; ob. ...

1320 Henry de Burghersh. Appointed 28 May, 1320; Lord
        Chancellor and Lord Treasurer; ob. Dec. 1340.

        Thomas le Bek is called the next Bishop,
        but it is uncertain when he succeeded; his
        will was proved 3 March, 1346.

1351 John Gynwell, or Gyndwelle, but called by Beatson,
        Heylen, and Isaacson, Simoin, Archdeacon of Nor-
        thampton. Confirmed 3 July, 1351; ob. 5 Aug. 1362.

1363 John Bokyngham. Appointed 5 April, 1363; Keeper
        of the Privy Seal; ob. 10 March, 1398.

1398 Henry Beaufort, Dean of Wells, Chancellor of Ox-
        ford. Appointed 19 July, 1398; Lord Chancellor;
        translated to Winchester in 1404.

1404 Philip de Repingdon, Abbot of Leicester, and Chan-
        cellor of Oxford. Appointed 19 Nov. 1404; he
        resigned 12 May, 1420, on being made a CARDINAL.

1420 Richard Flemying, Canon of Lincoln. Appointed 23
        May, 1420; ob. 25 Jan. 1431.

1431 William Grey. Translated from London 4 Aug. 1431;
        ob. Feb. 1436.

1436 William Alnwick. Translated from Norwich 9 Sept.
        1436; ob. 5 Dec. 1449.

1450 Marmaduke Lumley, Chancellor of Cambridge.
        Translated from Carlisle 28 Jan. 1450; ob. 1451.

1452 John Chedworth, Archdeacon of Wells. Appointed
        11 Feb. 1452; ob. 1471.

1472 Thomas Rotherham. Translated from Rochester 10
        March, 1472; Keeper of the Privy Seal, Lord Chan-
        cellor, Chancellor of Cambridge; Translated to
        York in 1480.

1480 John Russell, Archdeacon of Berks, Chancellor of Ox-
        ford. Translated from Rochester 9 Sept. 1480;
        Lord Chancellor; ob. 30 Jan. 1495.

1495 William Smith. Translated from Litchfield and Co-

ventry 6 Nov. 1495 ; Chancellor of Oxford, and President of Wales ; ob. 5 Jan. 1514.

1514 Thomas Wolsey, Bishop of Tournay, Almoner, Dean
of York. Appointed 6 Feb. 1514; Translated to
York in Sept. the same year.

1514 William Atwater, Dean of Salisbury. Appointed 15
Sept. 1514; ob. 9 Feb. 1520.

1520 John Longland, Principal of Magdalen Hall, Oxford.
Appointed 20 May, 1520; ob. 7 May, 1547.

1547 Henry Holbeach. Translated from Rochester 9
Aug. 1547; ob. 2 Aug. 1551.

1552 John Tailour, Master of St. John's College, Cambridge. Elected 18 June, 1552; deprived 20 March,
1553.

1554 John Whyte, Warden of Winchester. Appointed 2
May, 1554; translated to Winchester in 1556.

1557 Thomas Watson, Dean of Durham. Appointed 24
March, 1557; deprived 25 June, 1559.

1560 Nicholas Bullingham, Archdeacon of Lincoln. Elected 12 Jan. 1560; translated to Worcester 26 Jan.
1570.

1570 Thomas Cowper, Dean of Christ Church, Oxford.
Elected 4 Feb. 1570; translated to Winchester, 3
March, 1584.

1584 William Wickham, Dean of Lincoln. Elected 20
Nov. 1584; translated to Winchester 22 Feb. 1595.

1595 William Chaderton. Translated from Chester 5 April,
1595; ob. 11 April, 1608.

1608 William Barlow. Translated from Rochester 21 May,
1608; ob. 7 Sept. 1613.

1614 Richard Neyle. Translated from Litchfield and Coventry 17 Jan. 1614; translated to Durham 9 Oct.
1617.

1617 George Mountain, Dean of Westminster. Elected 21
Oct. 1617; translated to London 20 July, 1621.

1621 John Williams, Dean of Westminster. Elected 3
Aug. 1621; Lord Keeper; translated to York 4 Dec.
1641.

1641 Thomas Winniffe, Dean of St. Paul's. Nominated in
1641; ob. 1654.

THE SEE VACANT SIX YEARS.

1660 Robert Sanderson, Prebendary of Lincoln.   Elected
     17 Oct. 1660; ob. 29 Jan. 1663, æt. 76.
1663 Benjamin Laney. Translated from Peterborough 1
     March, 1663; translated to Ely 24 May, 1667.
1667 William Fuller. Translated from Limerick, in Ire-
     land 17 Sept. 1667; ob. 22 April, 1675.
1675 Thomas Barlowe. Elected 14 May, 1675; ob. 8 Oct.
     1691.
1691 Thomas Tennison. Elected 11 Dec. 1691; translated
     to Canterbury 16 Jan. 1694.
1694 James Gardiner, Sub-dean of Lincoln. Appointed 10
     March, 1694; ob. 1 March, 1705.
1705 William Wake, Dean of Exeter. Elected 4 Sept. 1705;
     translated to Canterbury, 16 Jan. 1716.
1716 Edmund Gibson, Archdeacon of Surrey. Nominated
     Jan. 1716; translated to London 1723.
1723 Richard Reynolds. Translated from Bangor 1723;
     ob. 1743.
1743 John Thomas, Bishop elect of St. Asaph.   Elected
     1743; translated to Salisbury 1761.
1761 John Green, Dean of Lincoln. Elected 1761; ob.
     1779.
1779 Thomas Thurlow, Dean of Rochester, and in 1781
     Dean of St. Paul's. Elected 1779; translated to
     Durham 1787.
1787 George Prettyman Tomline, Dean of St. Paul's.
     Elected 1787; translated to Winchester 1820.
1820 Hon. George Pelham. Translated from Exeter 1820.
     PRESENT Lord Bishop of Lincoln.

BISHOPS OF LITCHFIELD.

1067 Peter. Consecrated 1067; he removed the See to
     Chester; ob 1085.
1085 Robert de Limesey, Prebendary of St. Paul's.   Nomi-
     nated 25 Dec. 1085. He removed the See to Co-
     ventry 18 April 1102; ob. 30 Aug. 1117.

BISHOPS OF LITCHFIELD AND COVENTRY.

THE SEE VACANT NEARLY FOUR YEARS.

YEAR.

1121 Robert Peche, Chaplain to King Henry I. Consecrated 13 March, 1121; ob. Aug. 1127.

THE SEE VACANT TWO YEARS.

1129 Roger de Clinton, Archdeacon of Buckingham. Consecrated 22 Dec. 1129; ob. at Antioch, 16 April, 1148.

1149 Walter Durdent, Prior of Canterbury. Consecrated 2 Oct. 1149; ob. 7 Dec. 1161.

1162 Richard Peche, Archdeacon of Coventry. Consecrated 1162; ob. 6 Oct. 1182.

1183 Gerard la Pucelle. Consecrated 25 Sept. 1183; ob. 13 Jan. 1185.

1185 Hugh de Novant, or Minant, Prior of the Carthusians. Elected 1185; ob. 27 April, 1198.

1198 Geoffery de Muschamp, Archdeacon of Cleveland. Consecrated 21 June, 1198; ob. 6 Oct. 1208.

> On the Death of Bishop Muschamp the Monks chose Josbert their Prior; and the Canons of Litchfield, by the King's command, elected Walter de Grey, who, according to Godwin, held this See until 1214, when he was translated to Worcester; but Wharton asserts that Pandulph, the Pope's Legate, made void the election, and that afterwards, by consent of both Chapters

1215 William de Cornhull, Archdeacon of Huntingdon, was elected and consecrated 25 Jan. 1215; ob. 1223.

1224 Alexander de Stavenby. Consecrated 14 April, 1224; ob. 26 Dec. 1238.

> On the death of Bishop Stavenby, William de Rule, or Raleigh, was elected by both Chapters, but being about the same time elected Bishop of Norwich, he accepted of that

See. Disputes then arose between the Chapter of Litchfield and the Chapter of Coventry, the former having elected William de Manchestre their Dean, and the latter Nicholas de Farnham. After much controversy both parties, at the King's persuasion, agreed in the choice of

1239 Hugh de Patesbull, who was confirmed 25 Dec. 1239; ob. 7 Dec. 1241.

Richard, surnamed Crassus, was then elected, but he died at Riola, in Gascony, 8 Dec. 1242 before consecration, when Robert de Monte Pessulano was elected, but finding his appointment disagreeable to the King, he resigned the See into the Pope's hands, who substituted

1245 Roger de Wesebam, Dean of Lincoln. Consecrated 1 Jan. 1245; he resigned the See 4 Dec. 1256, and died 20 May, 1257.

1257 Roger de Longespee, or de Molend. Elected 31 Jan. 1257; ob. 16 Dec. 1295.

1296 Walter de Langton. Elected 20 Feb. 1296; Lord Treasurer, and Lord Chancellor; ob. Nov. 1321.

1322 Roger de Northburgh, Archdeacon of Richmond. Appointed 12 April, 1322; Lord Keeper, and Lord Treasurer; ob. Nov. or Dec. 1359.

1360 Robert Stretton, Canon of Litchfield. Elected 26 Dec. 1360; ob. April, 1385.

1386 Walter Skirlawe, Dean of St. Martin's. Elected 7 Jan. 1386; translated to Bath and Wells in the same year.

1386 Richard Scrope. Consecrated 19 Aug. 1386; translated to York 2 July, 1398.

1398 John Burghill. Translated from Landaff Sept. 1398; ob. May, 1414.

1415 John Ketterich. Translated from St. David's 1 Feb. 1415; translated to Exeter in 1419.

Query. James Cary, Godwin, p. 343.

1419 William Heyworth. Appointed 20 Nov. 1419; ob. 13 March, 1447.

YEAR.

1447 William Booth, Prebendary of St. Paul's. Appointed 26 April, 1447; translated to York 21 July, 1452.

1452 Nicholas Close. Translated from Carlisle 30 Aug. 1452; Chancellor of Cambridge; ob. ante 1 Nov. 1452.

1453 Reginald Butler. Translated from Hereford 7 Feb. 1453; ob. circa 1459.

1459 John Halse, or Hales, Prebendary of St. Paul's. Appointed 31 Oct. 1459; ob. 30 Sept. 1490.

1492 William Smith, Archdeacon of Surrey. Appointed 29 Jan. 1492; translated to Lincoln, 6 Nov. 1495.

1496 John Arundel, Dean of Exeter. Appointed 18 Sept. 1496; translated to Exeter 29 June, 1502.

1503 Geoffry Blythe, Dean of York. Appointed 26 Dec. 1503; ob. 1533.

1534 Rowland Lee, Chancellor and Prebendary of Litchfield, and Lord President of Wales. Elected 10 Jan. 1534; ob. 24 Jan. 1543.

1543 Richard Sampson. Translated from Chichester 19 Feb. 1543; Lord President of Wales; ob. 25 Sept. 1554.

1554 Ralph Bayne. Elected 10 Nov. 1554; deprived in 1559, and died soon afterwards.

1560 Thomas Bentham. Elected 15 Jan. 1560; ob. 19 Feb. 1579.

1580 William Overton, Prebendary of Winchester and Salisbury. Elected 10 Sept. 1580; ob. April, 1609.

1609 George Abbot, Dean of Winchester. Elected 27 May, 1609; translated to London 20 Jan. 1610.

1610 Richard Neyle. Translated from Rochester 12 Oct. 1610; translated to Lincoln in 1613.

1614 John Overal, Dean of St. Paul's. Elected 14 March, 1614; translated to Norwich in 1618.

1619 Thomas Morton. Translated from Chester 6 March, 1619; translated to Durham in 1632.

1632 Robert Wright. Translated from Bristol 30 Oct. 1632; ob. 1642.

1643 Accepted Frewen, Dean of Gloucester. Nominated 17 Aug. 1643; translated to York 22 Sept. 1660.

1661 John Hacket, Residentiary of St. Paul's. Elected 6 Dec. 1661; ob. 28 Oct. 1670, æt. 79.

1671 Thomas Wood, Dean of Litchfield. Elected 9 June, 1671; ob. 18 April, 1692.

1692 William Lloyd. Translated from St. Asaph 20 Oct.
1692; translated to Worcester in 1699.

1699 John Hough. Translated from Oxford 5 Aug. 1699;
translated to Worcester in 1714.

1714 Edward Chandler, Prebendary of Worcester. Elected
1741; translated to Durham 1730.

1730 Richard Smalbrooke. Translated from St. David's
1730; ob. 1749, æt. 76.

1749 Hon. Frederick Cornwallis, Canon of Windsor, and,
in 1766, Dean of St. Paul's. Elected 1749; translated to Canterbury 1768.

1768 Hon. John Egerton. Translated from Bognor 1768;
translated to Durham 1771.

1771 Brownlow North, Dean of Canterbury. Elected 1771;
translated to Worcester 1774.

1774 Richard Hurd, Master of the Temple. Elected 1774;
translated to Worcester, 1781.

1781 Hon. James Cornwallis. Succeeded his brother as
Earl Cornwallis in 1824; Dean of Durham; elected
1781; ob. 1824.

1824 Hon. Henry Ryder; translated from Gloucester 1824.
PRESENT Lord Bishop of Litchfield and Coventry.

BISHOPS OF LONDON.

1051 William the Norman. Consecrated Sept. 1051, living
1075.

1075 Hugh d'Orevalle, or De Orwell, a Norman. Appointed 1075; ob. 12 Jan. 1084.

1086 Maurice. Consecrated 25 Dec. 1086; Lord Chancellor; ob. 26 Sept. 1107.

1108 Richard de Belmis, or Rufus I. Consecrated 26 July,
1108; ob. 16 Jan. 1128.

1128 Gilbert, surnamed Universalis, Canon of Lyons. Consecrated 22 Jan. 1128; ob. Aug. 1134.

THE SEE VACANT FIVE YEARS.

1141 Robert de Sigello, Monk of Reading. Consecrated
1141; ob. 1150 or 1151.

YEAR.

1152 Richard de Belmis II. Archdeacon of Middlesex. Consecrated 28 Sept. 1152; ob. 4 May, 1162.

1163 Robert Foliot. Translated from Hereford 24 March, 1163; ob. 18 Feb. 1187.

THE SEE VACANT TWO YEARS.

1189 Richard Fitz-Neale, Dean of Lincoln. Consecrated 13 Dec. 1189; ob. 10 Sept. 1198.

1198 William de St. Maria, Prebendary of St. Paul's. Elected 16 Sept. 1198; resigned 26 Jan. 1221; ob. 1224.

1221 Eustace de Fauconberg. Elected 25 Feb. 1221; Lord Treasurer; ob. 1228.

1229 Roger Niger, Archdeacon of Colchester. Consecrated 10 June, 1229; ob. 29 Sept. 1241. CANONIZED.

1241 Fulk Basset, Dean of York. Elected Dec. 1241; ob. May, 1259.

1260 Henry de Wengham, Prebendary of St. Paul's. Consecrated 15 Feb. 1260; Lord Chancellor; ob. 13 July, 1262.

1262 Richard Talbot, Dean of St. Paul's. Elected 18 Aug. 1262; ob. Oct. 1262.

1262 Henry de Sandwich, Prebendary of St. Paul's. Elected 13 Nov. 1262; ob. 16 Sept. 1273.

1273 John de Chishull, Dean of St. Paul's. Elected 7 Dec. 1273; Lord Chancellor and Lord Treasurer; ob. 8 Feb. 1280.

Fulk Lovell was then elected, but he refused the dignity.

1280 Richard de Gravesend, Prebendary of St. Paul's. Consecrated 11 Aug. 1280; ob. 9 Dec. 1303.

1304 Ralph de Baldock, or Baudake, Dean of St Paul's Elected 23 Feb. 1304; ob. 24 July, 1313.

1313 Gilbert Segrave. Elected 17 Aug. 1313; ob. 18 Dec. 1316.

1317 Richard de Newport, Dean of St. Paul's. Elected 27 Jan. 1317; ob. 24 Aug. 1318.

1318 Stephen de Gravesend, Prebendary of St. Paul's. Elected 11 Sept. 1318; ob. 8 April, 1338.

1338 Richard de Wentworth, Prebendary of St. Paul's. Elected 4 May, 1338; Lord Chancellor; ob. 8 Dec. 1339.

YEAR.

1340 Ralph de Stratford, Prebendary of St. Paul's and Salisbury. Elected 26 Jan. 1340 ; ob. April, 1354.

1354 Michael de Northburg, Prebendary of St. Paul's. Elected April, 1354 ; ob. 9 Sept. 1361.

1361 Simon de Sudbury, alias Tybold, Chancellor of Salisbury. Appointed 22 Oct. 1361; translated to Canterbury May, 1375.

1375 William Courtenay. Translated from Hereford 12 Sept. 1375; Lord Chancellor, Chancellor of Oxford; translated to Canterbury Jan. 1381.

1381 Robert de Braybrooke, Dean of Salisbury. Appointed 9 Sept. 1381 ; Lord Chancellor; ob. 27 Aug. 1404.

1404 Roger Walden, Dean of York. Appointed 10 Dec. 1404; Lord Treasurer; ob. Jan. 1406.

1406 Nicholas Bubbewith, Prebendary of Salisbury. Appointed 13 May, 1406; Master of the Rolls, Keeper of the Privy Seal, and Lord Treasurer ; translated to Salisbury June, 1407.

1407 Richard Clifford. Translated from Worcester 13 Oct. 1407; ob. 20 Aug. 1421.

1421 John Kemp. Translated from Chichester 17 Nov. 1421 ; translated to York in 1426.

1426 William Grey, Dean of York. Consecrated 6 May, 1426; translated to Lincoln in 1431.

1431 Robert Fitz-Hugh, Archdeacon of Northampton, Chancellor of Cambridge. Consecrated 16 Sept. 1431 ; ob. 15 Jan. 1436.

1436 Robert Gilbert, Dean of York. Appointed 21 May, 1436 ; ob. 27 July, 1448.

1448 Thomas Kemp, Archdeacon of Middlesex, and Chancellor of York. Appointed 21 Aug. 1448 ; ob. 28 March, 1489.

1489 Richard Hill, Dean of the King's Chapel, and Prebendary of Salisbury. Elected 19 Aug. 1489; ob. 20 Feb. 1496.

1496 Thomas Savage. Translated from Rochester, 3 Aug. 1496 ; translated to York in April, 1501.

1502 William Warham, Prebendary of St. Paul's. Appointed ante Oct. 1502 ; Master of the Rolls, Lord Chancellor ; translated to Canterbury in 1503.

1504 William Barons, or Barnes. Appointed ante Novem-

YEAR.

ber 1504; Master of the Rolls; ob. 9 or 10 Oct. 1505.

1506 Richard Fitz-James. Translated from Chichester 1 Aug. 1506; ob. 15 Jan. 1522.

1522 Cuthbert Tunstall, Dean of Salisbury. Appointed 5 July, 1522; Master of the Rolls; translated to Durham in 1530.

1530 John Stockesley, Archdeacon of Dorset. Appointed 14 July, 1530; ob. 8 Sept. 1539.

1539 Edmund Bonner, Archdeacon of Leicester, Bishop-elect of Hereford. Elected 20 Oct. 1539; deprived Sept. 1549.

1550 Nicholas Ridley. Translated from Rochester 1 April, 1550; burnt 16 Oct. 1555.

1553 Edmund Bonner restored in 1553; deprived again 30 May, 1559; ob. 5 Sept. 1569.

1559 Edmund Grindall, Master of Pembroke Hall, Cambridge. Elected 26 July, 1559; translated to York May, 1570.

1570 Edwyn Sandys. Translated from Worcester 2 June, 1570; translated to York 1576.

1577 John Aylmer, Archdeacon of Lincoln. Elected 12 March, 1577; ob. June, 1594.

1594 Richard Fletcher. Translated from Worcester 25 Dec. 1594; ob. 15 June, 1596.

1597 Richard Bancroft, Prebendary of Westminster. Elected 21 April, 1597; translated to Canterbury in 1604.

1604 Richard Vaughan. Translated from Chester 24 Dec. 1604; ob. 30 March 1607.

1607 Thomas Ravis. Translated from Gloucester 18 May, 1607; ob. 14 Dec. 1609.

1610 George Abbot. Translated from Litchfield and Coventry 20 Jan. 1610; translated to Canterbury 1611.

1611 John King, Dean of Christ Church, Oxford. Elected 7 Sept. 1611; ob. 30 March, 1621, æt. 62.

1621 George Montaigne. Translated from Lincoln 20 July, 1621; translated to Durham in 1627.

1628 William Laud. Translated from Bath and Wells 15 July, 1628; Chancellor of Oxford; translated to Canterbury 19 Sept. 1633.

YEAR.

1633 William Juxon. Translated from Hereford, 23 Oct. 1633; Lord Treasurer; translated to Canterbury 20 Sept. 1660.

1660 Gilbert Sheldon, Prebendary of Gloucester. Elected 23 Oct. 1660; translated to Canterbury 31 Aug. 1663.

1663 Humphrey Henchman. Translated from Salisbury 15 Sept. 1663; ob. Oct. 1675.

1675 Henry Compton. Translated from Oxford 18 Dec. 1675; ob. 7 July, 1713.

1713 John Robinson. Translated from Bristol, 13 March, 1713; ob. 1723.

1723 Edmund Gibson. Translated from Lincoln 1723; ob. 1748.

1748 Thomas Sherlock. Translated from Salisbury 1748; ob. 1761.

1761 Thomas Hayter. Translated from Norwich 1761; ob. 1762.

1762 Thomas Osbaldeston. Translated from Carlisle 1762; ob. 1764.

1764 Richard Terrick. Translated from Peterborough 1764; ob. 1777.

1777 Robert Lowth. Translated from Oxford 1777; ob. 1787.

1787 Beilby Porteus. Translated from Chester 1787; ob. 1809.

1809 John Randolph. Translated from Bangor 1809; ob. 1813.

1813 William Howley. Elected 1813. PRESENT Lord Bishop of London.

BISHOPS OF NORWICH.

YEAR.

1094 Herbert Losinga, Abbot of Ramsay, Lord Chancellor. Consecrated Bishop of Thetford in 1091, and April 9, 1094, removed the See to Norwich; ob. 22 July, 1119.

1121 Everard, Archdeacon of Salisbury. Consecrated 12 June 1121; deprived 1145; ob. 15 Oct. 1149.

1146 William Turbus, a Norman, Prior of Norwich. Consecrated 1146; ob. 16 Jan. 1174.

YEAR.

1175 John of Oxford, Dean of Salisbury. Elected 26 Nov. 1175; ob. 1200.

1200 John de Grey. Consecrated 24 Sept. 1200; Lord Chief Justice; elected Archbishop of Canterbury in 1205, but set aside by the Pope; ob. 18 Oct. 1214.

THE SEE VACANT SEVEN YEARS AND A HALF.

1218 Pandulph Masca, the Pope's Legate and a CARDINAL. Elected 1218; ob. 16 Aug. 1226.

1226 Thomas de Blundeville, Clerk of the Exchequer. Elected 5 Nov. 1226; ob. 16 Aug. 1236.

1236 Ralph. Elected 28 Oct. 1236; ob. 1237.

THE SEE VACANT NEARLY THREE YEARS.

1239 William de Raleigh. Elected 10 April, 1239; translated to Winchester 1 Sept. 1242.

1243 Walter de Suthfield, alias Calthorp. Elected 1243; ob. 18 May, 1257.

1257 Simon de Wanton, or Walton, one of the King's Justices. Confirmed 2 Aug. 1257; ob. 2 Jan. 1265.

1265 Roger de Skerwyng, or Skerning, Prior of Norwich. Elected 23 Feb. 1265; ob. 22 Jan. 1278.

1278 William de Middleton, Archdeacon of Canterbury. Elected 24 Feb. 1278; ob. 1 Sept. 1288.

1288 Ralph Walpole, Archdeacon of Ely. Elected 11 Nov. 1288; translated to Ely 15 July, 1299.

1299 John Salmon, Prior of Ely. Appointed 15 July, 1299; Lord Chancellor; ob. 2 July, 1325.

Robert de Baldock, Archdeacon of Middlesex. Elected July 1325, but hearing that the Pope had reserved the presentation, he renounced the election 3 Sept. following; Lord Chancellor.

1325 William Ayremyn. Appointed in 1325; Lord Treasurer; ob. 27 March, 1336.

Thomas de Hemenhale was elected 6 April, 1336, but before consecration was removed to Worcester.

1336 Anthony de Beck. Appointed in 1336; ob. 19 Dec. 1343.

YEAR.

1344 William Bateman, Archdeacon of Norwich. Appointed
23 Jan. 1344; ob. 6 Jan. 1354.

1355 Thomas Percy. Elected 2 Jan. 1355; ob. 8 Aug.
1369.

1370 Henry Le Spencer, surnamed the Warlike. Appointed
3 April, 1370; ob. 23 Aug. 1406.

1406 Alexander Totington, Prior of Norwich. Elected 14
Sept. 1406; ob. 1413.

1413 Richard Courtenay, Dean of Wells, Chancellor of
Oxford. Appointed 11 Sept. 1413; he died at the
siege of Harfleur 14 Sept. 1415.

1416 John Wakering, Archdeacon of Canterbury. Confirmed 27 May, 1416; ob. 9 April, 1425.

1426 William Alnewick, Archdeacon of Salisbury. Appointed 27 Feb. 1426; Keeper of the Privy Seal;
translated to Lincoln 19 Sept. 1436.

1436 Thomas Brown. Translated from Rochester 19 Sept.
1436; ob. 6 Dec. 1445.

> John Stanberry, Provost of Eaton, was nomi-
> nated by the King, but set aside by the
> Pope.

1446 Walter Lybart, alias Hart, Provost of Oriel College,
Oxford. Appointed 24 Jan. 1446; ob. 17 May,
1472.

1472 James Goldwell, Dean of Salisbury. Appointed 17
July, 1472; ob. 15 Feb. 1499.

1499 Thomas Jane, or Jann, Archdeacon of Essex. Appointed 21 July, 1499; ob. Sept. 1500.

1501 Richard Nikke, or Nyx, Canon of Windsor, and Dean
of the King's Chapel. Confirmed 17 March, 1501;
ob. 14 Jan. 1536.

1536 William Rugge, or Repps, Abbot of St. Benedict in
Hulme. Elected 31 May 1536; ob. 21 Sept. 1550.

1550 Thomas Thirleby. Translated from Westminster 1
April, 1550; translated to Ely in 1554.

1554 John Hopton, Chaplain to Queen Mary. Elected 2
Oct. 1554; ob. circa 1559.

> Richard Cox. Elected 22 June, 1559, but be-
> fore consecration he was removed to Ely.

1560 John Parkhurst. Elected 13 April, 1560; ob. 2 Feb.
1575, æt. 63.

YEAR.

1575 Edmund Freke. Translated from Rochester 13 July, 1575; translated to Worcester in 1584.

1585 Edmund Scambler. Translated from Peterborough 5 Jan. 1585; ob. 7 May, 1594, æt. 85.

1594 William Redman, Archdeacon of Canterbury. Elected 17 Dec. 1594; ob. 25 Sept. 1602.

1603 John Jegon, Dean of Norwich. Elected 18 Jan. 1603; ob. 13 March, 1618.

1618 John Overall. Translated from Litchfield and Coventry 21 May, 1618; ob. 12 May, 1619.

1619 Samuel Harnset. Translated from Chichester 17 June, 1619; translated to York 26 Nov. 1628.

1629 Francis White. Translated from Carlisle 22 Jan. 1629; translated to Ely 8 Dec. 1631.

1632 Richard Corbet. Translated from Oxford 7 April, 1632; ob. 28 July, 1635.

1635 Matthew Wren. Translated from Hereford 10 Nov. 1635; translated to Ely 1638.

1638 Richard Montague. Translated from Chichester 4 May, 1638; ob. 13 April, 1641.

1641 Joseph Hall. Translated from Exeter 15 Nov. 1641; ob. 8 Sept. 1656, æt. 82.

1660 Edward Reynolds, Dean of Christ Church, Oxford. Elected 28 Nov. 1660; ob. 29 July, 1676.

1676 Anthony Sparrow. Translated from Exeter 19 Aug. 1676; ob. 19 May, 1685, æt. 74.

1685 William Lloyd. Translated from Peterborough 11 June, 1685, deprived for not taking the oaths 1 Feb. 1691.

- 1691 John Moore, Prebendary of Norwich. Nominated 23 April 1691; translated to Ely 31 July, 1707.

1708 Charles Trimnell, Prebendary of Norwich. Elected 23 Jan. 1708; translated to Winchester 1721.

1721 Thomas Green, Archdeacon of Canterbury. Elected 1721; translated to Ely 1723.

1723 John Leng. Elected 1723; ob. 1727.

1727 William Baker. Translated from Bangor 1727; ob. 1732.

1732 Robert Butts, Dean of Norwich. Elected 1732; translated to Ely 1738.

1738 Thomas Gooch. Translated from Bristol 1738; translated to Ely 1748.

YEAR.

1748 Samuel Lisle. Translated from St. Asaph 1748; ob. 1749.

1749 Thomas Hayter, Prebendary of Westminster. Elected 1749; translated to London 1761.

1761 Philip Yonge, translated from Bristol 1761; ob. 1783.

1783 Lewis Bagot. Translated from Bristol 1783; translated to St. Asaph, 1790.

1790 George Horne, Dean of Canterbury. Elected 1790; ob. 1792.

1792 Charles Manners Sutton, Dean of Peterborough, appointed Dean of Windsor in 1794. Elected 1792; translated to Canterbury 1805.

1805 Henry Bathurst, Prebendary of Durham. Elected 1805. PRESENT Lord Bishop of Norwich.

BISHOPS OF OXFORD.

This diocese constituted part of the diocese of Lincoln until 1541, when King Henry VIII. erected it into a Bishoprick, and endowed it out of the lands of the dissolved Monasteries of Abingdon and Osney.

1541 Robert King, the last Abbot of Osney. Created Bishop of Oxford on the erection of the See; ob. 4 Dec. 1557.

Thomas Goldwell, Bishop of St. Asaph, was designed for this See, but Queen Mary died before the translation could be perfected.

THE SEE VACANT TEN YEARS.

1567 Hugh Curwyn, or Coren, Dean of Hereford. Elected 26 Sept. 1567; ob. Oct. 1568.

THE SEE VACANT TWENTY-ONE YLARS.

1589 John Underhill, Chaplain to the Queen. Elected 8 Dec. 1589; ob. May, 1592.

THE SEE VACANT ELEVEN YEARS.

1603 John Bridges, Dean of Salisbury. Elected 4 Jan. 1603; ob. 26 March, 1618.

1618 John Howson. Elected 12 Sept. 1618 ; translated to Durham in 1628.

1628 Richard Corbet, Dean of Christ's Church, Oxford. Elected 24 Sept. 1628 ; translated to Norwich in 1632.

1632 John Bancroft, Prebendary of St. Paul's. Elected 12 May, 1632 ; ob. Feb. 1640.

1640 Robert Skinner. Translated from Bristol in 1640 ; translated to Worcester 1663.

1663 William Paul, Dean of Litchfield. Elected 14 Nov. 1663 ; ob. 24 May, 1665.

1665 Walter Blandford, Prebendary of Gloucester. Elected 7 Nov. 1665 ; translated to Worcester 2 June, 1671.

1671 Nathaniel Crew, Dean of Chichester. Elected 16 June, 1671 ; translated to Durham 22 Oct. 1674.

1674 Henry Compton, Canon of Christ Church, Oxford. Elected 10 Nov. 1674 ; translated to London 18 Dec. 1675.

1676 John Fell, Dean of Christ Church. Elected 8 Jan. 1676 ; ob. July 1686.

1686 Samuel Parker, Archdeacon of Canterbury. Consecrated 17 Oct. 1686 ; ob. 20 March, 1688.

1688 Timothy Hall, Rector of Horsington, in Bucks. Consecrated 7 Oct. 1688 ; ob. 10 April, 1690.

1690 John Hough, Prebendary of Worcester. Consecrated 11 May, 1690 ; translated to Litchfield and Coventry 5 Aug. 1699.

1699 William Talbot, Dean of Worcester. Consecrated 24 Sept. 1699 ; translated to Salisbury in 1714.

1715 John Potter, Canon of Christ Church, Oxford. Elected 9 May, 1715 ; translated to Canterbury 1737.

1737 Thomas Secker. Translated from Bristol 1737 ; translated to Canterbury 1758.

1758 John Hume. Translated from Bristol 1758 ; translated to Salisbury 1766.

1766 Robert Lowth. Translated from St. David's 1766 ; translated to London 1777.

1777 John Butler, Prebendary of Winchester, and Archdeacon of Surrey. Elected 1777 ; translated to Hereford 1788.

1788 Edward Smallwell, Canon of Christ Church, Oxford ; translated from St. David's 1788 ; ob. 1799.

YEAR.

1799 John Randolph, Canon of Christ Church, and Regius
     Professor of Divinity, Oxford. Elected 1799; trans-
     lated to London 1807.
1807 Charles Moss. Elected 1807 ; ob. 1811.
1812 William Jackson. Elected 1812 ; ob. 1815.
1815 Edward Legge. Elected 1815. PRESENT Lord Bishop
     of Oxford.

BISHOPS OF PETERBOROUGH.

This diocese is another of those erected by King
Henry VIII. and was wholly taken from the diocese of Lincoln.

YEAR.

1541 John Chambers, the last Abbot of Peterborough, was
     appointed Bishop of this See on its creation in 1541;
     ob. 1556.
1557 David Pole, or Poole, Archdeacon of Derby. Con-
     secrated 15 Aug. 1557 ; deprived in 1559, by Queen
     Elizabeth; ob. 1568.
1561 Edmund Scambler, Prebendary of Westminster and
     York. Elected 4 Feb. 1561 ; translated to Norwich
     , in 1584.
1584 Richard Howland, Master of St. John's College, Cam-
     bridge. Consecrated 16 March, 1584; ob. June,
     1600.
1600 Thomas Dove, Dean of Norwich. Succeeded in 1600;
     ob. 30 Aug. 1630, æt. 75.
1630 William Pierse, Dean of Peterborough. Elected 17
     Sept. 1630; translated to Bath and Wells Dec.
     1632.
1632 Augustine Lindsell, Dean of Litchfield. Elected 22
     Dec. 1632; translated to Hereford March 1634.
1634 Francis Dee, Dean of Chichester. Elected 9 April,
     1634; ob. 8 Oct. 1638.
1638 John Towers, Dean of Peterborough. Elected 21
     Nov. 1638; ob. 10 Jan. 1648.

THE SEE VACANT TWELVE YEARS.

YEAR.

1660 Benjamin Laney, Dean of Rochester. Elected 20 Nov. 1660; translated to Lincoln April, 1663.

1663 Joseph Henshaw, Dean of Chichester. Elected 15 April, 1663; ob. 9 March, 1679.

1679 William Lloyd. Translated from Landaff 28 March, 1679; translated to Norwich July, 1685.

1685 Thomas White, Archdeacon of Northampton. Elected 3 Sept. 1685; deprived for not taking the oaths 1 Feb. 1691.

1691 Richard Cumberland. Elected 20 May, 1691; ob. 1718.

1718 White Kennet, Dean of Peterborough. Elected 1718; ob. 1728.

1728 Robert Clavering. Translated from Landaff 1728; ob. 1748.

1748 John Thomas, Canon Residentiary of St. Paul's. Elected 1748; translated to Salisbury 1757.

1757 Richard Terrick, Canon Residentiary of St. Paul's. Elected 1757; translated to London 1764.

1764 Robert Lamb, Dean of Peterborough. Elected 1764; ob. 1794.

1769 John Hinchcliffe, Master of Trinity College, Cambridge. Elected 1769; ob. 1794.

1794 Spencer Madan. Translated from Bristol 1794; ob. 1813.

1813 John Parsons. Elected 1813; ob. 1819.

1819 Herbert Marsh. Translated from Landaff 1819. Present Lord Bishop of Peterborough.

BISHOPS OF ROCHESTER.

YEAR.

1058 Siward, Abbot of Abingdon. Consecrated 1058; ob. 1075.

1076 Ernostus, Monk of Becco, in Normandy. Consecrated 1076; ob. 15 July following.

1077 Gundulph, Monk of Becco. Consecrated 19 March, 1077; ob. 8 March, 1108.

1108 Ralph, Abbot of Say, in Normandy. Consecrated 9 Aug. 1108; translated to Canterbury 1114.

1115 St. Earnulph, Abbot of Peterborough. Consecrated 26 Dec. 1115 ; ob. 15 March, 1124 ; æt. 84.

1125 John, Archdeacon of Canterbury. Consecrated 24 May, 1125; ob. 20 June, 1137.

1137 John II. Consecrated 1137; ob. 1142.

1142 Ascelin, a Monk. Succeeded in 1142; ob. January, 1147.

1147 Walter, Archdeacon of Canterbury. Elected 1147; ob. 26 July, 1182.

1183 Walleran, Archdeacon of Baion. Succeeded in 1183 ; ob. 1184.

1185 Gilbert Glanville, Chief Justice. Elected 16 July, 1185; ob. 24 June, 1214.

1214 Benedict de Sansetun, Precentor of St. Paul's. Elected 13 Dec. 1214; ob. Dec. 1226.

1226 Henry de Sanford, Archdeacon of Canterbury. Elected 26 Dec. 1226; ob. 24 Feb. 1235.

1235 Richard de Wendover. Elected 26 March, 1235 ; ob. 12 Oct. 1250.

1250 Lawrence de St. Martin, Chaplain and Counsellor to the King. Elected 19 Oct. 1250 ; ob. June, 1274.

1274 Walter de Merton. Elected July, 1274 ; Lord Chancellor; ob. 27 Oct. 1277.

1278 John de Bradfield, Monk of Rochester. Consecrated 29 May, 1278 ; ob. 23 April, 1283.

> John de Kirkeby, Archdeacon of Coventry, was elected, but he refused the dignity.

1283 Thomas de Inglethorpe, Dean of St. Paul's. Elected 9 July, 1283; ob. May, 1291.

1291 Thomas de Wuldham, *alias* de Suthflete, Prior of Rochester. Elected, but refused the dignity ; being again elected he, however, accepted it, and was consecrated 6 Jan. 1291 ; ob. 28 Feb. 1316.

1316 Haymo de Hythe, Confessor to the King. Elected 18 March, 1316 ; ob. 4 May, 1352.

1352 John de Shepey, Prior of Rochester. Appointed 22 Oct. 1352 ; Lord Treasurer; ob. 19 Oct. 1360.

1360 William de Witlesey, Archdeacon of Huntingdon. Elected 23 Oct. 1360; translated to Worcester 6 March, 1363.

63 Thomas Trilleck, Dean of St. Paul's. Appointed 6 March, 1363; ob. Dec. 1372.

John de Hertley was elected, but he was set aside by the Pope.

1373 Thomas de Brinton, Confessor to the King. Appointed 31 Jan. 1373 ; ob. 1389.

John Barnet was elected, but he was set aside by the Pope.

1389 William de Bottlesham. Translated from Landaff 27 Aug. 1389; ob. Feb. 1400.

1400 John de Bottlesham, Prebendary of York. Consecrated 4 July, 1400; ob. April, 1404.

1404 Richard Young. Translated from Bangor 28 July, 1404; ob. Oct. 1418.

1419 John Kemp, Archdeacon of Durham. Elected Jan. 1419; translated to Chichester 28 Feb. 1421.

Thomas Spofford was then elected, but before consecration was removed to Hereford.

1421 John Langdon, Monk of Canterbury. Appointed 17 Nov. 1421 ; ob. 30 Sept. 1434.

1435 Thomas Browne, Dean of Salisbury. Consecrated 1 May, 1435; translated to Norwich 10 September, 1436.

1436 William Wells, Abbot of York, afterwards Provost of Beverley, Keeper of the Privy Seal. Consecrated 1 April, 1436; ob. 1443.

1444 John Lowe. Translated from St. Asaph 22 April, 1444; ob. 1467.

1468 Thomas Scot, surnamed Rotheram, Provost of Beverley. Appointed 27 March, 1468 ; translated to Lincoln in 1471.

1472 John Alcock, Dean of St. Stephen's, Westminster, Master of the Rolls. Appointed 17 March, 1472; translated to Worcester in 1476.

1476 John Russell, Archdeacon of Bucks. Appointed 20 Sept. 1476 ; translated to Lincoln in 1480.

1480 Edmund Audley, Prebendary of York. Appointed 18 Sept. 1480 ; translated to Hereford in 1492.

1492 Thomas Savage, Canon of York, and Dean of the King's Chapel. Appointed 3 Dec. 1492 ; translated to London 27 Oct. 1496.

1497 Richard Fitz-James, Prebendary of St. Paul's. Appointed 17 May, 1497; translated to Chichester 1503.

1504 John Fisher, Chancellor of Cambridge, and Master of Queen's College, CARDINAL. Appointed 14 Oct. 1504. Beheaded 22 June, 1535.

1535 John Hilsey, Prior of Dominican Friars in London. Appointed 4 Oct. 1535; ob. 1538.

1540 Nicholas Heath, Archdeacon of Stafford, Almoner. Elected 26 March, 1540; translated to Worcester 1543.

1544 Henry Holbeach, Dean of Worcester, Suffragan Bishop of Bristol. Elected 3 May, 1544; translated to Lincoln in 1547.

1547 Nicholas Ridley, Master of Pembroke Hall, Cambridge. Consecrated 5 Sept. 1547; translated to London 1 April 1550.

1550 John Poynet, Prebendary of Canterbury. Consecrated 29 June 1550; translated to Winchester 23 March 1551.

1551 John Scory. Consecrated 30 Aug. 1551; translated to Chichester May 1552.

THE SEE VACANT ABOVE THREE YEARS.

1554 Maurice Griffin, Archdeacon of Rochester. Consecrated 1 April, 1554; ob. 20 Nov. 1558.

1559 Edmund Gheast, Archdeacon of Canterbury. Elected 29 Jan. 1559; translated to Salisbury in 1571.

1571 Edmund Freake, Dean of Salisbury. Elected 26 Feb. 1571; translated to Norwich 1575.

1576 John Piers, Dean of Salisbury and [Christ Church, Oxford, Almoner. Elected 10 April, 1576; translated to Salisbury in 1577.

1578 John Young, Prebendary of Westminster. Nominated 31 Jan. 1578; ob. 10 April, 1605, æt. 71.

1605 William Barlow, Dean of Chester. Elected 23 May, 1605; translated to Lincoln in 1608.

1608 Richard Neyle, Dean of Westminster. Elected 2 July, 1608; translated to Litchfield and Coventry in 1610.

1610 John Buckeridge, President of St. John's College,

Oxford. Elected 29 Dec. 1610; translated to Ely in 1628.

1628 Walter Curle, Dean of Litchfield. Elected 22 July, 1628; translated to Bath and Wells in 1629.

1629 John Bowle, Dean of Salisbury. Elected 14 Dec. 1629; ob. 9 October, 1637.

1637 John Warner, Dean of Litchfield. Elected 13 Nov. 1637; ob. 14 Oct. 1666, æt. 86.

1666 John Dolben, Dean of Westminster. Elected 13 Nov. 1666; translated to York in 1683.

1683 Francis Turner, Dean of Windsor. Consecrated 11 Nov. 1683; translated to Ely 23 Aug. 1684.

1684 Thomas Sprat, Dean of Westminster. Consecrated 2 Nov. 1684; ob. 20 May, 1713.

1713 Francis Atterbury, Dean of Christ Church, Oxford. Appointed June, 1713; deprived and banished; he died in 1732.

1723 Samuel Bradford. Translated from Carlisle 1723; ob. 1731.

1731 Joseph Wilcocks. Translated from Gloucester 1731; ob. 1756.

1756 Zachariah Pearce. Translated from Bangor 1756; he resigned the Deanery of Westminster in 1768; ob. 1774.

1774 John Thomas, Dean of Westminster. Elected 1774; ob. 1793, æt. 83.

1793 Samuel Horsley. Translated from St. David's 1793; translated to St. Asaph 1802.

1802 Thomas Dampier, Prebendary of Durham. Elected 1802; translated to Ely 1808.

1808 Walter King. Elected 1808. PRESENT Lord Bishop of Rochester.

BISHOPS OF SALISBURY.

1046 Herman. Succeeded in 1046 as Bishop of Winton, and as Bishop of Shireburn in 1050. He removed the See to Salisbury; ob. ante 1080.

1078 St. Osmund de Seez, Earl of Dorset. Succeeded in 1078; Lord Chancellor; ob. Dec. 1099.

1102 Roger, Lord Chief Justice and Lord Treasurer. Elected 13 April, 1102; ob. 4 Dec. 1139.

THE SEE VACANT THREE YEARS.

1142 Josceline de Bailol, a Lombard, Archdeacon of Winchester, and Prebendary of York.   Consecrated
1142; ob. 18 Nov. 1184.

THE SEE VACANT FOUR YEARS.

1188 Hubert Walter, Dean of York. Elected 15 Sept. 1188;
translated to Canterbury 1193.

1194 Herbert Poore, called by Godwin *Robert* Poore. Elected 29 April, 1194; ob. 6 Feb. 1217.

1217 Richard Poore.   Translated from Chichester 1217;
translated to Durham 1228.

1228 Robert de Bingham, Prebendary of Salisbury. Elected
December, 1228; ob. 2 Nov. 1246.

1246 William of York, Provost of Beverley.   Elected 10
Dec. 1246 ; ob. 31 Jan. 1256.

1256 Giles de Bridport, Dean of Wells. Consecrated 11
March, 1256 ; ob. 13 Dec. 1262.

1263 Walter de la Wyle, Sub-chanter of Salisbury.   Elected
Feb. 1263; ob. 3 Jan. 1870.

1270 Robert Wykehampton, Dean of Salisbury.   Elected 6
March, 1270; ob. 24 April 1284.

1284 Walter Scammel, Dean of Salisbury. Appointed 24
May, 1284 ; ob. 25 Sept. 1286.

1287 Henry de Brandeston, Dean of Salisbury.   Elected
2 Jan. 1287 ; ob. 11 Feb. 1288.

Lawrence de Akkeburne, or De Hawkeborne.
Elected 10 May, 1288, but died 8 August
following, before confirmation.

1288 William de Corner.   Elected 25 Nov. 1288; in 1279
he was chosen Archbishop of Dublin, but set aside
by the Pope; ob. 1291.

1291 Nicholas Longespee, Prebendary of Salisbury.   Consecrated 16 March, 1291 ; ob. 18 May, 1297.

YEAR.

1297 Simon de Gaunt. Elected 31 July, 1297 ; ob. 31 May, 1315.

1315 Roger de Martival, Dean of Lincoln. Elected 11 June, 1315; ob. 14 March, 1330.

1330 Robert Wyvill. Succeeded 21 Aug. 1330; ob. Sept. 1375.

1375 Ralph Erghum. Appointed 12 Oct. 1375; translated to Bath and Wells 14 Sept. 1388.

1388 John Waltham. Appointed 3 April, 1388 ; Master of the Rolls, Lord Treasurer ; ob. Sept. 1395.

1395 Richard Metford. Translated from Chichester 25 Oct. 1395; ob. 1407.

1407 Nicholas Bubbewith. Translated from London 14 August, 1407; translated to Bath and Wells in 1408.

1408 Robert. Hallum, Archdeacon of Canterbury, CARDI-NAL, and Chancellor of Oxford. Appointed 22 June, 1408 ; ob. Sept. 1417.

1417 John Chaundeler, Dean of Salisbury. Elected 15 Nov. 1417; ob. July, 1426.

1427 Robert Neville, Provost of Beverly. Appointed 9 July, 1427 ; translated to Durham in 1437.

1438 William Aiscough, Clerk of the Council. Appointed 11 Feb. 1438 ; murdered 29 June, 1450.

1450 Richard Beauchamp. Translated from Hereford 14 Aug. 1450 ; the first Chancellor of the Garter ; ob. 1482.

1482. Lionel Woodville, Dean of Exeter, Chancellor of Oxford. Appointed 28 March, 1482; ob. 1485.

1485 Thomas Langton. Translated from St. David's 9 Feb. 1485 ; Chancellor of the Garter ; translated to Winchester in 1493.

1493 John Blyth, Master of the Rolls, Chancellor of Cambridge; Chancellor of the Garter. Appointed 22 Dec. 1493; ob. 23 Aug. 1499.

1500 Henry Deane. Translated from Bangor 22 March, 1500; translated to Canterbury 1501.

1502 Edmund Audley. Translated from Hereford 2 April, 1502; Chancellor of the Garter; ob. 23 August, 1524.

1524 Lawerence Campejus, CARDINAL. Appointed 2 Dec. 1524 ; deprived by act of Parliament 1534, for non-residence.

YEAR.

1335 Nicholas Shaxton, Treasurer of Sarum. Elected 22 Feb. 1535; he resigned in consequence of not subscribing to the Six Articles 1 July, 1539.

1539 John Salcott, or Capon. Translated from Bangor 31 July, 1539; ob. 6 Oct. 1557.

       Peter Petow, a CARDINAL, was provided to this See by the Pope, but the Queen would not allow him to enter the realm.

1558 Francis Mallet was nominated by the Queen 14 Oct. 1558; but he was set aside, on her death, in Nov. following.

1559 John Jewell. Elected 21 Aug. 1559; ob. 23 Sept. 1571.

1571 Edmund Gheast. Translated from Rochester 15 Dec. 1571; ob. 28 Feb. 1577.

1577 John Piers. Translated from Rochester 11 Oct 1577; translated to York 1588.

THE SEE VACANT THREE YEARS.

1591 John Coldwell, Dean of Rochester. Elected 2 Dec. 1591; ob. 14 Oct. 1596.

1598 Henry Cotton, Prebendary of Winchester. Elected 28 Sept. 1598; ob. 7 May, 1615.

1615 Robert Abbot, Master of Baliol College, Oxford. Elected 11 Oct. 1615; ob. 2 March, 1618, æt. 58.

1618 Martin Fotherby. Elected 26 March, 1618; ob. 11 March, 1620.

1620 Robert Tounson, Dean of Westminster. Elected 24 March, 1620; ob. 15 May, 1621.

1621 John Davenant, Master of Queen's College, Cambridge. Elected 11 June, 1621; ob. 20 April, 1641.

1641 Brian Duppa. Translated from Chichester in 1641; translated to Winchester 10 Sept. 1660.

1660 Humphrey Henchman, Precentor of Salisbury. Elected 4 Oct. 1660; translated to London 1663.

1663 John Earle. Translated from Worcester 19 Sept. 1663; ob. 17 Nov. 1665.

1665 Alexander Hyde, Dean of Winchester. Consecrated 31 Dec. 1665; ob. 22 Aug. 1667, æt. 70.

1667 Seth Ward. Translated from Exeter 5 Sept. 1667; Chancellor of the Garter; ob. 6 Jan. 1689.

1689 Gilbert Burnet. Consecrated 31 March, 1689; ob. 17 March, 1714.

1715 William Talbot. Translated from Oxford 23 April, 1715; translated to Durham 1722.

1722 Richard Willis. Translated from Gloucester 1722; translated to Winchester 1723.

1723 Benjamin Hoadley. Translated from Hereford 1723; translated to Winchester 1734.

1734 Thomas Sherlock. Translated from Bangor 1734; translated to London 1748.

1748 John Gilbert. Translated from Landaff 1748; translated to York 1757.

1757 John Thomas. Translated from Peterborough 1757; translated to Winchester 1761.

1761 Hon. Robert Drummond. Translated from St. Asaph 1761; translated to York same year.

1761 John Thomas. Translated from Lincoln 1761; ob. 1766.

1766 John Hume. Translated from Oxford 1766; ob. 1782.

1782 Hon. Shute Barrington. Translated from Landaff 1782; translated to Durham 1791.

1791 John Douglas. Translated from Carlisle 1791; ob. 1807.

1807 John Fisher. Translated from Exeter 1807. Chancellor of the Order of the Garter; ob. 1825.

BISHOPS OF WINCHESTER.

1070 Walkeline. Obtained his Bishoprick 23 May, 1070; ob. 3 Jan. 1098.

THE SEE VACANT TWO YEARS.

1100 William Giffard, Prebendary of St. Paul's, Lord Chancellor. Appointed 1100, but was not Consecrated until 11 Aug. 1107; ob. 25 Jan. 1129.

1129 Henry de Blois, CARDINAL, Abbot of Glastonbury, brother to King Stephen. Consecrated 17 Nov. 1129; ob. 6 Aug. 1171.

THE SEE VACANT THREE YEARS.

YEAR.

1173 Richard Tocliffe, *alias* More, Archbishop of Poictiers. Elected 1 May, 1173 ; ob. 1189.

1189 Godfrey de Lucy. Consecrated 1 Nov. 1189; ob. 1204.

1205 Sir Peter de Rupibus, Knt. Lord Chief Justice. Consecrated 25 Sept. 1205; ob. 9 June, 1238.

THE SEE VACANT FIVE YEARS.

1243 William de Raleigh, *alias* Radley, translated from Norwich 1243 ; ob. 1250.

1250 Gethelmar, Aymer, or Ludomare de Valencia, the King's half brother. Elected 1250 ; ob. 1261.

1261 John Exon, *alias* of Oxon, *alias* Gernsey. Consecrated 1261; ob. 20 Jan. 1268.

Richard Moore was elected, but set aside by the Archbishop of Canterbury.

1268 Nicholas of Ely; translated from Worcester 25 Feb. 1268; ob. 12 Feb. 1280.

1282 John de Pontissera, *alias* Sawbridge. Elected June, 1282; ob. 4 Dec. 1304.

1305 Henry Woodloke, *alias* de Merewell. Elected Feb. 1305 ; ob. 29 June, 1316.

1316 John de Sandale, Dean of St. Paul's, Chancellor of the Exchequer, Lord Chancellor, and Lord Treasurer. Elected 5 Aug. 1316 ; ob. Nov. 1319.

Adam .... was elected, but set aside by the Pope.

1320 Reginald de Asser, the Pope's Legate. Consecrated 16 Nov. 1320 ; ob. 12 April, 1323.

1323 John de Stratford. Appointed 20 June, 1323 ; Lord Chancellor and Lord Treasurer; translated to Canterbury 3 Nov. 1333.

1333 Adam de Orleton. Translated from Worcester 1 Dec. 1333; ob. 18 July, 1345.

John Devenesche, elected, but set aside by the Pope.

1345 William de Edindon, Lord Treasurer and Lord Chancellor. Succeeded in 1345; ob. 7 Oct. 1366.

1367 William de Wykeham. Consecrated 1367; ob. 27 Sept. 1404.

YEAR.

1405 Henry Beaufort, third son of John of Gaunt, Duke of
Lancaster, by Katherine Swinford. Translated from
Lincoln 14 March, 1405 ; CARDINAL and Lord Chan-
cellor ; ob. 11 April, 1447.

1447 William de Waynflete, *alias* Pattyn, Provost of Eton
College, Lord Chancellor. Appointed 10 May, 1447 ;
ob. Aug. 1486.

1487 Peter Courtenay. Translated from Exeter 29 Jan.
1487 ; ob. 22 Sept. 1492.

1493 Thomas Langton. Translated from Salisbury 24 June,
1493. Elected to Canterbury 22 Jan. 1500 ; but
died the 27th of that month, before his translation
was perfected.

1500 Richard Fox. Translated from Durham 17 Oct. 1500 ;
Lord Privy Seal ; ob. 14 Sept. 1528.

1529 Thomas Wolsey, Archbishop of York, CARDINAL, and
Lord Chancellor. Obtained leave to hold this See
in commendam, 6 April, 1529 ; ob. 29 Nov. 1530.

1531 Stephen Gardiner, Master of Trinity College, Cambridge. Appointed 5 Dec. 1531 ; deprived 1550.

1551 John Poynet. Translated from Rochester 23 March,
1551; resigned 1553.; ob. 11 April, 1556.

1553 Stephen Gardiner. Restored 1553, and made Lord
Chancellor ; ob. 12 Nov. 1555.

1556 John White. Translated from Lincoln 16 May, 1556;
Deprived circa 1560.

1561 Robert Horne, Dean of Durham. Consecrated 16
Feb. 1561 ; ob. 1 June, 1580.

1580 John Watson, Dean of Winchester. Elected 29 June,
1580 ; ob. 23 Jan. 1583, æt. 63.

1583 Thomas Cowper. Translated from Lincoln 12 March,
1583 ; ob. 29 April, 1594.

1595 William Wickham. Translated from Lincoln 7 Jan.
1595 ; ob. 12 June following.

1595 William Day, Dean of Windsor. Elected 3 Nov. 1595;
ob. 20 Sept. 1596.

1597 Thomas Bilson. Translated from Worcester 29 April,
1597 ; ob. 18 June, 1616, æt. 69.

1616 James Mountague. Translated from Bath and Wells
26 June, 1616 ; ob. 20 July, 1618, æt. 50.

1619 Lancelot Andrews. Translated from Ely 18 Feb. 1619;
ob. 21 Sept. 1626.

s s 2

YEAR.

1627 Richard Neile. Translated from Durham 10 Dec.
1627; translated to York Oct. 1632.

1632 Walter Curle. Translated from Bath and Wells.
Elected 26 Oct. 1632; ob. 1647.

THE SEE VACANT TEN YEARS.

1660 Brian Duppa. Translated from Salisbury 10 Sept.
1660; ob. 26 March, 1662, æt. 74.

1662 George Morley. Translated from Worcester 20 April,
1662; ob. 29 Oct. 1684.

1684 Peter Mew. Translated from Bath and Wells 22
Nov. 1684; ob. 9 Nov. 1706.

1707 Sir Jonathan Trelawney, Bart. Translated from Exeter 21 June, 1707; ob. 1721.

1721 Charles Trimnell. Translated from Norwich 1721;
ob. 1723.

1723 Richard Willis. Translated from Salisbury 1723; ob.
1734.

1734 Benjamin Hoadley. Translated from Salisbury 1734;
ob. 1761.

1761 John Thomas. Translated from Salisbury 1761; ob.
1781.

1781 Hon. Brownlow North. Translated from Worcester
1781; Prelate of the Order of the Garter; ob.
1820.

1820 George Pretyman Tomline. Translated from Lincoln 1820. PRESENT Lord Bishop of Winchester.
Prelate of the Order of the Garter.

BISHOPS OF WORCESTER.

1062 Wulstan. Consecrated 8 Sept. 1062; ob. 1095; æt.
circa 90.

1097 Sampson, Canon of Baion. Consecrated 15 June, 1097;
ob. 5 May, 1112.

1113 Theulph, or Theobald, Canon of Baion. Elected 28
Dec. 1113; ob. 1124.

1125 Simon, Chancellor to Queen Adeliza. Elected 8
May, 1125.

Alured. No date. *Quære de hoc.*

1151 John Pagham. Consecrated 4 March, 1151.

1163 Roger, son of Robert, Earl of Gloucester. Consecrated 26 Aug. 1163 ; ob. 9 Aug. 1179.

1181 Baldwin, Abbot of Ford. Consecrated 1181 ; translated to Canterbury 1184.

1186 Robert de Norball, Abbot of Gloucester. Consecrated 21 Sept. 1186; ob. 1190.

1191 Robert Fitz Ralph, Canon of Lincoln. Consecrated 5 May, 1191; ob. 1192.

1192 Henry de Soilly, Abbot of Gloucester. Consecrated 12 Dec. 1192; ob. 1196.

1196 John de Constantiis, Dean of Rouen, Archdeacon of Oxford. Consecrated 20 Oct. 1196; ob. Sept. 1198.

1199 Maugere, Dean of York. Nominated 24 Aug. 1199; ob. 1212.

1213 Walter Grey. Translated from Litchfield 1 13; Lord Chancellor; translated to York in 1216.

1216 Silvester de Evesham, Prior of Worcester. Elected 8 April, 1216; ob. 1218.

1218 William de Blois, or Bleys, Archdeacon of Bucks. Nominated 24 July, 1218; ob. 14 Aug. 1236.

1236 Walter de Cantilupe. Elected 9 Sept. 1236; ob. Feb. 1266.

1266 Nicholas de Ely, Archdeacon of Ely. Nominated 21 Feb. 1266 ; Lord Chancellor; translated to Winchester 1267.

1268 Godfrey Giffard, Archdeacon of Wells. Appointed 30 June, 1268; Lord Chancellor; ob. circa 1301.

John de St. German was elected, and obtained the Royal Assent, but it is doubtful if ever he was Consecrated.

1302 William de Gaynesburgh, a Friar Minor at Oxford. Appointed 4 Feb. 1302; living July, 1307.

Peter of Savoy. Nominated by the Pope, but set aside by the King.

1308 Walter Reynolds, Prebendary of St. Paul's. Appointed 6 April, 1308; Lord Chancellor and Lord Treasurer; translated to Canterbury 24 Sept. 1313.

1314 Walter Maydenstun, Prebendary of St. Paul's. Appointed 3 Feb. 1314; ob. 1317.

YEAR.

1318 Thomas Cobham, Sub Dean of Sarum. Appointed
20 Nov. 1318; ob. Aug. 1327.

> Wolstan, Prior of Worcester, was elected in
> Aug. 1327, had the Royal Assent, and the
> temporalities were restored to him, but ac-
> cording to Le Neve, "all these proceedings
> came to nothing."

1327 Adam de Orleton. Translated from Hereford Nov.
1327; translated to Winchester 1 Dec. 1333.

1333 Simon de Montacute, Archdeacon of Canterbury. Appointed 7 Dec. 1333; translated to Ely 1336.

1337 Thomas Hennibal, or Hemenhale. Consecrated 1337.
Godwin and Heylyn are the only writers (Le Neve
says) who notice him.

1338 Wolston de Brandsford, Prior of Worcester, apparently
the same person who was elected in 1327. Consecrated 1338; ob. 6 Aug. 1349.

> John de Evesham, Prior of Worcester, was
> elected in Sept. 1349, but he was never con-
> firmed.

1349 John Thoresby. Translated from St. David's 1349;
Lord Chancellor, CARDINAL; translated to York
Oct. 1352.

1352 Reginald Bryan. Translated from St. David's 1352;
ob. 1361.

1362 John Barnet, Archdeacon of London. Appointed 10
Jan. 1362; Lord Treasurer; translated to Bath
and Wells Nov. 1363.

1363 William Whittlesey. Translated from Rochester in
1363; translated to Canterbury in 1368.

1368 William de Lynn, or Lenne. Translated from Chichester Oct. 1368; ob. 18 Nov. 1373.

1375 Henry Wakefield, Archdeacon of Canterbury. Appointed 12 Sept. 1375; Lord Treasurer; ob. 11 Mar.
1394.

> John Green * was elected, but set aside by the
> Pope.

---

* By the will of John of Gaunt Duke of Lancaster, dated 3
Feb. 1397, "Johan' Evesq' de Wyrcestr,'" was appointed one
of that Prince's executors. *Vide* "Royal Wills," p. 163, and a
note there inserted relative to this Bishop.

YEAR.

1395 Tideman de Winchecumb. Translated from Landaff 25 Jan. 1395. " What became of him afterwards," says Le Neve, " I know not."

1401 Richard Clifford, Dean of York. Appointed 21 Sept. 1401? translated to London in 1407.

1407 Thomas Peverell. Translated from Landaff 30 Nov. 1407; ob. 1 March, 1418.

1419 Philip Morgan, Chancellor of Normandy. Appointed 19 June, 1419; translated to Ely 27 Feb. 1425.

1425 Thomas Polton. Translated from Chichester 28 Feb. 1425; ob. 1433.

1434 Thomas Bourchier. Appointed 9 March, 1434; translated to Ely in 1443.

1443 John Carpenter, Provost of Oriel College, Oxford, Chancellor of Oxford. Appointed 20 Dec. 1443. He resigned.

1476 John Alcock. Translated from Rochester 20 Sept. 1476; translated to Ely in 1486; Lord Chancellor.

1486 Robert Morton, Prebendary of York and Lincoln. Appointed 16 Oct. 1486; ob. 1497.

1497 John Gigles, Prebendary of St. Paul's, York, and Lincoln. Appointed 30 Aug. 1497; ob. 25 Aug. 1498.

1499 Silvester Gigles, nephew to the last Bishop. Appointed 17 March, 1499; ob. 16 April, 1521.

Julius de Medicis, CARDINAL, afterwards POPE CLEMENT VII. Was made Administrator of this See by the Pope 31 July, 1521, and resigned 1522.

1523 Jerome de Ghinucci, an Italian. Appointed 20 Feb. 1523. Deprived in 1534.

1535 Hugh Latimer. Consecrated Sept. 1585. Resigned 1 July, 1539; burnt 16 Oct. 1555.

1539 John Bell, Archdeacon of Gloucester. Elected 2 Aug. 1539; resigned 17 Nov. 1543; ob. 11 Aug. 1556.

1543 Nicholas Heath. Translated from Rochester 22 Dec. 1543. Displaced by King Edw. VI. and the see put in commendam.

1552 John Hooper, Bishop of Gloucester. Had leave granted him to hold this See in commendam in 1552; deprived 20 March, 1553.

1553 Nicholas Heath. Restored in 1553 by Queen Mary, and translated to York the same year.

1555 Richard Pate, Archdeacon of Lincoln and Winchester. Appointed 5 March, 1555. Deprived circa 1555

1559 Edwyn Sandys, Prebendary of Peterborough. Elected 25 Nov. 1559; translated to London 13 July 1570.

John Calfhill was nominated, but died before Consecration.

1571 Nicholas Bullingham. Translated from Lincoln 18 Jan. 1571; ob. 18 April, 1576.

1577 John Whitgifte, Dean of Lincoln. Nominated 24 March, 1577; translated to Canterbury 23 Sept. 1583.

1584 Edmund Freak. Translated from Norwich 26 Oct. 1584; ob. 21 March, 1590.

1592 Richard Fletcher. Translated from Bristol 24 Jan. 1592. Translated to London in 1594.

1596 Thomas Bilson, Prebendary of Winchester. Elected 20 April, 1596; translated to Winchester May, 1597.

1597 Gervase Babington. Translated from Exeter 30 Aug. 1597; ob. 17 May, 1610.

1610 Henry Parry. Translated from Gloucester 13 July, 1610; ob. 12 Dec. 1616.

1617 John Thornborough. Translated from Bristol 25 Jan. 1617; ob. 9 July, 1641.

1641 John Prideaux, Canon of Christchurch, Oxford. Elected 22 Nov. 1641; ob. 29 July, 1650; æt. 72.

THE SEE VACANT TEN YEARS.

1660 George Morley, Dean of Christchurch, Oxford. Elected 9 Oct. 1660; translated to Winchester 1662

1662 John Gauden. Translated from Exeter 23 May, 1662; ob. 10 Sept, following, æt. 57.

1662 John Earle, Dean of Westminster. Elected 1 Nov. 1662; ob. translated to Salisbury June 1663.

1663 Robert Skinner. Translated from Oxford 12 Oct. 1663; ob. 14 June, 1670, æt. 80.

1671 Walter Blandford. Translated from Oxford 2 June, 1671; ob. 9 July, 1675.

1675 James Fleetwood, Prebendary of Litchfield. Elected 26 July, 1675; ob. 17 July, 1683, æt. 81.

1683 William Thomas. Translated from St. David's 27 Aug. 1683; ob. June, 1689.

YEAR.

1689 Edward Stillingfleet, Dean of St. Paul's. Consecrated 13 Oct. 1689; ob. 27 March, 1699.

1699 William Lloyd. Translated from Coventry and Litchfield in 1699; ob. 1717.

1717 John Hough. Translated from Litchfield and Coventry 1717; ob. 1743.

1743 Isaac Maddox. Translated from St. Asaph, 1743; ob. 1759.

1759 James Johnson. Translated from Gloucester 1759; ob. 1774.

1774 Hon. Brownlow North. Translated from Litchfield and Coventry 1774; translated to Winchester 1781.

1781 Richard Hurd. Translated from Litchfield and Coventry 1781; ob. 1808.

1808 Foliot Herbert Walker Cornwall. Translated from Hereford 1808. PRESENT Lord Bishop of Worcester.

WESTMINSTER.

At the dissolution of monasteries, this Abbey was valued at 3,997l.; in 1539, King Henry VIII. erected it into a Deanery; and in 1540 into a Bishoprick, and appointed John Thirleby Bishop thereof. But he, having wasted the patrimony allotted by the King for the support of the See, was translated to Norwich, and with him ended the Bishoprick of Westminster. The Dean continued to preside until the accession of Queen Mary, who restored the Abbot; but Queen Elizabeth displaced the Abbot, and erected it into a Collegiate Church, of a Dean and twelve Prebendaries, as it still continues.

Westminster was erected into a Bishoprick by Henry VIII. 17 Dec. 1540.

I. 1540. Thomas Thirleby was consecrated Bishop of Westminster 19 Dec. 1540; sat ten years, and was the first and last that enjoyed this dignity. He was translated to Norwich 1 April, 1550; and King Edward VI. by letters patent, dated on the same day, dissolved this Bishoprick.

SUCCESSION

TO

THE PROVINCE OF YORK.

ARCHBISHOPS OF YORK.

YEAR.

1061 Aldred. Translated from Worcester in 1061 ; ob. 11 Sept. 1069.

1070 Thomas I. Canon of Baion. Succeeded in 1070 ; ob. 18 Nov. 1100.

1100 Gerard. Translated from Hereford in 1100 ; ob. 21 May, 1108.

1109 Thomas II. Bishop-elect of London ; but, before Consecration, was removed to this See, and Consecrated in June, 1109 ; ob. Feb. 1114.

1114 Thurstan, Prebendary of St. Paul's. Elected 15 Aug. 1114; but not Consecrated until Oct. 1119. He resigned 21 Jan. 1139.

1144 William, a kinsman of King Stephen. Consecrated 26 Sept. 1144, but was deprived by the Pope in 1147.

Hillary, Bishop of Chichester, was then elected by the greatest part of the Chapter, but the other part chose

1147 Henry Murdac, Abbot of Fountains, who was Consecrated Dec. 1147 ; ob. 14 Oct. 1153.

1153 William, who was deprived in 1147, was then restored; ob. 8 June, 1154.

1154 Roger of Bishopsbridge, Archdeacon of Canterbury. Consecrated 10 Oct. 1154; ob. Nov. 1181.

THE SEE VACANT TEN YEARS.

1191 Geoffrey Plantagenet, natural son of King Henry II. Archdeacon of Lincoln, Lord Chancellor. Consecrated 18 Aug. 1191 ; vacated the See 1207 ; ob. 18 Dec. 1212.

Simon de Langton, brother of Stephen, Archbishop of Canterbury, was elected, but was
set aside by the Pope.

1216 Walter de Grey. Translated from Worcester 27 March,
1216; Lord Chancellor; * ob. 1 May, 1255.

1255 St. Sewall de Bovill, Dean of York. Elected 1 Oct.
1255; ob. 10 May, 1258.

1258 Godfrey de Ludeham, Dean of York. Elected 25 July,
1258; ob. 12 Jan. 1264.

William de Langton, *alias* de Ruderfield, Dean of
York, was then elected, and had the Royal Assent,
but was set aside by the Pope, who gave it to Bona-
venture; but he soon afterwards resigned it into
the Pope's hands, when

1265 Walter Giffard was translated from Bath and Wells
15 Oct. 1265; Lord Chancellor; ob. 1279.

1279 William Wickwane, Chancellor of York. Elected 22
June, 1279. He quitted his Archbishoprick a short
time before his death, which took place 26 Aug.
1285.

1285 John le Romayne, Precentor of Lincoln. Elected 29
Oct. 1285; ob. 1296.

1296 Henry de Newerke, Dean of York. Elected 7 May,
1296; ob. 15 Aug. 1299.

1299 Thomas de Corbrigge, Prebendary of York. Elected
12 Nov. 1299; ob. 22 Sept. 1303.

1303 William Grenfeld, Dean of Chichester, Prebendary
of York. Elected 24 Dec. 1303; Lord Chancellor;
ob. 6 Dec. 1315.

1316 William de Melton, Provost of Beverley, Lord Chancellor and Treasurer. Elected 21 Jan. 1316; ob.
5 April, 1340.

1340 William le Zouch, Dean of York, Lord Treasurer.
Elected 2 May, 1340; ob. 19 July, 1352.

1354 John Thoresby. Translated from Worcester 8 Sept.
1354; Cardinal, Lord Chancellor; ob. 6 Nov.
1373.

1374 Alexander Neville, Archdeacon of Durham. Ap-

---

* Rapin, Vol. I. p. 354.

pointed 6 June, 1374; banished in 1387; ob. May, 1397.

1388 Thomas Fits-Alan, *alias* Arundel. Translated from Ely 3 April, 1388; translated to Canterbury 25 Sept. 1396; Lord Chancellor.

1397 Robert Waldby. Translated from Chichester 13 Jan. 1897; ob. 29 May following.

1398 Richard Scrope. Translated from Litchfield and Coventry 23 June, 1398; beheaded 8 June, 1405.

> Thomas Langley, Dean of York, was elected, and had the Royal Assent 8 Aug. 1405, but was set aside by the Pope.
> Robert Hallum was then nominated by the Pope; but the King not being agreeable, he was, before Consecration, removed to Salisbury.

1407 Henry Bowet. Translated from Bath and Wells 7 Oct. 1407; ob. 20 Oct. 1423.

1424 Richard Fleming. Translated from Lincoln 24 May, 1424; but the King and Dean and Chapter disapproving of his promotion, he was returned to his see of Lincoln, and

1426 John Kemp was translated from London 8 April, 1426; CARDINAL, and Lord Chancellor; translated to Canterbury April, 1451.

1452 William Booth. Translated from Litchfield and Coventry 21 July, 1452; ob. 20 Sept. 1464.

1465 George Neville. Translated from Exeter 17 June, 1465; Lord Chancellor; ob. 8 June, 1476.

1476 Lawrence Booth. Translated from Durham 1 Sept. 1476; ob. 19 May, 1480.

1480 Thomas Scott, *alias* Rotheram. Translated from Lincoln 3 Sept. 1480; Lord Chancellor; ob. 29 May, 1500, æt. 76.

1501 Thomas Savage. Translated from London 12 April, 1501; ob. 2 Sept. 1507.

1508 Christopher Bainbrigge. Translated from Durham 12 Sept. 1508; made a CARDINAL in 1511; ob. 14 July, 1514.

1514 Thomas Wolsey. Translated from Lincoln 5 Aug. 1514; Lord Chancellor, and a CARDINAL; ob. 29 Nov. 1530.

YEAR.

1531 Edward Lee, Chancellor of Salisbury, and Prebendary of York. Appointed 30 Oct. 1531 ; ob. 15 Sept. 1544, æt. 62.

1545 Robert Holgate. Translated from Landaff 10 Jan. 1545; Lord President of the North; deprived circa 1555.

1555 Nicholas Heath, late Bishop of Worcester. Appointed Feb. 1555; Lord Chancellor; deprived circa 1558 ; ob. 1579.

William May, Dean of St. Paul's. Elected, but died 12 Aug. 1560, before confirmation.

1561 Thomas Young. Translated from St. David's 27 Jan. 1561; Lord President of the North ; ob. 26 June, 1568.

1570 Edmund Grindall. Translated from London 11 April, 1570; translated to Canterbury 1575.

1576 Edwyn Sandys. Translated from London 25 Jan. 1576; ob. 8 Aug. 1588.

1589 John Piers. Translated from Salisbury 1 Feb. 1589; ob. 28 Sept. 1594.

1595 Matthew Hutton. Translated from Durham March, 1595; ob. 15 Jan. 1606.

1606 Tobias Matthew. Translated from Durham 26 July, 1606; ob. 29 March, 1628, æt. 82.

1628 George Monteign. Translated from Durham 16 June, 1628; ob. same year.

1628 Samuel Harsnet. Translated from Norwich 26 Nov. 1628 ; ob. 18 May, 1631.

1632 Richard Neyle. Translated from Winchester 28 Feb. 1632; ob. 31 Oct. 1640.

1641 John Williams. Translated from Lincoln 4 Dec. 1641; Lord Keeper; ob. 25 March, 1649.

THE SEE VACANT ABOVE TEN YEARS.

1660 Accepted Frewen. Translated from Litchfield and Conventry 22 Sept. 1660; ob. 28 March, 1664.

1664 Richard Sterne. Translated from Carlisle 28 April, 1664 ; ob. 18 June, 1683, æt. 87.

1683 John Dolben. Translated from Rochester 26 July, 1683; ob. 11 April, 1686.

1688 Thomas Lamplugh. Translated from Exeter 28 Nov. 1688; ob. 5 May, 1691, æt. 76.

1691 John Sharp, Dean of Canterbury.   Consecrated 5
　　　 July, 1691 ; ob. 2 Feb. 1714.
1714 Sir William Dawes, Bart. Translated from Chester 26
　　　 Feb. 1714.
1724 Lancelot Blackburn.   Translated from Exeter 1724 ;
　　　 ob. 1743.
1743 Thomas Herring.   Translated from Bangor 1743 ;
　　　 translated to Canterbury 1747.
1747 Matthew Hutton .   Translated from Bangor 1747 ;
　　　 translated to Canterbury 1757.
1757 John Gilbert. Translated from Salisbury 1757 ; ob.
　　　 1761.
1761 Hon. Robert Drummond.   Translated from Salisbury
　　　 1761 ; ob. 1776.
1776 William Markham. Translated from Chester 1776 ;
　　　 ob. 1807.
1807 Hon. Edward Venables Vernon.   Translated from
　　　 Carlisle 1807.   Present Lord Archbishop of York ;
　　　 Primate of England.

BISHOPS OF CARLISLE.

1133 Athelwold, or Athelward, the last Prior of St. Oswald's.
　　　 Consecrated 1133 ; ob. 1156.
1157 Bernard. Consecrated 1157 ; ob. 1186.

THE SEE VACANT THIRTY-TWO YEARS.

　　　 Though King John in 1200 granted this Bi-
　　　 shoprick to the Archbishop of Sclavonia for
　　　 his better support, and on the 8th June, 1203,
　　　 granted the See to Alexander de Lucy, but
　　　 the next regular Bishop was

1218 Hugh de Bello Loco, Abbot of Battel, in Sussex. Con-
　　　 secrated 24 Jan. 1218 ; ob. 1223.
1223 Walter Maclerk, Lord Treasurer. Elected 27 Oct.
　　　 1223 ; resigned 29 June, 1246 ; ob. 1248.
1246 Silvester de Everdon, Archdeacon of Chester. Elected
　　　 1246 ; Lord Chancellor ; ob. 13 May, 1254.
1255 Thomas Vipont. Elected 6 Nov. 1255 ; ob. Oct. 1256.
1258 Robert de Chause, or Chansey, or Cheverel, called by

Leland, Chaplain to the Queen. Consecrated 10 April, 1258; ob. Sept. 1278.

William de Rotberfeld, Dean of York, was elected 13 Dec. 1278, but he refused the dignity, and they elected on the next day

1278 Ralph de Ireton, Prior of Gisborne; ob. Feb. 1292.

1293 John de Halghton, Canon of Carlisle. Elected 23 March, 1293; ob. 1 Nov. 1324.

William Ayermin, Canon of York, was elected and obtained the Royal assent 17 Jan. 1325; but the Pope appointed

1325 John de Rosse, Canon of Hereford 20 Jan. 1325; ob. 1332.

1332 John de Kirkeby, Canon of Carlisle. Elected 8 May, 1332; ob. 1353.

John de Horncastle was nominated by the King, but set aside by the Pope, who appointed

1353 Gilbert de Wilton, 24 May, 1353; ob. 18 Jan. 1363.

1363 Thomas de Appleby, Canon of Carlisle. Consecrated 1363; ob. 5 Dec. 1395.

William Strickland was elected, but set aside by the Pope.

1396 Robert de Reade. Translated from Waterford in Ireland 30 March, 1396; translated to Chichester the same year.

1397 Thomas Merkes, *alias* of Newmarket, *alias* Sumestre. Consecrated 1397. He was deprived in 1399, and was afterwards Vicar of Sturminster, in Dorsetshire, and in 1404 became Rector of Todenham in Gloucestershire. He died about 1409.

1399 William Strickland. Appointed 15 Nov. 1399; ob. 30 Aug. 1419.

1420 Roger Whelpdale, Provost of Queen's College, Oxford. Appointed 17 March, 1420; ob. 4 Feb. 1423.

1423 William Barrow. Translated from Bangor 16 June, 1423; ob. 4 Sept. 1429.

1430 Marmaduke Lumley, Archdeacon of Northumberland, Lord Treasurer, Lord Chancellor, and Chancellor of Cambridge. Appointed 15 April, 1430. Translated to Lincoln in 1450.

YEAR.

1450 Nicholas Close, Archdeacon of Colchester. Appointed 14 March, 1450; translated to Litchfield and Coventry in 1452.

1452 William Percy, Prebendary of York, Lincoln, and Salisbury, Chancellor of Cambridge. Appointed 24 Oct. 1452; ob. 1462.

1462 John Kingscotes, Archdeacon of Gloucester. Appointed 12 July, 1462; ob. 1463.

1464 Richard Scrope. Appointed June 5, 1464; ob. 22 May, 1468.

1468 Edward Story, Chancellor of Cambridge. Appointed 1 Sept. 1468; translated to Chichester in 1478.

1478 Richard Bell, Prior of Durham. Appointed 24 April, 1478; ob. . . . . .

1495 William Siver, or Siveyer. Abbot of St. Mary, York. Appointed 11 Dec. 1495; translated to Durham 1502.

1502 Roger Leyburn, Archdeacon of Durham. Consecrated 10 Sept. 1503; ob. 12 Nov. 1504.

1509 John Penny. Translated from Bangor 26 June, 1509; ob. 1520.

1521 John Kite, Archbishop of Armagh, in Ireland. Consecrated 1521; ob. 19 June, 1537.

1537 Robert Aldrich, Provost of Eton College, and Canon of Windsor. Nominated 18 July, 1537; ob. 5 March, 1556.

1556 Owen Oglethorpe, Dean of Windsor. Appointed 27 Oct. 1556; deprived June, 1559.

1561 John Best, Prebendary of Wells. Consecrated 2 March, 1561; ob. 22 May, 1570.

1570 Richard Barnes, Chancellor, and Prebendary of York, styled Bishop of Nottingham. Elected to the See 25 June, 1570; translated to Durham May 1577.

1577 John Mey, Prebendary of Ely. Elected 9 Aug. 1577; ob. 1598.

1598 Henry Robinson, Provost of Queen's College, Oxford. Elected 27 May, 1598; ob. 19 June, 1616, æt. 64.

1616 Robert Snowden, Prebendary of Southwell. Consecrated 24 Nov. 1616; ob. 15 May, 1621.

1621 Richard Milbourne. Translated from St. David's in 1621.

1624 Richard Senhouse, Dean of Gloucester. Consecrated 16 Sept. 1624; ob. 1626.

YEAR.

1626 Francis White, Dean of Carlisle. Consecrated 3 Dec.
1626; translated to Norwich Jan. 1628.

1628 Barnabas Potter, Provost of Queen's College, Oxford.
Consecrated 15 March, 1628; ob. 1641.

1641 James Usher, Archbishop of Armagh. Had leave to
hold this See *in commendam*, and received the Ad-
ministration thereof 16 Feb. 1641; ob. 21 March,
1656.

THE SEE VACANT FIVE YEARS.

1660 Richard Sterne, Master of Jesus College, Cambridge.
Consecrated 2 Dec. 1660; translated to York in
1664.

1664 Edward Rainbow, Dean of Peterborough. Consecrated
10 July, 1664; ob. 26 March, 1684, æt. 76.

1684 Thomas Smith, Dean of Carlisle. Consecrated 29
June, 1684; ob. 12 April, 1702; æt. 88.

1702 William Nicholson, Archdeacon and Prebendary of
Carlisle. Consecrated 14 June, 1702; translated to
Derry, in Ireland, 1718.

1718 Samuel Bradford, Prebendary of Westminster. Elected
1718; translated to Rochester 1723.

1723 John Waugh, Dean of Gloucester. Elected 1723;
ob. 1734.

1734 Sir George Fleming, Bart. Dean of Carlisle. Elected
1734; ob. 1747.

1747 Richard Olbasdeston, Dean of York. Elected 1747;
translated to London 1762.

1762 Charles Lyttelton, Dean of Exeter. Elected 1762;
ob. 1769.

1769 Edmund Law, Archdeacon of Carlisle. Elected 1769;
ob. 1787.

1787 John Douglas, Canon-residentiary of St. Paul's. Elected 1787; translated to Salisbury 1791.

1791 Hon. Edward Venables Vernon. Elected 1791; translated to York 1807.

1808 Samuel Goodenough. Elected 1808. PRESENT Lord
Bishop of Carlisle.

BISHOPS OF CHESTER.

YEAR.

1542 John Bird. Translated from Bangor 13 April, 1542; deprived by Queen Mary in 1553; ob. 1556.

1554 George Cotes, Master of Baliol College, Oxford. Consecrated 1 April, 1554; ob. Dec. 1555.

1556 Cuthbert Scot, Prebendary of St. Paul's. Appointed 24 April, 1556, deprived by Queen Elizabeth circa 1560.

1561 William Downman. Prebendary of Westminster. Elected 1 May, 1561; ob. 3 Dec. 1577.

1579 William Chaderton, Prebendary of York and Westminster. Confirmed 7 Nov. 1579; translated to Lincoln in 1595.

1595 Hugh Bellot. Translated from Bangor 25 June, 1595; ob. 1596.

1597 Richard Vaughan. Translated from Bangor 23 April, 1597; translated to London in 1604.

1604 George Lloyd. Translated from Sodor and Man, 1604; ob. 1 Aug. 1615, æt. 55.

1616 Thomas Moreton, Dean of Winchester. Elected 22 May, 1616; translated to Litchfield and Coventry 1619.

George Massie was nominated, but died before consecration.

1619 John Bridgman, Prebendary of Litchfield. Elected 15 March, 1619; ob. 1657.

THE SEE VACANT THREE YEARS.

1660 Brian Walton, Prebendary of St. Paul's. Consecrated 2 Dec. 1660; ob. 29 Nov. 1661.

1662 Henry Ferne, Dean of Ely. Consecrated Feb. 1662; ob. 16 March following, æt. 59.

1662 George Hall, Archdeacon of Canterbury. Consecrated 11 May, 1662; ob. 23 Aug. 1668.

1668 John Wilkins, Prebendary of York. Consecrated 15 Nov. 1668; ob. 19 Nov. 1672.

1673 John Pearson, Prebendary of Salisbury and Ely. Consecrated 9 Feb. 1673; ob. July, 1686.

YEAR.

1686 Thomas Cartwright, Prebendary of Durham. Consecrated 17 Oct. 1686; ob. 15 April, 1689.

1689 Nicholas Strafford, Dean of St. Asaph. Consecrated
15 Sept. 1689; ob. 1708.

1708 Sir William Dawes, Bart. Prebendary of Worcester.
Consecrated 8 Feb. 1708; translated to York 1714.

1714 Francis Gastrell, Canon of Christ Church, Oxford.
Consecrated 4 April, 1714; ob. 1725.

1725 Samuel Peploe, Warden of Manchester. Elected
1725; ob. 1752.

1752 Edmund Keene. Elected 1752; translated to Ely
1771.

1771 William Markham, Dean of Christ Church, Oxford.
Elected 1771; translated to York 1777.

1777 Beilby Porteus. Elected 1777; translated to London 1787.

1787 William Cleaver, Prebendary of Westminster. Elected
1787; translated to Bangor 1800.

1800 Henry William Majendie, Canon Residentiary of St.
Paul's. Elected 1800; translated to Bangor 1809.

1809 Bowyer Edward Sparke. Elected 1809; translated to
Ely, 1812.

1812 George Henry Law. Elected 1812; translated to
Bath and Wells 1824.

1824 Charles James Blomefield. Elected 1824. PRESENT
Lord Bishop of Chester.

BISHOPS OF DURHAM.

YEAR.

1056 Egelwine. Succeeded in 1056. Expelled by William
the Conqueror in 1070, and died in prison in
1071.

1072 Walcher. Consecrated circa 1072; ob. 14 May, 1080.

1080 William de Kairlipho. Nominated 9 Nov. 1080; ob.
2 Jan. 1095.

THE SEE VACANT FOR ABOUT FOUR YEARS.

1099 Ralph Flambard, Lord Treasurer, and Lord Chief
Justice. Nominated 29 May, 1099; ob. Sept. 1128.

YEAR.

1129 Geoffery Ruffus.   Consecrated 6 Aug. 1129 ; Lord
       Chancellor ; ob. 6 May, 1140.

1142 William de St. Barbara, Dean of York.   Elected 14
       March, 1142 ; ob. 14 Nov. 1152.

1153 Hugh Pudsey, Treasurer of York, and Archdeacon of
       Winchester.   Consecrated 20 Dec. 1153 ;   ob. 3
       March, 1194, æt. 70.

1195 Philip of Poictiers.   Elected Nov. 1195 ; ob. 21 Sept.
       1208.

THE SEE VACANT ABOUT TEN YEARS.

1217 Richard de Marisco, Dean of Salisbury, Archdeacon
       of Northumberland.   Elected 29 June, 1217 ; Lord
       Chancellor ; ob. 1 May, 1226.

       Leave of Election was granted to William Scott,
       Archdeacon of Worcester, 25 May, 1226, but
       the King refused his assent.

1228 Richard Poore.   Translated from Salisbury 22 July,
       1228 ; ob. 15 April, 1237.

1240 Nicholas de Farnham.   Elected 2 Jan. 1240 ; he re-
       signed in 1248, and died in Feb. 1257.

1249 Walter de Kirkham.   Elected 21 April, 1249 ; ob. 9
       Aug. 1260.

1260 Robert Stitchell, Prior of Finchale.   Elected 30 Sept.
       1260 ; ob. 4 Aug. 1274.

1274 Robert de Insula.   Elected 24 Sept. 1274 ; ob. 7 June,
       1283.

1283 Anthony de Bek, Archdeacon of Durham, Patriarch
       of Jerusalem.   He had also from the King the
       Principality of Man.   Elected 9 July, 1283 ; ob.
       March, 1311.

1311 Richard de Kellawe.   Elected 30 March, 1311 ; ob.
       9 Oct. 1316.

1317 Lewis de Beaumont, Treasurer of Salisbury.   Elected
       Oct. 1317 ; ob. Sept. 1333.

1333 Robert de Greystanes.   Elected Oct. 1333, but was
       set aside by the Pope, and died soon after.

1333 Richard Angarville, *alias* de Bury, Dean of Wells,
       Lord Privy Seal, Lord Chancellor, and Lord Trea-
       surer.   Appointed 7 Dec. 1333 ; ob. April, 1345,
       æt. 58.

1345. Thomas de Hatfield, Prebendary of York and Lincoln,

Principal Secretary of State. Elected 8 May, 1345; ob. 7 May, 1381.

1381 John Fordham, Dean of Wells, Lord Treasurer. Appointed 9 Sept. 1381; translated to Ely 3 April, 1388.

1388 Walter Skirlaw. Translated from Bath and Wells 3 April, 1388; ob. March, 1406.

1406 Thomas Langley, Dean of York, Lord Chancellor: A CARDINAL. Elected 17 May, 1406; ob. 28 Nov. 1437.

1438 Robert Neville. Translated from Salisbury 27 Jan. 1438; ob. 8 July, 1457.

1457 Lawrence Booth, Dean of St. Paul's, Chancellor of Cambridge, Lord Chancellor. Consecrated 25 Sept. 1457; translated to York in 1476.

1476 William Dudley, Dean of Windsor. Appointed 14 Oct. 1476; ob. 1483.

THE SEE VACANT ALMOST TWO YEARS.

1485 John Sherwood, Chancellor of Exeter. Appointed 6 Aug. 1485; ob. 1492.

THE SEE VACANT TWO YEARS.

1494 Richard Fox. Translated from Bath and Wells 8 Feb. 1494; translated to Winchester in 1502.

1502 William Sever, or Siveyer. Translated from Carlisle 15 Oct. 1502; ob. 1505.

THE SEE VACANT TWO YEARS.

1507 Christopher Bainbridge, Dean of York and Windsor, Master of the Rolls. Appointed 17 Nov. 1507. Translated to York in 1508.

1509 Thomas Ruthal, or Rowthall, Dean of Salisbury, Lord Privy Seal. Appointed 3 July, 1509; ob. 4 July, 1523.

1523 Thomas Wolsey, Archbishop of York. Appointed to hold this See in commendam, 30 April, 1523; translated to Winchester April, 1529.

1530 Cuthbert Tunstall. Translated from London 25 March 1530. Deprived in 1552, and the Bishoprick

YEAR.

dissolved; restored in 1553; deprived again in 1559; ob. 18 Nov. 1559, æt. 85.

1561 James Pilkington. Elected 20 Feb. 1561; ob. 23 Jan. 1575, æt. 55.

1577 Richard Barnes. Translated from Carlisle 5 April, 1577; ob. 24 Aug. 1587, æt. 55.

THE SEE VACANT TWO YEARS.

1589 Matthew Hutton, Dean of York. Elected 9 June, 1589; translated to York in 1594.

1595 Tobias Matthew, Dean of Durham. Elected March, 1595; translated to York 18 Aug. 1606.

1606 William James, Dean of Durham. Appointed 1606; ob. 12 May, 1617.

1617 Richard Neyle. Translated from Lincoln Oct. 1617; translated to Winchester 1627.

1627 George Monteine, or Mountaigne. Translated from London in 1627; translated to York 1 July, 1628.

1628 John Howson. Translated from Oxford 18 Sept. 1628; ob. 6 Feb. 1632, æt. 75.

1632 Thomas Moreton. Translated from Litchfield and Coventry June, 1632; ob. 22 Sept. 1659, æt. 95.

1660 John Cosin, Dean of Peterborough. Consecrated 2 Dec. 1660; ob. 15 Jan. 1672, æt. 77.

1674 Nathaniel III.-3d Lord Crew. Translated from Oxford 22 Oct. 1674; ob. 1722.

1722 William Talbot. Translated from Salisbury 1722; ob. 1730.

1730 Edward Chandler. Translated from Litchfield and Coventry 1730; ob. 1750.

1750 Joseph Butler. Translated from Bristol 1750; ob. 1752.

1752 Honourable Richard Trevor. Translated from St. David's 1752; ob. 1771.

1771 John Egerton. Translated from Litchfield and Coventry 1771: ob. 1787.

1787 Thomas Thurlow. Translated from Lincoln 1787; ob. 1791.

1791. Hon. Shute Barrington. Translated from Salisbury 1791. PRESENT Lord Bishop of Durham.

BISHOPS OF MAN *.

" This Bishoprick was first erected by Pope Gregory
IV. and for its Diocese had this isle and the He-
brides, or Western Islands of Scotland ; but which
were called Sodoroc by the Danes, who went to
them by the north, from the Swedish, Sodor, Sail,
or Oar Islands, from which the title of the Bishop of
Sodor is supposed to have originated.   The Bishop's
seat was at Rushin, or Castletown, in the Isle of
Man, and in Latin is entitled *Sodorensis;* but when
this island became dependent upon the kingdom of
England, the Western Islands withdrew themselves
from the obedience of their Bishop, and had a
Bishop of their own, whom they entitled also *Sodorensis,* but commonly Bishop of the Isles.   The
patronage of the Bishoprick was given, together
with the island, to the Stanleys, by King Edward
IV. (and came by an heir-female to the late Duke
of Athol, whose only daughter, the present Duchess
of Athol, is Lady of the Isle of Man), who still
keeps it; and, on a vacancy thereof, they nomi-
nate their designed Bishop to the King, who dis-
misses him to the Archbishop of York for consecration. The above is a sufficient reason why the Bishop
is not a Lord of Parliament, as none can have suf-
ferage in that House who does not hold immediately of the King himself. By an act of Parliament, the 33d of King Henry VIII. this Bishoprick
is declared in the province of York."—*Beatson.*

YEAR.
1114 Wymundus, or Reymundus. Consecrated 1114 ; de-
       prived 1151.
1151 John. Succeeded in 1151.
1.... Michael, Bishop of Sodor ; ob. 1203.
1203 Nicolas de Meaux. Succeeded in 1203 ; ob. 1217.

* From Le Neve's *Fasti Ecclesiæ Anglicanæ,* whose list differs
very materially from Heylyn's.

YEAR,

1217 Reginald. Succeeded in 1217.

1230 J........, Bishop of Man and the Isles; witness to a deed dated 25 Sept. 1230.

1230 Simon. Succeeded in 1230; ob. 1249.

1249 Lawrence, Archdeacon of Man. Succeeded in 1249; ob. 1249.

THE SEE VACANT ALMOST TWO YEARS.

1252 Richard. He dedicated the Church of St. Mary's of Rushin, or Castletown, in 1260.

1289 Onachus.

1275 Mark of Galloway.

1305 Allen, or Onachus, of Galloway; ob. 15 Feb. 1321.

1321 Gilbert of Galloway. Succeeded in 1321; ob. 1324.

1324 Bernard, a Scott, Abbot of Kilwinning, in Scotland. Succeeded in 1324; ob. 1527.

1334 Thomas, a Scott; ob. 1348.

1348 William Russell, a Manksman, Abbot of Rushin. Consecrated 1348; ob. 21 April, 1374.

1374 John Donkan, a Manksman. Elected 31 May, 1374.

1381 Robert Waldby. Translated to Dublin in 1381; he is said by some writers to have been Bishop of this See in 1396, but Le Neve doubts it.

THE SEE VACANT MANY YEARS.

1429 Richard Pully. Omitted by Le Neve.

1448 John Green, or Sprotton, Vicar of Dunchurch, Warwickshire.

1455 Thomas Burton; ob. 1458.

1458 Thomas, Abbot of Vale Royal, Cheshire. Omitted by Le Neve.

1480 Richard Oldham, Abbot of Chester; ob. 1487.

1487 Huan Hisketh, or Blackleach. Consecrated 1487; ob. 1510.

1510 Thomas Stanley, Rector of Wigan. Deprived by Queen Mary.

Robert Farrer. Omitted by Le Neve; he is said to have been translated to St. David's in 1548.

1546 Henry Man, Dean of Chester. Elected 22 Jan. 1546; ob. 1556.

1558 Thomas Stanley. Restored circa 1558; ob. 1570.

1571 John Salisbury, Dean of Norwich. Elected circa 1571; ob. Sept. 1573.

   James Stanley. Le Neve says the See was vacant about three years, but Heylyn and Beatson state, that James Stanley was Bishop of Man from 1573 to 1576.

1576 John Merick, Vicar of Hornchurch, Essex. Appointed 13 April, 1576; ob. 1599.

1600 George Lloyd. Succeeded in 1600; translated to Chester in 1604.

1604 John Philips, Archdeacon of Cleveland and Man. Appointed 29 Jan. 1604; ob. 1633.

1634 William Forster, Prebendary of Chester. Confirmed 8 March, 1634; ob. 1635.

1635 Richard Parr, Rector of Eccleston, Lancashire. Appointed 13 June, 1635; ob. 1643.

THE SEE VACANT SEVENTEEN YEARS.

1661 Samuel Rutter, Archdeacon of Man. Omitted by Le Neve.

1663 Isaac Barrow. Consecrated 5 July, 1663; translated in 1669 to St. Asaph; but held this See two years *in commendam.*

1671 Henry Bridgeman, Dean of Chester. Consecrated 1 Oct. 1671; ob. 15 May, 1682.

1682 John Lake, Archdeacon of Cleveland. Consecrated December, 1682; translated to Bristol 12 August, 1684.

1684 Baptist Levinz, Prebendary of Winchester. Consecrated 1684; ob. 1693.

THE SEE VACANT FIVE YEARS.

1697 Thomas Wilson, of Trinity College, Dublin. Appointed 25 Dec. 1697; ob. 1755.

.755 Mark Hiddesley. Appointed 1755; ob. 1772.

YEAR.

1773 Richard Richmond. Appointed 1773; ob. 1780.

1780 George Mason. Appointed 1780; ob. 1783.

1784 Claudius Crigan. Appointed 1784; ob? 1813.

1813 George Murray. Appointed 1813. PRESENT Bishop
of Sodor and Man.

AN

ALPHABETICAL LIST

OF THE

KNIGHTS

OF THE MOST NOBLE

ORDER OF THE GARTER,

FROM THE INSTITUTION OF THE ORDER
TO THE PRESENT TIME.

ALPHABETICAL LIST

OF THE

KNIGHTS OF THE GARTER.

———◆———

In the following List of the Knights of the Garter, those Names printed in **black letter** were the Founders of the Order; those in SMALL CAPITALS, Sovereign Princes, and those in *italics*, the existing Knights. The figures exhibit the number of each Knight in the order of Election; but the proper number of those Knights who have been elected since 1770 has not been ascertained.

————

King Edward I. INSTITUTED THE ORDER 1349, ob. 1377.

THE SOVEREIGN.

... Abercorn, John James Hamilton, Marquess of, ob. 1818.

271 Abergavenny, George Nevill, Baron of, ob. 1535. Vide Bergavenny.

458 Albemarle, George Monk, Duke of, ob. 1670.

471 Albemarle, Christopher Monk, Duke of, ob. 1688.

505 Albemarle, Arnold Keppel, Earl of, ob. 1718.

561 Albemarle, William Anne Keppel, Earl of, ob. 1754.

... Albemarle, George Keppel, Earl of, ob. 1772.

... *Anglesey, Henry William Paget, Marquess of,*

261 Ap Thomas, Sir Rhys, temp. Hen. VII.

163 ARAGON, ALPHONSUS, KING OF, ob. 1458.

514 Argyle, John Campbell, Duke of, in Scotland; also Duke of Greenwich in England, ob. 1743.

476 Arlington, Henry Bennet, Earl of, ob. 1685.

314 Arundel, Henry Fitz-Alan, Earl of, ob. 1579.

36 Arundel, Richard Fitz-Alan, Earl of, ob. 1393.

95 Arundel, Thomas Fitz-Alan, Earl of, 1415.

106 Arundel, Sir William Fitz-Alan, *alias*, temp. Hen. IV.

144 Arundel, John Fitz-Alan, Earl of, ob. 1434.

202 Arundel, William Fitz-Alan, Earl of, ob. 1487.

209 Arundel, Thomas Fitz-Alan, Earl of, ob. 1524.

285 Arundel, William Fitz-Alan, Earl of, ob. 1543.

406 Arundel, Thomas Howard, Earl of, ob. 1646.
Astley, Sir John, temp. Henry VI.
23 Audley, James, Baron, ob. 1386.
304 Audley, Thomas, Baron (of Walden), ob. 1544.
... Austria, Francis II, Emperor of.
160 Avranches, Albo Vasques, Count of (in Normandy),
temp. Hen. VI.

411 Banbury, William Knollys, Earl of, ob. 1632.
55 Banister, Sir Thomas, ob. 1380.
122 Bardolph, William Phelip, generally called Lord ; ob.
1436.
45 Basset, Ralph, Lord (of Drayton), ob. 1390.
... Bath, Thomas Thynne, Marquess of, ob. 1796.
... Bath, Thomas Thynne, Marquess of.
... Bathurst, Henry Bathurst, Earl.
61 Bavaria, William, Duke of, ob. 1377.
11 Beauchamp John, ob. 1360.
158 Beauchamp, John, Baron (of Powyck); ob. 1475.
473 Beaufort, Henry Somerset, Duke of, ob. 1699.
516 Beaufort, Henry Somerset, Duke of, ob. 1714.
... Beaufort, Henry Somerset, Duke of, ob. 1803.
... Beaufort, Henry Charles Somerset, Duke of.
69 Beaumont, John, Baron, ob. 1396.
155 Beaumont, John, Viscount, ob. 1459.
39 Bedford, Ingelram de Couey, Earl of, ob. 1897.
90 Bedford, John Plantagenet, Duke of, ob. 1435.
176 Bedford, Jasper Tudor, Duke of, ob. 1495.
301 Bedford, John Russell, Earl of, ob. 1554.
349 Bedford, Francis Russell, Earl of, ob. 1585.
475 Bedford, William Russell, Duke of, ob. 1700.
508 Bedford, Wriothesley Russell, Duke of, ob. 1711.
561 Bedford, John Russell, Duke of, ob. 1771.
68 Bergavenny, William Beauchamp, Baron of, ob. 1410.
531 Berkeley, James, Earl of, ob. 1736.
422 Berkshire, Thomas Howard, Earl, ob. 1669.
179 Berners, John Bourchier, Baron, ob. 1474.
402 Bindon, Thomas Howard, Viscount, ob. 1582.
408 Bohemia, Frederick, King of, ob. 1632.
522 Bolton, Charles Paulet, Duke of, ob. 1722.
181 Bonvill, William, Baron, ob. 1460.
27 Bordeaux, Richard, afterwards King Richard II. ob.
1400.
380 Borough, Thomas, Lord, ob. 1597.
158 Boteler, Ralph Boteler, Lord (of Sudley). ob. 1473.

5 Bouch, Piers de Greilly, Captal de la, ob. circa 1376.
536 Bolton, Charles Paulet, Duke of, ob. 1754.
83 Bourchier, John, Baron, ob. 1400.
130 Bourchier, Hugh Stafford, Baron (jure uxoris), ob. 1421.
134 Bourchier, Lewis Robsart, Baron (jure uxoris), ob. 1431.
52 Boxbull, Sir Alan, ob. 1380.
456 Brandenburgh, Frederick William, Marquess of, ob. 1688.
557 Brandenburgh, Charles William, Margrave of, ob. 1745.
.... Brandenburg Anspach, Charles Frederick, Margrave of,
  ob. ...
515 Brandon, James Hamilton, Duke of, ob. 1712.
255 Bray, Sir Reginald, ob. 1503.
119 Borga, Duke of, temp. Hen. V.
452 Bristol, George Digby, Earl of, ob. 1697.
31 Britanny, John de Montfort, Duke of, ob. 1401.
305 Browne, Sir Anthony, ob. 1548.
165 Brunswick, William, Duke of, ob. 1482.
417 Brunswick, Christian II. Duke of, ob. 1626.
499 Brunswick Lunenburgh, Geo. William, Duke of, ob. ....
507 Brunswick Lunenburgh, George Lewis, Elector of,
  AFTERWARDS KING GEORGE I.
573 Brunswick Lunenburgh, Ferdinand, Duke of, ob. 1792.
... BRUNSWICK WOFFENBUTTLE, CHARLES, DUKE OF, ob.
  1806.
57 Bryan, Guy de, Baron, ob. 1390.
... Buccleugh, Henry Scot, Duke of (in Scotland), ob. 1812.
142 Buckingham, Humphrey Stafford, Duke of, ob. 1459.
208 Buckingham, Henry Stafford, Duke of, ob. 1485.
249 Buckingham, Edward Stafford, Duke of, ob. 1521.
413 Buckingham, George Villiers, Duke of, ob. 1629.
446 Buckingham, George Villiers, Duke of, ob. 1687.
479 Buckingham, John Sheffield, Duke of, ob. 1720.
... *Buckingham and Chandos, Richard Temple Nugent
  Brydges Chandos Grenville, Duke of.*
234 Burgh, Thomas, Baron (of Gainsborough), ob. 1496.
10 Burghersh, Bartholomew, Baron, ob. 1369.
137 Burgundy, Philip, Duke of, ob. 1467.
207 Burgundy, Charles, Duke of, ob. 1477.
77 Burley, Sir Simon, ob. 1388.
79 Burley, Sir Richard, temp. Richard II.
82 Burley, Sir John, temp. Richard II.
356 Burleigh, William Cecil, Baron, ob. 1598.
102 Burnell, Hugh, Baron, ob. 1420.
545 Burlington, Richard Boyle, Earl of, ob. 1735.
577 Bute, John Stuart, Earl of (in Scotland), ob. 1792.

434 Danby, Henry Danvers, Earl of, ob. 1643.
276 Dacre, Thomas, Baron (of Gillesland).
265 Darcy, Thomas, Baron, ob. 1538.
328 Darcy, Thomas, Lord (of Chicke), ob. 1558.
... Dartmouth, George Legge, Earl of, ob. 1810.
228 D'Aubeney, Giles Baron, ob. 1507.
 25 Daubricheourt, Sir Sanchet.
111 Daubricheourt, Sir John, temp. Hen. V.
269 De la Warr, Thomas West, Baron, ob. 1525.
324 De la Warr, Thomas West, Baron, ob. 1554.
124 DENMARK, ERIC, KING OF, ob. 1459.
256 DENMARK, JOHN, KING OF, ob. 1513.
364 DENMARK, FREDERIC II. KING OF, ob. 1588.
394 DENMARK, CHRISTIAN IV. KING OF, ob. 1648.
466 DENMARK, CHRISTIAN, KING OF, ob. 1699.
... DENMARK, *Frederick VI. King of.*
486 Denmark, George, Prince of, and Duke of Cumberland,
      ob. 1708.
... Denmark, Christopher of Bavaria, King of. Vide Anstis,
      vol. II. p. 18, seq.
... Denmark, Christierne, King of. Vide the same volume.
225 Derby, Thomas Stanley, Earl of, ob. 1504.
319 Derby, Edward Stanley, Earl of, ob. 1574.
359 Derby, Henry Stanley, Earl of, ob. 1592.
391 Derby, William Stanley, Earl of, ob. 1642.
451 Derby, James Stanley, Earl of, ob. 1651.
 41 Despencer, Edward, Baron, ob. 1375.
 78 D'evereux, John, Baron, ob. 1394.
251 Devonshire, Edward Courtenay, Earl of, 1509
386 Devonshire, Charles Blount, Earl of, ob. 1606.
496 Devonshire, William Cavendish, Duke of, ob. 1707.
513 Devonshire, William Cavendish, Duke of, ob. 1729.
547 Devonshire, William Cavendish, Duke of, ob. 1755.
568 Devonshire, William Cavendish, Duke of, ob. 1764.
... Devonshire, William Cavendish, Duke of, ob. 1811.
234 Dinham, John, Lord, ob. 1509.
 94 Dorset, John Beaufort, Marquess of, ob. 1409.
215 Dorset, Thomas Grey, Marquess of, ob. 1501.
241 Dorset, Thomas Grey, Marquess of, ob. 1530.
373 Dorset, Thomas Sackville, Earl of, ob. 1608.
420 Dorset, Edward Sackville, Earl of, ob. 1652.
497 Dorset, Charles Sackville, Earl of, ob. 1706.
524 Dorset, Lionel Sackville, Duke of, ob. 1763.

506 Dover, (and Queensbury in Scotland), James Douglas, Duke of ob. 1711.
194 Douglas, James, Earl of (in Scotland), ob. 1488.
 85 Dunstavil, Sir Robert, temp. Richard II.
178 Dudley, Edward Sutton, Baron, ob. 1530
195 Duras, Galliard, Lord of (in France), temp. Edw. IV.)
330 Dudley, Sir Andrew, temp. Eliz.
403 Dunbar, George Hume, Earl of (in Scotland), ob. 1611.

 24 Cam, Sir Henry.
110 Erpingham, Sir Thomas, temp. Hen. IV.
442 Espernon, Bernard de Foix, Duke of. Installed 1661.
168 Essex, Bourchier Henry, Earl of, ob. 1483.
243 Essex, Henry Bourchier, Earl of, ob. 1539.
300 Essex, Thomas Cromwell, Earl of, ob. 1540.
355 Essex, Walter Devereux, Earl of, ob. 1576.
369 Essex, Robert Devereux, Earl of, ob. 1600.
549 Essex, William Capel, Earl of, ob. 1743.
 63 Exeter, John Holland, Duke of, ob. 1400.
 92 Exeter, Thomas Beaufort, Duke of, ob. 1426.
116 Exeter, John Holland, Duke of, ob. 1446.
278 Exeter, Henry Courtenay, Marquis of, ob. 1539.
392 Exeter, Thomas Cecil, Earl of, ob. 1622.
430 Exeter, William Cecil, Earl of, ob. 1640.

140 Falstaffe, Sir John, ob. 1463.
105 Fanhope, John Cornwall, Baron, ob. 1443.
114 Felbrygge, Sir Simon, temp. Hen. V.
 49 Felton, Sir Thomas, temp. Edward III.
218 Ferrara, Hercules D'Este, Duke of, ob. 1505.
205 Ferrers, Walter Devereux, Baron (of Chartley), ob. 1485.
492 Feversham, Louis de Duras, Earl of, ob. 1709.
128 Fitz-Hugh, Henry, Baron, ob. 1424.
 16 Fitz-Simon, Sir Richard.
 47 Fitz-Warine, William, Baron, ob. 1361.
 51 Fitz-Warine, Fulke, Baron, ob. 1373.
292 FRANCE, FRANCIS I. KING OF, ob. 1547.
326 FRANCE, HENRY II. KING OF, ob. 1559.
348 FRANCE, CHARLES IX. KING OF, ob. 1574.
361 FRANCE, HENRY III. KING OF, ob. 1589.
374 FRANCE, HENRY IV. KING OF, ob. 1610.
     FRANCE, LOUIS XVIII. KING OF, ob. 1824.

... FRANCE, *Charles X. King of.*
87 Frane, Sir Sandich de, alias Sanchet de la Tour, temp.
   Ric. II.

308 Gage, Sir John, ob. 1556.
 60 Gelderland, William Duke of, ob. 1402.
 93 GERMANY, ROBERT, EMPEROR OF, ob. 1410.
117 GERMANY, SIGISMUND, EMPEROR OF, ob. 1437.
151 GERMANY, ALBERT II. EMPEROR OF, ob. 1439.
171 GERMANY, FREDERIC III. EMPEROR OF, ob. 1493.
235 GERMANY, MAXIMILIAN I. EMPEROR OF, ob. 1519.
351 GERMANY, MAXIMILIAN II. EMPEROR OF, ob. 1576.
363 GERMANY, RODOLPH II. EMPEROR OF, ob. 1612.
264 GERMANY, CHARLES V. EMPEROR OF.
279 GERMANY, FERDINAND, EMPEROR OF, 1558.
 58 Gloucester, Thomas Plantagenet, Duke of, ob. 1397.
 91 Gloucester, Thomas Plantagenet, Duke of, ob. 1397.
198 Gloucester, Richard Plantagenet, Duke of, (afterwards
    ᷄ KING RICHARD III.)
453 Gloucester, Henry Stuart, Duke of, ob. 1669.
501 Gloucester, Prince William, Duke of.—Generally so
    termed, though he died before the Patent passed the
    Great Seal. (Vide p. 270;) ob. 1689.
576 Gloucester, William Henry, Duke of, ob. 1805.
... *Gloucester, H. R. H. William Frederick, Duke of.*
511 Godolphin, Sidney Godolphin, Earl of, ob. 1712.
482 Grafton, Henry Fitz-Roy, Duke of, ob. 1690.
534 Grafton, Charles Fitz-Roy, Duke of, ob. 1723.
... Grafton, Augustus Henry Fitz-Roy, Duke of, ob.
    1811.
 84 Gramston, or Granston (temp. Ric. II.), Sir Thomas,
    ob. 1485.
562 Granville, John Carteret, Earl, ob. 1763.
457 Graville, John Gasper Ferdinand Count de, temp.
    Char. II.
 15 Grey, John, Baron (of Codnor), ob. 1392.
 71 Grey, Richard, Baron (of Codnor), ob. 1418.
129 Grey, Sir John (Earl of Tankerville in Normandy), ob.
    1421.
148 Grey, Sir John (father of Edmund Earl of Kent), temp.
    Hen. VI.
Greenwich. Vide Argyle.
288 Grey, William, Baron (of Wilton), ob. 1562.
252 Guildford, Sir Richard, temp. Hen. VII.

345 Hunsdon, Henry Carey, Lord, ob. 1596.
385 Hunsdon, George Carey, Lord, ob. 1603.
 40 Huntingdon, Guiscard d'Angouleme, Earl of, ob. 1380.
322 Huntingdon, Francis Hastings, Earl of, ob. 1560.
352 Huntingdon, Henry Hastings, Earl of, 1595.

410 Kellie, Thomas Erskine, Earl of, in' Scotland, ob. 1639.
157 Kendal, John de Foix, Earl of, temp. Hen. VI.
 14 Kent, Thomas Holland, Earl of, ob. 1360.
 97 Kent, Edmund Holland, Earl of, ob. 1407.
150 Kent, William Nevill, Earl of, ob. 1463.
260 Kent, Richard Grey, Earl of, ob. 1523.
517 Kent, Henry Grey, Duke of, ob. 1740.
... Kent. H. R. H. Edward, Duke of, ob. 1820.
258 Kildare, Gerald Fitz-Gerald, Earl of, ob. 1513.
303 Kingston, Sir William, ob. 1541.
532 Kingston, Evelyn Pierrepoint, Duke of, ob. 1715.
553 Kingston, Evelyn Pierrepoint, Duke of, ob. 1773.
 74 Knolys, Sir Robert, ob. 1407.
382 Knollys, Sir Francis, ob. 1596.
183 Kyriell, Sir Thomas, temp. Hen. VI.

  3 Lancaster, Henry Plantagenet, Duke of, ob. 1362.
 29 Lancaster, John Plantagenet, Duke of, ob. 1399.
 59 Lancaster, Henry Plantagenet, afterwards King Henry IV.
... Lansdowne, William Petty, Marquess of, ob. 1805.
 43 Latimer, William, Baron, ob. 1380.
    La Tour. Vide de Frane.
472 Lauderdale, John Maitland, Duke of (in Scotland), and Earl of Guildford, ob. 1682.
387 Lee, Sir Henry, ob. 1611.
481 Leeds, Thomas Osborne, Duke of, ob. 1712.
559 Leeds, Thomas Osborne, Duke of, ob. 1789.
342 Leicester, Robert Dudley, Earl of, ob. 1588.
414 Leicester, Robert Sydney, Earl of, ob. 1677.
395 Lennox, Lodowick Stewart, Duke of (in Scotland), and Richmond, ob. 1624.
416 Lennox, Esme Stewart, Duke of (in Scotland), and Earl of March, ob. 1624.
433 Lennox, James Stewart, Duke of (in Scotland), and Richmond, ob. 1655.

462 Lennox, Charles Stewart, Duke of (in Scotland), and Richmond, ob. 1672.

327 Lincoln, Edward Clinton, Earl of, ob. 1585.

565 Lincoln, Henry Fiennes Clinton, Earl of, ob. 1728..

429 Lindsey, Robert Bertie, Earl of, ob. 1642.

463 Lindsey, Montagu Bertie, Earl of, ob. 1666.

  9 Lisle, John, Baron (of Rugemont), ob. 1356.

283 Lisle, Arthur Plantagenet, Viscount, ob. 1541.

... *Liverpool, Robert Banks Jenkinson, Earl of.*

... *Lonsdale, William Lowther, Earl of.*

... Londonderry, Robert Stewart, Marquess of (in Ireland), ob. 1822.

156 Longueville, Gaston de Foix, Earl of (in Normandy), temp. Hen. VI.

101 Lovel, John, Baron, ob. 1408.

 20 Loring, Sir Nele, ob. 1385.

232 Lovel, Francis, Viscount, ob. 1487.

254 Lovel, Sir Thomas, ob. 1524.

464 Manchester, Edward Montagu, Earl of, ob. 1671.

 46 Manny, Walter, Baron, ob. 1372.

  8 March, Roger Mortimer, Earl of, ob. 1360.

416 March, Esme Stuart, Earl of, and Duke of Lennox in Scotland, ob. 1624.

453 Marlborough, Charles Spencer, Duke of, ob. 1722.

509 Marlborough, John Churchill, Duke of, ob. 1758.

... Marlborough, George Spencer, Duke of, ob. 1817.

270 Marney, Henry, Lord, ob. 1524.

397 Marr, John Erskine, Earl of (in Scotland), ob. 1634.

... Mecklenburgh Strelitz, Adolphus Frederick III. Duke of, ob. 1794.

193 Milan, Francis Sfortia, Duke of, ob. 1466.

 12 Mohun, John, Baron, ob. circa 1373.

467 Monmouth, James Scott, Duke of, ob. 1685.

335 Montacute, Anthony Browne, Viscount, ob. 1592.

187 Montagu, John Neville, Marquess, ob. 1471.

529 Montagu, John Montagu, Duke of, ob. 1749.

... Montagu, George Brudenell, Duke of, ob. 1790.

216 Montgomery, Sir Thomas, temp. Edw. IV.

404 Montgomery and Pembroke, Philip Herbert, Earl of, ob. 1650.

206 Montjoy, Walter Blount, Lord, ob. 1474.

289 Montjoy, William Blount, Lord, ob. 1535.

275 Monteagle, Edward Stanley, Baron, ob. 1523.
295 Montmorency, Anne, Duke de (in France), ob. 1567.
354 Montmorency Francis, Duke de (in France), ob. 1579.
450 Montrose, James Graham, Marquess of (in Scotland), ob. 1650.
... *Montrose, James Graham, Duke of (in Scotland).*
103 Morley, Thomas, Baron, ob. 1417.
435 Morton, William Douglas, Earl of (in Scotland), ob. 1648.
199 Mountgrysson, Lord (in Apulia), temp. Edw. IV.
381 Mulgrave, Edmund Sheffield, Earl of, ob. 1646.

86 Namur, Sir Robert de, temp. Ric. II.
192 NAPLES, FERDINAND II. KING OF, ob. 1496.
274 Nemours, Julian de Medici, Duke of, ob. 1516.
... NETHERLANDS, *William, King of the.*
44 Neville, John, Baron, ob. 1388.
206 Newblancb, Philip Chabot, Comte de (in France), temp. Hen. VIII.
449 Newcastle, William Cavendish, Duke of ob. 1676.
480 Newcastle, Henry Cavendish, Duke of, ob. 1691.
502 Newcastle, John Holles, Duke of, ob. 1711.
530 Newcastle, Thomas Pelham Holles, Duke of, ob. 1768.
... Newcastle, Henry Fiennes Pelham Clinton, Duke of, ob. 1794.
... *Newcastle, Henry Pelham Pelham Clinton, Duke of.*
64 Norfolk, Thomas Mowbray, Duke of, ob. 1413.
131 Norfolk, John Mowbray, Duke of, ob. 1432.
167 Norfolk, John Mowbray, Duke of, ob. 1461.
200 Norfolk, John Mowbray, Duke of, ob. 1475.
204 Norfolk, John Howard, Duke of, ob. 1485.
221 Norfolk, Thomas Howard, Duke of, ob. 1524.
263 Norfolk, Thomas Howard, Duke of, ob. 1554.
340 Norfolk, Thomas Howard, Duke of, ob. 1572.
406 Norfolk, Thomas Howard, Earl of, and Earl of Arundel and Surrey, ob. 1646.
489 Norfolk, Henry Howard, Duke of, ob. 1701.
33 Northampton, William Bohun, Earl of, ob. 1360.
312 Northampton, William Parr, Marquess of, ob. 1571.
400 Northampton, Henry Howard, Earl of, ob. 1614.
427 Northampton, William Compton, Earl of, ob. 1630.
212 Northumberland, Henry Percy, Earl of, ob. 1489.
242 Northumberland, Henry Algernon Percy, Earl of, ob.1527.

483 Salisbury, Cecil, Earl of, ob. 1683.
... Salisbury, James Cecil, Marquis of, ob. 1823.
Sanchet la Tour. Vide de Frane.
459 Sandwich, Edward Montagu, Earl of, ob. 1672.
277 Sandys, William Sandys, Baron (of the Vine), ob. 1542. ...
 72 Sarnsfield, Sir Nicholas, temp. Edw. III.
236 Savage, Sir John, ob. 1492.
333 Savoy, Emanuel, Duke of, ob. 1580.
... *Saxe Cobourg, Leopold, Prince of.*
556 Saxe Gotha, Frederick III. Duke of, ob. .....
470 Saxony, John George II. Duke of, ob. 1680.
139 Scales, Thomas Scales, Baron, ob. 1460.
539 Scarborough, Richard Lumley, Earl of, ob. 1740.
495 Schombergh, Frederick, Duke of, ob. 1690.
510 Scombergh, Mynhardt, Duke of, ob. 1719.
297 SCOTLAND; JAMES V. KING OF, ob. 1542.
375 SCOTLAND, JAMES VI. KING OF, ascended the throne as King of Great Britain, 1603.
190 Scrope, John Scrope, Baron (of Bolton), ob. 1494.
368 Scrope, Henry Scrope Baron (of Bolton), ob. 1592.
390 Scrope, Thomas Scrope. Baron (of Bolton), ob. 1612.
Scrope, Henry Scrope, Baron (of Masham).—Vide Anstis, v. II p. 13.
320 Seymour, Thomas Seymour, Lord, of Sudley, ob. 1549.
138 Shrewsbury, John Talbot, Earl of, ob. 1453.
172 Shrewsbury, John Talbot, Earl of, ob. 1460.
230 Shrewsbury, George Talbot, Earl of, ob. 1541.
316 Shrewsbury, Francis Talbot, Earl of, ob. 1560.
344 Shrewsbury, George Talbot, Earl of, ob. 1590.
376 Shrewsbury, Gilbert Talbot, Earl of, ob. 1616.
500 Shrewsbury, Charles Talbot, Duke of, 1718.
239 SICILY, ALPHONSUS, KING OF, ob. 1495.
350 Sidney, Sir Henry, ob. 1586.
 94 Somerset and Dorset, John Beaufort, Marquess of, ob. 1410.
147 Somerset, Edmund Beaufort, Duke of, ob. 1455.
152 Somerset, John Beaufort, Duke of, ob. 1444.
306 Somerset, Edward Seymour, Duke of, ob. 1552.
407 Somerset, Robert Car, Earl of, ob. 1645.
460 Somerset, William Seymour, Duke of, ob. 1660.
487 Somerset, Charles Seymour, Duke of, ob. 1748.
290 Southampton, William Fitzwilliam, Earl of, ob. 1543.
317 Southampton, Thomas Wriothesley, Earl of. ob. 155?

448 Southampton, Thomas Wriothesley, Earl of, ob. 1550.
478 Southampton, Charles Fitzroy, Duke of, 1730.
331 SPAIN, PHILIP II. KING OF, temp. Eliz.; he resigned the Order; ob. 1598.
... SPAIN, *Ferdinand VII. King of.*
... *Spencer, George, John Spencer, Earl.*
  6 Stafford, Ralph Stafford, Earl of, ob. 1372.
 38 Stafford, Hugh Stafford, Earl of, ob. 1386.
 96 Stafford, Edmund, Earl of, ob. 1403.
... Stafford, Granville Leveson Gower, Marquess of, ob. 1803.
... *Stafford, George Granville Leveson Gower, Marquess of.*
107 Stanley, Sir John, ob. 1413.
237 Stanley, Sir William, ob. 1494.
174 Stanley, Thomas Stanley, Baron, ob. 1458.
 17 Stapleton, Sir Miles, ob. 1373.
 80 Stapleton, Sir Bryan, temp. Edw. III.
438 Strafford, Thomas Wentworth, Earl of, ob. 1641.
465 Strafford, William Wentworth, Earl of, ob. 1695.
520 Strafford, Thomas Wentworth, Earl of, ob. 1739.
232 Strange, George Stanley, Baron (of Knokyn), ob. 1497.
 75 Sulby (or Sully) Sir John, temp. Edw. III.
 37 Suffolk, Robert Ufford, Earl of, ob. 1369.
 66 Suffolk, Michael de la Pole, Earl of, ob. 1389.
139 Suffolk, William de la Pole, Duke of, ob. 1450.
201 Suffolk, John de la Pole, Duke of, 1491.
253 Suffolk, Edmund de la Pole, Duke of, ob. 1513.
273 Suffolk, Charles Brandon, Duke of, ob. 1545.
316 Suffolk, Henry Grey, Duke of, ob. 1554.
384 Suffolk, Thomas Howard, Earl of, ob. 1626.
426 Suffolk, Theophilus Howard, Earl of, ob. 1640.
493 Sunderland, Robert Spencer, Earl of, ob. 1702.
533 Sunderland, Charles Spencer, Earl of, ob. 1722.
162 Surien, Sir Francis, temp. Hen. VI.
 62 Surrey, Thomas Holland, Duke of, ob. 1400.
307 Surrey, Henry Howard, commonly called Earl of, ob. 1546.
284 Sussex, Robert Ratcliffe, Earl of, ob. 1542.
332 Sussex, Henry Ratcliffe, Earl of, ob. 1556.
337 Sussex, Thomas Ratcliffe, Earl of, ob. 1583.
372 Sussex, Henry Ratcliffe, Earl of, ob. 1593.
388 Sussex, Robert Ratcliffe, Earl of, ob. 1629.

... *Sussex, H. R. H. Augustus Frederick, Duke of.*
424 SWEDEN, GUSTAVUS ADOLPHUS II. KING OF, ob. 1632.
469 SWEDEN, CHARLES XI. KING OF, ob. 1697.

100 Talbot, Gilbert Talbot, Baron, and Baron Strange of
  Blackmere, ob. 1419.
247 Talbot, Sir Gilbert, ob. 1516.
129 Tankerville, Sir John Grey, Earl of (in Normandy),
  ' ob. 1421.
454 Tarente, Henry, Charles de Tremouillé, Prince de,
  ob. 1672.
575 Temple, Richard Grepville Temple, Earl, ob. 1779.
540 Townshend, Charles Townshend, Viscount, ob. 1738.
226 Tunstal, Sir Richard, temp. Hen. VI.

 48 Ufford, Sir Thomas, temp. Edw. III.
  Ughtredé, alias Utreight, alias Wright. Vide Wright.
  (No. 54.)
108 Umfreville, Sir Robert de, ob. 1437.
211 Urbino, Frederick, Duke of (in Italy), ob. 1482.
257 Urbino, Guido, Duke of (in Italy), ob. 1508.
 56 Vache, Sir Richard de la, temp. Edw. III.
 73 Vache, Sir Philip de la, temp. Ric. II.
 50 Van Hall, Sir Francis, Knight Banneret, temp. Edward III.
154 Visco, Henry, Duke of (in Portugal), ob. 1460.

550 Waldegrave, James Waldegrave, Earl, ob. 1741.
572 Waldegrave, James Waldegrave, Earl, ob. 1763.
 18 Wale, Sir Thomas, ob. 1352.
  2 Wales, Edward, Prince of (the Black Prince), ob.
  vitâ patris 1376.
 27 Wales, Richard Plantagenet, Prince of, afterwards
  KING RICHARD II.
 88 Wales, Henry, Prince of, afterwards KING HENRY V.
175 Wales, Edward, Prince of, son of Henry V. ob.
  1471.
213 Wales, Edward, Prince of, afterwards KING EDWARD V.
240 Wales, Arthur, Prince of, son of King Henry VII. ob.
  1502, vitâ patris.
250 Wales, Henry, Prince of, afterwards KING HENRY VIII.
393 Wales, Henry Frederick, Prince of, son of James I. ob.
  1612, vitâ patris.

233 Widville, Sir Edward, ob. 1488.

383 Wirtemburgh, Frederick, Duke of, ob. 1608.

... Worcester, Thomas Percy, Earl of, ob. 1402.

186 Worcester, John Tiptoft, Earl of, ob. 1470.

244 Worcester, Charles Somerset, Earl of, ob. 1526.

353 Worcester, William Somerset, Earl of, ob. 1589.

379 Worcester, Edward Somerset, Earl of, ob. 1628.

54 Wright, alias Ughtrede, alias Utright,* Sir Thomas, temp. Edw. III.

19 Wrotesley, Sir Hugh, ob. 1380.

30 York, Edmund Plantagenet, Duke of, 1402.

65 York, Edward Plantagenet, Duke of, ob. 1415.

145 York, Richard Plantagenet, Duke of, ob. 1460.

214 York, Richard Plantagenet, Duke of, ob. 1483.

439 York, James Stuart, Duke of, afterwards King James II.

527 York, Ernest Augustus, Duke of, brother of King George I. ob. 1728.

564 York, Edward Augustus, Duke of, brother of King George III. ob. 1767.

... *York and Albany, H. R. H. Frederick, Duke of.*

---

* Query, if this personage was Thomas de Ughtrede, who was summoned to Parliament from 17 to 38 Edw. III. and died in 1365.

AN

ALPHABETICAL LIST

OF THE

KNIGHTS

OF THE MOST HONORABLE MILITARY

ORDER OF THE BATH,

FROM THE REVIVAL OF THAT ORDER IN 1725, TO ITS
ENLARGEMENT IN 1815;

AND OF THE

KNIGHTS GRAND CROSSES

FROM THAT YEAR TO THE PRESENT TIME.

ALPHABETICAL LIST

OF THE

KNIGHTS OF THE BATH.

◆

The Names in the following List which are printed in italics are the present Knights Grand Crosses.

———

Abercrombie, Sir Ralph, afterwards Lord Abercrombie, 1795; ob. 1801.
Abercrombie, Sir Robert.
A'Court, Sir William (CIVIL).
Albemarle, William Anne, Earl of, 1725; ob. 1754.
Alten, Count (HONORARY).
Amherst, Sir Jeffery, afterwards Lord Amherst, 1761.; ob. 1797.
Anglesey, Henry, Marquess of.
Antrim, William Randal, Marquess of, 1780; ob. 1791.
Auchmuty, Sir Samuel.

Bagot, Sir Charles, Hon. (CIVIL).
Baird, Sir David, Bart.
Banks, Sir Joseph, 1795, ob. 1820.
Barlow, Sir George Hillaro, Bart. (CIVIL).
Bateman, William, Viscount, 1732; ob. 1744.
Beaulieu, Edward, Earl of, 1753; ob. 1802.
Beckwith, Sir George.
Bellmont, Charles, Earl of, 1764; ob. 1800.
Bentinck, Lord William.
Beresford, William Carr, Viscount.
Blakeney, William, Lord, 1756; ob. 1761.
Blaquire, Sir John, afterwards Lord Blaquire; ob. 1812.
Blomefield, Benjamin, Lord (CIVIL).
Blucher, Field Marshal Prince (HONORARY).
Bolton, Charles, Duke of, 1753; ob. 1765.
Boyd, Sir Robert, 1784, ob. ...

Breadalbane, John, Earl of, 1723; ob. 1782.
Brownrigg, Sir Robert, Bart.

Calthorpe, Sir Henry, 1744.
Calvert, Sir Harry, Bart.
Cambridge, H. R. H. the Duke of, K. G.
Campbell, Sir Archibald, 1785.
Campbell, Sir James, 1742; ob. 1745.
Carnarvon, John, commonly called Marquess of,
    afterwards Duke of Chandos, 1732; ob. 1771.
Carysfort, John Lord, 1761; ob. 1772.
Catherlough, Robert, Earl of, 1770; ob. 1772.
Cholmondeley, George (commonly called Viscount Malpas),
    afterwards Earl of Cholmondeley, 1725; ob. 1770.
Christian, Sir Hugh Cloberry, 1796.
Clancarty, Henry, Earl of (Civil).
Clarence, H. R. H. the Duke of, K. G.
Clarke, Sir Alured.
Clavering, Sir John, 1777; ob. ...
Clifton, Sir Robert, 1725; ob. 1762.
Clinton, Hugh, Earl, 1725; ob. 1751.
Clinton, Sir Henry, 1777; ob. ...
Clinton, Sir Henry.
Clinton, Sir William Henry.
Clive, Robert Lord, 1764; ob. 1774.
Cochrane, Thomas, Lord, DEGRADED.
Cochrane, Hon. Sir Alexander Forrest.
Cockburn, Sir George.
Cole, Sir Galbraith Lowry.
Colpoys, Sir John, 1798, ob. ...
Colville, Hon. Sir Charles.
Combermere, Stapleton, Lord.
Coote, Sir Eyre, 1771; ob. 1783.
Coote, Sir Eyre, 1803; DEGRADED.
Cope, Sir John, 1742; ob. 1760.
Cornwallis, Hon. Sir William.
Cumberland, William Augustus, Duke of, 1725; ob. 1765.
Cumberland, H. R. H. the Duke of, K. G.

Dalhousie, George, Earl of.
Darcy, Sir Coniers, 1725; ob. 1758.
De le Warr, John, Earl, 1725; ob. 1776.
De le Warr, Sir Francis Blake, 1761; ob. 1771.
Deloraine, Henry, Earl of, 1725; ob. 1730.
Domett, Sir William.

Don, Sir George.
Dorchester, Guy, Lord, ob. 1808.
Downing, Sir George, Bart. 1732; ob. 1749.
Doyle, Sir John.
Draper, Sir William, 1765.
Drummond, Sir Gordon.
Duckworth, Sir John Thomas, Bart. 1801; ob. 1817.
Dundas, Sir David, 1802.

Elliot, Sir George Augustus, afterwards Lord Heathfield, 1783; ob. 1796.
Exmouth, Edward, Viscount.

Fawcett, Sir William, 1786.
Fitz-William, Richard, Viscount, 1744; ob. 1776.
Foley, Sir Thomas.
Frederick, Sir Charles, 1761.
Freemantle, Sir Thomas Francis, ob. 1819.
Frimont, Baron (HONORARY).

Gage, Sir William, Bart. 1725; ob. 1744.
Galway, Robert, Viscount, 1786.
Gambier, James, Lord.
Gibbons, Sir John, Bart. 1761; ob. 1776.
Gloucester, H. R. H. the Duke of, K. G.
Gordon, Sir William.
Graves, Sir Thomas, afterwards Lord Graves, 1801; ob. 1802.
Gray, Sir James, Bart. 1761; ob. 1773.
Grey, Sir Charles, afterwards Earl Grey, 1783; ob. 1807.
Griffin, Sir John Griffin, 1761; ob. 1771.
Gunning, Sir Robert, 1773.

Haldemand, Sir Frederick, 1785.
Halifax, George, Earl of, 1725; ob. 1739.
Hamilton, Sir William, 1772; ob. 1803.
Harbord, Sir William Morden, 1744; ob. 1770.
Harcourt, William, Earl of.
Harris, George, Lord.
Harris, Sir James, afterwards Earl of Malmesbury, 1779; ob. 1820.
Harvey, Sir Eliab.
Harvey, Sir Henry, 1800.
Hastings, Francis, Marquess of, K. G.

Hawke, Sir Edward, afterwards Lord Hawke, 1747; ob. 1781.

Henley, Morton, Lord (CIVIL).

Hewett, Sir George, Bart.

Hill, Rowland, Lord.

Hislop, Sir Thomas, Bart.

Hobart, Sir John, afterwards Earl of Buckinghamshire, 1725; ob. 1746.

Honywood, Sir Philip, 1742; ob. 1752.

Hood, Sir Alexander, afterwards Viscount Bridport, 1788; ob. 1814.

Hood, Sir Samuel, 1804; ob.

Hope, Hon. Sir Alexander.

Hopetoun, John, Earl of, ob. 1823.

Hotham, Sir Charles, Bart. 1772.

Howard, Hon. Sir Charles, 1749; ob. 1765.

Howard, Sir George.

Howard, Kenneth, Lord (of Effingham).

Howden, John Francis, Lord.

Howe, Hon. Sir, William, afterwards Viscount Howe, ob. 1814.

Hughes, Sir Edward, 1778.

Huntley, George, Marquess of.

Hutchinson, John Henry, Lord, 1801.

Inchquin, Earl of, 1725; ob. 1777.

Irwin, Sir John.

Johnson, Sir Henry, Bart.

Keene, Sir Benjamin, 1754; ob. 1757.

Keith, George, Viscount, 1794; ob. 1823.

Keith, Sir Robert Murray, 1772.

Keats, Sir Richard Goodwin.

Kempt, Sir James.

Kent, H. R. H. the Duke of, ob. 1820.

Keppel, Sir William.

Knowles, Sir Charles Henry, Bart.

Leicester, John, Earl of, 1725; ob. 1737.

Ligonier, John, Earl, 1742; ob. 1770.

Ligonier, Edward, Earl, 1781; ob. ...

Lindsey, Sir John, 1771; ob. 1788.

'ston, Right Hon. Sir Robert (CIVIL).

ndonderry, Charles William, Marquess of.

Long, Sir Charles, Right Hon. (Civil).
Lovel, Thomas, Lord, 1725, afterwards Earl of Leicester; ob. 1759.
Ludlow, George James, Earl, 1804.
Lynch, Sir William, 1771; ob. 1785.
Lynedoch, Thomas, Lord.
Lyttleton, Sir Richard. 1753; ob. 1770.

Macartney, Sir George, afterwards Earl of Macartney, 1773; ob. 1806.
Maitland, Sir Thomas, ob. 1824.
Malcolm, Sir John.
Malmesbury, James, Earl of, ob. 1820.
Manchester, Duke of, 1725; ob. 1739.
Mann, Sir Horatio.
Martin, Sir George.
Meadows, Sir William, 1792.
Methuen, Sir Paul, 1795.
Mitchell, Sir Andrew, 1765.
Mitchell, Sir Andrew, 1800.
Monson, Sir John, afterwards Lord Monson, 1748; ob. 1748.
Montague, Sir George.
Montagu, John, Duke of, 1725; ob. 1749.
Montague, Sir Charles, 1771.
Moore, Sir John, 1770.
Moore, Sir John, 1804; ob. 1809.
Mordaunt, Sir John, 1747.
Morgan, Sir William.
Mulgrave, Henry, Earl of.
Munro, Sir Hector, 1780.
Murray, Sir George.

Neale, Sir Harry.
Nelson, Sir Horatio, afterwards Viscount Nelson, 1797; ob. 1805.
Newton, Sir Michael, 1725; ob. 1743.
Nicol, Sir Charles Gunter, 1732; ob. 1733.
Northesk, William, Earl of, 1805.
Nugent, Sir George.

Oakes, Sir Hildebrand, ob. 1822.
Ochterlony, Sir David.
Onslow, Richard, Lord, 1752; ob. 1776.

Orange, H. R. H. the Prince of.
Oswald, Sir John.
Oughton, Sir James Adolphus.

Paget, Right Hon. Sir Arthur (CIVIL), 1804.
Paget, Hon. Sir Edward.
Pakenham, Hon. Sir Thomas.
Paulett, Lord Nassau, 1725 ; ob. 1741.
Payne, Sir Ralph, afterwards Lord Lavington, 1771 ; ob....
Peirson, Sir Richard, 1780.
Pitt, Sir William Augustus, 1792; ob. 1809.
Pocock, Sir George, 1761 ; ob. 1792.
Pole, Sir Charles Morice.
Pomfret, Thomas, Earl of, 1725 ; ob. 1743.
Powlett, Sir Charles Armand, 1747 ; ob. 1765.
Proctor, Sir William Beauchamp, 1761 ; ob. 1773.

Radstock, William Lord.
Richmond, Charles, Duke of, 1725 ; ob. 1750.
Robinson, Sir Thomas, afterwards Lord Grantham, 1742 ;
    ob. 1770.
Rodney, Sir George Bridges, Bart. afterwards Lord Rodney,
    1780 ; ob. 1792.
Rosslyn, James, Earl of.
Rowley, Sir William, 1753; ob. 1768.

St. Alban's, Charles, Duke of, 1725; ob. 1751.
St. Vincent, John, Earl of, 1782 ; ob. 1823.
Saumarez, Sir James, Bart. 1801.
Saunders, Sir Charles, 1761 ; ob. 1775.
Saunderson, Sir Thomas Lumley, afterwards Earl of Scar-
    borough, 1725; ob. 1742.
Saville, Sir John, afterwards Earl of Mexborough, 1747 ;
    ob. 1778.
Saxe Cobourg, R. H. R. Prince Leopold, of, K. G.
Schwartzenburgh, His Highness Prince (HONORARY).
Sherbroke, Sir John Cope.
Stewart, Hon. Sir William.
Sloper, Sir Robert, 1788.
Spencer, Sir Brent.
Stanhope, Sir William, 1725 ; ob. 1772.
Strachan, Sir Richard John, 1806.
Strangford, Percy, Viscount (CIVIL).

Stuart, Right Hon. Sir Charles (CIVIL).
Sussex, Talbot, Earl of, 1725; ob. 1731.
Sutton, Sir Robert, 1725; ob. 1746.

Tarleton, Sir Banastre, Bart.
Thompson, Sir Thomas Boulden, Bart.
Thornborough, Sir Edward.
Thornton, Right Hon. Sir Edward (CIVIL).
Tolly, Count Barclay de (HONORARY).
Torrington, George, Viscount, 1725; ob. 1733.
Trigge, Sir Thomas, 1801.
Tyrconnel, John, Viscount, 1725; ob. 1755.

Vaughan, Hon. Sir John, 1792.
Volkousky, His Highness General Prince (HONORARY).

Walker, Sir George Townsend.
Walpole, Sir Robert, afterwards Earl of Orford, 1725; ob. 1751.
Walpole, Hon. Sir Edward, 1753.
Warren, Sir George, 1761.
Warren, Sir John Borlase, Bart. 1794; ob. 1822.
Warren, Sir Peter, 1747; ob. 1752.
Wellesley, Hon. Sir Arthur, now Duke of Wellington, K. G. 1804.
Wellesley, Right Hon. Sir Henry (CIVIL).
Wentworth, Sir Thomas Weston, afterwards Marquess of Rockingham, 1725; ob. 1756.
Whitmore, Sir Thomas, 1744; ob. 1773.
Whitworth, Sir Charles (afterwards Earl Whitworth), 1793; ob. 1825.
Williams Sir Charles Hanbury, 1744; ob. 1759.
Williamson, Sir Adam, 1794.
Wills, Sir Charles, 1725; ob. 1746.
Wilmington, Spencer, Earl of, 1725; ob. 1743.
Woronzow, General Count (HONORARY).
Wrede, His Highness Prince (HONORARY).
Wurtemberg, Frederick, King of (HONORARY).

Yonge, Sir George, Bart. 1788; ob.
Yonge, Sir William, 1725; ob. 1755.

York, H. R. H. Frederick, Duke of, 1768.
York, Hon. Sir Joseph, afterwards Lord Dover; ob. 1792.
Young, Sir William.

Zieten, General Count (HONORARY).

THE END.

Printed by J. Nichols, and Son, 25, Parliament-street.

Lightning Source UK Ltd.
Milton Keynes UK
UKHW010811261118
332983UK00010B/1012/P

9 781528 114349